Dynamics of Banking

Dynamics of Banking

Edited by

Thomas M. Havrilesky
Duke University

Robert L. Schweitzer
University of Delaware

John T. Boorman
International Monetary Fund

Harlan Davidson, Inc.
Arlington Heights, Illinois 60004

Library of Congress Cataloging in Publication Data

Main entry under title:

The Dynamics of banking.

Includes bibliographies.
1. Bank management—Addresses, essays, lectures.
I. Havrilesky, Thomas M. II. Schweitzer, Robert L.
III. Boorman, John T.
HG1615.D96 1985 332.1′068 84-25157
ISBN 0-88295-411-3

PRINTED IN THE UNITED STATES OF AMERICA
91 90 89 88 87 2 3 4 5 6 7 8 9 10 MG

Contents

Preface

When the predecessor to this collection, *Current Perspectives in Banking,* appeared in early 1980, regulatory reform appeared to have been stymied. Since then a deluge of deregulation has swept over the financial services industry. At the same time, substantial innovations in the operations and marketing strategies of financial services firms have taken place. This, in turn, is provoking a thorough renovation of the roles of supervisory and regulatory bodies.

These changes are the major focus of this collection of readings. For example, in section I on bank management attention is not centered on traditional methods of separately managing assets, liabilities, and capital. Instead, the essays explore the newer concepts of simultaneous asset-liability-capital management—in theory *and* in practice—with emphasis on the related contemporary developments in gap management, bank hedging, and duration analysis. Section II is devoted to the subject of current financial innovation. How does innovation evolve? What changes are likely to emerge in the organization and regulation of the financial services industry?

The fourth section of this volume addresses the volatile topics of interstate banking, holding companies, and mergers. The readings are not concerned with the traditional definitions of banking markets or the nonbanking activities of bank holding companies. Indeed, the idea of distinct banking product and geographic markets and distinct nonbanking activities is rapidly becoming obsolete. Instead, the focus of section IV is on new markets for financial services and on the supervisory and regulatory reform that must occur as old geographic boundaries and product-line definitions dissolve while the desire to reduce risks imposed on the nation's payments system remains essentially intact. The remaining sections of this collection, on costs and profitability, international banking, and regulatory and supervisory reform, examine recent and likely future financial innovations and their impact on bank and regulatory behavior.

Recently, textbooks on money and banking, bank management, financial institutions management and financial institutions and markets have become increasingly specialized and fragmented. For example, many textbooks on money and banking provide standard coverage of LM-IS, aggregate demand/aggregate supply, macroeconomic models, and monetary policy, but devote little discussion to bank management and regulation. Likewise, texts on money and banking and bank management pay attention to traditional banking operations but fail to keep abreast of recent innovations and related domestic and international regulatory reform. Finally, few texts in money and banking, bank management, or financial institutions management provide rigorous coverage of recent developments in the theory and operations of the banking firm. *Dynamics of Banking* covers these and other important topics that are too often ignored or superficially treated in other texts.

This book, together with its companion volumes, *Contemporary Developments in Financial Institutions and Markets* and *Modern Concepts in Macroeconomics,* allows instructors to select a set of contemporary readings which complements their instructional needs. For example, the money and banking or bank management instructor whose textbook adequately covers the area of applied bank management but only briefly mentions recent banking innovations and regulatory reform would be attracted to this collection as a means of covering these topics in depth. The money and banking instructor who uses a textbook that emphasizes macroeconomic theory or monetary policy would find this volume an excellent way to provide students with detailed coverage of contemporary bank management and regulation. Thus this edition and its companion volumes can be used in various ways to meet each instructor's special needs and interests.

Moreover, even the most current textbook is usually constrained to cover the traditional material in bank management, history, and regulation. This often leaves little space to include current developments in such areas as financial services markets, innovations in banking operations, international banking, and supervisory and regulatory reform. This collection of readings, along with its companion volumes, provides an economical and convenient way of bringing students up to date with the latest developments in the field.

We would like to thank Edward Kane, Harvey Rosenblum, George Kaufman, Phillip Brock, Robert Eisenbeis, Stuart Greenbaum, Larry Freider, Vincent Apilado, Stephen Rhoades, Pam Powell, and Donald Puglisi for their suggestions, Chris Phelan, Barb Wagner, and Sherri Powell for their marvelous production assistance, and our editor, Harlan Davidson, for his unstinting cooperation and encouragement.

Thomas M. Havrilesky
Robert L. Schweitzer
John T. Boorman

Bank Management

I

A general rule of financial management for all firms is that a firm's asset configuration should shape financial and capital policy—that is, the liability and capital mix should reflect the risk, maturity, and liquidity of its assets. However, banking firms generally are viewed as being able to control their assets and liabilities simultaneously. Thus, the modern focus of bank management decisions is on assets *and* liabilities together.

The bank is usually regarded as an entity that can profitably intermediate by issuing checkable deposits in order to make longer-term loans. Thus, the bank typically has a "mismatched" balance sheet consisting of short-term liabilities and longer-term assets. As a result, banks have an acute need for sufficient liquidity.

At one time, short-term liquidity needs were met by reserve adjustments and the conversion of earning assets to cash. Today, however, the acquisition of new liabilities is an important source of liquidity. By managing short-term assets and liabilities, short-run liquidity adjustment patterns are determined by the preferences of bank management, subject to market, technological, and regulatory constraints.

For longer-term liquidity needs, bank management once focused exclusively on asset management. Most bank funds took the form of deposits from individuals located in the bank's market area. While these sources are still rather reliable, competition from other financial services firms and the payment of interest on checkable deposits have meant that traditional deposit sources cannot be taken for granted. Over the past two decades, therefore, banks have turned to purchased liabilities, including large-denomination certificates of deposit, Federal funds, repurchase agreements, acceptances, and, in the case of bank holding companies, Eurodollar loans and commercial paper. These sources are volatile and, under certain economic conditions, unreliable. The proper management of these sources together with the acquisition of capital determine a bank's scale of operations. Once the scale of operations is determined and the liability mix is known, the bank may decide how to allocate funds among various loans and investments.

Perhaps the most controversial area of concern in recent years has been bank capital adequacy. Rapid expansion has required heavy reliance on external debt. Equity financing has been shunned because of possible earnings dilution and the more attractive financial leverage provided by debt financing. Increased fixed-interest expenses, however, raise the risk of fluctuations in earnings at the same time that the debt-financed expansion raises credit risk.

The "mismatched" nature of a bank's balance sheet exposes it to the risk that interest rates will change the relationship between interest income and interest expense, creating a "gap" which modern bankers must learn to manage. Increasingly, *duration analysis* is being used to measure this gap. Once measured, however, there is considerable controversy over how to handle it. Can it be "managed" profitably by interest rate forecasting? Should the risk of interest rate changes be reduced by hedging? How should bank lending policy be affected?

In the opening selection of this volume, Thomas Havrilesky presents a survey of the microeconomic theory of the banking firm. He focuses on a theory of how banks who are not essentially risk averse in short-term and intermediate-term planning periods behave as profit maximizers. (A complementary model of the risk-averse banking firm is provided in the third reading by Drabenstott and McDonley). Havrilesky begins by reviewing the reasons underlying the existence of banks. Then, for the short-term planning period, he presents a model of liquidity management. For the intermediate-term planning period, the author provides a model of loan, investments, and deposits management. Both models require only a minimal math background and can be easily followed by most students. Havrilesky also gives introductory analyses of the problems of interest rate risk (gap management and hedging) and the bank capital decision. (These topics are developed in greater detail by other articles in this section.) Havrilesky's work is cross-referenced to recent literature in the field and includes an extensive bibliography.

While Havrilesky's opening article emphasizes *theory,* the remaining essays in this section offer more of an "applied" approach. The second reading by John Gildea, written especially for this volume, discusses the "how-to" of asset-liability management. Gildea surveys various methods of asset-liability management, paying particular attention to the ways in which banks handle the interest rate risk associated with mismatched balance sheets. Gildea's article provides a detailed discussion of the use of duration analysis to measure the gap, the possibility of managing the gap by forecasting interest rates, and the use of hedging to reduce interest rate risk. The discussion is also cross-referenced to recent literature in the field, and a basic bibliography is provided.

The opening selection in the book by Havrilesky treats the theory of the banking firm as though bank management is not essentially risk averse. Risk-averse models of bank behavior are cited but discussed only briefly. The third reading in this collection, by Mark Drabenstott and Anne O'Mara McDonley, is a simplified model of the bank firm whose management is assumed to be risk averse. Within this model, Drabenstott and McDonley provide a detailed example of bank hedging to reduce interest rate risk. Thus, this contribution is an excellent complement to the survey articles by both Gildea and Havrilesky.

The fourth article, by George Kaufman, continues this complementarity by providing a clear discussion of his seminal work (with Bierwag and Toevs) on duration analysis. His penetrating article adds rich detail to Gildea's thematic survey and serves as an excellent backdrop for the discussion of hedging by Drabenstott and McDonley.

Up to this point the readings have covered the bank's balance sheet as a whole, with special emphasis on problems associated with interest rate volatility. However, as indicated by Havrilesky's opening essay, bank management is also concerned with individual asset and deposit categories. In the fifth reading in this book, Randall Merris takes a detailed look at loan management practices of large banks. Consistent with Gildea's observations on asset-liability management to reduce interest rate risk, Merris cites a number of fascinating new methods for reducing interest rate risk through loan management. Merris' contribution is representative of many current innovations in banking operations.

One of the most revolutionary developments in loan management is the changing role of the prime rate of interest. In the modern era of volatile interest rates, the prime has assumed various meanings. In a most timely article, the sixth in this collection, Brian Gendreau discusses the latest developments in the prime rate convention. Gendreau's article can be profitably read in conjunction with all of the preceding articles on interest rate risk.

Theory-of-the-Firm Models of Bank Behavior

Thomas M. Havrilesky

1

Introduction

This article presents a theory of bank behavior from the perspective of the microeconomic theory of the firm in a manner which is both understandable to most students of banking and relevant to the competitive behavior of modern banking (financial services) firms. The approach is based on the assumption that the banking firm's only objective is to maximize profit (or the value of the bank's net worth to its stockholders). This assumption is the basis for models of the banking firm proposed by Klein (1971), Porter (1961), Wood (1975), and Orr and Mellon (1961).

An alternative approach is to assume that the banking firm behaves essentially like a risk-averse investor.[1] However, this alternative approach elicits two objections: first, it may be unrealistic and, second, it requires a knowledge of mathematical statistics which

[1]It may not be necessary to model bank management as being *essentially* risk averse. Risk may be hedged efficiently in the portfolios of investors in bank equity and, therefore, need not be systematically hedged by management of all banks. This view is challenged in papers by Fama (1980), Santomero (1983), and Draper and Hoag (1978) which present arguments that bank management can always and everywhere hedge more efficiently than investors and therefore is systematically rewarded for doing so. In light of these objections, a companion reading in this volume by Mark Drabenstott and Anne O'Mara McDonley models bank behavior from a risk-averse perspective. While they claim that risk averse behavior is more likely to be found in the management of smaller banks, their article is based on the seminal banking firm models of Parkin (1970), Pyle (1971), Hart and Jaffee (1971), Koehn and Santomero (1980), and Sealey (1980), which employ the view that all bank management is essentially risk averse.

Adapted for this volume from Thomas M. Havrilesky and John T. Boorman, *Monetary Macroeconomics* (Arlington Heights, IL: Harlan Davidson, Inc., 1978), pp. 83–86.

the general reader may not have. Therefore, the risk-averse approach is treated only briefly in this discussion. However, it is covered in more detail in a subsequent article by Drabenstott and McDonley.

The Existence of Banks

There are essentially three reasons for the existence of banking firms. First, as suggested by Klein (1973) and Kane and Buser (1979), the banking firm is able to transform, at low transactions cost, large denomination assets (bank loans and investments) into small, more liquid ones (bank deposits). Second, as pointed out by Pyle (1971) and Sealey (1980; 1983), the bank can exploit opportunities for expected profit because it is able to pay explicit interest rates on deposits that are less than rates earned on loans and investments. This differential, in turn, suggests that deposit customers substitute (liquid) depository services for explicit interest income.

These two reasons lead to the more general view of a bank as an *asset-transformer* with a mismatched balance sheet (consisting of short-term [liquid] depository liabilities and longer-term assets). Because its balance sheet is mismatched, the bank, rather than its depositors, must deal with the risk of interest rate changes, that is, interest rate risk. This risk may be dealt with by different means, such as interest rate forecasting and hedging. Such methods are discussed later in this article and in subsequent essays in this section by Gildea, Kaufman, and Drabenstott and McDonley.[2] The mismatched balance sheet also requires the bank to deal with the risk of borrower default, that is, credit risk.

A third reason for the existence of banking firms is that, as indicated by Leland and Pyle (1977), Campbell and Kracaw (1980), Diamond (1982), and Boyd and Prescott (1983), banks have an informational advantage in evaluating loan applicants which enables them to intermediate profitably. In this sense, the bank serves as a *broker* who provides information (about borrowers) for ''resale'' to its depositors at a profit. We may conclude, therefore, that banks exist because they serve as *asset-transformers* and *brokers*.

In today's environment of financial deregulation, competitive forces are obliterating traditional patterns of institutional specialization. Banking firms are spreading their operations into product lines that transcend the old loans-and-deposits categories. Increasingly, routine financial services such as depository services are being delivered electronically. This approach creates economies of scale and scope with a smaller number of firms serving nationwide markets without the need for labor-intensive methods. (Nonroutine services, such as fixed rate commercial lending, underwriting, and insurance, will probably continue to be labor intensive.) Unable to finance fixed-term commercial loans with short-term variable rate deposit funds, banks will seek to enter markets for long-term fixed rate liabilities such as insurance and pension funds. The traditional separation of banking from certain nonbanking areas may gradually break down under these pressures.

[2]The article by John Gildea surveys the applied literature on managing mismatched balance sheets. Gildea also surveys the recent work by Desmukh, Greenbaum and Kantas (1983), which integrates the applied literature on mismatched balance sheets into the theory of the banking firm. The Kaufman essay shows how *duration analysis* is applied to measuring the mismatch. The selection by Drabenstott and McDonley demonstrates a *hedging approach* to dealing with the mismatched balance sheet.

Nevertheless, as long as an institutional link exists between profitable liquidity (depository) service activities and profitable lending activities, the generic concept of "banks" will continue to survive (perhaps only as operationally separable subdivisions of financial services firms such as the one just described). Of course, much of the continued existence of this link is closely related to the fact that such "banks" are protected from competition by regulatory restrictions. These include (1) restrictions on free entry by nonbanks into "banking's" geographic and product markets (such as limits on chartering of depository institutions); (2) restrictions on free entry by one bank into another "bank's" geographic market (such as branching restrictions); (3) restrictions on "banking" firms' entry into nonbanking markets (such as bank holding company restrictions); and (4) regulatory subsidies in the form of deposit insurance where the premiums are not adjusted for risks assumed by bank management and lender-of-last-resort loans and other assistance to troubled "banks."

Regulatory restrictions and subsidies are likely to go hand in hand, because once government insures deposits in this way and acts as lender-of-last-resort, it encourages bank management to assume more risk. Part of this risk is borne by government. Regulatory restrictions are often intended to reduce the risk imposed by bank management on government. Thus, restrictions will persist as long as government insists on protecting the nation's depository services system. This insistence often seems based on the belief that banking is an inherently unstable industry.

As Diamond and Dybvig (1982) have shown, there is indeed reason to believe that fractional reserve banking will periodically lead to the classic phenomenon of a bank run in which the "output" of the banking industry is abruptly reduced. It should be remembered that, in the absence of entry and exit restrictions, natural market barriers to entry into banking markets (such as huge capitalization requirements) are small. Therefore, as basic microeconomic theory teaches, adjustments in output occur through the entry *and exit* of firms. Exit of banking firms is often seen as damaging to the nation's payments mechanism. Therefore, there is a strong likelihood that government regulatory restrictions will continue to isolate these deposit-taking, asset-transforming/brokering firms, or "banks," thus fostering their survival as separate entities.

A Theory of Asset-Liability Management

"Banks" have profitable opportunities for meeting customer loan demands while maintaining adequate liquidity. In order to meet customer loan demands and satisfy liquidity needs, a bank can attract funds from a wide spectrum of sources.

A useful way to view this process is to see the bank attracting funds from deposits and other sources until the marginal cost of attracting those funds (marginal cost includes interest costs and resource [production] costs borne by the bank) is equal to the marginal return on investments. This marginal return is adjusted downward to reflect legal reserve requirements, if any, on each source of funds. Having determined the total level of funds and the optimal scale of bank operations, management would allocate funds across alternative classes of loans and investments until their respective marginal returns, adjusted for any risk aversion on the part of bank management, are equal.

This view suggests a theory-of-the-firm model of bank behavior. As it involves the manipulation of both assets and liabilities by bank management it may be referred to as a *theory of asset-liability management*.

The simplified model of asset-liability management to be presented here has its roots in the microeconomic theory of the firm. Expected profit maximization is assumed to be the goal of bank management, with the present net worth, loans, and deposits of the bank assumed given over its short-term planning period. However, over a single intermediate-term planning period only net worth is assumed given.[3]

The following balance sheet is given:

$$\bar{L} + V_s + \overline{RR} + FF = \overline{DD} + \overline{TD} + \overline{NW} \tag{1}$$

where: $\bar{L}$ = loans, V_s = short-term government securities, $\overline{RR}$ = required reserves, FF = Federal funds borrowing, $\overline{DD}$ = checkable deposits, $\overline{TD}$ = time deposits, and $\overline{NW}$ = net worth. (A bar over a variable indicates that it is given at the beginning of the planning period.)

Asset-Liability Management: Short-Term Planning (Liquidity Management)

Short-term liquidity management is viewed as an ongoing process that occurs *within* the context of an intermediate-term planning period. Expected cash drains that arise from expected deposit shifts and currency withdrawals and from expected variations in loan repayments and loan demand determine a bank's liquidity needs. The bank then satisfies its net short-term liquidity needs from the multiplicity of sources: excess reserve balances, Federal funds purchases, repurchase agreements, borrowing from the Fed, offerings of short-term negotiable CDs, issues of bank-related commercial paper, Eurodollar borrowing, and the sale of short-term Treasury bills. Net liquidity needs are met from each source until the rising marginal cost of obtaining liquidity from each source is equal to the (fixed) penalty cost at which the bank borrows from the Fed, including all implicit costs perceived by the borrowing bank.

A highly simplified model of short-term liquidity management might be sketched, after DePamphilis (1974), as follows. We assume that required reserves are fixed proportions ρ of checkable deposits and b of time deposits.

$$RR = \rho DD + bTD,\ 0 < \rho,\ b < 1 \tag{2}$$

The legal reserve requirement is an important constraint on bank portfolio management because it requires a bank to hold a certain amount of its assets in a nonearning form.

Uncertainty is built into our model through random aspects of deposit supplies and loan demands. Important constraints on bank management have to do with the volatility of deposit shifts and currency withdrawals, and variations in customer loan demand. These random factors lead to expected cash drains that determine the bank's short-term liquidity

[3]Longer term balance sheet management involving optimal net worth (capital) is considered below. Multi-period planning models are more realistic. Examples of these are described by Goldfeld and Jaffee (1970), Wood (1975), Flannery (1982), and Blackwell and Santomero (1982).

needs. In a more sophisticated model, we could assume that a probability distribution of expected cash drains exists and that the cost associated with an expected level of cash drains rises with the level of deposits and falls with the level of reserves. In such a model there could be implicit and explicit costs to the bank that vary directly with expected cash drains. Explicit costs might include the penalty rate at which banks with reserve deficiencies can borrow reserves from the Federal Reserve. Implicit costs might include the "embarrassment" felt at borrowing from the Fed. However, in the present case our model will be a bit simpler.

We assume that expected cash needs vary in direct proportion to the level of checkable deposits and the level of time deposits. Let these factors of proportionality be α and β, respectively. Assume further that expected cash needs also vary proportionately with the level of loans by a factor γ. The *gross* liquidity needs of the banking firm Q_g are therefore

$$Q_g = \alpha \cdot \overline{DD} + \beta \cdot \overline{TD} + \gamma \cdot \overline{L} \tag{3}$$

where the bars indicate intermediate-term equilibrium values.

Assume for simplicity that instead of the wide array of sources of liquidity cited above there are only three: required reserves, RR; short-term government securities, V_s; and Federal funds purchases, FF. (This truncated set of sources does not affect the realism of the model's implication.) Thus the *sources* of the banking firm's gross liquidity are:

$$Q_g = RR + V_s + FF \tag{4}$$

As required reserves are defined in Equation (2), we may substitute Equation (2) into Equation (4) and the result into Equation (3). Rearranging allows us to equate *net* liquidity needs, Q_n to the means by which these net needs may be satisfied.

$$Q_n = \overline{DD} \cdot (\alpha - \rho) + \overline{TD} \cdot (\beta - b) + \overline{L} \cdot \gamma = V_s + FF \tag{5}$$

Net liquidity needs may be met either by the bank's selling short-term securities, V_s, or by its borrowing in the Federal funds market, FF. A short-run optimum position is obtained where the increasing marginal (interest-opportunity and transactions) cost of selling securities is equal to the given rate at which Federal funds may be borrowed. If considerable liquidity is needed for only a few days, it might be quite costly to sell (and to repurchase) short-term securities. Conversely, if funds were needed for a longer period, repeated Federal funds borrowing might be more costly than the sale of short-term securities.[4]

[4]The theoretical literature in *reserve management* predates and is a subset of the theory of liquidity management. Reserve management considers only the optimal quantity of primary or secondary reserves (RR and V_s in Equation [4], above) to be held subject to losses described in Equation (3) above. The literature includes papers by Orr and Mellon (1971), Poole (1968), Cooper (1971), Frost (1971), Baltensperger (1972, 1974), Brown (1972), Knobel (1977), and Ratti (1979).

Literature on *asset allocation* and *conversion-of-funds* (the matching principle) approaches to bank liquidity management represent specific *applications* of the theory of short-term asset-liability management and liquidity management discussed in this article. A companion article by Gildea in this volume surveys these and other applications of the theory of asset-liability management. Gildea shows how *hedging* and *duration analysis* are applied to gap management.

Within an intermediate-term planning period there are a number of short-term planning periods. Deposit and customer loan variability and the various interest rates will change between short-run periods. Thus, for example, the bank could be a lender of Federal funds and a purchaser of short-term securities in one short-term period and a borrower of Federal funds and a seller of short-term securities in another.

While the distinction between short-term and intermediate-term planning periods is an artificial one, it has the advantage of simplifying our discussion. In reality, the bank's balance sheet undergoes a dynamic adjustment to shocks. For example, if a bank is successful at increasing its level of deposits, it may first hold excess reserves and then loan out these reserves in the Federal funds market. Next, if the new level of deposits persists, it may purchase short-term securities. Finally, if in the intermediate term it regards these deposits as secure, it may fully adjust its portfolio by increasing its loans.[5]

Asset-Liability Management: Intermediate-Term Planning

We focus now on a model of intermediate-term planning. Over the intermediate term, we shall assume for simplicity that cumulative costs of loan and deposit variability and excess or deficient reserves, holdings of short-term securities for liquidity purposes, and Federal funds purchased or sold are zero.

Loans

All loans are assumed to be negotiated directly with bank customers at the beginning of the planning period and to fall due on the last day of the period. There are no loan carryovers from the preceding period and no turnovers during the period. The public's demand curve for loans facing the bank may be viewed as the aggregate of individual demand curves of customers deemed viable by the bank.[6] The demand curve for loan funds is shown in Figure 1. It is assumed that the bank charges a uniform explicit rate to all loan customers at each level of quantity demanded.

The assumption of a uniform loan rate is quite a simplification as it implies that the bank charges the same rate for all loans, provided customers' qualifications exceed some minimum standard.[7] Therefore, one could view this rate as representing the interest rate the

[5]The process of dynamic portfolio-theoretic adjustment to exogenous forecasted changes in deposits using a variety of estimation techniques is discussed by Hester and Pierce (1975).

[6]The loan market is modeled monopolistically here, following suggestions that (1) banks have an informational advantage in local and regional lending as discussed above, (2) banks are protected from competition in this activity by regulatory restrictions on free entry into ''banking's'' geographic and product-line markets, and (3) regulatory subsidies help a bank gain customers. This type of model is also described in Porter (1961), Shull (1963), Klein (1971) and Stillson (1974). In contrast, some risk-aversion models of bank behavior, such as Pyle (1971), Hart and Jaffee (1974), Parker (1970), and Sealey (1980), model the loan market competitively. A subset of the monopolistic model—sticky rate and tied-product models of the loan market—is discussed under *Credit Rationing* below.

[7]Because the demand curve is an aggregate of the demands of individual customers, an increase in the bank's loan standards, a decrease in the credit worthiness of loan customers (say because of a change in default risk), or a decrease in the expected deposits of loan customers could shift the loan demand curve leftward. This would reduce the quantity of loans at any level of the rate. The credit standards of a bank could thus become another variable controlled by bank management. In the interest of simplicity, we ignore this consideration. For a more detailed treatment, see Luckett (1970).

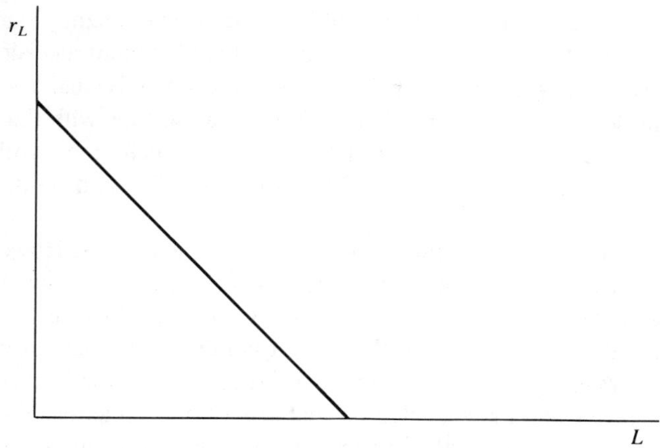

FIGURE 1 Demand for Loans Facing the Bank

bank charges for loans, net of the cost of credit investigations, processing and administering loans; and maintaining relationships with customers. In this analysis the probability of loss through customer default is assumed to be built into each individual customer's loan demand curve.[8] Thus, after holding enough loans to capture the risk-reducing, return-increasing benefits from diversifying the loan portfolio, risk-averse bank managers would hold smaller loan portfolios than risk-neutral ones. (For reasons given at the outset of this article, bank managers are not assumed to be always and everywhere risk averse.)

The linear loan demand relationship shown in Figure 1 is expressed as:

$$r_L = r_0 + a \cdot L \tag{6}$$

where r_0 is the intercept and a is the negative slope parameter; $a < 0$. The dollar level of loans is L, and r_L is the expected rate of return on loans. The magnitudes of these measures, indeed the form of the relation, depend on the factors discussed above: the risk characteristics of bank customers, the production costs of the bank, and the competitive structure of the loan market. Costs of loan variability are not included as they are part of the short-term liquidity management problem discussed earlier. Interest rate risk, the risk that interest rates will undergo significant and unexpected change during the planning period is discussed below in the section entitled *Interest Rate Risk*.

Credit Rationing

As an alternative to the approach used here, we could assume that the bank is confronted by several different classes of loan customers. Further, it is constrained by its legal, social,

[8]Dealing explicitly with default risk would require specifying the probability of loan repayment for each customer. See Broaddus (1972) for an example. Our demand curve represents a cumulative array of customer loans ranked according to their expected rate of return, net of all loan costs including expected default costs. For a model of how such ranking might be derived, see Murphy (1969).

or competitive environment not to charge different profit-maximizing loan rates to each loan class. Therefore, the bank may have to make credit-rationing decisions—rationing credit among the customers it deems viable. In this case each individual customer's default risk and the expected profitability of other business relationships with that customer (for example, expected deposits) are used to determine how much credit will be offered at every possible loan rate. As a result, a "loan offer curve" could be drawn in (r_L, L) space.

The loan offer curve would be upward sloping at lower loan rates. However, as default risk increases with the size of the loan payments, the offer curve would change to a negative slope at higher rates. If the amount of credit demanded by a customer exceeds the amount offered at the going loan rate, then credit is rationed to that customer. Thus the rationing decision will depend upon the marginal expected return on loans to the customer as well as on loan risk and the expected profitability of other relationships with the customer. Obviously, these factors will vary among customers.[9] It is important to note that in this type of model credit rationing relates to the size of a customer's (potential) deposit balance as well as the other continuing business relationships the customer maintains with the bank or related nonbank affiliates.[10]

Securities

The rate of return on United States government securities, r_V, is determined in the market for these securities where the bank is only one of many participants. Therefore, the bank cannot influence this rate; it may acquire whatever volume of government securities it desires at the going market rate, $\bar{r}_V$. It is assumed that the bank does not intend to sell these securities during the intermediate-term planning period. It is further assumed that securities transactions are costless, that securities prices and coupon yields do not change significantly during the planning period, and that securities are held primarily for income purposes.[11] Interest rate risk, the risk that interest rates will change in an unanticipated way during the planning period and thereby affect bank profit, will be discussed below in the section entitled *Interest Rate Risk*.

[9]The model described here is derived from the traditional credit-rationing literature, which includes Freimer and Gordon (1965), Kane and Malkiel (1967), Modigliani and Jaffee (1969), and Slovin and Sushka (1983). This literature has been criticized by Blackwell and Santomero (1982) and others because of the unrealistic assumptions of exact knowledge by banks of loan customer risk characteristics and of stickiness in interest rates. Recent improvements over the traditional literature, Jaffee and Russell (1976), Barro (1976), Stiglitz and Weiss (1981), and Wette (1983), involve informational "adverse selection" models. In these models bank management prefers to clear the loan market by charging a lower-than-equilibrium rate and then rationing credit, rather than clear the market by charging a higher rate and discouraging preferred low-risk borrowers but not high-risk ones.

[10]The credit-rationing approach often underscores the fact that banking loan and deposit markets are not strictly independent. The availability of credit to a loan customer is "tied in" to the size of his or her deposit balances and other continuing relationships with the bank. The classic statement of this view is Hodgman (1961); see also Murphy (1969). For an excellent critique of the credit-rationing approach, see Baltensperger (1978). For an alternative model of the link between loans to customers and subsequent deposits from them based on the "customer relationship," see Wood (1975).

[11]The traditional concentration of commercial banks on customer lending and the volatility of deposits create liquidity problems. As discussed earlier, short-term government securities are one way of satisfying a bank's liquidity needs. However, securities are also a source of income. While the distinction between holding securities for income and holding them for liquidity is not clear-cut, liquidity management is viewed here as a short-term planning problem. In the intermediate-term planning context of this article, securities are held for income.

By these assumptions, the probability of default or temporary unmarketability is virtually nil and the rate of return on government securities is less than or equal to the marginal expected rate of return on loans. This reflects in a fairly simplistic fashion another fundamental constraint on bank portfolio management—a constraint imposed by the nature of the bank's earning assets. The relationship shown in Figure 2 is expressed as:

$$r_v = \bar{r}_v \tag{7}$$

where $\bar{r}_V$ is the money market-determined rate on United States government securities. In essence, securities are available in perfectly elastic supply.[12]

Deposits

Whether one uses theory-of-the-firm models, as we do here, or risk-aversion models, one can no longer realistically regard the level and mix of bank liabilities as given, with all management decision-making focused on the asset side. Today, banks actively compete for funds with other financial services firms in a great many markets. Indeed, short-term liability management is part of the liquidity management problem discussed earlier. Here we are examining liability management within the context of an intermediate-term planning period.

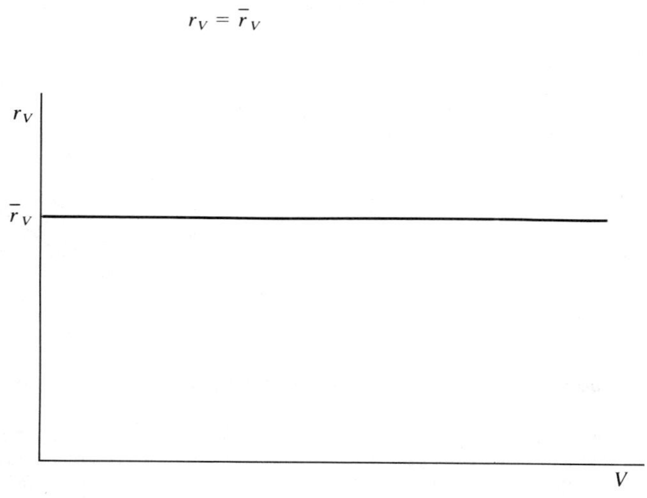

FIGURE 2 Supply of Government Securities Facing the Bank

[12]It has been suggested that Federal funds sales (and purchases) would perform the same role as securities in this context. The validity of the infinite elastic supply curve in the (purely competitive) securities market assumption has been challenged by Pringle (1973) and Miller (1975).

As mentioned at the outset, in the present theory-of-the-firm model, any risk characteristics relevant to an individual bank's management are assumed to be "built in" to the demand and supply relations facing the banking firm, and expected profit is maximized. In contrast, in the risk-aversion approach to bank modeling, the risk-return characteristics of each asset (loans and securities) are exogenously determined and all banking firms are seen as making the standard expected utility-maximizing choice, *a la* mean-variance portfolio theory.

Figure 3 reflects this competitive situation in a fairly simplistic fashion. It depicts the two areas in which banks actively attempt to "attract" funds: the market for checkable deposits and the market for time deposits. We assume that the average total cost of attracting checkable deposits, C_{DD}, and the average total cost of attracting time deposits, C_{TD}, vary positively and linearly with checkable and time deposit volume, respectively. We further assume that these costs are expressed as pure numbers, that is, the average number of cents expended per dollar, such as explicit interest payments on deposits and real resource (production) costs. (Production costs could include account maintenance and service costs not fully charged to the customer, and advertising and promotional expenditures.) However, costs of deposit variability associated with short-term planning are not included as they are part of the liquidity management problem discussed earlier.[13] In the interest of simplicity we assume that all deposits are zero at the outset of the planning period and are attracted by the bank during the period.[14]

The relations shown in Figure 3 are expressed as follows:

$$C_{DD} = C_{DD_0} + g \cdot DD \tag{8}$$

$$C_{TD} = C_{TD_0} + m \cdot TD \tag{9}$$

where $C_{DD_0} < 0$, $C_{TD_0} < 0$, and $g > m > 0$. The parameter, C_{DD_0}, reflects the fact that checkable deposits would be positive even if a bank expended nothing to attract them and that it could attract some deposits even if it paid zero interest, charged customers for all

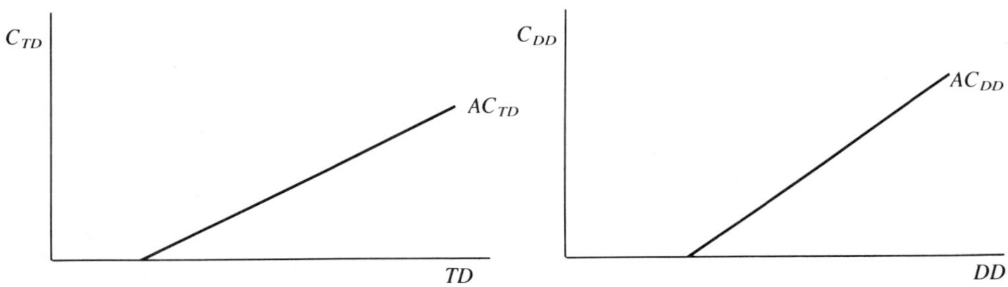

FIGURE 3 Supply Curves of Time and Checkable Deposits Facing the Bank

[13]We abstract from the problem that some costs of attracting deposits vary with the *number* of deposit accounts rather than their *size* and that many costs cannot be attributed separately to either checkable deposits, time deposits, or loans. That is, the cost relations, in reality, are unlikely to be independent and may include elements of overhead. The inclusion of per-account production costs and/or overhead is associated with the work of Klein and Murphy (1971) and Sealey and Lindley (1977).

Within the framework of interdependent deposit and loan cost functions, it is impossible to separate asset decisions from liability structure decisions. Adar, Agmon, and Orgler (1975) suggest a new departure in this area: the specification of joint production costs. For a multi-period planning model of the joint loan/deposit relationship see Wood (1975).

[14]Time and deposit variability may be viewed either separately or as related processes. They can be measured either as the dispersion of deposit balances about some average level during the planning period (see Broaddus [1972]), or as deposit turnover (see Klein and Murphy [1971]). Deposit (and loan) variability were considered part of the short-term, liquidity management problem discussed earlier.

depository services, and did not advertise or promote these services. The parameter, $0 < g < \infty$, reflects the fact that the supply of checkable deposit funds is not infinitely elastic at a rate determined in a purely competitive market.

This situation occurs in part because entry into and exit from the business of producing depository services is limited by various government restrictions. (These include bank holding company regulations, chartering and branching restrictions, and other means of limiting entry by other financial services firms into the "bank's" geographic and deposit product-line markets.) In addition, the supply of checkable deposit funds is not infinitely elastic because government provides low-cost deposit insurance and lender-of-last-resort subsidies to these institutions. Each depository institution, therefore, has a degree of "monopoly power." The positive parameter, C_{TD_0}, reflects the notion that a bank would have a small residual level of time deposits even if it paid no interest on these funds and expended no resources in attracting them. This situation occurs because the bank's monopoly power in the checkable deposit and loan markets enables it to attract some time deposit funds from its checkable deposit customers, even if it does not pay interest on its time deposits. The parameter, $0 < m < \infty$, reflects the fact that the supply of time deposit funds is not infinitely elastic at a rate determined in a purely competitive market.

Both relations have positive slopes, but the average cost of "attracting" time deposits rises less quickly than the average cost of attracting checkable deposits. The graphs reflect a comparatively lower elasticity of supply for checkable than for time deposits. These differences are accounted for by the existence of somewhat more intensive price and nonprice competition for time deposit funds among financial services firms and issuers of marketable securities.[15]

The Capital Decision

Since ours is an intermediate-term model, we do not cover planned longer term borrowing by banks to sustain an increase in bank lending and investing activity. Thus, the capital or net worth position of the banking firm is assumed to be given. In the long run, bank capital can be increased either through retained earnings or through the issuance of new securities or long-term subordinated debt. Like the deposit relations, these sources of bank capital would vary positively with average cost. Of course, as pointed out by Modigliani and Miller's seminal work (1958), in a perfectly competitive unregulated environment no optimal capital structure exists. Therefore, we could introduce banking regulation to our model by imposing a "bank soundness constraint." This constraint would weight each asset, liability, and capital category by parameters imposed by regulatory authorities. The model could then be solved subject to this additional constraint (see Mingo and Wolkowitz [1977]).

[15]Because of the competitive structure of deposit markets, as yields on marketable securities rise, commercial banks may reduce service charges on checkable deposits and/or increase advertising and promotional efforts to attract time and checkable deposits. See Havrilesky and Schweitzer (1975).

Where costs of deposit account activity are shared by customer and bank, Mitchell (1979) shows that implicit interest payments result, and Flannery (1982) demonstrates that such an arrangement accounts for less volatility in explicit deposit rates of interest. This type of literature is probably obsolete because the era is past of underpricing depository services to counter legal ceilings on deposit interest rates, and thereby attract deposits.

Alternatively, where loan and deposit markets are not perfectly competitive, as in the present model, resulting excess profits imply that capital can be attracted at less than the given risk-adjusted competitive market rate, r_v. An optimal level of capital may then be found where the resulting rising marginal cost of capital satisfies the profit-maximizing condition discussed below. Where the level of capital consistent with the "bank soundness constraint" exceeds this optimum level, the firm might attempt to offset the effect of this limit by absorbing more risk in its asset/liability configuration. This reasoning suggests that effective banking regulation should be premised on a familiarity with the theory of the banking firm.[16]

Interest Rate Risk

In today's environment of volatile interest rates it is, of course, unrealistic to assume that interest rates earned on loans and securities and paid on deposits will not change significantly in the planning period of the bank. When interest rates do change, the subsequent impact on bank earnings depends on whether assets are more rate sensitive than liabilities—reflecting the rate-sensitive funds gap. For instance, when the level of interest rates rises significantly and unexpectedly within the intermediate-term planning period and if deposits are more rate sensitive than loans and securities (that is, if the gap is negative), then bank profits suffer. Conversely, if loans and securities are more rate sensitive and can be turned over at a lower cost than deposits (that is, if the gap is positive), then bank profits would improve.

Within a "gap" framework, once the gap is defined, the banking firm has a number of options. One option is *managing* the difference between rate-sensitive assets and rate-sensitive liabilities (that is, managing the gap), depending on interest rate forecasts. Another option is *hedging* in futures markets to reduce unanticipated changes in profits. However, there are a number of theoretical and empirical criticisms regarding the plausi-

[16]Optimal capital models based on less-than-competitive loan and deposit markets include Pringle (1974), Taggart and Greenbaum (1978), and Orgler and Taggart (1983). A risk-aversion, portfolio approach to similar optimal capital calculations is provided by Kahane (1977), while O'Hara (1983) describes a dynamic model. Essays by Koehn and Santomero (1980), Talmor (1980), and Santomero and Vinso (1977) integrate the probability of failure considerations into the optimal capital decision.

Central to these discussions is the insistence of government on protecting the nation's payments mechanism. As a lender of last resort, government provides banks with the incentive to substitute earning assets for cash, thereby endangering bank solvency at any level of bank capital and passing risk on to taxpayers. As a result of this precarious situation, government imposes various entry, pricing, product-line, and geographic restrictions on banks to inhibit their risk-assuming activities. As an insurer of deposits, government eliminates default risk for depositors, thereby reducing a bank's need for capital and passing more risk on to taxpayers. Taxpayers become, in essence, risk takers and, hence, *de facto* equity owners of the nation's banking system. This, in turn, has led to further governmental, product-line, supervisory, and monitoring restrictions on banks, again to inhibit their risk-assuming activities.

The extensive literature on bank capital adequacy, bank monitoring, disclosure of bank risk taking, and bank failure is closely related to this discussion. For further information, see the articles in this volume by Greenbaum and Higgins on financial innovation; Benston and Ehlen (1983) on capital adequacy; Putnam (1983) on monitoring; Gilbert (1983) on disclosure; and Mayer (1975) on bank failure. In addition, articles in this volume by Greenbaum and Higgins, Kane, and Eisenbeis suggest that the aforementioned regulatory restrictions often encourage rather than inhibit risk-assuming activities by banks.

bility of both these options. Suffice it to say that the problem of interest rate risk significantly modifies the theory of the banking firm presented here.[17]

Profit Maximization

We assume that the objective of bank management is to maximize profit during its intermediate-term planning period. Profits or losses associated with short-term planning are not considered here as they are part of the liquidity management problem discussed earlier. The planning period is defined to be long enough to permit the bank to control all of its decision variables. This time span can be fairly short, perhaps no more than three months. If we assume that all profit is retained (none is paid out as dividends), we can also assume that the bank maximizes the increase in its net worth. In order to maximize profit, funds must be attracted in both deposit markets until the marginal cost of attracting deposit funds in both markets is equal to the marginal rate the bank can earn on the earning assets it can obtain with these funds.

We may derive the profit-maximizing levels of both types of deposits. First we multiply average total cost, expressed as a pure number, an average (interest) rate, per dollar of deposits in Equations (8) and (9), by the level of deposits in order to obtain the total cost relation in dollars:

$$DD \cdot C_{DD} = C_{DD_0} \cdot DD + g \cdot DD^2 \tag{10}$$

$$TD \cdot C_{TD} = C_{TD_0} \cdot TD + m \cdot TD^2 \tag{11}$$

The marginal costs of attracting deposits, expressed as marginal (interest) rates, are the first derivatives of the quadratic total cost functions, the right-hand sides of Equations (10) and (11).

$$\frac{d(DD \cdot C_{DD})}{dDD} = C_{DD_0} + 2 \cdot g \cdot DD \tag{12}$$

$$\frac{d(TD \cdot C_{TD})}{dTD} = C_{TD_0} + 2 \cdot m \cdot TD \tag{13}$$

The profit-maximizing bank will attract deposits until the marginal cost of each type of deposit is equal to the marginal rate at which earnings can be generated from that source of funds. There are two factors which determine the marginal rate. The first is the rate of interest determined in the market for United States government securities. This interest

[17] A sizable applied literature has grown around this subject and is surveyed in the companion article in this volume by John Gildea. Following the survey, Mark Drabenstott and Anne O'Mara McDonley develop a model of *hedging* behavior by a risk-averse bank as a means of dealing with the gap. Finally, George Kaufman in his article shows how *duration analysis* may be used to measure the gap.

rate is used because, while both loans and securities are earning assets, in equilibrium loans are made until the marginal loan rate is equal to the given market rate on securities. The second factor, which determines the percentage of each dollar of deposit funds that can be invested in earning assets, is the legal reserve requirement on each type of deposits. Thus one dollar of checkable deposits can be invested in only $(1 - \rho)$ of a dollar of earning assets, and one dollar of time deposits can be invested in $(1 - b)$ of a dollar of earning assets. Therefore, the profit-maximizing condition may be expressed as:

$$C_{DD_0} + 2 \cdot g \cdot DD = \bar{r}_V(1 - \rho) \tag{14}$$

$$C_{TD_0} + 2 \cdot m \cdot TD = \bar{r}_V(1 - b) \tag{15}$$

The resulting expressions may be rearranged in order to solve for the profit-maximizing levels of checkable and time deposits, denoted as $\overline{DD}$ and $\overline{TD}$, respectively.[18]

$$\overline{DD} = \frac{\bar{r}_V(1 - \rho) - C_{DD_0}}{2 \cdot g} \tag{16}$$

$$\overline{TD} = \frac{\bar{r}_V(1 - b) - C_{TD_0}}{2 \cdot m}. \tag{17}$$

The sum of these two sources of funds plus the net worth at the beginning of the period were given earlier on the right-hand side of Equation (1).

$$L + V_s + RR + FF = \overline{DD} + \overline{TD} + \overline{NW} \tag{1}$$

This provides the scale of the banking operation, that is, the level of its total assets.

Figure 4 shows graphically that the profit-maximizing levels of time and checkable deposits are found where the marginal cost of attracting each class of deposits is equal to the rate earned on United States government securities times one, minus the legal reserve requirement on that class of deposit. Figure 4 also reflects the notion, expressed in Equation (1), that these deposit sources plus net worth determine the total assets of the banking firm.

Not all deposit funds so obtained are available to be invested in earning assets. Equation (2) indicated earlier that portions of checkable and time deposits must be held as required reserves.

$$RR = \rho DD + bTD, \; 0 < \rho, \; b < 1 \tag{2}$$

Substituting Equation (2) into Equation (1) and rearranging the terms leaves the remainder:

[18]Formally, we are maximizing profit (the increase in net worth).

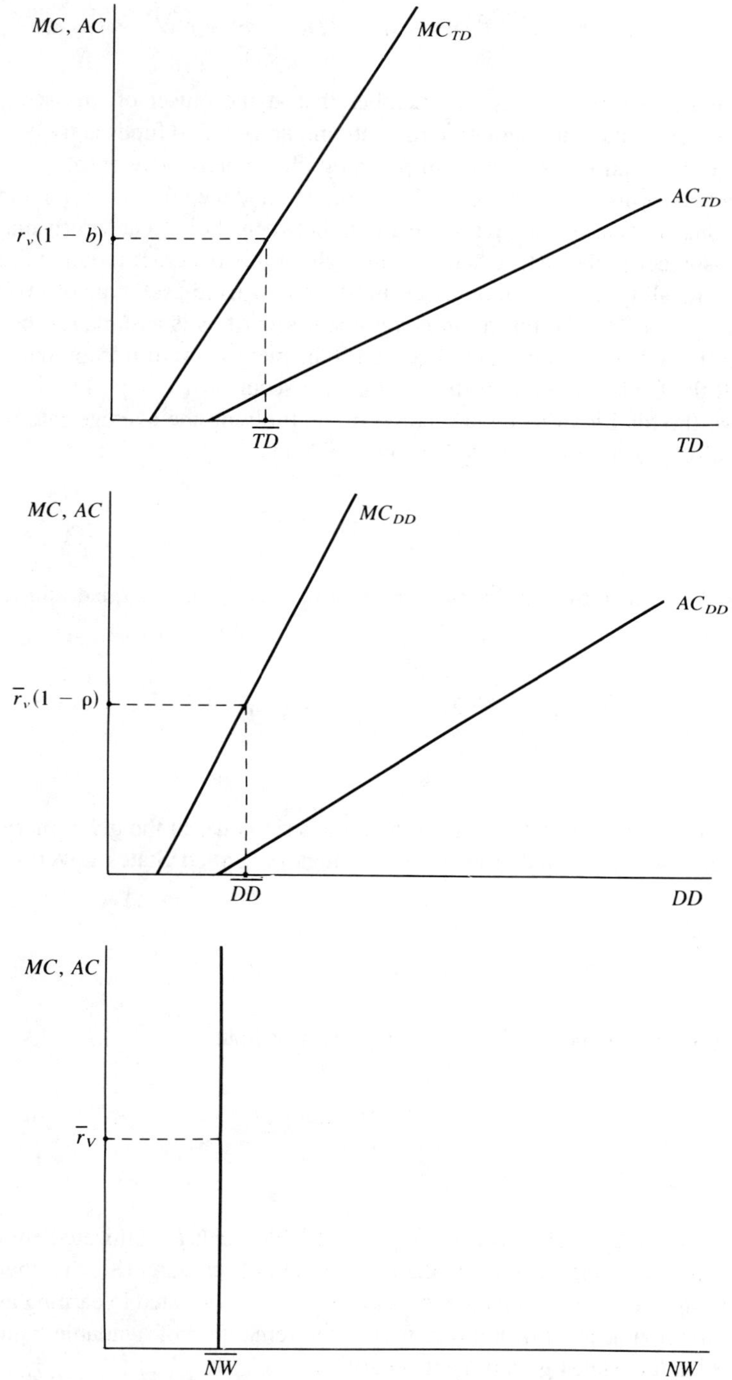

FIGURE 4 Determination of the Profit-Maximizing Level of Time and Checkable Deposits

$$L + V = \overline{DD}(1 - \rho) + \overline{TD}(1 - b) + \overline{NW} \tag{18}$$

to be invested as earning assets. (Remember that at the outset of this section, it was assumed that during the intermediate-term planning period, Fed funds activity, excess and deficient reserves, and other short-term planning phenomena were zero).

There are two forms of earning assets in our model, and the profit-maximizing bank will make a rational allocation of investable funds between them. The profit-maximization condition is subject to the risks discussed throughout this paper. It requires that funds be allocated across all types of earning assets until the returns to each type of investment are equal at the margin. As the return on government securities is assumed to be given, the profit-maximizing bank will invest in loans until the marginal return from loans is equal to the rate that the bank can earn on these long-term securities.

We derive the total loan revenue relation by multiplying the average rate of return on loans, Equation (6), by the total dollar value of loans:

$$r_L \cdot L = r_0 \cdot L + aL^2 \tag{19}$$

The marginal rate of return on loans is the first derivative of this quadratic function:

$$\frac{d(r_L \cdot L)}{dL} = r_0 + 2 \cdot a \cdot L \tag{20}$$

where a is a negative parameter. This derivative is set equal to the given marginal rate at which earnings are generated from bank holdings of United States government securities,

$$r_0 + 2 \cdot a \cdot L = \bar{r}_V \tag{21}$$

and we may solve for the profit-maximizing level of loans $\bar{L}$:

$$\bar{L} = \frac{\bar{r}_V - r_0}{2 \cdot a} \tag{22}$$

Figure 5 shows graphically how the bank's available funds are allocated among earning assets to maximize profits. It reflects the fact, given in Equation (18), that there is a total funds constraint—only a certain amount is available to be invested in earning assets. After the profit-maximizing level of loans is found, the remainder of available bank funds are allocated to United States government securities.

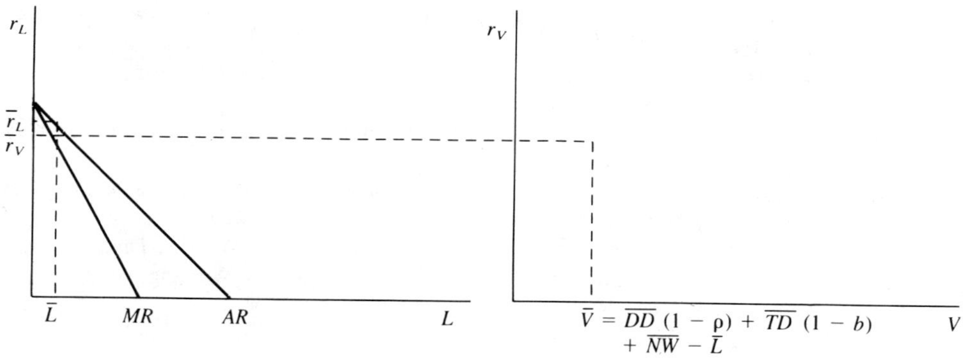

FIGURE 5 Profit-maximizing Allocation of Earning Assets

Concluding Comment

In this article, we presented simple models of a theory of bank asset and liability management. The models are centered on planning periods of short and intermediate lengths. We also discussed bank management's capital decision and credit rationing, the joint selling of credit and depository services, and the problem of mismatched balance sheets and interest rate volatility.

The present analysis indicates how bank management decision making must focus simultaneously on assets and liabilities. It defines the role of the costs of attracting deposit funds and the return on loans and investments. It also explains how profitability considerations impinge upon the decisions of bank management. While in this case bank management is not modeled as being always and everywhere risk averse, because of our model's rather general nature, it can serve as a basis for further study of the theory of the banking firm.

BIBLIOGRAPHY

ADAR, ZVI, TAMIR AGMON, and YAIR E. ORGLER, "Output Mix and Jointness in Production in the Banking Firm," *Journal of Money, Credit and Banking,* 7 (May 1975), 235–43.

AIGNER, DENNIS J., and WILLIAM R. BRYAN, "A Model of Short-Run Bank Behavior," *Quarterly Journal of Economics,* 85 (February 1971), 97–118.

BALTENSPERGER, ERNST, "Economics of Scale, Firm Size and Concentration in Banking," *Journal of Money, Credit and Banking,* 4 (August 1972a), 467–88.

BALTENSPERGER, ERNST, "Costs of Banking Activities—Interactions Between Risk and Operating Costs," *Journal of Money, Credit and Banking,* 4 (August 1972b), 595–611.

BALTENSPERGER, ERNST, "The Precautionary Demand for Reserves," *American Economic Review,* 64 (March 1974), 205–10.

BALTENSPERGER, ERNST, and HELLMUTH MILDE, "Predictability of Reserve Demand, Information Costs, and Portfolio Behavior of Commercial Banks," *Journal of Finance,* 31 (June 1976), 835–43.

BALTENSPERGER, ERNST, "Credit Rationing: Issues and Questions," *Journal of Money, Credit and Banking,* 10 (May 1978), 170–83.

BALTENSPERGER, ERNST, "Alternative Approaches to the Theory of the Banking Firm," *Journal of Monetary Economics,* 6 (January 1980), 1–37.

BARRO, ROBERT J., "The Loan Market, Collateral and Rates of Interest," *Journal of Money, Credit and Banking,* 4 (May 1972), 397–413.

BLACKWELL, NORMAN R., and ANTHONY M. SANTOMERO, "Bank Credit Rationing and the Customer Relation," *Journal of Monetary Economics,* 9 (January 1982), 121–29.

BOYD, JOHN H., and EDWARD C. PRESCOTT, "Financial Intermediaries," Working Paper, 1983.

BROADDUS, ALFRED, "A General Equilibrium Model of Bank Decisions," Working Paper, Federal Reserve Bank of Richmond, 74 (April 1972).

BROWN, GEORGE F., JR., "Optimal Management of Bank Reserves," *Journal of Financial and Quantitative Analysis,* 7 (December 1972), 2031–54.

BRUCKER, ERIC, "A Microeconomic Approach to Banking: Reply," *Journal of Finance,* 27 (June 1982), 724–26.

CAMPBELL, TIM S., "A Model of the Market for Lines of Credit," *Journal of Finance,* 33 (March 1978), 231–44.

CAMPBELL, TIM S., and WILLIAM A. KRACAW, "Information Production, Market Signalling and the Theory of Financial Intermediation: A Reply," *Journal of Finance,* 37 (September 1980), 1097–99.

CHAN, YUK-SHEE, "Information Production, Market Signalling and the Theory of Financial Intermediation: A Comment," *Journal of Finance,* 37 (September 1982), 1095–96.

CHARNES, A., and STEN THORE, "Planning for Liquidity in Financial Institutions: The Chance-Constrained Method," *Journal of Finance,* 21 (December 1966), 649–74.

COHEN, KALMAN J., and FREDERICK S. HAMMER, "Linear Programming and Optimal Bank Asset Management Decisions," *Journal of Finance,* 22 (May 1967), 147–68.

COOPER, J. PHILLIP, "Stochastic Reserve Losses and Expansion of Bank Credit: Note," *American Economic Review,* 61 (September 1971), 741–45.

DAELLENBACH, HANS G., and STEPHEN H. ARCHER, "The Optimal Bank Liquidity: A Multiperiod Stochastic Model," *Journal of Financial and Quantitative Analysis,* 4 (September 1969), 329–43.

DALEY, GEORGE G., "Financial Intermediation and the Theory of the Firm: An Analysis of Savings and Loan Association Behavior," *Southern Economic Journal,* 37 (January 1971), 283–94.

DEPHAMPHILIS, DONALD, "A Microeconomic Analysis of the Short-Term Commercial Bank Adjustment Process," *Research Report,* Federal Reserve Bank of Boston, 55 (April 1974).

DIAMOND, DOUGLAS W., "Financial Intermediation and Delegated Monitoring," Working Paper, 1982.

DIAMOND, DOUGLAS W., and PHILLIP H. DYBVIG, "Bank Runs, Deposit Insurance and Liquidity," *Journal of Political Economy,* (December 1982), 340–71.

DRAPER, DENNIS W., and JAMES W. HOAG, "Financial Intermediation and the Theory of Agency," *Journal of Financial and Quantitative Analysis,* 13 (November 1978), 595–611.

EDGEWORTH, FRANCIS Y., "The Mathematical Theory of Banking," *Journal of Royal Statistical Society,* 51 (March 1888), 113–27.

EHLEN, JAMES G., "A Review of Bank Capital and Its Adequacy," *Economic Review,* Federal Reserve Bank of Atlanta (November 1983), 54–60.

EMERY, JOHN T., "Risk, Return and the Morphology of Commercial Banking," *Journal of Financial and Quantitative Analysis,* 6 (March 1971), 763–76.

FAMA, EUGENE F., "Banking in the Theory of Finance," *Journal of Monetary Economics,* 6 (January 1980), 39–57.

FLANNERY, MARK, "Retail Bank Deposits as Quasi-Fixed Factors of Production," *American Economic Review,* 72 (June 1982), 527–36.

FREIMER, MARSHALL, and MYRON J. GORDON, "Why Bankers Ration Credit," *Quarterly Journal of Economics,* 79 (August 1965), 397–416.

FRIED, JOEL, "Banking Portfolio Selection," *Journal of Financial and Quantitative Analysis,* 5 (June 1970), 203–17.

FRIED, JOEL, and PETER HOWITT, "Credit Rationing and Implicit Contract Theory," *Journal of Money, Credit and Banking,* 12 (August 1980), 471–87.

FROST, PETER A., "Banks' Demand for Excess Reserves," *Journal of Political Economy,* 79 (July/August 1971), 805–25.

GILBERT, GARY, "Disclosure and Market Discipline: Issues and Evidence," *Economic Review,* Federal Reserve Bank of Atlanta (November 1983), 70–76.

GOLDBERG, MICHAEL A., "The Impact of Regulatory and Monetary Factors on Bank Loan Charges," *Journal of Financial and Quantitative Analysis,* 16 (June 1981), 227–46.

GOLDFELD, STEPHEN M., and DWIGHT M. JAFFEE, "The Determinants of Deposit-Rate Setting by Savings and Loan Associations," *Journal of Finance,* 25 (June 1970), 615–32.

GOLDFELD, STEPHEN M., and DWIGHT M. JAFFEE, "Deposit Rate Setting by Savings and Loan Associations: Reply," *Journal of Finance,* 26 (December 1971), 1158–60.

GOLDFELD, STEPHEN M., and EDWARD J. KANE, "The Determinants of Member-Bank Borrowing: An Econometric Study," *Journal of Finance,* 21 (September 1966), 499–514.

HART, OLIVER D., and DWIGHT M. JAFFEE, "On the Application of Portfolio Theory to Depository Financial Intermediaries," *Review of Economic Studies,* 41 (January 1974), 129–47.

HAVRILESKY, THOMAS M., and ROBERT L. SCHWEITZER, "A Model of Non-Price Competition in Banking," *Journal of Bank Research,* 6 (Summer 1975), 113–21.

HODGMAN, DONALD R., "The Deposit Relationship and Commercial Bank Investment Behavior," *Review of Economics and Statistics,* 42 (August 1961), 257–68.

HODGMAN, DONALD R., *Commercial Bank Loan and Investment Policy* (Bureau of Business and Economic Research, University of Illinois, 1963).

JAFFEE, DWIGHT M., and FRANCO MODIGLIANI, "A Theory and Test of Credit Rationing," *American Economic Review,* 59 (December 1969), 850–72.

JAFFEE, DWIGHT M., and THOMAS RUSSELL, "Imperfect Information, Uncertainty, and Credit Rationing," *Quarterly Journal of Economics,* 90 (November 1976), 651–66.

JAMES, CHRISTOPHER, "Self-Selection and the Pricing of Bank Services: An Analysis of the Market for Loan Commitments and the Role of Compensating Balance Requirements," *Journal of Financial and Quantitative Analysis,* 16 (December 1981), 725–46.

KAHANE, Y., "Capital Adequacy and the Regulation of Financial Intermediaries," *Journal of Banking and Finance,* 1 (October 1977), 207–18.

KALAY, AVNER, and RAMON RABINOVITCH, "On Individual Loans Pricing, Credit Rationing and Interest Rate Regulation," *Journal of Finance,* 33 (September 1978), 1071–85.

KANE, EDWARD J., and STEPHEN A. BUSER, "Portfolio Diversification at Commercial Banks," *Journal of Finance,* 34 (March 1979), 19–34.

KANE, EDWARD J., and BURTON MALKIEL, "Deposit Variability, Bank-Portfolio Allocation and the Availability Doctrine," *Quarterly Journal of Economics* (February 1965), 55–69.

KLEIN, MICHAEL A., "A Theory of the Banking Firm," *Journal of Money, Credit and Banking,* 3 (May 1971), 205–18.

KLEIN, MICHAEL A., The Economics of Security Divisibility and Financial Intermediation,'' *Journal of Finance,* 28 (September 1973), 923–31.

KLEIN, MICHAEL A., and NEIL B. MURPHY, ''The Pricing of Bank Deposits: A Theoretical and Empirical Analysis,'' *Journal of Financial and Quantitative Analysis,* 6 (March 1971), 747–61.

KNOBEL, ABRAHAM, ''The Demand for Reserves by Commercial Banks,'' *Journal of Money, Credit and Banking,* 9 (February 1977), 32–47.

KOEHN, MICHAEL, and ANTHONY M. SANTOMERO, ''Regulation of Bank Capital and Portfolio risk,'' *Journal of Finance,* 35 (December 1980), 1235–44.

KOLODONY, RICHARD, PETER SEELEY, and MURRAY E. POLAKOFF, ''The Effect of Compensating Balance Requirements on the Profitability of Borrowers and Lenders,'' *Journal of Financial and Quantitative Analysis,* 12 (December 1977), 801–15.

LELAND, HAYNE E., and DAVID H. PYLE, ''Information Asymmetries, Financial Structure and Financial Intermediation,'' *Journal of Finance,* 32 (May 1977), 371–87.

LUCKETT, DUDLEY, ''Credit Standards and Tight Money,'' *Journal of Money, Credit and Banking,* 2 (November 1970), 420–34.

MILLER, STEPHEN M., ''A Theory of the Banking Firm: Comment,'' *Journal of Monetary Economics,* 1 (January 1975), 123–28.

MINGO, JOHN J., and BENJAMIN WOLKOWITZ, ''The Effects of Regulation on Bank Balance Sheet Decisions,'' *Journal of Finance,* 32 (December 1977), 1605–16.

MITCHELL, DOUGLAS W., ''Explicit and Implicit Demand Deposit Interest,'' *Journal of Money, Credit and Banking,* 11 (May 1979), 182–91.

MITCHELL, DOUGLAS W., ''The Effects of Interest-Bearing Required Reserves on Bank Portfolio Riskiness,'' *Journal of Financial and Quantitative Analysis,* 17 (June 1982), 209–16.

MODIGLIANI, FRANCO, and MERTON H. MILLER, ''The Cost of Capital, Corporation Finance and the Theorem of Investment,'' *American Economic Review,* 48 (June 1958), 261–97.

MONTI, MARIO, ''Deposit, Credit and Interest Rate Determination Under Alternative Bank Objective Functions,'' in *Mathematical Methods in Investment and Finance,* edited by Giorgio P. Szego and Karl Shell (Amsterdam: North Holland Publishing Company, 1972), pp. 430–54.

MURPHY, NEIL B., ''A Study of Wholesale Banking Behavior,'' *Research Report,* Federal Reserve Bank of Boston, 44 (1969).

O'HARA, MAUREEN J., ''Property Rights and the Financial Firm,'' *Journal of Law and Economics* (October 1981), 371–82.

O'HARA, MAUREEN J., ''A Dynamic Theory of the Banking Firm,'' *Journal of Finance,* 38 (March 1983), 127–40.

ORGLER, YAIR E., and ROBERT A. TAGGART, JR., ''Implications of Corporate Capital Structure Theory for Banking Institutions,'' *Journal of Money, Credit and Banking,* 15 (May 1983), 212–21.

ORR, DANIEL, and W. G. MELLON, ''Stochastic Reserve Losses and Expansion of Bank Credit,'' *American Economic Review,* 51 (September 1961), 614–23.

PARKIN, M., ''Discount House Portfolio and Debt Selection,'' *Review of Economic Studies,* 37 (October 1970), 469–97.

POOLE, WILLIAM, ''Commercial Bank Reserve Management in a Stochastic Model: Implications for Monetary Policy,'' *Journal of Finance,* 23 (December 1968), 769–91.

PORTER, RICHARD C., ''A Model of Bank Portfolio Selection,'' *Yale Economic Essays,* 1 (Fall 1961), 323–59.

PRATT, J. W., ''Risk Aversion in the Small and in the Large,'' *Econometrica,* 32 (January 1964), 15–27.

PRINGLE, JOHN J., "A Theory of the Banking Firm: A Comment," *Journal of Money, Credit and Banking,* 5 (November 1973), 990–96.

PRINGLE, JOHN J., "The Capital Decision in Commercial Banks," *Journal of Finance,* 28 (June 1974), 779–95.

PUTNAM, BARRON, "Early Warning Systems and Financial Analysis in Bank Monitoring," *Economic Review,* Federal Reserve Bank of Atlanta (November 1983), 6–13.

PYLE, DAVID H., "On the Theory of Financial Intermediation," *Journal of Finance,* 26 (June 1971), 737–47.

PYLE, DAVID H., "Descriptive Theories of Financial Institutions Under Uncertainty," *Journal of Financial and Quantitative Analysis,* 26 (December 1972), 2009–31.

RATTI, RONALD A., "Stochastic Reserve Losses and Bank Credit Expansion," *Journal of Monetary Economics,* 5 (April 1979), 283–94.

SANTOMERO, ANTHONY M., "The Role of Transaction Costs and Rates of Return on the Demand Deposit Decision," *Journal of Monetary Economics,* 5 (July 1979), 343–64.

SANTOMERO, ANTHONY M., *Current Views of the Bank Capital Issue* (Washington D.C.: Association of Reserve City Bankers, 1983).

SANTOMERO, ANTHONY M., "Fixed Versus Variable Rate Loans," *Journal of Finance,* 38 (December 1983), 1571–79.

SANTOMERO, ANTHONY M., and JOSEPH D. VINSO, "Estimating the Probability of Failure for Commercial Banks and the Banking System," *Journal of Banking and Finance,* 1 (September 1977), 1267–82.

SEALEY, C. W., JR., "Deposit Rate-Setting, Risk Aversion and The Theory of Depository Financial Intermediaries," *Journal of Finance,* 35 (December 1980), 1139–54.

SEALEY, C. W., JR., "Valuation, Capital Structure, and Shareholder Unanimity for Depository Financial Intermediaries," *Journal of Finance,* 38 (June 1983), 857–71.

SEALEY, C. W., JR., and JAMES T. LINDLEY, "Inputs, Outputs and a Theory of Production and Cost at Depository Financial Institutions," *Journal of Finance,* 32 (September 1977), 1251–66.

SHULL, BERNARD, "Commercial Banks as Multiple Product Price Discriminating Firms," in D. Carson, ed., *Banking and Monetary Studies* (Homewood, IL: Richard D. Irwin, 1963). Slovin, Myron B., and Marie Elizabeth Sushka, "A Model of the Commercial Loan Rate," *Journal of Finance,* 38 (December 1983), 1583–96.

STARTZ, RICHARD, "Competition and Interest Rate Ceilings in Commercial Banking," *Quarterly Journal of Economics,* 98 (May 1983), 255–65.

STIGLITZ, JOSEPH E., and ANDREW WEISS, "Credit Rationing In Markets with Imperfect Information," *American Economic Review,* 71 (June 1981), 393–410.

STIGUM, MARCIA L., "Some Further Implications of Profit Maximization by a Savings and Loan Association," *Journal of Finance,* 31 (December 1976), 1405–26.

STILLSON, RICHARD T., "An Analysis of Information and Transaction Services in Financial Institutions," *Journal of Money, Credit and Banking,* 6 (November 1974), 517–35.

TAGGART, ROBERT A., JR., and STUART I. GREENBAUM, "Bank Capital and Public Regulations," *Journal of Money, Credit and Banking,* 10 (May 1978), 158–69.

TALMOR, ELI, "A Normative Approach to Bank Capital Adequacy," *Journal of Financial and Quantitative Analysis,* 15 (November 1980), 785–811.

THAKOR, ANJAN V., "Toward a Theory of Bank Loan Commitments," *Journal of Banking and Finance,* 6 (March 1982), 55–83.

THAKOR, ANJAN V., STUART I. GREENBAUM and HAI HONG, "Bank Loan Commitments and Interest Rate Volatility," *Journal of Banking and Finance,* 5 (December 1981), 471–510.

TOWEY, RICHARD W., ''Money Creation and the Theory of the Banking Firm,'' *Journal of Finance,* 29 (March 1974), 57–72.

WEBER, G. S., ''Interest Rates on Mortgages and Dividend Rates on Savings and Loan Shares,'' *Journal of Finance,* 21 (September 1966), 515–21.

WETTE, HILDEGARD C., ''Collateral in Credit Rationing in Markets with Imperfect Information,'' *American Economic Review,* 73 (June 1983), 170–83.

WOOD, JOHN, *Commercial Bank Loan and Investment Behavior* (New York: John Wiley and Sons, 1975).

VOJTA, GEORGE, *Bank Capital Adequacy* (New York: Citicorp, 1973).

ASSET/LIABILITY MANAGEMENT

John Gildea

2

The responsibility for profitably allocating assets and liabilities to achieve consistently high after-tax rates of return on equity while providing for sufficient liquidity and an adequate capital base remains the *raison d'être* of bank managers. What has changed in recent years, however, is the environment in which bank managers find themselves performing their duties. Since 1970, the U.S. economy has been subject to a continual barrage of private supply and government deficit demand shocks coupled with an erratic and unpredictable monetary policy. In addition, the removal of ceilings on deposit interest rates, technological improvements in the cost of transferring funds, and related depository innovations such as money market deposit accounts have reduced the interest elasticity of the demand for money. One result of this scenario has been a dramatic increase in the volatility of interest rates. For example, the prime rate changed more times in the four-year period 1970–1973, inclusive, than in the previous thirty-five years. Moreover, the rate swings have been as large as an 850 basis point drop in 68 days during the second quarter of 1980.

This article was written especially for this volume. I would like to thank Thomas Havrilesky for his suggestions and comments.

Interest rate instability, however, is just one of the many factors that have contributed to the changing environment confronting the banking industry. In the 1970s Regulation Q ceilings, greater depositor sophistication with respect to cash management techniques, and the introduction of money market mutual funds led to disturbing amounts of disintermediation. In the deregulated environment of the 1980s, increased competition from thrift institutions and other financial services firms including financial supermarkets, money market funds, and money management accounts has intensified the pursuit of low-cost funds. Add to this the growing burden of noninterest expense (production costs) on banks' income statements in this era of geographic and product-line proliferation, the decreasing propensity to save in the economy, and the recent reregulatory reaction and one begins to understand the strains being felt in the banking industry.

To deal with these evolutionary changes, bank managers now stress the importance of coordinated management of both assets and liabilities. Increasingly, banks rely on an overall planning strategy for the acquisition and allocation of funds to provide for maximum earnings while ensuring adequate liquidity and capital. The purpose of this article is to review five of the asset/liability management methods currently being practiced by banks so as to provide an understanding of how bankers are adapting to their changing environment. We discuss the experience method, the asset allocation method, the conversion of funds method, the liability management method, and the gap management method.[1] The gap management method is analyzed in greater detail because it promises to be the most fruitful path for bank management to follow. The use of futures markets within a gap management framework affords a particularly profitable and efficient means for management to deal with risk and therefore is included in this discussion. Also within this framework, the concept of duration as it applies to a financial institution's assets and liabilities is examined as another measure of interest rate risk.

While each method is presented separately, one should not infer that banks must rely on only one asset/liability management method. Depending upon the sophistication of bank management and the resources available, several of these methods may be compatible with one another and thus may be employed simultaneously.

I. Experience Method

The experience method of asset/liability management is the least demanding in terms of both analysis and cost. Basically, banks that rely on this method believe strongly in the ability of a few strategically placed people not only to assess market conditions and industry trends but also to make common sense decisions, sometimes on a case-by-case basis, that will maintain desired income, liquidity, and capital levels. Generally, banks that use this approach are smaller institutions which are constrained by their rudimentary accounting systems and thus have limited quantitative information but which possess a thorough knowledge of their clientele and local economic environment.

[1]This classification and discussion draws on material presented by James V. Baker in "Asset Liability Management," *Banking*, June-October 1978.

Not so surprisingly, these smaller banks perform quite well in their local markets. While some of the credit should rightfully be given to the expertise of their managers, much of it is attributed to the less-than-competitive environment these firms enjoy. An established smaller bank has a sound deposit base built upon years of trust and convenience with which more remote larger banks and other financial service firms cannot immediately and directly compete. However, as bank and nonbank financial service firms begin to penetrate the smaller markets and offer more diverse product lines, smaller banks will have to adopt more aggressive and sophisticated strategies. To do so, they must first develop or tie into in-depth accounting procedures and quantitative forecasting techniques.[2]

II. Asset Allocation Method

The asset allocation method is both straightforward and relatively simple to implement. It is quite compatible with the experience method discussed above. To understand asset allocation one simply needs to consider the priorities inherent in this approach. A bank manager using this method is mainly concerned with maintaining an adequate liquidity level. After allocating sufficient capital for the fixed assets necessary to support a banking operation, the manager then sets aside funds to meet the legal reserve requirements. Since these funds will be in noninterest-bearing form such as cash and Federal Reserve deposits, they are kept to a minimum. The manager's next concern is to provide for the liquidity needed to respond to the variability of loan demand and deposit levels. This is done by forecasting the future amounts of these variables and then allocating sufficient funds into various short-term marketable securities.[3]

Having thus provided for the bank's liquidity needs, the bank manager's next concern is to generate income. Funds are now channeled into the booking of those loans from creditworthy customers which yield higher rates of return than those available on long-term securities of similar risk. Any funds remaining after this step are simply invested into these longer-term securities.

While this approach is relatively easy to understand, it is clearly not optimal with respect to the link between interest rate risk and bank earnings. This method would have bank managers investing in securities when loan demand, and thus interest rates, are low and selling securities when loan demand, and thus interest rates, are high. The more volatile the interest rates, the larger the capital losses banks will be forced to write off. With interest rates becoming more volatile in recent years, bank managers prescribing to the asset allocation method are putting bank earnings and bank stockholders in a very precarious position.

[2]The articles in sections II and III of this book discussed geographic and product-line expansion and the technologies that financial services firms, large and small alike, are likely to adopt in the future.

[3]The preceding article by Havrilesky in this volume describes the theory and application of liquidity management. His discussion is consistent with methods two, three, and four in this article.

III. Conversion of Funds Method

Similar to the asset allocation method, the conversion of funds method of asset/liability management also tacitly assumes that the bank's liquidity concern is the number one short-run priority of bank managers. However, this approach differs from the asset allocation method in how funds are handled. Instead of allocating liquid assets to meet deposit and loan variability, the conversion of funds method attempts to match long-term assets to stable liabilities and stable loan demands and short-term assets to volatile liabilities and volatile loan demands. This application of the matching principle is accomplished by classifying each liability and loan type according to its volatility over time. For example, small checkable and time deposits are typically more stable in terms of dollar amounts over time than are large checkable and time deposits. Accordingly, a high percentage of the stable checkable and time deposits are used to fund the longer-term liabilities such as home mortgages while the more volatile liabilities are used to purchase short-term money market instruments. In this way a bank is limited in its asset funding by the volatility of its liabilities and loan demands.

For this approach to work well a great deal of flexibility is required. The percentages of funds allotted to certain assets may need frequent adjustments as loan demands, liability volatility, credit risk, and the level of interest rates change. Allowing for this flexibility, the conversion of funds method more thoroughly insulates bank earnings from a changing financial market environment than does the asset allocation approach. However, both approaches still neglect the bank's need to respond to possible interest rate risk. The revaluation of assets and liabilities within as short a time span as ninety days because of unexpected interest rate changes may adversely affect bank earnings in the short run.

IV. Liability Management Method

The liability management method was developed in response to the problem of meeting a bank's increasing loan demand in the 1960s and 1970s. During that period

(1) deposit growth was stagnant because of competition from other financial services firms and the high rates of interest on marketable securities,

(2) government securities as a source of bank liquidity were in short supply because of their prior liquidation from bank portfolios, and

(3) liquidation of remaining government securities entailed capital losses due to rising interest rates.

Banks needed a new source of funds to maintain good relations with loan customers and the stable deposits that accompany these loan accounts. The solution, as designed by some of the large money center banks in New York City, was to repackage the bank's liabilities.

In 1961 large denomination negotiable certificates of deposit (CDs) were introduced. This allowed banks for the first time to compete for funds with the issuers of high-yielding, short-term marketable securities. Also in the 1960s, the Federal funds market gained stature as a primary source of short-term funds, and the Comptroller of the Currency allowed national banks to sell uninsured debentures. The emergence of these three sources of funds not only provided banks with ways to meet new loan demands but also gave them new techniques to cover fluctuations in reserve requirements and temporary cash drains. The growing aggressive attitude toward buying funds by these, and other, means in order to expand asset volume was based on the assumption that funds would always be available at reasonable cost. This optimistic assumption was soon severely tested.

Between 1966 and 1968 market interest rates rose above the legal ceiling on rates payable on large CDs as dictated by Regulation Q. Banks were forced to find another source of funds in a hurry. The solution this time was to acquire Eurodollar deposits and for subsidiaries of bank holding companies to sell non-FDIC-insured commercial paper in the open market. Shortly thereafter, the Penn Central crisis undermined the reliability of uninsured commercial paper as a source of bank funds and prompted regulatory officials to raise and then suspend ceiling rates on CDs. This step revived banks' ability to use insured CDs as a source of short-term funds.

After this episode banks which continued aggressively to purchase short-term money to fund asset expansion soon found themselves caught in another credit crunch. Between 1973 and 1974 short-term interest rates skyrocketed and for most of this period remained above comparable long-term rates. Many banks which neglected to consider the possibility of a sharp rise in funds could no longer acquire them at profitable spreads. Consequently, during this period they saw their profits decline. In addition they saw their capital cushions erode as assets in highly leveraged balance sheets fell in value.

This painful episode along with the previous credit crunch exposed some of the dangers inherent in liability management. In light of these pitfalls, many banks have chosen to avoid liability management altogether or at least to relegate it to an emergency method of raising funds. Still others, mainly the larger banks, have come to rely upon liability management to provide a core source of funds to support asset expansion. The development and growth of certain purchased liabilities in the late 1970s (especially repurchase agreements) and the continued guarantee of deposit safety by the FDIC have greatly aided this reliance.

The experience gained through liability management has been extremely instructive in the evolution of asset/liability management. Liability management allows for the aggressive management of a significant portion of a bank's balance sheet previously thought untouchable. However, the approach still neglects the crucial, sometimes fatal, problem for management of interest rate risk. Financing long-term fixed rate loans with short-term liabilities, as we have seen, may leave the bank with a highly leveraged balance sheet in the precarious position of rolling over debt at ever-increasing interest rates. When this happens, bank earnings are negatively impacted and the confidence of uninsured creditors, stockholders, and regulators is weakened. The result is often increased withdrawals, higher borrowing costs, and pressure from regulatory authorities—all of which severely compound the banking community's problems. To avoid or limit these problems, bank managers must opt for a better coordinated management strategy.

V. Gap Management Method

The gap management method is the most sophisticated of the asset/liability management methods discussed here. It attempts to outline a coordinated strategy on the positioning of both assets and liabilities to achieve high and steady bank performance when threatened with the possibility of interest rate risk. This method differs from the previous methods in that it explicitly recognizes the effects that volatile interest rates have on bank earnings. It provides one of the most effective techniques banks have at their disposal to insulate themselves from a volatile interest rate environment. While any size bank can use this method, larger banks are able to exploit the opportunities presented in gap management more fully.

To implement this method, a bank must first develop a highly sophisticated accounting system. The greater the detail in categorizing accounts at the beginning, the more it will be possible to fine-tune expected income at the end. Once this classification system is established, current and forecasted future values must be used to calculate both the interest and interest rate spreads between assets and liabilities over a short-run time horizon, such as one year. These all-important spreads are what management will try to protect or enhance in the face of potential interest rate risk.

Interest rate risk is estimated by classifying each asset and liability according to how sensitive its cash flows are to changing short-term interest rates. Specifically, those assets and liabilities which may be repriced within a ninety-day period are classified as interest rate sensitive. Examples of interest rate-sensitive assets include short-term federal funds sold, short-term securities, and variable rate loans. Examples of rate-sensitive assets are short-term federal funds purchased and time deposits maturing in the stated ninety-day period.

The difference between rate-sensitive assets and rate-sensitive liabilities is called the *rate-sensitive funds gap*. If the funds gap is positive (or if the ratio of rate-sensitive assets to rate-sensitive liabilities is greater than one) this indicates that more assets will be repriced compared to liabilities for a given interest rate change. This situation is illustrated in Figure 1.

Similarly, when the funds gap is negative, more liabilities will be repriced compared to assets. Thus the funds gap is a crude measure of the interest rate exposure a bank is positioned to bear. It is crude because interest rates on assets and liabilities do not usually move in tandem; thus the speed and magnitude of repricing is not usually proportional.

Once identified, a bank's exposure may be manipulated by management which uses its interest rate forecast in order to stabilize or increase bank profits. If short-term interest rates are rising, a positive funds gap will mean that more assets will increase in earning power compared to liabilities. Conversely, a negative funds gap with short-term interest rates rising will mean that the cash flows associated with rate-sensitive liabilities will be larger than the cash flows associated with rate-sensitive assets. If short-term interest rates are falling, a positive funds gap will similarly decrease bank earnings, while a negative funds gap will increase bank earnings.

The choice of size and sign of the funds gap will depend on the bank managers' confidence in their interest rate forecasts, their control over the adjustment of the funds gap, and their preferences toward risk and return. Bank managers mainly interested in stable

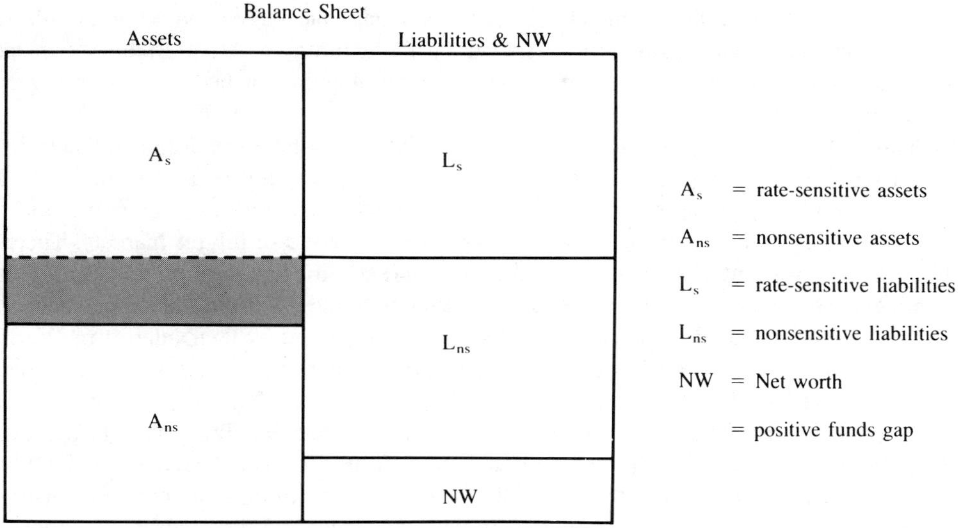

FIGURE 1 Positive Funds Gap

earnings will want to avoid extreme gap positions. They may feel they are incapable of outpredicting the market when it comes to interest rate forecasts. On the other hand, bank managers who are willing to bet on an increase in short-term interest rates will want to create a large positive funds gap by making more variable rate loans, shortening the maturity of the bank's assets, and increasing the maturity of the bank's liabilities. In practice, however, these steps may prove difficult, because other market participants may have similar interest rate forecasts and may not want to accept the types of assets and liabilities offered by the bank.[4] Similarly, a bank might find itself in an environment where it has little control over the types and maturities of assets and liabilities it is able to offer, no matter what the interest rate forecast. Critics often question the effectiveness of the gap management method on these grounds. They argue that a funds gap cannot be adjusted quickly enough, thus forcing banks to endure their interest exposure. While this is no doubt true for many banks, there is a partial solution to this problem for those banks which are familiar with the working of futures markets.

Futures Markets and Hedging

Within the gap management framework of asset/liability management, the futures market can provide an excellent opportunity for a bank to protect itself from unexpected changes in earnings due to interest rate risk. A bank which finds itself unable to match its rate-sensitive assets and liabilities due to its customers needs can, at a very low cost, transfer the risk of unanticipated interest rate changes by agreeing to buy or sell an appropriate

[4]According to rational expectations analysis of modern economic theory, a kissing cousin of the efficient markets hypothesis in the theory of finance, market participants cannot systematically outguess the markets. If an individual participant's forecast methods are successful, they will be adopted quickly by others. Thus, the basis for systematically outperforming the market will disappear.

futures contract. By doing so, the unexpected loss or gain due to the exposed funds will be offset to an extent by the gain or loss associated with the futures contract. In this way bank managers can change a positive or negative funds gap into a hedged position very quickly.

It should be noted that the use of interest rate futures by banks is designed solely for defensive purposes. A positive funds gap, for example, may not be transformed into a negative funds gap through the use of futures contracts. Banking regulations prohibit a bank from increasing its interest rate exposure through the use of futures markets. Therefore, all mismatching must be done in the cash market prior to entering into any futures contracts. This is an important point, because even with the use of futures contracts bank managers may be unable to achieve the desired gap suggested by their interest rate forecast. At most, then, exercising a futures contract can bring about only a matched book.

Given this constraint, implementing a futures market strategy is fairly straightforward. To protect a positive funds gap (or a portion thereof) from unexpected decreases in interest rates, a long hedge must be performed. This entails buying a futures contract of an instrument closely related to the types exposed for the same amount of the funds gap (or for the portion for which protection is desired) with the intention of offsetting this transaction later by selling another contract for the same instrument with the same delivery date. Once the initial purchase is made, the bank managers have locked in an interest spread. If interest rates decrease during the length of the futures contract, the losses accrued to the lower yields on the bank's positive funds gap will be offset by the gains registered on the unexpected higher-priced futures contract when the hedge is closed out. Analogously, if interest rates increase, the gains experienced from the higher yields on the unmatched assets will be offset by the losses registered on the unexpected lower-priced futures contract when the hedge is once again closed out.

The analysis works in reverse for a bank which wants to protect a negative funds gap from unanticipated increases in interest rates. This time a short hedge must be carried out. To do this, bank managers must sell a futures contract of an instrument closely related to the types exposed for the same amount of the funds gap with the intention of offsetting this transaction later by purchasing an identical contract. If interest rates increase during the time period the futures contract is in effect, the losses realized on refinancing the many liabilities will be offset by the profit booked when an identical futures contract is purchased at a lower than expected price. If interest rates fall, the gains realized on refinancing the exposed funds will be offset by the losses registered when the futures contract is purchased at a higher than expected price. No matter what happens to interest rates, the interest rate risk to which a funds gap is exposed will be eliminated.

Of course, all this does not come free. An old saw in economics and finance states, "There is no such thing as a free lunch." First of all, as described above, potential gains on the exposed funds will be eliminated just as potential losses have been. Higher returns will have been traded for lower risk. Secondly, entering into futures contracts to hedge a position introduces a new type of risk called *basis risk*. What this risk represents is the unproportional changes in yields that may occur among those instruments which make up the funds gap and the instrument used to hedge the position. In other words, there is a chance that the basis point spread between the instruments in the cash market and instruments in the futures market may change from beginning to end. If this happens, the losses in one market will not be offset exactly by the gains in the other market. While this is usually the case, it is generally believed that this type of risk is substantially less than the associated interest rate risk.

Thirdly, since futures contracts are marked to market daily, the losses or gains realized in the futures markets are likely to show up sooner on income statements than the offsetting gains and losses of the cash market. If this happens, current reported income may not accurately reflect the true profitability of the bank's position. Inasmuch as regulators are usually concerned with book values, a perfectly hedged position may still produce a great deal of anxiety.

Finally, the ability of bank borrowers to prepay their loans when interest rates are falling may leave a bank with only a loss position in the futures market. If banks do not require a prepayment penalty, they may be adding a degree of risk back into their asset/liability strategy that they had not anticipated.

Whether these drawbacks, in conjunction with bank managers' general unfamiliarity with futures contracts, are enough to circumvent the extended use of futures markets remains to be seen.

Asset/Liability Committee (ALCO)

Given that a practical and proficient asset/liability management framework has been pieced together and put into place it now has to be implemented and continually reviewed as conditions warrant. The execution of these formidable tasks are ordinarily the responsibility of the Asset/Liability Committee. ALCO is customarily composed of the chairman and president of the bank, the senior loan and investment officers, the chief financial officer, and the bank's chief economist. Usually, it is the senior investment officer who is designated chairman of this committee because of the officer's oversight of the most flexible part of the bank's balance sheet. This committee may convene as often as once a week or as little as once a month depending upon the bank and market conditions.

It is essentially the duty of ALCO to adjust the maturity and terms of the bank's loans, investments, and borrowings in view of the national and local economic outlooks and the forecasts for loan demand, deposit balances, and liquidity needs. ALCO attempts to position the bank so as to take full advantage of the changing economic environment. It examines and suggests possibilities for maintaining and improving the bank's interest rate spread in view of the risks involved. To this end, flexible guidelines are established for the desired levels of mismatch between rate-sensitive assets and rate-sensitive liabilities.

To assist these asset/liability committees in performing their complex duties several ''how-to'' models have been developed over the years. State-of-the-art optimization techniques have been employed to individually optimize a bank's assets, liabilities, or portfolio subject to various risk, liquidity, time, and information constraints. Only recently, however, has the entire asset/liability management problem been modeled within the theory-of-the-firm framework and been presented rigorously as a two-sided problem.

Recent Theoretical Developments

Much of the recent modelling of the asset/liability problem has employed the concept of asset and liability duration.[5] Very simply, duration summarizes the present value cash flow characteristics of an asset or liability in one variable so as to serve as a measure of the interest rate risk accompanying that instrument. Macaulay in 1938 defined duration (D) as:

$$D = \frac{\sum_{t=1}^{N} \frac{C_t\,(t)}{(1+r)^t}}{\sum_{t=1}^{N} \frac{C_t}{(1+r)^t}}$$

where

C_t = interest and/or principal payments at time t
(t) = length of time to the interest and/or principal payments
N = the length of time to final maturity
r = yield to maturity[6]

As defined, the denominator is the present value of the interest and principal payments while the numerator is the present value of the cash flows, where each payment is weighted by the time at which the payment is expected. This new variable is thus a measure of the average life of an asset's or liability's cash flows measured in units of time.

If a bank were now to calculate the duration of its assets and liabilities (including net worth), it would have measures of the interest rate sensitivity of all of its assets and all of its liabilities. The interest rate risk to which a bank is exposed is then approximated by the difference between the duration of its assets and the duration of its liabilities. This new gap takes into account the interest rate sensitivity of the entire balance sheet and not just those assets and liabilities which are subject to revaluation within ninety days due to a change in interest rates. A financial institution can now actively manage this duration gap in order to achieve desired expected risk and return levels. For example, a financial institution predicting interest rates to rise above market expectations should have the duration of its assets less than the duration of its liabilities. Higher interest rates will lower the prices of the bank's longer-duration liabilities more than the prices of the bank's assets and thus produce an increase in the bank's net worth. This is analogous to a bank having more rate-sensitive assets than rate-sensitive liabilities at a time when interest rates are rising. More assets will be turned over at higher rates than will maturing liabilities.

Conversely, if a bank expects interest rates to fall below market expectations, it should position its assets and liabilities so that the duration of its assets is greater than the duration of its liabilities. This essentially locks in the high interest rates for more assets than liabilities.

[5]Another article in this volume, by George Kaufman, addresses this subject in much greater detail.
[6]Frederick R. Macaulay, *The Movement of Interest Rates, Bonds, Yields, and Stock Prices in the United States Since 1865* (New York: Columbia University Press, 1938), pp. 44–53.

As a third option, as Redington has shown, a bank can completely immunize its balance sheet against interest rate risk by setting the duration of its assets equal to the duration of its liabilities.[7] While this immunization is only for parallel shifts in the yield curve, it still provides more complete protection of a bank's assets and liabilities than do previously discussed methods.

Having briefly explained the concept of duration, it is now possible to discuss how researchers have applied duration to model the entire asset/liability management problem within the theory-of-the-firm context. In an important article, Deshmukh, Greenbaum, and Kanatas (1983) describe a bank as an asset transformer or a broker depending upon whether interest rate uncertainty is present when borrowing. They show that an expected profit-maximizing intermediary will reduce its inventory of loanable funds and hence move towards a broker's mode of operation when there is increased uncertainty regarding the intermediary's lending or borrowing rate. In other words, the increased uncertainty of interest rate movements is an incentive for intermediaries to minimize their loanable funds inventory and thus avoid mismatching duration measures. On the other hand, a reduction in interest rate uncertainty or an increase in borrowing or lending interest rates will induce an intermediary to hold a larger loanable funds inventory and thus provide more asset transformation. In duration terms, this implies greater mismatching of assets and liabilities.

In a closely related article (1983b), these authors demonstrate the effects of interest rate uncertainty on lending policies. As the uncertainty over interest rates increases, intermediaries will move closer toward functioning as a stylized broker that books less loans because of stricter credit standards.

In another recent paper, Bierwag, Kaufman and Toevs (1982) outline the development of a portfolio which is immunized from interest rate shifts through duration matching. Unlike the previous formulation by Redington which uses the Macaulay measure of duration to immunize a portfolio for parallel shifts in the yield curve, these authors derive a more complex duration measure. This more complex measure may be employed to immunize a portfolio if the stochastic process of interest rate changes is known, and makes riskless arbitrage opportunities unavailable. Since the actual stochastic process of interest rate changes is generally not known with certainty, the authors conclude elsewhere (1983) that the simple Macaulay measure of duration performs reasonably well and appears to be cost effective.

As these new models, methods, and strategies are disseminated, bank managers will find it advantageous to incorporate them into their way of thinking. Thus, not only will the strategies, methods and models used by bank managers have to adapt to a changing economic environment, the managers themselves must be able to assimilate modern and innovative ideas.

[7]F. M. Redington, "Review of the Principle of Life-Office Valuations," *Journal of the Institute of Actuaries*, 78 (1952), pp. 286–340. Reprinted in Gabriel A. Hawawini (ed.), *Bond Duration and Immunization: Early Developments and Recent Contributions* (New York: Garland Publishing, 1982).

BIBLIOGRAPHY

ALLENDOERFER, CARL W., and HEMPEL, GEORGE H., "Improving Gap Management for Controlling Interest Rate Risk," *Journal of Bank Research,* Summer 1982, pp. 109–115.

BAKER, JAMES V., "Asset Liability Management" *Banking,* June 1978–October 1978.

———, "Riding the Rates, or Asset/Liability Management Revisited," *Banking,* August 1980, pp. 57–59.

BAUGHN, WILLIAM H., and WALKER, CHARLES E., *The Bankers Handbook* (Homewood, IL: Dow-Jones-Irwin, Inc., 1966).

BIERWAG, G. O., "Immunization, Duration and the Term Structure of Interest Rates," *Journal of Financial and Quantitative Analysis,* December 1977, pp. 725–741.

———, "Measures of Duration," *Economic Inquiry,* October 1978.

BIERWAG, G. O., KAUFMAN, GEORGE G., and TOEVS, ALDEN, "Single Factor Duration Models in a Discrete General Equilibrium Framework," *Journal of Finance,* 37 May 1982, pp. 339–48.

———, "Duration: Its Development and Use in Bond Portfolio Management," *Financial Analysts Journal,* July–August 1983, pp. 15–35.

BINDER, BARRETT F., "Asset Liability Management," *Magazine of Bank Administration,* November 1980–January 1981 and June 1981.

———, "New Initiatives in Asset/Liability Management," *Magazine of Bank Administration,* June 1981, pp. 56–64.

BUDZEIKA, G., "The Effect of Liability Management by Banks on their Lending Policies," Research Paper 8007 (1980), Federal Reserve Bank of New York.

———, "A Study of Liability Management by New York City Banks," Research Paper 7608 (1976), Federal Reserve Bank of New York.

BRANCH, RENE O., JR., and STIGUM, MARCIA L., *Managing Bank Assets and Liabilities* (Homewood, IL: Dow Jones-Irwin, Inc., 1983).

CHAMBERS, D., and CHARNES, A., "Inter-Temporal Analysis and Optimization of Bank Portfolios," *Management Science,* 7 July 1961, pp. 393–410.

COHEN, KALMAN, J., "Dynamic Balance Sheet Management: A Management Science Approach." *Journal of Bank Research,* 2, Winter 1972, pp. 9–19.

COHEN, KALMAN J., and HAMMER, FREDERICK S., *Analytical Methods In Banking* (Homewood, IL: Richard D. Irwin, Inc., 1966).

———, "Linear Programming and Optimal Bank Asset Management Decision," *Journal of Finance,* 22, May 1967, pp. 147–165.

CORNS, MARSHALL, *Practical Operations and Management of a Bank* (Boston, MA: Bankers Publishing Company, 1962).

CROSSE, HOWARD D., and HEMPEL, GEORGE, *Management Policies for Commercial Banks,* 2nd ed. (Englewood Cliffs, NJ: Prentice-Hall, Inc., 1973).

DESHMUKH, SUDHAKAR D., GREENBAUM, STUART I., and KANATAS, GEORGE, "Lending Policies of Financial Intermediaries: Brokers Versus Quantitative Asset-Transformers," Banking Research Center Working Paper No. 75, October 1981.

———, "Interest Rate Uncertainty and the Financial Intermediary's Choice of Exposure," *Journal of Finance,* 38, March 1983, pp. 141–147.

———, "Lending Policies of Financial Intermediaries Facing Credit and Funding Risk," *Journal of Finance,* 39, June 1983, pp. 873–882.

DEW, JAMES KURT, and MARTELL, TERRENCE F., "Treasury Bill Futures, Commercial Bank Lending and the Synthetic Fixed-Rate Loan," *Journal of Commercial Banking Lending,* June 1981, pp. 27–38.

DOWRIE, GEORGE W., *American Monetary and Banking Policies* (New York: Longmans, Green and Co., 1930).

FISHER, LAWRENCE, and WEIL, ROMAN L., "Coping with the Risk of Interest Rate Fluctuations: Returns to Bondholders from Naive and Optimal Strategies," *Journal of Business,* October 1971, pp. 408–431.

FLANNERY, MARK J., "Market Interest Rates and Commercial Bank Profitability: An Empirical Investigation," *Journal of Finance,* 36, December 1981, pp. 1085–1101.

______, "Some Further Evidence on Market Interest Rates and Bank Profitability," *Journal of Money, Credit and Banking,* 15, August 1983, pp. 355–362.

GOLDSMITH, RAYMOND W. *Financial Institutions,* New York: Random House, 1968.

HALEY, C. W., "Interest Rate Risk in Financial Intermediaries: Prospects for Immunization," Working Paper, University of Washington, 1981.

HAYWOOD, CHARLES F., *The Pledging of Bank Assets: A Study of the Problem of Security for Public Deposits* (Chicago, IL: Association of Reserve City Bankers, 1967).

HAYES, DOUGLAS A., *Bank Lending Policies-Domestic And International,* 2nd ed. (Ann Arbor, Michigan: Division of Research, Graduate School of Business Administration, The University of Michigan, 1977).

HO, THOMAS S. Y., and SAUNDERS, ANTHONY, "The Determinants of Bank Interest Margins: Theory and Empirical Evidence," *Journal of Financial and Quantitative Analysis,* 16, November 1981, pp. 581–600.

KANE, E. J., "The Three Faces of Commercial Bank Liability Management," In R. Lombra and H. Kaufman (eds.), *The Political Economy of Policymaking.* (Beverly Hills, California: Sage Publications, 1979), pp. 149–174.

KEEN, HOWARD JR., "Interest Rate Futures: A Challenge for Bankers," *Business Review,* Federal Reserve Bank of Philadelphia, November-December 1980, pp. 13–22.

MACAULAY, FREDERICK R., *The Movement of Interest Rates, Bonds, Yields, and Stock Prices in the United States Since 1865* (New York: Columbia University Press, 1938), pp. 44–53.

McCABE, GEORGE M., and McLEOD, ROBERT W., "Regulation and Bank Trading in the Futures Market," *Issues in Bank Regulation,* 3, Summer 1979, pp. 6–14.

______, "The Use of Financial Futures in Banking" in *Commercial Banking* by John R. Brick, (Michigan: Systems Publications Inc., 1984).

MEEK, PAUL, *U.S. Monetary Policy and Financial Markets,* Federal Reserve Bank of New York, 1982.

MORRISON, GEORGE R., and SELDEN, RICHARD T., *Time Deposit Growth and the Employment of Bank Funds* (Chicago: Association of Reserve City Banker, 1965).

NADLER, PAUL S., *Commercial Banking in the Economy* (New York: Random House, 1968).

REED, EDWARD W., COTTER, RICHARD V., GILL, EDWARD K., and SMITH, RICHARD K., *Commercial Banking* (Englewood Cliffs, NJ: Prentice-Hall Inc., 1976).

ROBINSON, ROLAND I., *Money and Capital Markets* (New York: McGraw-Hill Book Company, 1964).

______, *The Management of Bank Funds* (New York: McGraw-Hill Book Company, 1962).

ROSENBLUM, HARVEY, "Interest Rate Volatility, Regulation Q and the Problems of Thrift Institutions," *Proceedings of a Conference on Bank Structure and Competition,* Federal Reserve Bank of Chicago, May 1980, pp. 16–42.

SILBER, WILLIAM L., *Portfolio Behavior of Financial Institutions* (New York: Holt Rinehart and Winston, Inc., 1970).

SMITH, PAUL F., *Economics of Financial Institutions and Markets* (Homewood, IL: Richard D. Irwin, Inc., 1971).

STIGUM, MARCIA, *The Money Market: Myth, Reality and Practice* (Homewood, IL: Dow Jones-Irwin, Inc., 1978).

TYLER, WAT H., *Developing a Better Perspective for Managing the Asset/Liability Mix* (New York: McKinsey and Company Inc., 0000).

VOJTA, GEORGE J., *Bank Capital Adequacy* (New York: Citibank, N.A., 1973).

VON FURSTENBERG, GEORGE M., "The Equilibrium Spread Between Variable Rates and Fixed Rates on Long-Term Financing Instruments," *Journal of Financial and Quantitative Analysis*, 8, December 1973, pp. 807–819.

WEIL, ROMAN L., "Macaulay's Duration: An Appreciation," *Journal of Business*, October 1973, pp. 589–592.

The Effect of Financial Futures on Small Bank Performance

Mark Drabenstott and Anne O'Mara McDonley

3

Commercial banks have always encountered risks in their normal course of business. However, the volatility of interest rates in recent years has increased the risk of mismatching interest-sensitive assets and liabilities. Small community and agricultural banks, it has been found, have felt the effects of this risk more than their larger urban counterparts.[1] As a result, many small banks might use financial futures to reduce the risks of interest rate volatility if they knew how such use would affect their performance.

This article employs an economic model of a representative rural bank to demonstrate the possible effects that the use of financial futures can have on bank performance. The first section discusses a conceptual framework for the small banking firm and introduces financial futures to the framework. The second section presents an empirical economic model of a bank based on this conceptual framework. The model is then used to show how the representative bank performs when futures are used in various situations. The final section draws some implications for potential users of financial futures and summarizes the findings of the article.

Reprinted from *Economic Review* (November, 1982): 15-31 by permission of the Federal Reserve Bank of Kansas City and the authors.

[1]For a fuller discussion of financial futures and their applications for agricultural banks, *see* Drabenstott and McDonley, "The Impact of Financial Futures on Agricultural Banks," *Economic Review,* Federal Reserve Bank of Kansas City, May 1982, pp. 19-30.

The Small Banking Firm

The ownership of small banks usually differs significantly from the ownership of large banks. Most small banks are closely held corporations, often with only one major stockholder. The major owners of small banks, therefore, exert considerable influence over the management of the bank. Large banks, by contrast, are normally publicly held corporations with many stockholders, none usually holding a strong majority position. Thus, a separation of ownership and management is characteristic of large banks.[2]

Because of these differences in ownership, the operating objectives of large and small banks are usually different. A large bank tries to maximize the total value of bank stock holdings. This objective is consistent with the goals of both stockholders and management. The operating objective of a small bank, however, more directly reflects the goals of a small group of owners. Their goals tend to include greater risk avoidance along with profit maximization. Thus, the operating objective of a small bank can be defined as simultaneously satisfying the goals of profit maximization and risk avoidance.

Utility maximization is another way of describing the operating objective of a small bank. In this context, utility can be defined as the satisfaction owners receive from achieving profits and avoiding risk. The choice of an operating strategy that maximizes utility depends on the owners' preferences between risk and profit and the bank's feasible performance—the various portfolio combinations of profit and risk that the bank can achieve.[3]

A small bank that follows a utility maximization objective faces one danger. If the owners are too cautious and bank earnings fall low enough, the bank may be bought by someone that perceives that the bank's profit performance can be improved. In effect, this amounts to the bank being operated at a value below market expectations. For a large bank, low performance would be reflected directly in a drop in the price of its stock. But for a small bank, because its stock is not actively traded, a utility maximizing course that drives down earnings will be revealed eventually when a buyer offers to take over the bank at a premium price. This premium will be determined by the difference between current value and the perceived value that could be achieved under a value maximization objective.

Bank Utility Functions

The utility function combines the satisfaction gained from achieving all the bank's goals into one calculation and reflects the bank owners' preferences among these goals. Given a

[2]Another important distinction is that, unlike the shares of stock of large banks that trade on major exchanges, shares of small banks typically trade in local imperfect markets.

[3]The distinction between a value (or profit) maximizing objective for publicly held banks and a utility maximizing objective for closely held banks is discussed extensively in economic literature. For a discussion of alternative theories of the banking firm, see E. Baltensperger, "Alternative Approaches to the Theory of the Banking Firm," *Journal of Monetary Economics,* 6 (1980), pp. 1-27. For an example of a model that deals with a value maximizing bank, see M. Flannery, "Market Interest Rates and Commercial Bank Profitability: An Empirical Investigation," *Journal of Finance,* 36 (1981), pp. 1085-1101. For an example of a model that deals with a utility maximizing bank, *see* L. Robison and P. Barry, "Portfolio Adjustments: An Application to Rural Banking," *American Journal of Agricultural Economics,* 59 (1977), pp. 311-20.

bank's goals of profits and risk avoidance, a utility function quantifies the bank's risk aversion. In other words, the utility function indicates the amount by which earnings must increase for the bank to accept additional risk.

A graphic presentation clarifies the utility function concept. A bank measures profits by the expected net spread of its portfolio—the difference between its asset earnings and liability costs. Risk is measured by the variability associated with this expected return. Measured in these terms, the utility function depicts combinations of profit and risk that provide the bank with a constant level of utility.

Because the bank does not prefer any one combination, the locus of points that represents the complete set of risk-return combinations is called an indifference curve. Thus, curve I_0 in Figure 1 represents one indifference curve. The bank receives the same utility from either combination *A* or *B*. The bank shows its risk aversion by being willing to accept the higher risk at *B* only by gaining a higher rate of return.[4] The bank receives more satisfaction when it can operate on curve I_1 since combination *C* provides a higher rate of return than combination *A*, but with the same level of risk.

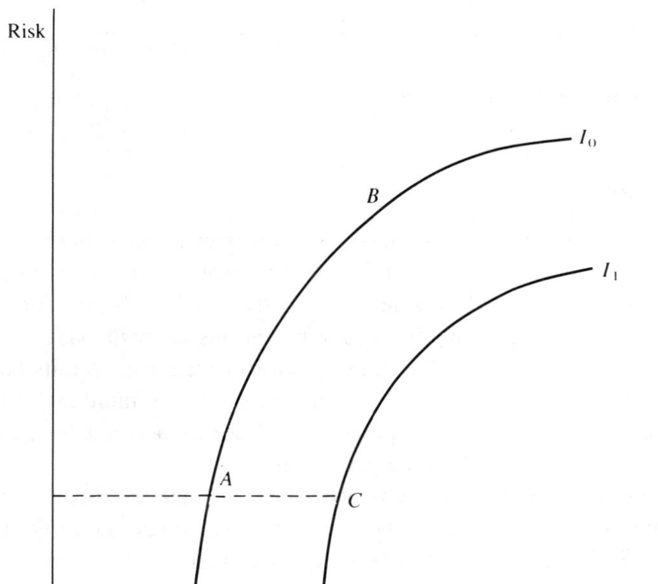

FIGURE 1 Bank Owner Indifference Curves

[4]The utility function illustrated in Figure 1 is a quadratic function that exhibits the property of increasing relative risk aversion. Alternative utility functions would, of course, imply different graphic representations.

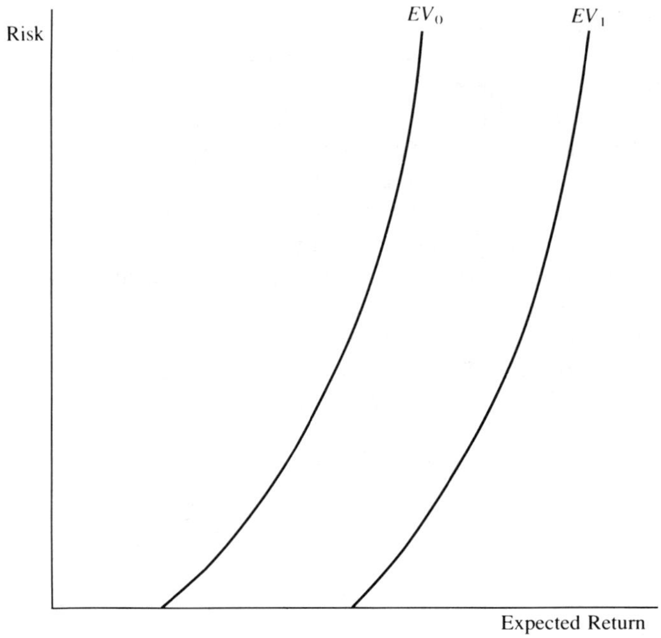

FIGURE 2 Bank *EV* Frontiers

Bank Performance

Feasible bank performance determines the utility a bank can achieve. In the context of this article, bank performance is defined as the maximum profit a bank can earn for a given level of risk. Conversely, it is the lowest level of risk that can be achieved for a given profit level. Improved performance, by the first definition, means the bank has increased profits without increasing the level of risk. Decreased performance means profits have declined from the same level of risk. These definitions differ from more traditional financial measures of performance, such as return on equity, that do not account for risk. A bank's utility, therefore, depends on its feasible performance.

Two factors determine the best performance a bank can attain—operating constraints and the substitution of risk for return. The operating constraints that affect bank performance are numerous, including such things as equity capital, asset returns, liability costs, regulatory environment, and investment alternatives. For example, because a bank keeps an equity reserve proportional to its total assets, the amount of equity capital effectively constrains the size of the bank's portfolio. A bank can try to increase profits, but only if it is willing to accept greater risk. Conversely, portfolio risk can be reduced by more conservative lending and investing policies, but the portfolio return will decline as a result. Risk and return, therefore, are substitutes for each other, and the substitutions made help shape feasible bank performance.

A bank's feasible performance can be plotted graphically in an analogous manner as the utility function. Curve EV_0 in Figure 2 represents the best performance the bank can attain

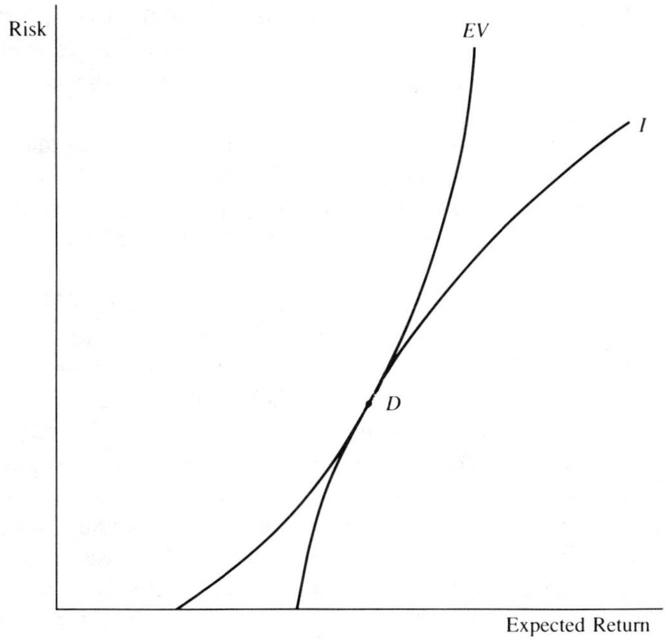

FIGURE 3 Utility Maximization for the Small Bank

over the full range of risk-return tradeoffs available to it, given a certain set of operating constraints. Every point on the curve represents one possible portfolio combination that produces an expected return at a particular risk. Curve EV_0 is called an expected return-variance *(EV)* frontier because the bank cannot improve its performance any further, given its operating constraints and its possible substitutions between risk and return.[5] A relaxing of one of the operating constraints would allow the bank to improve its performance to the higher level represented by EV_1. This might occur, for example, if there were an infusion of additional equity capital.

To determine the one specific portfolio combination that maximizes utility, the bank combines its utility function with its *EV* frontier (Figure 3). By arranging its portfolio so that is is consistent with point *D,* the bank is able to maximize the satisfaction of its owners, given the best performance the bank can achieve. A more thorough discussion of *EV* frontiers and an analysis of financial futures are in the Technical Appendix.

Volatile Interest Rates and Hedging

The effect that interest rate volatility has on small banks can be demonstrated within the framework of utility maximization. By increasing the variability of asset returns and

[5]J. A. James, ''Portfolio Selection with an Imperfectly Competitive Asset Market,'' *Journal of Finance and Quantitative Analysis,* 11 (1976), pp. 831-46, has demonstrated that an EV frontier has the shape shown in Figure 2 when one of the assets in question is bought and sold in an imperfect market. This shape has been used here because small banks typically price their loans in an imperfect local market.

liability costs, volatile interest rates increase the risk of bank portfolios, forcing banks to accept higher risks for the same expected returns. The result is a reduction in the best performance a bank can attain. Increased volatility, therefore, corresponds to a leftward shift of the *EV* frontier.[6]

Increased volatility affects a bank in two ways. First, with a loss in the performance it can attain, the bank can no longer achieve the same utility. In short, bank owners suffer a loss in satisfaction. Second, with increased portfolio risk, the bank is encouraged to reduce risk by substituting assets with less risk, resulting in a reduced rate of return on the portfolio.

A bank can use financial futures, however, to counter the effects of increased interest rate volatility. Hedging allows a bank to reduce the interest rate variability of the asset or liability being hedged.[7] Thus, hedging shifts the *EV* frontier to the right. The reduction in the interest rate variability improves the best attainable bank performance. Hedging cannot remove all the increased risk of interest rates, because basis risk is substituted for interest rate risk. The basis is the difference in price between a futures contract and the cash market value of the financial instrument on which the contract is based. Risk is involved because the price differential fluctuates in response to several market stimuli, including market expectations concerning the future course of interest rates. Because basis risk is smaller and more predictable than interest rate risk, hedging can effectively reduce the variability of portfolio returns. Thus, financial futures offer the bank an opportunity both to reduce utility loss and avoid substitutions to less profitable assets.

In summary, small banks with interdependent goals of profitability and risk avoidance seek to maximize utility. The choice of a utility maximizing portfolio combination depends on the bank's utility function and its best attainable performance. Greater volatility in interest rates leads to a loss of utility and portfolio substitutions away from assets that are higher yielding but riskier. Financial futures offer banks a strategy for reducing these effects of interest rate volatility.

Model of a Representative Agricultural Bank

The economic model selected to analyze the effects of using futures on bank performance is based on the utility maximization framework discussed above.[8] The model maximizes

[6]In addition to making a bank's portfolio spread more variable, interest rate volatility can also cause the spread to widen over time. The result of decreased bank performance assumes that a bank has a mismatch in the maturities of its assets and liabilities. Banks with matched asset and liability maturity structures automatically insulate themselves from the effects of interest rate volatility.

[7]Hedging substitutes basis risk for cash market interest rate risk through the purchase or sale of financial futures contracts. Hedging a particular asset or liability is referred to as microhedging, while hedging a bank's net portfolio interest rate exposure is called macrohedging. For further discussion of hedging as a risk-management tool and a comparison of macrohedging and microhedging, see Drabenstott and McDonley, "The Impact of Financial Futures on Agricultural Banks."

[8]The model used in this research is an adaptation of one developed by Freddie Barnard in a Ph.D. thesis at the University of Illinois (1982), "An Evaluation of the Effects of Regulation Q on Farm Lending by Agricultural Banks." His model has been extended to examine the effects of financial futures on bank performance. For an earlier application of quadratic programming models see Linden Robison and Peter Barry, "Portfolio Adjustments: An Application to Rural Banking," *American Journal of Agricultural Economics,* 59 (1977), pp. 311-20.

the utility of a representative agricultural bank, given the operating constraints the bank faces. The model follows a mathematical procedure, known as quadratic programming, to find the portfolio combination that earns the bank the highest income for a given level of risk. Risk is measured in the model as the variance of bank earnings.[9] By varying the level of risk, the model determines the best tradeoff the bank can make between risk and return—that is, the *EV* frontier.[10]

The model is designed to capture the operating conditions of a typical small agricultural bank, assumed to have total assets of slightly less than $15 million and equity capital of slightly more than $1 million. The bank earns income from agricultural and nonagricultural loans and from investing in Treasury securities and nontaxable municipal securities. The bank is assumed to operate in an imperfect local market, which means it has some control over the interest rates it charges on loans. By comparison, the bank would have no control over its loan interest rates if it operated in a perfectly competitive market. Allocable funds are acquired through several sources: demand and savings deposits, $100,000 certificates of deposit (CD's), 30-month CD's, 6-month money market certificates (MMC's), federal funds, and borrowings from a Federal Reserve Bank.[11]

The bank represented in the model (the model bank) faces several operating constraints. Corporate income taxes must be paid on net taxable income, and the bank pays a 30-percent after-tax dividend. A capital to total assets ratio of 8 percent constrains the size of the asset portfolio. Reserves against deposits must be maintained in accordance with Federal Reserve requirements. Also, bank liabilities are limited by the funds available in the local market. The model accounts for limitations in the local market by constraining the distribution of liability sources to reflect the experience of average agricultural banks of comparable size (Table 1).

The model contains data reflecting financial market conditions in 1980. Asset returns and liability costs are averages for that year expressed as nominal interest rates. Corporate income taxes also represent 1980 rates. Operating costs correspond to those listed for average banks in the Federal Reserve's 1980 Functional Cost Analysis.[12]

Model Results

This section discusses the model results dealing with how bank performance is affected by hedging the cost of issuing money market certificates. The money market certificate was selected as the instrument to be hedged because most agricultural banks have grown

[9]Quadratic programming models have some shortcomings. They measure risk as the variance of interest rates. Other measures of risk, such as coefficient of variation and other distributional characteristics, are not accounted for in this model. Also, the model incorporates the assumptions of expected utility theory. These assumptions include the ability to order preferences, use continuous (as opposed to discrete) utility functions and make decisions independent of others.

[10]Selection of a quadratic programming model for the purpose of this article can be justified for several reasons. Quadratic programming models are used extensively for risk analysis and are well recognized in economic literature. By accounting explicitly for portfolio variability, the model can easily be extended to include hedging. Finally, the model reflects the utility maximizing theoretical framework that characterizes the management of small, closely held banks.

[11]Federal Reserve borrowings are not related to the bank's hedging activity. Rather, they represent a normal source of funds for a typical agricultural bank under the Federal Reserve's seasonal borrowing privilege.

[12]*Functional Cost Analysis,* 1980 Average Banks, Board of Governors of the Federal Reserve System, Washington, D.C.

Table 1 Distribution of Liability Sources for the Model Bank

	Percentage of Total Liabilities
Demand Deposits	28.99
6-Month Money Market Certificate of Deposit	25.36
Savings Deposits	19.57
Time Deposits	12.32
$100,000 Certificates of Deposit	8.70
30-Month Certificates of Deposit	3.62
Federal Funds Purchased	.72
Federal Reserve Borrowings	.72
Total	100.00

Source: Freddie Barnard, "An Evaluation of the Effects of Changes in Regulation Q on Farm Lending by Agricultural Banks," Ph.D. thesis, University of Illinois, 1982. This distribution was derived from a sample of 67 agricultural banks.

increasingly dependent on MMC's as a source of funds. Their relatively short maturity, moreover, means that volatility in interest rates quickly change the bank's portfolio spread. The results that follow represent the effects of hedging this one specific liability item. Hedging strategies for other balance sheet items, however, would generate results reinforcing the conclusions reached here.

A key assumption in these results is that the bank is hedging its overall balance sheet gap. The results assume that the bank's total MMC position is not matched by an asset of equal maturity. Thus, the bank can hedge its MMC position and reduce total balance sheet risk. Regulators' guidelines, including those of the Federal Reserve System, allow banks to use financial futures only in situations that reduce total balance sheet interest rate exposure. These guidelines appear in a 1980 joint Federal Reserve-Federal Deposit Insurance Corporation-Comptroller of the Currency policy statement that states the following:

> In managing their investment portfolio, banks should evaluate the interest rate risk exposure resulting from their overall activities to insure that the positions they take in futures...markets will reduce their risk exposure. Pairing a transaction in the spot market with an offsetting position in futures...contracts can be an effective way to reduce interest rate risk. However, policy objectives should be formulated in light of the bank's entire asset and liability mix.[13]

A few assumptions underlie the model results that follow. Hedging strategies are assumed to be 75-percent effective, which means the bank can successfully offset three-fourths of the volatility in the rates it pays for MMC's. When interest rates are rising, for

[13]Board of Governors of the Federal Reserve System, *Policy Statement Concerning Forward Placement of Delayed Delivery Contracts and Interest Rate Futures Contracts,* Janurary 1, 1980. For a discussion of financial futures regulation and micro vs. macrohedging, see Drabenstott and McDonley, "The Impact of Financial Futures on Agricultural Banks," *Economic Review,* Federal Reserve Bank of Kansas City, May 1982, pp. 26–29.

example, the bank can negate three-fourths of the rise in borrowing costs from the time the hedge is placed. If the hedge were perfect, it would offset 100 percent of the volatility. The 75-percent level was chosen because it seems consistent with the experience of many banks.[14]

Results are presented for the full range of market environments under which hedging can take place: when MMC rates rise, fall, and remain constant after the hedge is placed. In analyzing hedging under these alternative market situations, the sequence of events is important. The results that are present are based on the assumption that the bank places a hedge, rearranges its portfolio accordingly, and then interest rates change. Comparisons are drawn between the bank performance that resulted from the bank hedging and what performance would have been in the absence of hedging. For the sake of comparison, all three market environment solutions are based on the same transactions costs. Results also are presented for other transaction costs.

Two types of model results are presented under each of these four headings. First, the effect of hedging on feasible bank performance is shown by comparing model generated EV frontiers. The comparison allows general conclusions to be drawn about the value of hedging. Second, the effect of hedging on bank earnings, portfolio size and selection, and return on equity are presented for one arbitrarily selected level of risk-return preference. Selecting this one level of risk-return preference amounts to choosing a point along the *EV* frontier where the owners' tradeoff between risk avoidance and profits is fixed. Holding this tradeoff constant for a number of model solutions provides results that demonstrate the portfolio adjustments that occur as a result of hedging. Because these results represent bank performance for an arbitrary point, they cannot be interpreted as precise measures of the effects of hedging. Rather, they provide an indication of whether the effects are positive or negative.

Interest Rates Rise

Hedging the cost of issuing MMC's benefits the bank most when MMC interest rates are rising. The interest rate for MMC's in the base solution is 12.7 percent, the actual average for 1980. This rate was increased to 13.5 percent to analyze the effects of hedging when borrowing costs subsequently rise. When the rate rises and the bank has not hedged, the bank's optimal performance declines relative to the base level because portfolio net returns fall. The higher MMC rate, therefore, shifts the bank's *EV* frontier to the left (Chart 1). However, if the bank hedges when interest rates are still 12.7 percent, its best attainable performance exceeds even the base level. Thus, hedging shifts the bank's *EV* frontier to the right and places the bank in a much better position in terms of performance and utility.

The performance benefits of hedging can be further demonstrated by comparing the different degrees of risk that result from hedging when the bank tries to maintain the same level of income. For example, if the bank wanted to earn income of $400,000 at the initial level of interest rates, it would have to accept risk equivalent to a standard deviation in

[14]No written documentation of hedging effectiveness is available. The 75-percent level was determined through an informal phone survey of banks that are currently hedging and represents the midpoint of the 50 to 95-percent range determined in the survey.

earnings of $47,000 (Chart 1).[15] When interest rates rise to the new level and the bank has not hedged, earnings of $400,000 have a standard deviation of $89,000. This increase in portfolio risk occurs because to maintain earnings of $400,000, the bank must increase its lending volume to offset a narrower spread. On the other hand, if the bank hedged before interest rates rose, $400,000 in earnings implies a standard deviation of only $32,000. Risk is reduced because hedging lowers the variability of MMC rates and, consequently, allows the bank to increase loan volume without raising total portfolio risk. In short, hedging allows a bank to improve performance by achieving the same amount of earnings at a lower level of risk.

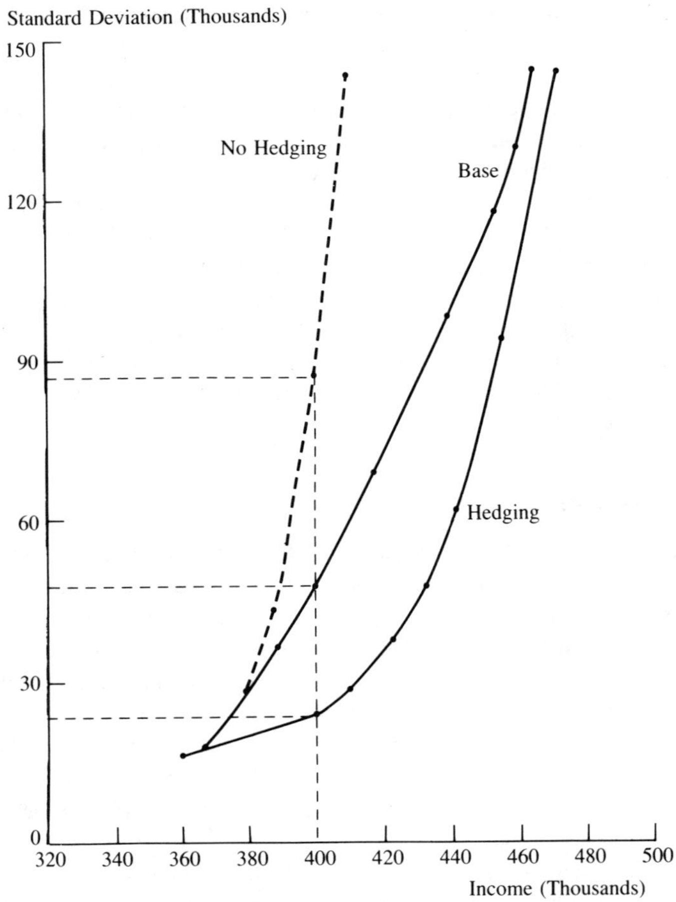

CHART 1 Hedging When Interest Rates Rise

[15]Standard deviation is a measure of risk that describes the tendency of individual values to differ from the mean. In this case, the bank could reasonably expect bank earnings to fall within a range of $400,000 ± $47,000 if it was aiming at a $400,000 earnings target.

For the specific level of operation, bank performance improves substantially as a result of hedging. Both income and return on equity are higher than when the bank did not hedge (Table 2). When the bank has not hedged, it chooses to eliminate MMC's from its portfolio as interest rates rise and lending volume declines as a consequence. Hedging also allows the bank to issue more MMC's than it could at the base level, boost its loan volume, and increase earnings. Thus, hedging the cost of borrowing when rates are rising enables the bank to increase overall portfolio size over what it would have been and significantly raise its earnings.

Interest Rates Fall

Falling interest rates mitigate some of the benefits of hedging borrowing costs. A bank might still be better off by hedging, however, even if interest rates declined. To analyze the usefulness of hedging under falling interest rates, the interest rate charged on MMC's was dropped to 12.0 percent. The bank can achieve greater performance with this lower rate than it could have in the base solution (Chart 2), but hedging interest rates at their original level still offers higher performance than not hedging when rates are falling.

Table 2 Bank Performance Under Alternative Interest Rate Levels

	Base	No Hedging Rising Interest Rates	Hedging MMC Rising Interest Rates	No Hedging Falling Interest Rates	Hedging MMC Constant Interest Rates
Expected Income	$ 397,708	$ 374,527	$ 431,886	$ 409,553	$ 434,413
Standard Deviation	45,575	37,992	46,510	49,916	46,510
Return on Equity	29.5%	27.8%	32.0%	30.4%	32.2%
Assets					
Federal Funds Sold	$ 502,121	$ 227,727	$ 564,926	$ 614,246	$ 564,926
1-Year Treasury Bill	0	0	0	0	0
Nontaxable Securities	0	0	0	0	0
Agricultural Loans	6,462,031	5,989,573	7,518,470	6,599,321	7,418,470
Reserves	554,681	525,001	565,392	565,392	629,999
Total Assets	$11,548,943	$10,300,000	$13,800,000	$11,946,410	$13,800,000
Liabilities					
Federal Funds Purchased	$ 0	$ 100,000	$ 100,000	$ 0	$ 100,000
Demand Deposits	4,000,000	4,000,000	4,000,000	4,000,000	4,000,000
Savings Deposits	2,700,000	2,700,000	2,700,000	2,700,000	2,700,000
Time Deposits	1,700,000	1,700,000	1,700,000	1,700,000	1,700,000
$100,000 CD's	116,220	1,200,000	1,200,000	0	1,200,000
6-Month MMC	2,432,723	0	3,500,000	2,946,410	3,500,000
30-Month CD's	500,000	500,000	500,000	500,000	500,000
Federal Reserve Borrowings	100,000	100,000	100,000	100,000	100,000
Total Liabilities	$11,548,943	$10,300,000	$13,800,000	$11,946,410	$13,800,000

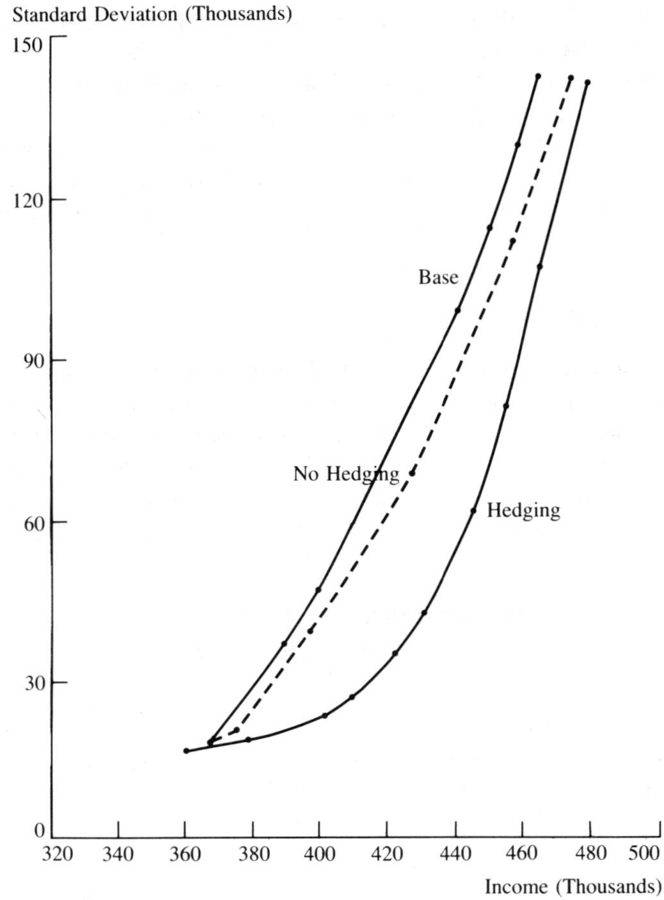

CHART 2 Hedging When Interest Rates Fall

The result that hedging improves performance even when interest rates fall does not seem logical for a firm earning profits. It can be explained, however, for a utility maximizing bank. Because the bank has goals of avoiding risks as well as earnings profits, the risk reducing benefits of hedging can offset the profit reducing effects. Even though hedging causes the bank to pay a higher rate for its MMC's, the reduction in the variability of portfolio returns that comes from hedging outweighs the higher liability costs. Therefore, hedging borrowing costs can improve the bank's optimal performance, even when interest rates are falling.

Results for the specific level of risk-return preference indicate that bank performance is higher when the bank hedges. Income is slightly higher as a result of hedging while the return on equity also improves (Table 2). By reducing the variability of MMC rates through hedging, the bank is encouraged to expand its loan portfolio, providing returns from increased lending that outweigh the relatively higher cost of borrowing. Thus, model results suggest that hedging borrowing costs when interest rates are falling may improve bank performance. For some greater decline in interest rates, the resultant higher relative costs of borrowing could presumably negate the risk-reducing benefits of hedging.

Interest Rates Remain Constant

Hedging the cost of issuing MMC's has pronounced benefits for the model bank, even when MMC rates do not change after the hedge has been placed. A comparison of model generated *EV* frontiers shows the bank can increase its utility by hedging. Hedging reduces the variations in the interest rates that must be paid on MMC's and shifts the bank's *EV* frontier to the right (Chart 3). By hedging, the bank improves on the best performance it had been able to achieve, earning more at the same risk.

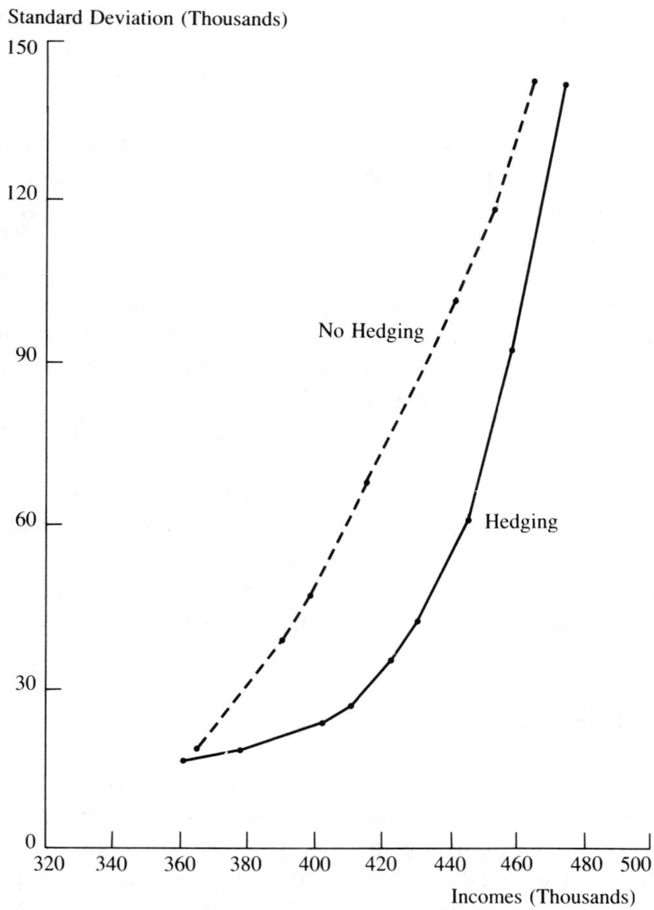

CHART 3 Hedging When Interest Rates Remain Constant

Comparisons of bank performance for a specific risk-return preference further demonstrate the benefits of using financial futures. Hedging boosts the bank's performance by increasing income, return on equity, and the total size of the portfolio (Table 2). The improvement in earnings comes from increased lending, because with less variability in interest rates, the bank is encouraged to issue more MMC's—a primary source of loanable funds. Moreover, the size of the bank's portfolio expands as much as available equity capital allows. In summary, model results indicate that hedging the borrowing costs during a period of constant interest rates can improve all measures of bank performance.

Alternative Transaction Costs

The transaction costs of hedging are important to banks that use financial futures, especially small banks that may not hedge often. Transaction costs for such banks may not be confined to trading costs alone. Because many small banks do not have the resources to manage their own hedging program, they may employ an advisory service to help develop hedging strategies. Total transaction costs for hedging may then include not only the actual trading costs but also a consulting fee for advice used in implementing the hedge and other aids in analysis.

The results discussed in previous sections were based on transaction costs of $40 per contract. That figure, which includes placing and lifting the hedge—a complete futures contract turn—represents an average of current trading costs for futures contracts. To analyze the extent that higher transaction costs might reduce the benefits of hedging, other model solutions were derived using different transaction costs. The model bank was forced to pay first $100 and then $200 per futures contract. All these model solutions were based on the assumption that MMC interest rates remained constant after the hedge was placed. Because the higher transaction costs had minimal effect on bank performance, only the results for the specific risk-return preference are discussed.

Model results suggest that the advantages of hedging far outweigh the cost, even when the costs are substantial. Higher levels of transaction costs did not discourage the bank from continuing to hedge. Nor did they force the bank to reduce its portfolio or cut back on the MMC's it issued, even when they reached a substantial $200 per contract (Table 3). The only noticeable effect of the higher hedging costs is a modest reduction in bank income. These results indicate that the benefits that come from a reduction in portfolio variability more than counterbalance even high transaction costs.

Implications of Hedging

Model results provide an empirical framework for testing whether hedging improves bank performance. The model used in this analysis shows financial futures can make significant improvements in several measures of bank performance. Hedging the risk involved in issuing MMC's clearly placed the model bank in a better position both when interest rates remained unchanged and when they rose. When borrowing costs fell, optimal performance was greater with hedging than without it, except when interest rates had declined signif-

Table 3 Bank Performance Under Alternative Transaction Costs

	$40 Transaction Cost	$100 Transaction Cost	$200 Transaction Cost
Expected Income	$ 434,413	$ 434,360	$ 434,227
Standard Deviation	46,510	46,510	46,510
Return on Equity	32.2%	32.2%	32.2%
Assets			
Federal Funds Sold	$ 564,926	$ 564,926	$ 564,926
1-Year Treasury Bill	0	0	0
Nontaxable Securities	0	0	0
Agricultural Loans	7,518,470	7,518,470	7,518,470
Nonagricultural Loans	5,986,605	5,986,605	5,986,605
Reserves	629,999	629,999	629,999
Total Assets	$13,800,000	$13,800,000	$13,800,000
Liabilities			
Federal Funds Purchased	$ 100,000	$ 100,000	$ 100,000
Demand Deposits	4,000,000	4,000,000	4,000,000
Savings Deposits	2,700,000	2,700,000	2,700,000
Time Deposits	1,700,000	1,700,000	1,700,000
$100,000 CD's	1,200,000	1,200,000	1,200,000
6-Month MMC	3,500,000	3,500,000	3,500,000
30-Month CD's	500,000	500,000	500,000
Federal Reserve Borrowings	100,000	100,000	100,000
Total Liabilities	$13,800,000	$13,800,000	$13,800,000

icantly. Results indicate, therefore, that under most market conditions hedging offers substantial rewards.

Although the results of this study apply to a small rural bank, the general conclusions can be extended to other closely held banks. Adapting the model to another such bank would require changing portfolio size and income, but the bank's feasible set of portfolio combinations would show similar risk-return tradeoffs. Thus, model results demonstrating the effect of financial futures on the performance of a larger bank would show more absolute changes in measures of bank performance, but the direction of the changes would be the same as for the size of bank modeled in this study.

One implication of the results is that when interest rates are volatile hedging gives banks more flexibility in selecting their optimal portfolio. By hedging, the model bank could enlarge its portfolio and maintain or even increase the MMC's it issued. Without hedging, the interest rate risk associated with MMC's forced the bank to cut back on this liability and lending volume was curtailed as a result. Thus, hedging largely offsets the risk of volatile interest rates and gives a bank more freedom in selecting a higher yielding portfolio. Hedging also gives the bank another management tool for reducing risk.

Another implication to be drawn from the results is that transaction costs are probably a comparatively minor consideration for small banks. Even when transaction costs are raised to a high level, hedging still improves bank performance. This suggests that small banks that lack the resources to manage their own hedging programs might be able to achieve higher levels of performance by employing capable advisory services to carry out hedging programs than by not hedging at all.

The implications of hedging go well beyond the benefits that accrue to a small bank and its owners. To the extent that use of financial futures reduces bank risks, hedging has implications for depositors, borrowers, and the general economy. Not only do depositors face less risk of loss when overall bank risk has been reduced, but with less risk the cost of insuring deposits may decline for a bank that successfully hedges. Model results also indicate that hedging encourages increased lending, with the result that farmers and other rural borrowers benefit from the greater availability of loan funds. Finally, by allowing banks to transform risks in the economy more efficiently, hedging benefits society in general.

Summary and Conclusions

This article has examined the effects of financial futures on bank performance. Beginning with a conceptual framework of the banking firm, the article presented an economic model to test the effect of hedging money market certificates on the performance of a representative small agricultural bank. The results suggest that hedging significantly improves bank performance whether measured by income, return on equity or portfolio size. Furthermore, these beneficial effects hold even under some adverse financial market conditions.

The advantageous effects demonstrated in this article raise the question of why more banks are not using financial futures as a risk-management tool. The likely answer is that many banks, especially small banks, lack the expertise to carry out an effective hedging program. As banks become more aware of the benefits of hedging, increased use of financial futures markets might be expected.

Technical Appendix

The expected return-variance *(EV)* frontier traces out the most efficient tradeoffs a bank can make between risk and return (Figure A1). The *EV* frontier is efficient in that the expected return on the bank's portfolio cannot be improved for a given level of expected return.[1] Every point along curve, EV_0 represents a different portfolio combination. Point *A*, for example, represents total investment in such almost riskless investments as Treasury bills. Point *B* represents more aggressive commercial lending with limited investment in securities.

The frontier shifts in response to changes in the bank's operating parameters. Equity capital, for example, affects the size of the bank's asset portfolio. By allowing more lending and investing, an infusion of more equity causes the *EV* frontier to shift in parallel to the right from EV_0 to EV_1. If the bank suddenly has an increase in the return on one of its risk assets, the *EV* frontier also shifts to the right, but as shown in the movement from EV_0 to EV_2, the shift is not parallel.

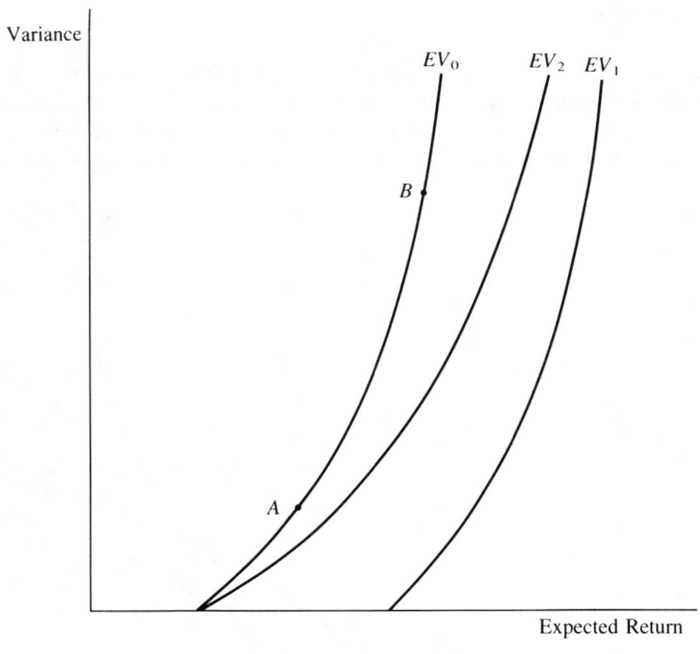

FIGURE A1 Bank *EV* Frontiers

[1]Portfolio analysis for an individual has its theoretical roots in the work first pioneered by James Tobin, "Liquidity Preference as Behavior Towards Risk," *Review of Economic Studies,* 25 (1958), pp. 65–86 and Harry Markowitz, "Portfolio Selection," *Journal of Finance,* 7 (1952), pp. 71–91. For a further discussion of portfolio theory as applied to the bank firm, see J. M. Mason, *Financial Management of Commercial Banks,* New York: Warren, Gorham, and Lamont, 1979.

Interest Rate Volatility

The impact that interest rate volatility has on commercial banks can be demonstrated within a utility maximization framework. Volatile interest rates increase the variability of both asset returns and liability costs. The result for most banks has been more variability in their net portfolio spread. This corresponds to a leftward, nonparallel shift in the *EV* frontier, shown in Figure A2 as the movement from EV_1 to EV_0. The bank then adjusts its portfolio combination to be consistent with point *E* instead of point *C*.

The total impact of increased volatility on the bank's operation can be divided into two components—the income and substitution effects. The income effect is the net loss in utility that results from greater volatility. This is shown in Figure A2 as a move from point *C* to point *D*. The shift to EV_0 also causes the bank to hold fewer risky assets that it had. This substitution for assets with lower risks corresponds to the movement from point *D* to point *E*. An increase in the volatility of interest rates, then, not only reduces utility but also encourages banks to reduce their holdings of risky assets.

Using Financial Futures

The same framework can be used to demonstrate the effect of financial futures. If interest rates become more volatile, a bank's *EV* frontier effectively shifts to the left. This corresponds to the movement from EV_0 to EV_2 (Figure A3). If the bank keeps the new portfolio arrangement, point *C*, utility drops from I_0 to I_2 and the bank readjusts its portfolio to include fewer risky assets.

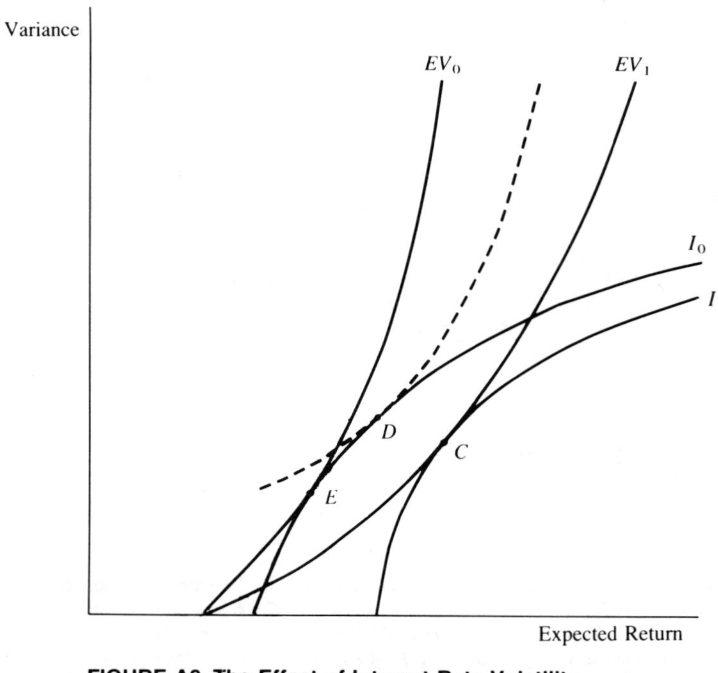

FIGURE A2 The Effect of Interest Rate Volatility

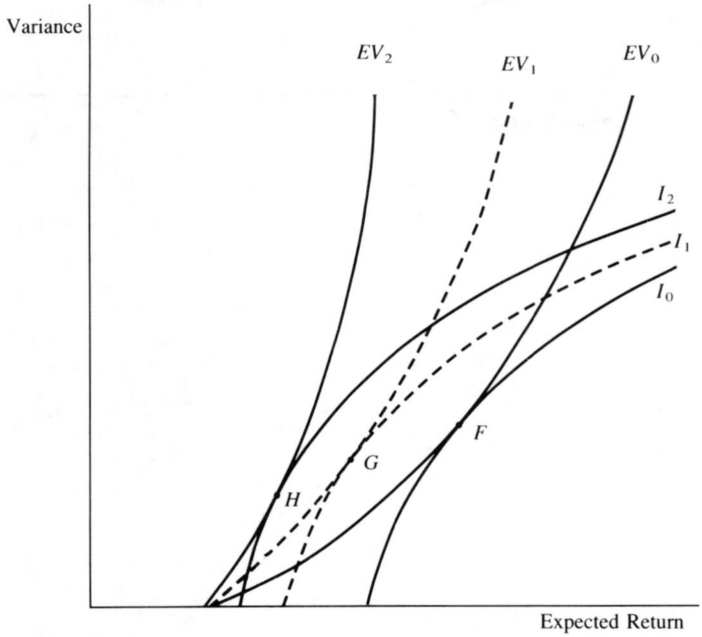

FIGURE A3 The Effect of Hedging

Both the utility loss and the portfolio adjustments can be mitigated by use of financial futures. Suppose that instead of accepting point C as its new point of operation, the bank anticipates the increased volatility in interest rates and places a macrohedge in an effort to keep the portfolio variability associated with point F. This hedge, if properly placed, will shift the EV frontier back to the right, to some new value, EV_1. The frontier shifts to the right because portfolio variance has been reduced and the bank can earn a higher return for any given level of risk. The exact location of EV_1 will depend on the effectiveness of the hedge—how well basis risk is managed—and transaction costs. The more effective the hedge, the closer EV_1 will lie to the initial frontier, EV_0. The net effect of using financial futures, then, is that the bank now operates at point G instead of point H, providing the bank with more utility and fewer portfolio adjustments than it could have achieved without hedging.

Measuring and Managing Interest Rate Risk: A Primer

George G. Kaufman

4

Losses from unexpected changes in interest rates have become an increasing problem at depository institutions over the past decade, as interest rates have become more volatile and have climbed to unprecedented levels. Such losses occur when unexpected increases in interest rates decrease the market value of an institution's assets more quickly than the market value of its liabilities—deposits and other borrowed funds. This differential change in market values occurs if the institution's assets are less *interest sensitive* than its deposits, that is, if the earnings rate on assets adjusts more slowly to market changes in interest rates than does the payout—the coupon or contract rate—on deposits. Under the same balance sheet condition, the institution experiences a gain when interest rates decline unexpectedly.

The more quickly an asset or liability adjusts to market rate changes, the more interest sensitive it is said to be. Institutions expose themselves to interest rate risk whenever the interest sensitivity of the two sides of their balance sheet is not equal.

The problems of interest rate risk are well-known, but accurate measurement of risk exposure is not easy. And, without such measurements, reliable management of this risk is not possible. This article describes a new technique for measuring in one number or factor the degree of risk exposure an institution assumes, and develops simple hypothetical examples to demonstrate the implications of various interest rate changes for depository

Reprinted from *Economic Perspectives* (January/February, 1984): 16–29 by permission of the Federal Reserve Bank of Chicago and the author.

institutions. The article also discusses alternative strategies for managing or controlling interest rate risk and the pros and cons of the new technique relative to more commonly used procedures.

A Hypothetical Bank Balance Sheet

The implications of interest rate changes may be analyzed most easily with a simplified bank balance sheet. The same principles apply to more complex and realistic situations. Here, we describe an institution that has only three types of assets:

1. Cash reserves (C)
2. 2½-year business loans, amortized monthly (BL), and
3. 30-year mortgage loans, amortized monthly (ML).

It also has only two types of deposits (P):

1. 1-year single payment certificate of deposit (CD1) and
2. 5-year single payment certificate of deposit (CD5).

These deposits make no coupon payments and may not be redeemed before maturity. The remaining item on the right side of the balance sheet is net worth or capital (K). The balance sheet shown in Table 1 describes an institution with total footings of $1,000. All accounts are valued at market. Cash is $100; business loans are $400; mortgage loans are $500; one-year CDs are $600; and five-year CDs are $300. The bank's capital is valued at $100, and its capital-to-asset ratio is 10 percent.

For the sake of simplicity, interest rates are assumed to be the same for all terms to maturity for all securities and deposits of a given default risk class. That is, the yield curve is assumed to be flat. All interest rates are compounded monthly. All payments are to be made on schedule; there are no assumed defaults, prepayments, or early deposit withdrawals. The interest rate on all business loans is initially assumed to be 13 percent and on all deposits, 11 percent. Cash reserves are assumed not to bear interest initially. The projected net income of the bank for the year may be computed by multiplying the market value of each account by the appropriate interest yield. This is shown in the summary income statement in Table 1.[1] The bank's initial net income (NI) projected for the year is 1.8 percent on assets. This income will be realized if interest rates do not change during the year. The expected return on capital is 18 percent.

If interest rates change, they are assumed to change by equal percentage points (basis points) for all securities. After a change in interest rates, all bank accounts are marked to their new market (present) values—the price for which the accounts could be sold, if necessary. The balance sheet is designed so that accounts are not equally sensitive to interest rate changes.

[1]This definition of net income reflects economic income. All gains and losses due to changes in interest rates are recognized immediately. In practice, banks do not use this accounting system and do not recognize these gains and losses unless securities are sold before maturity. Nevertheless, economic income provides the most meaningful picture of a bank's income condition.

Table 1 Initial Conditions

Balance sheet

Assets	Dollars*	D (yrs.)†	Liabilities	Dollars*	D (yrs.)†
Cash	100	0	CD (1 yr.)	600	1.0
BL (2½ yr.)	400	1.25	CD (5 yr.)	300	5.0
ML (30 yr.)	500	7.0	Net worth (*K*)	100	5.5
Total	1,000	4.0	Total	1,000	2.65

Deposit duration

$$D_p = \frac{600\ (1) \times 300\ (5)}{900} = 2.33 \text{ years}$$

Projected annual income statement for year

	Interest yield	Market value ÷ total assets	Interest ÷ total assets (percent)	
Revenues				
Cash	0	.1	0	
Loans	13	.9	11.7	11.7
Expenses				
Deposits	11	.9	9.9	9.9
Net income				1.8

Summary accounts

$K = \$100$
$K/A = 10\%$
$NI = 1.8\%$

*All accounts are valued at market (present value).

†Approximate.

Interest rates increase by 200 basis points

Now let interest rates increase 200 basis points across the board. This reduces the market value of all accounts. The new balance sheet and income statements are shown in Table 2. It is obvious that the accounts do not change by equal amounts. Longer-term accounts decline more in value than shorter-term accounts. For example, the market value of the business loan declines from $400 to $390, while that of the longer-term mortgage loan declines from $500 to $437. Total assets decline to $927. Likewise, the market value of the one-year CD declines from $600 to $589, the five-year CD from $300 to $272, and total deposits from $900 to $861. The value of capital, which is the difference between the value of total assets and deposits, declines 34 percent from $100 to only $66. Capital as a

Table 2 Assume Interest Rate Increase of 200 Basis Points

Balance sheet

Assets	Dollars* Actual	Dollars* Approx'd.†	Liabilities	Dollars* Actual	Dollars* Approx'd.†
Cash	100	100	CD (1 yr.)	589	588
BL (2½ yr.)	390	390	CD (5 yr.)	272	270
ML (30 yr.)	437	430	Net worth (*K*)	66	62
Total	927	920	Total	927	920

Projected annual income statement for year

	Interest yield	Market value ÷ total assets	Interest ÷ total assets (percent)	
Revenues				
Cash	2	.11	0.2	
Loans	15	.89	13.4	13.6
Expenses				
Deposits	13	.93	12.1	12.1
Net income				1.5

Summary accounts

$K = \$66$

$K/A = 7.1\%$

$NI = 1.5\%$

*All accounts are valued at market (present value).

†By equations 2 or 4.

ratio of total assets declines from 10 percent to 7.1 percent. The increase in interest rates also decreases the projected annual net income by increasing the interest cost of deposits more than the revenue from assets, even though cash is now assumed to yield a small interest return. This occurs because deposits now account for proportionately more of total footings than before, so that interest expense has increased in relative importance. The projected net income declines to 1.5 percent of total assets from 1.8 percent. It is evident that the increase in interest rates has harmed the institution.

An equal decrease in interest rates of 200 basis points would have opposite effects. As can be seen from Table 3, the values of all bank accounts except cash increase. Capital increases to \$147, the capital to asset ratio to 13.5 percent, and net projected income to 2.0 percent of total assets. The institution is better off than it was before.

Table 3 Assume Interest Rate Decrease of 200 Basis Points

Balance sheet

Assets	Dollars* Actual	Dollars* Approx'd.†	Liabilities	Dollars* Actual	Dollars* Approx'd.†
Cash	100	100	CD (1 yr.)	612	612
BL (2½ yr.)	410	410	CD (5 yr.)	331	330
ML (30 yr.)	580	570	Net worth (K)	147	138
Total	1,090	1,080	Total	1,090	1,080

Projected annual income statement

	Interest yield	Market value ÷ total assets	Interest ÷ total assets (percent)	
Revenues				
Cash	−2	.09	−0.2	
Loans	11	.91	10.0	9.8
Expenses				
Deposits	9	.87	7.8	7.8
Net income				2.0

Summary accounts

$K = \$147$

$K/A = 13.5\%$

NI = 2.0%

*All accounts are valued at market (present value).
†By equations 2 or 4.

Duration analysis

Changes in a bank's financial position due to interest-rate changes can be looked at with the help of *duration analysis*. Duration is a measure of the average life of a security. In its simplest form, it is computed by multiplying the length of time to each scheduled payment by the ratio of the present value of that payment to the total present value or price of the security and summing, or

$$D = \frac{\sum_{t=1}^{m} t \cdot PVF_t}{\sum_{t=1}^{m} PVF_t} \tag{1}$$

where:

D = duration

t = length of time (number of months, years, etc.) to the date of payment

PVF_t = present value of the payment (F) made at (t), or $\frac{F_t}{(1+i)^t}$

$\sum_{t=1}^{m}$ = summation from the first to the last payment (m).

This measure of duration is referred to as Macauley's Duration, and is named after Frederick Macauley, who first computed it in 1938 in his seminal study of the history of interest rates in the United States. Duration is a single number that is measured in units of time, e.g., months or years. For securities that make only one payment at maturity, duration is equal to maturity; for all other securities, it is shorter than term to maturity. Duration effectively converts a coupon security into its zero coupon (single payment or bullet) equivalent. For coupon bonds, for example, duration is equal to the term to maturity of an equivalent zero coupon bond that makes the same total payments and yields the same interest rate. The properties of duration have been described elsewhere.[2] Most importantly for our purposes, at first approximation, duration relates changes in interest rates and percentage changes in bond prices linearly as follows:

$$\frac{\Delta S}{S} = -D\frac{\Delta i}{(1+i)} \approx -D\Delta i \qquad (2)$$

where:

S = price of a security

i = yield to maturity

Δ = change from previous value.

Equation 2 is more accurate the smaller are the interest rate changes.

Now we can readily see why the value of each account changed when interest rates increased. All we need to do is compute the duration for each account by Equation 1 and multiply by the 200 basis point increase in interest rates. The duration of each account is shown in Table 1. (For ease of following the analysis, the durations shown are rounded.)

[2]G. O. Bierwag, George G. Kaufman, and Alden Toevs, "Duration: Its Development and Use in Bond Portfolio Management," *Financial Analysts Journal,* July/August 1983 and "Management Strategies for Savings and Loan Associations to Reduce Interest Rate Risk," *New Sources of Capital for the Savings and Loan Industry: Conference Proceedings* (Federal Home Loan Bank of San Francisco), December 1979. A more technical analysis appears in George G. Kaufman, G. O. Bierwag, and Alden Toevs, eds., *Innovations in Bond Portfolio Management: Duration Analysis and Immunization,* Greenwich, Conn.; JAI Press, 1983 and in Gabriel A. Hawawini, ed., *Bond Duration and Immunization,* New York; Garland Publishing, 1982.

As was noted earlier, the duration of securities that generate periodic flows before maturity is less than their term to maturity. Thus, the initial duration of the 30-year monthly amortized mortgage yielding 13 percent is only seven years (7.14 years precisely). The durations of the single payment CDs are equal to their maturities. Because the bank will generate a constant stream of earnings as shown in the projected income statements unless interest rates change, the return on capital is projected to be constant. Thus, the duration of capital is the same as the duration of a fixed-coupon perpetual bond (consol) and approximates $1/i$. The initial return on capital is \$18 per \$100 or 18 percent, and its initial duration is approximately 5½ years.[3] The longer are the durations, the proportionately greater will be the price change predicted by Equation 2 for a given change in interest rates. Note also that: 1) duration, unlike maturity, has a linear relationship with price sensitivity and 2) the longer the duration of a security, the smaller is its interest sensitivity as defined at the beginning of this article.

The change in the market value of each account predicted by Equation 2 is shown in Table 4. Changes in interest rates of 200 basis points are large relative to the capabilities of Equation 2. As a result, the predictions are only rough approximations and will be less accurate with longer durations. In actuality, changes of 200 basis points are unlikely to occur all at one time. In addition, the predictions are distorted because rounded rather than precise values of duration are used. The approximate changes in values will approach the actual changes in value as the assumed interest rate changes decrease in size and the precise values of duration are used. Nevertheless, for all the accounts except capital and total liabilities, the computed dollar changes are reasonably close to the actual changes

Table 4 Using Duration to Measure Risk Exposure for Individual Accounts

Approximate changes in the market value of balance sheet accounts for 200 basis point *increase* in interest rates (see equation 2):

BL:	−1.25	(+200)	=	− 2.5%,	(−\$10)
ML:	−7.0	(+200)	=	−14.0%,	(−\$70)
1 yr. CD:	−1.0	(+200)	=	− 2.0%,	(−\$12)
5 yr. CD:	−5.0	(+200)	=	−10.0%,	(−\$30)
K:	−5.5	(+200)	=	−11.0%,	(−\$11)*
TA:	−4.0	(+200)	=	− 8.0%,	(−\$80)
TL:	−2.65	(+200)	=	− 5.3%,	(−\$53)*

*Price effect (PE) only. But there is also an income effect (IE) = $(TA_{PE} - TL_{PE}) = (80-53) = \$27$

Thus, total effect = PE + IE = :

TL: $-53 + (-27) = -\$80$

K: $-11 + (-27) = -\$38$

[3]If the bank's earnings are expected to increase, duration would be greater than the consol value, as can be seen from Equation 1. If earnings are expected to decrease, duration will be shorter. Although capital has no maturity date, its duration is not constant. It changes when interest rates change.

between Tables 1 and 2. For example, the actual decline in the market value of the 5-year CD is $28 (from $300 to $272) and the approximated decline is $30 (from $300 to $270). To the extent that changes in prices reflect the degree of interest rate risk assumed, duration represents a good first-approximation measure of risk because it is proportional to the price change. For example, the price of the five-year CD will change five times as much for a given change in interest rates as the price of the one-year CD. This makes it five times as risky, which is reflected in a duration five times as great.

For capital and total liabilities, the computed declines are substantially smaller than the actual declines. This occurs because the approximated market value of the assets declines by $80 when interest rates increase by 200 basis points, while the sum of deposits and capital declines by only $53 (42 + 11), or $27 less. The additional $27 loss must be charged against capital. When this is done, the approximated value of capital declines by $38, directly by $11, as shown in Table 4, and indirectly by $27, from the additional loss in assets. (The actual value of capital declines by $34.) The sharp decline reflects the combined effects of the 200 basis point increase in the discount rate on capital from 18 to 20 percent and the decline in projected earnings on capital from 18 to 15 percent. Now also the approximated market value of total liabilities declines by $80 (53 + 27), the same amount as the decline in assets, and the two sides of the balance sheet balance. Thus, as formulated, Equation 2 cannot be used directly for approximating changes in the value of capital.

With a small adjustment, however, durations can be used to measure the overall interest rate exposure of the institution. As is evident from analyzing the changes in the balance sheet and income statement above, the increase in interest rates did not affect every account equally. It is thus necessary to specify precisely what account is most important to the institution. The selection of such a target account whose value is to be controlled and the assumption of a particular degree of risk exposure in that account is the function of the bank's senior management. In this article, we will focus on only two accounts: 1) the nominal value of capital and 2) the capital-to-asset ratio.[4] The first is most likely of primary concern to the shareholders of the bank and the second, to bank examiners. While the interest rate sensitivity or risk of individual accounts is related to the duration of the account, the interest rate risk of a target account is related to the difference, or gap, between the average duration of the assets of the institution and the average duration of the deposits. The duration gap measures for the two accounts discussed above are:

$$\begin{aligned} &K\colon (D_A - wD_P) \\ &\frac{K}{A}\colon (D_A - D_P) \end{aligned} \qquad (3)$$

where:

[4]It is also possible to use net income as a target account and to develop appropriate measures of duration gap. The duration gap measure for economic income is complex and has been derived by G. O. Bierwag. A duration gap measure for net income using current bank accounting practices has been derived in Alden Toevs, "Gap Management: Managing Interest Rate Risk in Banks and Thrifts," *Economic Review* (Federal Reserve Bank of San Francisco), Spring 1983.

D_A = average duration of assets

D_P = average duration of deposits

w = a weight defined as $P/P+K = P/A$

The proofs for these relationships are derived in the Appendix.

The average durations for the measure of duration given in Equation 1 are obtained by weighting the durations for the individual securities by their relative market values. Substituting into Equation 3 the appropriate values of duration from Table 1 yields the values of the duration gap for each account. These are shown in Table 5. Note that the duration gaps differ for the two accounts, reinforcing the need for the bank to identify a primary target account. The gap is 1.9 years for capital and 1.7 years for the capital-to-asset ratio.

The estimated impact of interest rate changes on the target accounts can be obtained by substituting the relevant duration gap into Equation 2, as follows:

For capital:

$$\begin{aligned}\frac{\Delta K}{A} &= -(D_A - wD_P)\Delta i \qquad (4)\\ &= -(4 - .9 \times 2.3)\Delta i\\ &= -1.9\Delta i\end{aligned}$$

or

Table 5 Using Duration Gap to Measure Interest Rate Risk Exposure for Target Accounts

Duration gap formulas:

K: $(D_A - wD_P) = 4.0 - .9(2.3) = 1.9$ years

$\frac{K}{A}$: $(D_A - D_P) = 4.0 - 2.3 = 1.7$ years

where $w = \left(\frac{P}{A}\right)$

Approximate changes in market values for 200 basis point increase in interest rates (see equation 4):

K: $-1.9(+200) = \$-38$

$\frac{K}{A}$: $-1.7(+200)\ (0.9) = -3.1\%$

Formulas for immunization ($IRR = 0$):

K: $D_A = wD_P$

$\frac{K}{A}$: $D_A = D_P$

$$\frac{\Delta K}{K} = -(D_A - wD_P)\left(\frac{A}{K}\right)\Delta i$$
$$= -(1.9)(10)\Delta i$$
$$= -19\Delta i \qquad (4)$$

For capital-asset ratio:

$$\Delta\left(\frac{K}{A}\right) = -(D_A - D_P)\left(1 - \frac{K}{A}\right)\Delta i \qquad (4)$$
$$= -(4 - 2.3)(.9)\Delta i$$
$$= -1.5\Delta i$$

Multiplying each duration gap by the 200 basis point increase in interest rates yields the decrease in the value of the respective account as a percent of total footings. Capital now decreases by 3.8 percent of total assets, or the full \$38, a combination of the \$11 price effect and the \$27 income effect (See Table 4).

The above examples clearly demonstrate that the actual changes in the market value of the balance sheet accounts attributed to interest rate changes are proportional to the duration of the accounts. Accurate measures of duration yield close approximations of these actual changes.

The institution can change its degree of interest rate exposure to any extent it wishes by changing the composition of its balance sheet in such a way as to obtain the desired duration gap for its target account. The greater the duration gap, the greater is the institution's risk exposure for a particular target account; and conversely, the smaller the gap, the smaller its exposure. Moreover, the relationship is linear. For example, if in the above example the duration gap for capital were twice as large, say 3.8 years, then the value of capital would decline twice as much, or \$76 for a 200 basis point increase in interest rates.

An institution can also eliminate its risk exposure to zero by setting its target account duration gap to zero. This can be seen by using a value of zero in Equation 4. The bank is then said to be "immunized," and unexpected interest rate changes will not change the market value of the target account. The decision on how much interest rate risk exposure to assume and the strategy of how to achieve this is referred to as interest rate risk management and is discussed in the next section.

Before introducing risk management, it is useful to emphasize a number of points:

1. If the institution does not specify a target account, it cannot measure its interest rate risk exposure accurately.
2. Interest rate exposure is directly related to the absolute size of the duration gap for the target account; the greater the gap, the greater the risk exposure.
3. Interest rate exposure can be removed or immunized in a target account by setting the appropriate duration gap to zero.
4. If the market value of total assets changes more or less with changes in the price level, maintaining a constant capital-to-asset ratio (immunizing) maintains a constant real value of capital.

5. Although the bank balance sheet used in our examples includes only securities traded on the cash market, duration analysis applies equally well to securities traded on the futures and options markets. The durations of these securities can be computed and included in the appropriate duration gap measure to measure the overall interest rate exposure of the bank.

Managing interest rate risk

Like any private business firm, a depository institution attempts to maximize its profits. However, profit maximization presumes a desired level of risk exposure. Expected profit and risk are directly related. The greater the risk of loss assumed, the greater must be the expected profit required to compensate for the higher likelihood of loss, and, conversely, the smaller the risk exposure assumed, the smaller can the expected profit be. The desired risk-return trade-off for an institution is determined by its senior management and may be expected to differ from bank to bank. Interest rate risk is only one type of risk a bank assumes. It generally also assumes credit quality risk, liquidity risk, foreign exchange rate risk, and so on. Thus, managing interest rate risk is part of overall risk management.

To manage any risk accurately, a bank must predict the probability of possible outcomes of undertaking the risky activity. To manage interest rate risk, it is necessary to predict, at minimum, the direction of interest rate changes. The effect of an interest rate change will differ depending on whether the bank has a positive gap (the duration of assets is greater than the duration of the appropriately weighted deposits) or a negative gap in the relevant target account. As may be seen in Equation 2, decline in interest rates will increase the nominal value of a bank's capital account if its capital duration gap is positive and decrease the value if its gap is negative. An increase in interest rates will have the opposite effect, decreasing the nominal value of the capital account if the duration gap is positive and increasing it if it is negative. The greater the gap, the greater will be the gain or loss. Thus, the bank must determine both the direction and the size of its gap on the basis of its predicted interest rates. Correct predictions will increase capital and incorrect predictions will decrease capital. A bank may pursue two interest rate risk strategies; a passive (immunization) strategy or an active strategy.

IMMUNIZATION

For whatever reasons, a depository institution may wish to maintain a constant nominal value of its target account regardless of changes in interest rates and immunize its interest rate risk exposure. This is a complete hedging strategy. It should be noted that banks generate profits if they assume interest rate risk and manage it correctly, and that this income may be reduced or lost altogether when it decides to immunize. On the other hand, by immunizing the bank also decreases its chances of suffering losses if the risk is mismanaged. As discussed earlier, to immunize fully the bank needs to set the appropriate duration gap to zero.

Assume that the bank chooses the nominal value of capital as its target account and wishes to immunize its current market value. In our example in Table 1, the initial value of capital is \$100. To immunize capital, the bank needs to restructure its balance sheet so that from Equation 3:

$$D_A - wD_P = 0 \tag{5}$$

Initially $D_A = 4$ years, $D_P = 2.3$ years and P/A = .9. This yields a duration gap of 4 − .9 (2.3) = 1.9 years. The bank is not immunized. It can reduce the gap to zero either by shortening the duration of its assets by 1.9 years to 2.1 years or by lengthening the duration of its deposits to 4.4 years so that .9 (4.4) = 4 years. It can do so either on the cash or the futures market. We will assume that the bank prefers to lengthen its deposits on the cash market. It can do so by reducing the dollar volume of its one-year CDs from \$600 to \$125 and increasing the volume of its five-year CDs from \$300 to \$775. As is shown in Table 6, this increases the duration of the deposits from 2.3 to 4.4 years and satisfies Equation 5.

Now let interest rates increase 200 basis points as before. (For the sake of ease in tracing the mechanics, the examples are created using the approximate duration values rather than

Table 6 Immunize K and Set *DGAP* = 0 Years When $D_A = 4$ and $D_P = 2.3$

Strategy: Set $D_A - \left(\frac{P}{A}\right)D_P = 0$

Currently: $D_A = 4, \left(\frac{P}{A}\right)D_P = 2.1$ years

$DGAP_K = 4 - 2.1 = 1.9$ years

Can satisfy by:

1. By shortening *TA* to $D_A = 2.1$ years
2. Lengthening *P* to $D_P = 4.4$ years
   $\left[\left(\frac{P}{A}\right)D_P = .9\ (4.4) = 4.0\right)\right]$

Can act on:

1. Spot market
2. Futures market

Assume *lengthening P* on *cash* market by changing mix:

Assets	Dollars*	*D* (yrs.)†	Liabilities	Dollars*	*D* (yrs.)†
Cash	100	0	CD (1 yr.)	125	1
BL (2½ yr.)	400	1.25	CD (5 yr.)	775	5
ML (30 yr.)	500	7.0	Net worth	100	5.5
Total	1,000	4.0	Total	1,000	2.65

Deposit duration

$$D_P = \frac{125\ (1) \times 775\ (5)}{900} = 4.44 \text{ years}$$

Table 6 Immunize K and Set *DGAP* = 0 Years When $D_A = 4$ and $D_P = 2.3$ (Continued)

If interest rates increase by 200 basis points:

	Dollars*			Dollars*	
Assets	Actual	Approx'd.‡	Liabilities	Actual	Approx'd.‡
Cash	100	100	CD (1 yr.)	123	122
BL (2½ yr.)	390	390	CD (5 yr.)	704	698
ML (30 yr.)	437	430	Net worth	100	100
Total	927	920	Total	927	920

Projected annual income statement

	Interest yield	Market value ÷ total assets	Interest ÷ total assets (percent)	
Revenues				
Cash	2	.11	0.2	
Loans	15	.89	13.4	13.6
Expenses				
Deposits	13	.89	11.6	11.6
Net income				2.0

Summary accounts

$K = \$100$

$K/A = 10.8\%$

$NI = 2.0\%$

Analysis (duration gap)

$K: 4 - .9(4.44) = 0$ yrs.

$K/A: 4 - 4.44 = -.44$ yrs.

*All accounts are valued at market (present value).

†Approximate.

‡By equations 2 or 4.

the precise duration values. Thus, the bank will not be perfectly immunized in actuality). Except for capital, which remains at $100, the approximated market value of each account declines. Because the composition of assets was not changed, the decline in their market value is the same as in Table 2. The composition of the deposits was changed, however, by reducing the proportion of shorter-term deposits. As a result, the decline in the value of total deposits is greater than before. Capital remains unchanged because the decline in the market value of the deposits is now exactly equal to the decline in the market value of the assets. Although capital remained unchanged, the values of the other two summary accounts did not. The capital-to-asset ratio increased to 10.8 percent, and net income increased to 2.0 percent of assets. Thus, immunization of the capital account does not imply immunization of other accounts. As shown in Table 6, the gap for the capital-to-asset ratio is −0.44 when the gap for capital account is 0.

Because, as can be seen from Equation 1, the change in interest rates changes the duration of all securities, Equation 5 is no longer satisfied after the change in rates. Thus, the bank is no longer immunized and must restructure its balance sheet so that it is immunized against the next interest rate change. Moreover, as may also be seen from Equation 1, the durations of securities decline, even if there is no interest rate change, just from the passage of time. To remain immunized, the bank must continually restructure its balance sheet to offset this duration ''drift''. For larger institutions that buy or sell Fed funds daily in the normal course of their business, this is not a problem. It is more of a problem for smaller institutions.

It is important to note that even though an immunized institution as a whole does not assume interest rate risk, the durations of the individual securities on the bank's balance sheets need not be matched, and the institution may still engage in interest rate intermediation in individual accounts. In our example, the bank has 30-year mortgages financed in part by one-year deposits. The reduction in overall risk exposure is achieved through diversification across individual securities with different durations. A portfolio of a given average duration can be structured from an almost infinite number of individual securities with different durations.

ACTIVE MANAGEMENT

Many banks do not wish to eliminate interest rate risk altogether, but prefer to manage it. Because accepting risk exposure assumes that the bank will suffer losses if interest rates change in the wrong direction, the decision to accept such exposure presupposes that the bank is willing to predict interest rates and believes it can do so successfully. (If it is not, it is better off to immunize and to assume no risk for the same expected return.) Indeed, to determine the desired direction and magnitude of the duration gap, it is necessary, at minimum, for the bank to forecast the direction in which interest rates will change. If rates are predicted to increase, the gap should be negative, so that the average duration of the assets is shorter than that of the weighted deposits. This would make the bank behave as if it were a net liability, whose value declines as interest rates rise. The bank will benefit from an interest rate rise. On the other hand, if rates are predicted to decline, the institution would be better off if the gap were positive. Then the bank behaves like a net asset, whose value increases as interest rates decline.

Assume the bank predicts that interest rates will decline. It will restructure its portfolio to obtain a positive duration gap. The precise value of the gap it chooses depends on its risk-return preferences. The larger the gap, the higher the potential return but the higher also the risk of loss. The decision as to the precise risk-return matrix to assume and thus the value of the gap to achieve is generally made by the bank's top management in consultation with the Asset and Liability Management Committee. Assume that the bank predicts that interest rates will decline in the next period and prefers to accept risk in the value of its capital consistent with a value of a positive duration gap of 1 year so that:

$$D_A - wD_P = 1 \tag{6}$$

It can achieve this value in our example either by shortening the duration of its assets from 4 to 3.1 years or by lengthening the duration of its deposits from 2.3 to 3.3 years. (We again use the approximate durations.) For every 100 basis points interest rates decline, the bank's capital value will rise by $10 (100 basis points × 1 year gap = 1% of total assets).

In Table 7, the bank lengthens the duration of its deposits on the cash market to 3.3 years by reducing the dollar amount of one-year CDs from $500 to $375 and increasing the dollar amount of five-year CDs from $300 to $525. Now, contrary to the bank's expectations, let interest rates increase by 200 basis points rather than decrease. The bank is worse off. Assets again decline to $927 as before, but the market value of capital declines by $17 to $83. The bank has lost its bet on interest rates and has paid the price. At the same time, its capital-to-asset ratio declines to 9.0 percent and its net income remains basically unchanged. Each of these changes is easily predictable using duration analysis and assuming alternative interest rate scenarios. As was noted earlier, to win with an active policy, the bank must both predict interest rates and be right. As before, the interest rate increase changes the durations of the accounts differently and thus the value of the duration gap. To maintain a gap of 1 year, or any other target amount, the bank must restructure its balance sheet accordingly.

The changes in the values of the different summary accounts for a 200-basis-point increase in interest rates for alternative value of the duration gap in terms of capital are

Table 7 Set *DGAP* for K = 1 Year When $D_A = 4$ and $D_P = 2.3$

Strategy: Set $D_A - \left(\frac{P}{A}\right) D_P = 1$ year

Currently: $D_A = 4$, $\left(\frac{P}{A}\right) D_P = 2.1$ years

$DGAP_K = 1.9$ years

Can satisfy by:

1. Shortening *TA* to $D_A = 3.1$ years
2. Lengthening *P* to $D_P = 3.3$ years

$$\left[\left(\frac{P}{A}\right) D_P = 3.3 \text{ and } .9D_P = 3\right]$$

Can act on:

1. Spot market
2. Futures market

Assume *lengthening P on cash* market by changing mix:

Assets	Dollars*	D (yrs.)†	Liabilities	Dollars*	D (yrs.)†
Cash	100	0	CD (1 yr.)	375	1
BL (2½ yr.)	400	1.25	CD (5 yr.)	525	5
ML (30 yr.)	500	7.0	Net worth	100	5.5
Total	1,000	4.0	Total	1,000	3.5

Table 7 Set *DGAP* for $K = 1$ Year When $D_A = 4$ and $D_P = 2.3$ (Continued)

Deposit duration

$$D_P = \frac{375\ (1) \times 525\ (5)}{900} = 3.33 \text{ years}$$

If interest rates increase by 200 basis points:

Assets	Dollars* Actual	Dollars* Approx'd.‡	Liabilities	Dollars* Actual	Dollars* Approx'd.‡
Cash	100	100	CD (1 yr.)	368	367
BL (2½ yr.)	390	390	CD (5 yr.)	476	473
ML (30 yr.)	437	430	Net worth	83	80
Total	927	920	Total	927	920

Projected annual income statement

	Interest yield	Market value ÷ total assets	Interest ÷ total assets (percent)	
Revenues				
Cash	2	.11	0.2	
Loans	15	.89	13.4	13.6
Expenses				
Deposits	13	.91	11.8	11.8
Net income				1.8

Summary accounts

$K = \$83$

$\frac{K}{A} = 9.0\%$

NI = 1.8%

Analysis (duration gap)

K: $4 - 3 = 1$ yr.

$\frac{K}{A}$: $4 - 3.3 = 0.7$ yr.

*All accounts are valued at market (present value).

†Approximate.

‡By equations 2 or 4.

summarized in Table 8. The changes may even be in different directions. For example, if the duration gap for capital is set at 0.5 years, the market value of capital will decline by

Table 8 Changes in Summary Accounts for Alternative Duration Gaps Targeting Capital Account when Interest Rates Increase by 200 Basis Points

GAP	Approximate changes in summary accounts*		
(years)	*K*	(*K*/*A*)	NI
1.9	$−38	−3.1%	−0.2%
1.0	−20	−1.2	0.0
0.5	−10	−0.2	+0.1
0	0	+0.8	+0.2

*Using Equation 4.

about $10 when interest rates increase by 200 basis points, the capital-to-asset ratio declines somewhat by 0.2 percentage points, and net income increases by .08 percentage points.

Practical Problems with Applying Duration Gap Analysis

Although theoretically appealing, duration gap analysis has some practical problems that have limited its use to date. Duration gap analysis imposes strenuous data demands. It requires complete data on each account (security) or, at minimum, each homogeneous group of accounts on the bank's balance sheet, including not only information on contract (coupon) interest rate and maturity but also on when a variable rate account (security) can be repriced (its contract rate changed) before maturity and any constraints on the amount by which it can be repriced. In addition, data on prepayment and other call provisions; due-on-sale, early deposit withdrawal, and other put provisions; and any other options that are included and the conditions for when and how they may be exercised are required. This information requires full access to the bank's account origination files. The less information on individual accounts that is available, the less reliable will be the computed duration gaps.

Variable rate contracts and contracts that contain option provisions have effective maturities that are shorter than their nominal maturities. For example, if a 10-year variable rate bond can be repriced at $100 at the beginning of every year, its price behavior resembles that of a one-year bond rather than a 10-year bond. Likewise, a 10-year bond with a call option permitting the borrower to buy back (prepay) the bond at no more than a maximum price will behave like a shorter term bond when interest rates decrease so that the probabilities of a call are sufficiently high. The computation of durations for cash flows that involve either repricing or the exercise of option provisions requires forecasts of interest rates to determine when the cash flow pattern will be changed and by how much. The best forecasts to use for this purpose are the rate forecasts that are implicit in the term structure of interest rates at the time.[5]

[5]For example, if the current interest rate on one-year fixed rate bonds is 10 percent and on two-year bonds is 11 percent, the implied rate on a one-year bond for delivery next year is approximately 12 percent.

A number of types of bank deposit accounts, such as demand deposits, savings, NOWs, SNOWs, and MMDAs, do not have specific maturity dates. Depositors may redeem these accounts at any time at par value. The accounts effectively have a put option exercisable by the holder on the bank at any time. What are the durations of such deposit accounts?

On the one hand, it may be argued that these are one-day accounts. If market rates of interest increase and the bank does not raise its deposit rates accordingly, either in cash or in services, the depositor may withdraw the funds. This is particularly likely in a world of increasing deregulation in which institutions across the street are able and likely to compete by offering market rates. The deposits may be effectively viewed as variable rate accounts that are repriced at par every day. Unlike our earlier examples, their market value will never decline below par value as interest rates rise. Their durations would be one day. This treatment makes it difficult for a bank to structure its balance sheet to produce zero or even small positive or negative duration gaps.

On the other hand, in the old world of regulation and deposit rate ceilings and to some extent even today, all deposits are not equally interest sensitive. If a bank's deposit rates lag increases in market rates, all deposits will not leave the bank immediately. "Core" deposits will remain for some time and flow out only slowly. It may be possible to assign accurate probabilities to the timing of the net outflows, depending on the difference between the market and deposit rates. From this it is possible to compute the effective decline in the market value of the remaining deposit accounts by assuming them to be equivalent to certificates of deposits with maturity dates equal to the predicted outflow dates. Their durations would also be equivalent and thus would be longer than one day. If interest rates increase, it is then possible to value these deposits at less than their par value.

However, the correct duration to assign these deposits cannot be determined arbitrarily by the desirability of the assumptions. Rather, the actual price behavior of the accounts when interest rates change must be used. Otherwise the interest rate sensitivity of the bank is misgauged. The correct duration awaits additional research. (To the extent that interest rate deregulation has increased the availability of deposit accounts without specific maturity dates, it may have made it more difficult for banks to structure small positive or negative duration gaps and to decrease their interest rate exposure.)

Because the value of a security's duration is determined by the interest rate, changes in interest rates change its duration and may force a restructuring of the portfolio in order to maintain the desired duration gap. Moreover, even if interest rates did not change, periodic restructuring is necessary in a dynamic framework because the durations of coupon securities do not decline or age at the same rate as does time. They generally decline more slowly, although at times duration can increase as time passes. Thus, the durations of the two sides of the balance sheet are unlikely to change equally over time and continual updating or restructuring of the balance sheet is required. Restructuring, of course, is costly. But most depository institutions operate, at least in the Fed funds market, daily, so that restructuring at the margin should not be much of a burden.

In effect, every day is a new day for managing the gap. Although there may be long duration accounts on the balance sheet, the relevant time horizon for asset and liability management is only to the next restructuring date. Only in this interval is the interest rate exposure of the institution uncertain. The disposition of cash flows beyond this interval is of no immediate concern for ongoing institutions. Through time, long duration accounts become shorter duration accounts and maturing accounts are, at maturity, either removed from the balance sheet or rolled over into the same or other accounts, whose durations are then included in the gap measure. At any moment, only an account's interest sensitivity matters.

We have made a number of simplifying assumptions in the analysis. One of these was to assume that the yield curve is flat and that when interest rates change, they all change by the same amount. This is highly unlikely. But the duration measure defined in Equation 1 is dependent on it. Different and more complex assumptions about the shape of the yield curve and changes in interest rates yield different and more complex measures of duration. If the actual process that governs interest rate changes, referred to as the stochastic process, were known, the correct duration formula could be used. But this process is not known with certainty. The theory, however, assumes that the correct duration measure is used. Moreover, securities of different default risk classes may be subject to different stochastic processes. Thus, the bank is likely to use an incorrect measure of duration and this introduces a source of error.[6]

In addition, the theory applies strictly only to securities that are free of the risk of default. Yet, many bank accounts, particularly on the asset side, have default risk. This introduces additional inaccuracies into the computation of the correct duration measure. Lastly, the analysis abstracts from transactions costs and taxes. Introduction of these complicates the analysis further.

Advantages of Duration Gap Analysis

Despite these disadvantages, duration gap analysis has substantial advantages over alternative techniques for measuring interest rate risk exposure accurately. The most widely used alternative measure technique involves classifying all asset and liability accounts by their terms to maturity or to first permissible repricing, whichever comes first.[7] The accounts are grouped in a number of maturity-period "buckets;" e.g., one day, one to three months, three to 12 months, one to five years and so on. Net balances, or maturity gaps in dollars, are computed for each bucket. The larger are the net balances in the shorter maturity buckets, the more interest sensitive and less price sensitive the institution.

Duration analysis considers the timing of coupon and other intermediate cash flows as well as the timing of the final payment at maturity. This is particularly important for mortgages and other amortized loans for which the intermediate flows are significantly larger than the final payment. Yet the maturity bucket approach classifies such accounts only by the date of the final payment or of the first permissible repricing.

For practical purposes, the number of maturity categories must be limited. What should be the maturity cutoffs for each bucket? Should the shortest-term bucket include accounts

[6]The nature of this risk is discussed in G. O. Bierwag, George G. Kaufman, and Alden Toevs, "Bond Portfolio Immunization and Stochastic Process Risk," *Journal of Bank Research,* Winter 1983.

[7]Alden L. Toevs, *op. cit.;* Barrett F. Binder and Thomas W. F. Lindquist, *Asset/Liability and Funds Management at U.S. Commercial Banks,* Rolling Meadows, IL; Bank Administration Institute, 1982.

maturing or eligible for repricing in 1–30 days, 1–60 days, or 1–90 days? The same question applies to the other bucket categories. Changing the limits of the buckets can give a different picture of a bank's interest rate sensitivity. Table 9, which groups the accounts in the balance sheets shown in Tables 1 and 6 in a number of alternative ways, illustrates this problem.

The more limited the number, the wider the category. But the wider the category, the less accurate is the informational content of each category. For example, a category of 6 to 12 months is frequently used, e.g., on the new Federal Reserve call report. This category would encompass 182-day securities as well as 364-day securities. If these were zero coupon single payment instruments so that the terms to their maturities were equal to their durations, Equation 2 indicates that the price sensitivity of the 364-day security to a given interest rate change is exactly twice that of the shorter security. Thus, if the 182-day security was the only security on the asset side of the balance sheet and the 364-day security the only security on the liability side, the maturity bucket would indicate no gap and no interest sensitivity. Yet the bank's liability side would in fact be twice as price sensitive as the asset side. In reality, there will be larger numbers of securities with different maturities in all the buckets so that the average maturity in each is unlikely to be at one extreme of the maturity range. Nevertheless, accuracy is sacrificed.

As noted, the maturity gap analysis yields a number of gap values equal to the number of maturity categories used. These individual gaps cannot be simply summed. The overall degree of risk exposure is thus difficult to summarize. It is not readily observable, for example, from any of the alternative maturity gap groupings in Table 9 that the balance sheet is one that immunizes the dollar value of capital. The gap in any one bucket, even the shortest one, is unlikely to be representative of the overall interest rate sensitivity of the institution. The impact of the value of the gap in the shortest term bucket can be more than offset by the value of the gap in the next shortest bucket, so that the longest gaps can be in the same direction as the shortest gaps. More importantly, measured this way, the risk exposure is difficult to manage. A different strategy is required for each bucket. To immunize, for example, cash flows must be matched in each bucket. This involves considerable management and transactions costs. It is reasonable to assume that some of the bucket gaps are internally offsetting and that the use of external transactions to achieve the same objective is inefficient. In contrast, duration analysis yields a single number and only a single gap to manage. Any internal cancelling is already accounted for.

Maturity bucket gaps must generally be managed with securities in the same maturity category; e.g., a gap in the 6 to 12-month bucket can be changed most easily by buying or selling other securities in this maturity range. This constrains management. The larger the number of buckets used to gain greater accuracy, the more constrained is management. On the other hand, duration gaps can be managed with a very wide range of maturities. For example, as was seen earlier, the duration of a 30-year amortized fixed rate mortgage when interest rates are 13 percent is nearly equivalent to that of a seven-year zero coupon bond. Moreover, even durations on individual securities on the two sides of the balance sheet need not be equal or different by the size of the gap as long as the average durations of all securities are. The desired target gap value may be achieved by diversifying among individual securities of different but offsetting durations. Thus, bank management has an

Table 9 Alternative Maturity Gap Measures

Maturity bucket	Assets	Liabilities	Gap	Assets	Liabilities	Gap	Assets	Liabilities	Gap	Assets	Liabilities	Gap
A. Balance sheet from Table 1 *(dollars)*												
0-3 mos.	100	0	+100									
3-6 mos.	0	0	0	100	600	−500	100	600	−500			
6 mos.-1 yr.	0	600	−600							500	600	−100
1-2½ yrs.	400	0	+400	400	0	+400	400	300	+100			
2½-5 yrs.	0	300	−300	0	300	−300						
5-10 yrs.	0	0	0	0	0	0	500	100	+400	500	400	+100
>10 yrs.	500	100	+400	500	100	+400						
Total	1,000	1,000	0	1,000	1,000	0	1,000	1,000	0	1,000	1,000	0
B. Balance sheet from Table 6 *(dollars)*												
0-3 mos.	100	0	+100									
3-6 mos.	0	0	0	100	125	− 25	100	125	− 25		125	+375
6 mos.-1 yr.	0	125	−125							500		
1-2½ yrs.	400	0	+400	400	0	+400	400	775	−375			
2½-5 yrs.	0	775	−775	0	775	−775						
5-10 yrs.	0	0	0	0	0	0	500	100	+400	500	875	−375
>10 yrs.	500	100	+400	500	100	+400						
Total	1,000	1,000	0	1,000	1,000	0	1,000	1,000	0	1,000	1,000	0

almost unlimited choice of maturities and can continue to provide a range of interest rate intermediation services to its customers within a given degree of net interest rate risk exposure to the institution. Even if the bank wishes to immunize itself, it may still engage in a wide range of interest rate intermediation for individual securities; it does not have to match cash flows in each maturity bucket. That is, a bank can simultaneously engage in macro immunization and micro interest rate intermediation and continue to accommodate its customers, who have a wide range of maturity preferences, with an equally wide range of products.

Lastly and perhaps most importantly, the strenuous data demands made by duration analysis are not any more severe than those that alternative systems, including maturity gap analysis, would impose if they were to be equally accurate. All measuring techniques must forecast interest rates to know when repricing will occur and options will be exercised. The relative simplicity claimed for some alternative systems cannot be obtained by sweeping such problems under the rug. Only a complete and thorough cost-benefit analysis can differentiate among the alternative techniques. Simplicity and reduced cost is likely to be achieved only at the cost of reduced accuracy. And, because once a computerized information system is in place it is costly to change, banks should plan their systems for asset and liability management models of the future. Duration-based models are in a relatively early stage of development and require further refinement. They appear, however, a most promising tool for accurate asset and liability management.

Summary

Interest rate risk continues to be a problem of increasing importance to many depository institutions. In order to manage this risk correctly, it is first necessary to measure it accurately. This article has discussed how the recently developed technique of duration analysis can be applied to this problem. Duration gap is both an accurate measure of an institution's interest rate risk exposure and, because it is a single number, a simple concept to manage. But its application is complex, and the data required is costly. However, most of these complexities and costs also apply to alternative measures of interest rate risk, if they are to be equally accurate, including maturity gap analysis. Banks and other depository institutions should consider the use of duration analysis to measure and manage their interest rate exposure reliably and to maximize their long-run profits.

Appendix follows

Appendix

Approximate proofs of duration gap measures*

Assume:

1) In market values: $A = P + K$ and $\Delta A = \Delta P + \Delta K$
2) All interest rates for same default risk class securities are the same and all changes in interest rates are equal.

1. Target account K

Let $\Delta K = 0$ (immunize)

Then from above assumptions: $\Delta A = \Delta P.$

Recall the basic equation: $$\frac{\Delta A}{A} = -D_A \Delta i$$

or $$\Delta A = -D_A \Delta i_A.$$

Thus as $\Delta i_A = \Delta i_P$ $$D_A A = D_P P$$

or $$D_A = \left(\frac{P}{A}\right) D_P$$
$$= wD_P$$

It follows that *DGAP* is: $(D_A - wD_P)$

2. Target account: K/A

Let $\Delta(K/A) = 0$ (immunize)

Define $$\left(\frac{K}{A}\right) = c$$

so $$K = c\text{A}.$$

Then from above assumptions: $$A = P + cA$$
$$\Delta A = \Delta P + c\Delta A$$
$$A(1 - c) = P$$

And $$\Delta A(1 - c) = \Delta P$$

Using the basic equation with $\Delta i_A = \Delta i_P$:

$$D_A A(1 - \text{c}) = D_P P$$

or $$D_A = D_P$$

It follows that *DGAP* is: $(D_A - D_P)$

*More detailed proofs are found in F. M. Redington, "Review of the Principle of Like-Office Valuations," *Journal of the Institute of Actuaries,* 1952, pp. 286-340 (reprinted in Gabriel Hawawini, ed., *Bond Duration and Immunization,* New York: Garland Publishing Co., 1982, pp. 286-340); Myron A. Grove, "On 'Duration' and the Optimal Maturity Structure on the Balance Sheet," *The Bell Journal of Economics,* Autumn 1974, pp. 698-709; and the references cited in footnote 2.

Business Loans at Large Commercial Banks: Policies and Practices

Randall C. Merris

5

Commercial bank lending was once a fairly simple business. Business loans were nearly all short term and carried fixed interest rates. Any other details, except possibly collateral requirements, were left to informal agreements between a bank and its customers.

Business lending began getting more complex in the 1930s as many banks started making term loans—loans with maturities of more than a year. Relations between banks and business borrowers have been growing more complex—and more formal—ever since, the formality of term loans now being applied to many short-term loans as well.

Part of the push for more complicated loan arrangements—and, therefore, a greater variety in the kinds of agreements—has been the need for banks and borrowers to protect themselves from movements in interest rates over the credit cycle. Increases in market rates boost bank costs of funding outstanding loans. They also increase the opportunities for more lucrative new credits elsewhere. Reductions in market rates lower the interest costs of other debt financing available to bank loan customers.

Floating rates have probably been the most important innovation in bank lending since the advent of the term loan. Provisions for adjusting loan rates periodically give banks and borrowers some protection against market rate fluctuations. By combining some of the advantages of term and short-term loans, floating rates have allowed banks to compete effectively for their share of the business credit market—even in the face of increased

Reprinted from *Economic Perspectives* (November/December, 1979):15–23 by permission of the Federal Reserve Bank of Chicago and the author.

competition from the commercial paper market and other nonbank credit suppliers. At the same time, use of floating rates has encouraged changes in the other terms and conditions of business lending.

This article examines business lending practices at large banks, especially toward commercial and industrial loans. These loans to businesses other than financial institutions most clearly reflect the recent directions in bank lending policy. Pricing, maturities, and other lending terms depend on the particular bank and borrower negotiating the credit, as well as the use of the loan proceeds—such as, to provide working capital, cover accounts receivable, or finance expenditures on plant and equipment.

Term Loans

Term loans range in maturity from just over a year to more than ten years. Banks once held loans with maximum maturities of five to seven years. For customers that needed longer terms, banks participated with other lenders. A bank might, for example, take the first five years of credit, with an insurance company taking the rest to maturity, often under different terms and conditions. Banks are more inclined now to take all the term credits themselves or to participate with other banks, each taking part of the loan for the whole maturity.

With the future always uncertain, lengthening the maturity structure of bank loan portfolios might seem to mean banks were taking more risks. But at least half the term lending at large banks calls for periodic adjustment of loan rates.

Costs are nearly always higher for initiating term loans than short-term loans. Considerable negotiation is required, usually at top levels of management and often with legal staffs representing the bank and the borrower. And voluminous documentation is needed to cover both the terms and conditions of the loan. Administrative costs are also high, especially in the frequent situations where the bank and borrower need to keep in touch throughout the life of the loan.

Agreement has to be reached not only on the amount of the loan and its price but also any number of other points:

Loan commitment—an arrangement for the borrower to draw down loans and sometimes even a schedule for disbursing the funds. As the funds are made available to the borrower whether he uses them or not, a fee is sometimes charged on the amount of the commitment not used.

Fall of the Real Bills Doctrine . . .

Though term loans were sometimes made for special purposes, most banks offered only short-term credit until well into this century. This was because bank policies were based on the commercial loan theory of credit, an American adaptation of the Real Bills Doctrine in England.

According to this doctrine, the only appropriate bank loans were short-term, self-liquidating notes. By self-liquidating, bankers meant loans that led to enough increase in sales and near-term profits to cover repayment. Loans for plant and equipment did not usually qualify, the reasoning being that several years might be needed before returns on fixed capital were enough to retire the debt.

Some business loans were renewed routinely, even as early as the 1830's, with the result that nominally short-term credit arrangements were actually long term. Not until the 1920s, however, was the commercial loan theory seriously challenged. The idea that loans needed to be self-liquidating began losing credibility for several reasons:

- The realization that the commercial loan theory did not provide the monetary policy advantages its proponents claimed.
- The practice of financing long-term projects by borrowing from one bank to pay off another—sequential bank financing.
- The emergence of the view that banks could gain liquidity better from their nonloan assets and their liabilities.

Proponents of the Real Bills Doctrine had long argued that the requirement that bank loans be self-liquidating made the money supply expand and contract with the needs of business. However, bankers became increasingly aware, especially in looking back on the Panic of 1907, that the policy did not prevent severe contractions, bank deposit runs, or bank failures.

Many banks, meanwhile, had imposed the rule that customers had to have all their loans at the bank paid up sometime during the year. This clean-up rule, meant to strengthen the commercial loan theory, actually had the opposite effect. Annual cleanups tended to encourage short-term borrowing first at one bank, then another, and then back at the first bank—all to extend effective credit periods for fixed-capital purposes.

Renewals, sequential financing across banks, and the clean-up rule together debased the short-term loan doctrine. It took a new theory of bank management, however, to utterly discredit the commercial loan theory.

The new theory took the view that as most business loans were not actually liquid, they did not serve as a funding cushion against unexpected deposit withdrawals. In place of short-term loans, the theory turned for liquidity to other assets—such as government and corporate securities, bankers' acceptances, and commercial paper—that could be sold with little loss of their capital value. A forerunner to modern liability management, the new theory also noted that banks could acquire liquidity through Federal Reserve borrowings and interbank sale of bonds under repurchase agreements.

Together, these changes both in attitude and in the structure of banks' short-term investment portfolios helped foster some growth of term lending in the 1920s.

Instalment schedule—a timetable for paying down the principal and interest. Payments are most often due monthly, quarterly, or semiannually.

Supporting balance requirement—the borrower's obligation to maintain demand deposits that help offset the cost of funding the loan. A bank may require that even a loan commitment be backed by demand deposits.

Collateral—property put up against a loan. Banker and borrower must agree on the physical nature of the collateral, its value, and the care to be taken in its handling and protection.

Protective covenants—a requirement that the borrower do certain things, as for example, keep working capital above some minimum level during the credit term or furnish the bank periodic financial reports. Covenants can also require that the borrower not do certain things without the bank's approval—for example, expand its fixed assets, undertake further external financing, enter a merger, or acquire an affiliate.

Some of the costs of initiating and administering term loans are charged directly to borrowers as fees. But there is, of course, an interest rate at which banks are willing to absorb the remaining costs of term lending.

. . . and rise of term lending

Although Real Bills persisted into the 1930s, events gave impetus to term lending.

- The slack demand for short-term loans during the Depression—even at a prime rate of 1½ percent from 1933 on—gave banks incentives and opportunities to shift into some higher yielding term loans.
- The Banking Acts of 1933 and 1935 limited bank activities in corporate security markets, leading banks to substitute term lending.
- The establishment of deposit insurance in 1933 reduced the likelihood of financial panics and deposit runs, encouraging some lengthening of the maturity of bank loan portfolios.
- A change in Federal Reserve rules in 1933 allowing loans of all maturities to be used as assets for discounts and advances at Federal Reserve banks increased the liquidity of term loans.
- Under the revision of bank examination standards in 1934, term loans were no longer routinely classified as "slow."
- With modern amortization gaining general acceptance, term loans, which had usually called for payment of principal and interest at maturity, were made payable in annual, semiannual, quarterly, or monthly instalments. Instalment payments smoothed the flow of interest and principal back to the bank and, by demonstrating a borrower's ability to repay, helped banks monitor term loans and identify problem credits.
- Banks were encouraged to help finance the recovery, and followed the examples set by the Federal Reserve and Reconstruction Finance Corporation in making direct term loans to business.

The change was marked. A Federal Reserve survey in 1939 showed term loans accounted for a fourth of the dollar volume of business loans at the banks sampled—39 percent at the banks sampled in New York. More than a third of the banks, however, showed no more than five term loans on their books. A 1946 survey of member banks showed term lending accounting for more than a third of the dollar volume of business loans.

Revolving credits

Revolving credits were once treated as short-term loans, which followed the banking convention that all loans had to be paid up sometime during the year—the annual cleanup rule. They now fall somewhere between term loans and short-term loans. Customers with revolving credits can borrow and repay repeatedly over the life of the agreement (usually two or three years) as long as the debt outstanding does not exceed the amount originally agreed on.

As many banks have relaxed the clean-up rule, however, allowing continuous indebtedness, revolving credits often qualify now as an intermediate form of term lending. Some contracts, in fact, include conversion clauses that allow credits to continue as term loans when the revolving credit agreement expires. Under such contracts, the period of revolving credit is often viewed as the first years of a term loan.

Short-term and term loans as substitutes

Distinctions between term and short-term loans have sometimes been misleading. The most detailed survey of continuous indebtedness through renewal of short-term loans were conducted nearly 25 years ago in the Cleveland Federal Reserve District. The survey showed that half of the dollar holdings of short-term business loans outstanding at member banks in the district were obligations of borrowers continuously in debt to the same bank for at least two years. A fourth of the short-term credit was owed by businesses in debt to the same bank continuously for at least five years. Only 8 percent of this credit was to customers in debt to the same bank no longer than three months.

As long as loans are renewable, some borrowers with long-term financing needs might actually prefer short-term loans. Initiation costs are lower. And as the contracts are less detailed, they are less likely to put operating constraints on the borrower.

Continuous indebtedness of this kind may not be to the bank's advantage, however, especially if it has to renew credit to prevent a loan default or bolster future demand for loans or other bank services. The prospects of renewal requests increase uncertainties for the bank. A borrower may feel that the loan can be renewed. But the bank cannot be sure renewal will be requested. Even if a bank has done very well in predicting renewal requests and sorting out the loans it feels obligated to renew, this ability is a poor second for certain knowledge of the length of indebtedness agreed on when the credit was first made.

Floating loan rates . . .

Banks have been devising alternatives to fixed-rate pricing of business loans for decades. Graduated rates on some term loans appeared in the late 1930s. This scheme, applying progressively higher rates to later years of maturity, did not provide floating rates, of course. Term premiums to be added to the loan rate for later years were set when the loan was originated. The loan rate did not move with market rates, and the bank had no influence on it over the life of the loan.

Floating rates came into use in the late 1940s, with the introduction of formulas involving the addition of a quarter of a percentage point or more to the Federal Reserve discount rate. Floating rates were not widely used, however, as long as the discount rate and other rates remained fairly stable.

When the discount rate began changing more often in the early 1950s—and lagging hikes in the prime rate—banks switched the floating-rate base to the prime, a rate more closely reflecting market forces. Floating rate provisions, limited almost entirely to term loans, were not nearly as common as today.

The big change came in the mid-1960s, with the advent of modern bank liability management, growth of money-market funds, and more changes in short-term rates. Floating rates gave banks a way of making sure returns on outstanding loans—both long and short term—moved with the costs of funds.

Short-term loan renewals can, of course, be appropriate at times, as for example, when the need for long-term credit was not anticipated. But the flexibility of term loans nowadays reduces the need for renewals. The term loan itself can be written to capture one of the main advantages of short-term loan renewal—periodic adjustment in the interest rate. Floating rates substitute directly for the privilege of banks to change the interest rate when a short-term loan is renegotiated at maturity.

Both bank and borrower find advantages in negotiating the *effective* maturity at the outset instead of a *nominal* maturity that can be renewed. Sure of the maturity of a loan, a bank can absorb some of the other risks elsewhere in a loan agreement or lower the average loan rate. Assured of credit for the full term, a borrower is spared the real (albeit sometimes small) risk that a renewal request might be denied.

Loan commitments

Loan commitments, once informal credit lines available to customers that kept adequate balances at a bank, are now more apt to be firm agreements laying out a bank's obligation to provide credit in the future (including the amount of the credit and the rate to be

. . . and the formulas for computing them

Essentially two types of prime-based formulas are used in calculating floating rates:

- Prime-plus. The more conventional of the two, this method calls for an add-on factor to adjust for default risk and provide a term premium for long-term credit. An example is the prime rate plus 2 percentage points—"prime *plus* 2."
- Times-prime. Becoming more common, this method calls for multiplication of the prime by a factor to adjust for credit risk and a term premium. An example is the prime multiplied by 1.2—"1.2 *times* prime."

With either example, a prime rate set initially at 10 percent results in a floating loan rate of 12 percent.

Differences follow, however, if the prime rate is any rate other than 10 percent. With reductions in the prime rate, floating rates based on times-prime pricing decline faster than plus-prime rates. And increments in the prime result in faster increases in times-prime rates than in plus-prime rates.

Suppose, for instance, that an initial 10 percent prime is hiked to 12 percent. The prime-plus-2 loan rate moves from 12 percent to 14. The 1.2-times-prime rate moves from 12 percent to 14.4. If the prime is lowered from 10 percent to 8, the plus-prime rate falls from 12 percent to 10, but the times-prime rate drops to 9.6 percent.

Banks sometimes combine the two methods. An example is 1.09 times the *sum* of prime plus 1 percentage point—a floating rate equal to 1.09 *times* the prime plus 1.09 percentage points. Again, if the prime rate is set initially at 10 percent, the combination method leads to about the same floating rate at the basic methods—for example, 1.09 times 10 percent plus 1.09 percentage points, or roughly 12 percent. Effects for the combination method at any other prime, however, are the same as times-prime pricing, given the same multiplicative factors in the formulas.

As times-prime rates vary more than plus-prime rates over the interest-rate cycle, they have greater implications for changing bank loan revenue and, therefore, total profits.

One of the main reasons for times-prime pricing is that when the prime rate is raised, bank costs of funding outstanding loans in interest-sensitive markets may go up faster than the prime. The greater-than-proportional increase in the loan rate from times-prime pricing helps compensate banks for lagged upward responses of the prime rate.

The drift away from compensating balances also helps explain the growing use of times-prime pricing. The trend toward higher loan rates and lower required demand-deposit balances has, in fact, been a major factor in the use of more complicated floating-rate formulas.

The idea is to raise the loan rate enough to offset the loss of loanable funds when compensating balance requirements are eased. But the cost to a bank of foregoing these balances varies over interest-rate and credit cycles. When credit demand rises and banks scramble for ever more costly money-market funds, earlier reductions in compensating balances become increasingly costly. If rates are adjusted by the times-prime formula, explicit reimbursement to the bank increases as the prime rate rises. That is, an escalating rate premium replaces the supporting deposit balances.

Against these advantages of floating rates must be set the main disadvantage—the greater variation in loan revenue over the credit cycle. The disadvantage of floating rates becomes most apparent when market rates are falling. If formula loan rates are geared to fall as fast as money market rates or even faster, bank profit margins on outstanding loans can be squeezed. Banks can immunize part of their business-loan portfolios from movements in money-market rates and the prime by continuing to make fixed-rate loans to customers interested primarily in loan-rate certainty.

charged) and often the customer's obligation to pay fees on the credit availability. The change has come with the growth of both term loans and revolving credits and the greater use made of formal commitments for short-term lending.

The Federal Reserve Survey of Loan Commitments at Selected Large Banks for April 1979 showed $68 billion outstanding in unused formal agreements. Of these unused formal commitments, 16 percent was for term loans, 71 percent was for revolving credits, and the remaining 13 percent was mostly for short-term credits. Loans that had been made under formal commitments totaled $76 billion.

Despite the trend toward formalization of loan commitments, informal but confirmed lines of credit still accounted for much of the unused commitments. A total of $95 billion in unused credit was available to business borrowers under informal but confirmed lines, compared with $68 billion in formal commitments. Use of informal lines was much less, however. Loans outstanding under confirmed lines amounted to $29 billion, compared with $76 billion in loans that had been made under formal commitments.

Compensating balances

Although many banks still require compensating (or supporting) balances, with the trend toward explicit pricing of bank services, less emphasis is put on these balances than in the past. As a result, required balances are being replaced in many cases by explicit fees and increases in lending rates.

Where demand-deposit balances are still used, the requirement is usually stated as an average deposit balance equal to a percentage of the loan or commitment. A typical requirement is an average balance of 15 percent of the loan. Another is 10 percent of the loan, plus 10 percent of the unused commitment—10 percent of the total commitment.

Negotiations sometimes result in higher requirements on the loan commitments than on the loans themselves. In other cases, balance requirements are set higher on loans than on commitments.

Pressure from a credit customer to shift the balance requirement one way or the other gives a bank some indication of how the commitment is to be used. If the borrower wants the balance requirement on the commitment reduced enough to have the loan requirement raised an equal amount, he clearly expects to make little use of the loan commitment—less than half of it on average. If he expected to use most of the commitment, he would want the opposite, with more of the balance requirement on the unused commitment.

Loan prepayments

Prepayment provisions in loan contracts spell out the penalty costs (premiums) charged for paying a loan before it matures. Until the 1960s, banks usually did not charge premiums when loans were paid off (or paid down) before maturity, provided the funds came from operating earnings or other internal sources. Although substantial premiums were often imposed on prepayments financed from other borrowing, especially from other banks, many banks in the 1950s actually encouraged prepayments from a firm's retained earnings.

Banks today often impose substantial penalties on the prepayment of fixed-rate loans, the intentions being to hold borrowers to the full terms of their contracts in return for the banks' having to risk a rise in interest rates.

If term borrowers could prepay their loans at will, with no direct or implied costs, they would in effect control maturities. As banks could not be sure of the repayment dates, prime-setting decisions would have to be based on probable prepayments, with banks undoubtedly charging more to compensate for the uncertainty.

Prepayment of floating-rate loans is seldom a problem. Borrowers have little incentive to prepay loans when the rates move with the costs of credit generally. Even if other interest rates fall a little faster than the floating rate, or rise a little slower, the substantial costs of originating other credit are apt to lock a customer into the existing loan.

Whether the rates are fixed or floating, then, most term loans run to maturity. And as a result, outstanding term loans are essentially immune to changes in the prime rate.

There are limits, of course, to the changes that can be made in prime rates. If floating rates went up too much or did not respond to drastic reductions in market rates, borrowers would stand the prepayment penalties and term loans outstanding would fall.

Secured loans

Although large corporations with top credit ratings routinely receive unsecured bank loans, many business borrowers have to post collateral. The amount of collateral and the type depend on the customer's credit rating, the size and maturity of the loan, and the

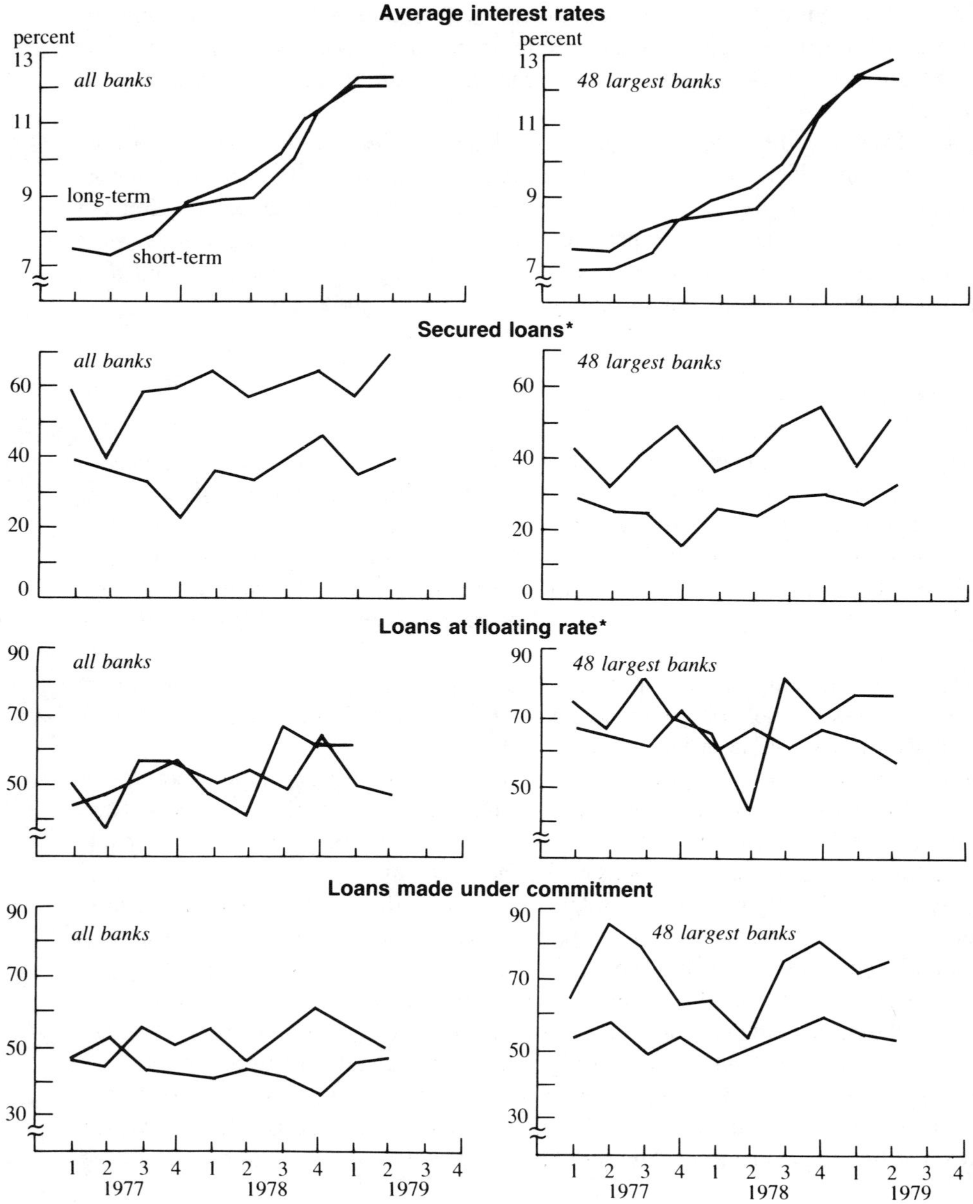

Profile of commercial and industrial loans

*Proportions of total dollar volumes

Source: Federal Reserve Survey of Terms of Bank Lending. The survey data are taken from about 340 banks selected to represent all sizes of banks. The data are collected from one business week in the middle month of each calendar quarter. Short-term loans have original maturities of less than one year, and term loans have maturities of one year or more.

purpose of the credit. Because of risk factors involved in some types of term credit, term loans are more apt to be secured than are short-term loans.

The most recent trend in secured bank lending is the kind of asset-based lending long handled by commercial finance companies. Large banks and their holding companies have become active in this specialized form of secured lending by acquiring existing finance companies, establishing new commercial-finance affiliates, and restructuring their own lending policies for closer management and monitoring of the collateral behind secured loans. The inroads large banks have made into asset-based lending represent a competitive response—especially to attract small business borrowers—and awareness of the need for adequate collateralization as an adjunct to the risk-bearing business of modern bank lending.

Recent pricing tactics

When loan demand eases and money-market rates fall, large money-center banks come under pressure to lower their prime-rate quotations in an effort to attract more new business loan customers. This was the situation in 1976 and 1977. Because of floating-rate provisions in outstanding business loans, however, reductions in the prime rate aimed at bolstering new loans call for forfeitures of revenue on floating-rate loans already on the books. Bank concern over loss of this revenue can slow the lowering of the prime.

When two large banks in a money-center have significantly different proportions of their loan portfolios in floating-rate loans—especially if the loans are priced by different formulas (see box)—the one with the larger proportion may well be at a disadvantage in lowering its prime. These interbank differences in floating-rate loans help to explain split-rate primes—different prime rates at various money-center banks.

Large banks have tried several loan pricing policies aimed at bolstering loan demand and at the same time protecting profit margins on outstanding loans. One policy, dating from the 1950s, specifies ranges in which floating rates can be revised, as for example, an initial loan rate of 6 percent with the rate floating from 4 percent to 8 percent.

Some banks redesigned the cap-rate feature a few years ago by offering floating rates that would not average more than an agreed-on rate over the life of the loan. Because these cap rates combined the borrowing advantages of both fixed rates and floating rates, they gained some customer acceptance in 1971 and 1972.

When open-market rates rose, in 1973 and 1974, however, pushing up funding costs, profit margins on outstanding cap-rate loans dwindled. The upper limit on average interest costs became a ceiling that made further rate increases impossible. Banks have paid little attention to this type loan since. They have also shown few inclinations to adopt minimum-rate features that would limit the decline in loan rates when the prime was lowered.

Another technique for bolstering loan demand while protecting bank loan income has been floating rates tied to base rates other than the prime. This pricing feature is often tailored to the needs (and competitive environment) of large multinational corporations with access to credit markets abroad.

One of the rates that moves somewhat independently of the regular prime rate quotations governing other floating rates is the London Interbank Offering Rate (LIBOR), a short-term European money-market rate. Although this is the most common formula rate for these loans, such U.S. money-market rates as the commercial paper rate and secondary certificate of deposit rate are also used. In some cases, large banks have revised their overseas lending policies to provide credit in the European market at rates tied either to their U.S. prime rate or to LIBOR, depending on the expected changes in the prime-LIBOR rate spread.

Business lending strategies refined at large banks during a time of rising interest rates will be tested when demand for loans eases and interest rates fall. As pressures build for banks to lower their prime rates from the above-15 percent levels of recent months, a large part of their current loan portfolios will still be on the books.

Banks have been preparing for an eventual downturn by diversifying their business loans, interspersing fixed-rate loans with loans written to various formula rates based on prime and other rates. Their success in pursuing this diversification strategy will be reflected in how well their prime rates follow declines in market rates.

Since revisions in prime rates usually lag behind changes in market rates, the tendency is for the spread to widen when rates fall rapidly. If, after adjustment for the lag, the prime rate still responds sluggishly to easing market conditions, banks may have to rethink some of their explicit pricing methods for business lending.

When Is the Prime Rate Second Choice?

Brian C. Gendreau

6

Not long ago, little controversy surrounded the prime rate convention. The prime rate was understood to be the rate banks charged on loans to their most creditworthy corporate customers. Other corporate borrowers paid a rate marked up over the prime. Though prime-related loans were generally floating-rate loans—such that borrowers' loan rates changed with the prime—the prime rate usually rose and fell gradually, giving customers a measure of stability in their borrowing costs.

Banks still post prime rates, and changes in the prime continue to be reported on national newscasts and greeted by bursts of trading activity in securities markets. But now the prime seems to change faster in response to market interest rate movements. Moreover, many loans are being made at rates below the prime. According to a Federal Reserve Board survey of the terms of all short-term business loans granted by 48 of the nation's banks, in the first week of November, 1982, over 92 percent were at rates below the prime.

Consequently, many commentators now doubt that the prime is a useful benchmark loan rate. After the staff of the House Banking Committee studied lending practices at ten large banks in early 1981, Chairman Ferdinand St. Germain concluded that "the prime rate has been so often misused, abused, and tortured in recent years that the phrase now seems beyond repair." Secretary of the Treasury Donald Regan concurs that the prime rate no longer reflects loan costs accurately, and recently proposed creating in its stead a "watch

Reprinted, with deletions, from *Business Review* (May/June, 1983):13–23 by permission of the Federal Reserve Bank of Philadelphia and the author.

rate'' set at half a percentage point above the commercial paper rate—the interest rate firms pay on short-term notes sold in money markets. Why have bank lending practices changed? What kinds of loans are being made below prime? What does the prime rate mean today? The answers depend in part on the characteristics of the prime, and especially on the manner in which prime rate changes are determined.

The Prime: A Curiously Sticky Rate

Popular definitions of the prime rate usually distinguish it from other rates by the credit quality of the underlying loan. The prime rate also differs importantly from other interest rates, however, in the way it reacts to changes in credit market conditions. While rates on money market instruments such as Treasury bills and commercial paper change with trading throughout each day, the prime rate changes less frequently. In past years, when interest rates were more stable, the prime rate did not change for months or even years on end. Now the prime rate changes more often, but it still lags changes in market rates.

The stickiness in the prime rate is easily seen in Figure 1, which compares the movements of the prime rate, the 3-month commercial paper rate, and their difference from 1972 through 1982. The prime rate adjusts fully to short-term interest rate movements, but

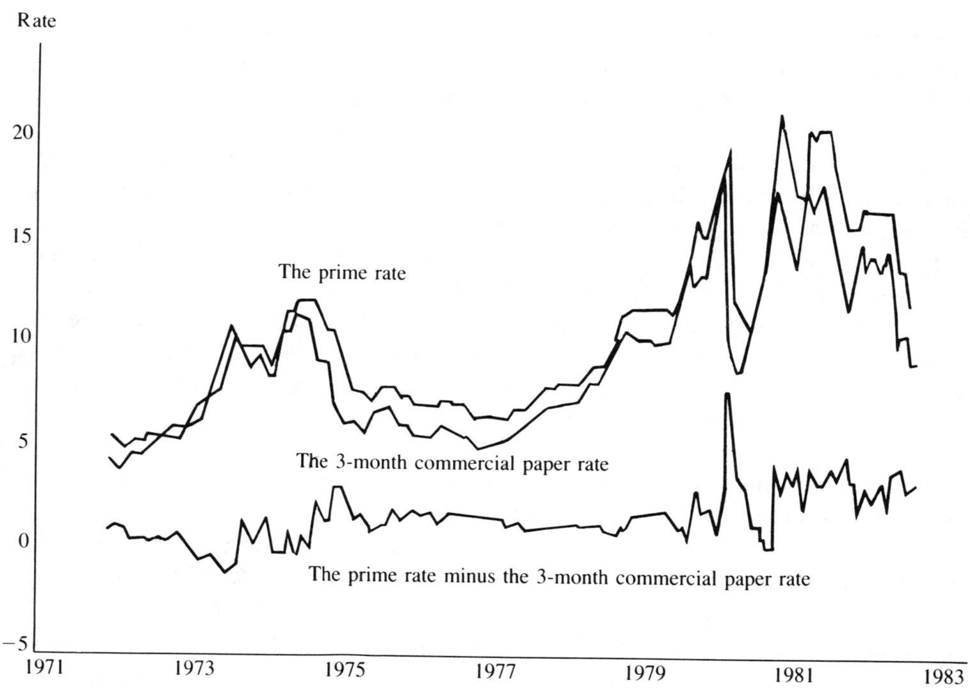

FIGURE 1 The Prime Rate Responds Slowly to Changes in Market Interest Rates

only after a substantial lag. When short-term rates rise, the prime rate initially does not keep pace, and the spread between the prime and short-term rates narrows and occasionally becomes negative. Conversely, when interest rates fall, the prime rate lags behind, and the spread between the prime and market rates widens appreciably.

The stickiness in the prime rate can be traced to a corresponding stickiness in banks' cost of attracting new funds from so-called *core deposits*—demand deposits and those time deposits subject to binding interest rate ceilings. Since Congress prohibited the payment of interest on demand deposits and authorized the Federal Reserve to limit the rates paid on time deposits in the Banking Act of 1933, banks have competed for core deposits by paying implicit interest in the form of services provided below cost. These services, which are provided on core deposits to this day, include check clearing, gifts, the convenience of a multitude of bank branches, extended hours, credit lines, and, for firms, payroll and cash management systems (see ***Nonrate Competition and the Prime***).

Nonrate Competition and the Prime

An industry-wide prime rate first emerged in 1934, shortly after Congress prohibited the payment of interest on demand deposits. Banks, having suffered three consecutive years of losses (in the aggregate) by 1934, welcomed the legal restrictions against deposit rate competition and began to compete for deposits by paying implicit interest in services, as they do to this day. The timing of the inception of the prime rate suggests that the prime is closely connected to nonrate deposit competition. But why would banks prefer nonrate to rate competition? And how is the prime linked to nonrate competition?

When banks engage in interest rate competition for deposits, they must pay the competitive rate on all deposits. This rate is highly visible, and can be compared with other banks' rates with ease. In contrast, with nonrate competition customers must undertake a costly search among banks to find the best loan and deposit service bundles. Once interest rate competition is prohibited, banks can take advantage of the imperfect information customers have about each other's services to reduce services below the competitive level. Moreover, by competing for deposits with services banks are able to reduce their costs by offering less in services to customers who are relatively insensitive to the return on their deposits than to more return-sensitive customers.

The prime rate is connected with nonrate deposit competition because many bank depositors are also borrowers. The most effective way to pay implicit interest to depositor-borrower customers is through loan rate concessions. Widespread loan rate concessions, however, would have wiped out the benefits of nonrate competition provided by deposit rate ceilings. Hence banks attempted to preserve nonrate competition by adopting a uniform rate for loans to their best customers—the prime rate—that served as a floor rate for industry-wide loan pricing.

Banks Adjust Implicit Deposit Rates Slowly. . . When interest rates are low and stable, banks have little difficulty in attracting core deposits by paying implicit interest. But when interest rates move higher and become more variable, bank deposit and loan pricing becomes more complicated. The problem is that implicit interest payments cannot be changed quickly in response to interest rate movements. It takes time to build new branches, to run or pull advertising campaigns, to mail out notices of changes in service charges (and to decide to do these things). Banks cannot hope to match frequent fluctuations in short-term interest rates with costly, cumbersome changes in service. Nonetheless, banks that fail to adjust their implicit interest payments to meet a permanent change in market rates risk losing customers.

Unable to change services quickly, yet compelled by competition to match eventually a sustained change in market rates, banks have little choice but to adjust implicit interest payments gradually to changes in market interest rates. Economists' estimates of the implicit interest rates paid by banks are consistent with this kind of rate setting behavior. Two estimated implicit interest rate series are presented in Figure 2. These estimates show that implicit rates respond to changes in market rates, but do not adjust on a one-to-one basis with changes in current period, short-term interest rates.[1]

. . .Making the Prime Rate Sticky. In seeking to maximize profits, banks adjust their loan rates to reflect changes in their costs in raising new funds. As long as some of these funds are obtained by paying implicit interest on core deposits, banks' costs in attracting additional funds will change only gradually in response to market rate movements. Since loans are priced as a markup over these costs, loan rates will also change gradually.[2]

In the process of adjusting their loan rates, banks use the prime rate as an industry-wide pricing guide. Because there is no objective indicator of when bank costs have changed permanently, banks are likely to disagree over when the prime rate should change. But once a large money center bank has signaled its judgment that a given level of interest rates will be sustained by changing its prime rate, and other banks have ratified that change, a new guideline exists for loan pricing.

[1]See Richard Startz, ''Implicit Interest on Demand Deposits.'' *Journal of Monetary Economics* 5 (1979). pp. 515–534, and Edward J. Stevens. ''Measuring the Service Return on Demand Deposits.'' Federal Reserve Bank of Cleveland Working Paper No. 7601 (December, 1976). Startz's series is an estimate of the average implicit interest rate paid on all demand deposits, and is available through 1976. Stevens' series is an estimate of the implicit rates paid to attract extra (marginal) demand deposits, calculated under the assumption of perfect competition, and is available through 1974.

[2]An added benefit to banks in making loan rates more in tandem with their costs of raising new funds from all sources is that by following such a strategy bank earnings will be unaffected by interest rate movements. Slow loan and deposit rate adjustment, moreover, is consistent with empirical evidence that, on the whole, bank profits are not very responsive to changes in market interest rates. See Mark J. Flannery. ''How Do Changes in Market Interest Rates Affect Bank Profits?'' *Business Review*, Federal Reserve Bank of Philadelphia (September-October, 1980) pp. 13–22.

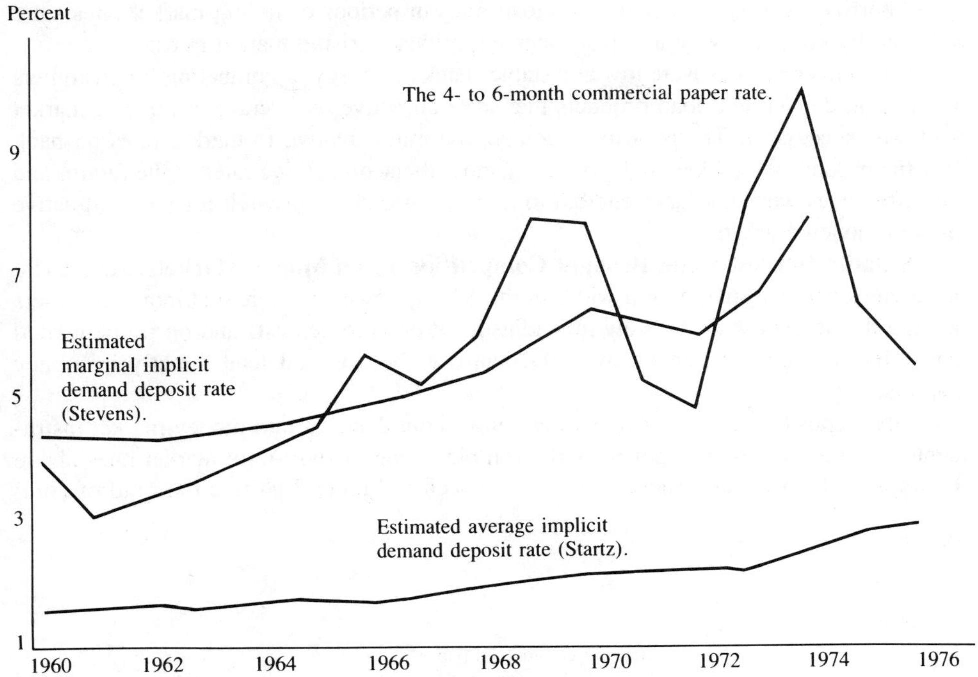

FIGURE 2 Estimates of the Implicit Interest on Demand Deposits

Source: See footnote 1 in the text.

Why is the Prime Rate Convention Changing?

Throughout the post-war period, the critical ingredient in banks' slow deposit and loan rate adjustment was their ability to attract core deposits when market rates were rising relative to implicit interest rates, and to retain loan customers when money market rates were falling relative to the prime rate. Though banks could not adjust services quickly to short-term interest rate fluctuations, they did attempt to attract deposits by offering a stable level of services that was attractive, on average, over the interest rate cycle. In some periods—particularly when interest rates were rising—implicit interest rates on core deposits fell below short-term market rates. But in periods of falling interest rates, implicit interest payments remained high relative to short-term money market returns.[3] Similiarly, because the stickiness in implicit deposit rates was reflected in the prime, banks gave prime borrowers rates that were competitive with market rates, on average, over the interest rate

[3]Twice in the 1970s money market rates fell below passbook savings account rates. Because banks also paid implicit interest on savings deposits, these deposits must have been quite attractive to customers in these periods. For an analysis reconciling temporarily high core deposit costs with bank profit maximization, see Mark J. Flannery, "Retail Bank Deposits as Quasi-Fixed Factors of Production." *American Economic Review*. 72, (June 1982), pp. 527–536.

cycle: borrowers' relatively high bank loan rates in periods of falling market rates were followed by comparatively low loan rates in periods of rising market rates.

When interest rates were low and stable, banks' strategy of competing for customers by offering deposit and loan products that were attractive on average relative to market rates was successful. Temporarily uncompetitive rates relative to market rates on bank deposits or loans were likely to be offset by more than competitive rates in the future, and the differences were not large enough to induce customers to search for more attractive rates in money markets.

Volatile Interest Rates Brought Competition From Money Markets. As interest rate swings became sharper and wider in the 1970s, however, more and more customers became dissatisfied with the slow rate adjustment on core deposits and on prime-related loans. Increasingly, customers bypassed banks to borrow and lend directly in money markets.

On the deposit side, customers shifted out of core deposits into money market instruments, such as commercial paper, with each big swing in short-term market rates above the implicit deposit rate. These shifts can be seen in Figure 3. where the ratio of com-

FIGURE 3 Favorable Returns Have Encouraged the Growth of Commercial Paper Relative to Demand Deposits

Source: See footnote 1 in the text.

mercial paper to demand deposits outstanding together with the spread between the 4-to-6 month commercial paper rate and estimates of the implicit rate paid on demand deposits have been graphed from 1960 to 1976. Initially, most of these shifts were by corporations. The rapid growth of money market mutual funds after the mid-1970s, however, facilitated households' shifts out of core deposits by opening the money markets to small investors previously unable to buy large denomination financial instruments. Once investors overcame costs involved in placing their funds in money markets, they never went back to holding as much of their assets in the form of core deposits, as reflected in the steady decline in the share of core deposits among large bank liabilities visible in Table 1.

On the loan side, the spreads between the sluggish prime and the commercial paper rate widened to several hundred basis points during declines in market rates in the 1970s and 1980s, motivating large firms to incur the startup costs necessary to tap the money markets. About 500 new companies began to issue commerical paper in the years after 1974,

Table 1 Demand and Savings Deposits Have Fallen Relative to Interest-Sensitive Funds in Large Banks' Liabilities

	Percent of Total Liabilities		
Date	Demand and Savings Deposits	Interest-Sensitive Funds[a]	Other Liabilities
1972	52.3	28.8	18.9
1973	45.9	38.3	15.8
1974	40.9	45.3	13.8
1975	41.7	44.1	14.2
1976	46.7	39.0	14.3
1977	45.4	40.0	14.6
1978	42.3	43.7	14.0
1979	39.1	47.2	13.7
1980	36.1	48.2	15.7
1981	33.1	50.9	16.0
1982	28.6	53.8	17.6

Data are for Large Weekly Reporting Banks with Assets of $2 billion or more in 1972 dollars as of June of each year.

[a]Interest-sensitive funds are defined as the sum of federal funds purchased, time deposits in accounts of $100,000 or more, and other borrowings (including liabilities to foreign branches as a proxy for Eurodollar borrowings).

Source: Weekly Report of Assets and Liabilities for Large Banks, Board of Governors, Federal Reserve System.

boosting the amount of paper outstanding in that market from $50 billion in 1974 to almost $180 billion by mid-year 1982.[4]

Banks Responded By Moving Towards Market Rate Pricing. To replace the core deposits that could no longer be relied upon as their principal source of loanable funds, banks issued liabilities carrying market rates of interest such as domestic and Eurodollar certificates of deposit (CD's), money market certificates, and federal funds. By 1981, large banks were raising more than half their funds from interest-sensitive liabilities. As banks attracted fewer funds from the core deposits that were responsible for the sluggishness in deposit costs, they changed their loan rates faster in response to fluctuations in market interest rates. The average lag in the response of the prime rate to money market rates fell markedly between 1970 and 1982, from over 8 weeks in the early 1970s to slightly over 4 weeks in the 1979–1982 period.

In addition to speeding up the pace of prime rate changes, banks hastened their move towards market rate loan pricing by offering loans tied to money market rates to customers with the ability to draw on the commerical paper market. These new loans—called money market loans—are typically for short maturities (one month or less), and are matched by the bank to the size, rate, and maturity of a specific liability. A bank may, for example, issue a 30-day CD and use the funds to make a 30-day loan to a customer at a fixed rate over the CD rate. By matching the loan to a specific liability with the same maturity, bank earnings on the transaction are unaffected by interest rate fluctuations over the life of the loan. When the loan matures, the liability matures, too, and a new transaction can be made at the new market rates.[5] Money market lending is often carried out in close cooperation with the bank's financial instrument trading desk to ensure that the pricing and maturity matching on the transaction are precise. Because the rate on money market loans must be close to money market rates to be competitive, bank profit margins are small, and large transactions are necessary to cover the costs of arranging the loan.

What Accounts for Below-Prime Lending?

In experimenting with money market lending in recent years, banks have offered corporate customers with good credit standing a choice between a variety of short-term credits tied to money market rates as well as prime-related loans with longer maturities. Given the stickiness in the prime rate, it was inevitable that rates on short-term loans tied to money market rates would fall below the prime when interest rates declined. In those periods, firms tried to reduce their borrowing costs by taking fixed-rate, short-term credits instead of prime-related loans. The responsiveness of fixed-rate borrowing to the spread between

[4]See Evelyn M. Hurley, "The Commerical Paper Market Since the Mid-Seventies," *Federal Reserve Bulletin* (June 1982).

[5]Not all money market loans are fixed-rate credits. Indeed, banks are now offering large customers an exotic variety of loans pegged to different short-term rates and adjustable (repriced) at different intervals. For example, some banks are making five-day loans with rates pegged to the daily federal funds rate. Others are making one-year loans priced as a markup over the 3-month Treasury bill rate, but repriced quarterly. These hybrid credits are likely close substitutes for and have rates highly correlated with those on the more numerous fixed-rate, short-term credits. No distinction is made in the text among the varieties of money market loans.

the prime and the 30-day commercial paper rate can be seen in Figure 4. The peaks in the proportion of large loans made with fixed rates occurred when the commercial paper rate fell below the prime. The peaks in fixed-rate lending in Figure 4 also mark periods of widespread below-prime lending. In both the first weeks of May, 1980 and November, 1981, for example, the weighted average rate on all commercial loans at surveyed banks was below the ruling prime rate. In those weeks the prime rate was over 800 basis points and 330 basis points, respectively, above the 30-day commercial paper rate. Given these cost differences, it should not be surprising that customers with the ability to take out loans at money market rates did so.

The recent episodes of fixed-rate lending and below-prime lending cannot be dismissed as mere aberrations from normal prime-related lending patterns. Since late 1979, as Figure 4 shows, a trend towards more below-prime lending developed at large banks, reflecting the trend toward more fixed-rate lending in large credits. Yet it would be premature to conclude that the prime rate is no more than an artifact of past lending practices. Assuming that the majority of floating-rate loans are prime-related, and that most large fixed-rate loans represent money market credits, Figure 4 shows that in many periods large banks make more floating-rate loans (in dollars of credit extended) than money market loans, and that even in periods of massive fixed-rate lending large banks still make some prime-

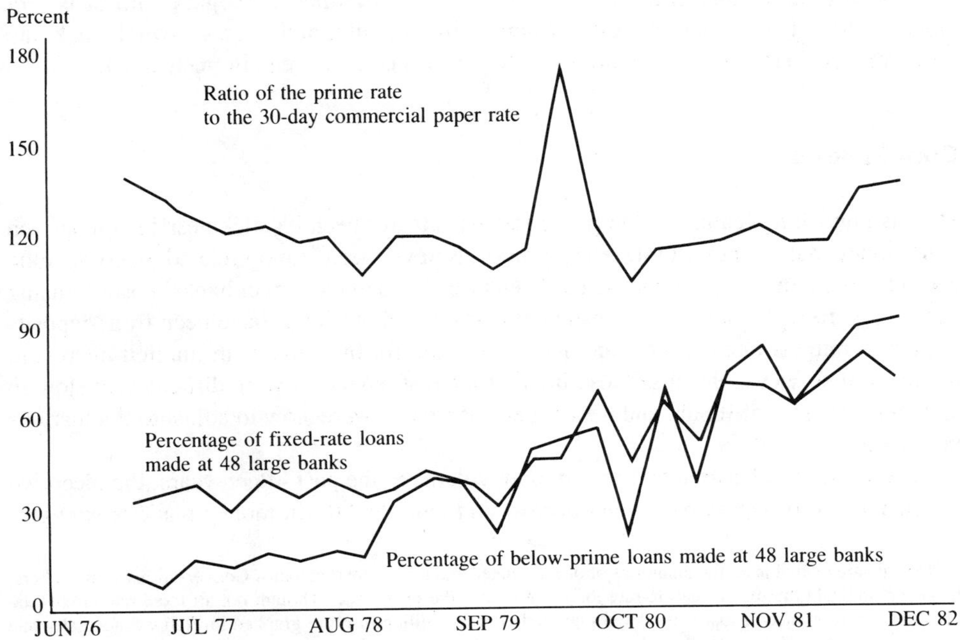

FIGURE 4 Below-prime Lending and Fixed-rate Lending Varies with the Ratio of the Prime to Money Market Rates

Source: *Federal Reserve Bulletin* and unpublished portions of the Survey of Terms of Bank Lending.

related loans.[6] Data collected in the Federal Reserve's Survey of the Terms of Bank Lending indicate, moreover, that fixed-rate lending and below-prime lending are not as widespread at small and medium-sized banks as at large banks.

The reason prime-related loans coexist with money market loans is that not all loan customers can substitute money market loans for prime-related credits, and those who can do not find them to be perfect substitutes. Prime-related loans today, as in past years, are generally floating-rate loans, usually repaid in 60 to 90 days, that are used as working capital by businesses.[7] A firm will not substitute money market loans or commercial paper for prime-related loans if its funding needs are small, because only large money market credits and commercial paper issues will overcome the fixed costs of going to the market. If a firm's credit is less than impeccable, it will not be able to sell its commercial paper, and will have little power in bargaining for a money market loan from its bank. Even firms with funding needs and a credit standing allowing them to obtain money market loans will not always do so, because it is not always clear that a string of short-term credits at market rates will be less expensive than a single prime-related loan. If interest rates were to take an unexpected upturn over the firm's borrowing horizon, for example, the rate increases on market-related credits could outstrip the more slowly changing costs of prime-related credit.

For these reasons, small firms without access to the commercial paper market and larger firms with less than flawless credit are likely to find prime-related loans attractive. Large, creditworthy firms, furthermore, can be expected to continue to bargain with banks for money market loans when interest rates are falling rapidly, and to try to switch back into prime-related loans when rates are rising or are expected to remain unchanged.

Conclusions

The distinguishing feature of the prime rate has always been its stickiness in comparison with money market interest rates. The prime has never been closely related to any specific current short-term rate, but instead has been priced as a markup over banks' cost of raising new funds from all sources. A substantial portion of these funds have been from deposits subject to interest rate ceilings, and have been paid for by banks with implicit interest in the form of services. Because these implicit interest payments were difficult and slow to adjust banks' cost of funds, and hence their loan rates, were slow to adjust to fluctuations in market rates.

As interest rates became higher and more volatile in the past fifteen years, the incentive for customers to bypass banks and borrow and lend directly in money markets strength-

[6]No data are available on the quantities of prime-related and money market loans. Conversations with bankers, however, indicate that most floating-rate loans are tied to the prime rate. Though not all fixed-rate credits are short-term money market loans, the fixed-rate credits of $1 million or more graphed in Figure 5 generally had average maturities of one month or less, and thus may be considered money market loans.

[7]Prime-related loans are commonly made with a variety of fixed maturities, as well as on demand. A precise average maturity for prime-related loans thus cannot be provided. Survey data and conversations with bankers, though, indicate that 60 to 90 days is a reasonable approximation of the normal effective maturity of prime-related loans.

ened. Banks responded by issuing liabilities carrying market rates of interest to finance their loans, by speeding up changes in the prime rate, and by offering customers loans with rates tied to the rates on money market instruments. Much of the below-prime lending in recent years occurred when the rates on these money market loans fell below the more slowly moving prime during a decline in interest rates.

With the advent of a large quantity of below-prime lending, the prime no longer represents the lowest rate at which banks are extending credit. But prime-related lending is far from gone. Firms without the credit standing or funding needs to tap money markets are likely to receive prime-related loans for some time in the future. And even those firms with the ability to issue their own paper in the market are likely to find prime-related loans attractive when interest rates are unchanged or rising.

As deposit rate ceilings are phased out and demand and savings deposits are replaced by banks' new money market accounts, bank loan rates will move more closely with market rates. Banks and their customers are likely to find a reference rate for the cost of short-term credit like the prime useful in the future, but it will probably be a faster moving, more closely market-related rate than today's prime.

Financial Innovation

II

The confluence of financial re-regulation and competitive forces is erasing outmoded patterns of specialization in the financial services industries. Technological developments have made physical distances between financial services firms and their potential customers increasingly irrelevant. Therefore, traditional geographic market definitions are becoming more and more obsolete. Highly volatile interest rates provide firms with the need to combine financial services in ways that reduce risk. The breakdown of regulation provides firms with the opportunity to produce financial services more efficiently in combination rather than on a stand-alone basis. These *economies of scope* explain why the product lines of financial services firms are merging and traditional product market definitions are becoming obsolete.

A wide array of financial services once produced in a highly labor-intensive manner by compartmentalized departments within specialized firms are now provided by multiple service firms through electronic transactions and record keeping. Efficient production requires that financial services firms share customers and equipment. Thus, these firms belong to networks that both compete with and serve one another. Financial organizations will adapt and change to complement these emerging networks, developing new services to fill specific customer needs.

Within this changing market and organizational environment there is considerable social and political interest in maintaining sound depository institutions through regulation. However, regulated firms often manage to stay steps ahead of their regulators. Regulated firms change their organizational form in order to circumvent regulations that cramp the pursuit of profit. While it often entails increased risk, this process of *structural arbitrage* puts considerable pressure on regulators to reduce regulatory burdens. Regulators must concern themselves with the discomfiting combination of increased risk taking (in the form of inter-industry mergers, product-line expansion, and disappearing geographical boundaries); reduced regulation; and the ongoing commitment of government to make safe the nation's payments mechanism by insuring deposits at prices which do not adequately reflect the risks taken by depository institutions and by acting as a lender of last resort.

This section serves several purposes. First, to provide a basic understanding regarding the *evolution* of the market behavior of financial services firms. Second, to give the reader an idea of the *form* of present and likely future financial services competition and regulation. Third, to describe how electronic transactions are generating competitive product-line expansion as well as cooperation among firms. Finally, to project these new forms of competition and cooperation into the future and examine the implications. These are demanding objectives and require the investigation of some fundamental questions. Why do banking institutions exist? Why does regulation of these institutions exist? What synergy of factors brings about financial evolution? Where is this synergy likely to lead? The articles in this section, written by four of the most brilliant financial scholars of our time, answer these questions in a refreshingly candid yet comprehensive manner.

The seventh selection in this book and the opening article in this section by Stuart Greenbaum and Bryon Higgins is appropriately titled "Financial Evolution." In this masterful essay, the authors not only offer an explanation of why banks, financial systems, and their regulation exist, they also evaluate the inflationary, regulatory, and technological forces that have stimulated recent changes. Greenbaum and Higgins chart the rapidly changing financial landscape and provide the reader with reliable bearings in this revolutionary era. Greenbaum and Higgins close their contribution with an excellent review of different theories of financial innovation.

Greenbaum and Higgins' analysis of how binding regulatory constraints actually *increase* the risk imposed on the government deposit insurance system is closely related to the important articles by Eisenbeis in Section IV of this volume. The authors' views also provide an interesting perspective for the various regulatory and supervisory reform measures proposed in Section VI.

One of the most provocative theories of financial innovation surveyed by Greenbaum and Higgins is Edward Kane's theory of the *regulatory dialectic*. In the eighth article in this book, Kane provides a commanding overview of the evolution of the market behavior of financial institutions and the regulatory environment. Kane's viewpoint affords an analytical perspective from which to understand the inevitable struggle between the innovative behavior of firms and the ''catch-up'' efforts of regulatory agencies—a classic dialectical process. He contends that firms exploit *economies of scope* based on technological change and deposit insurance subsidies to engage in innovative forms of risk bearing. These innovations involve firms restructuring their organizations in order to avoid government regulation. Kane provides a model of how this process of structural arbitrage works.

Where does electronic technology fit into the state of affairs masterfully analyzed by Greenbaum and Higgins and placed in perspective by Kane? Indeed, what are the current manifestations of that technology? Where is electronic funds transfer technology likely to lead? The ninth article in this book, by Paul Horvitz, provides answers to these questions in a sweeping examination of the recent history of funds transfer systems. Horvitz gives the reader some pithy, down-to-earth insight on the likely effects of the coming electronic revolution in the payments' mechanism on a myriad of factors including the future roles of commercial banks and the Federal Reserve, the competitive structure of the financial services industry, the efficacy of monetary policy and the risk and privacy of electronic transactions.

The future of financial services market competition and its regulation depends on the types of feasible technological opportunities that are available but not yet in place. Will the opportunities permit new economies of scope? Will these economies preclude competition and hasten cooperation among firms? What will be the dominant organizational forms, e.g., financial supermarkets, networking, and the like, that will govern future systems? What will be the competitive structure of financial services markets? What are the likely responses of the regulatory bodies? The fourth section of this volume, Constraints on Geographic and Product-Line Expansion by Financial Services Firms, provides further insight into these questions.

Financial Innovation

Stuart I. Greenbaum and Bryon Higgins

7

Introduction

Financial evolution is a process by which the financial system adapts to environmental shocks such as changes in technology, demand, and public regulation. This adaptation is manifested in the mix of claims produced, the delivery systems through which these claims are marketed, and the organizational forms and industrial structure of the financial services industry. When external shocks are moderate relative to the adaptive capability of the financial system, we observe smooth passages from one state to the next without disruption of financial or related "real-sector" activities. However, when shocks are large or when the financial system's adaptive capability is impaired, disturbances result in financial crises, recessions, and related symptoms that capture public attention and often ignite social upheaval. Whether disturbances result in trauma or smooth transitions, the process of adaptation inevitably affects the prices and availability of financial services, the allocation of other resources, and the distribution of income and wealth.

The adaptive process is illustrated by the U.S. experience of the past decade, during which massive real resources were diverted to financial applications such as cash management. In addition, credit contracts were redesigned, shortening durations in line with the eclipse of capital markets. At the same time, deposit-type intermediaries lost their "core" deposits, a major source of bank capital, thereby impairing their ability to with-

Reprinted from *Financial Services,* George J. Benston, ed., © 1983 by The American Assembly. Published by Prentice-Hall, Inc., Englewood Cliffs, NJ 07632.

stand external shocks. These changes have been spurred by a stubborn inflation and by technological advances in data processing and telecommunications. The upshot is a financial system undergoing profound change with its future contours only vaguely defined. The questions raised by this flux transcend the financial services industry. Property rights are affected, of course, as is the distribution of risk among the public, industry, and government. In addition, the industry's traditional role as a conduit of monetary policy casts the issues in a still more expansive context. These issues motivate this article on the causes and consequences of financial innovation.

This article is organized in seven sections. For background, the next section describes the traditional functions of the financial system. This is followed by a description of the financial system in terms of the claims produced, the delivery systems used to market these claims, and the organizational forms and structure of the financial services industry. The subsequent section addresses inflation's effects on the financial system in terms of the allocation of real resources, the conduct of monetary policy, the pace of technological advance in the financial system, the subversion of public regulation, and the public's growing financial sophistication. The next section addresses the rationale and appropriate scope for public regulation of financial institutions. In particular, we examine the government's role as guarantor of the financial system and then consider the implications of sanctioning this government intervention in financial arrangements. The next to last section describes three theories of the financial innovation process, all of which are linked to inflation and public regulation. The final section presents conclusions.

Functions of the Financial System

Financial intermediaries perform two closely related functions: they process information and risk. The informational function is illustrated by the "best-efforts" contract of the investment banker. As a broker, the banker matches transactors but need not incur risk. A broker simply produces information for resale. The broker's only possible risk arises from uncertainty regarding the demand for the information it supplies.

The potential reuseability of information is the broker's raison d'être. By centralizing the collection and processing of information, the broker reduces resources used in search and related informational activities. Viewed in this way, the need for brokerage is both compelling and fundamental, especially in large and complex environments. When the object of search is well-defined and readily observable, the brokerage function can be performed mechanically and quite simply. Only if the attributes about which information is desired are subtle, as in the cases of personality or default risk, do the brokers' skills and reputation become important. Thus, the larger the grid over which the search is to be performed, the more compelling the need for brokers, irrespective of skills. The less observable or well-defined the object of search, for any given grid, the greater the return to search skills and reputation.

Risk-processing, the second basic function of the financial system, relates to qualitative asset-transformation. Whereas a broker can maintain a balance sheet with perfectly matched assets and liabilities, the asset-transformer has a mismatched balance sheet, thereby altering the attributes of the claims held by its clientele. Furthermore, in accepting the mismatched balance sheet, the asset-transformer incurs interest rate risk. The widely noted withdrawal risk faced by depository institutions is a special form of interest rate risk, often resulting from a ceiling on deposit interest rates. If the transformation is across currencies, the risk relates to exchange rates. Credit risk, still another form of exposure, arises when the intermediary fails to shift default risk directly from borrowers to ultimate lenders. For example, the depositor does not directly or completely assume the credit risk inherent in the bank's earning assets.

The qualitative asset-transformer may shift risk to a third party, in which case it evolves toward the hedged position of the broker. Alternatively, the asset-transformer may simply absorb risk or dissipate it through diversification. In general, asset-transformation encompasses a variety of processes, forms of exposure, and claim attributes (e.g., liquidity, divisibility, reversibility, use as a unit of account, acceptance in exchange, and degree of default risk). However, the standard example is that of a depository intermediary funding long-term loans with short-term liabilities. In this case, the asset-transformer accepts default risk and also shortens the duration of publicly held claims. Setting aside default considerations, the intermediary assumes the risk of rising short-term interest rates and is presumably compensated by a liquidity premium imbedded in the term structure of interest rates. Indeed, the liquidity premium provides the incentive for duration-reducing asset-transformation which, in turn, reduces the premium in the term structure of interest rates. Thus, duration transformation evidences an underlying liquidity premium, but it also confounds its measurement.

Still another, perhaps even more basic, rationale for asset-transformation derives from indivisibility of claims. Suppose a fixed cost inhibits all but the largest nonfinancial firms from fractionating their liabilities. That is, only if the potential number of claim holders is very large can average costs be low enough to warrant the distribution of many small dividend and interest checks and the maintenance of necessary ownership and tax records. Because of these fixed costs, smaller firms find it optimal to issue their claims *en bloc,* as in private placements or bank loans. In such a setting, asset-transformers emerge for the purpose of purchasing the issues of smaller nonfinancial firms with the proceeds of their own, more divisible, liabilities. The asset-transformer thereby permits constrained wealth-owners, the ultimate investors, to diversify without financial leverage. In performing this service, the asset-transformer accepts a form of balance sheet mismatching owing to the need for an inventory in any such activity (Deshmukh, Greenbaum, and Kanatas, 1983).

Although many taxonomic treatments of financial intermediation focus on other services, such as the maintenance of the payments mechanism (provision of a medium of exchange) or the temporal transfer of consumption, the broker/asset-transformer description subsumes most of these alternative descriptions as special cases. For example, moneyeyness can be viewed as a claim attribute that asset-transformers provide by assuming various forms of exposure, particularly funding and credit risk. Alternatively, money can be viewed as an intermediary in its own right, directly providing brokerage services as in the case of J. Niehans's (1971) trading-stations argument. Similarly, Irving Fisher's (1930) explanation of credit markets as instruments for the temporal adjustment of consumption to arbitrarily timed endowments is readily interpreted as a form of brokerage activity. Still another example is provided by the specialist in the organized exchange or the market-maker in any "over-the-counter" market. The market-maker typically provides a combination of brokerage and asset-transformation services. Without an inventory the client obtains a pure low-skill brokerage service. With an inventory, the market-maker sustains risk and provides liquidity, divisibility, and price-smoothing services.

Three Facets of the Financial System

As mentioned earlier, we view the financial system as being composed of claims, delivery systems, and organizations. Claims can be thought of as embodiments of various combinations of attributes. Thus we can visualize an attribute continuum with as many dimensions as there are relevant attributes. Each produced claim can be represented as an address, in this hyperspace, and the introduction of a new claim is nothing more than a change of the attribute mix to occupy a previously vacant address. The proliferation of claims reduces the gaps between existing claims and tends to complete the market. The menu of produced claims may increase because of interest rate or wealth increases, technological advances, or because public regulation provides incentives to innovate. The production of a new claim imposes a new mix of exposures on the intermediary and thereby presents a new risk-management challenge. However, it is difficult to imagine that this form of innovation can generate inordinate fixed costs. Nor are the welfare implications of claim proliferation entirely clear.

In contrast, a delivery system is a nonfinancial asset used for marketing purposes. In the present context, financial claims are the objects being marketed. Delivery systems typically involve substantial development costs along with subsequent depreciation costs. A system is usually capable of distributing a wide array of financial services to a particular market. Thus, delivery systems tend to be market-specific rather than product- or service-specific.

Retail commercial banking has traditionally employed a brick and mortar delivery system that many now believe to be obsolete. Life insurance companies and commercial lending have relied for the most part on labor-intensive personalized selling. Mutual funds use phone, mail, and wire distribution systems. Credit and debit cards represent yet another distribution technology, whereas automated teller machines (ATMs) are a robotic substitute for full-service branches. Each of these systems is designed to serve a particular niche in the market, with inevitable overlap resulting in competition and even potential eclipse of outmoded systems. Since the functional rationalization or coalescence of the older delivery systems has been inhibited by legal and regulatory barriers, circumvention of these barriers has resulted in the development of newer systems in much the same way that interest rate ceilings have led to development of new claims.

Public regulatory restrictions on organizational forms, particularly spatial and functional limitations, have constrained the types of delivery systems. Without these restrictions, the technology of brick and mortar probably would have led to the development of extensive branching systems such as those in the United Kingdom, Canada, and Israel. Similarly, real estate, securities distribution, accounting and legal services, and insurance might have been distributed through the same brick and mortar delivery system were it not for legal restrictions. However, the American financial tradition has been characterized by narrowly focused delivery systems with sharp product line and geographic distinctions. This has led to excessive investment in banking plant and equipment, and also to low market entry barriers. Indeed, regulatory entry restrictions can be viewed as compensating for the artificially low market entry barriers resulting from regulation-mandated spatial and functional restrictions and from governmental deposit insurance.

Relaxation of public regulation of organizational forms seems to be a major contemporary theme. The recent expansion, some would say rationalization, of delivery systems has been variously ascribed to technological advances and to the growing impotence of public regulation, both of which are attributable in part to inflation. Whatever the ultimate explanation, the restructuring of organizational forms and delivery systems has had far-reaching manifestations, including franchising, networking, and shared ATM systems. The interstate expansion of thrifts and bank loan production offices (LPOs) and the entry of both thrifts and banks into discount brokerage provide still other examples. On yet another level, the striking international integration of banking is a manifestation of the changing relationship between organizational form and delivery systems. Money market mutual funds and credit (debit) card systems, perhaps the first nationwide retail banking distribution systems, constitute yet other examples.

The continuation of this trend toward increased scale and scope of delivery systems points to an industry organized around tiers of firms, with a small number of worldwide systems challenging the regulatory hegemony of nation states. A small number of nationwide delivery systems will serve mass markets without brick and mortar or labor-intensive technologies. These nationwide systems will be complemented by a larger number of specialized distribution systems for specialized segments of the market. Routine financial services will undoubtedly be delivered electronically, but commercial lending, underwriting, and many forms of insurance will continue to require more labor-intensive distribution methods. Banks engaged in commercial lending will find it increasingly compelling to offer fixed-rate term loans in order to permit their commercial borrowers to achieve a tolerable degree of protection against interest rate exposure. Unable or unwilling to fund these loans with short-term purchased money, the banks will come under increasing pressure to develop markets for term liabilities. The most likely candidates are insurance and pension liabilities. Thus we can expect a powerful tendency for coalescence between commercial banks on the one hand and insurance companies and pension fund managers on the other. Although this coalescence could be achieved indirectly through the use of futures markets, the more direct joining of complementary functions is likely to be less costly, especially for larger institutions. The traditional separation of banks and their trust departments is likely to be reexamined.

Brick and mortar will continue to play a significant role in serving "downscale" markets where verification requirements are substantial, credit lines are small, and educational levels are low. Nevertheless, the development of national and even transnational delivery systems will raise serious questions of public policy. Retail intermediation services may come to look increasingly like public utilities. Entry costs will undoubtedly escalate, perhaps reducing the degree of competition. Furthermore, multinational financial institutions are uniquely equipped for arbitrage across regulatory domains, thus requiring a higher degree of international cooperation among governments.

Organizational form, the third facet of the financial system, is perhaps most ephemeral. It can be viewed as the outcome of tension between the technology of production and public regulation. A wide variety of organizational designs is probably consistent with almost any technology. Thus a nationwide electronic funds transfer system could be a monopoly, as in the case of our telephone system, or a competitive industry with several firms. Decisions regarding organizational forms are often substantially political but have important economic implications. The tradition of mutuality in the thrift industry provides a good example. Despite deep historical roots, the mutual form of organization among thrifts seems to be in eclipse as a result of a moderately sustained period of economic adversity. The relative disadvantage of mutual institutions is their unfavorable access to capital markets and their high operating costs (Deshmukh, Greenbaum, and Thakor, 1982). Some argue that the mutual form of organization also impedes adaptation because of the division between de jure and de facto ownership.

In any case, we are confronted with difficult political choices regarding organizational forms, including choices between public and private ownership. However, these choices will need to be made in light of more fundamental economic considerations relating to delivery systems and claim menus.

Inflation's Effects on the Financial System

The U.S. financial system is based on contracts written in nominal rather than real terms. Moreover, many financial assets offer more or less fixed nominal returns. In such a setting, inflation—especially if unanticipated—inevitably savages the system by encouraging substitution away from those claims offering lower real rates of return. Since interest rate ceilings are applied to existing claims, whereas yields on unproduced claims are unconstrained, inflation typically spurs proliferation of claims. This is perhaps the most fundamental effect of inflation on the financial system. It explains the proliferation of money substitutes, such as money market mutual funds, as well as the growth of federal funds, repurchase agreements, C/Ds, and the like.

The counterpart of this claim proliferation is the increasing use of real resources for cash management. The combination of legal reserve requirements and interest rate ceilings induces efforts to reduce the holding of rate-constrained claims, thereby increasing the velocity of money (Niehans, 1982). This explains the Federal Reserve's recent frustration in its conduct of monetary policy. The heightened volatility of interest rates and the confusion regarding monetary aggregates are the concomitants of the massive substitution away from traditional monetary forms. Hence, we have observed the elevation and expansion of the financial function in nonfinancial firms as well as the dramatic growth in the past decade in all manner of financial service enterprises.

Interest and exchange rate volatility has also contributed to the striking growth of risk-shifting instruments, such as forward exchange, options, financial futures, loan commitments, letters of credit, and bankers acceptances (Wolkowitz, et al., 1981). The implications of bank contingent (and often off-balance sheet) liabilities for banks' management of solvency risk and the central bank's monetary management are serious, but barely grasped. For a discussion of the management issues, see Thakor, Hong, and Greenbaum (1981). The perverse effects of loan commitments on monetary policy are explained by Deshmukh, Greenbaum, and Kanatas (1982) and Ricart i Costa and Greenbaum (1983A).

Less widely appreciated are inflation's effects on technological advances and the speed of their adoption. Basic computer and telecommunications technology probably was not substantially influenced by recent inflation. However, financial applications certainly were stimulated by high nominal interest rates and the associated turbulence in financial markets. Illustrations include the development of same-day clearing for international payments, the spreading use of ATM systems, improved wire-transfer systems, videotex systems, and money market mutual funds. Many of these advances simply speed payments and reduce float. They are merely symptoms of the cash management syndrome referred to earlier. Thus many innovations thought to be exogenous are in part the result of inflation. Innovative applications of new technology are often responses to the more basic motive to husband assets bearing diminishing real returns because of inflation.

Just as inflation hastens the application of new technology, it also stimulates the search for means of circumventing regulation. These two phenomena are closely related in that both technology and regulation constrain the transformation of inputs into financial services. They differ in that technological constraints are natural in origin, whereas regulatory constraints are artificial. With both, inflation elevates the shadow price of a constraint and thereby stimulates the search for means of circumvention. Illustrations include the expanded use of nonreservable bank liabilities such as Eurodollars, federal funds, and repurchase agreements. Claims also were designed to circumvent Regulation Q, and even the modest deposit insurance premium. The growth of bank contingent liabilities, particularly off-balance sheet items, resulted in part from attempts to avoid regulatory constraints relating to liquidity and financial capital.

The nationwide spread of LPOs was a palpable circumvention of the intent of the McFadden Act and the Douglas Amendments to the Bank Holding Company Act, although the connection with inflation is somewhat oblique. The spread of LPOs was part of a broader phenomenon involving the international integration of financial markets (Porzecanski, 1981). Nonetheless, this integration was rooted in the inflationary pressures that varied across countries and were so important in escalating the volatility of exchange rates.

Differences between the financial regulatory agencies of the 1960s and those of today are also striking. Whether correct or not, public regulators previously believed they could shape the direction of change. All acknowledged regulators' power to discipline their constituents. Today we find the central bank unable to define money and uncertain of its ability to control it, however defined. We find regulators preoccupied with financial institutions seriously weakened by the loss of core deposits and deterioration of asset quality. For the first time in forty years, failing institutions are an overriding concern. Even the vaunted governmental deposit insurance system is being challenged for the first time in its history. Moreover, major pieces of the financial system have either drifted away from regulatory control or have grown up outside the regulators' sphere of influence. We find a severely shaken community of public regulators, with badly strained and overextended resources, especially in examination, supervision, and deposit insurance.

Some would add yet another effect of inflation to our list. Investors of all stripes have allegedly begun to ascend a learning curve that irreversibly sensitizes them to financial change. Financial markets may become increasingly erratic, reacting to every scintilla of information, misinformation, or disinformation. The increased awareness of asset-holders helps explain the increase in real resources dedicated to financial management. It also suggests that important aspects of financial change are irreversible (i.e., the system is permanently destabilized by the heightened sensitivity and growing sophistication of investors). The learning curve paradigm implies that a return to lower inflation and lower nominal interst rates may not reverse the flow of resources into financial management or allow return to a financial system stabilized around idle balances together with some lender exploitation.

Public Regulation of the Financial System

In the span of U.S. history, the financial system has always been the object of substantial public regulation. Despite numerous explanations, there remains considerable controversy as to the motive and necessity for public intrusion into private financial arrangements. The currently fashionable view of regulation as an instrument for organizing commerce in governmentally dispensed privileges seems incomplete at best (Stigler, 1975). More localized forces seem to explain pervasive public regulation of the financial sector. Special treatment of the financial sector is almost certainly traceable to the putative fragility of the financial system and to its monetary functions. The system's strategic position is further heightened by its role as a conduit for monetary policy, although activist monetary policy is a recent phenomenon extending back at most to the formation of the Federal Reserve System.

This interpretation raises two questions. Is the financial system unstable? If it is unstable, does its monetary role warrant regulation? The latter question can be formulated in terms of the real costs of turbulent financial markets. Some scholars have argued that the financial system performed without catastrophe for protracted periods, such as from the demise of the Second Bank of the U.S. in 1836 to the Civil War period, with only minimal governmental intervention (Hammond, 1957; Friedman and Schwartz, 1963). To be sure, bank failures were quite common during this period. Nevertheless, the effects were more or less isolated without the major externalities associated with contagious and cumulative runs (Rolnick and Weber, 1983; Rockoff, 1974). Moreover, firms come and go in other industries without major social costs. If markets work, as they assuredly do most of the time, firms that choose to operate with high risk are evaluated accordingly by investors. Thus, even if failures of financial firms are numerous, the money and capital markets should price deposits and other financial assets appropriately, and the public can exercise its preferences without impediment. The failure of firms need not imply the failure of markets. It is the latter type of failure that must be demonstrated to justify public intervention.

An alternative view is that informational asymmetries inhibit the working of the financial system as just described. Information costs and consequent informational asymmetries among potential transactors are thought to be especially important in rental markets, among which labor and financial markets are notable examples. The services traded in these markets tend to be especially heterogeneous, thus posing problems of observability, breaches of contract, and moral hazard. These problems tend to undermine the efficient working of rental markets and inhibit trade. The singular vulnerability of rental markets to failure owing to informational asymmetries provides a brokerage role for government. In the financial realm, this role has been expressed in a variety of ways, e.g., "to provide a stable environment to facilitate private contracting," "to maintain a stable money," "to stabilize the financial system," and "to provide a uniform commercial code." These are all means of resolving informational asymmetries that frustrate contracting and thereby impede commerce and production. Moreover, long placid periods without public regulation did not preclude occasional explosive disruptions, such as those in 1907 and 1929, that not only paralyzed commerce and production, but also threatened political upheaval.

We turn now to the question of why the financial system may be singularly unstable. First, it should be noted that generations of business cycle theorists have explained economic instability in terms of the periodic collapse of the financial system (Mitchell, 1927). Thus, the idea of financial sector fragility is not novel. There seem to be two related reasons for this alleged fragility. First, as explained by Diamond and Dybvig (1982), a fractional reserve banking system is characterized by multiple equilibriums: one is a tenable equilibrium whereas another is characterized by a "run," the ultimate form of withdrawal risk. According to his analysis, the process of liquidity production via private asset-transformation inherently gives rise to the possiblity of a "runs equilibrium" because of the associated limited liability and credit risk. A 100 percent reserve banking system, as recommended by Simons (1948), would remedy the problem but would also preclude private production of liquidity.

A second reason for the alleged instability of the financial system arises from the technology of intermediation. Financial intermediation requires little specific physical or financial capital. To see this, one need only compare the balance sheet of a randomly selected financial institution with that of a similarly selected nonfinancial firm of the same asset size. Entry into financial intermediation requires little more than the ability to borrow. The low natural barriers to entry have meant that considerable adjustment in the industry's equilibrium output is effected by the entry and exit of firms. This method of adjusting output is considerably more disruptive than output changes by existing firms, since it involves breaches of contracts. Indeed, one advantage of permitting the industry to become more concentrated is that the number of firms might be stabilized because of the associated increase in barriers to entry. It is presumably more difficult to enter an unprotected market and compete directly with Citicorp than it would be to open a bank next to The First Bank of Hazard in a countywide market area. Thus the nexus between private liquidity production and bank runs on the one hand, and the low natural barriers to entry, on the other, helps explain the fragility of the financial system. Moreover, informational asymmetries can result in market failures that may warrant a role for government as a broker and guarantor in financial markets. However, the extent of governmental intervention justified by informational considerations is an open question.

We now turn to the locus of governmental intervention in financial markets and its implications. The most basic governmental intrusions are those of lender-of-last-resort and guarantor of bank liabilities. To be sure, bank regulation has many other manifestations, but most can be understood as deriving from these two basic activities. Moreover, these two activities are inextricably linked in much the same way as liquidity and solvency are linked. The history of public regulation and guarantee of the banking system reflects the same confusion and contradictions found in the economics literature on the relationship between liquidity and solvency. For example, Keynes (1936) tried with limited success to define precisely what liquidity is. Tobin (1958), one of Keynes's foremost interpreters, clarified the issues. However, there is still no clearly accepted definition of liquidity and no clear distinction between the concepts of liquidity and solvency. Moreover, the concept of solvency of financial institutions, is itself subject to disparate interpretations.

The lender-of-last-resort is the most time-honored of central banking functions. Indeed, it was the unquestionable need for such a facility that led to the creation of the Federal Reserve System. The introduction of the quasi-governmental lender-of-last-resort in 1913 immediately raised questions regarding the appropriate terms and availability of credit extended through this facility.

Two questions were uppermost. First, given that the discount window was intended to augment liquidity rather than to remedy problems of asset quality, what were the appropriate availability restrictions? Second, in light of the narrowly circumscribed role of the discount window, how should advances be priced? The first question was addressed by defining eligible paper—essentially an asset quality restriction related to solvency—and by delimiting the legitimate purposes of discount borrowing, which proved difficult to administer in all but the most egregious cases. The pricing issue is traceable to the idea that the window was to serve as an emergency facility. Consequently a "penalty" discount rate would discourage abuse. It was thought that banks should never be presented with arbitrage opportunities involving discount window advances. However, the Federal Reserve has never accepted this pricing principle, preferring to post a lower rate and thereby placing a heavier burden on "administration" of the discount window. Certainly, this facet of Federal Reserve behavior is consistent with Stigler's (1975) theory of public regulation.

However, even with a penalty discount rate, a subsidy inheres in the discount window giving rise to a moral hazard problem that helps explain many other facets of bank regulation. Given the possibility of a bank being "rationed out of the market," any discount facility guaranteeing a finite rate of interest presents its clientele with a subsidy. By eliminating the possibility of banks being confronted with an infinite marginal borrowing rate, the discount window inevitably reduces banks' voluntary holdings of liquidity reserves. This reduction in reserves, attendant to the introduction of the discount window, shifts part of the profit from money creation to the private banks and thereby constitutes a form of moral hazard (Greenbaum, 1983).

The Federal Reserve is in much the same position as the fire insurance carrier whose clients do not install sprinkler systems. The introduction of a lender-of-last-resort provides an incentive for banks to substitute earning assets for cash. This substitution not only shifts deposit seigniorage from govennment to the banks, but also results in increased risk of insolvency for any given level of bank capital. To be sure, the shift in seigniorage tends to increase bank capital, offsetting to some extent the greater risk of insolvency. Nevertheless, the government is faced with a loss of tax revenue together with increased bank risk as a result of its accepting the lender-of-last-resort responsibility. It therefore responds by introducing risk-abatement regulations together with monitoring of compliance. The discount window therefore provides a rationale for reserve requirements, asset proscriptions, capital requirements, bank examinations, and entry restrictions. If one accepts the argument that high funding costs lead banks to acquire riskier assets, then the discount window can also explain deposit interest rate ceilings.

After twenty years of experience, it was agreed that the lender-of-last-resort was not the panacea some of its most ardent supporters had thought. It became apparent that the public's confidence in banks could be eroded despite the presence of a discount facility with virtually unlimited resources. The problem was one of solvency, not liquidity; the discount window was confined to a narrowly defined role. Political forces demanded that government's role in banking be expanded from deep involvement to total immersion. This meant guaranteeing bank liabilities in addition to liquefying bank assets. The introduction of federal deposit insurance meant that the government's risk exposure arising from private decisions took a quantum leap. Banks were no longer borrowing against their own liabilities. They were now selling contingent liabilities of the U.S. government, much like the debt issues of U.S. government agencies such as the Federal National Mortgage Association. The expanded guarantor role resulted in additional moral hazard and thereby subjected the government to further potential exploitation and abuse.

Before the introduction of deposit insurance, bank capital served three distinct functions. It provided a buffer against bankruptcy costs associated with insolvency, a direct source of funds, and an indirect source of funds. In this last role, capital reduced the cost of selling debt by reducing the default risk sustained by depositors. In principle, each bank would weigh the cumulative benefits of capital against its cost in order to determine the optimal amount of financial capital. The introduction of deposit insurance virtually eliminated the indirect-source-of-funds function of bank capital by eliminating default risk on deposits. Insured deposits became perfectly interchangeable across banks because they were seen as contingent liabilities of the U.S. government. The elimination of one of its three functions meant that capital became less valuable. As a result, banks would be expected to reduce their capital and thus increase their financial leverage.

This phenomenon is equally apparent from another point of view. Bank capital serves as a deductible on the deposit insurance policy in that the government sustains losses only after the bank's capital is exhausted. Hence, at an unchanged insurance premium, the value of the policy is increased with a reduction in bank capital. The introduction of deposit insurance, therefore, provided banks with an incentive to reduce their capital and incur higher risk of insolvency, while at the same time increasing the government's contingent liability. This moral hazard problem is aggravated by the structure of deposit insurance premiums, which are approximately proportional to a bank's total (not insured) deposits.

Despite criticism of the insurance pricing system and frequent calls for more risk-sensitive pricing, the regulators have until very recently not endorsed such proposals. To be sure, many of the recommendations have been unduly facile in failing to recognize the difficulties of risk measurement (Ricart i Costa and Greenbaum, 1983B). On the other hand, the regulators' demonstrated lack of enthusiasm for risk-sensitive premiums—most recently in response to the deposit insurance study mandated by Section 712 of the Garn-St Germain Depository Institutions Act of 1982—is probably related to their similar lack of enthusiasm for a penalty discount rate. This seems to reflect a regulatory preference for administrative rather than pricing remedies for incentive compatibility problems. Rather than attempting to price the risk and thereby reduce the necessary scope of regulation, the regulators choose to deal with moral hazard problems by employing rules and proscriptions with the attendant necessity for monitoring through supervision and examination. This, of course, expands the resources dedicated to regulatory activities.

To summarize, the government's guarantee system involves two related activities, the lender-of-last-resort function and deposit insurance. Although these guarantees are separated for administrative, and even occasionally for analytical purposes, the two are conceptually inextricable because liquidity protection is inseparable from solvency protection. Any liquidity-augmenting innovation reduces the probability of insolvency. Similarly, any measure to protect depositors against default risk increases banks' liquidity. Indeed, when considered as a single entity, the pricing of the government's guarantee is less risk-insensitive than focusing exclusively on deposit insurance premiums would suggest.

Both guarantees provide banks with incentives to assume added risk which could be mitigated, but probably not eliminated, by alternative pricing structures. This residual moral hazard provides the most compelling justification for public regulation and monitoring of banks. As long as the government serves as guarantor of the financial system, there will be moral hazard warranting some regulation and monitoring. However, the scope of regulation has been unnecessarily magnified by the regulators' bias against incentive-oriented pricing policies.

The necessity for public regulation, given the government's role as guarantor of the financial system, provides a basic motivation for financial innovation. To the extent that regulation constrains private initiatives, entrepreneurs will weigh the cost of compliance against the cost of circumvention. This cost comparison serves as the trip-switch for the introduction of new claims, new delivery systems, and new organizational forms.

Theories of Financial Innovation

The recent turbulence in financial markets has stimulated academic interest in explaining financial evolution. This work is still in an embryonic stage of development. Much of it is fragmentary and conjectural, and to speak of theories of financial evolution is a form of intellectual hyperbole. Nevertheless, three related strands of thought are identifiable: the linear programing approach, associated with Silber (1975); the Hegelian dialectic, associated with Kane (1981); and the regulatory explanation, associated with Greenbaum and Haywood (1971). These three explanations are by no means mutually exclusive. Indeed, they differ more in explanatory style and emphasis than in substance.

Silber's explanation is clearly most general. It is virtually axiomatic and probably also is incapable of being empirically rejected. He views the financial system as maximizing some (linear) objective function, subject to a set of constraints. The constraints have shadow prices, i.e., implicit prices of violating (or just satisfying) the constraints. These constraints can be regulatory in origin, like a legal reserve requirement or a capital requirement; they may be technologically based, like a production function parameter; or they may be rooted in the tax code. In Silber's view, financial innovation is a systemic response to rising shadow prices. Thus, as the cost of satisfying a particular constraint increases, resources are devoted to circumventing or overcoming it. The culmination of this effort is a change in the financial system in the form of a new claim, delivery system, or organizational form.

The generality of Silber's approach derives from the fact that shadow price increases can be attributable to a wide variety of stimuli, including changes in demand, tax laws, regulation, or technology. The theory, therefore, says little more than that financial innovation is an adaptive response by the financial system to some external shock that expresses itself in terms of an increase in the system's cost of satisfying some constraint. As such, the theory is difficult to quarrel with; however, it provides limited illumination.

Kane explains innovation in dialectical terms. The protagonists are the financial system on the one hand and public regulators on the other. The latter seek to restrain the financial system through the imposition of some constraint—a price ceiling, a reserve requirement, or an asset proscription. The system adapts in order to circumvent the regulatory initiative. The regulators respond by imposing yet another restriction, thereby prompting yet another adaptive initiative. The process continues ad infinitum resulting in an ever-expanding regulatory system together with an increasingly complex financial system. The implication is that both represent a squandering of societal resources with a welter of perverse effects.

Kane's characterization of innovation focuses on the undeniable tension between the governmental and private participants in the financial system. It constructively suggests, but does not pursue, a game-theory approach to explaining both regulation and the system's adaptation to regulation. But it also leaves a good deal unanswered. For example, why doesn't the regulator eventually learn to anticipate the system's responses and vice versa? Why doesn't the process converge to an equilibrium? Why is there public regulation to begin with, and what makes the system so readily adaptable? Periods of rapid change, including occasional crises, seem to alternate with others that are relatively placid. Can the theory explain the conditions giving rise to alternate periods of rapid and gradual evolution?

Greenbaum and Haywood argue that new claims are brought into existence largely because of secular increases in real income and cyclical increases in interest rates. The growth of real income creates a demand for a wider variety of financial claims, and the system duly responds by producing an ever-wider array of claims. This explanation merely asserts that increasing income results in increased demand for all claims, whether produced or not. Hence, rising income should gradually pull more and more claims from the unproduced to the produced category.

Rising interest rates also increase the demand for unproduced claims, because these are the claims without ceiling interest rates. As rates rise and we substitute away from claims with constrained rates, new claims come into existence. The problem with this substitution-effect argument is the absence of any clear long trend in interest rates that would help explain a secular proliferation of claims. Cyclicality in interest rates presumably should carry some of the burden of expanding the secular growth in the menu of claims. The explanation originally offered by Greenbaum and Haywood was that after claims are brought into existence, owing to high interest rates, they become candidates for regulatory protection. More plausibly, claims do not become candidates for regulatory protection, but firms producing claims do. Thus, claims can disappear as readily as they appear, provided their disappearance does not threaten the population of firms in the financial system. When new claims are produced by specialized new firms, there will be a tendency toward irreversibility. However, when new claims are produced by existing firms that provide a wide array of claims, we would expect a cyclical reversal in interest rates to lead to the disappearance of the new claim. Thus, a drop in interest rates is much more likely to eclipse the federal funds, retail repurchase agreements, and sweep accounts of commercial banks than it is to lead to the disappearance of, say, money market mutual funds.

Because regulation is skewed toward protecting firms in the financial system, it tends to relegate innovation to the periphery. The proscriptions that are central to regulation inhibit existing firms from leading the innovation process. New claims, therefore, tend to spawn new firms and sometimes even new delivery systems. By pushing innovation to the system's periphery and then protecting financial firms, the public regulator may foster secular proliferation of claims growing out of interest rate cyclicality. This view of the innovation process also suggests a financial and regulatory system of ever-increasing complexity and fragility. One might imagine this process culminating in collapse owing to the sheer weight of the system's elephantine structure. Collapse and crisis can be expected to prompt basic reform as illustrated by the Banking Act of 1933 (creating the FDIC), the Federal Reserve Act, the National Bank Act, and the legislation giving birth to the First and Second Banks of the U.S.

Before leaving this topic we should note that government and public regulation are not the sole possible sources of irreversibilities in the financial system. Others have emphasized the importance of investor learning, as mentioned earlier. Once the public has learned about money market mutual funds, it is claimed that they are not likely to return to passbook savings accounts, even if interest rates retreat quite considerably. Although there may be considerable force in this argument, it incorporates an element of implausibility. Rather than prompting an educational revolution, high interest rates dictate a diversion of real resources to financial management, and low rates can be expected to reverse the resource flow. It would therefore seem plausible to anticipate the reemergence of idle balances and even our traditional, civilized obliviousness to issues of "float." This reversion is not a return to naivete; rather it constitutes a rational response to altered opportunity costs. Indeed, we have forgotten how to ride horses, except in Hollywood movies and on polo fields. The concept of float only became *au courant* in the frenetic 1970s.

Still another possible irreversibility stems from the recent development of costly and expansive delivery systems. In order to avoid the discarding of these assets, their owners have an incentive to maintain the system's level of throughput. Thus, one might imagine operating the system even at a loss in order to avoid redevelopment costs the next time a profitable product opportunity becomes available. Effectively, this is what Citicorp was doing for years with their credit card system. They correctly anticipated that the card would become the foremost mass market delivery system for financial services and that it would ultimately operate profitably. They did not shrink from this vision, despite years of negative spreads and huge operating losses.

Conclusion

In a brief ten years, inflation has destabilized our financial system and set it on an evolutionary path of uncertain direction and terminal points. Although inflation has abated, at least temporarily, the financial system continues to lurch erratically, posing a variety of disquieting policy questions. Barring new governmental initiatives and fundamental reform, we will need to learn to live with a financial system stripped of much of its financial capital, a system much more akin to that of the 1920s than to that of the 1950s or 1960s. This will mean more frequent failures among financial institutions, together with a growing tendency toward concentration among financial firms. It will also mean less scope for subsidizing socially mandated investment in housing and other areas. In addition, we can anticipate higher credit standards in general and less unsecured lending (the recent growth of asset-based lending is symptomatic). Total deregulation is unlikely, but the locus of regulation can be expected to shift toward the major sources of exposure in intermediation, i.e., credit and funding risk. This may well mean an expanded intrusion of public regulation into the treasury function of financial institutions, perhaps in lieu of legal reserve requirements.

These changes may necessitate compromises in public convenience and in managerial prerogatives, and they will almost certainly elevate the importance of management skills. The industry will have to husband and rationalize these resources much more intensively. But this more fragile financial system may prove workable and may even allocate society's resources more intelligently. The great danger is that a return to higher inflation may result in major disruptions with attendant economic trauma and chaos.

BIBLIOGRAPHY

DESHMUKH, SUDHAKAR D., STUART I. GREENBAUM, AND GEORGE KANATAS, "Bank Forward Lending in Alternative Funding Environments," *Journal of Finance,* 37 (September 1982), 925–40.

______, "Lending Policies of Financial Intermediaries Facing Credit and Funding Risk," *Journal of Finance,* 38 (June 1983).

DESHMUKH, SUDHAKAR D., STUART I. GREENBAUM, AND ANJAN V. THAKOR, "Capital Accumulation and Deposit Pricing in Mutual Financial Institutions," *Journal of Financial and Quantitative Analysis,* 17 (December 1982), 705–26.

DIAMOND, DOUGLAS W., AND PHILIP H. DYBVIG, "Bank Runs, Deposit Insurance and Liquidity," *Journal of Political Economy,* 1982.

FISHER, IRVING, *The Theory of Interest as Determined by Impatience to Spend Income and Opportunity to Invest It.* New York: Macmillan, 1930.

FLANNERY, MARK J., "A Method for Empirically Assessing the Impact of Market Interest Rates on Intermediary Profitability," in *Proceedings of a Conference on Bank Structure and Competition,* Federal Reserve Bank of Chicago, 1980A, pp. 1–15.

———, "How Do Changes in Market Interest Rates Affect Bank Profits?" *Business Review,* Federal Reserve Bank of Philadelphia, September/October 1980B, pp. 13–22.

FLANNERY, MARK J., AND JACK M. GUTTENTAG, "Problem Banks: Examination, Identification and Supervision," in *State and Federal Regulation of Commercial Banks,* Federal Deposit Insurance Corporation, Washington, D.C., 2 (1980), 169–226.

FORD, WILLIAM F., "Banking's New Competition: Myths and Realities," *Economic Review,* Federal Reserve Bank of Atlanta, January 1982, pp. 3–11.

FRIEDMAN, MILTON, AND ANNA J. SCHWARTZ, *A Monetary History of the United States, 1867–1960.* Princeton, New Jersey: Princeton University Press, 1963.

GREENBAUM, STUART I., "Legal Reserve Requirements: A Case Study of Bank Regulation," *Journal of Bank Research,* 14 (Spring 1983).

GREENBAUM, STUART I., AND CHARLES F. HAYWOOD, "Secular Change in the Financial Services Industry," *Journal of Money, Credit and Banking,* 3 (May 1971), 571–89.

HAMMOND, BRAY, *Banks and Politics in America: From the Revolution to the Civil War.* Princeton, New Jersey: Princeton University Press, 1957.

KANE, EDWARD J., "Accelerating Inflation, Technological Innovation and the Decreasing Effectiveness of Banking Regulation," *Journal of Finance,* 36 (May 1981), 355–67.

———, *The Gathering Crisis in Federal Deposit Insurance: Origins, Evolution and Possible Reforms* (in progress).

MITCHELL, WESLEY C., *Business Cycles: The Problem and Its Setting.* New York: National Bureau of Economic Research, 1927.

NIEHANS, JÜRG, "Money and Barter in General Equilibrium with Transactions Cost," *American Economic Review,* 61 (December 1971), 773–83.

———, "Innovation in Monetary Policy: Challenge and Response," *Journal of Banking and Finance,* 6 (March 1982), 9–28.

PORZECANSKI, ARTURO C., "The International Financial Role of U.S. Commercial Banks: Past and Future," *Journal of Banking and Finance,* 5 (December 1981), 5–16.

RICART I COSTA, JOAN E., AND STUART I. GREENBAUM, "Bank Forward Lending: A Note," *Journal of Finance,* 39 (September 1983A).

———, "The Pricing of Deposit Insurance," Banking Research Center, J. L. Kellogg Graduate School of Management, Northwestern University, Working Paper 88, 1983B.

ROCKOFF, HUGH T., "The Free Banking Era: A Re-examination," *Journal of Money, Credit and Banking,* 6 (May 1974), 141–67.

ROLNICK, ARTHUR J., AND WARREN E. WEBER, "The Free Banking Era: New Evidence on Laissez Faire Banking," *American Economic Review,* 73 (1983).

SILBER, WILLIAM L., "Towards a Theory of Financial Innovation," in *Financial Innovation,* ed. William L. Silber. Lexington, Massachusetts: D. C. Heath, 1975.

SIMONS, HENRY C., "A Positive Program for Laissez Faire: Some Proposals for a Liberal Economic Policy," in *Economic Policy for a Free Society.* Chicago: University of Chicago Press, 1948.

STIGLER, GEORGE, *The Citizen and the State: Essays on Regulation.* Chicago: University of Chicago Press, 1975.

STRACHAN, S., " 'Congenerics' Draw Enough Buyers to Spark Sound Rally in Equities," *American Banker,* July 8, 1968.

THAKOR, ANJAN V., HAI HONG, AND STUART I. GREENBAUM, "Bank Loan Commitments and Interest Rate Volatility," *Journal of Banking and Finance,* 5 (December 1981), 497–510.

TOBIN, JAMES, "Liquidity Preference as Behavior Towards Risk," *Review of Economic Studies,* 25 (March 1958), 65–86.

WOLKOWITZ, BENJAMIN, PETER LLOYD-DAVIES, BRIAN C. GENDREAU, GERALD A. HANWECK, AND MICHAEL A. GOLDBERG, "Below the Bottom Line: The Use of Contingencies and Commitments by Commercial Banks," Board of Governors of the Federal Reserve System, Washington, D.C., Staff Study 113, 1982.

Technological and Regulatory Forces in the Developing Fusion of Financial Services Competition

EDWARD J. KANE

8

Although the term is applied almost universally to events in the financial-services industry, deregulation has become a misleading catchword for the evolutionary fading away of lines of market cleavage that delimit inherited patterns of competition. Jimmy Durante's signature line, "*Every*body wants to get into the act," sums up the landscape of contemporary financial competition. With and without the explicit blessing of specialized financial regulators, deposit institutions, brokerage firms, and insurance companies are feverishly expanding into one another's traditional bailiwick. Providing opportunities for customers to transact these diverse lines of financial business in a single-statement framework is restructuring front-office and back-office work flows. It is turning a growing number of banking lobbies into pinstriped caricatures of Istanbul's famous covered bazaar and back offices into electronic transactions and communications centers.

1. An Introductory Overview

In at least two ways, deregulation misrepresents the nature of the adjustments taking place. First, it locates the impetus for change in the political arena to the exclusion of the economic one. It intimates that *exogenous* governmental policy decisions are causing nontraditional competitors to enter geographic markets and product lines from which exclusion-

Reprinted from the *Journal of Finance* vol. 39, no. 3 (July 1984):759–772 by permission of the American Finance Association and the author.

ary laws drafted by clever lawyers had previously shut them out. Such a perspective fails to acknowledge the prior breakdown of the inherited system of exclusionary regulation or to raise the issue of why society would suddenly reveal a preference for abandoning rather than rebuilding legal barriers to entry in the financial-services industry. To analyze these issues, one must focus on scope economies and on opportunities for structural arbitrage. By structural arbitrage, I mean adaptive changes in a firm's organizational form designed to lighten its tax and regulatory burdens. In turn, one must recognize that structural arbitrage creates costs and benefits for government officials that require reactive changes in operative tax codes and regulations. Contemporary realignment of federal and state regulatory frameworks is largely a process of competitive reregulation.

The second way that deregulation misleads is in suggesting that the process involves the complete abandonment of regulation rather than its selective and partial relaxation. Talking about deregulation diverts attention from regulations that are being tightened or left unaltered and from reallocations of regulatory authority. Particularly with respect to destabilizing incentives established by deposit-insurance pricing and coverage, unchanged and tightened restrictions play at least as important a role in shaping financial market structures as the particular regulations undergoing relaxation.

Endogeneity of Market Structure.

Rationalizations for laws intended to segment interinstitutional competition presume that, while scale economies may be important in finance (so that small firms need to be protected), scope economies are not. Contemporary events and a conjectural reading of cross-section evidence on the jointness and U-shapedness of commercial-bank costs functions (Benston, Berger, Hanweck, and Humphrey, 1983) suggest that both halves of this presumption are wrong. In the financial-services industry scope has always been correlated with firm size, making it hard to isolate the role played by economies of joint production in the growth and profitability of successful firms.

This article depicts the fusion of financial-services competition as confirming the contestability model of multimarket competition (Baumol, Panzar, and Willig, 1983). Contestability theory maintains that, far from being an exogenous determinant of industry performance, market structure adapts through entry and exit to permit customer demand to be served at minimum cost. The desegmentation of financial markets involves the expansion of low-cost producers at the expense of high-cost ones.

Regulatory interference slows the rate of adaptation by imposing entry restrictions and corresponding avoidance costs on particular firms. But in a free society in which multiple legislatures and regulatory agencies compete—under jurisdictions that overlap—for regulatees, tax receipts, and/or budget funds, authorities cannot induce either great or long-lasting divergences between the actual and the cost-minimizing market structure.

Implications for Deposit Insurance.

In the financial-services industry, any act of regulatory avoidance or reregulation sets into motion two interacting processes (Kane, 1981):

1. Adaptive responses by competing state and overlapping federal regulators (and their supporting political coalitions) to reoptimize their spheres of control by adjusting the rules under which the financial-service game is played;
2. Adaptive responses by various types of financial institutions (including foreign ones) to minimize regulatory burdens by arbitraging differences in applicable regulatory structures.

Because the inherited system of deposit insurance is not rationally priced, changes in organizational form and expansions in financial-institution product lines may also arbitrage differences between the price of risk-bearing in capital markets and implicit and explicit premiums imbedded in federal deposit insurance (Buser, Chen, and Kane, 1981). Since at least the late 1970s, structural arbitrage has increased FDIC and FSLIC risk exposure faster than these agencies have been able to reset their conceptions of contingent claims on their resources. The resulting subsidy to risk-bearing creates a growing need for fundamental deposit-insurance reform. Although we lack the space to discuss them here, the shifting of these subsidies explains a series of anomalous features in the contemporary pattern of financial-services competition.

2. Exclusionary Rules, Avoidance, and the Cost of Multiproduct Operation

To model the costs of multiproduct operation and of laws meant to enforce product specialization, it is sufficient to posit two goods, X_1 and X_2. (By interpreting X_1 as a vector of N-1 outputs, the formulation can easily be generalized to any number of outputs.) Economies of scope exist when the total costs of producing the two goods jointly, $C(X_1,X_2)$, is less than the combined cost, $C_1(X_1)+C_2(X_2)$, of producing the same amounts of each good separately. Economies of scope are economies of joint production. They occur when two outputs share one or more capital or labor inputs in the production process. A traditional example concerns unallocable joint costs that occur in constructing and operating a multipurpose dam to produce electricity, flood control, and recreational services. Abstracting from offsetting costs of managerial coordination, a financial intermediary's computer, communications network, and branch-office system should make it cheaper for it to offer standardized deposit, loan, brokerage, and insurance products in combination than a series of specialized producers could produce the same products on a stand-alone basis.

During the last 15 years, technological change (in the form of the computerization of record-keeping and transacting, the robotization of teller functions, and expanding telecommunications links with customers, services, and financial markets) has increased the role of multipurpose capital equipment in producing financial services. The desirability of spreading the costs of operating this ''telemation'' equipment across additional product lines underlies the rapid progress toward homogenization of function observed for different types of financial intermediaries. It also explains the attraction of nonfinancial firms (particularly those in data-processing and communications) into financial services.

The Generic Financial-Services Firm.

Homogenization in the product lines of formerly specialized financial institutions leads to the concept of the all-purpose *financial-services firm:* a generic reconceptualization of financial-industry boundaries broad enough to encompass the range of activities being undertaken by contemporary institutional competitors. The financial-services firm (FSF) produces informational and transactional products for a base of customers with whom it has established relationships. Informational products include advice, data-processing, and communications services. Transactional products include execution of trading and payment orders, bidirectional funds rental, and risk-bearing services.

To deliver any financial service, an FSF must exchange information with its customers. Customers and FSFs exchange information by means of information media, which today include: personal contacts, paper evidences (such as loan agreements, checks, and deposit slips); telephonic messages; magnetic entries on striped plastic cards, tapes, or discs; and keyboard-actuated video displays. These media connect the customer with the particular FSF product he wishes to use.

Increasingly, financial services register on and occur through an electronic transactions and record-keeping system. This system employs three kinds of productive processes: (1) techniques for maintaining and communicating with remote data bases; (2) techniques for executing transactions; and (3) techniques for delivering services to customers. Because the first two types of technology are known as back-office technology, the third type is called front-office technology. Elements of front-office technology confront the customer every day: brick-and-mortar offices, automated teller machines, drive-in teller windows, and home-based electronic equipment such as telephones and computer terminals.

Among the elements that the customer does not see are the complicated interfaces that connect FSFs across the transactions system. Efficient production requires that FSFs belong to networks in which they both compete with and serve one another. With respect to back-office services, competing banks have always shared some resources. Interbank cooperation is exemplified by such developments as regional clearinghouses, check standardization, ATM networks, and loan syndications. At the same time that brokerage firms and correspondent banks act as wholesalers of back-office services to FSF customers, they compete with these customers for front-office business. Federal Reserve Banks play a quadruple role. They not only supply correspondent and communications services to firms they compete against, they are even empowered to regulate their competitor's activities. Moreover, as regulators they compete against other federal agencies and state banking departments.

Costs of Exclusionary Rules.

This section states a condition for exclusionary rules to be successful and develops a measure of these rules' social cost. A key component of both equations is $C_{a',r}$, the cost of perfectly circumventing or avoiding a given set of restrictions against multiproduct operation in the most efficient way known at the time. Opportunities for circumvention act as a brake on the welfare burden of regulation, keeping this burden lighter than it would otherwise be.

By construction, $C_{a,r}$ is nonnegative. Avoidance costs may be conceived as the incremental costs of creating an unregulated substitute product or institutional arrangement. Examples include the extra costs of running a zero-balance sweep operation to circumvent the prohibition against paying explicit interest on demand deposits or the extra costs of offering a prohibited product through a subsidiary corporation or holding-company affiliate. Whether X_1 and X_2 are produced jointly or singly depends on which of the following costs is smaller:

$$C(X_1,X_2) + C_{a,r} \textit{ versus } C_1(X_1)+C_2(X_2). \tag{1}$$

This condition confronts only half of the resource waste inherent in effective regulation. The social cost of a regulatory exclusion is the sum of two items: (1) administrative costs of promulgating and enforcing the restriction and (2) the lesser of $C_{a,r}$ and the forfeited economies of scope $[C(X_1)+C(X_2)-C(X_1,X_2)]$.

The Impact of Technological Change.

Technological change lowers *both* components of the lefthand side of condition (1). It increases the role of multipurpose ''telemation'' equipment in financial-services production and makes it easier for management to coordinate unregulated substitute arrangements such as sweep accounts or the activities of an array of subsidiary firms. Hence, it makes product-line homogenization increasingly likely.

Unless regulators increase administrative and avoidance costs to offset technological change, exclusionary rules would tend to lose their effectiveness. However, the social costs of regulation could rise, fall, or remain the same. We look at constraints that regulatory competition places on the behavior of regulators in Section 3.

This paragraph illustrates numerically how technological change might undermine exclusionary rules. Let us suppose that prior to a change in technology $C(X_1,X_2)$ equalled 8 and $C_{a,r}$ was 3, while $C_1(X_1)+C_2(X_2)$ was 10. Because scope economies of 2 fall short of avoidance costs, the exclusionary rule would succeed and specialized producers would be observed. The social cost of regulation would be the sum of forgone economies of scope (2) and administrative costs (which we arbitrarily assume to be 3). Next, let us assume that innovation drives the costs of joint production to 7 and avoidance costs to 2, without affecting the costs of specialized operation. This change makes the exclusionary rule unenforceable, because it increases the costs of forgone economies of scope to 3 while reducing avoidance costs to 2. To minimize the burden of regulation, product-line homogenization would develop. If regulator costs remained unchanged at 3, the social costs of regulation would stay at 5, but avoidance costs would now register in place of forgone scope economies.

Scope Economies Are Partly Rooted in the Mispricing of Deposit-Insurance.

Mispricing deposit-insurance guarantees provides an unintended subsidy that reduces an insured institution's exposure to risk in product-line expansions. When brokers and insurers incorporate a deposit institution into their operation and when deposit institutions diversify into brokerage and insurance activities, some of the blessing of deposit insurance extends to these firms' nondepository affiliates. This is because, as a practical matter, it is impossible for deposit-insurance bureaucrats to prevent an insured deposit institution from assisting its troubled affiliates and subsidiaries whenever management perceives such assistance to be in its own best interest (Eisenbeis, 1983a).

Currently federal deposit insurance fully guarantees an institution's deposit accounts up to $100,000 per distinct combination of accountholders, with accounts held singly and jointly and accounts held in different institutions each afforded a separate insurance status. To exploit the opportunity for individuals to multiply their coverage, funds brokers have developed software and communications facilities that distribute multimillion-dollar concentrations of wealth across individual institutions in $100,000 pieces. In recent months, such brokers are said to have played a significant role in funneling deposits to seriously troubled banks and thrifts eager to pay a premium rate on $100,000 CDs.

Deposit-insurance guarantees are supported by *explicit* premiums of $\frac{1}{12}$ of one percent of total (insured and uninsured) deposits booked at domestic offices. Currently, this premium is rebatable in part for FDIC clients, but not for FSLIC customers.

Because this pattern of explicit pricing is not sensitive to differences in either interest-rate volatility or an FSF's leverage, asset, or affiliated-institution risk, client risk-taking must be regulated directly. It is convenient to view capital adequacy requirements and back-up regulatory penalties for excessive risk-taking as *implicit* premiums that agency managers vary to control these and other bureaucratically recognized forms of risk-taking.

Three things are wrong with this coverage and pricing system. First, it is *allocationally inefficient:* By underpricing risk, it wastes scarce resources. Second, it is *distributionally unfair:* It overcharges conservatively managed deposit institutions and forces them to stand ready to bail out high-flying competitors. Third, it fosters *financial instability:* It subsidizes deposit-institution risk-taking *most* when markets are most volatile and loads the burden for financing this subsidy onto both conservatively managed deposit institutions that are sure to survive any crisis and taxpayers at large. The implicit liability facing surviving institutions is underscored in the still-unresolved failure of a state-insured institution in Lincoln, Nebraska in the fall of 1983. When the state insurance fund was revealed to have only $2 million to cover $70 million in guarantees, politicians immediately proposed assessing surviving financial institutions for the difference.

FDIC and FSLIC premium structures subsidize *unregulated* forms of risk-bearing. They lead dynamically to a continual search for (and expansion of) such new forms of risk-taking as entry into futures markets, investment banking, or insurance underwriting. They also make bureaucratic conceptions of operative categories of deposit-institution risk-taking play the pivotal role in preventing a system breakdown.

Federal deposit insurers would not end up subsidizing risk-taking if they were quick to adapt their regulatory policies to emerging problems (Bierwag and Kaufman, 1983). But this is merely a counsel of perfection. Unless bureaucratic incentive systems can be made to mimic those of profit-oriented enterprises, this counsel of perfection has no empirical importance. Bureaucrats are inherently slower in responding to changes in interest-rate volatility and other emerging forms of risk than private insurers would be. Politically appointed agency heads typically have short horizons and are sensitive to political constraints that overlay an agency's strictly economic interests in the decisions it makes. This leaves government bureaucracies markedly lower in *adaptive efficiency* than value-maximizing firms. Given this relative weakness and a financial-services environment changing as rapidly as our own, it is poor public policy to require an agency to follow policies that thrust its adaptive efficiency in protecting its economic interests into a pivotal role. Such an agency spends its energy playing catch-up, much like a sprinter who is habitually late out of the starting blocks or a baseball pitcher who slips persistently behind in the count.

3. Structural Arbitrage and Competitive Reregulation

Through structural arbitrage and the threat of structural arbitrage, value-maximizing managers of U.S. deposit institutions may to a large extent choose the set of laws and the particular regulatory bodies by which they are governed. This is because the set of restrictions applicable to their business operations and the particular agencies assigned to oversee their behavior vary with how they resolve a series of options concerning the institution's structural form.

Structural Options.

The broadest set of options concerns the type of *charter* under which a deposit institution elects to operate. First, it may charter or recharter itself as a commercial bank, a savings-and-loan association (S&L), or a savings bank (MSB). Rechartering may be accomplished by charter conversion or by merging into an institution that already has the desired charter type. Second, each type of charter is available alternately from state or federal authorities. While commercial banks and S&Ls are chartered in all 50 states, MSB charters are available in only 17. Whenever the location of an institution's offices is not predetermined, these options generate a space of as many as 120 ($=2\times51+18$) different regulatory "micro-climates."

Most of these micro-climates involve multiple regulators and dimensions of additional choice. For example, federally chartered commercial banks (national banks) have the Comptroller of the Currency as their primary regulator, but are subject to additional oversight from the Federal Reserve and the FDIC. Although under the primary direction of its state banking department, a state-chartered commercial bank typically subjects itself to federal co-supervision. This occurs whenever it is federally insured, with an even richer regulatory climate coming on line if it chooses to become a member of the Federal Reserve System.[1]

[1]Only in about three states may a new bank elect against FDIC insurance and the additional balance-sheet regulation that comes with it. Until universal reserve requirements dictated by Depository Institutions Deregulation and Monetary Control Act (DIDMCA) of 1980 are fully phased in, member banks face higher reserve requirements than nonmembers do.

Until 1979, all savings banks were state-chartered and insured either by the FDIC, a state insurance fund, or both. Federal charters have gained in popularity since the Garn-St Germain Depository Institutions Act (DIA) of 1982, which permits a converting MSB to retain FDIC insurance. Prior to the DIA, federal savings banks had to be insured by the FSLIC, which meant that a MSB could convert only when the prior insurer(s) and the FSLIC could agree on compensation for shifting the liability associated with the insurance guarantee over to the FSLIC.

Micro-climates for S&Ls are in some respects richer than for MSBs. First, S&Ls have an institutionally specialized federal regulator (the Federal Home Loan Bank Board or FHLBB) and deposit-insurance fund (the FSLIC). In addition, most states have separate agencies regulating banks and S&Ls. Five states also operate insurance funds for state-chartered thrifts (Massachusetts, Maryland, North Carolina, Ohio, and Pennsylvania).

A second variety of option concerns the *form* of institutional ownership. For managers who elect against seeking a commercial-bank charter, the opportunity exists to operate under either stockholder or mutual ownership. The outcome of this election affects the incentive structure under which management functions, in that managers of stockholder institutions are subject to SEC disclosure requirements and to possible dismissal in proxy fights and unfriendly takeovers, on the one hand; but are able to work out a rich variety of stock-based compensation schemes or even to participate in leveraged buyouts, on the other. For existing institutions, the conversion option is effectively one-way: from mutual to stock ownership.

For stock firms, the most important option is whether or not to allow the stock to be owned by a holding company (i.e., to interpose a layer of indirect ownership—a corporate stockholder—between the deposit institution and its ultimate owners). Deposit-institution holding companies (HCs) are differentially taxed and regulated as compared to deposit institutions themselves. Deposit-institution HCs are subject in some states to additional state regulation and to federal regulation of permissible activities under the Fed or FHLBB. However, under special provisions of federal law, S&L HCs are currently exempted from the layer of FHLBB regulation as long as the HC chooses to own only one S&L. Deposit-institution HCs are also subject to disclosure regulation by the SEC from which deposit institutions themselves are exempt, but HCs may avoid SEC oversight by keeping the HC's value of equity and number of stockholders within legislated limits. Notwithstanding this exposure to incremental regulation, the HC device provides opportunities to circumvent many restrictions on deposit-institution activities. Nonbank affiliates may undertake activities that deposit institutions cannot. Moreover, tax and regulatory burdens even on permissible activities may be lightened in important ways.

A similar set of options exists even for non-HC institutions. This concerns whether or not to use *subsidiary corporations* (or, in the case of deposit-institution subsidiaries of HCs, affiliated corporations) to operate various lines of deposit-institution business. Spinning off some product lines may lighten the burden of federal capital-adequacy requirements and, not only circumvent interstate and intrastate restrictions on office locations, but allow individual product lines to be produced in the micro-climate in which they can generate the highest after-tax profit.

Competition Among Legislatures and Regulatory Bodies.

Markets for regulatory services should be regarded as nearly as contestable as those of regulatees. This contestability makes applicable laws and the regulatory postures of different authorities partly endogenous. Deposit institutions' structural choices have economic consequences for legislatures and for regulatory agencies. Their desire to influence the outcomes of regulatee choices leads these bodies to compete for the "regulatory business" of potential clients. This competition gives deposit-institution lobbyists political leverage with which to play authorities off against each other to win regulatory forbearance for circumvention activities and to educe favorable changes in legislation or agency rules.

Competition between overlapping federal and state regulators looks in the short run like wasteful duplication, but leads in the long run to better-adapted regulatory rules. When the opportunity cost of an exlusionary rule rises, pressures develop to soften the rule. It is unlikely that laws meant to hold deposit institutions out of brokerage and insurance activities and brokers and insurance companies out of deposit-institution markets can stand up indefinitely against opportunities to reduce product costs created by growing scope economies. While it is natural for lobbyists from each industry to fight a rearguard political action to delay change, American politics and ideology favor innovation over regulation in many ways. In one way or another, low-cost schemes for producing and distributing products are able to push aside high-cost ones. This is partly because reregulation is a competitive process that responds to *economic* as well as political forces.

Banks' recent success in winning favorable product-line regulation in Delaware and South Dakota illustrates the process. Legislatures in these states have given specialized subsidiaries of out-of-state HCs long-desired freedoms and powers, particularly with respect to credit-card and insurance operations. Especially if (as I contend) economies of joint production are increasing over time, scope economies give deposit institutions an incentive to probe nationwide for political weak points in exclusionary policies. At the same time, the tax, budget, and employment benefits of winning regulatory refugees from other jurisdictions give bureaucrats and legislatures an incentive to trade in regulatory relaxation.

Similar pressures are fueling the drive for legislation permitting reciprocal interstate banking at least within collections of neighboring states. Limited-reciprocity laws have already passed the Massachusetts, Connecticut, and Rhode Island legislatures, and are actively being considered by state officials in other regions. Maine and New York permit acquisitions by out-of-state banking organizations from any state that grants reciprocal privileges to banks in their state, while Alaska allows virtually unconditional acquisition of *existing* institutions by out-of-state organizations. Lawsuits have been brought against the limited-reciprocity laws on several grounds, including the claim that the Constitution's interstate-commerce clause precludes states from imposing conditions on interstate entry. But by the time that these suits wend their way fully through the courts, odds are good that either Congress will have already blessed these regional experiments or interstate operation of deposit institutions will (as NOW accounts and remote ATMs were in 1980) prove politically too well-established to be undone.

By realigning its organizational structure, a financial firm not only can reorganize its regulatory environment, it can also create pressure on legislatures and regulators to rewrite the regulations under which it has to play. Competitive reregulation occurs not only among officials in different states, but also between state and federal officials and between managers of different federal agencies. Regulators try to forestall changes in organizational form that would transfer some or all of their traditional regulatees' business from their dominion to that of another agency. When an agency suffers a cumulative loss of regulatees, it maneuvers both administratively and in the legislative arena to recapture its clientele, usually by lowering the net burden its regulations place on its clients. Federal Reserve (and eventually Congressional) response to the Fed's membership problem of the 1960s and 1970s and the granting of new powers for state-chartered institutions by state banking departments and legislatures in response to the DIDMCA of 1980 exemplify the typical pattern of defensive reaction.

But it must never be forgotten that some regulatory agencies and legislatures have capacities for a punitive retightening of regulations, with the U.S. Congress having the greatest capacity of all. Congress can vote retaliatory *preemptions* of state laws able to nullify particular legislative and regulatory actions in every state. It can also enact lengthy *moratoria* that suspend the opportunity to effect particular types of organizational change. With the courts, Congress serves as the final arbiter of disputes over alternative agencies' dominion and power.

Such disputes arise frequently at the federal level, especially between the SEC and banking regulators (e.g., over who should be entitled to regulate brokers of $100,000 CDs or discount-brokerage subsidiaries of deposit-institution HCs) and between the Federal Reserve and other federal regulators of deposit institutions. In such contests, the Fed has special clout with Congress. This clout grows out of the Fed's responsibilities for macroeconomic stability and its willingness to be scapegoated for unfavorable macroeconomic events. The Bush Commission's difficulties in dispersing the Fed's existing regulatory authority among more specialized deposit-institution agencies provides renewed evidence of the Fed's special primacy in the arena of financial regulation.

Distressing Implications for Financial Stability and Public Policy Toward the Nonbank Bank.

Pre-existing conflicts over regulatory turf have been heightened in the 1980s by cross-industry merger activity and product-line expansion by brokerage, insurance, and deposit firms. The ongoing robotization and electronification of systems for producing and delivering financial services is extending the boundaries of regional competition and sweeping the activities of individual deposit institutions into new states and into the orbits of securities and futures-market regulators and state insurance departments. These same forces are simultaneously thrusting the activities of securities, futures, and insurance firms into the orbits of state and federal deposit-institution regulators.

If the scope economies that are driving financial change did not include subsidies to risk-bearing rooted in the mispricing of risk in federal deposit insurance, structural arbitrage and competitive reregulation would shape up as unambiguously resource-saving activities. However, until federal deposit insurers explicitly price such unregulated risks as those associated with borrower default, asset maturity, balance-sheet leverage, affiliated institutions, and technological change, social welfare is served by regulatory action to limit risk-taking by insured firms. Although this concern justifies authorities' search for ways to constrain and supervise a deposit institution's portfolio positions as well as risky activities undertaken by any holding-company affiliates, it in no way proves the optimality of the particular policies actually adopted.[2]

In the short run, bureaucratic competition for jurisdiction is leading various state and federal regulators to facilitate forms of structural arbitrage that undermine the inherited system of federal deposit insurance. Although this arbitrage is vastly increasing the risk exposure of the FDIC and FSLIC, political pressures and competition from other regulators have deflected the deposit-insurance agencies from bringing these new risks under administrative control.

Holding-company arbitrage is a game that may be played by brokers and insurers, too. The existence of patterns for circumventing regulatory restrictions on deposit-institution activities makes deposit institutions more attractive candidates for takeover by nondepository firms. Just as deposit-institution HCs can acquire nondepository firms, nondepository financial institutions (such as Merrill Lynch, Dreyfus Corp., and Prudential Insurance) and even nonfinancial firms (such as Sears Roebuck, J.C. Penney, National Steel, and the Parker Pen Co.) can acquire a stockholder-owned deposit institution. If the acquired firm is a thrift institution or is converted into one, its parent can avoid specialized federal oversight at the holding-company level as long as it meets the definition of a unitary savings-and-loan holding company. If the acquired firm is a bank, spinning off either the demand-deposit or the commercial-loan side of the business makes it possible in principle for the parent firm to elude Fed regulation as a bank HC. The hybrid operation that results is known paradoxically as a "nonbank bank." In terms of the operative definitions of the Bank Holding Company Act, the institution becomes a "nonbank," even though as the holder of a bank charter it may continue to gather time and savings deposits and to have these deposits insured by the FDIC. Moreover, it even seems possible to circumvent restrictions on interstate banking (or at least it seemed possible to the management of Dimension Corp.) by operating a network of limited-service banks in different states.

To some deposit-institution regulators and trade associations, the freedom afforded nonbank banks and unitary S&L HCs represents a glaring pair of loopholes in the legislative fabric of exclusionary regulation (Eisenbeis, 1983b). During 1983, Fed Chairman Volcker, citing a growing threat to the traditional separation of banking from commerce and investment banking, repeatedly urged Congress to pass a temporary moratorium on nondepository acquisitions of deposit institutions and on state and federal actions that allow different types of financial-services firms to expand beyond their traditional lines of business.

[2]Kane (1983) discusses how deposit-insurance subsidies are shifted to selected borrowers and depositors, and suggests a series of reforms ranging from market-value accounting for insured institutions to changes in FDIC and FSLIC risk management, coverages, and pricing. Any subset of the reforms would allow scope economies to be pursued without surrendering control of the aggregate risk to which the FDIC and FSLIC are exposed.

Volcker's position on the desirability of separation was not supported by other federal regulators of deposit institutions. Although in 1983 and 1984 the Comptroller of the currency imposed his own moratorium on applications for *de novo* national-bank charters by securities firms and other nonbanking businesses, his stated goal was to give Congress time to redraw industry boundaries. His office continued to process pending applications and to permit nondepository firms to acquire *existing* national banks. In even sharper contrast, the FDIC and FHLBB encouraged their regulatees to undertake various forms of securities activities, with the FHLBB asymmetrically delaying action on applications by brokerage firms and insurance companies to acquire thrifts.

Lack of consenus among federal regulators and among financial-industry trade associations left Congress reluctant to legislate. Congress hates to choose sides in contests in which the social costs and benefits of alternative solutions are highly uncertain. For this reason, Congress appeared willing to permit structural arbitrage to set the future parameters of financial-services competition and to accept any resulting strains on the deposit-insurance system.

Unwilling to accept these same strains, in late 1983 the Federal Reserve Board launched a bold reregulatory counterattack whose ultimate legality remains uncertain. Frustrated by Congressional inaction, the Board unilaterally broadened its interpretation of what activities it holds to be "commercial loans" and "demand deposits" under the Bank Holding Company Act. Its definition of commercial loans now includes sales of federal funds, extension of call loans to brokers, and purchases of commercial paper, certificates of deposit and bankers acceptances, while the category of demand deposits now includes NOW and super-NOW accounts.[3] These redefinitions force nonregistered corporate owners of most nonbank banks to confront a pair of nested dilemmas. They must either further narrow the product lines of their nonbank-bank subsidiary (e.g., by focusing on MMDAs and noncheckable deposit accounts, repurchase agreements, and consumer and mortgage loans) or, within two years, either divest themselves of the nonbank bank or register with the Fed as a bank HC and accept Fed dominion over its activities. Sugaring the pill, the Fed simultaneously added five new powers to the list of permissible activities for nonbanking subsidiaries of bank HCs: issuing money orders; arranging equity financing for real estate; underwriting and dealing in government and specified money-market obligations; providing foreign-exchange advisory services; and performing as a futures commission merchant.

In contrast to the customary regulatory practice of exempting or grandfathering all combinations undertaken under the old rules, the new definitions are retroactive. However, the Fed proposed to permit combinations established before December 10, 1982 to apply for exemptions based on hardship and fairness. The cutoff date coincides with a Board ruling that Dreyfus Corp. would have to register as a bank HC before it acquired a New Jersey bank (a ruling Dreyfus later circumvented by acting under state authority).

These actions increase the expected value and the variance both of the Fed's own administrative costs and of costs for unconventional entrants of circumventing Fed regulation of bank holding companies. If Fed officials were truly confident in the Board's

[3]This act of redefinition recalls the Comptroller's unsuccessful attempt to rule that off-premises ATMs were not legally branch offices whose locations were subject to regulation under existing branch-banking laws.

authority to close the nonbank-bank loophole on its own, one must suppose that Chairman Volcker would not have allowed a problem that so obviously distressed him to fester for so long. The most logical way to read the Board's action is as a forcing move designed to make Congress and the federal courts referee the game of HC reregulation. Effectively, the Fed has demanded that Congress and the Courts either sustain or overrule its redefinitions and choice of cutoff date. Unlike Chairman Volcker's polite pleas for legislative action, this public challenge raises constitutional questions that cannot be turned aside. No matter what the referees finally decide, their merely having the issue under advisement and the threat of additional unilateral action by the Fed promise to reduce for the duration prospective net benefits to brokers and insurers from entering the banking business.

4. Summary

On the TV show, *You Bet Your Life,* a minister once thanked Groucho Marx for all the joy his work had brought into the world. Without missing a beat, Groucho in turn thanked the minister for all the joy his work had taken *out* of it. For brokers, insurance companies, and Dimension Corp., Chairman Volcker has taken some of the joy out of the world of finance. The Board's action leaves the opportunity for deposit institutions to enter brokerage and insurance asymmetrically much greater than the opportunity for insurers and brokers to enter banking. The disadvantaged parties should lobby with greater vigor for a legislative rebalancing of regulatory subsidies. As brokers and insurers come to appreciate the size of deposit-insurance subsidies and their role in lessening the risks of product-line extension by deposit institutions, they may tip the balance of lobbying pressure toward deposit-insurance reform.

As long as scope economies and deposit-insurance subsidies remain substantial, almost "everybody" should still want to get into each other's act. The Fed's redefinition of its regulatory domain temporarily reduces the product-line flexibility of nonbank financial-services firms relative to banks. In raising the costs of interstate and nonbank entry into banking markets and forcing the hand of Congressional and judicial referees, the Fed transformed a routine regulatory price war into a constitutional struggle over the limits of the Fed's power as financial regulator and stabilizer of last resort.

REFERENCES

BAUMOL, WILLIAM, PANZAR, JOHN C., and WILLIG, ROBERT D., "On the Theory of Perfectly Contestable Markets," Bell Laboratories Discussion Paper No. 268 (June 1983).

BENSTON, GEORGE J., BERGER, ALLEN N., HANWECK, G. A., and HUMPHREY, D. B., "Economics of Scale and Scope in Banking," in *Proceedings of Conference on Bank Structure and Competition,* Chicago: Federal Reserve Bank of Chicago, 1983.

BIERWAG, GERALD O. and KAUFMAN, GEORGE G., "A Proposal for Federal Deposit Insurance with Risk-Sensitive Premiums," in *Proceedings of Conference on Bank Structure and Competition,* Chicago: Federal Reserve Bank of Chicago, 1983.

BUSER, STEPHEN, CHEN, ANDREW H., and KANE, EDWARD J., "Federal Deposit Insurance, Regulatory Policy, and Optimal Bank Capital," *Journal of Finance,* 36 (March 1981), pp. 51–60.

EISENBEIS, ROBERT A., "Banking Holding Companies and Public Policy," in George J. Benston (ed.), *Financial Services: The Changing Institutions and Government Policy,* Englewood Cliffs, NJ: Prentice-Hall, Inc. for the American Assembly, 1983(a), pp. 127–155.

EISENBEIS, ROBERT A., "Policy Issues Raised by the Expansion of Nonbank Banks," unpublished manuscript, University of North Carolina, Chapel Hill, 1983(b).

KANE, EDWARD J., "Accelerating Inflation, Technological Innovation, and the Decreasing Effectiveness of Banking Regulation," *Journal of Finance,* 36 (May 1981), pp. 355–367.

KANE, EDWARD J., "A Six-Point Program for Deposit-Insurance Reform," *Housing Finance Review,* 2 (July 1983), pp. 269–278.

Payments System Developments and Public Policy

Paul M. Horvitz

9

Economic historians have always placed great emphasis on the invention of money as a necessary step in allowing a primitive economy to develop into one based on exchange in which specialization is feasible. As an economy becomes more complex, the existence of money is not sufficient: an efficient mechanism for transferring money—a payments system—is essential.

Even in advanced economies, most small payments will be made with coin and currency, but security considerations make this less desirable for larger transactions and not feasible when payments must be made at a great distance. Further, when large transactions are involved, the time and risk involved in moving coin and currency (or other paper-based means of payment) may represent a significant cost.

For the first hundred years of U.S. history, coin and currency—much of it issued by private banks—was the primary payments medium. Over the last hundred years, we have seen the development of an efficient payments system based primarily on the paper check. It has become increasingly common to make large payments, particularly involving financial transactions, through the use of electronic communications systems, and we are moving toward greater use of electronic means of handling consumer payments.

The writing of checks on commercial bank demand deposits became a significant payments system in the U.S. in the 1870s and has developed since that time in response to initiatives taken by individual banks, by banker associations and committees, and as a

Reprinted from *Financial Services,* George J. Benston, ed., © 1983 by The American Assembly. Published by Prentice-Hall Inc., Englewood Cliffs, NJ 07632.

result of policies adopted by the federal government. Development of an efficient check payments system was more difficult in the United States than in other countries. As distinct from other countries, the U.S. banking system consisted of a very large number of banks, most of them very small, spread across a very large area. During the last half of the nineteenth century a number of clearing houses developed where local banks could exchange checks on each other promptly and cheaply. Collection of intercity checks was slower and more cumbersome. Banks developed networks of correspondent relationships to facilitate collections, though a number of banks imposed exchange charges on checks delivered to them by mail. While improvement was steady, round-about and inefficient means of collecting checks persisted into this century.

The establishment of the Federal Reserve System in 1913 represented a quantum leap forward. Though the emphasis today is on the monetary policy responsibilities of the Federal Reserve, a major purpose of the Federal Reserve Act was the creation of a national check collection and settlement system. Federal Reserve member banks were able to deposit checks with their Federal Reserve Bank for collection (including checks drawn on nonmember banks), receiving credit in accord with a firm schedule. Nonmember banks were able to obtain such services indirectly by arrangements with a correspondent bank that was a Federal Reserve member.

Over the next forty years there was further improvement in the speed and efficiency of the check collection system. The volume of check payments grew at an annual rate of about 7 percent (except for the interruption of the Great Depression), and the number of checks handled by the Federal Reserve System grew at a somewhat faster rate, representing an increase in its role in the check payments system. Handling the growing volume of checks has always required the use of the most modern equipment available. But because checks generally pass through more than one bank, a decision on processing methods and equipment frequently involves agreement among all participants in the system. During the 1950s representatives of the commercial banking industry, the Federal Reserve, and equipment manufacturers agreed on magnetic ink character recognition (MICR) as the standard for automated check handling. The agreement was rapidly implemented, and by 1963 almost 85 percent of all checks handled by the Federal Reserve carried MICR encoding. The use of highspeed check sorters based on MICR greatly reduced the time and cost of check processing at both commercial banks and the Federal Reserve, with an estimated doubling of the productivity of such operations from the 1960s to 1979.

Despite the improved productivity in handling paper checks, concern was expressed during the 1960s and early 1970s about the ability of the banking system to handle the ever increasing volume of checks. Check volume was continuing to increase at about a 7 percent annual rate, which implies a doubling in about ten years. Analogies were frequently drawn with the securities industry which came close to a breakdown in the 1960s as increased stock trading volume threatened to swamp back-office capabilities. Several efforts at developing electronic payments systems were justified on the basis of fears that the paper-based check payments system would not be able to handle the growth in volume, though there is some dispute about the reality of that fear. Thus, one expert on the payments system, Edwin Cox (1974) of Arthur D. Little, stated at a Federal Reserve Bank of Boston Conference that "concern with the payment system was rooted in the fear that growing check volumes posed a threat to the continued satisfactory performance of the system'' (p. 16). Similarly, at the same conference, John Reed of Citicorp referred to ''the driving force of many involved in the early EFTS (Electronic Funds Transfer System) efforts to seek an alternative to the check processing system based on the view that the system was potentially fragile.''

On the other hand, Robert H. Long (1974) of the Bank Administration Institute argued that, ''Since the implementation of MICR, I have found no EFTS implementor who believed that check volume was a serious problem. Rather, I believe this fear was and is a straw man, a useful prod that EFTS promoters used to arouse some degree of cooperation and support from the industry at large'' (p. 32). In any case, subsequent developments have tended to support the views of those who believe that the banking system will be able to keep up with the increasing volume of paper checks. Basic change in the system has not seemed to be required to keep up with normal growth.

In recent years, however, several major changes have occurred in the economy and the financial system which have profound impacts on the payments system. These changes in the economy suggest that major changes in the payments system are inevitable and that these changes may have public policy implications. That is, it may not be appropriate to allow the payment system to evolve solely in accord with the needs and interests of the providers of payments services.

The purpose of this chapter is to describe briefly the present payments system of the United States, to describe the forces impinging on the payments system and the changes they are likely to bring to it, to discuss the public policy issues raised by these changes, and to consider the appropriate public response to these problems.

The Present U.S. Payments System

Currency

Payments are made in a variety of ways in the U.S. economy. Obviously a very large number of transactions are made with currency. This is now and will remain the principal means of payment for the majority of small transactions made by consumers. For such transactions this is convenient and efficient. While good data exist on the volume of currency in circulation, there are no reliable data on the actual volume of transactions, though there is some evidence of an increase in the use of currency for larger transactions. The lack of data on currency transactions, reflecting the anonymity of such transactions, may be related to the possible increasing use of currency for illegal transactions (particularly drug trafficking) and its use in the ''underground economy,'' where otherwise legal transactions involve payment in cash to evade income taxes. While there are some public policy issues involved in the growing use of currency for these purposes, they are not related to the efficiency of the payments mechanism itself. Consequently, these issues are not discussed further in this chapter.

Checks

Apart from payments made with currency, nearly all payments in the United States at the present time are made by check. Recent intensive study of the check payment system conducted by the Federal Reserve Bank of Atlanta and the Bank Administration Institute found that 32 billion checks were written on commercial banks in 1979, with an additional 1 billion government checks and money orders. The annual rate of growth in the number of checks written has been declining over the past decade, from slightly above 7 percent ten years ago to about 5 percent in 1982. Over 70 percent of all checks require processing by more than one bank, with the average check handled by 2.4 institutions.

While most checks are handled efficiently on an automated basis, some items, such as NSF checks (drawn on accounts with insufficient funds), involve hand processing with higher labor costs and long delays. The danger of losses from acceptance of bad checks adversely affects the willingness of merchants and others to accept checks. Further, despite extensive automation of the process, paper checks still involve significant labor, transportation, and space costs. Some of these costs could be avoided if it were not necessary to return checks to the original writer of the check. A number of banks, and many thrift institutions with checking accounts, have truncated the process by holding the checks rather than returning them to their depositors. This saves postage and some sorting costs, though the bank must be able to retrieve the check at a customer's request if needed for proof of payment. These savings are modest as compared with the potential of truncation at the bank of first deposit. If such a system were in effect, the information from the check would be moved electronically, but physical transportation of checks would no longer be necessary. Consumers seem reluctant to give up the security of the paper check as a legal receipt, but this is the direction in which the system is moving.

An important attribute of the paper check system is that the collection of checks takes time. This gives rise to "float"—a difference between the time a check is presented in payment of an obligation and the time at which the payee actually receives good funds. All during that time one party to the transaction is, in effect, providing free credit to another party. There has been much conflict over the years among depositors, their banks, correspondent banks, and the Federal Reserve as to who will reap the benefit from that float. Part of the consumer's reluctance to adopt electronic payments devices is concern that he will lose the float he had previously been enjoying. While float is frequently treated as an inefficiency in the system, it should be noted that it involves no net cost to society—one party's loss is someone else's gain—and reducing float through use of more labor, equipment, or transportation facilities involves real social costs. (Of course, float can involve some real costs. An increase in the length of time it takes to collect a check increases the risk that the check writer will fail before the check is collected. The greater the volume of checks in the collection pipeline, the greater the total risk in the system.)

The current state of the checking system was accurately summed up in a study of the payments system conducted by Arthur D. Little, Inc. (1982) for the Association of Reserve City Bankers: "Checking services are . . . reliable, accurate, and timely. It is a readily accepted means of funds transfer in most sectors of society. As such, it acts as a standard against which other payments systems are and will continue to be measured" (p. 114). The check payment system has been firmly established in our legal system, which means that the allocation of risks in the system is well understood by all participants in the process. While this is easily taken for granted, the allocation of risks is not settled in all electronic systems.

Wire Transfers

There are several systems by which funds can be transferred by wire. The oldest and largest is the Fed Wire system, which began with a leased telegraph system linking Federal Reserve Banks and branches in 1918 and has been upgraded several times since. In 1980, $80 trillion was transferred over the Fed Wire in 43 million transactions (an average of over $1.8 million per message). While the number of transactions is a small fraction of the 34 billion checks written during the same period, the dollar amount of wire transfers greatly exceeded the $19 trillion of check payments.

An important feature of the Fed Wire system from the point of view of participating commercial banks is that it is the only element of the payment system on which all transactions are instantaneous and final. A bank receiving funds via this means knows that the transaction cannot be reversed because of the failure to deliver by any participant in the system. The bank receiving a paper check cannot be certain that the funds are good because of the possible failure of the writer of the check or the bank on which the check is written. Probably the Federal Reserve is the only institution that can make such a guarantee.

The New York Clearing House Interbank Payments System (CHIPS) began operations in 1970 to facilitate transfers of funds for international customers of the members of the New York Clearing House. Banks other than clearing house members, both domestic and foreign, are now participants in the system. In 1980 CHIPS handled about 13 million transactions involving $37 trillion, and system volume has been growing at a rate of about 20 percent per year. Settlement of net debits and credits among the participants is handled at the close of business each day. This ''same-day'' settlement was designed to minimize risks to participants, but some risk remains. Consider the bank that receives a message with a credit for a customer of the bank. If the customer is allowed immediate use of the funds, and the sending bank fails before the settlement at the end of the day, then the receiving bank is at risk. While these risks are extremely small on an individual basis, the volume of transactions is very high, with amounts equal to many times the bank's total capital flowing into and out of the bank in the course of a single day.

There are two other operating communications networks—BankWire and the Society of Worldwide Interbank Financial Telecommunication (SWIFT). BankWire was organized in 1952 by a group of large commerical banks. SWIFT includes about 900 members in 39 countries. Up to now, these systems have been for communication rather than funds transfer, though the majority of messages relate to the transfer of funds. Actual transfer requires a means of settlement which, for all practical purposes, requires Federal Reserve participation and agreement. BankWire has negotiated such arrangements with the Federal Reserve and will soon begin operating a network that will be a full competitor of the Fed Wire System.

While the wire systems have agreements among their members with respect to the allocation of risks and potential losses, the legal status of bank customers in such transactions does not have the settled precedents of the older check payments system. In an important case in 1981, an Illinois federal court held that a bank could be liable for consequential damages of $2.1 million for failing to process a $27,000 telex message in a timely manner. While the finding was reversed on appeal, this suggests that banks may be liable for some failures of the system. In addition to risks from failure of a participant in the system before settlement, there are also fraud risks of a generally unknown magnitude in wire transfer systems. It is not clear whether adequate insurance is available for such risks.

Automated Clearing Houses

The automated clearing house (ACH) is a means of reducing the cost of handling paper checks by putting the information that would normally be found on a paper check in a machine-readable form. A typical ACH transaction would involve a large employer putting payroll information on magnetic tape that would be delivered to the ACH. The ACH would combine the information from that tape with tapes from other employers and sort by payee bank. Each bank that is a member of the clearing house would receive a tape with information on the amounts to be credited to the accounts of its depositors. Actual transfer of funds would be made by the bank of the employer.

ACH volume has been growing rather rapidly, but the principal originator of transactions has been the U.S. Treasury Department. Social Security benefits are paid through ACHs, as are many government salary payments, but private sector use of automated clearing houses has grown slowly. Over thirty automated clearing houses serve most of the country. With the exception of the New York ACH, all of these are operated by the Federal Reserve Banks.

There is no inherent advantage or aesthetic superiority to a computer-based payment system over a paper-based system. The real issue is one of cost, and at the present time the cost of an ACH transaction is far above that of paper checks. The attraction of the ACH is that there appear to be large economies of scale in the process, so that as volume grows, the cost per transaction will fall. The cost of transporting and mounting a reel of magnetic tape is the same regardless of the number of records it contains, and existing volumes are very low in relation to the capability of the system. These decreasing costs with increases in volume contrast with the paper check system, which faces diseconomies of scale.

Bank Cards

Credit card transactions rank next to the check in the volume of transactions. In 1980 Visa and MasterCard, the two bank card systems, accounted for a total of 1.3 billion transactions. The two systems have about 120 million cardholders, so that for a large segment of the population the bank card has become a familiar vehicle with which to access the payments system.

While credit cards were heralded in their early days as the means to a "checkless society," they do not eliminate paper. Consumers sign credit slips which the merchant deposits in his bank. The paper processing is truncated at that bank, with information transmitted electronically from that point forward. Cardholders receive a monthly statement listing transactions, but without the original sales slips. This "descriptive billing" was controversial when first introduced, but now is routinely adopted. As we have noted, there are great potential savings from truncation of the check payment system if that could be introduced and accepted.

The familiar plastic card has been the key to use of other payments services. The "debit card" is used to authorize a payment charged to the cardholder's checking account. It is similar to a check payment but with the card issuer, in effect, guaranteeing the merchant will receive payment. This system represents a step toward the use of point-of-sale (POS) terminals to effect instantaneous transfer of funds from the deposit account of the consumer to the account of the merchant. Some experimental POS systems have been developed, and the equipment exists to implement such systems, but operational POS systems are virtually nonexistent. While there are reasons to believe that this may indeed represent the payments system of the future, there are also reasons why it is not the system of the present. These reasons lie in economic considerations, consumer psychology, and government regulation, rather than in technology, and will be discussed in more detail later in this chapter.

The plastic card has also been the method of access to automated teller machines (ATM). The number of ATMs in use has grown dramatically in recent years, and the average usage of each machine has also risen as consumers have become more familiar with the systems. The amount of usage has been enhanced by the development of shared systems so that the consumer's card can be used at many locations. These systems represent a means by which financial institutions can economize on the need for labor and for brick-and-mortar branches, rather than a means of making payments generally. However, with an enhanced ability of consumers to obtain cash with which to make payments, the need for check or credit card transactions may be reduced.

Home Banking

In the future, a significant portion of consumer payments may be made through home-based systems. These systems include payments by telephone, computer, or cable television. Pay-by-phone systems are currently in operation, but most of these still involve a heavy labor component. The full potential of such systems will not be achieved until the customer's communication is directly with the bank's computer without human intervention. Volumes have generally not been high enough to make the systems cost-effective for most banks, while users find the systems economic when the benefits of postage savings are taken into account.

Experiments have been launched based on computers and cable television. While there is some long-run potential in such systems, at the present time and for a number of years into the future, too few households will have computers or interactive cable systems to make such systems economically viable (though there are some estimates that over 50 percent of U.S. households will have interactive television by 1990).

This brief review of the various components of our payments system suggests that there is little reason for public concern with its development. The mainstay of the system—the paper check—is functioning smoothly with no danger of an imminent breakdown. Other payments systems reflect technological developments and incorporate new technology when they become economic. The interests of the providers of payments services lie with lowering costs and improving efficiency, and competition is a stimulus to such improvements.

Unfortunately, the sanguine conclusion that the public can ignore the payments system is no longer warranted. Several recent developments threaten some participants in the payments process and may affect the ability of the system to move toward greater efficiency at the optimal pace. These recent developments are described in the following section.

Factors Affecting Payments System Development

The progress of payments system development has been affected in recent years by several important changes in the economy and society. These changes include higher and more volatile interest rates, rapid advances in technology, increased competition, regulatory reform, and increased consumer sophistication. These changes are interrelated—interest rate developments may have stimulated regulatory changes and have increased consumer awareness of rate differentials—but it is not necessary for our purposes to separate cause and effect. What is relevant is that all these changes have had significant impact on the payments system.

The increase in interest rates has made the public—consumers and business firms—reluctant to hold wealth in the form of non-interest-earning financial instruments. Traditionally, the check payment system in the U.S. has been based on transfers of ownership of demand deposits on which, under existing laws, banks cannot pay interest. The earnings on these interest-free funds were sufficient so that banks usually did not charge for the costs of handling transactions. Put another way, since banks were not allowed to compete for deposits on a rate basis, they competed by offering services free or at a low cost.

This system was workable as long as market interest rates were low, but higher interest rates stimulated bank customers to economize on their demand deposit balances. High interest rates, combined with legal interest rate ceilings, led to the development of the money market mutual fund industry. Most of the money market mutual funds combined a going market rate on shares with the ability to write checks on the fund balance (though there were usually restrictions on the check writing privilege).

High interest rates also increase the problem of float. Some float may be inevitable in the check collection process, but high interest rates have led some participants in the payments system to seek an artificial increase in float to their benefit by writing checks on banks in remote locations. Obviously, float is more valuable with high interest rates. On the other hand, it may be wasteful to use additional real resources—labor, computer time, or transportation services—to speed up the transfer of ownership of funds from one holder to another, with no net creation of value.

Technology, particularly in the computer and communications fields, has been changing at a rapid rate. These changes have lowered the cost of information processing and, perhaps more important, have reduced the size and cost of equipment for smaller installations. A variety of means of handling transactions is now technologically feasible. Plastic cards are not merely the means of instituting a paper-based credit transaction, but can, through magnetic-stripe or other technology, contain information that can be used on an on-line basis. Point-of-sales terminals exist, as do home computers and interactive cable television systems that have the capability of use for transactions purposes. The number of alternatives poses problems, because it is difficult to foresee which method will win out, and there are substantial risks in backing the wrong technology.

Changes in regulation have probably been the most significant factor affecting the course of the payments system. The Depository Institutions Deregulation and Monetary Control Act of 1980 (DIDMCA) has several provisions that relate directly or indirectly to the payments process. That legislation authorized negotiable order of withdrawal (NOW) accounts on a national basis for both commercial banks and thrift institutions. NOW accounts represent a checking account that pays interest, and this tends to reduce the incentive for households to economize on checking account balances (corporations are not allowed to have NOW accounts). However, from the time NOW accounts were authorized in January 1981 until January 1983, the Depository Institutions Deregulation Committee set the ceiling rate on such accounts so far below open market rates that the incentive to economize on transaction balances remained strong. NOW accounts, however, did allow for a substantial entry into the transaction business by savings and loan associations, thus providing substantial new competition for commercial banks.

The DIDMCA requires all depository institutions to meet reserve requirements imposed by the Federal Reserve and also gives all these institutions—nonmember banks, mutual savings banks, savings and loan associations, and credit unions, as well as Federal Reserve member banks—access to Federal Reserve services (primarily check collection services). The act also requires the Federal Reserve to charge for these services, which formerly were provided free to member banks. The charges must be sufficient to cover the full costs of providing the services, so as to allow room for competition from the private sector. The Federal Reserve does not pay interest on reserves, and this puts institutions subject to such reserve requirements (primarily commercial banks) at a cost disadvantage as compared with institutions not subject to reserve requirements (such as brokerage firms).

These legal changes disrupted the existing process of check collection. Many member banks had previously used the Federal Reserve for check collection services since they were available at no cost. With pricing, these institutions now have an incentive to seek alternatives in the private sector. Similarly, correspondent banks which made great use of Federal Reserve services are developing alternate check collection paths (such as establishment of new local clearing houses). On the other hand, many nonmember banks had previously relied on correspondent banks for such services since they did not have access to the Federal Reserve. Moreover, these banks were usually subject to state reserve requirements, which could be met with deposits at correspondent banks. These balances (at zero interest rates) are highly desirable to correspondent banks, which compete for them by providing check collection and other services at low cost. Nonmember banks must now meet Federal Reserve reserve requirements, rather than state requirements, and this allows them to economize on their balances with correspondents. Since they now have access to Federal Reserve services (though at a price), some of their activity will be shifted to the Federal Reserve.

Perhaps as a result of these economic and regulatory developments, consumers have become much more sophisticated and knowledgeable about financial instruments, interest rates, and financial services. While inertia still plays an important role in financial decisions, the general public has become more aware of the difference between rates available on market instruments and the rates on some types of accounts at depository institutions. This has been stimulated, of course, by the very high market interest rates of recent years, but the increased knowledge is permanent. That is, the consumer who shifts funds from a 5 percent passbook account to a money market mutual fund paying 15 percent will probably not shift back to the passbook when the yield on the money market fund drops to, say, 9 percent.

These considerations have led to a substantial decline in the proportion of bank and thrift institution funds accounted for by demand deposits, savings accounts, and other low-yielding consumer time deposits. Both households and business firms have economized on demand deposits at commercial banks, but banks and, more importantly, thrift institutions have held some low cost funds through the growth of NOW accounts—transaction accounts that are interest-bearing. The new Money Market Deposit account and the "Super-NOW" account have accelerated the conversion of funds from low-rate accounts to those paying market rates.

The full effects of the development of NOW accounts have yet to be felt by the financial system. NOW accounts were pioneered in Massachusetts in the early 1970s, and, despite great popularity with customers, their spread was rather slow. While many thrift institutions were anxious to have authority to offer NOW accounts as a means of entering the payments business, commercial banks feared that the need to pay interest on checking accounts (which had been non-interest-bearing) would be devastating to profits. (Massachusetts commercial banks were among the least profitable in the country.) Many savings and loan officials opposed NOW accounts because of their concern that obtaining checking account powers would be linked to an end to the 0.25 percent interest ceiling differential which they enjoyed as compared with commercial bank ceilings. In their view, the differential was an important competitive advantage that outweighed the benefits of offering transaction accounts.

The debate over NOW accounts was heated during the late 1970s, but when NOW accounts became legal on a nationwide basis in 1981, market interest rates were so high that NOW accounts, even with a 5.25 percent interest rate, represented a rather cheap source of funds. As market interest rates declined in late 1982, the cost of NOW accounts became a matter of growing concern to commercial banks, a concern that increased as the rate ceiling was removed in early 1983. Banks and thrift institutions face the cost of handling transactions as well as the interest cost of such accounts. Moreover, for many institutions the gathering of household deposits has rested on a system of branch offices (or holding company subsidiaries). The substantial cost of this deposit-gathering infrastructure could be justified when banks were forced to compete on the basis of convenience, but branches may be a burden in competing on a rate basis. The future payments system will reflect the effects of these changes in the financial system. The implications of these developments will be discussed in a later section.

Future Problems of the Payments System

While progress is evident, the developments described in the previous section of this article suggest some problems that will eventually face the payments system. Past problems of the payments system have been resolved by a mixture of governmental and private efforts. Private firms have incentives to make improvements in the payments system. They may profit from faster collection of funds or by selling improved service to customers. The government also has a legitimate role in the payments system. The Constitution specifically allocates responsibility for control of money to the federal government. The key question to be addressed in the remainder of this chapter is whether the problems to be faced by the payments system require additional government intervention, or whether we can rely on competitive market forces to shape the payments system in an optimal manner.

The Role of Commercial Banks in the Payments System

For nearly all of our history commercial banks have been virtually the only institutions active in the transactions business. In recent years, mutual savings banks, savings and loan associations, and credit unions have provided checking accounts services for households, primarily through the NOW account and share-draft account of the credit unions. Money market mutual funds have provided for access to funds and transfer of funds through wire transfer and checks, though the ability to write checks on most such funds is limited. Some brokerage firms have combined the money market fund with a broader ability to write checks and carry out other financial transactions. The Merrill Lynch Cash Management Account was the first, and it has been most successful in attracting customers—as well as attracting several imitators.

So far, the money market funds (and the cash-management-type accounts) have handled transactions through commercial banks. That is, the money market fund drafts are written on zero-balance accounts at commercial banks, and then are cleared through the traditional paper check mechanism. If this continues, commercial banks will maintain their predominance in the check clearing system, though whether that continued role will be profitable will depend on whether the commercial banks can charge appropriately for their services. But it is by no means clear that that predominance will continue. When thrift institutions entered the transaction business through NOW accounts, the resulting drafts were handled exclusively by commercial banks. The DIDMCA gave thrift institutions direct access to Federal Reserve services, with the opportunity to clear checks without going through commercial banks. The money market funds and brokerage firms do not have direct access to Federal Reserve services, but they can gain such access by establishment or acquisition of a commercial bank. Acquisition by a brokerage firm of a nonmember bank that does not make commercial loans does not violate either the Bank Holding Company Act or the Glass-Steagall Act. This opportunity for access to the payments system, as well as competitive pressures among commercial banks, suggests that the ability of commercial banks to earn substantial profits from payments services provided to other institutions will be limited in the future. That is, they will be able to maintain a predominant role in the payments process only to the extent that they price their services no higher than the cost of a nonbank firm doing the work itself.

Further, as electronic payment spreads into the consumer sector, nonfinancial firms may assume a major role in that process. Such firms may operate POS or ATM systems, with the banks playing a role only in settlement. Cable television companies may provide basic services which banks will buy. A number of scenarios are possible which involve only a subsidiary role for commerical banks.

The possibility that the future will see a diminished role for commercial banks in the payments system is clearly a matter of concern to the banking industry and to individual commercial banks. But this is not a matter of broader public policy concern. As long as payments services are generally available and are provided at reasonable cost, the public has little need for concern as to which institutions provide those services. The increased competition that will result from nonbank entry into the payments business will benefit consumers.

Elimination of Deposit Interest Rate Ceilings

A general conclusion of economic analysis is that efficient resource allocation requires that the prices of goods and services equal the marginal costs of producing those goods. The financial services business, like many other regulated industries, has operated with a great deal of *cross-subsidization,* where some services are priced below cost, subsidized by high profits on other services. For several reasons this cross-subsidization is likely to disappear, resulting in severe strains on the traditional means of operating the payments system.

Cross-subsidization has resulted from the prohibition of interest on demand deposits and the regulatory ceiling on interest on time deposits. As we have noted, banks have not been allowed to compete for demand deposits on a rate basis. They have competed by providing services free or at less than full cost, and they have also competed on the basis of convenience by opening multiple offices. Even where banks have charged for checking services, the pricing system generally involves free checking accounts for balances above some amount, with a flat charge for accounts below the minimum. In this case, less active accounts subsidize active accounts. As interest rate ceilings are phased out, and particularly when the prohibition of interest on checking accounts is eliminated completely, the opportunity for cross-subsidization will disappear, as depositors will not hold large idle balances at below market interest rates.

Until the DIDMCA, Federal Reserve membership involved a similar form of cross-subsidization. The Federal Reserve imposed reserve requirements on member banks, paid no interest on these reserve balances, but provided various services (primarily related to check collection) free of charge for member banks. As noted earlier, correspondent banks could recoup some of the cost of reserve requirements by providing services to other banks with much of the cost borne by the Federal Reserve. The DIDMCA changes the ground rules by applying reserve requirements to all depository institutions and requiring the Fed to charge for services (with access to all). The opportunity to repackage Federal Reserve services and resell them at a profit is thereby limited. (Federal Reserve pricing of services involves a significant cross-subsidy in that collection of checks on banks in remote locations is done at below cost, in a manner analogous to the U.S. Postal Service's rural delivery program.)

The current legal framework will put commercial banks at a disadvantage in competing for transactions business with nondepository institutions as these other firms expand in this area—banks will be faced with the burden of reserve requirements with no offsetting advantage in access to Federal Reserve services. This could be resolved if the Federal Reserve paid interest on reserve balances—a change that would have merit for other reasons which will be explored later.

Cross-subsidization affects consumers of financial services in a manner that leads to inefficiency. Under the present situation, most consumers receive payments services—checking accounts—at no explicit cost. Consumers have no incentive to economize on the number of checks. Equally important, consumers have no incentive to seek out lower cost payments methods. The banker who seeks to introduce a cost-saving innovation, say, truncation, faces a very difficult time in persuading his customers of the advantages. The customer cannot be offered a higher interest rate on a demand deposit account (the ceiling is fixed by law), and he cannot be offered a lower cost (the service is already free). It is not easy to persuade the customer to switch from a familiar, satisfactory system to a new one simply to save money for his banker.

We have already noted that the eventual phase-out of interest rate controls will end the opportunities for cross-subsidization. This process is now well under way, particularly with the end of ceilings on NOW accounts in January 1983 (these accounts are available to households but not to business firms at the present time). But the need for explicit pricing in a free market will be very difficult for many banks used to the protection of the regulatory umbrella. It is likely that a number of institutions will make mistakes in their pricing and marketing of services and, in a competitive environment, will fail. While this is a problem for poorly managed banks and their stockholders, it is not a matter of broad social concern. This existing deposit insurance system should be sufficient to preserve the soundness of the financial system despite some increase in the number of bank failures. There is no reason to believe that such an increase in failures would bring about a loss of confidence in the system. Further, the disappearance of a number of banks will have no implications for the efficiency of the payments system itself.

The Federal Reserve Will Lose Market Share in the Payments System

The response of the Federal Reserve and depository institutions to the DIDMCA has led to a significant decline in the number of checks processed by the Federal Reserve. The Federal Reserve has attempted to retain its role in the check collection system within the constraints of the act (which requires that Federal Reserve prices cover the full cost of providing such services) through marketing efforts aimed at persuading financial institutions to use its services and by improving its processing and transportation schedules.

Despite these efforts, the loss of business by the Federal Reserve appears irreversible. While this is apparently a matter of serious concern to the Federal Reserve, it does not necessarily have important implications for the efficiency of the payments process. This turns on whether there are significant economies of scale in the check processing business and whether the Federal Reserve is more efficient than other providers of such services.

If there are economies of scale, a decline in volume for the Federal Reserve will increase its average costs. Under the DIDMCA, the increase in average costs requires an increase in prices, which will lead to a further loss in volume. This process would ultimately result in the Federal Reserve being forced out of the check clearing business and in higher costs of check collection services.

There is substantial evidence, however, that check processing is not characterized by economies of scale. If that is correct, a loss in volume by the Federal Reserve need not increase average costs (though in the short run, where much of the cost is fixed, a decline in volume can temporarily increase average costs). The Federal Reserve can retain that business which it can handle more efficiently than its private sector competitors. This competition results in an efficient allocation of resources and lower costs for users of checks.

It is important to consider, however, whether there are other public policy implications of a changed role for the Federal Reserve in check processing. Bankers competing with the Federal Reserve argue that there is a conflict of interest in the Fed's dual role as a supervisor of the banking system and as a competitor. In their view, the Federal Reserve has taken advantage of its position as holder of the banks' reserve accounts to offer processing schedules that cannot be matched by private competitors. Moreover, the Federal Reserve's regulatory decisions reflect concern for preserving of its role in check processing rather than for the interests of users of checking accounts. Competing bankers contend that the public interest would best be served by total Federal Reserve exit from check processing, or by its taking a role solely as a "clearer-of-last-resort." In any case, they oppose any effort by the Federal Reserve to set its prices below full costs.

The Federal Reserve believes that it must maintain a major role in check processing to assure that banks throughout the country, even those in relatively remote areas, have access to service on an economical basis. They argue that profit-oriented correspondent banks will have little incentive to provide such services, which are necessary to maintain a unified, national financial system in which checks are accepted at par. The argument is similar to that over the subsidization of rural postal service. Critics argue that while Americans may choose to live in remote areas that generate inefficiently low volumes of checks to process, they cannot expect the general public to subsidize that choice.

It appears that a major factor in the Federal Reserve determination to hold processing volume is a concern about personnel. The Federal Reserve employs thousands in the check processing function and is understandably reluctant, on both humanitarian and efficiency grounds, to see this trained work force disbanded. But there are other good reasons for the Federal Reserve to maintain some operational role in the payments system. It has an essential role to play in settlement. The most convenient means for net settlement, even of payments systems in which the Federal Reserve plays no other operational role (such as credit card drafts or CHIPS) is on the books of the Federal Reserve where all banks maintain accounts. Further, the Fed Wire is the only payments system on which transfers are immediate and final, with no risk of default. It is desirable that such a system exist, and no private party is in a position to make the same guarantees as the Federal Reserve.

A broader operational role for the Federal Reserve may be appropriate in ACH systems. The evidence indicates that ACH operations are subject to economies of scale (Humphrey, 1981), and, until a private operator is willing to take on this function (as has been done by the New York Clearing House Association, for example), there are benefits to the Federal Reserve assuming this responsibility. None of these considerations, however, indicates that a major role for the Federal Reserve in check processing is necessary or even desirable. If the competitive forces that result from the DIDMCA, with its pricing and access provisions, result in a reduced role for the Federal Reserve, or eliminate it entirely, that is consistent with efficiency in the payments system. It is important to make sure that the Federal Reserve does not take advantage of its unique monetary and regulatory powers to preserve a role in check processing beyond what is necessary for efficiency.

Risk in the Payments System

As a result of the economic and technological developments discussed earlier, the rate of turnover of bank assets has increased greatly. In 1970, the annual turnover rate of demand deposits of New York City banks was 155 times. By 1981 that figure increased to 1,326 times. That is, every day more funds flow into and out of the bank than the total assets of the bank. This very high volume of transactions per dollar of transactions balances means an increased degree of risk. Over a great many years banks have developed means of dealing with risk in the payments system. The risks are greater now in the wire transfer systems, and we have less certainty as to our ability to deal with this risk.

Loss in payments transactions can arise from mistake, fraud, delay, or credit risk. The frequency and seriousness of these problems differ from one type of payments mechanism to another. Fraud is a common problem in credit card transactions but is very rare in wire transfer systems. However, while the amount at risk in an individual fraudulent credit card transaction is relatively small, a single wire transfer fraud may involve millions of dollars. Failure of an institution can involve losses to other institutions receiving messages (checks, wire transfers) from the failed institution for which good funds have not yet been received. Bank A may receive a wire from Bank B indicating a transfer of funds to a customer of Bank A. If A allows the customer to draw on those funds before settlement is made by B and if B fails before payment is made, A faces a potential loss. CHIPS has reduced the length of exposure by moving to same-day settlement rather than waiting until the following day for settlement. Checks, on the other hand, are in the collection pipeline for a longer period during which failure could occur. But individual checks are for smaller amounts, and banks have rather well-established rules that prevent most customers from drawing on deposited checks until they are determined to be good.

An Arthur D. Little (1982) study of the payments system done for the Association of Reserve City Bankers noted several serious issues relating to risk in wire transfer systems.

> The banking industry has no comprehensive industry data on the frequency and size of fraud losses relating to wire transfers. . . . Many wire system risks are generally not covered by contract, statute or insurance. . . . Prices for wire transfer do not now reflect a full allowance for risk and cannot until responsibility for losses is resolved. . . . If losses from failing institutions are to be limited, participation in payments systems may have to be restricted to credit worthy institutions (p. 43).

These problems are related—it is difficult for an insurer to offer insurance protection in the absence of information on risk and without clear understanding of the allocation of responsibilities of the various parties in case of failure or loss. In the case of checks, credit card transactions, and ACH operations, risks tend to be fully allocated among the participants by contract, statutory law, or years of experience in which virtually every possible eventuality has been litigated and resolved. With some wire transfer transactions, it is not clear for which fraud a given bank is responsible, as opposed to those that are the responsibility of its customers or the other banks which participated in the transaction.

It is an appropriate governmental responsibility to establish the legal framework necessary to protect consumers as they participate in payments transactions. The Uniform Commercial Code does this fully with respect to the check system, and existing law spells out consumer rights with respect to a variety of EFT systems. The relationships among the financial and communications firms involved in wire transfers or other electronic payments systems can be resolved by contract among the parties, but there may be need for additional law. Work is currently being done to develop a "Payments Code" for all types of payment (except cash) to supplement or replace the Uniform Commercial Code and other state and federal laws.

Implications for Competition

The paper check system is a highly competitive business, albeit one laced with a heavy dose of regulation and governmental involvement. Bank and thrift institutions offer their own checking accounts at prices they determine (though restricted as to the payment of interest on business accounts) and with services and conditions they specify. Various vendors compete to provide services to banks to facilitate the check collection process. These participants include correspondent banks, computer service bureaus, courier services, the Federal Reserve System, and the U.S. Postal Service.

The credit card business is also a competitive one, although the situation in which many banks offered proprietary cards has changed to one in which two credit card systems, Visa and Master-Card, account for nearly all of the bank credit cards issued. Competition exists within those systems, however. Each participating bank decides to whom cards will be issued and sets the terms of payment. Some banks charge an annual fee; others, a transaction charge; some charge interest from date of purchase, while others provide a grace period. Each determines the interest rate charged on credit balances (subject to usury ceilings) and sets the discount rate charged to merchants. Other firms, such as American Express, Sears, and other retailers, compete in the credit card business.

Despite these examples, there has been concern that competition may not work in electronic-based consumer payment systems, particularly ATMs and POS systems. The concern is that costs of developing and operating such systems are so large, and economies of scale so prevalent, that only the largest banks could afford to offer such systems. If that is the case, many analysts seem to prefer the model of a regulated utility (i.e., local telephone or electric power delivery), rather than relying on competitive forces to protect consumers. Where service might be provided by joint ventures of potentially competing institutions, access to the system must be assured to smaller institutions through mandatory sharing rules.

Participants in the market may be too quick to assume that a natural monopoly exists. As Donald Baker (1974) has put it:

> Businessmen are, in the main, fairly cautious with their money. When they are faced with a new and untried system that requires a large capital outlay, they are very much given . . . to assume that anything so large and new and difficult should be handled jointly by all competitors. In effect, they try to turn it into a monopoly in order to minimize their own competitive risks. If the new system works, they are guaranteed a piece of the reward; if it fails they are not hurt very badly; but, above all, no one else will be able to take away their share of the business. A joint venture is a form of insurance against risk (p. 50).

With such joint ventures or shared systems there is less incentive to innovate or expand. Several competing banks may have an incentive to establish a new ATM in a location if they see an opportunity to gain new business and enhance their market share. But if that new equipment must be shared with competitors, there is less to be gained and the incentive to expand is reduced. Traditional antitrust considerations hold that those who jointly control an essential facility must grant access to it on reasonable terms to all in the trade. This applies to a local clearing house, for example. But it is a question of fact as to what facilities are essential. Furthermore, the traditional mandatory sharing approach applies to joint venture rather than to individually owned facilities.

The public generally benefits from competition. It may still be too early to judge which electronic systems involve economies of scale that require treatment as natural, shared monopolies. In several cases, state laws have prejudged the situation with mandatory sharing rules that seem more designed to protect small banks and their market share than to stimulate competition so as to provide the best service to consumers. There is an important public policy interest in seeing that competition prevails to the maximum extent feasible, but existing law and oversight by the Justice Department may be adequate. In the past public policy has erred in the direction of not allowing full opportunity for competition in the provision of financial services. Restrictions on competition still exist, and we should avoid additional laws that may work to preserve competitors rather than competition.

Privacy

The concept of an ultimate electronic payments system, with all income and expenditures of an individual recorded in the giant computers of a nationwide financial utility, raises the spectre of what civil libertarians have condemned as an ''Orwellian horror delight.'' As Alan F. Westin (1979) has put it:

> The automated data base of individual accounts would allow managers of the system—and anyone else allowed to use it or able to penetrate it unlawfully—to accomplish unprecedented feats of surveillance: to locate individuals at a given moment, to track their movements over time, develop profiles of their spending and saving habits, monitor whether their use of government or private funds met various regulatory or program requirements, identify their money-based political, religious, civic, or sexual affairs, and impose various controls over access to funds that could have enormous regulatory consequences for various economic and social groups in the population (p. 300).

This image of tracing the private life of an individual through the trail of payments permanently emblazoned on the memory of a huge computer is a vivid one, and one that will be technologically feasible eventually (if not now). It is less clear that there will ever be economic incentives to create and maintain a permanent payments record. As Westin notes: "One of the most important findings of the National Academy of Sciences' Project on Computer Data Banks was that there are enormous organizational, legal, competitive, social, and cost-effective constraints on the adoption of technologically possible computer and communications systems" (p. 301).

Of course, a paper trail of payments has long existed with checks, but retrieval of these without the cooperation of the subject is difficult. Analogous issues of privacy and control of records have arisen with respect to credit bureaus, an area in which there were documented cases of serious abuse. These problems were dealt with in the Fair Credit Reporting Act, which, among other provisions, guarantees consumers access to their own records and the opportunity to correct erroneous information.

Appropriate public policy must walk a fine line in this area. Nearly everyone, and not just devoted civil libertarians, supports the concept of a right to privacy. Yet most would not want to shield the records of illegal activities from appropriate law enforcement officials. Construction of appropriate safeguards is not easy, but the issue must be resolved before the system can be developed in an optimal manner. It is possible that concern over privacy will affect the public's willingness to use electronic payments techniques.

Monetary Policy

A basic assumption of monetary policy is that there is some set of assets in the economy, which we designated as "money," whose volume can be controlled by the monetary authority. Monetary policy rests on the existence of a fairly stable relationship between that volume of money and total spending in the economy. There are different views as to the best definition of money, the best means of controlling its supply, and the mechanism by which changes in supply affect spending.

The developments we have discussed that affect the payments system also have important implications for monetary policy. The introduction of NOW accounts has given savings deposits a transaction capability. Money market mutual funds are not only highly liquid assets; they can be used, within limits, for transactions. Products similar to the Merrill Lynch Cash Management Account have full payments capability, with the power to draw on securities as collateral for credit card transactions. While it was possible at one time to define the money supply meaningfully as consisting solely of currency and demand deposits, that concept is no longer useful. This problem has been greatly exacerbated by the removal of interest rate ceilings on NOW accounts. With these accounts paying market rates, consumers have an incentive to combine transactions balances and investment or savings funds in one account. The relationship between various measures of the money supply becomes permanently altered.

More important than the definitional problem, however, is the dramatic increase in the turnover of deposits, particularly at large banks. This suggests the possibility of a substantial change in the relationship between money supply and spending in the economy. Statistical studies seem to indicate that the velocity of M1 (the relationship between gross national product and the narrowly defined money supply) has been increasing at about its historical rate, while the velocity of M2 (a broader definition of the money supply) has been relatively stable. If this finding is valid, then monetary policy can continue to operate as it has. Other analysts argue, however, that the changes in the payments system, such as the development of the "Super-NOW" account, will require the Federal Reserve to abandon its efforts to focus on something called "money," and emphasize rather some other variables in the economy, such as interest rates or aggregate credit. There are shortcomings to either of these variables as the basis of monetary policy.

This problem should not be confused with the matter of the Federal Reserve's operating role in the payments system. As we have noted, continuation of the Federal Reserve's operating role is not important for efficiency in the payments system if there are cheaper alternatives, while maintenance of its monetary policy powers is an important social need. There is no evidence that the likely changes in the payments system over time will interfere with the Federal Reserve's ability to conduct monetary policy. In particular, there is no evidence that a continued role for the Federal Reserve in the payments business is essential for monetary policy.

Conclusions

This chapter has described the present status of the payments system and has discussed some potentially serious problems that the payments system faces in the years ahead. These problems arise now because of economic, technological, sociological, and regulatory developments that have changed the pace of the normal evolution of payments systems. The key question raised by these developments is simply whether we can continue to rely primarily on competitive market forces and the development of technology to result in the optimal payments system, or whether some additional governmental/regulatory shaping of the system is necessary.

If we could determine today what the optimal payments system of the future should look like, it would be appropriate public policy to adopt policies that would steer the financial system toward the optimal structure. We cannot, however, have sufficient confidence in any such forecast. There are a number of promising avenues that are being explored simultaneously in a competitive system. The Federal Reserve has attempted to spur the growth of the automated clearing house by subsidizing its processing of such transactions, but that has correctly been criticized by private market participants. Such subsidy tends to promote not only ACH development, but also Federal Reserve monopoly operation of the ACH. Even if the ACH is the correct way to go, there is no assurance that a dominant Federal Reserve role in the ACH is optimal. The odds are that any attempt to steer the payments system in a particular direction will turn out to have been the wrong choice.

The preceding section has discussed a number of specific problems. For the most part, these problems are serious from the point of view of particular participants in the payments system: the Federal Reserve may lose its role in the payments system operations; the role of commercial banks may shrink; various participants face significant risks in the newer electronic payments techniques. These problems should be faced by the participants, with government providing only the necessary legal framework and background for private contracts and for protection of competitive forces. Legislation should make clear the responsibilities of various parties to payments transactions and should protect consumers' rights, including rights of privacy. The competitive process should be assured through antitrust standards that are appropriate to the nature of the problem and that do not prematurely assume that electronic funds transfer systems are natural monopolies. Competition is enhanced by the existing rules that prevent the Federal Reserve from competing with the private sector with below-cost pricing. Efficiency would also be enhanced by eliminating the prohibition of interest on checking accounts of businesses.

The one major public policy issue posed by payments system development is the threat to the ability of the Federal Reserve to conduct monetary policy in its traditional manner. Resolving this issue may require some change in the ground rules. An example might be the payment of interest on reserves held by depository institutions with the Federal Reserve. The requirement to hold such reserves at zero interest forces banks to economize on such balances, but still puts them at a competitive disadvantage with respect to institutions not facing such requirements. That cost advantage can lead to the development of payments systems outside the banking system, not because the outside provider of services is more efficient, but simply because it is not subject to the costly requirement. While this issue cannot be resolved in this chapter, it is possible that payment of interest on reserves combined with the payment of interest on demand deposits may reverse the increase in the rate of turnover of deposit accounts that poses a threat to the operations of monetary policy.

There is no guarantee that the payments system will develop smoothly and without problems in the years ahead. There is reason to believe, however, that a competitive system will provide benefits to users of the payments system, with greater efficiency and lower cost. There is little justification for increased governmental intervention into the evolution of the system. Government intervention to protect individual institutions, particular types of institutions, or particular means of payment seems unnecessary and undesirable.

BIBLIOGRAPHY

ARTHUR D. LITTLE INC., *Report on the Payments System,* Report to the Association of Reserve City Bankers, Washington, D.C., 1982.

ATKINSON, THOMAS R., *Trends in Corporate Bond Quality*. New York: National Bureau of Economic Research, 1967.

BAKER, DONALD I., "Competition, Monopoly and Electronic Banking," in *The Economics of a National Electronic Funds Transfer System,* Federal Reserve Bank of Boston Conference Series #13, 1974, pp. 47–64.

COX, EDWIN B., "Developing an Electronic Funds Transfer System: Incentives and Obstacles," in *The Economics of a National Electronic Funds Transfer System,* Federal Reserve Bank of Boston Conference Series #13, 1974, pp. 15–31.

HUMPHREY, DAVID B., "Scale Economies at Automated Clearing Houses," *Journal of Bank Research,* 12 (Summer 1981), 71–81.

INTERAGENCY TASK FORCE ON SMALL BUSINESS FINANCE, "Overview of a Series of Papers on Financing Small Business," in *A Report to Congress,* Board of Governors of the Federal Reserve System, Comptroller of the Currency, Federal Deposit Insurance Corporation, Washington, D.C., February 1982.

LONG, ROBERT H., "Discussion," in *The Economics of a National Electronic Funds Transfer System,* Federal Reserve Bank of Boston Conference Series #13, 1974, pp. 32–38.

WESTIN, ALAN F., "Privacy Aspects in EFT Systems," in *Issues in Financial Regulation,* ed. Franklin Edwards. New York: McGraw-Hill Book Company, 1979.

Costs and Profitability

III

Readings in the previous sections demonstrate the growing fusion among financial services firms. As the boundaries between financial institutions are erased, depository institutions will be able to offer a fuller line of financial services to households and business firms. Besides these traditional competitors, nondepository institutions have entered markets with an expanding variety of financial services.

How many firms will survive? What will the survivors look like? Will larger financial institutions enjoy lower costs than smaller ones? The answers depend in part on whether larger institutions enjoy ''economies of scale.''

The first study in this section, and the tenth selection in this book, by George J. Benston, Gerald A. Hanweck, and David B. Humphrey finds that larger size does not seem to give a bank a significant competitive advantage. The authors reveal that costs per account for banks larger than \$50 million in deposits increase with bank size, while costs decline with bank size for banks with less than \$25 million in deposits. This suggests there is a niche in tomorrow's financial markets for small banks.

In the previous section, Paul Horvitz examined payments system technology and discussed the forms of organization likely to evolve to handle that technology. In the second essay in this section, number eleven in this volume, Paul F. Metzker forsees substantial and growing economies of scale in the future production of payments services. Consistent with the findings of Benston, Hanweck, and Humphrey, he expects small institutions to capture the benefits of scale by sharing the networks of larger ones.

Operating Costs in Commercial Banking

George J. Benston, Gerald A. Hanweck and David B. Humphrey

10

Reasons for Concern with Banks' Operating Costs

In most businesses, operating costs are a private matter. In banking, though, these costs receive wider attention. A bank's managers and owners clearly are concerned with costs since they profit if costs are controlled. A bank's customers also are concerned, since banking costs ultimately are passed on to users of the bank's services. In addition, legislators and those charged with bank regulation have a derivative concern; the more efficiently banks are operated, the larger the earnings flows that may improve safety by absorbing losses, the more efficiently the nation's payments system works and the more efficiently savings are channeled into investment.

Large versus Small Institutions

Legislators and regulators also have a direct concern with banks' operating efficiency, because efficiency may influence the way specific regulations are enforced. In particular, if larger banks produce a given level and quality of services at a lower cost than smaller banks—that is, if banking is subject to economies of scale—then larger banks could offer lower prices or more service than smaller banks. In an unrestricted environment, larger

Reprinted from *Economic Review* (November, 1982): 6–21 by permission of the Federal Reserve Bank of Atlanta and the authors.

banks might well displace the small banks, reducing competition. If these economies of scale are large enough, the savings of resources might offset anticipated reductions in competition. However, if economies of scale aren't significant, a policy of unrestricted chartering (free entry) would probably not result in failure of new banks due to their inherent inability to compete successfully with larger banks. Instead, failure would be associated more with management skill and specific economic events than with the scale of operation.

Form of Organization—Branching and Holding Companies

Financial institutions' operating costs also may be related to their form of organization. Information on this relationship is important for states trying to decide what type of bank branching and bank holding companies they will allow, and for the federal government as it considers various proposals for interstate banking. Branches, independent banks and bank holding company subsidiaries may all have different relationships between size and operating costs per unit of output. Branches, in particular, may be more or less costly to run than similar sized unit banks (banks without branches). Or very small branches may be more efficient than small unit banks, while large branches may be less efficient than similar sized unit banks. And, even if branches were most costly to operate, they might permit a bank to grow and take advantage of economies of scale, the savings from which could offset the presumed extra costs of branching. Considering the costs of holding companies' operations is important, since they are an alternative to branching.

Multiple Products

Banks produce multiple products. To answer some of the above questions, cost information on individual products is required; some other questions require information on the bank as a whole. In some cases, the costs and amounts of various services must be separated so that institutions producing different types and quantities of outputs can be compared meaningfully. Estimates of the production cost of a specific service, such as mortgage lending, are desirable in a market analysis for a particular product. For example, in considering competition between commercial banks and savings and loan associations, the possibilities for economies of scale in mortgage lending and time deposits are of primary concern; the costs of many other banking services may not be important.

Aggregating the costs of multiple banking services is necessary to determine if a financial institution as a whole is subject to economies of scope. These economies occur when several products (such as time and demand deposits or demand deposits and business loans) are produced together at a lower total cost than when produced separately. If there were significant economies of scope in producing, say, business, consumer and mortgage loans in one operation, specialized institutions such as S&Ls would be less efficient than full-service commercial banks. The common production of transactions in corporate and government securities also could give rise to economies of scope. This has implications for public policy regarding the powers allowed thrift associations and commercial banks as well as for mergers between different types of institutions.

Results of a Current Bank Cost Study

This study reviews research on bank costs and reports on a recently published study by the authors. Consecutive sections address the technical problems of defining and measuring operating costs and output, estimating operating efficiency, and obtaining appropriate data for cost analysis. The article then reports the findings of our latest study and discusses them in relation to other recent studies of bank operating costs. Results and implications of the analysis are summarized at the conclusion of this reading.

The important objectives of bank cost studies have been to determine:

1. the extent that the scale of bank operations affects bank costs
2. the effects of branching and holding company organization on costs
3. the cost effects of banks producing multiple services; and
4. the effects of different types of bank customers on bank costs.

A number of fundamental problems are common to all bank cost studies as well as cost studies of other industries. Fortunately, measurement problems are not great using data from the Federal Reserve's Functional Cost Analysis (FCA) program.

The most recent research (using 1975–78 FCA data, a more flexible estimating functional form, and a theoretically supportable index number method of aggregating the various banking outputs) generally confirms many of the results of previous research. New results are summarized as follows:

1. Banks with more than $50 million–$75 million in deposits in unit banking states experienced diseconomies of scale—that is, average costs increased as the banks increased in size.
2. Banks of all sizes in states that allow branch banking experienced economies of scale with respect to the numbers of deposits and loan accounts.
3. When the mode of expansion—increasing the number of accounts or the number of offices for branching banks but only expanding the number of accounts for unit banks was accounted for, banks in both branching and unit states above $50 million–$75 million in deposits experienced diseconomies of scale.
4. Economies of scale appeared to be unchanged over the 1975–78 period.
5. Larger account sizes for both types of banks increased costs less than proportionately.
6. Average costs (unadjusted for certain differences in branch and unit banks) were similar for banks with up to $75 million in deposits in branch and unit states; larger banks in branching states had considerably lower average costs than similar banks in unit states.
7. Taking into account the different ways that branch and unit state banks can expand—by increasing offices or average account size, respectively—average costs were similar among banks of similar size in unit and branching states.
8. Bank holding company affiliation was found to have little effect on bank costs.

Definition and Measurement of Operating Costs and Output

Measuring Operating Costs

Public and private policy questions require numbers that meaningfully reflect economic values rather than accounting measurements. Regulators and bankers should be concerned with "opportunity costs," the value of resources given up because of a decision to do one thing rather than another. For example, the cost of making and servicing a mortgage loan is the dollar value of resources that, as a consequence, cannot be used for the next best opportunity. Where outlays are made in cash or in close equivalents (e.g., the present value of promises to pay cash in the future) for such expenses as salaries, supplies and computer services, the accounting numbers reflect economic values well, since the amount of cash used for the stated purpose is no longer available for another.

Other costs may not be so well reflected, however. For example, the economic cost of the space occupied by the mortgage loan department is not well measured in accounting statements. These statements include depreciation, an essentially arbitrary allocation of a portion of the original cost of the building and equipment to a given activity over a specific time period. These figures seldom provide valid estimates of the present economic cost of using the building. This cost is measured by the bank's next best opportunity. This would be the amount that it would receive if it rented out the space occupied by the mortgage department or the amount it could save by giving up space occupied by another function that could be moved into the mortgage department's space. Other costs that may be similarly misstated are inventories valued at acquisition cost and salaries and other tax deductible compensation that are substituted for dividends. Clearly, opportunity costs involved in these situations are very difficult and often impossible to measure.

Even when costs are measured reasonably well, it often is very difficult to assign them to specific types of output with reasonable accuracy. For example, the cost of employing the bank president might be measured correctly if the present value of his pension and other fringe benefits were accounted for along with his salary. But how much of the president's compensation should be charged to demand deposits, business loans, mortgage loans, and the other banking functions? Even if one could keep track of the president's time, there is no reason to expect a direct relationship between the time spent with a department and the value of the president's services to the bank. Similar problems beset the allocation of other overhead costs.[1]

Fortunately, the divergence of the numbers that can be obtained (accounting data) from those that one wants (economic values) is relatively small for financial institutions. Salaries, which can be measured by accounting numbers, comprise about 52 percent of commercial banks' operating costs (excluding interest and loan and security losses). Occupancy expense, including building depreciation, represents only 9 percent of those costs.[2] The cost of supplies and goods sold, a large part of most other enterprises' costs, is

[1]See Benston (1982) for a more complete description of the difference between economic values and accounting numbers.

[2]Federal Reserve. *Functional Cost Analysis: 1978 Average Banks*, p. 20. The percentages are almost the same for other years. 1978 figures are used here because data for this year are analyzed further below.

negligible for financial institutions. Thus, except for a relatively small amount of depreciation and the inherent difficulty of assigning costs to specific outputs, the accounting numbers recorded on financial institutions' books, provide reasonably good proxy measures of economic values.

Further problems arise because not all costs of producing financial services are recorded on the institutions' books; however, these problems are considerably less than those for cost studies of other firms. Two problems specific to financial institutions' costs arise from the possible tradeoffs between revenues and expenses included in operating costs. With respect to lending operations, for instance, higher expenses for monitoring and collecting loans can substitute for higher loan losses. To the extent that this substitution is made, operating expenses will be higher, since actual loan losses are not considered operating costs, but are charged to reserves. As an alternative, higher loan losses could be compensated for with higher interest and fee income. In this event, not only must loan losses be excluded from operating expense, but higher losses need not even be associated with lower monitoring (operating) expenses.

Interest and other payments for deposits present the second problem. These payments are returns to depositors on their investments, as much as dividends and capital gains on mutual funds shares are returns to shareholders. The bank is merely an intermediary, as is a mutual fund. While interest is an important outlay to the bank, it is determined by market forces that reflect alternative investments available to depositors. Thus interest is not an operating expense for purposes of measuring banks' efficiency. However, the amount a bank can pay its depositors in the form of interest is constrained by law. For this and other reasons such as personal income taxes and administrative efficiency, banks may pay customers for their deposits in the form of ''free'' services, preferred lending arrangements (including lower interest charges) or more convenient banking facilities. ''Free'' services result in higher operating costs while preferred lending arrangements result in lower revenue. A similar problem may affect the recorded expenses of banks that get services from other banks in exchange for compensating balances.

Differences in incurring and recording operating costs may produce misleading conclusions about bank efficiency if the differences are related systematically to the size or organizational form of the institution. Fortunately, this seems not to be the case, at least with respect to the size of banks. For banks with deposits up to $50 million, from $50 to $200 million and over $200 million, occupancy expenses average 9.0 percent, 9.7 and 9.7 percent of total operating expenses.[3] For these same bank size groupings, the five-year average amount of loan losses, expressed as percentages of loans outstanding are .15 percent, .16 percent and .21 percent. The reported gross yields on loans for these banks average 9.8 percent, 9.8 percent and 10.2 percent.[4] Thus the relatively larger loan losses at banks with deposits over $200 million appear to be compensated for by higher yields.

Nor does the understatement of respondent banks' operating expenses (since they pay for some correspondent bank services with compensating balances rather than with fees) appear to distort the cost data with respect to bank size. In two previous studies, the opportunity cost of these balances was computed and added to the banks' operating

[3]Ibid.

[4]Ibid., p. 5

expenses; this adjustment had no significant effect on the estimates of economies of scale.[5] Hence, we conclude that bank operating costs, as usually reported, measure economic values reasonably well and, to the extent they do not, appear not to bias economies of scale estimates. A major problem is the exclusion of the cost of customer inconvenience when there are too few banking offices available due to legal restrictions on banking.

Measurement of Output—What Do Banks Really Produce?

Measuring output is a more difficult problem. One's view of what banks produce depends on one's interests. Economists who are concerned with economy-wide (macro) issues tend to view the banks' output as dollars of deposits or loans. Monetary economists see banks as producers of money—demand deposits.[6] Others see banks as producing loans, with demand and time deposits being analogous to raw materials.[7] Thus banking statistics are reported and banks described in dollar terms, as a ''million-dollar bank.'' Customers also often describe the output of a bank in dollar terms, since they hold so many dollars in deposits or want to borrow a given amount of money.

But banks do not incur operating costs directly as a function of the number of dollars of deposits or loans they process. The cost of accepting and collecting a deposited check is affected only slightly by the number of digits that appear around the decimal point. While a $10,000 check involves somewhat more risk to process than a $10 check, the extra cost is not 1,000 times greater. Similarly, a $100,000 loan may involve more careful administration than a $10,000 loan, but not by a factor of 10. Indeed, with respect to operating costs, a bank is best described as a recordkeeping and processing ''factory.'' The key cost-causing output variable is the number and types of pieces of paper and electronic signals processed.

Though not proportionately so, the dollars written on the paper processed are also relevant. The risk, should a deposit be mishandled, a check not collected, a loan not repaid, or a security defaulted, is related positively to the amount of the check, loan or security. The amount of services a bank is willing to give to its depositors in lieu of direct interest payments (which are legally prohibited or restrained) also is a function of the value of the deposit. Therefore, to be complete, the dollar amount as well as the number of items and accounts processed should be considered operative cost-causing factors.

Which particular variables are taken to measure output? It depends on the question asked. For the regulatory and bank management questions posed above, the preferred measure is that which yields answers to such questions as, ''what are the operating costs of large compared to small banks, of branches compared to unit banks, automated teller machines compared to bank offices, of banks compared to thrift associations, and of combinations of financial institutions?'' To answer these questions, we must attempt to relate the costs incurred by various institutions to the same set of cost-causing activities.

[5]Flannery (1981) and Benston. Hanweck and Humphrey (1982). Dunham (1982) also made this correction but did not estimate total bank cost output elasticities for the bank as a whole.

[6]For example, see Goldschmidt (1981).

[7]Studies that employ this definition (e.g., Greenbaum, 1967) are reviewed below.

For these purposes, it is meaningless to report that a large bank enjoys lower costs per dollar of loans than a small bank if this "economy" is achieved because the large bank makes larger loans. Most operating costs are related to the loan, as such, rather than to its amount. Comparing the efficiency of a large and small bank in this manner is like comparing costs per dollar of sales of a wholesaler selling by the case and a retailer selling by the item.

Measurements of operating costs per dollar can be useful, however, since the lower cost per dollar loaned may explain why interest rates are lower on larger loans. But unless the size of loans or deposits is expected to change as a consequence of a regulatory or business decision, the variables used to measure output should refer to the ongoing factors that generate operating costs.

Any analysis of the output of financial institutions, then, should be multifaceted, and should include the numbers of deposit items processed and loans made and serviced. Collateral banking services, such as trust and safe deposit boxes, also should be accounted for. If different institutions are compared, differences in the levels and qualities of their outputs should be considered. And, because the costs incurred are functions of local economic conditions and the value of the dollar over time (when data for different time periods are used), the recorded costs should be adjusted for the effect of price-level factors.

Problems of Estimating Operating Efficiency

Two basic problems beset researchers who would analyze operating cost. One is accounting for differences among banks with respect to the amounts of costs recorded and the types of outputs produced. The second is accounting for differences in costs related to unique attributes of specific banks or markets rather than to general attributes, such as size and type of organization. For instance, a bank may have grown large because it was run efficiently, possibly because of the genius of particular individuals. Their compensation for superior abilities would not be included in current operating costs if it was paid for with stock options or if it occurred in the past. The cost of these factors may have been expensed in the past or may have been fortuitously acquired. That such banks currently achieve low operating costs and have grown large does not necessarily mean banking is characterized by economies of scale. Similarly, lower operating costs and, say, small size, could be associated jointly with characteristics of the markets in which banks operate. Thus small towns may have both lower wages and small banks. This relationship is not an indication of economies of scale, since banks in small towns cannot effectively serve customers who live in distant large cities.

Fortunately, these problems are not serious for studies of financial institutions' costs. The technology and managerial methods used by banks are generally well-known and available. Furthermore, branching and chartering laws restrict banks to given geographic areas for deposit services. Except for large business loans, their markets are constrained by the cost to customers of dealing with banks far outside their communities and the cost to banks of acquiring information about and monitoring distant customers. Thus banks tend to be large or small because of the markets in which they operate. The operating cost and output data, therefore, are likely to trace out cost curves from intersections of supply and demand curves rather than tracing out demand curves.

The problem of accounting for factors that produce differences among banks in recorded costs and types of output is dealt with in two ways. With respect to cost, one way is to assume, usually implicitly, that these differences either are trivial or are not systematically related to bank output. Operating cost, then, is taken to be adequately measured by the amount reported in the banks' earnings statements. The bias in this simple "solution" is not likely to be serious, at least with respect to bank size. However, differences among individual banks should be kept in mind. In situations where differences may be important, the data should be adjusted and checked to see if perceived differences are systematically related to the variables at issue.

With respect to output, two approaches of measuring comparative bank efficiency have been followed. In one, differences among banks are assumed to be unimportant. Total costs of producing outputs such as deposits or loans are divided by total outstanding amounts of these outputs. This gives costs per dollar of output, which are taken to be a valid measure of operating efficiency. The unit costs are presented in tables (tabular analysis) comparing banks grouped according to a variable of interest (for example, deposit size). The second approach uses the statistical method of multiple regression analysis to account for differences in output in order to isolate the scale effect from other cost-causing factors. The advantages, shortcomings, and findings of each type of analysis are presented in the next two sections.

Data for Cost Analyses

All Bank Aggregate Data

Since all chartered financial institutions regularly report income, expense and balance sheet data, measuring operating efficiency as total recorded costs divided by total deposits, loans and securities, or assets has considerable advantages. In studies using this method, costs per dollar typically are averaged for banks grouped by deposit size and compared in tables (hence, tabular analysis). This procedure was followed by Alhadeff (1954), who published the first study of bank operating costs, using California data from the years 1938–1950. But this comparison does not account for differences among banks, such as the composition of their earning assets, deposits, type of organization, and location. Horvitz (1963) replicated Alhadeff's study with data from all Federal Reserve member banks for 1949–1960. He subdivided the 1959 data into branch and unit banks and into three groupings according to the ratio of time to total deposits. Other variables were not accounted for. Assuming that these other variables are not important or are unrelated to size, Horvitz found (as did Alhadeff) that "once a bank reaches the relatively small size of $5 million in deposits, additional size does not result in reduced costs to any great extent until a bank reaches the giant size of over $500 million," and that branch banks have uniformly higher costs per dollar of loans and investments than unit banks. But, as the more complete statistical analyses reported below indicate, the assumptions necessary for this exercise are not likely to be valid.

FCA Data

One important shortcoming of the data used in these early studies is the lack of detail with respect to specific banking outputs. Fortunately, a rich source of data on the costs of major banking functions has been available since the late 1950s. The Federal Reserve provides banks with a Functional Cost Analysis (FCA) service in which the banks allocate costs and revenue to specific banking functions. These figures are then structured into a standard format that may be compared to other reporting banks. The FCA program is voluntary, with 780 banks responding nationwide in 1978.

Among the data allocated to the banking functions are itemized revenue, expense, dollars of deposits and assets (averages of 12 month end amounts), and the number of accounts opened and items processed. Thus, these data provide a wealth of detail that permits the analyst to improve upon potentially misleading tabular analyses.

However, even though FCA figures are aggregated by three bank deposit sizes, a comparison of the numbers must rest on several possibly untenable assumptions. One is that the banks' organizational structure is not relevant, since branch and holding company banks are not distinguished from unit banks in the published results. Another is that the location of a bank (e.g., urban or rural) does not affect its costs. Third, the analyst either must remove the allocated overhead expenses or accept the essentially arbitrary allocations made in the FCA data. Perhaps most important for a measure of efficiency is that output can be measured with only one variable for each type of product—number of accounts serviced, number of items processed, or dollars of account balances outstanding. The joint effect of items processed, accounts serviced and dollars outstanding cannot be simply measured. In order to assess the joint effect of these variables, economists who have used these and other data employ multiple regression analysis.

Findings of a Recent Study[8]

The Model

We recently specified and estimated a bank cost function using multiple regression analysis. We used annual Federal Reserve FCA data for the years 1975 through 1978 involving from 747 to 852 banks, amounting to about 15 percent of the Federal Reserve members. Since this program is voluntary, the banks included are likely to be more conscious than most of the value of cost control. The banks range up to $1 billion in deposits, since the few banks in the FCA panel larger than this were excluded. Thus, the sample covers the range of U.S. banks except the giants, and it is perhaps overrepresentative of more efficient banks due to the voluntary nature of the FCA program.

Operating cost was defined to exclude interest and loan losses—since only the outputs of the banking deposit and loan functions were analyzed, the direct and allocated costs of the functions of safe deposit box, trust, customer computer services and investments were also excluded. The included outputs account for more than 72 percent of total operating costs.

[8]Details of this study may be found in Benston, Hanweck and Humphrey, 1981 and 1982.

We measured output using the average number of deposit and loan accounts serviced, augmented with information on the average balances of the accounts. Since we wanted to estimate the relationship between total operating cost and output (and other variables), we had to construct an index to represent the multiple products produced by banks. For this purpose we employed the technique suggested by aggregation theory (see Diewert, 1976 and Barnett, 1981) to construct a Divisia multilateral index number of bank output. In effect, we weighted the number of accounts of each of the five types of output (demand deposits, time and savings deposits, real estate loans, installment loans, and business loans) by their proportionate share in total operating costs using the FCA data.[9] The Divisia Index number of accounts provides a valid measure of the aggregate cost-causing transactions undertaken by banks for their customers. Including the average size of accounts serves as a control for activities that are related primarily to the dollar amounts of the accounts.

Differences among the banks in the prices of inputs were accounted for with variables that measured the average annual salaries plus fringe benefits paid per employee and an index of regional office floor space rental costs—the opportunity cost per square foot of bank building space.

Two types of organizational differences were recognized. The effect of multibank holding company (MBHC) affiliation on operating cost was captured with two variables, one of which measures its effect on total cost and the other its interaction between branching and MBHC affiliation. The costs of branching also were accounted for in two ways. First, the data were analyzed separately for banks in unit banking states and banks in states that permitted branch banking. This procedure avoids forcing the estimated parameters to be equal for branch and unit state banks, a common (but incorrect) assumption of other studies. Second, interactions between the number of offices and output were specified so that the effect of branching was not measured as merely a simple and constant percentage of total cost. We believe that absence of this more general branching specification seriously mars the findings of previous studies whose effect was to assume that the cost of adding a branch office was a constant percentage of total operating costs. Thus the cost to a larger bank of adding a branch of a given size would always be proportionately greater than the cost of adding the same size branch to a smaller bank.[10] Our specification allows the cost of an additional branch, as a percentage of operating costs, to vary across different sized banks.

Finally, the functional form fitted, the translog cost function, is designed to permit increasing and/or decreasing costs to be measured as output increases, as well as to provide estimates of economies of scale, of branching, and of account size that are permitted to vary by size of bank. It is not constrained to meet the requirements of a particular production function, such as the Cobb-Douglas function which was almost exclusively used in earlier studies.

Three principal shortcomings of this study must be emphasized. One is that the data include only the fraction of U. S. banks that participate in the FCA program. The other

[9]See Benston, Hanweck and Humphrey, 1982, for details

[10]For example, Longbrake and Haslem (1975. Table 2) estimate the demand deposit cost of an additional branch at a bank having from two to five branches as $1,253 while the same sized additional branch at a bank having between twenty-five and fifty branches is $3,760

shortcomings are that estimates of economies of scope have not been separated from estimates of economies of scale and that scale economies of individual banking functions are not separately estimated. These analyses are in progress.

Since economies of scale and average costs per account can and do differ for each bank, derived estimates of economies of scale and other parameters from the regression estimates were based on unit and branch banking state subsamples for nine deposit-size groups. The relevant measures were then calculated for the (geometric) average bank in each group. The following findings may be drawn from our analysis.[11]

Economies of Scale

- Banks in unit banking states above $50 million–$75 million in deposits experienced **diseconomies** of scale with respect to the Divisia number of accounts. The smaller banks in these states had scale economies or constant costs. The elasticities range from .95 to 1.23.[12] (See Table 1, column 1.)
- Banks in branching states of all sizes experienced economies of scale with respect to the Divisia number of accounts. The elasticities range from .81 for the smallest deposit size group to .92 for the largest. These elasticities were calculated for each deposit size group, so the fact that larger branch banks have more branches was taken into account. (See Table 1, column 1.)

The economies of scale experienced by banks in branching states appear to result from the ability of branch banks to operate out of many smaller offices, avoiding the diseconomies associated with a large number of accounts per office.

To account for differences in the mode of branch bank expansion (by adding branches each with a given number of accounts) versus that for unit banks (by adding more accounts at a single office), we calculated augmented elasticities, where the effect on costs of changes in the number of offices as well as the number of accounts serviced is accounted for. These augmented elasticities (not shown in Table 1) show that:

- Banks in unit states with deposits below $25 million enjoyed economies of scale. The middle-sized banks ($75 million to $300 million in deposits) had significant diseconomies of scale and the others had insignificant scale diseconomies. (The numbers are almost the same as those given in Table 1 for the unaugmented measure.)
- Banks in branching states with more than $25 million in deposits experienced statistically significant diseconomies of scale (using the number of accounts as output). The elasticities range from 1.09 for banks with $25 million to $50 million in deposit size group to 1.16 for the largest. Smaller banks experienced approximately constant costs.

Thus, when the normal path of expansion is accounted for, branch and unit state banks experienced similar scale economy or diseconomy values. Other results indicate that:

[11]The numbers presented are for the analysis of 1978 data. The analysis of the 1975, 1976 and 1977 data yields similar results. See Benston, Hanweck and Humphrey (1982) for details.

[12]An elasticity is the proportional change in cost associated with a given proportional change in output. For example, an elasticity of .95 means that a 100 percent increase in output is associated with a 95 percent increase in cost. Since cost increases less than proportionately, the banks are said to experience economies of scale.

Table 1. Scale Economy (Elasticity) Estimates, Unit and Branch States Banks, 1978 FCA Data

Deposit Size Group ($ millions)	Operating Cost Number of Accounts	Excluding Interest Dollars of Accounts	Operating Cost Number of Accounts	Including Interest Dollars of Accounts
A. Unit State Banks				
$0–10	.95	.73*	.95	.96°
10–25	1.01	.82*	.98	.95*
25–50	1.07	.88*	1.00	.96*
50–75	1.11*	.92°	1.01	.98*
75–100	1.13*	.96	1.03	1.00
100–200	1.19*	1.01	1.05	1.02
200–300	1.19*	1.06	1.08°	1.09*
300–400	1.24*	1.06	1.06	1.13*
400+	1.23*	1.12	1.09	1.13*
Total Sample	1.09*	.92°	1.01	.97*
B. Branch State Banks				
$0–10	.81	.63*	.81*	1.01
10–25	.89°	.74*	.95*	1.02
25–50	.93*	.81*	1.02	1.02*
50–75	.93*	.84*	1.04*	1.02*
75–100	.92*	.85*	1.05*	1.01*
100–200	.94	.89*	1.06*	1.01
200–300	.92	.90	1.06*	1.00
300–400	.93	.93	1.05	.99
400+	.92	.94	1.04	.99
Total Sample	.92*	.84	1.04*	1.02*

Notes: a Source - Benston, Hanweck and Humphrey 1981 and 1982
*(°) indicates elasticities different from 1.0 (constant costs) at the .05(.10) confidence level in a two tail t-test.

- Economies of scale appear to be unchanged over the period 1975 through 1978, since the elasticities computed are either very similar or show unsystematic changes over the years.
- With respect to the average size of accounts, banks in both unit and branching states experienced considerable economies of scale. Elasticities averaged between .28 and .50 over the four years studied. The elasticities increase considerably for the larger deposit size groups of banks. In particular, the smallest banks had almost no additional cost associated with larger account sizes, but the cost of the largest deposit size banks (particularly the unit state banks) almost doubled when their average account sizes doubled. This finding indicates that the larger banks, which have larger loans and deposit accounts, incur proportionately larger costs, probably arising from monitoring the loans and attracting the deposits.

Average Cost per Account

For many policy questions, average costs per account are more relevant than economies of scale. It may be that unit banks experience diseconomies of scale but their costs per account serviced might be lower than those for branch banks.

Average cost per account was calculated in several ways. First, the average (geometric mean) values of input prices, holding company affiliation, size of account, and number of offices of each of the nine deposit size groups were used for the calculation. Thus the calculated average cost per account is the average experienced for each size group. These are plotted in Chart 1 and show:

- Similar average costs for banks in unit and branch states up to $75 million in deposits.
- Greatly increasing average costs for larger banks in unit states. Costs incurred by the largest banks were more than double those for the middle size group.
- Higher average costs for larger banks in branching states that, nevertheless, are considerably below those for similar sized banks in unit states.

For most policy questions (for example, mergers and unit versus branch banking), the average size of accounts is not relevant. Presumably, bank customers would demand loans and hold deposits that met their convenience rather than the bank's. Consequently, we extended our analysis to abstract from this difference among banks, by holding the average

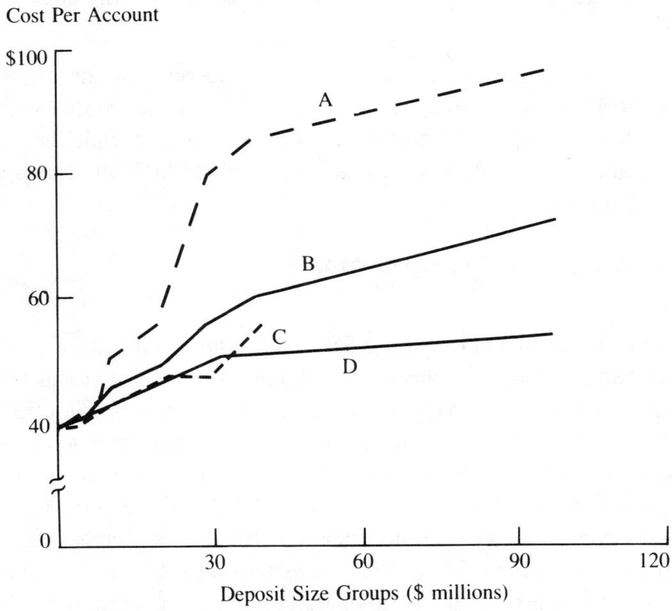

CHART 1 Average Cost per Account, 1978 FCA Data, At Unit and Branch State Banks

A - unit state banks, variables at means of deposit size group.

B - branch state banks, variables at means of deposit size groups.

C - unit state banks, variables at branch state bank. Means for entire sample, except number of accounts and offices. Deposit size group $400–1,000 is omitted since none of the unit state banks had numbers of accounts of the magnitude serviced by branch state banks.

D - branch state banks, variables at means for entire sample, except number of accounts and offices.

size of account constant at the mean values for the entire branching state bank sample. Input prices and holding company affiliation also were held constant at the branching state sample means; however, the number of offices operated was not held constant. Branch banks tend to expand by opening more offices; therefore, it would be unrealistic to assume that higher output could be achieved without branch expansion. Unit banks, though, must expand at a single full-service office.

To compare average costs of banks in unit states with average costs of banks in branching states, we substituted branching state cost determinants in the unit states' cost equation. We entered averages of number of accounts, number of offices, account size and holding company affiliation. Average number of offices in branching states could not be entered in the unit state equation; thus, this cost determinant was ignored. We emerged from this exercise with an estimate of the average costs of unit banks with all of the characteristics of branch banks but multiple offices. These calculations (plotted in Chart 1) show:

- Somewhat higher average costs for larger banks.
- Very similar average costs for similar sizes of banks in unit and branching state banks.

These results indicate that when we take proper account of the current difference between unit and branch state banks, these two classes of banks would experience similar average costs. This reinforces the earlier reported similarities with the scale economy results when account is taken of the different expansion methods used by unit and branch banks (due to regulatory constraints).

Cost of Branching and Holding Company Affiliation

We can also compare estimated operating costs of a branch with those of a similar sized unit bank. Such comparisons are relevant to public choice of unit versus branch banking and of methods of interstate banking. The typical branch serves from 5,000 to 11,000 accounts. The operating costs of unit banks with the same output are \$210,000 and \$462,000.[13] Branches serving the same number of accounts at smaller branch banking organizations have estimated costs of \$213,000 and \$483,000, respectively. Similar sized branches at larger banking organizations are estimated to have increasingly higher operating costs (for example, an 11,000-account branch of a bank with \$300 million to \$400 million in total deposits costs \$650,000 to operate). Thus, small unit banks appear able to compete successfully with branches, particularly those operated by large banks.

We found the effect on operating costs of bank holding company affiliation to be insignificant. Not only were the coefficients of relevant variables generally statistically insignificant, but calculations of average costs that included or excluded consideration of these variables produced numbers that were almost identical.

[13] 1978 data (as are the following numbers). The amounts for the other years studied (1975–1977) are similar though lower due to the effects of inflation over the same period. See Benston, Hanweck and Humphrey, 1981, Table 6 for the individual year amounts.

Implications of the Studies and Conclusion

At this point, only a few implications can be drawn concerning commercial banks' operating costs. To date, we are unable to weigh the possibilities and magnitudes of economies of scale or the cost savings from producing bank services jointly rather than separately. However, studies using data from 1959 through 1970 provide us with some evidence on banks' costs to produce individual services, such as demand deposits and installment loans. Unfortunately, the functional forms used appear to have understated the costs for larger banks. Also, their old data may not reflect present cost conditions. Thus we are unable at this time to go much beyond saying it is unlikely that there are large, if any, economies of scale in producing the most important banking services. (Business loans may be an exception.)

However, it does appear safe to conclude that branch and unit banks incur about the same costs per account, after we adjust for the higher cost of servicing customers with larger accounts. Small branch and unit banks, though, appear to be more efficient than larger banks.

We should emphasize that customer-borne costs, such as inconvenience, are not accounted for, nor is the benefit to customers of using collateral services offered by an individual bank. Presumably, the effect of these factors should be reflected in banks' revenues. Considering these caveats, our analysis of the presently available data leads us to conclude that smaller banks are, at the least, not at an operational disadvantage with respect to large banks. As a result, mergers appear unlikely to result in operating cost savings. Whether or not other benefits or costs flow from a policy of freer entry, or branching, or a more liberal merger policy is beyond the scope of this analysis.

Appendix
Regression Studies of Bank Operating Costs

Before considering the implications of these findings for the policy questions delineated above, we review briefly the previously published regression studies of bank operations costs. These studies may be grouped according to the type of data used, which, in large measure, determined the researchers' definition and measurement of output. The first group used balance sheet and income statement data, with output defined as dollars of assets, while the other used FCA data, with output defined as number of accounts.

Output as Dollars of Earning Assets

Three of the six regression studies that use dollars of assets as output report economies of scale. (Two of these employed specifications that imparted a strong bias towards this result.) One study (Powers) found some evidence of diseconomies and two others (Schweitzer and Kalish and Gilbert) found strong evidence of U-shaped average cost curves, that is, decreasing costs at lower output levels and increasing costs at higher levels. The use of dollars of earning assets as the measure of output appears to have biased the findings of the studies away from showing higher costs for larger banks and deemphasizes the U-shape of the average cost curves. We reach this conclusion in part because when our present study is recast roughly in terms of these previous analyses, the findings are rather similar to theirs. All the studies found branch banking organizations as having higher costs than unit banks. The two studies that included measures of holding company affiliation report conflicting findings.

The first two studies that employed multiple regression analysis measured costs as total operating expenses (including interest) divided by year-end total assets (Schweiger and McGee (1961) and Gramley (1962)). This cost measure was regressed on bank size as measured by deposit size groups by Schweiger and McGee and total assets by Gramley. Other variables used to hold bank characteristics constant were the ratios of time to total deposits, various types of earnings assets as a percent of total assets, and whether a bank was a unit or branch bank. Schweiger and McGee used all member bank data for 1959 and Gramley used a sample of Tenth (Kansas City) District member banks. Both studies found evidence of large economies of scale. Schweiger and McGee also reported higher costs per dollar of assets for branch banks (Gramley's sample included only unit banks). Unfortunately, the use of costs per dollar of assets to measure unit costs imparted strong bias toward the finding of economies of scale. The use of dollars of assets as the output measure requires the implicit and incorrect assumption that large and small loans are equally costly per dollar outstanding. Thus banks with larger average loan sizes appear more efficient. Equally important is the fact that neither study included variables that could identify U-shaped cost curves nor made a formal determination that a U-shaped curve was not necessary to properly describe the data they used.

Four studies defined output as loans and securities, with deposit services being considered an input. Greenbaum (1967), Powers (1969) and Schweitzer (1972), and Kalish and Gilbert (1973) reasoned that the "social" value of these earning assets is equal to the amount people are willing to pay to obtain them. Hence, except for Powers, they weighed each bank's dollars of loans and securities outstanding by the average gross yields on these assets over all banks in the sample to abstract from the effect of local market conditions. Powers used the rates charged at each bank rather than the average rate for all banks because he believed that a loan's social value is measured best by its actual local price. Thus output is equal to gross revenue or a variant thereof. Cost is defined as total operating cost, including interest, less fees for deposit services.[14]

Greenbaum (1967) analyzed 1961 data of 745 and 413 insured banks in the Tenth (Kansas City) and Fifth (Richmond) Federal Districts. He found U-shaped average costs in both districts; however, 98 percent of the banks are on the portion of the cost curve that showed economies of scale. The Fifth District sample was analyzed separately for branch and unit banks. When thus separated, both groups have downward sloping average costs. The unit banks have lower and more rapidly declining costs than the branch banks, but the unit banks are much smaller. Greenbaum concludes that banks grow larger by branching because large unit banks may be more costly to operate.

Powers (1969) analyzed 1962 data from all insured banks in the Seventh (Chicago) Reserve District. He stratified his sample of 2,411 banks into 24 subsamples, according to asset size, current operating revenue to total output (which he defined as total revenue), lending output to total output, and branch versus unit. Of these sub-samples, five have some suggestion of a U-shaped cost curve within the range of the data. With respect to the branch versus unit dichotomy, Powers finds that the branch banking organizations generally (but far from uniformly) have higher average costs than do unit banks.

Schweitzer (1972) analyzed 1964 data from 1,325 Ninth (Minneapolis) District banks. Unlike Greenbaum and Powers, he included the following additional variables: time deposit rate paid, two dummy variables for city location to account for input price differences among banks, and dummy variables measuring the effect of Federal Reserve membership and bank holding company affilia-

[14]Greenbaum did not deduct deposit service fees from costs.

tion. The data were sub-categorized into four size of loans and securities groups. Schweitzer reports "scale economies for banks with total assets under $3.5 million, constant returns to scale for banks between $3.5 and $25.0 million, and decreasing returns for larger banks." (p. 265). He also found significant economies associated with large holding company affiliation, except for banks over $25.0 million in assets. Small bank holding company affiliation indicated economies that are not statistically significant.

Kalish and Gilbert (1973) analyzed 1968 data from 898 FCA banks, using a method that traced out costs with observations from the most efficient banks. The banks were separated into sub-samples of 86 holding company affiliates, 353 branch banks and 460 unit banks. They report U-shaped average cost curves for all three groups, with unit banks having the lowest costs (except for the very largest banks). Branch banks above $1 million in adjusted revenue (or $10 million in loans and investments) show lower costs than holding company subsidiaries and smaller branch banks had higher costs than similar sized holding company affiliates.

The four studies that allowed for finding of diseconomies of large scale found them.[15] However, the evidence of eventually upward sloping curves is slight in Greenbaum's study and mixed in Power's study. The four studies that included measures of branch versus unit banking report higher costs for branch banks. Results on holding company affiliation are conflicting. Using 1964 data, Schweitzer found holding company affiliates to have lower costs (Schweitzer, 1964 data); using 1968 data Kalish and Gilbert found them to have higher costs (Kalish and Gilbert, 1968 data).

Before these results can be accepted as meaningful, at least with respect to the banks and time periods analyzed, we must consider the extent to which the more important misspecifications may bias these findings. The three principal problems are (1) exclusion of variables that account for differences in input prices and types of deposit services, (2) inclusion of interest in operating expenses, and, most important, (3) output defined as dollars of assets outstanding.

The exclusion of input price differences in the studies does not appear to be serious, at least with respect to the calculation of elasticities and average costs, where the banks are ordered by size and by type of organization (branch and unit). We calculated these numbers for our samples holding these factor prices constant over the entire sample; the changes in the scale economy estimates and average costs were slight and did not affect any of the conclusions. However, ignoring differences in types of deposits is likely to be serious, since about half of the total operating expenses (excluding interest) are due to deposits.[16] Furthermore, the proportion is higher at the small banks (those with deposits under $50 million): 53 percent compared to 49 percent for banks with $50 to $200 million in deposits and 46 percent for banks with over $200 million in deposits. The smaller banks also have relatively more demand deposit expense (39 percent versus 36 and 35 percent). This misspecification probably overstates the average costs of smaller banks.

Exclusion of interest from operating expenses might understate the costs of large banks, since they generally purchase a greater proportion of their funds in the market. We tested this hypothesis by including interest in operating expenses in our data and recalculating the cost functions. The recalculations showed greater economies of scale for all the banks (See Table 1, column 3). With interest included and the Divisia number of accounts as the measure of output, the larger banks (over $25 million in deposits) in unit states had nearly constant costs. The smaller (under $25 million in deposits) branch banks had statistically significant economies of scale, and the medium-sized ($50 million to $300 million in deposits) banks in branching states had small, but statistically significant, diseconomies of scale. Thus, inclusion of interest could account, in part, for the larger economies or lower diseconomies of scale for larger banks found in the other studies.

[15]Schweiger-McGee and Gramley employed different methods which, we feel, biased their measures of scale (as discussed above).

[16]1978 Functional Cost Analysis data.

Finally, measuring output with assets (weighted by revenues in most of the studies) may impart a bias for banks that service larger accounts, showing them as being more efficient. We tested for this bias by recalculating the elasticities and average costs with dollars of deposits and loans as the output measure instead of the number of accounts and average size of account. These elasticities are considerably lower for all size groups of the unit banks and for all but the larger (up to $200 million to $300 million in deposits) branch banks (see Table 1, column 2). With interest included as part of operating expenses, the middle-sized banks in both unit and branch states show diseconomies of scale, a finding similar to those reported in the studies that similarly measured cost and output (see Table 1, column 4). Thus using dollars of deposits is equivalent to measuring output by the number of accounts while assuming that the size of accounts is uniform among banks. This assumption biases the elasticity estimates towards greater economies of scale particularly at the large unit banks. This effect also is reflected in the average cost per dollar of deposits and loans (not shown): the cost curve is less U-shaped.

Output as Numbers of Accounts and Average Size of Accounts in a Cobb-Douglas Production Function

Benston (1965A) is the first study to use the FCA data, which permitted him to specify output as the average number of accounts serviced and the average size of accounts, and to analyze costs of separate banking functions. He analyzed each of the five functions—demand deposits, time and savings deposits, real estate loans, installment loans, business loans, and securities—and overhead costs. Overhead was regressed on total assets rather than the number and average size of accounts. For most of the analyses, Benston used a functional form that can show only continuously rising, falling, or flat average cost curves. But by including higher powers on the output measure he also tested for the presence of U-shaped cost curves. This study used data from some 80 banks in the Boston Federal Reserve District for 1959, 1960 and 1961 and found economies of scale for all except the business loan function and the overhead costs. Slight U-shaped curves were present for installment loans only. The estimated elasticities (averaged over the three years) ranged from .74 (securities) and .87 (demand deposits) to 1.0 (business development and overhead). However, the largest bank included had $55 million in assets (1961 price level), so the data did not cover the full range of bank output. Branch banks were found to have higher operating costs than unit banks that serviced the same number of accounts (Benston 1965B), but because the cost effect of branching was misspecified the validity of this finding is questionable.

Bell and Murphy (1968) extended Benston's work considerably. They analyzed data from 210 to 283 banks in the Boston, New York and Philadelphia Federal Reserve Districts that reported FCA data for 1963, 1964 and 1965. They did not explicitly test the data for the presence of U-shaped cost curves, since they explicitly based their analysis on the Cobb-Douglas production function. They estimated elasticities (averaged over the three years) ranging from .83 (securities) and .86 (real estate loans) to 1.0 (safe deposits and trust department). They constructed an overall measure of economies of scale by weighing the individual elasticities by the average cost of each function and type of overhead expense. This yielded a total elasticity of .93. Branch banks were found to have higher operating costs than unit banks, but Bell and Murphy calculated that expansion of branch banks did not generate greater average costs, since the higher cost of branching, in their calculations, was offset almost exactly by economies from a larger volume of output.

Murphy (1972) replicated and further extended this work with a larger sample (967 banks) of large banks (up to $5.5 billion in deposits) nationwide for 1968. The only important difference between the elasticities measured with these data compared to the earlier (1965) results is the change from significant economies of scale in demand deposits to approximately constant costs. Most of the other functions showed only small economies of scale, so that the estimated total elasticity for the 1968 sample is .95.

Longbrake and Haslem (1975) also used these data (1968 FCA banks, nationwide), but restricted the analysis to direct demand deposit costs, emphasizing the effect on these costs of organizations structure. They separated the sample of 767 banks into four sub-sets: unit banks and branch banks, each affiliated or not affiliated with holding companies. They found statistically significant economies of scale (elasticities of .93 for unit affiliates and branch non-affiliates and .82 for branch affiliates) for all except the unit bank non-affiliates, which had constant costs (elasticity of 1.03). In general, the branch banks (particularly the larger ones) had higher estimated costs per account or dollar of deposit than did the unit banks, the affiliated unit banks had higher costs than the unaffiliated unit banks, but the affiliated branch banks had lower costs than the unaffiliated branch banks.

Mullineaux (1975) also separated a 1970 sample of 196 FCA banks in the Boston, New York and Philadelphia Reserve Districts, into branch (167) and unit (29) banks, to test the hypothesis that the estimated coefficients differ by type of organization. Elasticities were estimated for each of the five principal banking functions and the hypothesis was accepted. For most functions, unit banks had economies of scale and branch banks had diseconomies. As the previous studies found, branch banks appeared to have higher operating expenses than similar unit banks.

Benston and Hanweck (1977) reported preliminary findings of a study of nationwide FCA banks for the years 1968 through 1974 (904 banks in 1974). The direct costs of the five principal banking functions were analyzed separately. Unlike the other studies which used the Cobb-Douglas cost function, a quadratic cost function was estimated which permitted estimation of U-shaped cost curves.[17] They report finding scale economies for most years only for business loans. Little indication of systematic economies or diseconomies was found for the real estate, installment loan or time deposit functions. The demand deposits function, though, exhibited diseconomies of scale starting at low output levels.

The effect of holding company affiliation was tested by separating the sample into affiliated and independent banks. The affiliated banks exhibited somewhat lesser scale economies than the independents. But average costs per account at the affiliates were lower, particularly with respect to demand deposits. For 1974, demand deposits costs averaged 4 percent lower for banks affiliated with a small holding company and 17 percent lower for banks affiliated with a large holding company. Branch and unit banks were not separately identified and this misspecification may have confounded the results somewhat.

Finally, a recent study by Dunham (1982) used 1978 FCA data for three Federal Reserve Districts (Boston, New York and Chicago). The Cobb-Douglas form was used and separate estimation was performed for five banking functions—demand deposits, time deposits, commercial and agricultural loans, installment loans and mortgage loans. Operating costs were adjusted for correspondent services paid for with non-interest bearing balances by imputing a cost based on the three-month Treasury bill rate applied to net "due from" balances. Output was measured by the number of accounts for each function. When operating costs are not adjusted for the imputed cost of correspondent services, the demand deposit function exhibited constant costs while the other functions showed significant scale economies. After costs were adjusted, the demand deposit function also exhibited significant economies of scale. In addition, this study also found that branch banks had higher costs than unit banks with the same characteristics. Thus, the results are similar to those of Benston, Bell and Murphy.

These studies offer some important insights into costs of individual bank outputs and changes in banks cost structure over time. The analyses indicated economies of scale in the early 1960s for all

[17]The variables were divided by output to correct for heteroscedasticity.

banking functions and departments except safe deposit boxes and trust. The late 1960s and early 1970s data revealed a change to constant costs for the important demand deposit function, at least for unit banks not affiliated with holding companies. Affiliated unit banks and branch banks were found to have economies of scale in demand deposit operations similar to those computed with earlier data. Data for 1970 yielded approximately constant direct costs for branch banks but economies of scale for unit banks. However, one study that used data through 1974 found diseconomies of scale. This study (Benston-Hanweck) is the only one using data covering a broad range of bank sizes that specified a cost function to test for U-shaped cost curves. Thus, the earlier findings of continuous slight economies of scale might be due to this misspecification or to a change over time in the cost function faced by commercial banks.

It also is important to note that none of these studies tested for economies of scale for banks as entire entities. Where overhead costs were analyzed, these costs were regressed on output measured as total assets. Hence, the elasticities of banks that serviced larger average size accounts appear to be biased downward. This problem could have resulted in a finding of economies of scale or constant costs when, in fact, diseconomies of scale were experienced.

To test for the possible misspecification effect of not allowing for U-shaped cost curves and of not analyzing the banks as an entire entity, and as a means of separating the effects of sample and specification differences, we reestimated our 1978 findings using the Cobb-Douglas cost function. This functional form yields the following elasticities: branch state banks, .93*, unit state banks 1.07*, and for the entire sample, 1.01 (an asterisk indicates elasticities statistically significantly different from 1.0—constant costs—at the 95 percent confidence level.) These are almost the same as the mean elasticities computed with our more complex translog cost function which allows for a U-shaped cost curve. But, as Table 1, column 1 shows, the mean elasticity value masks the finding of lower elasticities for smaller banks and higher elasticities for larger banks. Combining unit and branch banks in a single sample also masks important and statistically significant differences between them. Furthermore, as the augmented measure of branch bank elasticities presented above shows, ignoring the way in which branch banks actually expand understates the elasticities experienced by branch banks when one wishes to determine the scale economy of the entire organization rather than of a single office.

With respect to branch banking, most of the studies reported higher branching costs that appeared to be offset by measured economies of scale. Studies that calculated average costs found them to be higher for branch banks, with larger branching systems having even higher costs per account. Those findings are consistent with our more current study, with one exception. We found branch and unit banks to have very similar costs per account when differences between them, in terms of their mode of expansion, were accounted for properly.

REFERENCES

1. ALHADEFF, DAVID A. *Monopoly and Competition in Banking*. Berkeley, California: University of California Press, 1954.
2. BARNETT, WILLIAM A. "Divisia Indices." *Encyclopedia of Statistical Sciences,* New York, New York: Wiley and Sons, 1981.
3. BELL, FREDERICK W., and NEIL B. MURPHY *Costs in Commercial Banking: A Quantitive Analysis of Bank Behavior and its Relation to Bank Regulation*. Federal Reserve Bank of Boston, Research Report No. 41, 1968.
4. BENSTON, GEORGE J. "Economies of Scale and Marginal Costs in Banking Operations." *The National Banking Review,* 2 (June 1965A), 507–49.

5. BENSTON, GEORGE J. "Branch Banking and Economies of Scale." *The Journal of Finance,* XX (May 1965B), 312–31.
6. BENSTON, GEORGE J. "Accounting Numbers and Economic Values." *The Antitrust Bulletin,* XXVII (Spring 1982), 161–215.
7. BENSTON, GEORGE J. and GERALD A. HANWECK "A Summary Report on Bank Holding Company Affiliation and Economies of Scale." *Proceedings of a Conference on Bank Structure and Competition,* Federal Reserve Bank of Chicago, 1977.
8. BENSTON, GEORGE J., GERALD A. HANWECK, and DAVID B. HUMPHREY "Scale Economies in Banking: A Restructuring and Reassessment." Working Paper. Federal Reserve Board, November 1981.
9. BENSTON, GEORGE J., GERALD A. HANWECK, and DAVID B. HUMPHREY "Scale Economies in Banking: A Restructuring and Reassessment." *Journal of Money, Credit, and Banking,* XIII (November 1982, Part 1).
10. DIEWERT, W. ERWIN "Exact and Superlative Index Numbers." *Journal of Econometrics,* 4 (May 1976), 115–145.
11. DURHAM, CONSTANCE "Commercial Bank Costs and Correspondent Banking." *New England Economic Review,* Federal Reserve Bank of Boston (September/October 1981) 22–36.
12. FLANNERY, MARK J. "Correspondent Services and Cost Economies in Commercial Banking." Research Paper No. 77, Federal Reserve Bank of Philadelphia, November 1981.
13. GOLDSCHMIDT, AMMNON "On the Definition and Measurement of Bank Output." *Journal of Banking and Finance,* 5 (1981), 575–585.
14. GREENBAUM, STUART I. "Banking Structure and Costs: A Statistical Study of the Cost-Output Relationship in Commercial Banking." *National Banking Review,* 4 (June, 1967), 415–34.
15. GRAMLEY, LYLE E. *A Study of Scale Economies in Banking.* Federal Reserve Bank of Kansas City, 1962.
16. HORVITZ, PAUL M., "Economies of Scale in Banking." *Private Financial Institutions,* Englewood Cliffs, N.J.: Prentice-Hall, Inc., 1963, 1–54.
17. KALISH, LIONEL and R. ALTON GILBERT "An Analysis of Efficiency of Scale and Organizational Form in Commercial Banking." *Journal of Industrial Economics,* 21 (July 1973), 293–307.
18. LONGBRAKE, WILLIAM A. and JOHN A. HALSLEM "Productive Efficiency in Commercial Banking: The Effects of Size and Legal Form of Organization on the Cost of Producing Demand-Deposit Services." *Journal of Money, Credit and Banking,* 7 (August 1975), 317–330.
19. MULLINEAUX, DONALD J. "Economies of Scale of Financial Institutions: A Comment." *Journal of Monetary Economics,* 1 (April 1975), 233–240.
20. MURPHY, NEIL B. "A Re-estimation of the Benston-Bell-Murphy Cost Functions for a Larger Sample with Greater Size and Geographical Dispersion." *Journal of Financial and Quantitative Analysis,* 7 (December 1972), 2097–105.
21. POWERS, JOHN A. "Branch Versus Unit Banking: Bank Output and Cost Economies." *Southern Economic Journal,* 36 (October 1969), 153–64.
22. SCHWEIGER, IRVING and JOHN S. MCGEE "Chicago Banking: The Structure and Performance of Banks and Related Financial Institutions in Chicago and Other Areas." *Journal of Business,* 34 (July 1961), 203–366.
23. SCHWEITZER, A. A. "Economies of Scale and Holding Company Affiliation in Banking." *Southern Economic Journal,* 39 (October, 1972), 258–266.

Future Payments System Technology: Can Small Financial Institutions Compete?

Paul F. Metzker

11

According to many studies of payments system technology, the difference between unit operating costs at large and small financial institutions has been insignificant in the recent past. Even though small financial institutions appeared to have slightly lower unit costs for some payments system services, large institutions appeared to enjoy a slight unit cost advantage in others. Taken together, the respective ''comparative advantages'' seem to even out, making both large and small financial institutions formidable competitors.

Do these trends remain in effect? Will the historical trend of unit operating cost ''parity'' continue through the rest of the decade? This article addresses these questions and develops a model for the most likely source of payments system services offered by small financial institutions.*

Reprinted from *Economic Review* (November, 1982): 58–67 by permission of the Federal Reserve Bank of Atlanta and the author.

*This article's focus is not on large financial institutions versus small institutions in all facets of their operations; instead, it concentrates on payments system-related products and services offered by large and small financial institutions. It explores the impact of future technology on the traditional unit cost parity in payments systems among financial institutions of all sizes.

Generally speaking, this article refers to small financial institutions as commercial banks with less than $150 million in assets, savings, and loan institutions with less than $250 million in assets, and credit unions. Large financial institutions generally consist of commercial banks and savings and loan associations with assets in excess of the small financial institution's limits.

The Situation Today

Other research on this subject suggests that small banks enjoyed a slight edge in their payments system unit costs during the 1970s. What kinds of unit cost differences exist today?

Data in the Federal Reserve System's Functional Cost Analysis (FCA) show that similar trends continue. Recently released data for 1981, covering 614 commercial banks nationwide, show that:

> Interest-bearing checking accounts were most profitable at the smaller banks (deposits of $50 million or less), earning them $11.22 monthly per account. . . .
>
> Medium-sized banks (deposits of $50 million to $200 million) earned $8.35 each month per account. . . .
>
> The largest banks (more than $200 million in deposits) earned $5.77 per month on the accounts. . . .
>
> The cost of administering a NOW account grew in all size groups over the previous year. Smaller banks again had the lowest administrative expenses. The accounts cost the smallest banks $6.06 monthly per account to handle. The medium banks had expenses of $6.69 per month per account. And it cost the largest banks $8.59 per account.[1]

A review of other FCA data shows that the lowest-cost mantle varies between large and small financial institutions in the other payment systems. Time and savings deposits functions show variation too. Thus, when performance in all of these payments and deposit generating activities is netted out, the traditional overall parity remains generally intact.

The historical evidence implies that, so far anyway, payments system technology has not given either large or small financial institutions an insurmountable advantage in the delivery of such products as checking accounts, savings accounts, credit cards, and ATMs. Technological change during the 1970s and early 1980s did not appear to alter materially the unit cost parity between large and small financial institutions in payments system service.

The Status Quo Is Under Attack

During the rest of the 1980s, though, both the payments system (as now structured) and the traditional unit cost parity among financial institutions are expected to be altered in several respects. First, the Federal Reserve System has begun to charge for its services and will

---

This article assumes that references to small banks in their payments system behavior are also generally applicable to the behavior of other small financial institutions. It assumes a similar relationship for large commercial banks and their large counterparts in other segments of the industry.

The term "technology" here refers to computer hardware and software, terminal devices, and electronic communication networks.

Finally, the article does not attempt to compare large and small financial institutions on a point and counterpoint basis. The emphasis is on whether payments system technology will be a friend or foe of small financial institutions in the 1980s.

[1] Carson, Teresa. "Interest Bearing Accounts Gain, and So Does Their Profitability." *American Banker* (New York), August 19, 1982, p. 3

charge even more as attempts intensify to price all Fed float. Second, as Regulation Q is phased out, interest expenses on all kinds of deposits should escalate. Third, interstate banking is progressing on a de facto basis and is likely to become a legal activity before the decade is over. Fourth, savings and loan associations, mutual savings banks and credit unions are now providing such products as checking accounts, credit cards, ATMs and debit cards. Fifth, new players, offering payment services of one sort or another, are entering the arena—Sears, Merrill Lynch, and American Express to name a few. Sixth, backroom operations in the paper-based payment systems are labor and energy intensive. Costs in paper-based systems are expected to continue spiraling.

When itemized, these trends may sound foreboding to bankers. Yet such lists usually cite payments system technology as the salvation of financial institutions from these threatening trends. The general thrust of the technology argument is that computer and communications advances offer lower cost electronic alternatives to the paper-based payment systems and their gloomy future. Even more exciting, the argument contends that new, innovative alternatives to today's narrow, "me too" product lines can be designed and marketed electronically, at lower cost and with higher profit margins.

Explicit or implicit in many of these upbeat, technology-inspired forecasts is a suggestion that the future success of financial institutions will not only require use of this technology, but also use of large, networked payment systems. In other words, large financial institutions will be in the best position to reap the technological windfall and gain a unit cost superiority.

Many forecasts of this genre imply that electronic banking concepts are an important weapon in efforts to improve the nation's payments system. Such scenarios envision a necessary and desirable shakeout period as small, inefficient financial institutions are forced to merge or fold. The following prediction is typical of those anticipating much greater concentration in the industry:

> The financial services industry of the future is unlikely to consist of the same familiar types of institutions that we know today. It is not ordained that all or most commercial banks, savings and loans, mutual savings banks, credit unions, insurance companies, investment bankers and others of the old forms of financial institutions will survive. It is more likely that many of them will not.[2]

According to the shakeout theory, only large organizations have the capital and technical expertise to support large, complex electronic networks. One disagreement among proponents of this theory is the rate at which the transition will occur. In any case, the projected result for small financial institutions is an inevitable death—fast as with an electric chair or slow as with a Chinese water torture.

Such forecasts seem logical, tidy, neat and clean. But another scenario, just as plausible, is emerging to challenge the shakeout theory. The concepts embodied in the alterna-

[2]Kaufman, George, Larry Mote and Harvey Rosenblum, "Product Lines in Geographic Markets." *Bankers Monthly Magazine*. Volume 94 (May 15, 1982), p. 22. This article, as do others that it is representative of, does not suggest that all small financial institutions are expected to survive. By contrast, there is another school of thought, which the divisibility theory supports, that believes that a very large number of small financial institutions will survive—if they elect to do so and are well managed.

tive theory are not new or unique. They have been evident in many other industries.[3] The alternative is based on the ease with which electronic products can be produced in large quantities for several smaller customers on a pooled or shared basis.

The divisibility theory, as it will be called here, suggests that the foreseeable technological trends are not the private preserve of an elite large few. Instead, the divisibility features of the new technology could offer even more unit cost competition between all sizes of financial institutions. More importantly, the new technology could lead to greater service differentiation and market segmentation than is now possible.

Likely Technological and Unit Cost Trends During the 1980s

To visualize fully the impact of payments system technology on financial institutions during the rest of this decade, let's review some of the general technological and cost trends expected during the 1980s. The review provides a preface for a more specific discussion of how technology can impact the payments system services of small financial institutions.

Inexpensive, powerful, computer hardware.

Computing power will be less expensive and more accessible to households, small businesses, and small financial institutions. Whether we look at trends in the price-performance of large mainframe computers, minicomputers, or microcomputers, the cost of computing per calculation is declining. This article, for example, is being written with a

[3]A review of the history of the retail grocery industry provides another example of the divisibility theory.

In the early years of this century, separate retail outlets typically sold separate lines of groceries, e.g., meat markets sold meat, dry goods grocers sold canned/packaged food products, and produce markets sold vegetables and fruits. Many of these outlets were proprietorships and often the owner lived on the premises.

Then in the 1930s when the supermarket chain concepts began evolving, many industry forecasters predicted a shakeout of all proprietorships and specialized stores. The demise was expected to occur because small retailers were not expected to achieve the economies of scale available to the supermarket chains with their centralized buying, warehousing and distribution systems.

These forecasts ignored the easy divisibility of these centralized functions into lots usable by several smaller retailers on a cooperative basis. Wholesalers and cooperatives were established to support independent supermarkets as well as corner stores or "mom and pop" operations. The divisibility theory enabled "independents" to achieve chain store economies of scale without the massive capital investment of a chain. The pooled resources of all the wholesaler's users/cooperatives's members were sufficient to compete with the large chain's economies of scale.

Granted the era did see the decline of the corner store concept in most areas of the country. Ironically another mutation, in the 1960s and 1970s, revived the corner store concept in a slightly different format and in a chain structure. The mutation is the convenience store where premium prices are charged for access to many supermarket items at locations or during hours when easy access to a supermarket is not possible.

Today, the retail grocery industry is a mixture of chain supermarkets, chain convenience stores, independent supermarkets, independent convenience stores, and specialty outlets such as meat markets and produce markets. Their coexistence demonstrates how an easily divisible product, food, can be provided by organizations with many different organizational structures, with either similar shelf prices or with extra convenience at a premium price.

microcomputer and word-processing package that together cost less than $2,500. The memory capacity of this microcomputer equals the combined memory capacity of the IBM 1401 computers in four check reader-sorters, costing thousands of dollars per year in the early 1970s, at the Federal Reserve Bank of Atlanta.

Price-performance improvements are being accompanied by miniaturization. The four reader-sorters of 1970 required a large room with special electrical wiring, humidity control and temperature control. Today, memories of comparable size and power are available in desk-top and smaller computers requiring none of the special environmental support of earlier years.

These trends during the 1980s should produce an exponential growth in the sales of cheap memory and data storage devices. As a result, computing power will represent an exception to the resource scarcity now being faced with energy, strategic minerals, and even water. The surfeit of computing power will provide electronic payments with a significant price-performance advantage over more-labor intensive payment systems.

Inexpensive, user-friendly, computer programs.

Canned, easy-to-use software for general management, as well as for payments products and services, will be readily available at reasonable prices. Much current literature on bank operations points out that programming costs are escalating rapidly and possibly threatening the economies that arise from automation and electronic payments.

These concerns are based on a traditional reliance on the in-house development of software. The rationale for in-house software development has been that a particular financial institution is unique and cannot possibly use software written for another financial institution. Unfortunately for those adhering to the in-house philosophy, some small financial institutions are living proof that several organizations can use the same software and even share a large computer system. Instead of owning the entire rock, so to speak, small financial institutions are finding ways to own just the pieces of a larger rock that they need in their organization.

Thus the idea that software development costs are rising and will continue to rise needs to be tempered with the realization that an individual financial institution may actually reduce software expenses during the 1980s by moving from proprietary, in-house software to canned or shared software concepts.

Inexpensive electronic communications.

Advances in communications technology will lead to less expensive movement of information between locations. As energy and other air or surface transportation costs continue to rise, electronic transmission of information will become a greater bargain.

Wide-scale networking.

Intelligent terminals, costing under $200 a unit, should facilitate electronic access of households and small businesses to a wide array of products and services. Such terminals, linked to inexpensive computer hardware, user-friendly software, and inexpensive electronic communications networks, will create an electronic network with inestimable impact. Among the products and services readily adaptable to such a network are those often referred to as "home banking" services.

New concepts of "branch" banking.

The cost advantages of electronic banking will lead to the demise of extensive networks of brick-and-mortar, full-service banking facilities. Many facilities will be replaced with a wider distribution of ATMs, home terminals, and point-of-sale (POS) systems.

More sophisticated households, workers, and small businesses.

Over time, the nation's population is being exposed to a more electronic world. Today's children, are growing up in a more computerized world. The work force and household bases of 1990 will be more receptive to price-competitive electronic alternatives for existing services, in general, and payments services in particular.

Tomorrow's small businessman and consumer will be more knowledgeable and sophisticated in selecting and using credit, payment, and investment vehicles. Idle, non-earning balances left with financial institutions will continue their movement into easily accessible accounts/investment vehicles. Widespread use of such vehicles should virtually eliminate demand deposits as a low-cost source of funds for financial institutions. Accordingly, financial institutions can be expected to rely less on spread income and more on fee income.

Finally, the trend throughout American industry and trade will continue to be away from blue collar jobs toward technical and white collar occupations. In the financial industry, the trend translates to less reliance on clerical work forces and more emphasis on technically skilled professional staffs that are comfortable working with a more computerized environment.

These technological trends will drastically change the unit cost structure for financial institutions. Donald G. Long, a finance industry consultant with the IBM Corporation, recently summarized the anticipated impact of these technological trends on the unit cost of several payments system products. The following unit cost trends are excerpted from his recent article in the *Journal of Bank Retailing:*

> **Branch Automation.** In the traditional office, an average transaction accepted by a teller over the counter without on-line capability at the teller station cost 61 cents in 1981. At a conservative 6 percent compound rate of growth, the cost will be 82 cents in 1986. Providing full function on-line capability at the teller window could reduce that cost by approximately 21 percent to 48 cents. . . .
>
> **Automated Teller Machines (ATMs).** While the figure is not directly comparable to the above because of differences in transaction mix, the cost per transaction of an ATM doing 6,000 transactions per month exclusive of inquiries is approximately 28 cents. . . . A major additional consideration is that the very high component of technology involved in this service delivery mechanism can significantly reduce the rate of cost growth. Based on this, I estimate that the same volume and transaction mix on the ATM in 1986 will average 30 cents per transaction. . . .

> **Point-of-Sale.** At the merchant point-of-sale, the current cost of a check accepted for goods or services is approximately 39 cents of merchant cost (57 cents general merchandise retailer and 33 cents supermarket skewed to reflect the majority of such checks in supermarkets) and 9 cents net bank cost (13 cents handling and processing less 4 cents deposit charges per item). This POS financial transaction cost could be reduced to about 31 cents (27 cents merchant cost and net 4 cents bank cost) through the use of an on-line debit card system providing both electronic authorization and data capture. . . .
>
> **The Automated Clearinghouse. . . .** A recent study sponsored by the Bank Administration Institute estimated the cost to the bank of an EFT deposit at 7 cents versus 24 cents for an over-the-counter teller deposit and 59 cents for a bank-by-mail deposit. . . .
>
> **Home Banking. . . .** The net cost to the payor, biller, and bank of a payment made by mail exceeds 65 cents. Providing a "Model T" capability, such as telephone bill payment, can reduce that net cost to less than 30 cents.[4]

Clearly, payments system technology is positioned to play a strong role in the unit costs of financial services and products as the decade unfolds. Yet as formidable as these technological trends and the unit cost projections may seem, they still skirt the original question: What does technology hold in store for unit costs at small financial institutions?

Impact of Payments Technology On Small Financial Institutions' Unit Costs

Small financial institutions probably will not generate sufficient volumes in electronic payment systems to develop proprietary, completely in-house hardware, software, and communications functions. But, just as obviously, the divisibility theory permits shared efforts that can achieve, collectively, the break-even volumes to be price-competitive with larger financial institutions.[5] Let's explore some of the implications of the divisibility theory further.

First, regulators have tended to require small banks to maintain higher capital ratios than large banks. One often-stated reason is that small financial institutions experience more risk because of their size. However, one risk not usually discussed is the relative automation investment of large versus small financial institutions.

Table 1 shows the primary sources of computer processing for small, medium and large banks as determined from responses to the American Bankers Association's Operations and Automation Surveys in 1974, 1977 and 1980. Large banks typically use in-house

[4]Long, Donald G. "The Business Case for Electronic Banking." *Journal of Retail Banking*. Volume 4 (June 1982), pp. 19-20.

[5]Please see Appendix A, Transaction Volumes and Unit Costs, for a more thorough description of the concepts involved in economies of scale for an electronic payment product/service and how the divisibility theory makes these economies available to small financial institutions.

Table 1. Primary Source of Computer Processing
Percent of banks by asset size in millions of dollars

Processing source	Under $100			$100–$500			$500 and above		
	1974	1977	1980	1974	1977	1980	1974	1977	1980
On-premise operations	9%	15%	24%	62%	58%	45%	77%	82%	75%
Holding co. arrangement	10	12	12	12	17	19	17	13	18
Correspondent bank	58	52	41	7	7	11	1	0	1
Joint venture	5	4	2	6	5	4	0	1	1
Facilities management	8	5	6	10	6	9	5	3	4
Servicing by non-bank	8	10	13	3	9	10	0	1	0
Other	0	0	2	0	0	2	0	0	1

Source: "Operations/Automation Scoresheet compare your bank with its peers." *ABA Banking Journal*. vol. 74 (Feb. 1982), p. 98.

equipment and much in-house software. Small banks rely much more frequently on third-party sources. Conversations with vendor representatives indicate that, with few exceptions, small banks use canned software even if they have in-house processing capability.

Exhibit 1 (chart and table) shows the much larger percentage increase in expenditures for hardware and software that large banks anticipate in comparison with small banks. At a time when banks are experiencing new competitive pressures and squeezed profit margins, it appears that a significantly greater proportion of large bank expense and investment resources will be tied up in automation efforts. In contrast, small banks are buying what they need, in the quantity they need, when they need it. The latter approach would seem to carry less risk.

Why? A large bank is likely to be heavily committed and heavily invested in a software/hardware system that becomes prematurely obsolete from the rapid innovation spawned by a highly competitive marketplace. As a result, it will feel management pressure either to continue offering an obsolete product or service until the initial investment has been recouped or to drop the incompletely depreciated product taking a heavy loss on the initial investment. On the other hand, a small bank, using third-party suppliers, can change products or services as the market dictates with much less internal financial impact. Divisibility, in a sense, decreases small bank automation risk and increases small bank ability to respond to a rapidly changing marketplace.

EXHIBIT 1 Projected Hardware/Software Expenditures per Bank - 1982

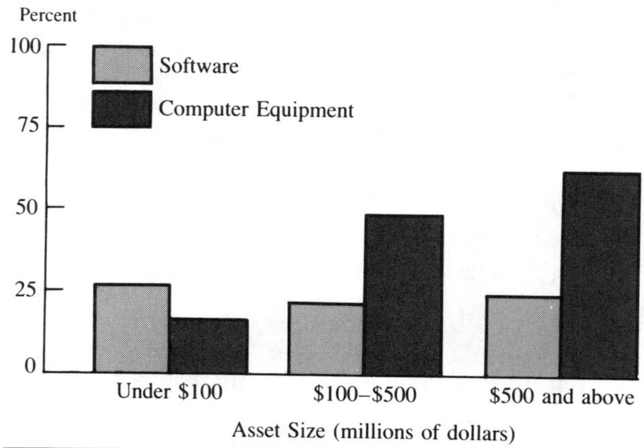

Average Hardware/Software Expenditures per Bank

	Asset Size (millions of dollars)		
	Under $100	$100–$500	$500 and Above
Computer Equipment	($000s)	($000s)	($000s)
1980–actual	39	198	1,978
1981–budgeted	48	222	2,229
1982–anticipated	50	242	2,482
Sotware			
1980–actual	11	24	180
1981–budgeted	11	33	258
1982–anticipated	13	36	298

Source: "Operations/Automation Scoresheet: Compare your bank with its peers." ABA Banking Journal Vol 74 (Feb. 1982), p. 96

Second, there are several indications that the economies of scale in payment systems now require volumes larger than are achievable even at large financial institutions. For example, during the past year several large financial institutions have turned their Visa and/or Mastercard backroom operations over to a third party. Almarin Phillips, Professor of Economics, Law and Public Policy at the University of Pennsylvania, recently predicted:

> Economies of scale in funds management, distribution, and in the electronic and mechanical aspects of clearing mean that many institutions will be unable independently to enter new markets with new products, or indeed, competitively to maintain their old services in their old markets. . . . In many respects, the sharing of product offerings, with compatible hardware and software and general customer recognition is highly procompetitive. It keeps in the marketplace numbers of firms that would otherwise disappear; it also makes entry easier if procompetitive, non-exclusionary participations are allowed.[6]

[6]Phillips, Alamarin, ''Financial Institutions in a Revolutionary Era,'' *Journal of Credit Union Management and Economics,* Volume 2 (Spring 1982), p. 17.

Perhaps it is the large financial institutions that will become more like their small brethren with respect to automation resources. Perhaps it is the small institution's approach to harnessing automation resources that kept its unit costs so competitive during the last decade. If so, the small financial institution is really the automation model for the 1980s, not the large financial institution. If so, the divisibility theory actually has a broader application than once visualized.

Third, networking opens up markets for smaller financial institutions that were not profitably serviceable in the traditional payments system environment. William S. Anderson, chairman of NCR Corporation, observes that:

> A score of regional EFT networks in the United States—each capable of providing retail banking services over a broad geographic area—have now been organized. It is only a matter of time until full-scale national networks of this type, as well as international networks, will be in operation. When that occurs, any bank regardless of location or size will at least theoretically have the entire world as its market.[7]

In this respect, technology opens new doors of opportunity for small financial institutions. Surely it would be naive to believe that small institutions can provide mass-market products nationally or internationally. But it does not seem naive at all to think that small financial institutions could use this technological windfall in certain well-defined market segments.

A good example of how new technology can be accessed by large and small institutions is the sweep and invest feature now being marketed by several large and small institutions in conjunction with their checking accounts for large balance customers. The size of the financial institution does not appear to be a deterrent to offering this feature. In fact, the sweep and invest feature offered by many large and small institutions is being obtained from the same third-party source.

Fourth, the literature in support of the shakeout theory seems to ignore a major question: Where will large financial institutions obtain the financial wherewithal to go on a merger binge? Raoul D. Edwards, senior editor, *United States Banker,* suggests that a source is not available. Therefore, he observes:

> What has happened is a new and less certain economic pattern, marked increasingly by shrinking earnings margins, escalating labor costs, increasing pressures on the bottom line—and a consequent reluctance to make the kind of massive commitment implicit in major acquisitions. Some deals will still get made; the joining of a good sized pair of banks as equals, where no dilution of value occurs, for example. But no one in today's environment wants to go out and buy up a bunch of smaller institutions at book-and-a-half or two-time book, especially if their own stock is selling under book.[8]

According to Edwards, a major shakeout of small financial institutions is unlikely. What is likely is that technology will be the tool with which all financial institutions will attempt to

[7]Anderson, William S. "Electronic Funds Transfer is Reaching the Point-of-Sale," *American Banker* (New York), July 28, 1982, p. 58.

[8]Edwards, Raoul D. "The Vendor and Changing Worlds," *United States Banker,* Volume 93 (May 1982), p. 68

offer products and services equal to or better than those in the past, but at a lower price and, hopefully, a better profit margin.

The same article that presented Edwards' scenario touched on a point that bears amplification here as a potential advantage for small financial institutions in the competition of the 1980s:

> This (trend) means that the vendor of products will increasingly find his market opening up at the bottom. Moreover, the range of services he can sell will broaden. . . .
> The vendor who recognizes this and prepares for the new market is going to find it large and growing; the banker who understands this will find his options will be far greater, far more useful, than ever before.[9]

If vendors behave in this manner, small financial institutions will find more, not fewer, potential sources of supply for their hardware, software, technical, product, and service support in the 1980s than they can find now. If we assume that more vendors mean more price competition, then small financial institutions could find more of a ''buyer's market'' when shopping for suppliers than will large financial institutions deeply engrossed in more complex, longer lead time efforts to develop proprietary products and services. If so, intense price-performance competition among vendors will help cap potential cost increases for small institutions. If so, the divisibility theory provides them yet another benefit.

Fifth, minicomputers—and now microcomputers—constitute new technological weapons for small businesses and small financial institutions. Their full benefit has not been tapped yet by small institutions. Admittedly, their impact transcends the payments system functions of financial institutions.

Until the advent of microcomputers, only large businesses and financial institutions could afford automated planning and control. Robert H. Long, president of Long, Inc., and editor of Microbanker, recently wrote in *The Southern Banker* that:

> The microcomputer is one of the first pieces of technology that places a potent competitive weapon in the hands of community bankers—a piece of technology that can help them competitively serve the more profitable markets and reposition themselves for success in a deregulated environment. Large banks will use them the same way, but the effect will not be as dramatic.[10]

Stated another way, large financial institutions achieved the major planning and control software on their large computer systems during the last decade. Thus, for large banks, microcomputers will essentially serve as ''fine tuning'' devices. But microcomputers provide the first reasonable method for small financial institutions to achieve the management and operations improvement economies available from scientific planning and control processes. The ''quantum leap,'' so to speak, could help small financial institutions improve their efforts to control expenses and to make better product/service decisions.

[9]Ibid., pp. 68 and 71.

[10]Long, Robert H. ''Welcome Micro Technology,'' *The Southern Banker,* Volume 158 (July 1982), p. 26.

In the process, the comparative advantages of sophisticated management processes at large financial institutions will trickle down to small institutions. As a result, large financial institutions would lose one of their significant comparative advantages in unit cost control. The ability of small financial institutions to compete would be enhanced as this aspect of the divisibility theory materializes.

Will Unit Cost Parity Be Sustained in the 1980s?

Unfortunately, our research uncovered little quantitative data that address the question. Much qualitative information was found to structure a logical argument for or against continued unit cost parity. Technology, as represented in the divisibility theory, appears to provide small financial institutions with an enhanced ability to compete. The preceding discussion suggests that technology in the 1980s will trickle down to small financial institutions bringing many of the beneficial management control processes and systems once the province of large financial institutions with large computer installations.

The divisibility theory also suggests that the sourcing model for financial institutions during the 1980s will not be the in-house proprietary route so often favored by large financial institutions during the 1970s. Instead, the most cost-effective alternative appears to be the third-party, shared systems concepts practiced so effectively by small financial institutions during these years. The small financial institution's approach is also more flexible and more capital conservative, no small considerations in the volatile, unpredictable marketplace of the 1980s.

On the basis of the qualitative information we have reviewed, it appears that unit cost parity is possible for small financial institutions in the 1980s. More significantly, evidence suggests that small financial institutions could even enjoy a unit cost advantage over large institutions during the 1980s.

If the number of small financial institutions contracts during the 1980s, the contraction should not be caused by a lack of state-of-the-art technology at competitive prices for small institutions. Other causes will need to be sought if such a contraction occurs.

The Bottom Line

Future payments system technology appears unlikely to prevent small financial institutions from competing effectively during the 1980s. In fact, there are several indications that the benefits of the divisibility theory are so attractive that small institution sourcing arrangements will become the norm with many large financial institutions as well. The available quantitative evidence, albeit sparse, indicates that future payments system technology should not hinder the competitiveness of small institutions.

But any elation over this conclusion needs strong qualification. Technology will not save a financial institution—large or small—that is not well managed. Harnessing new technology is just one of the many responsibilities that management must oversee. Payments system technology is merely a tool by which an organization can achieve results in its payments activities. Without sound management, technological advances will not achieve the cost benefits potentially available to all financial institutions.

Appendix
Transaction Volumes and Unit Costs

The following discussion is excerpted from an article by David A. Walker, associate professor, Georgetown University, titled "Electronic Funds Transfer Issues and Experience: What Credit Unions Should Consider," and published in the *Journal of Credit Union Management and Economics,* Volume 2 (Spring 1982), pp. 5–6.

> Besides the absolute costs of developing EFT systems, the per unit costs are a major concern. The average cost per transaction (total costs divided by total transactions) over the long run is used to judge whether or not there are economies of scale associated with an economic activity. If average costs decline as output (transactions) increase, economies of scale exist and the marginal cost per unit (additional cost for an additional transaction) is below the average cost in this transaction range.
>
> Two economic approaches have been applied to developing cost models for financial services. One approach assumes that average costs decline, or remain constant, or increase throughout the relevant output range; and curve is selected, from among ones shaped like *AA′*, *BB′*, or *CC′*, respectively, in Figure A1. The relevant marginal cost relationships for these three cases are *aa′*, *bb′*, or *cc′*, respectively. The second, broader approach is to assume that average costs decline at low output levels (0 to Q^*) and then begin to rise beyond some higher output level ($\bar{Q}$); in this approach, instead of selecting one of the three possibilities from Figure A1, all three are presumed to represent parts of the relationship as shown in Figure A2.
>
> The empirical evidence on the average and marginal costs per EFT transaction is very meager. . . . It appears that average costs per transactions decline as cash dispenser and automated teller transactions increase (as shown in Figure 2). Lower average costs are expected to be observed until approximately 45,000 transactions per month (Q^* in Figure A2) occur at a particular retail terminal.

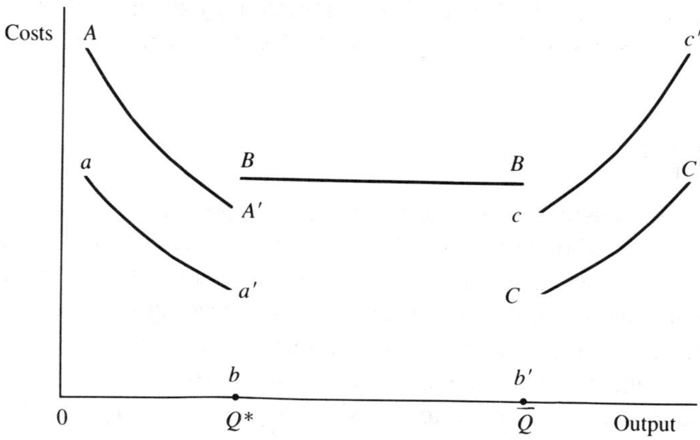

FIGURE A1

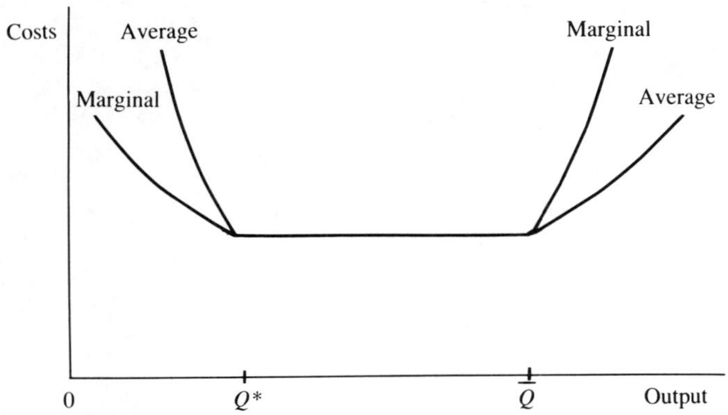

FIGURE A2

0 to Q^*	average costs may decrease as output increases *(economies of scale);*
Q^* *to* $\overline{Q}$	average costs may remain constant as output increases *(constant returns to scale);*
above $\overline{Q}$	average costs may increase as output increases *(diseconomies of scale).*

The preceding discussion shows how economies of scale can be measured in an EFT system. Walker's example pertains to a single cash dispenser or ATM. The same basic rationale applies to a payment product, overall, offered by a financial institution. More importantly, using Figure A2 in Walker's discussion, it is possible to show how the divisibility theory benefits small financial institutions.

A small financial institution quite possibly can only generate a volume of transactions in the range of 0 to less than Q^*. If so, the small institution is not operating in the portion of the cost curves that allows its unit costs to be most competitive with larger competitors. But, if several small financial institutions use a third-party source, their combined transaction volume will more than likely allow them to operate in the Q^* to 0 range of the cost curves. In this range, each of the small financial institutions will achieve unit costs that are competitive with larger institutions.

Constraints on Geographic and Product-Line Expansion by Financial Services Firms

IV

The traditional, and still most common, forms of geographic expansion by banks are branching and mergers. In some jurisdictions the only way to establish a branch is by acquiring an already operating bank. Another vehicle for geographic and product-line expansion by banks is the bank holding company. Regulation of branching, bank holding companies, and mergers places binding constraints on geographic and product-line expansion by financial services firms.

In the first reading of this section, the twelfth in this volume, E. Gerald Corrigan forcefully contends that "banks"—financial services firms that offer transactions depository services and lend the proceeds—are special. Whatever the technological, competitive, and organizational environment, Corrigan asserts that entities which provide transactions depository services and invest the funds procurred deserve special regulatory and supervisory consideration because of the traditional need to provide for the safety of the nation's payments mechanism. Corrigan's thoughtful article stands in contrast to many of the previous readings in this book which describe why and how banks are rapidly transcending this narrow conceptual role and must now be treated differently by regulators. (Fast-growing financial institutions are extending their operations into even broader geographic regions with even broader product lines.) Using his "safety first" attitude as a premise, Corrigan derives policy implications with regard to banking powers, banking markets and bank holding company subsidiaries that are in contrast with those proposed in other articles in this section.

One of the hottest topics in the area of bank geographic and product-line expansion is interstate banking. Although interstate banking is prohibited by the McFadden Act and the Douglas Amendment to the Bank Holding Company Act, banks for some time have been offering financial services on an interstate basis. They are doing so because ''grandfather'' provisions of banking legislation allow some banking firms to maintain full-service banks in more than one state. In addition, the Garn-St. Germain Act of 1982 allows banks and savings and loan associations to acquire depository institutions across state lines. The Bank Holding Company Act also permits bank holding companies to establish or acquire certain kinds of nonbank subsidiaries across state lines and to establish banking subsidiaries in states which permit such entry. Recently, more and more states have passed laws that sanction interstate banking on a regional basis.

In the thirteenth article of this volume, Robert A. Eisenbeis, one of the leading authorities on interstate banking and bank holding companies, analyzes the mounting pressure to relax geographic restrictions on banking, including the interstate competition of nonbanking enterprises. Eisenbeis' discussion can best be understood in the context of the articles on financial innovation by Greenbaum and Higgins, and Kane and Horvitz—in section II—which examine why these pressures are emerging. Eisenbeis closes his article by discussing the effect of increased interstate banking on the state of concentration and competition in banking markets. His analysis provides valuable insight into the system of regional interstate banking that is emerging in the mid-1980s.

An excellent companion piece to the preceding contribution by Eisenbeis is the fourteenth selection, by Paul M. Horvitz. While Eisenbeis clearly identifies the forces behind the interstate movement, Horvitz delves deeply into its pros and cons. He demonstrates that the effects on competition and concentration depend on whether interstate banking occurs through branching, liberalization of bank holding company restrictions, or some other means. Horvitz notes that impediments to interstate banking, such as regulatory attitudes toward mergers and acquisitions, will persist even if legal barriers are completely removed.

Next, we turn our attention to bank holding company regulation. The article by Robert Eisenbeis ranks as a seminal contribution. Eisenbeis persuasively demonstrates that the expansion of bank holding companies is an integral part of the process of financial innovation, explored with such insight by Greenbaum and Higgins, Kane and Horvitz in the second section of this volume. To avoid binding regulation and to compete effectively with unregulated competitors, banking firms have shifted traditional activities to the less regulated subsidiaries of their holding companies. This exposes the system of government deposit insurance to more risk and elicits suggestions for regulatory reform (such as those reviewed in Section VI). Eisenbeis concludes that regulatory-induced evolution of the financial system and all the attendant regulatory problems will continue unless necessary regulatory reforms take place. He proposes the treatment of banking organizations as consolidated entities for risk-assessment purposes. Eisenbeis' views are in concert with those of Greenbaum and Higgins and are complemented by the selections in section six of this volume.

The pressures for geographic and product-line expansion are often said to have rendered obsolete the traditional concepts of banking markets used by regulators. Nowhere is this obsolescence more apparent than in the regulation of banking mergers. The author of the sixteenth selection in this book, Elinor Solomon, argues with great conviction that commercial banking is no longer a separate line of commerce; she presents three likely scenarios for the evolution of financial services markets. Her article provides further insight into new types of financial services firms likely to emerge from the new deregulated environment. (Her contribution is closely related to the selections in Section II on financial innovation and can be profitably read in conjunction with those articles.) She closes by assessing issues related to the potential increases in the market power that arise from financial product deregulation.

Reading number seventeen by Robert Eisenbeis probes the consequences of the failure of regulatory agencies to redefine banking's line of commerce in a manner that is consistent with the marketplace realities so forcefully portrayed by Solomon. Eisenbeis warns that such failure might erase the gains that increased competition has generated for the public.

The pressures cited by Solomon and Eisenbeis are provoking new definitions of banking markets and new measures of banking concentration. The eighteenth selection in this volume, by Margaret Guerin-Calvert, reflects the attempt by the U. S. Department of Justice to cope with these pressures. Most significant, perhaps, is a new methodology for defining geographic and product markets and its implication for disaggregating banking services into multiple product lines. It is unlikely that the new guidelines will be the final word on this matter.

Are Banks Special?

E. Gerald Corrigan

12

Introduction

The recent evolution of the financial structure in the United States has produced two competing points of view regarding the proper direction for further change. On the one hand, there is the view that the "financial services industry"—encompassing banks, thrifts, brokers, investment banks, and insurance companies—should be looked at as a single entity. According to this view, efforts to distinguish among kinds of institutions are both futile and unnecessary. This view of the financial services industry is based on the belief that many financial services offered by various classes of institutions are so complementary to (or such close substitutes for) one another that institutional distinctions are rendered useless. Implicit in this view is the assumption that banks are not special.*

The competing, if not opposing, view is that banks are indeed special. This view holds that specialization of financial institutions has worked well and, at least in some cases, specialization may still be more efficient and also better serve the public interest. This

Reprinted from *Annual Report 1982* by permission of the Federal Reserve Bank of Minneapolis and the author.

*In this essay, the term "bank" is used in a generic way that makes no effort to distinguish commercial banks from thrifts and other depository institutions. This is done merely to simplify the discussion. However, in considering the essential functions of "banks" in light of the Depository Institutions Deregulation and Monetary Control Act of 1980 and the Garn-St Germain Depository Institutions Act of 1982, it is clear that in substance there are no longer meaningful differences. To be sure, differences in powers, in regulatory treatment, and in tax status remain, but the basic characteristics that distinguish banks from other classes of financial and nonfinancial enterprises now seem to apply to thrifts as well as to commercial banks.

view is associated with the historical separation of banking from commerce and from investment banking. In general, this "separation doctrine" in banking grew out of concerns about concentration of financial power, possible conflicts of interest, and the appropriate scope of risks banks should incur in the face of the special trusteeship falling on institutions that engage in the lending of depositors' money. In a shorthand way, as pertains to banks and the banking system, these concerns are typically captured by the phrase, "safety and soundness."

These two points of view do not necessarily represent mutually exclusive approaches to financial market structure. For example, in the context of a large financial services holding company, banks could be legally separated from nonbanks, but it is not clear that such separation would necessarily provide the kinds of protections that are currently built into federal banking laws.

Thus, assessing the merits of these two competing views must start with some very basic questions: Are banks "special" or are they simply another provider of financial services? Does it matter what kinds of risks banks incur? Does it matter who owns banks? Is "safety and soundness" a cliche, or should it have genuine and substantial meaning for banks, for bank regulators, and for the public at large?

While banking practices have naturally evolved over time, recently a combination of events has shifted that process to one of an almost revolutionary character. Amidst this process of rapid change, with market innovation and new sources of competition, there is a perception that banks' competitive position—and presumably their market share—has slipped. Casual observation of the growth of the commercial paper market, the thrift industry, money market mutual funds (MMMFs), and the de facto trend toward ownership of banks by securities firms and commercial enterprises, tends to support that perception. Indeed, there are numerous instances in which nonbanks have been able to provide "bank-like" services at a lower cost (or a higher rate of return) to the individual or corporate customer, thereby drawing business away from banking institutions.

High on the list of reasons that are cited for this perceived shift of market position from banks to nonbank competitors is the extra burden of regulation on banks. The fact of a heavy regulatory burden on banks is beyond dispute, but in some cases it is also true that regulation—relating to, for example, deposit insurance or access to the discount window—provides powerful incentives for individuals and businesses to maintain relationships with banks. While it is difficult to judge the net competitive results of differing degrees of regulation, it does seem clear that of all the regulatory burdens on banks, there have been two that stand out in terms of their impact on banks' competitive position over time: Regulation Q and limitations on the scope of bank services. This is not to suggest that other regulations on banks—ranging from reserve requirements to community reinvestment—have not been costly. But, at the cutting edge of market position or market share, it is Regulation Q and service line restrictions that have been the most critical restraints on banks.

Despite these regulatory restraints, banks have not stood still in the face of changing financial markets and new sources of competition. By using the flexibility provided by the Bank Holding Company Act, by developing sophisticated liability management techniques, by major expansions abroad, and by creative and innovative adaptations of "conventional'' banking services, banks have actually fared rather well in terms of preserving their overall market position. It is not easy to measure what has happened to the relative position of banks over time. Allowing for the inherent measurement problems in such an exercise—to say nothing of the data limitations—analysis simply does not bear out the perception noted earlier that banks have lost ground in the domestic marketplace over the past three decades. (While not captured by the data, banks have, of course, made major expansions abroad during this period.) The analysis does not, however, imply that heavy regulation has not constrained the growth of banks and their market share, for it is quite possible that absent such regulations, banks' position would have risen rather than essentially held steady. Nor does the analysis indicate whether a rising or falling bank share is good, bad, or indifferent from the perspective of the public interest. To some extent these issues depend upon whether, in fact, there is something special about banks that is worth preserving. Indeed, if banks are special, it would not be in the public interest for the features or functions that make banks special to be eroded by competitive, regulatory, or legislative forces. By the same token, if what is special about banks dictates a *relatively* heavy dose of regulation, public policymakers should not be goaded into eliminating *necessary* regulation simply because bank market share might grow to some higher level without that regulation.

What Makes Banks Special?

Reduced to essentials, it would appear that there are three characteristics that distinguish banks from all other classes of institutions—both financial and nonfinancial. They are:

1. Banks offer transaction accounts.
2. Banks are the backup source of liquidity for all other institutions.
3. Banks are the transmission belt for monetary policy.

These three essential bank characteristics and the interrelationships between them are discussed below. Of necessity, the discussion treats each factor separately. However, it is clear that these essential characteristics are highly complementary and furthermore that it is the relationship among them that best captures the essence of what makes banks special.

Issuance of Transaction Accounts

Only banks issue transaction accounts; that is, they incur liabilities payable on demand at par and are readily transferable by the owner to third parties. The owner of a transaction account can demand and receive currency in the face amount deposited in the account; write a check in the full amount of the account; or, perhaps most importantly, the owner of the account can transfer the full amount of the account to a third party almost instantaneously by wire transfer. The liquidity, mobility, and acceptability of bank issued transaction accounts permit our diverse economic and financial system to work with the relative ease and efficiency to which we are accustomed. Moreover, in periods of financial stress, the capacity to quickly move transaction account balances to third parties takes on special significance by providing elements of flexibility and certainty in making and receiving payments that help to insure that financial disruptions do not spread. Individual banks can also create these highly liquid and mobile balances through their lending function. The capacity to "create" liabilities with these characteristics is vital to the ongoing needs of commerce, but it takes on special significance in periods of financial stress.

Because of the peculiarities of law and regulation, not all classes of transaction accounts have the same precise legal or regulatory characteristics. The "demand deposit" is the purest form of transaction account, since, for example, negotiable order of withdrawal (NOW) accounts and some share drafts at mutual organizations have restrictions on the extent to which they are payable on demand. However, from the perspective of both the issuing institutions and their customers, these differences appear to be without substance since the accounts are perceived and treated as transaction accounts both by the issuing institution and by the public. For this reason, a contemporary definition of "transaction" accounts—at least for purposes of identifying and defining special characteristics of banks—should focus on functional characteristics rather than existing legal or regulatory distinctions. If a financial asset satisfies the functional test of being payable on demand at par and readily transferable to a third party, it should—for those purposes—be a "transaction" balance.

A case can be made that nonbank financial institutions incur liabilities that appear to have some or all of the characteristics of a transaction account issued by a bank. However, on close inspection it appears that such instruments—whether MMMFs, retail repurchase (RPs) agreements, customer credit balances with brokers, sweep accounts, etc.—do not, at least in a technical sense, in fact possess the characteristics associated with the bank issued transaction account. However, as is discussed later, making the distinction is particularly difficult in the case of MMMFs. In all of these cases, including money market mutual funds, instruments which appear to have bank transaction account characteristics take on those characteristics in part because the acquisition or disposition of such assets involves, at some point, the use of a transaction account at a bank. However, technology makes it possible to manage these financial assets in a way in which their ultimate dependence on a bank account is not apparent to the individual holder of the asset.

As long as banks issue transaction accounts they, by definition, incur a form of "term structure" risk. That is, the presence of transaction balances on the books of a bank makes it difficult, if not impossible, to match the maturities of assets and liabilities, particularly in a contemporary setting in which bank holdings of liquid assets have shrunk and in which some assets, traditionally considered as liquid, may not, in fact, be all that liquid. Indeed, the asset side of the balance sheet for at least some banks provides a small margin of functional liquidity that can readily be brought to bear to meet large and sudden deposit outflows. In this setting, the inherent term structure mismatch on the books of banks is one of the realities that gives rise to concerns about strains on bank liquidity and sudden drains on bank deposits.

Banks and bank regulators have long since recognized the importance of banks acting in ways that preserve public confidence in banks' capacity to meet their deposit obligations, thereby minimizing the likelihood of large, sudden drains of bank deposits. Deposit insurance and direct access to the lender of last resort are uniquely available to banks to reinforce that public confidence. Indeed, deposit insurance and access to the lender of last resort constitute a public safety net under the deposit taking function of banks. The presence of this public safety net reflects a long-standing consensus that banking functions are essential to a healthy economy. However, the presence of the public safety net—uniquely available to a particular class of institutions—also implies that those institutions have unique public responsibilities and may therefore be subject to implicit codes of conduct or explicit regulations that do not fall on other institutions.

Experience suggests rather strongly that public confidence in a bank—with or without deposit insurance and the Fed's discount window—is ultimately related to public perceptions about the financial condition of banks and specifically about the quality of banking assets, liquidity, capital, and the capacity to absorb short-run shocks. Sudden drains on bank deposits occur when depositors conclude that loan losses or other circumstances might jeopardize a bank's ability to meet its deposit obligations. The evidence is overwhelming, for example, that most "problem" bank situations in recent years involved concerns growing out of losses or perceived losses associated with lending, securities activities, foreign exchange activities, and/or poor management. In this regard, it should be noted that even when "problem" bank situations have been resolved with a minimum of costs to the individual institution, these situations have, on occasion, involved high costs in terms of generalized financial market disruption. Thus, while deposit insurance and access to the lender of last resort may rightly be viewed as the public policy safety net under banks' deposit taking function, the integrity of the deposit taking process and therefore the strength of the public safety net process depend to a substantial degree on the prudent management and control of risks on the part of the banking system as a whole.

Looked at in this perspective, the critical difference between banks and other classes of financial institutions rests with the capacity of banks to incur (and to create) liabilities that are payable on demand at par and that are readily transferable to third parties. The resulting mismatch of the maturities of assets and liabilities makes banks particularly vulnerable to sudden drains on deposits that can jeopardize their solvency. In practice, depositors—reinforced by the public policy safety net—have demonstrated tendencies to drain deposits from particular banks only when confronted with the reality or the perception of losses growing out of asset management problems and/or poor management of banking organizations. Thus, while the deposit taking function of banks is what makes them unique, the integrity of that process depends upon the risks, real and perceived, associated with the lending and related activities of the banking system as a whole and its capacity to absorb shocks in the short run.

Backup Sources of Liquidity

As discussed above, the fact that banks issue transaction deposits is the key factor that distinguishes them from other classes of financial and nonfinancial institutions. However, experience also suggests that public confidence in the ability of banks to meet their deposit obligations is ultimately related to the quality of bank assets and to the overall financial condition of the bank. This relationship takes on additional importance when it is recalled that banks can also create, through their lending activities, transaction deposits. Indeed, in a very real way, banks are the primary source of liquidity for all other classes and sizes of institutions, both financial and nonfinancial.

The extent to which banks play this role cannot be judged simply by looking at the number and value of loans on the books of banking organizations. For these purposes, contingent credit obligations of banks, such as loan commitments and standby letters of credit, must be considered in virtually the same light as direct loans. These standby credit facilities are, for example, the arrangements which permit most financial markets and institutions to function as they do. It is highly unlikely that the commerical paper market would function very well were it not for the presence of standby bank credit facilities obtained by those corporations that issue commercial paper. Similarly, it is very difficult to imagine that even the best managed and capitalized broker/dealers could handle their day-to-day business with the efficiency that is now so common without ready access to bank lines of credit. The same, of course, applies to nonfinancial corporations. Indeed, while all such institutions may, over time, have access to a wide variety of funding sources, direct or standby bank credit facilities are the cornerstone upon which these alternative sources of credit rest. If there are problems in one segment of the credit network, institutions will simply shift their borrowing activities elsewhere in the network. However, if the problem is in the banking sector, banks must either turn to each other or to the central bank.

Even in the "normal" course of events, the direct and standby credit facilities provided by banks are the foundation upon which other credit markets depend for their vitality. This relationship takes on special significance, however, in periods of selective or generalized financial stress. For example, in virtually every case of "selective" financial shock in the 1970s and early 1980s, troubled institutions—financial and nonfinancial, bank and nonbank—turned to the banking system to provide at least a bridge until more lasting solutions to the problem could be worked out. At the very least, these bridging arrangements helped to contain problems and prevent them from spreading to other institutions or to the financial system generally.

Banks' ability to supply credit and liquidity, particularly in situations where other institutions or markets may be unwilling or unable to do so, arises because the deposit creating function of banks (in tandem with banks' relationship with the central bank) provides an element of credit and liquidity elasticity which is not immediately available to other institutions. In point of fact, the extent and frequency with which banks have had to directly rely on extraordinary funding by the central bank (either through the discount window or via open market operations) have been quite limited. In the normal course and even in periods of stress, individual banks and the banking system as a whole are able to provide necessary liquidity because of their ability to quickly fund loans through a variety of market sources including the domestic and foreign interbank market, RPs, the issuance of large certificates of deposit (CDs), and so on. For many banks, access to these markets has become the primary source of bank liquidity.

Banks' access to these markets—and by extension, banks' ability to function as backup sources of liquidity—occurs in a context in which individual suppliers of such funds—whether federal funds, CDs, Eurodollars, etc.—make judgments about the strength and vitality of individual banks and the banking system as a whole. Experience is clear, for example, that individual banks experiencing problems with classified assets, earnings, and so on, often see that phenomenon first manifest itself in the form of having to pay a risk premium over the "going" rate for federal funds and large CDs. Similarly, when concerns about the banking system arose in 1974–1975 and more recently in 1982, an early manifestation was a widening of the interest rate spread between bank and treasury liabilities of comparable maturities. In the extreme cases of severe problems with individual banks, widening spreads ultimately result in these sources of funding being cut off, with a consequent need to either contract the size of the bank, borrow from the Fed's discount window or, in some cases, close or merge the bank.

The point is, of course, that the ability of a bank to fulfill its role as a backup supplier of liquidity to the financial and business communities depends on easy access not only to traditional sources of deposit liabilities, but also to markets for nondeposit sources of funding. The same applies to the banking system as a whole, because while one or a few banks can turn to the London market to fund themselves in times of adversity, it is clear that the banking system as a whole cannot. Thus, as with the preservation of the integrity of the deposit taking function described earlier, experience clearly suggests that the ability of banks to provide the essential function of a backup source of liquidity is ultimately dependent on market judgments as to the quality of the banks' assets and overall financial strength.

Looked at in this light, the ability of banks to fulfill their role as standby sources of liquidity and credit rests importantly on the quality and consistency of credit judgments made by banks. This is particularly true in periods of stress when banks may be called on to supply credit to borrowers who, for one reason or another, temporarily do not have access to other sources of funds or to make the even more difficult decisions as to which borrowers are experiencing problems of a fundamental or irreparable nature. It is in these particular circumstances that banks must be in a position to make rigorous, impartial, and objective credit decisions, because it is precisely in such circumstances that the potential for compromise in the impartiality of the credit decision making process is greatest and the potential for asset quality deterioration is the largest. It is in this light that considerations about the commingling of banking and other interests and concerns about the ownership and control of banks become compelling.

To summarize, virtually all other financial markets and other classes of institutions are directly or indirectly dependent on the banking system as their standby or backup source of credit and liquidity. Banks can fulfill this function for a variety of reasons, including their relative ease of access to deposit and nondeposit sources of funding. However, experience suggests that the capacity to provide this function or, more directly, to provide access to these markets and sources of funding—like the integrity of the deposit taking function—is ultimately related to the overall financial strength of banks and the quality of bank assets. This role of banks as a standby source of liquidity takes on special significance in periods of stress and in this light underscores the importance of rigorous and impartial credit judgments by banks. This, in turn, provides a particularly relevant context in which concerns about the commingling of banking and other interests should be evaluated.

Transmission Belt for Monetary Policy

As the preceding discussion suggests, there is a direct link between banks and the central bank arising in part from the central bank's lender of last resort function. More broadly, the fact that banks are subject to reserve requirements places the banking system in the unique position of being the "transmission belt" through which the actions and policies of the central bank have their effect on financial market conditions, money and credit creation, and economic conditions generally. To put it somewhat differently, the required reserves of the banking system have often been described as the fulcrum upon which the monetary authority operates monetary policy: The reserves in the banking system also serve the complementary purpose of providing the working balances which permit our highly efficient financial markets to function and to effect the orderly end-of-day settlement of the hundreds of billions of dollars of transactions that occur over the course of each business day.

Some have argued that neither monetary policy nor the payments mechanism are dependent on the relationship between reserves and the banking system. There have been, or are, schemes for conducting monetary policy and operating a payments mechanism that do not use bank reserves and the banking system in the way the U.S. system currently operates. However, it is also true that any of these alternative arrangements would entail major institutional changes and run the risk that they might not work as efficiently as the current framework or the possibility that they might not work at all. In short, to justify departure from the current arrangement the weight of evidence should be overwhelming that the current system is not working or that some alternative system would work decidedly better.

In fact, the current system seems to work rather well, although recent developments may have introduced elements of slack into the transmission belt. For example, the proliferation of close substitutes for bank-issued transaction accounts narrows the effective scope of reserve coverage. The narrowed reserve coverage can introduce more slippage into the process of monetary control, and it also means that a relatively smaller reserve base is supporting a larger flow of payments. Similarly, the deregulation of the liability side of banks' balance sheets seems to imply that, in order to achieve a given degree of monetary restraint, a higher level of market interest rates is required than might otherwise have been the case. Further, increased leverage of banking organizations may work in the direction of introducing slippage into the monetary control process, in that a larger volume of credit flows may be associated with some given rate of growth of "money." Finally, higher leverage and greater risk exposure may weaken the capacity of the banking system to adjust to and to absorb the changes in credit market conditions that must accompany periodic monetary restraint.

As suggested above, these and other forces may already be working to introduce a larger margin of slack into the transmission belt. While the slack evident today is of manageable proportions, the future design of the banking and financial system must leave intact a strong yet adaptable mechanism through which monetary policy and the payments mechanism can function. This imperative underscores the case for attempting to segregate essential banking functions into an identifiable class of institutions and seeking to ensure that these institutions have the financial strength and vitality to perform their essential functions and to absorb changes in the credit market and economic conditions associated with periods of monetary restraint.

Defining a Bank

From the previous discussion, it should be clear that there are in fact certain special and unique functions of banks and that they are essential to the functioning of an efficient and safe financial and economic system. However, it also seems likely that if "banks" did not provide these essential functions, someone else would—just as it is abundantly clear that the process of market innovation has already produced services which are close substitutes for essential bank services. Given these considerations, the threshold question that arises is whether it is still desirable, from a public interest point of view, to attempt to segregate essential banking functions into an identifiable class of institutions and, if that is the case, whether it is possible to define a bank in a manner that is both functionally and intellectually satisfactory.

Putting aside for the moment practical problems of definition, it would seem that the case for segregating *essential* banking functions into an identifiable class of institutions is every bit as powerful today as it was in the 1930s. If anything, concerns regarding financial concentration, conflicts of interest, and the fiduciary responsibilities associated with lending depositors' money may be more relevant today than they were 50 years ago. To be sure, the lines of distinction may not have to be drawn in the same way and in the same place that they were in the past, but the earlier discussion of the essential functions of banks serves as a powerful argument for separation at some point. Indeed, to reject the notion of separation would—as a matter of logic—require that deposit insurance and access to the lender of last resort, together with the associated supervisory and regulatory apparatus, either be done away with altogether or be made universally available to any institution that provides essential banking functions—irregardless of what other types of business or commerce it might be engaged in. However, as a practical matter, the case for separation is only viable if we are able to provide a satisfactory definition of a bank.

Over time, a variety of tests have been used for the purpose of defining a bank. These tests ranged from a charter test to the functional test of issuing demand deposits *and* making commercial loans. At one time, each of these tests was satisfactory. However, currently neither existing statutes nor regulations seem to contain a definition that is satisfactory.

A satisfactory definition of a bank must start with a clear recognition of the essential functions provided by such institutions. From the earlier discussion, it is clear that *the* single characteristic of banks that distinguishes them from other classes of institutions is that they issue transaction accounts; that is, accounts that in law, in regulation, or in practice are payable on demand at par and are readily transferable to third parties. A powerful case can be made that the definition of a bank should stop right there: a bank is any organization that is *eligible* to issue transaction accounts. If an institution meets this test, it would (1) be eligible for government deposit insurance; (2) have direct access to the discount window; (3) be subject to the Fed's reserve requirements; and (4) have direct access to the Federal Reserve's payments services, particularly the wire transfer system. For these purposes, an appropriate statute would have to redefine transaction accounts. At a minimum, such a definition would have to include conventional demand deposits, NOW accounts, and share drafts. It might also include the new money market deposit accounts (MMDAs) and, depending on the standards of definition, perhaps even MMMFs or other nonbank institutional arrangements that provide ''check'' writing capabilities.

On the surface, this definition of a bank may seem inadequate because it contains no corollary asset or lending test; it focuses only on the liability side of the balance sheet. This seeming inadequacy arises in part because the current Bank Holding Company Act's definition requires that a bank issue demand deposits *and* make commercial loans. More substantially, the absence of a lending test seems to fly in the face of arguments made earlier concerning the critical link between the deposit taking function and the lending or asset acquisition functions of banks. However, it is precisely because of the nature of the relationship between deposit taking and asset acquisition that the essential definition of a bank should be couched in terms of its deposit taking function—without regard for the particular distribution or classification of its loans and/or investments. Taken by itself, there is nothing unique or special about the asset side of a bank's balance sheet, except for the limits on the scope of asset acquisition powers discussed below. Concerns about the nature and risk characteristics of bank assets arise in the context of the unique nature of bank liabilities, the need to preserve the integrity of the deposit taking function, and the special trusteeship growing out of that function. Thus, while it may be appropriate from the standpoint of public policy to limit the asset powers of banks to certain less risky activities, the definition of a bank need only deal with the liability side of the balance sheet.

The absence of an asset test might, however, create a definitional loophole. That is, ''banks'' could conceivably refrain from issuing transaction deposits while funding their asset acquisition activities with insured time and savings deposits. However, this problem could be minimized by reliance on such an institution's *eligibility* to issue transaction accounts. If so eligible, it would be defined and regulated as a bank even though, in practice, it refrained from issuing transaction accounts. An institution that was not eligible to issue transaction accounts would not be a bank and would not be eligible for deposit insurance, access to the Fed, and so on.

By this definition, existing commercial banks, thrifts, and credit unions would be considered ''banks.'' Similarly most of the ''nonbank'' banks formed in recent years under the Bank Holding Company Act (by not engaging in commercial lending) would be banks, as would, depending on state laws, some "industrial" banks. Treating thrifts and certain other institutions as "banks" raises a host of difficult and politically charged issues relating to regulatory treatment, tax status, divestiture, and grandfathering arrangements. However, for purposes of this discussion, the fact that certain "nonbank" financial institutions are, for a variety of reasons, banks does not require immediate or perhaps even parallel regulation. Rather, the suggestion would be that there is an essential core of regulation that should apply more or less equally to this broader class of institutions which provides essential banking functions.

The issue of whether money market mutual funds fit the definition of a bank—even at a conceptual level—is not so easy to deal with. Many such funds certainly appear to have all the characteristics of bank transaction accounts. In the case of the money market mutual fund, the critical distinction relative to a bank transaction account appears to be the extent to which the liabilities in question are payable at par. In the case of a bank deposit, deposit insurance, the capital of the bank, and the bank's access to alternative sources of short-run funding provide assurances that a depositor can withdraw dollar-for-dollar from the bank the principal amount deposited—even when changes in interest rates may have reduced the market value of bank assets.

In the case of the money market mutual fund the ability to pay out dollar-for-dollar the amount of the initial "deposit" is less certain. The fund itself does not have capital as such, and in the short-run it cannot easily tap alternative sources of liquidity to pay out to some shareholders thereby buying time for assets to mature or for interest rates to reverse course. As a related matter, the fund is not insured so that even though the risk of loss to the individual shareholder is small, it does exist. The fact that in recent months a number of money market mutual funds have taken steps in the direction of securing some form of private insurance would suggest that some fund managers perceive that there is an important distinction to be drawn between the fund shares and bank deposits. The irony of this, of course, is that to the extent funds obtain insurance, they come even closer to possessing bank-like characteristics.

From a competitive viewpoint, the question of whether a money market mutual fund is a bank is far less important today than it was before the introduction of MMDAs at banks. Indeed, if being a "bank" is equated with deposit insurance, access to the Fed's discount window, and payments services—the costs of reserve requirements notwithstanding—some money funds might not object at all to being called a bank in the current market setting. Moreover, if the power of banks or bank holding companies was expanded to permit such institutions to offer mutual funds, the question, from a competitive point of view, would be even less pressing.

However, in terms of intellectual consistency, the question of whether money market mutual funds (or similar arrangements which permit "check" writing) should fall within the definition of a bank does not disappear simply because current competitive conditions render the issue less compelling. On technical grounds, it would seem that the distinction arising from the payment at par principle could justify treating money funds as nonbanks. On functional grounds, however, and particularly from the perspective of the shareholder, the check writing features of some funds simply may create too much of a "look alike" situation to make a meaningful distinction on the technical grounds of payment at par. It may therefore be necessary to place certain restrictions—such as limits on the number of third-party transfers (as with bank-issued MMDAs) and/or reserve requirements—on "nonbank" financial instruments or institutions that provide check writing features. Of course, if MMDAs were defined as transaction accounts, then the case for treating MMMFs as banks would become powerful.

Bank Powers and Structure

If a bank can be satisfactorily defined along the lines suggested above, there are three related questions which must be answered in order to sketch out a reasonable approach to the future scope and structure of banking activities and banks. They are: (1) What kinds of subsidiary powers should banks have? (2) What restraints, if any, should be placed on the ownership or control of banks? (3) Is it important, from a public policy perspective, whether the subsidiary activities of banks are performed in the bank, a subsidiary of the bank, or in a subsidiary of a bank holding company?

The answers to each of these questions must be guided by the earlier discussion of what it is that makes banks special and the relationship between the integrity of the deposit taking function, the financial strength of the bank, and ultimately the strength of the financial system. That discussion implied that in thinking about asset powers, ownership, and the organizational structure of banks, substantial weight needed to be given to safety and soundness considerations, the special trusteeship of banks and the objectivity and impartiality of the credit decision making process. This is not to suggest that other factors such as concentration and public convenience and need are not important from the perspective of public policy. Indeed, these things may be very important, but their importance—in the context of questions relating to banking powers, ownership, and structure—is secondary to the safety and soundness factors.

Having said that, a case can be made that whatever weight safety and soundness and related criteria have been given in the past, these factors should be given less weight in the future. Better information and management systems, more efficient markets, greater disclosure, improved supervision, and the presence of the public safety net, all seem to work in the direction of reducing public policy concerns about the safety and soundness of banks.

However, there are strong forces working in the opposite direction. Financial affairs generally are much more complex and more interdependent than they once were. One consequence of this is that when problems arise they are more difficult to isolate and contain than in the past. Perhaps more importantly, the combination of liability management techniques and deregulation has significantly altered the overall liability structure of banks. Stable and low cost core deposits are virtually a thing of the past. These developments have, in combination with more sophisticated and interest-rate conscious corporate treasurers and individuals, increased the term structure risk at banks and made banks more susceptible to sudden deposit shifts. At the same time, "spread management"—whereby banks attempt to float the rate of return on assets in some reasonably fixed relationship to changes in the cost of funds—may, subtly but insidiously, be working to undermine the traditional disciplines of both borrowers and lenders. Finally, the far-flung international activities of banks have introduced new elements of risk into the equation. While it is a matter of judgment as to whether this crosscurrent of events is working to reduce or to increase the risks associated with the activities of banks, it does seem prudent to conclude that they are working in the direction of creating greater risks.

Bank Subsidiary Powers

As suggested earlier, to preserve and protect the *essential* functions of banks, banks must be competitively viable institutions. This means, among other things, that banks must be able to offer a sufficiently wide and competitive range of services to maintain profitability, attract capital, and preserve a de facto monopoly on the transaction account business. Without delving into the specific types of powers banks should have, the preceding discussion is suggestive of the general criteria which should be used in making judgments about the scope of banking powers. While a number of factors may be relevant in this regard, the essential functions of banks as described earlier suggest the primacy of two general criteria. They are: subsidiary banking activities should not entail excessive risk of loss *and* should not impair the impartiality of the credit decision making process. This dual criteria, while conceptually useful, is operationally ambiguous. To some extent, it becomes more clear in a context in which secondary criteria relating to competition/concentration considerations are introduced. Similarly, as a practical matter, defining the extent of appropriate subsidiary banking powers can be guided by policies governing bank ownership. That is, logic would seem to dictate that a particular set of powers be vested in banks only to the extent that there is a willingness to permit another institution engaging in those activities to own and/or control banks. For example, if we are willing to permit banks to engage in commerce generally (that is, the acquisition, manufacture, or distribution of goods and nonfinancial services), then we should be prepared to say that firms engaged in such business, whether oil companies or shoe stores, can own and control banks. The converse also should follow: if we are unwilling to permit banks to engage in such activities, then logic would seem to dictate that such commercial firms should not own banks. The symmetry of this argument is important, for it lends weight to the apparent consensus that the separation of banking from commerce generally is appropriate and should be maintained in both directions.

However, even in the realm of so-called financial services, the risk/impartiality criteria do not provide unambiguous insights as to how far banking powers should be extended. For example, if there is a consensus that the risk/impartiality test should not preclude banking organizations from engaging in the sale and distribution of mutual funds shares or in the distribution and brokerage of securities, it is by no means clear that such a consensus would extend to activities relating to the underwriting of stocks and corporate bonds generally or to taking positions in commodities. The point is, of course, that while it is a fairly easy matter to conclude that a continued separation of banking and commerce makes sense, it is not nearly so easy to conclude—as a matter of public policy—that the full range of financial services should be fair game for banking organizations. At the very least, the risk/impartiality criteria suggested above and the bank ownership/control questions discussed below suggest that we should not be indifferent to the scope of financial services offered by banking organizations.

Bank Ownership

If there is some agreement (1) that the segregation of essential banking functions into identifiable classes of institutions makes sense; (2) on the definition of a "bank"; and (3) on the appropriate scope of powers to be housed within banking organizations, then dealing with the question of bank ownership becomes fairly easy. That is, nonbanking organizations would be permitted to own banks only insofar as the activities of such entities match the activities in which banking organizations would otherwise be permitted to engage. For example, a securities firm whose activities did not go beyond the activities directly permissible to banks and bank holding companies could own a bank, but in the process that organization would become a bank holding company. On the other hand, financial or nonfinancial firms could not own a bank unless they were willing to divest those activities which fall outside the list of permissible activities for banks and bank holding companies. Thus, depending on the determination of the scope of banking powers—which, as noted earlier, should be undertaken primarily within the context of the risk/impartiality criteria—this approach would require that a number of existing situations involving the ownership of "banks" by financial and nonfinancial firms would have to be grandfathered or, perhaps in some cases, divestiture arrangements would have to be worked out over a period of time.

Banking Structure

Finally, in this context, questions will inevitably arise as to whether it matters, from the perspective of public policy, if particular subsidiary activities of banks are carried out in the bank, in a subsidiary of the bank, or in a subsidiary of the bank's holding company. Given the earlier discussion about the importance of segregating essential banking activities and the importance of the risk/impartiality criteria for purposes of evaluating the appropriate scope of banking activities, it would seem to follow that there is a powerful case for placing some subsidiary activities of banking organizations into affiliates of bank holding companies. This case is reinforced by the protections against self-dealing, which are made possible by certain provisions of the Bank Holding Company Act and by the de facto segregation of capital that is made possible by the holding company structure.

However, it does not follow from the above that we can be indifferent as to the degree of risk associated with such activities simply because they may be housed in a separately organized and separately capitalized subsidiary of a bank holding company. To the contrary, experience suggests rather clearly that in times of peril it may not be possible to insulate the bank from the problems of its sister organizations—even when such problems arise in affiliated organizations, including subsidiaries of bank holding companies. While there are good and sufficient public policy reasons for concluding that at least some "nonbank" activities of banking organizations should be housed in subsidiaries of bank holding companies, such organizational arrangements are not likely to produce a situation in which the bank is immune from the problems, risks, or losses that might develop in such subsidiaries. In short, the holding company structure is neither a substitute for prudent management nor a fail-safe device for containing risk.

In Conclusion

This essay started out with a seemingly straightforward question: Are banks special? Having answered that question in the affirmative, it does seem appropriate that the current debate about the powers and structure of banks be framed in a context that gives greater weight to the underlying issues of what banks are, and what, from the perspective of public policy, we want them to be. Looked at in that light, and with a firmer grasp on what it is that makes banks special, it becomes somewhat easier to grapple with the very difficult questions relating to the definition of a bank, the scope of banking powers, the ownership and control of banks, and the structure of banking organizations. This approach—entailing as it does an element of going back to square one—can help to ensure that bankers, regulators, and legislators approach successive steps in the reshaping of our financial system in a manner which helps to preserve the unique functions and characteristics of banks while at the same time encouraging those elements of competition and innovation that will permit the banking system and the financial system more generally to safely and efficiently meet the needs of a growing and stable domestic and international economy.

ECONOMIC AND POLICY ISSUES SURROUNDING REGIONAL AND NATIONAL APPROACHES TO INTERSTATE BANKING

Robert A. Eisenbeis

13

Introduction

Over the past decade, market pressures have precipitated significant changes in the structure and regulation of the financial service industry. Financial innovations such as NOW accounts and money market mutual funds (MMMFs) were critical factors in passage of the Monetary Control Act of 1980 and the Garn-St. Germain Act of 1982 which mandated the elimination of deposit rate ceilings and broadened the asset and liability powers of thrift institutions. Similar financial innovations and the resulting market pressures that flow from successful innovation are causing bankers, legislators, and regulators to reassess the feasibility of retaining existing McFadden Act and Douglas Amendment restrictions on interstate banking.

This article briefly details these market trends and discusses why market forces are generating changes by individual states in their prohibitions on interstate banking and bank holding company operations. It then describes recent state efforts to promote regional approaches to interstate banking. Finally, it evaluates some of the key policy issues and implications of the alternative ways that have been suggested to relax interstate banking prohibitions.

Reprinted from a report prepared for the New York State Bankers Association, Febuary 4, 1984 (revised May 1984), by permission of the author and the New York State Bankers Association.

Innovations to Avoid Interstate Banking Restrictions

In spite of the 1927 McFadden Act limitations on interstate branching, banking organizations have been very successful during the late 1960s and early 1970s in innovating ways to establish physical presences across state lines.[1] Table 1 shows that there are over 7,800 offices of out-of-state banking organizations already in place. Banks have employed loan production offices, Edge Act Corporations, corporate calling officers, and EFT facilities to expand interstate.[2] Larger banks have adopted the bank holding company form of organization to facilitate the operation of nonbanking subsidiaries, such as consumer finance companies, industrial banks, mortgage banking firms and trust companies throughout the country.

Similarly, many key classes of customers have found it profitable and attractive to incur the costs and inconvenience to deal with nonlocally based suppliers of financial services. Large corporate customers have long operated in the national and international markets, and the establishment of a relationship with a nonlocal financial institution also has meant that all or a portion of both loan and deposit balances flowed into the national market.

To a significant extent, then, the prohibitions on intra- and interstate banking have become progressively eroded by financial innovations. But it is also significant that, except for the largest customers, most of these innovations have affected lending activities. The principal area that has remained less affected by these developments has been the retail deposit market.

Recently, however, significant developments have taken place that are breaking down the insulation of retail deposit markets. For example, the Monetary Control Act of 1980 and the Garn-St. Germain Act of 1982 broadened the range of asset and liability powers of thrifts to enable them potentially to become full competitors with commercial banks for the retail consumer business. Increasingly, S&Ls have been permitted to expand nationwide as troubled S&Ls have been merged to form interstate networks, and it is likely that the Federal Home Loan Bank Board may permit unrestricted interstate expansion.[3] In addition, numerous unregulated suppliers have sprung up offering close substitute services for those offered by commercial banks on an interstate basis. Lastly, the growth of money market mutual funds, perhaps more than any other innovation, has served to move previously locally limited consumers into the national market.

[1]See for example, Eisenbeis (1980), Whitehead (1983), Kane (1981) Department of the Treasury (1981), Peter Merrill Associates (1981) and Golembe Associates (1979).

[2]There are now over 100 shared and proprietary EFT systems that allow a customer to obtain cash by drawing down funds in an account across state lines. In addition, several bank and nonbank sponsored EFT systems now enable consumers to shop and arrange for a mortgage on a nationwide basis without even entering a depository institution (see LaGesse [1984]).

[3]No change in federal law would be required.

Table 1 Summary of Interstate Activity

Location	Grandfathered								
	Domestic			Foreign*			Foreign Banks		
	Holding* Companies[A]	Banks	Branches	Holding* Companies[A]	Banks	Branches	Agency	Edge	Branch
Alabama									
Alaska									
Arizona	1	1	161						
Arkansas									
California				8	8	148	63	2	2
Colorado	1	3	7						
Connecticut									
Delaware	12	12	40						
District of Columbia									1
Florida	2	2	188				22	6	
Georgia							10		
Hawaii				1	1	15	2		
Idaho	2	2	107						
Illinois	1	3	4	1	1	1		3	36
Indiana									
Iowa	1	11	50						
Kansas									
Kentucky									
Louisiana							1		
Maine									
Maryland	1	2	30						
Massachusetts									4
Michigan									
Minnesota									
Mississippi									
Missouri									
Montana	3	25	48						
Nebraska	1	5	39						
Nevada	1	1	66						
New Hampshire									
New Jersey									
New Mexico	1	5	35						
New York	1	2	27	3	3	39	18	2	37
North Carolina									
North Dakota	3	34	110						
Ohio									
Oklahoma									
Oregon	1	1	169						
Pennsylvania									7
Rhode Island									6
South Carolina									
South Dakota	3	12	80						
Tennessee	2	2	27						
Texas								9	
Utah	1	1	35						
Vermont									
Virginia	1	6	63						
Washington	1	1	85						10
West Virginia									
Wisconsin	3	6	22						
Wyoming	2	4	4						
TOTALS	45	141	1,397	13	13	203	116	22	103

○ • These states allow entry of limited purpose banks

□ • These states allow expansion of interstate grandfathered banks

Table 1 Summary of Interstate Activity

States* With Reciprocal Agreement	Preferred* Stock Deals Filed With Board	Interstate* S&Ls	Offices of 4(c) 8 Subs	Loan Production Offices	Edge Act Corporations	Total Offices per State
	1	1	107	1		108
√			4	1		5
			159			321
			3			3
		2	521	22	23	787
		1	158	14		182
	1		64	1		65
○			27	3	5	87
		2	2	3		6
□	1	7	372	6	25	621
	1	2	253	8	5	276
		2	39			57
		1	47			156
□		1	132	21	11	212
			99	1		100
□	1		42	2		105
		1	78			78
		1	61			61
			164	4	1	170
√	1		1			1
		2	82	7		121
√	2	1	68	6	3	81
			58	2		58
	1		34	5	4	43
			89			89
		1	75	6	2	83
		2	28	1		102
			28	2		74
		1	21			88
			20	1		21
			110	2		112
			44			84
√	4	3	156	16	31	331
			367	3		370
			23	1		168
	2		310	8	4	322
	1		76	3		79
		4	83	7	3	270
	2		320	7	2	335
			13			13
	1		229			229
○			16			108
			159	14		202
	1	5	289	19	17	334
√		1	37	1		74
			4			4
		1	227	1		297
		2	114	3	6	219
			40			40
			39		1	68
		1	10			18
10	20	45	5,500	202	143	7,840

* • These columns are not included in total number of offices

A • Six of the foreign bank holding companies own only one bank, but the bank is located outside the home state of the foreign banking organization

Interstate Expansion by Nonbank Competitors

In the early 1980s the combination of extremely high interest rates and binding deposit rate ceilings stimulated the entry of unregulated institutions into the financial service industry. These firms have developed innovative ways both to take retail deposits across local markets and on an interstate basis and to offer a wide range of financial, investment, and insurance services not available to commercial banks.

The principal innovation that evolved to collect consumer deposits on an interstate basis was the money market mutual fund. At the time of the Garn-St. Germain Depository Institutions Act of 1982, noninstitutional deposits in these funds approached $183 billion or about 15% of bank and thrift small time and savings deposits.[4] The real importance of money market mutual funds, however, is that they served to break down the dependence of previously locally limited customers on local depository institutions for financial services. The rapid growth of these funds during the early '80s indicates that when the opportunity costs to consumers resulting from regulatory constraints, such as deposit rate ceilings, are sufficiently high (1) to overcome the inconvenience and search costs associated with seeking higher rate alternatives, (2) to breakdown the resistance to dealing with nonlocal institutions, and (3) to compensate for holding a greater portion of their financial assets in the form of uninsured liabilities, consumers will shift their funds into alternative investment instruments. Confirmation of this fact is the return of consumer funds to banks and thrifts following the offering of the MMDA and Super-NOW accounts authorized by the Garn-St. Germain Act and the inflow of funds into banks and thrifts as the phase-out of deposit rate ceilings has been nearly completed. In the lower rate environment of 1983 and 1984, these flow reversals have resulted because the combination of convenience and deposit insurance were sufficient to overcome the relative rate advantage of the money funds. One should not conclude that these flow reversals are permanent should depository institutions find themselves unable to pay market rates again in the future.

As distinct from the supply and delivery oriented methods banks have developed to avoid restrictions on interstate banking, the growth of money market mutual funds has affected the structure of both the demand and supply of deposit funds. Clearly, these funds increased the number of alternative suppliers of deposit-type services offering near-money market rates. In addition, their growth and customer acceptance signaled fundamental changes in the nature of the demand for deposit and other financial services. Once customers are no longer dependent on local sources of supply for deposit service, the geographic market ceases to be local; and in this case it has become an interstate market with price and terms determined by broader market forces. Under these circumstances, any benefits that might have accrued previously to in-state banks from prohibitions on intra-or interstate banking—by protecting local deposit markets from actual entry or the threat of entry by out-of-state banks—are completely dissipated.

[4]Even the subsequent authorization of the $2,500 minimum deposit Super-NOW account and the MMDA account, which were both free of interest rate ceilings, did not reduce the importance of money market mutual funds. To be sure, the phenomenal growth of these two new accounts suggests that, *ceteris paribus,* consumers prefer insured to uninsured accounts. However, it was estimated that only $10 billion of this initial growth came from money market mutual funds.

Four other recent interrelated financial innovations have served to bring existing interstate banking restrictions into question by increasing the competitive presence of nonlocal suppliers in consumer markets. The first is the joining together of independent firms to provide services that the participants could not legally or economically provide individually.[5] The classic example is the Merrill Lynch Cash Management Account. It combines a margin account at a brokerage firm, a captive money market mutual fund, a Visa debit card, and a servicing arrangement through BankOne of Ohio. Variants and refinements of this service are being offered by numerous other brokerage firms. Not only do these services capitalize on the fact that consumers have learned that they can obtain financial services from nonlocal and nontraditional firms, but also some of these firms have extensive interstate presences which are being developed into additional consumer service centers.

The second of the four financial innovations was the creation of the broker-bankers. Recent combinations of American Express-Shearson, Bache-Prudential and Sears-Dean Witter-Coldwell Banker, just to name a few, have resulted in a whole new class of financial service firms.[6,7] These firms are internalizing certain symbiotic financial arrangements to take advantage of potential synergistic or scope economies. The broker-bankers are also positioning themselves to offer a wide range of consumer and corporate financial, brokerage, and insurance services.[8] Thus the potential competitive threat of these broker-bankers and other unregulated competitors spreads far beyond their immediate activities with money market mutual funds and cash management accounts.

The third recent financial innovation that heightens the interstate competitive threat to commercial banks has been the recent wave of acquisitions of nonbank banks. Brokerage firms, insurance companies, retailers, money market funds, and financial conglomerates have discovered that they can diversify into either the commercial banking or consumer banking business outside the present scope and jurisdiction of the Bank Holding Company Act by acquiring insured commercial banks and divesting either the demand deposit or commercial loan business. Such an entity—although federally insured and regulated as a commercial bank—does not meet the technical legal definition of a bank for purposes of the Bank Holding Company Act. Therefore, it may be acquired by any nonbanking or nonfinancial firm without subjecting the acquiring firm to the restrictions of the Bank Holding Company Act or to regulation or supervision by the Federal Reserve.[9,10] Because of the potential for linking brokerage, commercial, and industrial activities with interstate deposit taking, the expansion of nonbank bank acquisitions should be perceived as a real competitive concern to banks under the present regulatory system.

[5]See Eisenbeis (1981a, 1981b).

[6]For a detailed listing of such combinations see Rosenblum and Siegel (1982) or Rosenblum and Pavel (1983).

[7]Sears has most recently announced its intention to use its Sears World Trade, Inc., subsidiary to market financial services worldwide.

[8]See Murphy and Brunner (1981).

[9]Acquisition of more than 10% of such a bank's stock must still be approved by the appropriate federal bank regulator under the Change in Bank Control Act. To date, such approvals have been given by all three federal regulators. Recent changes in the Federal Reserve's Regulation Y broadening the definition of a bank may reduce, somewhat, nonbank bank expansion (see *Banking Expansion Reporter* [1984]).

[10]Of course such banks would still be prohibited from branching interstate, but interstate companies could be created. Fleet Financial, for example, has proposed to expand into Massachusetts.

The fourth innovation has been the recent expansion of activity by money brokers. Brokerage firms and other institutions are brokering insured deposits for customers, both individual and corporate, and placing them in federally insured accounts across the country. Because of federal insurance, risk is irrelevant to the depositor and so funds flow to the highest bidder.[11] The effect is to create a national market for insured deposits.

Summary of Innovations to Avoid Interstate Banking Prohibitions

Several important observations arise from this brief analysis of recent financial innovations to avoid branching constraints. First, banks, thrifts, and nondepository institutions have evolved numerous ways to supply bank-type services across state boundaries to nearly all classes of customers. Second, the unexploited potential of the broker-bankers, the nonbank banks, and other similar institutions suggest that further expansion of nontraditional suppliers into the banking business is extremely likely and raises important regulatory and competitive equity issues. Third, the growth of money market mutual funds, cash management type accounts, and money brokers indicates that, like the large corporate customers, significant groups of consumers are no longer limited to local markets for many of their financial services.

The logical conclusion which follows from these developments is that the main parties now likely to be adversely affected by the existing restrictions on geographic expansion are commercial banks which are increasingly being forced to compete with nonbank and thrift institutions not subject to similar restrictions on the geographic scope of their operations. Existing inter- and intrastate banking prohibitions are no longer protecting local banks from outside competition as they once did. Instead, they are preventing banks from following their customers or attracting new customers over the same geographic range as their competitors except by resorting to less efficient and more costly methods. In fact, the recent success of the Securities Industry Association in the U.S. District Court of Washington in applying McFadden Act restrictions to the operation of offices of national bank discount brokerage subsidiaries across state lines suggests the very real possibility that similar restrictions might be applied to operations of other bank subsidiaries as well.

It may be concluded that interstate banking prohibitions are no longer limiting nationwide flows of funds or significantly reducing competition in local markets to the extent that they once did, and that they are harming those very banks the restrictions were once designed to protect.

Changing State Attitudes

Competitive pressures and obvious inequities are beginning to force the realization that it may no longer be in the long-run best interests of banks or their shareholders, or of the

[11]Both the Federal Home Loan Bank Board and FDIC have proposed limiting federal deposit insurance coverage on brokered funds so as to discourage the activity and to limit the agencies' risk exposure, but no final action has yet been taken (see McCue [1984]).

states in which these institutions are located, to maintain the status quo with respect to branching policy. A few states have liberalized recently their policies toward intrastate expansion.[12] This includes Illinois, Florida, Oklahoma, and Arkansas; more important, 19 states have also enacted legislation allowing out-of-state banking organizations to enter.[13] These 19 states may be divided roughly into three categories based upon the type of outside entry permitted.

South Dakota, Delaware, Virginia, Maryland, Nevada and Nebraska allow the acquisition of only single office, limited-purpose banks by out-of-state bank holding companies.[14] In each state, however, minimum initial capital requirements are specified. These limited-purpose banks also must employ a minimum number of employees. There are additional restrictions to prevent these institutions from conducting a general purpose banking business, thereby posing a competitive threat to indigeneous banks. Several of these states (especially, Delaware and South Dakota) are attractive for entry by outside bank holding companies because of favorable usury ceilings and accommodating tax laws. As a result, banking organizations, such as those in New York and Pennsylvania, have relocated their credit card and certain other activities. In addition, part of the motivation for attracting outside entry was rooted in attempts to promote local economic development and employment.[15]

The second group, consisting of Washington and Oregon, represents an attempt to facilitate the takeover of institutions which were in financial distress. This legislation cannot be interpreted as a change in state policy toward interstate banking; rather, it was an attempt to avoid the costs—both explicit and implicit—of bank failure.[16]

The remaining ten states, Kentucky, Georgia, Maine, New York, Massachusetts, Rhode Island, Connecticut, Florida, South Carolina and Alaska, place no restrictions on the kinds of banking business that may be conducted. But each does restrict either the types of entry and/or the locations of those companies seeking to enter. For example, Alaska prohibits the acquisition of *de novo* banks and requires that entry be accomplished by acquisition of banks that have been in existence for at least three years. The Alaska law, however, does not mandate reciprocal entry legislation on the part of the entering holding

[12]The Douglas Amendment to the Bank Holding Company Act of 1956 prohibits interstate acquisitions of banks unless the acquired bank's state explicitly has enacted legislation permitting such acquisitions.

[13]Iowa, Illinois, Nebraska and Florida are often included as states that permit out-of-state banking organizations to acquire instate banks. But in each instance, the applicable statute merely grandfathered existing out-of-state operations. Only one bank holding company in Iowa and Illinois and only three (one Canadian) in Florida are affected. In Florida, one of the three companies has begun a substantial expansion campaign, one has agreed to sell to another Florida company, and one has not expanded as of yet.

[14]South Dakota recently passed legislation permitting banks to engage in insurance activities that they would be prohibited from engaging in through subsidiaries of bank holding companies. This has already kindled additional interest in outside entry by banking organizations into South Dakota and intensified the legislative activities of the insurance industry to close this loophole.

[15]See Moulton (1983).

[16]Utah also has a provision permitting out-of-state banking organizations to acquire failing in-state institutions.

Minnesota passed a similar law to permit the acquisition of a troubled savings bank which was subsequently absorbed by an in-state organization. Since only one savings bank existed in Minnesota, the law is now moot.

company's home state. New York permits banking acquisitions by out-of-state bank holding companies provided these holding companies are located in states with reciprocal legislation permitting entry by New York bank holding companies, respectively. Massachusetts, Rhode Island, and Connecticut, the most recent states to permit outside entry, have a similar reciprocal clause, but only for bank holding companies headquartered in other New England states. Georgia's reciprocal law limits entry to banking organizations located in ten southern states, and similar legislation has been enacted in South Carolina and Florida. Limiting entry to institutions from particular geographic areas is a forerunner, and may be symptomatic, of a growing trend toward cooperative regional approaches to the problem of relaxing interstate banking restrictions; Kentucky's new law, for example, limits entry to contiguous states, but this provision will be dropped in two years. Golembe (1983) reports that 39 states are, or have considered, changing their laws. Interest in regional compacts is also increasing.[17] Unfortunately, part of the rationale for such regional approaches lies in the desire to avoid significant changes that may affect adversely the competitive positions of local banks or that may result in outflows of funds (especially core deposits) from the area.[18] This view ignores, however, the significant structural developments in financial markets in recent years that are eliminating core deposits and that have evolved to collect and reallocate funds efficiently throughout the country. Thus these compacts will be eroded by market forces just as state prohibitions are being broken down today.

Policy Issues Pertaining to Interstate Banking

The Carter Administration's report on interstate banking identified several policy issues to be considered when changes in interstate banking restrictions are proposed.[19] These include the implications of any proposed changes for:

1. the level and quality of services to local communities,
2. the viability of smaller banks,
3. the safety and stability of the system, and
4. competition and concentration of resources.[20]

[17]See *American Banker* (1984).

[18]In New England, a strong desire exists to exclude the large New York banks from possible expansion throughout New England. While New York banks can, and have, expanded into Maine, the new Massachusetts law explicitly excludes New York banks from using their Maine subsidiaries to leapfrog into New England markets. Not all New England banks, however, share this desire and Northeast Bancorp. has brought suit against the Connecticut law which voided a planned merger with Bank of New York. Citicorp has filed a similar suit against the Massachusetts law.

[19]See Department of the Treasury (1981). For an excellent discussion of why national as opposed to regional interstate banking may be preferred, see Savage (1984).

[20]The Administration's report identified a fifth issue which concerned the division of supervisory and regulatory responsibilities among state and federal authorities. This issue is primarily political as opposed to economic, and therefore, is not addressed in this paper.

The consequences for the first three of these areas are largely the same, almost regardless of the alternative methods proposed for liberalizing branching and interstate bank expansion, be it regional or national in scope. Therefore, these issues will be treated in general terms before moving to a discussion of the other issues or to particular policy options.

Level and Quality of Service

In evaluating the possible effects of liberalizing interstate banking restrictions on the level and quality of services in local markets, it is useful to focus on three classes of customers: consumers and small businesses, middle market firms, and municipalities.[21] Generalizing on the evidence from intrastate banking studies, interstate banking would not be expected to reduce significantly the number of organizations in metropolitan areas (presuming entry was not limited to *de novo* expansion), and in the longer run the number of offices in rural and nonmetropolitan markets should increase slightly.[22] These conclusions follow because most interstate expansion (entry) would take place by acquisition of banks in metropolitan markets, simply replacing locally based banks with nonlocal firms.[23] Over the long run, since these new entrants would tend to be larger organizations, greater branch expansion would be expected in adjacent nonmetropolitan and rural areas, thus increasing the number of competitive alternatives and consumer convenience in these smaller markets.[24] Also, because of the larger relative size of these new entrants, the range of services would increase.[25] More important, the research evidence suggests that the availability of credit, in the aggregate, to small and middle-market businesses and to consumers, would increase, as would the allocation of funds to municipalities. This conclusion follows because larger banks tend to have higher lending limits and loan-to-deposit ratios than smaller banks and hold a greater proportion of state and local obligations. It has also been argued that large banks, by virtue of their access to lower costs of funds—both long and short term—would lower the cost of credit to borrowers. But this supposed advantage, if it exists, may be less relevant because financial innovations and technology have opened national credit markets to even small borrowers. Moreover, if the regulatory agencies continue to pursue their revised capital standards, some of the cost advantage traceable to increased leverage by large banks may be erased.

On the other side, there is also no evidence to support the contention that multioffice banking would tend to syphon funds from rural or more local metropolitan markets into the

[21]National market firms would be unaffected since they are not confined in their search for services to local markets. See also Horvitz (1983).

[22]For a review of these studies see McCall (1980). The presumption has always been that relaxing intrastate banking restrictions results in increased statewide concentration. Recent unpublished evidence indicates that states with the greatest increases in statewide concentration have simultaneously had declines in local market concentration.

[23]The recent experience in Pennsylvania is also consistent with this conclusion.

[24]For evidence supporting these conclusions see Guttentag (1976) and Jessup and Stoltz (1975).

[25]Whether these services would be demanded or used is another matter. For example, increased access to international services in rural areas may be irrelevant to the customers in those areas.

national money markets.[26] In any case, the growth of the Federal Funds market, money market mutual funds, and money brokers means that methods have already evolved to reallocate funds, albeit less efficiently, from surplus to deficit areas.

Horvitz (1983) suggests that a smaller local bank acquired by a larger outside organization may become less locally oriented, but at this time there is no systematic evidence supporting this possibility.* Finally, it is also worth noting that smaller banks tend to have relatively lower loan deposit ratios and greater proportions of Federal funds sold and investments in Treasury obligations than larger banks. In fact, small banks are net suppliers of Federal funds and represent one of the principal channels by which funds are collected from local markets and directed into the national market.

Although these general net benefits of interstate banking may exist, the critical question concerns the incremental value of relaxing the restrictions on a nationwide basis as compared with selective relaxation on a regional basis. Given the numerous methods that out-of-state organizations have exploited to enter many states (see Table 1) and the recent expansion of asset and liability powers of thrift institutions in the Garn-St. Germain Act and the Monetary Control Act, one can probably conclude that the incremèntal effect on the level and quality of banking services of relaxing interstate banking restrictions, while positive, is small. Slightly greater incremental benefits may accrue in those markets in which national and regional firms are located if nationwide interstate banking were permitted as compared with regional interstate banking, more convenient access to the national market and a wider potential array of services may be available, but again the benefits would be small.

Viability of Small Banks

Notwithstanding the widespread fears of smaller banking organizations, interstate branching or bank holding company expansion would not pose a threat to the viability of small banks. Numerous small banks already operate in major metropolitan markets in head-to-head competition with large banks. Moreover, there is no evidence that these large banks enjoy cost or scale economies over small banks.[27] Furthermore, small banks have tended consistently to outperform large banks in recent years, whether measured by returns on assets or equity, despite the supposed pressures of deregulation.[28] And this comparative performance advantage of small banks has held in even the most competitive markets.[29] In fact, the research results imply that entry of large banks by acquisition of large banks

[26]One of the studies which failed to find evidence of parasitic behavior was by Kohn, Carlo, and Kaye (1973) which looked at the effects of entry by large banks into local markets in New York State.

**Editors' Note: The Horvitz article discussed here is reprinted as the next reading in this volume.*

[27]For reviews of the scale economy literature see Humphrey (1983), Benston, Berger, Hanweck, and Humphrey (1983) or Benston, Humphrey, and Hanweck (1982). *Editor's Note: The Benston, Humphrey, and Hanweck article is reprinted in Section III of this volume.*

[28]See Opper (1981–83), Wall (1983) and Mallinson (1983).

[29]Savage and Rhoades (1981) have examined the performance of small banks in major metropolitan markets.

within a market tend to be associated with declining market shares rather than market dominance.[30]

Safety and Soundness

Safety and soundness issues also do not appear to be a determining factor in considering interstate banking issues. To the extent that competition, loan-to-deposit ratios, and leverage are increased, then one might conclude that bank risk would be increased. This increased risk, however, is counter-balanced by a number of factors including the opportunities for greater product and geographic diversification and the ease in facilitating the takeover of weak or failing institutions.[31] Studies reveal little effect of enlarged opportunities for geographic expansion on bank closings. Overall, fewer multi-office banks or bank holding companies appear on the regulatory agencies' problem lists than do unit banks.[32]

It has been suggested that the foreign debt or other problems that might occur in major center banks would be transferred to those small or regional banks that affiliated with them, thereby increasing the risk exposure of the domestic banking system.[33] There are a number of factors, however, which serve to diminish or limit this concern. First, existing law requires the responsible federal banking agency to consider the effects of a proposed bank holding company acquisition or bank merger on safety and soundness of the surviving institution. Second, the banking agencies have heightened their surveillance activities and increased capital requirements for larger banking organizations. Third, to the extent that market discipline is, or can ever be, an important constraint on bank behavior, then the shareholders of proposed acquired firms would be expected to perceive this possible increased risk and should demand increased compensation for any increased risk they might assume by swapping their shares for those of the acquiring firm. Higher prices would reduce the attractiveness of such acquisitions to the larger firms or else induce risk-reducing behavior in order to increase the attractiveness of merger to the acquired firm's shareholders.[34]

Competition and Concentration

The most controversial issues surrounding consideration of modifying interstate banking laws deal with the implications of proposed changes for competition and concentration of resources. There is little doubt that restrictions on geographic expansion have, in the past,

[30]See Rhoades (1978). This result is not consistent with the claims that large banks are superior competitors or have competitive advantages over small banks.

[31]In the case of large banking organizations and thrift institutions, the Garn-St. Germain Act now provides for a suspension of interstate banking limitations by permitting the acquisition of large qualifying institutions in financial difficulty by out-of-state banking organizations. It was in such cases that Citicorp gained entry into California, Illinois, and Florida; however, future expansion by these acquired thrifts is McFaddenized by the Garn-St. Germain Act.

[32]See McCall and Lane (1980)

[33]See Rivard (1983).

[34]The benefits of introducing more market discipline have formed a critical part of the banking agencies and Federal Home Loan Bank Board's recommendations for deposit insurance reform.

insulated many local markets from competition and have restricted economic growth. While casual inspection of the data suggests that states with more liberalized policies toward intrastate banking have generally had higher economic growth rates than unit banking states, empirical studies show no convincing relationship between banking structure and economic development.[35]

On the other hand, there is also the legitimate concern that wider geographic expansion will be associated with increased consolidation of the banking system. And this consolidation is likely to take place—as it has already begun in Pennsylvania and in New England—by first combining the largest competitors rather than ensuring that a large number of same-sized competitors are formed and allowed to compete head to head.

The Carter administration expressed the fear that existing antitrust laws and policies may not be adequate to guide the transition from a regional and local banking system to one that permits wide geographic expansion with the consequence that the financial system would be dominated by a very few giant organizations. This is one of the principal arguments for many of the regional approaches to liberalizing interstate banking restrictions. It is argued that such proposals allow the growth and consolidation of regional institutions into larger firms and thus promise to increase the number of firms that can compete effectively at the national level. But the cost may be increased concentration of resources and economic power within the regions. Furthermore, if regional barriers are then relaxed, continuing consolidation of the banking system would be facilitated since out-of-region organizations could acquire dominant positions by acquiring the dominant firms within a region that had been formed. In fact, a strong case could be made that using regional interstate banking as a transition to national interstate banking would result in fewer competitors and more concentrated and less competitive structure than simply moving directly to full interstate banking. It is these issues and the implied tradeoffs that suggest any interstate banking proposals be given careful consideration before certain options are excluded. The remaining sections of this article analyze these factors as they affect four of the more common methods that have been adopted by individual states around the nation to deal with the economic pressures to change the interstate banking laws.

Alternative Ways to Permit Interstate Banking

Because of McFadden Act prohibitions on interstate branching and the revealed reluctance to date of Congress to take up the issue of interstate banking as a matter of national policy, the focus of the interstate banking issue has shifted to the individual states. In particular, the focus has been on whether individual states should enact legislation, as permitted under the Douglas Amendment to the Bank Holding Company Act of 1956, to authorize out-of-state bank holding companies to operate banks within their boundaries. There are, in fact, an almost infinite number of ways to structure such activity, and the recent actions of several states provide a reasonable menu of the practical alternatives. These include 1. permitting regional reciprocity, such as Georgia, South Carolina, Massachusetts and Con-

[35]More detailed study would have to be done to determine whether this is just a matter of correlation or causation.

necticut; 2. allowing nationwide reciprocity, such as Maine and New York; 3. permitting unrestricted entry, such as Alaska; and 4. maintaining the status quo. The implications of each of these options are discussed below.

Maintain the Status Quo

Those states that have not chosen to act have adopted implicitly the policy, at least in the short run, of maintaining the status quo. This means a continuation of the present trends in the evolution of individual state's banking structure. In particular, out-of-state organizations (both bank and nonbank alike) will attempt to avoid interstate banking restrictions and exploit financial innovations to expand their activities. Banking organizations, for example, will continue to expand their existing activities in the form of nonbanking activities of bank holding companies, loan production offices, and Edge Act Companies.

Competitively, these activities would tend to concentrate in providing services to the major nonlocally limited business firms, foreign trade related commerce, and consumer credit. In addition, however, recent developments permitting the operation of industrial banks by many states, recent expansion by the Federal Reserve of permissible nonbanking activities for bank holding companies, and the successful acquisition of troubled S&Ls by Citicorp suggest that inroads into the consumer deposit markets are to be expected despite best efforts to prevent them. In addition, a new avenue was opened up by the Federal Reserve in the U.S. trust decision on March 23, 1984, which allowed the establishment of the equivalent of nine bank banks across state lines for bank holding companies. More than twenty institutions have applied to establish over one hundred of these subsidiaries across the country. Most of this activity would probably be centered in the major metropolitan areas. Thus, maintaining the status quo would not affect the competitive situation in local and more rural markets in individual states. This implies that the competitive impacts would be greatest on those firms operating in the larger markets and those attempting to serve larger and middle-market customers, which are typically the larger local and regional banking organizations. The main beneficiaries of such a policy would be those aggressive in-state organizations seeking to grow by consolidation which would experience somewhat reduced competition for acquisitions and somewhat lower prices for those mergers that are consumated. Maintaining the status quo will not prevent out-of-state organizations from making stake-out investments in anticipation of future changes in state laws. In short, the end result may only be postponed rather than avoided.

Nationwide Reciprocity or Unrestricted Nationwide Entry

There is little substantive difference between a policy of nationwide reciprocity, such as that enacted by Maine, or unrestricted entry, such as that enacted by Alaska. The principal effects would be to increase acquisition activity. If the patterns set in Maine continue to be followed, then acquisitions would first involve the state's largest organizations which would be prime acquisition targets for out-of-state firms.

Carried to its extreme, either policy would tend to lead to a banking structure more dominated by out-of-state organizations. However, banking structure would be less concentrated in terms of the competitive alternatives available to local and regional type firms and to banks purchasing correspondent services, and hence, one would expect that the resulting structure would be more competitive in its performance. Such a structure would evolve because there would be fewer incentives for consolidations among in-state firms whose shareholders would likely receive higher prices by accepting offers from nonlocal firms. It has been reported in the financial press that bank share values in New England states which passed reciprocal interstate banking laws have appreciated in value by as much as 40%. In such circumstances, the nationwide unrestricted policy would be preferable to a reciprocal policy for two reasons. First, it would ensure a more geographically dispersed representation of out-of-state organizations operating in local and regional markets. Secondly, the nationwide policy would increase the number of bidders and lead to higher share prices in acquisitions.

This scenario is one that is not viewed as attractive by many in those states facing the problem of how to modify their policy. However, there also is an important set of market-related factors that will tend to limit the extent that money center and other large banks will be able successfully to buy dominant institutions in many states around the country. These factors relate to the relative earnings performance of the nation's largest banking organizations compared to the target regional companies and to the practical problems of assimilating a large number of large acquisitions in a short period of time. Because regional banking organizations tend to be both better capitalized and higher earners than the money center organizations, the prices that will have to be paid in terms of ownership dilution and capital outlays will make otherwise attractive alternatives too costly and limit the number of feasible acquisitions. This is especially true since the federal banking agencies are concerned about the capital adequacy of the nation's large organizations.
In addition, the logistic and technical problems of integrating newly acquired firms and the associated drain on managerial resources will also limit the number of feasible acquisitions.[36] These factors should limit significantly the pace at which the nations' largest organizations could acquire large regional companies and should instead tend to favor combinations among more equal-sized and stronger performing regional organizations.

Regional Reciprocity[37]

Regional reciprocity with other similarly situated states is seen by many as being a middle ground between maintaining the status quo and the nationwide options. The supposed benefits of this option, however, are either questionable or equally applicable to the nationwide options. It is argued, for example, that regional reciprocity would preserve regional control of banking organizations and permit the major organizations within the region to grow to a size to compete with money center organizations. There is little evidence, however, that size conveys cost or other competitive advantages to larger firms.

[36]Fleet Financial has chosen to establish a *de novo* nonbank bank in Massachusetts because high share prices have made entry by acquisition too costly.

[37]This discussion leaves aside the constitutionality issues of such legislation presently in the courts (Northeast Bancorp Inc. *v.* Woolf, NO. H-83-654; D.C., Conn., filed July 29, 1983). It also does not explore the variety of regional options that might be considered, such as, contiguous state expansion, EFT expansion, or expansion by entry in SMSAs crossing state boundaries. For discussion of these options see Department of the Treasury (1981).

Another possible benefit to locally controlled firms might be greater local orientation with respect to their accommodation of middle market firms and municipalities, but there is no empirical evidence to support such contentions; moreover, the links to economic development are also uncertain.[38] Regional reciprocity would also permit banking organizations to expand their representation in their ''natural markets'' from which they had been excluded by antiquated branching policies. This situation would increase the service convenience offered local customers. On the other hand, to the extent that regional reciprocity encouraged consolidations among larger firms within the regional some competition for regional loan and correspondent business would be eliminated.[39] In general, however, regional reciprocity would have little impact in local consumer and small business markets for the reasons noted when discussing the nationwide reciprocity proposals. Bank shareholders would gain, however, from appreciation in their stock as competition for acquisitions increased, but this appreciation would not be as great as with the nationwide options.

Lastly, it has been argued that regional reciprocity would serve as a useful transition to full interstate banking. But to the extent that it encouraged consolidation among regional firms that might then be consolidated into large national organizations, the resulting structure could produce greater local concentration and less competition than the unrestricted options.

The chief beneficiaries of regional reciprocity would be the managers of those institutions that would otherwise be prime acquisition targets and who might suffer as a result of a sale and reorganization. If regional reciprocity provides the opportunity for these institutions to grow and not be subject to a takeover, then these managers will prosper relative to how they might fare under more permissive policies.

Conclusions

From the long-run point of view of improving competition, enhancing the quantity and quality of financial services, and providing for more efficient allocation of financial resources, a persuasive argument can be made that the present limitations on interstate banking are unduly restrictive. On the other hand, the press of market forces and the evolution of ways to avoid these restrictions have facilitated the collection of funds at the local level and their reallocation nationally, making the additional benefits from a more liberal policy toward interstate banking smaller than they would have been a few years ago. These developments combined with recent changes in federal law broadening the powers of thrifts have significantly increased competition in financial markets, be they national, regional, or local in scope. Despite these reduced benefits, however, it is still

[38]It was for these reasons, for example, that the Southern Growth Policies Board recommended that regional reciprocity be used as a transition to national reciprocity (see Skinner, 1982). Rhode Island has adopted this model.

[39]It has been common to argue against regional and intrastate banking on the grounds that it would be anticompetitive based on the theory of linked oligopoly. See recent work by Whitehead (1984) and Rhoades (1983).

clear that maintaining the existing restrictions is not now working to the best interests of commercial banks and the ability to compete against less regulated competitors. Furthermore, they are unduly restricting those investors wishing to sell their stock to the highest bidder. On these grounds, consideration should be given to relaxing the restrictions on interstate banking. Which policy option (regional, national, or status quo) to select hinges mainly on the tradeoffs made between the interests of managers and their desire to maintain control of their institutions against the interests of shareholders rather than on overriding public benefits or competitive consideration favoring one option over another.

REFERENCES

AMERICAN BANKER, "Interstate Banking Picks up Steam on Three Fronts," Thursday, January 19, 1984.

AMERICAN BANKERS ASSOCIATION, "State Legislation on Interstate Acquisitions by Bank Holding Companies," memo of November 23, 1983.

BANKING EXPANSION REPORTER, "Fed Approves Reg Y Revision," January 2, 1984.

BENSTON, GEORGE J., ALLEN BERGER, GERALD HANWECK, and DAVID B. HUMPHREY, "Economies of Scale and Scope in Banking," Research Papers in Banking and Financial Economics No. 64, Board of Governors of the Federal Reserve System, July 1983.

———, GERALD A. HANWECK, and DAVID B. HUMPHREY, Operating Costs in Commercial Banking, *Economic Review,* Federal Reserve Bank of Atlanta, November 1982.

DEPARTMENT OF THE TREASURY, *Geographic Restrictions on Commercial Banking in the United States,* The Report of the President, Department of the Treasury, 1981.

EISENBEIS, ROBERT A., "Financial Innovation and the Role of Regulation: Implications for Banking Organization, Structure and Regulation," Board of Governors of the Federal Reserve System, February 1980.

———, "Interstate Banking: Federal Perspectives and Prospects," Proceedings of a Conference on Bank Structure and Competition, Federal Reserve Bank of Chicago, May 1981a.

———, "Regulation and Financial Innovation: Implications for Financial Structure and Competition Among Depository and Non-Depository Institutions," *Issues in Bank Regulation,* Vol. 4, No. 3, Winter, 1981b.

FEDERAL RESERVE, "Bank Holding Company Acquisition of Thrift Institutions: A Study by the Staff of the Board of Governors of the Federal Reserve System, September 1981.

GOLEMBE ASSOCIATES, "A Study of Interstate Banking by Bank Holding Companies," prepared for the Association of Bank Holding Companies, May 25, 1979.

GUTTENTAG, JACK M., "Branch Banking in Alabama," mimeo, February 1976.

HORVITZ, PAUL M., "Alternative Approaches to Interstate Banking," *Economic Review,* Federal Reserve Bank of Atlanta, May 1983.

HUMPHREY, DAVID B., "Costs and Scale Economies in Financial Intermediation," Board of Governors of the Federal Reserve System, July 1983.

JESSUP, PAUL F., and RICHARD STOLTZ, "Customer Alternatives Among Rural Banks," *Journal of Bank Research,* Summer 1975.

KANE, EDWARD J., "Accelerating Inflation, Technological Innovation, and the Decreasing Effectiveness of Bank Regulation," *Journal of Finance,* May 1981.

KOHN, ERNEST, CARMEN J. CARLO, and BERNARD KAYE, *Meeting Local Credit Needs,* New York State Banking Department, 1973.

LAGESSE, DAVID, "Mortgage Networks Arrange Loans on Computers," *American Banker,* Monday, January 23, 1984.

MCCALL, ALAN S., "The Impact of Bank Structure on Bank Service to Local Communities," *Journal of Bank Research,* Summer, 1980.

______, and JOHN T. LANE, "Multi-Office Banking and the Safety and Soundness of Commercial Banks," *Journal of Bank Research,* Summer, 1980.

MC CUE, LISA J., "Money Brokers Imperil Insurance System, Gray Says," *American Banker,* Wednesday, February 1, 1984.

MALLINSON, EUGENIE, "Profitability of Insured Commercial Banks in the First Half of 1983," Federal Reserve *Bulletin,* December 1983.

MOULTON, JANICE M., "Delaware Moves Toward Interstate Banking: A Look at the FCDA," *Business Review,* Federal Reserve Bank of Philadelphia, July–August 1983.

MCNEIL, CHARLES R., and DENISE M. RECHTER, "The Depository Institutions Deregulation and Monetary Control Act of 1980," Federal Reserve *Bulletin,* June 1980.

MURPHY, C. WESTBROOK, and THOMAS W. BRUNNER, "Will Anyone Try to Block Amexco?" *American Banker,* Thursday, April 13, 1981.

OPPER, BARBARA NEGRI, "Profitability of Insured Commercial Banks in 1980," Federal Reserve *Bulletin,* September 1981.

______, "Profitability of Insured Commercial Banks in 1981," Federal Reserve *Bulletin,* August 1982.

______, "Profitability of Insured Commercial Banks in 1982," Federal Reserve *Bulletin,* July 1983.

PETER MERRILL ASSOCIATES, "The Effect of Bank Holding Companies on Competition in U.S. Banking Markets," prepared for the American Bankers Association, January 1981.

RHOADES, STEPHEN A., "The Effect of Bank Holding Companies on Competition," in *The Bank Holding Company Movement to 1978: A Compendium,* Board of Governors of the Federal Reserve System, September 1978.

______, "The Effect of Multimarket Interdependence on Market Performance and Rivalry," Board of Governors of the Federal Reserve System, 1983.

RIVARD, RICHARD J., "An Independent Analysis of the Implications of Interstate Banking for Florida," *Florida Banking,* April 1983.

ROSENBLUM, HARVEY, and CHRISTINE PAVEL, "Financial Services in Transition: The Effects of Nonbank Competitors," Federal Reserve Bank of Chicago, 1984.

______, and DIANE SIEGEL, "Competition in Financial Services: The Impact of Nonbank Entry," Federal Reserve Bank of Chicago, 1982.

SAVAGE, DONALD T., and STEVEN A. RHOADES, "Can Small Banks Compete?" *Bankers Magazine,* January–February 1981.

______, "Regional Interstate Banking—Better than the Alternatives?" forthcoming *Issues in Bank Regulation,* 1984.

SKINNER, ALTON, "Report of the Southern Regional Banking Committee to the Executive Committee of the Southern Growth Policies Board," Southern Growth Policies Board, November 14, 1982.

WHITEHEAD, DAVID D., "Interstate Banking: Taking Inventory," *Economic Review,* Federal Reserve Bank of Atlanta, May 1983.

______, "Can Interstate Banking Increase Competitive Market Performance? An Empirical Test," *Economic Review,* Federal Reserve Bank of Atlanta, January 1984.

WALL, LARRY D., "Will Bank Capital Adequacy Restrictions Slow the Development of Interstate Banking?" *Economic Review,* Federal Reserve Bank of Atlanta, May 1983.

Alternative Avenues to Interstate Banking

Paul M. Horvitz

14

Observers of the U.S. financial scene generally agree that broadened interstate banking activity is coming. We will focus on the *differences* in the impact of interstate banking depending on the way it comes about. The effect on financial institutions and on their customers will differ depending on whether interstate banking comes through liberalization of the McFadden Act (branching), elimination of the Douglas Amendment (bank holding company acquisition), or through greater exploitation of other devices.

While there is a presumption that interstate banking eventually will be allowed nationwide, a number of proposals have advocated *limited* interstate banking, either permanently or as a means of phasing in the eventual nationwide system. These proposals include regional interstate banking, limits on the number of interstate acquisitions, or limitations on the method of entry into interstate markets—*de novo* (starting a new bank) or through acquisition of existing institutions.[1]

Reprinted from *Economic Review* (May, 1983): 32–39 by permission of the Federal Reserve Bank of Atlanta and the author.

[1]Various approaches to interstate banking are also discussed by Alan S. McCall and Donald T. Savage in "Branching Policy. The Options," *Journal of Bank Research,* Summer 1980, pp. 122-126.

Different Avenues Have Different Effects

In analyzing the impact of different methods of interstate banking, it is useful to consider the effect on four types of bank customers—large corporations, middle-market firms, small businesses, and consumers.

The easiest to deal with are the large national firms. Competition for their business is already national in scope. The largest banks in the country are seeking the business of Fortune 500 or 1,000 firms, regardless of location of either the bank or the corporation. This competition does not require a local branch or subsidiary bank. Thus, money center banks can compete for Lockheed's business without maintaining a branch in Atlanta. If physical presence is desirable, a loan production office, legal under existing law, is usually adequate.

Small businesses are now served exclusively by local lenders. The small firm in Orlando obtains banking services from Orlando banks. The small businessman from Orlando who seeks credit at a Miami bank will be greeted with courtesy, no doubt, but also with suspicion as to why he is unable to meet his needs in his own locality. For that small Orlando firm, seeking financing in Atlanta is out of the question.

The devices that currently allow interstate activity, such as loan production offices or Edge Act corporations, are not an efficient means of serving the small business borrower. Loan production offices are staffed with lending officers experienced in seeking business from large corporations. The offices are not set up to make smaller loans and, in any case, they are not allowed to take deposits. Part of the consideration involved in a bank lending transaction is the opportunity to obtain a borrower's deposit account. If the nonlocal bank cannot compete for the deposit account, it is at a disadvantage in competing with local institutions. Some subsidiaries of out-of-state bank holding companies, such as finance companies or leasing subsidiaries, can extend credit to a small business; but they too lack the opportunity to handle its deposit account. The effect on the local small business of a change to allow interstate banking will depend heavily on the specific form of the change.

De novo entry (establishment of a new bank) by an out-of-state bank generally will benefit small business customers more than entry through acquisition. *De novo* entry adds to the small firm's sources of service while entry by acquisition merely substitutes one bank for another. This substitution is not without effect, however, and the effect of a *de novo* establishment of an out-of-state bank's branch differs from a *de novo* bank holding company subsidiary.

An important distinction between a branch and a bank subsidiary of a bank holding company is that the branch's lending limit is based on the capital of the entire bank, while the subsidiary is limited by its own capital. Thus, the branch of a money center bank established in Atlanta or Birmingham can make a multi-million dollar loan to large local firms. An important implication is that an out-of-state branch can emphasize service to larger businesses in an area, while the bank subsidiary of a bank holding company must be oriented toward small business customers and consumers.

It follows, therefore, that small businesses may be benefitted more by establishment of a bank holding company's subsidiary than by its branches. Analogously, the competitive position of small local banks may be more affected by entry of subsidiary banks than by branches. This is an interesting consideration because it is frequently asserted—as in the Carter administration report on the McFadden Act—that interstate bank holding company expansion is less disruptive to the existing competitive banking structure than interstate branching.

Acquisitions have a somewhat different impact. When a sizable local institution is taken over by an out-of-state institution (whether to be operated as a subsidiary or as a branch), it may become less locally oriented in its lending policy. If so, change would not benefit local small business but, conversely, it would represent less of a competitive threat to local small banks.

The effect of interstate activity on smaller banks also varies depending on location. Small banks in major cities already face stiff competition from large banks. Small banks in Atlanta, Tampa or Miami compete with the largest institutions in their state. Evidence suggests that small firms prefer to deal with smaller banks, and small banks have long operated profitably in this competitive environment. Thus, *de novo* interstate branching or bank holding company expansion is unlikely to represent a significant change in the competitive structure of those cities. And if a large local competitor is acquired by an out-of-state institution, the small local bank's competitive position is probably improved.

The bank in a smaller city or town may be affected significantly by entry of a large out-of-state bank, but such banks are unlikely to enter *de novo* into smaller cities. There are limits to the pace at which even the most aggressive bank can expand following a change in the law—limits that we will discuss later. The small-city bank is most likely to find itself in direct competition with an out-of-state institution if that institution acquires an existing competing bank or its parent. Thus, an independent bank in Macon may find itself competing with a subsidiary of a money center bank holding company if a New York or Chicago bank acquires a local competitor or the parent of a local competitor. But the local bank's ability to compete with the money center bank for small business customers is at least as good as its ability to handle existing competition.

The banks most likely to be affected by interstate competition appear to be larger institutions doing business with locally based middle-market firms. Those firms, the best customers of the larger in-state banks, will be the principal targets of out-of-state entrants into the market. In many states, these firms already have access to many of the larger banks in the state, and they may not have much to gain from new competition. On the other hand, in some smaller states or those with a concentrated banking structure, these middle-market firms may see a significant improvement in their access to bank services.

Potential interstate entrants much prefer branch expansion over holding company acquisitions because it allows them to tailor expansion to the particular market being entered. It is feasible to establish a wholesale oriented branch at lower cost—requiring less capital, modest office space and few employees. Such an operation may be little more than a deposit-taking loan production office. If interstate banking comes about through change in the Douglas Amendment allowing only *de novo* bank holding company subsidiaries, the cost and difficulty of raising sufficient capital will hold down the number of interstate ventures.

Effects on Consumers

When interstate expansion's objective is consumer business, analyzing the alternative types of interstate expansion becomes more complex. First of all, a major objective of interstate consumer banking has been attracting low-cost core deposits. Consumers traditionally have maintained sizable demand deposits (on which no interest is paid), NOW accounts and saving deposits (with interest at 5¼ percent), and other fixed-maturity time deposits with below-market interest rates. The phase-out of interest rate ceilings and the recent creation of money market accounts and super-NOW accounts at competitive market rates may make consumer business less profitable to commercial banks in the future. Thus, some of the motive for interstate expansion in this market may have lessened or disappeared.

Second, it is unclear whether **any** change in the law is necessary to conduct consumer business on an interstate basis. On the lending side, finance company subsidiaries of bank holding companies have the necessary powers and already can operate interstate. Savings and loan associations have gained full consumer banking powers, both in lending and deposit-taking (including checking accounts). If bank holding companies were allowed to own S&Ls on an interstate basis, change in the McFadden Act or the Douglas Amendment would not be needed to bring about full interstate competition in consumer banking. Loan limits are not a problem in consumer lending, so a branch is not a more attractive vehicle for interstate entry than a holding company subsidiary.

The Federal Reserve already has authorized bank holding company acquisition of an S&L in a few exceptional cases, the most dramatic being Citicorp's acquisition of Fidelity Savings and Loan in California.[2] A Federal Reserve staff study recommended that the savings and loan business be considered an appropriate activity under Section 4(c)(8) of the Bank Holding Company Act, but the Board has sought congressional guidance before making a general decision in this controversial area.[3] The 1982 Garn-St Germain Act authorized interstate and inter-industry acquisitions of failing thrift institutions. The legislation clearly treats such acquisitions as exceptional, which can be interpreted as a congressional intent that such acquisitions should not be allowed under "normal" (non-failure) circumstances.

Even without the S&L vehicle, existing mechanisms may be sufficient for carrying out consumer banking business interstate. Banks can and do solicit credit card business nationwide. Banks can also solicit deposits by mail on an interstate basis, and a number of large banks have begun to do so in connection with the new money market accounts. Money market mutual funds familiarized consumers with the idea of handling liquid asset portfolio transactions by mail with distant institutions, and the large commercial banks now are taking advantage of that familiarity. Customers of out-of-state banks can be given local access to their funds through automated teller machines. Shared interstate ATM networks

[2]See "Citicorp's Acquisition of Fidelity Federal Saving and Loan Association of San Francisco," Federal Reserve Bulletin, October 1982, pp. 656–660, and "Interstate Financial Corporation's Acquisition of Scioto Saving Association, Columbus, Ohio," Federal Reserve Bulletin, May 1982, pp. 316–318.

[3]"Bank holding company acquisitions of thrift institutions"—staff study prepared for the Federal Reserve Board September 1981.

are being expanded. Consumers will still probably prefer to keep their checking account local, however.

Regardless of any change (or lack of change) in federal law, then, consumer banking appears likely to become less locally limited. If local market conditions are not competitive, or if local banks are inefficient or unable to provide modern services, out-of-state banks will be able to solicit business successfully. Local offices may be less necessary in the future than they have been in the past. Interest rate ceilings have prevented banks from competing on rates, so convenience has represented the most important dimension of competition. But that is no longer the case.

It is difficult to predict just how consumer financial services will be delivered in the future. Rather than seeking a local presence, large, consumer-oriented banks may franchise or sell sophisticated services to local banks. The non-local vendor may be able to extract much of the potential profit from consumer business through service fees paid by the local bank. In any case, competition for consumer business is becoming more intense. The consumer, except in relatively isolated communities, may not need further change in the law.

Implications for Intrastate Branching

These consumer banking considerations have implications for the desirability of intrastate as well as interstate branching. One of the most controversial aspects of interstate banking has been its effect on state control over banking structure, particularly the extent of branching within a state. We have noted that the McFadden Act defers to state law with respect to geographical limits on branching by national banks. But this may be less important in the future, as extensive branching becomes less profitable.

Consumer banking traditionally has involved collecting funds from depositors at low interest cost on the basis of convenience. Where state law has allowed, convenience has been provided through extensive (and expensive) branch facilities. If banks have to pay market rates for these funds, they no longer will be able to afford the cost of such facilities—estimated at perhaps 2 percent of funds collected. Direct deposit, automated clearing houses, and automated teller machine networks may provide consumer convenience in the future, and the longstanding debate over branch banking may fade away.

If branching continues to be a matter of controversy, however, changing the Douglas Amendment would do much less violence to traditional state control over intrastate branching than would liberalization of the McFadden Act. This consideration apparently was given heavy weight in the Carter administration McFadden Act Report, which recommended the Douglas rather than the McFadden route to interstate banking.

Restraints on Interstate Expansion

There seems to be a widespread belief that removal of the McFadden Act or Douglas Amendment immediately would spark a tremendous expansion of interstate branching or holding company activity. This rests on the assumption that the sole barrier to interstate activity is the legal one, and hence if that barrier were removed interstate activity could proceed unencumbered. However, other factors will tend to limit interstate holding company activity even after legal barriers are removed.

Three types of constraints that will persist include considerations relating to the profitability of the target area, constraints based on the capacity of the expanding bank, and legal/regulatory constraints. A bank holding company does not expand interstate in the abstract; it must have a particular market in mind. However, there are only a limited number of attractive banking markets—markets in which the expanding bank can expect to operate profitably. Atlanta, for example, may appear to be an attractive location for a money center holding company to organize a new bank or acquire an existing bank. But it is less attractive considering the possibility that five or ten or more other holding companies may try to do the same thing. This problem exists with either a *de novo* bank or an acquisition. A rash of *de novo* banks would increase competition and reduce profitability. The acquisition route would not directly add to the number of competing institutions in the market. But if a number of potential acquirers pursue a limited number of attractive acquirees, the price of their stocks will be bid up. Earning a profit on an acquisition requiring a substantial premium would prove difficult.

Even if there are attractive opportunities available to aggressive bank holding companies, the holding companies remain subject to their own internal limitations. The most important are likely to be capital and management shortages. Few money center banks have more capital than supervisory agencies view as marginally adequate. Expansion through *de novo* holding company subsidiaries requires additional capital. While acquisition of an existing bank through an exchange of stock does not necessarily require new capital, its feasibility turns on the capital market's valuation of the stock involved. The key issue in all cases is the holding company's ability to tap the capital markets. While capital considerations do not necessarily constrain interstate expansion, the current state of both equity and debt markets will make it difficult for most large banks to generate the additional capital needed to finance a substantial expansion.[4] Capital will be a more serious constraint on holding company expansion than on branching.

For many banks considering nonlocal expansion, the pace of such expansion will be limited by management talent. This has, in fact, already limited the pace of expansion by some banks, which see the opportunity for profitably establishing additional loan production offices but lack the qualified lending officers to staff them. That problem becomes more severe when an entire bank must be staffed. Of course, the problem is less if an existing bank with competent management is acquired. Yet, unless the acquiring bank is able to devote some managerial expertise to the acquisition, it is likely to represent merely a financial investment, not a true merging of the acquired institution providing real operating economies or advantages.

[4]During the heyday of conglomerate merger expansion, the market's tendency to put high price-earnings ratios on stock of aggressive conglomerates enabled them to acquire firms with lower price-earning ratios at prices attractive to shareholders of the acquired firm yet which increased earnings of the acquirer. The situation in the banking industry today is just the opposite. Many banks in attractive growth markets are selling at higher prices relative to earnings than the money center banks. Such acquisitions would involve a significant degree of dilution to shareholders of the money center banks.

Even with change in the Douglas Amendment or McFadden Act, other delays and constraints are inherent in the regulated nature of the banking business. Organization of a *de novo* subsidiary bank or branch or an acquisition requires at least one regulatory approval, and usually more. The pace of much regulatory agency decision making can be slow, particularly when applications involve controversial issues. That certainly will be the case with applications for interstate charters or acquisitions. There are really two separate problems involved: first is simply the supervisory agencies' ability to handle the flow of paper if 100 or 200 applications for interstate operations are added to a volume that already strains the agencies' resources; second is the difficulty the agencies will face in making necessary policy decisions on the applications.[5]

Since sizable acquisitions are likely, we must also consider the role of the Justice Department and the courts under antitrust laws. Some applications of antitrust concepts to banking have been rather clearly resolved. A series of bank merger cases decided by the Supreme Court in the 1960s (in particular, Philadelphia, Lexington, and Phillipsburg), combined with the 1966 amendments to the Bank Merger Act, set clear limits on horizontal bank mergers—mergers involving banks in direct competition in the same market. These standards have been applied consistently by the banking agencies, and have been understood by banks and their counsel, so mergers that would be prohibited by these guidelines are rarely even proposed.

The courts have spoken less clearly in the case of ''market extension'' mergers—those involving the issue of ''potential competition.'' In these cases, the two parties to the merger are not in direct competition in the same market. The acquiring bank is alleged to have the capacity and the interest in entering the market of the acquired bank on a *de novo* basis, or through a merger with a smaller bank now in the market (a ''toehold'' acquisition), thus encouraging competition. It is also often argued that the acquiring bank is already affecting the market because banks in the area, aware of the competitor ''waiting in the wings,'' refrain from pricing strategies that would encourage entry. The Justice Department has brought suit in several cases on the grounds of ''potential competition'' and ''probable future competition,'' but has lost every time. Debate over the applicability of potential competition has been intense, both in banking and other contexts. Courts generally have acknowledged applicability of the argument in principle, but have never found the facts sufficient to rule for the Justice Department. The result is a great deal of uncertainty as to what is allowable and what is not.

Bank acquisition cases involving potential competition have been a relatively minor factor in changing bank structure. But this issue will come to the fore if barriers to interstate banking are eliminated. Virtually all acquisitions in such a framework would be

[5]Several methods of reducing this problem warrant attention by the Congress. Congress can put a deferred effective date on legislation authorizing interstate banking. During this period, perhaps a year or longer, the agencies can determine policy and establish procedures to be used when the applications are received. Congress could provide some guidance as to policies to be followed by the agencies. Congress could also impose a firm deadline for decision making, as it has done with bank holding company acquisitions handled by the Federal Reserve. The agencies could accept applications during the interim period and decide them all as of the effective date of the legislative change. A similar approach was used when Florida first authorized branching, avoiding the inequity that results when Bank A has its application approved and gains a head start on Bank B, whose equally meritorious application happens to fall later in the queue of cases.

market extension acquisitions that would raise potential competition issues. Most of the banks that would seek interstate acquisitions are large and probably would prefer to acquire banks that have a significant market share. There is nowhere a bank can turn to obtain accurate guidance as to which possible acquisitions will meet the test of the antitrust laws and which will be barred.[6]

Uncertainty does inhibit mergers. Many mergers make economic sense if they can be handled smoothly, but are not worthwhile if they require huge legal costs to complete. Thus, inhibited mergers are not simply those that agencies or the courts would rule unacceptable, but also many that would, if carried to a final Supreme Court decision, be found to be legal. While some advocates of a strong anti-merger policy view this inhibiting effect as desirable, uncertainty of the law scarcely promotes economic efficiency.

These considerations suggest that even if there is a change in the law to allow unlimited interstate banking, the pace of such expansion will remain subject to important constraints.

The Role of Foreign Banks

While these considerations will limit the pace of interstate expansion by U. S. banks, foreign banks should be considered separately. Before the International Banking Act of 1978 (IBA), foreign banks were allowed to operate full-service banking offices in more than one state. Several operated in both New York and California. Such activity was frozen by the IBA, but many foreign banks retain an interest in interstate expansion if the law should allow it. A number have already taken advantage of liberalized restrictions on Edge Act Corporations to establish such operations in several cities, with Miami and Houston the preferred locations.

Some foreign banks are interested in consumer business, a traditional strength of the British banks. Several Japanese banks have been successful in consumer banking in California. Yet most foreign banks are interested in middle-market firms that may have links to their home country or that may have use for a foreign bank's particular expertise. For example, many middle-sized Texas firms are suppliers to oil operations in the North Sea, the Middle East or Latin America, and banks from these areas may seek an office in Houston or Dallas. With the exception of foreign banks interested in consumer banking, the type of business contemplated can be more efficiently handled with a branch rather than a holding company subsidiary.

This aspect of interstate banking is significant because there are probably more foreign banks interested in interstate expansion in the United States than there are domestic banks capable of such activities. Of the 500 largest banks in the world, 403 are non-U.S. banks, and 142 of these are already operating in the United States.[7] While the IBA attempted to put foreign and domestic banks on an equal competitive basis (removing the foreign banks'

[6]For a further discussion of antitrust issues in interstate banking, see Steve A. Halbrook and Donald T. Savage, "Interstate Commercial Banking: The Antitrust Issues." *Banking Law Journal,* September 1981, pp. 747-767.

[7]*American Banker,* July 28, 1982, p. 41.

freedom from reserve requirements, for example), foreign banks may still enjoy some advantages in interstate expansion. Most important is in the regulation of capital. Many foreign banks are allowed to operate with lower capital ratios than U.S. banks (substantially less than the *regional* U.S. banks they will compete against). If a foreign bank establishes a branch in the United States, it may be feasible for U.S. authorities to police the capital adequacy of that office, but more difficult to regulate the capital of the entire organization. It is easier to regulate the capital of a bank holding company subsidiary (it is a domestic bank), but it is not clear whether the Federal Reserve can or should attempt to regulate the capital adequacy of a consolidated foreign bank holding company as it does with domestic bank holding companies.

If interstate banking is authorized, the share controlled by foreign banks will increase substantially, particularly if branching rather than holding company expansion is authorized. While several studies have failed to find any detrimental effects associated with an increased foreign bank role in the U. S. banking system, this is likely to become at least a political issue.

Proposals for Limited Interstate Banking

Despite evidence that much interstate banking already exists, many consider too drastic any change in U.S. law to allow full service nationwide banking. Some argue that limited interstate banking can provide the advantages cited for nationwide banking with fewer disruptive effects, while others argue for a limited approach temporarily to cushion the impact of a change to nationwide banking.

The most restrictive approach would be to allow branching (or holding company acquisitions) only within standard metropolitan statistical areas, or SMSAs. The Hunt Commission urged that states be progressive in changing their laws in recognition of the fact that several banking markets are divided by state lines.[8] The New York City SMSA includes portions of New Jersey and Connecticut, while the Washington SMSA includes several counties of Virginia and Maryland. Other SMSAs include portions of a second state. Because current banking economics make extensive branching within a SMSA less attractive, this proposal has less to recommend it now than in the past. ATMs can accomplish nearly all the benefits previously attributed to intra-SMSA branching.

There are many proponents of regional interstate banking, particularly among the large regional banks. At one level it is easy to dismiss such suggestions as self-serving. The regional banks naturally want the opportunity to move into attractive banking markets in nearby states, while keeping the money center banks out of their territory. But basic economic similarities among groups of states could provide economic efficiencies from limited interstate banking. The bank serving textile manufacturers in Georgia, for instance, can bring experience and expertise to similar customers in the Carolinas that a Minneapolis bank cannot. Lending to wheat growers in Kansas is similar to lending to wheat growers in South Dakota; oil drilling in Wyoming is similar to drilling in Colorado.

[8] See The Report of the President's Commission on Financial Structure and Regulation, December 1971, p. 62.

In particular, smaller firms may benefit from increased competition that can result from regional interstate banking. The small furniture manufacturer in Virginia may not be a customer sought by a money center bank moving into that state, but may be desirable to the North Carolina bank already familiar with the business. On the other hand, banks from nearby states may already be a competitive force in the market.

The basic problem with proposals for regional banking is that no one has been able to define regions on a logical and consistent basis. In an attempt to overcome the essentially arbitrary nature of regional classification, many have seized on the concept of contiguity. Neighboring states are usually similar in economies. But this basis is also arbitrary and clearly inequitable in its treatment of banks in different states. Contiguous state branching would give Florida banks access only to Georgia and Alabama, while Nevada banks would have access to California, Oregon, Utah, Idaho and Arizona. In fact, such a limitation would encourage the artificial shifting of headquarters. A Florida bank could enter Georgia and make Georgia its headquarters, thus enabling it to enter states not open to it from Florida. This artificial movement has taken place in Pennsylvania under that state's contiguous county branching law. Again, this approach bases treatment of banks on their location rather than on their efficiency or ability to operate on an interstate basis. While such a limited approach to interstate banking might be justified as a step toward eventual nationwide banking, it is not a reasonable permanent solution.

A final approach involves limiting the number or the method of interstate operations, rather than the location. Our current banking structure grew out of a traditional American fear of concentrated financial power. No other country has so many commercial banks. Those who see this as an attribute of the U.S. financial structure fear that nationwide banking could lead to a wave of mergers creating a concentrated banking system such as that of England or Canada.

One means of preventing this, while gaining the benefit of broader interstate banking, would be to allow interstate expansion on a *de novo* basis only. Entry under such a rule necessarily would increase competition rather than concentration. The ultimate effect of such an approach is not clear, however. Many banking markets are already competitive. Additional new entry could require the exit of existing firms. If banks were precluded from selling out to out-of-state institutions, we would see an increase in intrastate mergers. The ultimate net effect on concentration might be the opposite of what is intended. Further, interstate mergers offer an efficient means of resolving problems of failing institutions. Barring such mergers would sacrifice a major potential advantage of interstate banking.

For directly opposite reasons, some favor interstate banking through merger only. Proponents of this approach argue that the U. S. banking system is too fragmented, with many banks too small to achieve economies of scale. Interstate acquisitions could reduce the number of banks without necessitating mergers between directly competing institutions. (Some believe the approach taken in the Garn-St Germain Act is ideal in that it allows such mergers only when necessary to prevent a failure.)

This proposal has a political advantage. Many bankers oppose interstate banking because they fear increased competition from giant out-of-state institutions. Interstate banking limited to mergers may remove their fear of a money center bank opening an office next door and may offer investors a greater number of potential buyers when it comes time to sell their bank.

Fear of the disruptive impact of liberalized interstate banking on the competitive structure clearly is the principal reason such activity has been restricted. Proposals for limited interstate banking attempt to deal with this problem. An alternative means of cushioning the immediate impact of a change is to limit the number of interstate ventures that each bank can undertake. Banks could be restricted to a few acquisitions or *de novo* entries per year. Over time banks would be allowed to operate nationwide, but restrictions in the early years would enable the regional banks to strengthen their operations while facing only limited direct competition from money center banks.

Economic and regulatory constraints are probably sufficient to obviate such legal restrictions. It is unlikely that even the largest banks in the country could plan, negotiate, and finance several major interstate ventures in the first year such activity is legalized. Nevertheless, a legal constraint may provide comfort for some who otherwise might oppose interstate banking.

Conclusion

Because interstate banking has long been a matter of intense controversy, it is important that advantages and disadvantages be discussed thoroughly. But much of that discussion necessarily takes place in the abstract in terms of interstate banking generally rather than focusing on the effects of specific approaches to interstate banking. Our purpose has been to suggest that those effects differ depending on the route chosen toward interstate banking. Any discussion of the merits of changing the McFadden Act or the Douglas Amendment must recognize that many means of engaging in interstate banking already exist, and that such activity will increase even without change in fundamental restrictions on interstate activity.

Bank Holding Companies and Public Policy

Robert A. Eisenbeis

15

Introduction

The decade of the 1970s saw the emergence of bank holding companies (BHCs) as the dominant form of organization in the U.S. banking system, culminating an evolutionary process begun before the turn of the century. Almost all of the nation's top fifty banks have converted to the bank holding company form, and these companies presently control about 75 percent of U.S. banking resources and about 33 percent of its banks. This proportion and number of banks has more than doubled since passage of the 1970 Amendments to the Bank Holding Company Act of 1956. Not only have bank holding companies come to control a majority of banking resources, but also they have begun to provide an expanded array of intermediary and other bank-related services.

Many of these services are close substitutes for those provided by insured banks and thrifts and by less regulated suppliers. Consequently, the future role and function of bank holding companies in the U.S. financial system and how they should be supervised and regulated have become important public policy issues. These issues have been elevated to a high profile as the result of Treasury Department proposals in 1982 to expand the permissible nonbanking activities of bank holding companies and to restructure holding company regulation. These issues have been further complicated by passage of the Garn-

Reprinted from *Financial Services*, George J. Benston, ed., © 1983 by The American Assembly. Published by Prentice-Hall, Inc., Englewood Cliffs, NJ 07632.

St Germain Depository Institutions Act of 1982, which expanded bank authority to establish service corporations and to engage in activities generally permissible to bank holding companies.

This chapter discusses the issues raised by the changing role of bank holding companies in the U.S. financial system and explores their implications for future regulatory policies toward these organizations. The chapter begins with a discussion of the historical evolution of bank holding companies and why banks have been induced to adopt the holding company form of organization.

The Evolution of Bank Holding Companies

The explanation for why bank holding companies evolved lies in understanding how regulation affects banking organizations and how they respond to binding regulatory constraints. Early U.S. financial history proved that our economy could not function smoothly with a rapidly expanding money supply followed by financial panics. Therefore, because of the unique role banks and their deposit liabilities play in our economy, they traditionally have been heavily regulated. Restrictions have been placed on the scope of their assets and liabilities, on the geographic locations at which business may be conducted, and on their capital structure to ensure that banks are operated in a safe and sound manner. In addition, deposit rate and usury ceilings have been imposed to redirect credit flows. Finally, Federal Reserve member bank reserve requirements and related regulations have been imposed, first, to maintain the liquidity and safety of the banking system, and then to facilitate the conduct of monetary policy.

Kane (1981) and others (see Eisenbeis, 1980) have convincingly argued that regulation imposes costs and limits profit-making alternatives and, therefore, has provided powerful economic incentives for banks to innovate to avoid as many of the costs of regulation as they can. The consequences of these regulatory-induced financial innovations have been numerous and far reaching; they have radically affected the structure and functioning of financial markets. For example, these innovations have altered the array of financial services provided to the public and have substantially increased the number of close money substitutes. An unintended consequence has been to complicate the measurement of the monetary aggregates and the implementation of monetary policy. Avoidance efforts have also increased banks' reliance on shorter term, more interest sensitive sources of funds. This in turn implies greater earnings variability over interest rate cycles and hence greater risk over business cycles, which appear to have increased in both frequency and amplitude. The process of financial innovation has also broken down traditional barriers to competition between banks and thrifts and has opened the door to new unregulated purveyors of financial services.

Most important, however, from the perspective of this chapter, are the effects of financial innovation and regulation on the organization, structure, and operations of banking firms. In particular, banks were induced to form bank holding companies because of that form's advantages in facilitating regulatory avoidance. As such, the evolution of bank holding companies may be viewed as part of the broader process of financial innovation designed to avoid regulation. The early history of the bank holding company movement, discussed in the next section, suggests that the ability to avoid state and federal limitations on branching was the primary reason for the expansion of bank holding companies until 1956 (see Savage, 1978, and Fischer and Golembe, 1976). Thereafter, restrictions on geographic and product expansion were but two of several important stimuli accelerating bank holding company formation. These included deposit rate ceilings, reserve requirements, tax considerations, and capital adequacy requirements (see Eisenbeis, 1980).

Bank Holding Companies Before 1956

The pre-1956 growth of bank holding companies is closely rooted in federal and state policies toward bank branching and geographic expansion. In particular, the National Banking Act of 1864, while apparently silent on the issue of branching, was interpreted by the Office of the Comptroller of the Currency (OCC) as prohibiting nationally chartered banks from operating branches. This interpretation, coupled with generally restrictive state branching laws, meant that unit banking dominated the scene well into the 1920s. (By 1920, for example, only 530 of the 30,291 banks in existence operated branches, of which 60 percent were located in the same city as the head office.)

Multioffice banking, however, existed in other forms besides branching. In particular, even before 1900, individuals began acquiring interests in more than one bank and linking them together in chain relationships. Similarly, once several states began relaxing prohibitions on corporate ownership of stock in the late 1800s, bank holding companies came into existence. But significant growth in bank holding companies did not occur until the 1910–30 period which coincided with heightened economic pressures stimulating the expansion of branch banks.

As urbanization, income growth, and customer mobility increased, the inability to branch on the part of national banks and state banks in states with restrictive branching laws inhibited banks from serving customers within their natural markets. The resulting loss of profit alternatives increased pressures to relax restrictions on branching and stimulated the growth of group and chain banking. In the face of these forces, individual states began to relax their limits on branching for state banks. This placed national banks at a competitive disadvantage because of the restrictive interpretation of the National Banking Act of 1864, which stimulated conversions of national banks to state bank status. The competitive inequity and concern for the viability of the national banking system resulted in compromise federal legislation in the form of both the McFadden Act of 1927, permitting national banks to branch within their head office city, and the Banking Act of 1933, allowing national banks to branch intrastate on the same basis as state banks.

Despite this liberalizing trend of state and federal policies toward branching, however, more than half of the states still prohibited any form of branch banking as late as 1929. And it was especially in those states (such as Texas, Illinois, Colorado, and Wisconsin) that chain and group banking flourished.

In addition to the ability to expand in states with restrictive branching laws, several other factors have been cited by Savage (1978) as being important in explaining bank holding company expansion. For example, the series of bank failures in the 1920s made geographical diversification desirable and affiliation with bank holding companies attractive. Second, the general wave of business mergers during the period undoubtedly carried over to banking as well, probably motivated in part by the desire of banks to achieve greater size to serve larger businesses. Also, the upward surge of the stock market in the 1920s probably enhanced bank holding company access to capital markets and made further expansion possible. Although data are not generally available on the extent of banking company and chain banking relationships, it is known that by the end of the decade there were nearly 300 group and chain organizations controlling more than 2,000 banks.

During the 1930s, many group and chain banking organizations failed; however, the failure rate was about half that of commercial banks in general. Savage has indicated that between 1930 and 1934, the failures included 201 banks in 40 bank groups having resources of about $1.5 billion. However, about half of the total resources of these failed banks were accounted for by only two companies in Detroit. In some instances, bank groups actually expanded during the thirties due to their generally sounder condition which led to supervisory and other mergers and acquisitions.

The growth of bank holding companies during the thirties was also accompanied by legislative attempts at both the state and federal level to expand supervision and regulation of bank holding companies and to limit the concentration of economic power. The Banking Act of 1933 extended, for the first time, federal regulation to bank holding companies; those companies with a majority interest in a member bank were required to obtain Federal Reserve approval to vote their stock. In granting voting approval, the Federal Reserve usually required such companies to be subject to examination, to publish financial reports, to divest themselves of their securities activities, and to adhere to several other restrictions as well.

Passage of this act did not eliminate concern over bank holding companies for several reasons. Holding company formation and expansion were not subject to regulation. Moreover, since the restrictions in the act applied only to companies with a majority interest in Federal Reserve member banks, it was easy for companies to avoid regulation by reducing their ownership and by acquiring nonmember banks. As a result several legislative initiatives were undertaken that were designed to increase bank holding company regulation and to eliminate many of the deficiencies of the Banking Act of 1933, including the definition of control.

Although numerous efforts were undertaken between 1935 and 1956, no further legislation was enacted until passage of the Bank Holding Company Act of 1956. The failure of the Supreme Court to sustain the Federal Reserve Board's charges that Transamerica Corporation violated Section 7 of the Clayton Act by acquiring banks in five western states finally crystallized congressional concern that bank holding company expansion should be regulated. Among the more significant of the 1956 act's provisions were those prohibiting interstate expansion unless the host state explicitly permitted entry by out-of-state holding companies (the Douglas Amendment), extending regulation to include those companies controlling 25 percent of the stock of two or more insured banks, limiting expansion without regulatory approval, and prohibiting ownership in nonbanking firms engaged in activities, other than Federal Reserve-approved, bank-related activities. The act did not apply however, to companies owning only one bank.

Bank Holding Company Formation Following the Bank Holding Act of 1956 and the Role of Deposit Rate Ceilings and Reserve Requirements

The credit crunch of 1959-60 ushered in a new set of stimuli, in addition to the desire to avoid restrictions on geographic and product diversification, which contributed to bank holding company growth. More specifically, accelerating inflation coupled with binding deposit rate ceilings increased the opportunity costs to large corporations and individual depositors of holding temporarily idle cash balances in demand deposits. The more sophisticated of these depositors sought higher returns in the open market from less regulated competitors. The resulting disintermediation placed commercial banks in a liquidity squeeze. In response, banks began to create new instruments in attempts to reclaim existing deposits and attract new funds by offering market rates to their most interest-sensitive customers.

Successful innovation, however, did not go unnoticed by the Federal Reserve, other regulators, and Congress. Often, out of concern for housing and the stability of financial markets, one or more of these groups stepped in and either attempted to shut down the innovation or ratified it by raising interest rate ceilings on close substitutes offered by banks and thrifts. The general process being described, then, is a continuous evolutionary cycle involving banks, thrifts, unregulated suppliers of financial services, money markets, and the regulators, all interacting in response to market pressures. And the principal economic force sustaining these pressures was inflation, accompanied by rising interest rates.

The persistence of the pressures stimulating financial innovation during the late 1960s and early 1970s and the variety of institutional responses is quite striking. For example, the development of the Eurodollar, federal funds and repurchase agreements (R/P), and large certificate of deposit (C/D) markets are all examples of innovations that expanded as the result of disintermediation pressures. It was also during this period that the first of the financial innovations having significant implications for the growth and expansion of bank holding companies developed.

Shut out of the Eurodollar and other markets and pressed for funds in late 1969 and early 1970, as interest rate ceilings again became a significant constraint, banks began to exploit the holding company organizational form by issuing nonreservable commercial paper as a liability of the holding company and downstreaming funds to subsidiary banks. (Commercial paper sales by banks were already reservable.)

There is little, if any, direct evidence to suggest that banks had perceived the financing advantage of bank holding companies when the first wave of formations occurred following Citicorp's announcement of its intention to form a one-bank holding company in July of 1968. It is interesting to note, however, that the great bulge in interest in the one-bank holding company organizational form occurred over the last half of 1968 when the gap between Regulation Q (savings and time deposit interest rate) ceilings and commercial paper rates widened by over 250 basis points. Between September 1 and December 31, 1968, seven banks with $14.1 billion in deposits formed one-bank holding companies, and another seventy-six banks with deposits of $71.8 billion—including thirty-four of the nation's one hundred largest banks—announced their intentions to form one-bank holding companies (see U.S. Congress, 1969). This compares with the $17.8 billion in deposits in the 684 companies existing prior to September 1, 1968 (Table 1).

Over the last two and one-half quarters of 1969 and the first half of 1970, commercial paper issued by the bank holding companies became a major source of funds to banks. Sales of bank-related commercial paper increased from about $1.9 billion in July of 1969 to a high of $7.8 billion a year later in late July of 1970. The significance of this source of funds is placed in better perspective when it is recognized that banks lost over $13 billion in C/Ds between November of 1968 and September of 1969 but were able to recover nearly 20 percent through commercial paper sales over that period.

Bank holding companies' sales of commercial paper remained high over the summer of 1970 until they began a slight downward trend in late August. On September 18, 1970, following a Federal Reserve Board proposal made a year earlier, Regulation D (member bank reserve requirements) and Regulation Q were amended to cover commercial paper sales by bank holding companies and their subsidiaries whenever the proceeds were used to supply funds to bank affiliates; a 10 percent marginal reserve requirement applied. The effect of this regulatory change was to price banking organizations out of the commercial paper market.

Commercial paper sales were not the only vehicle for bank holding companies to finance their activities free from Regulations D and Q. Beginning in July of 1974 Citicorp and other holding companies began issuing a series of small denomination floating rate notes. Congress acted by promptly passing Senate Bill 3838 in October of 1974 giving the Federal Reserve Board authority to regulate nearly all bank holding company note issues and to subject them to Regulations D and Q. At first, these regulations were not applied by the Federal Reserve to bank holding company note issues. But finally to shut down a series of note issues designed to be just outside existing Regulation Q ceilings, all bank holding company note issues were gradually brought under Regulations D and Q (the last being in 1979 during the Credit Restraint Program) regardless of whether the funds were used to fund banking subsidiaries or nonbanking affiliates.

Table 1 Existing One-Bank Holding Companies 1955–70 and Proposed Formations September-December 1968

Year	Number of One-Bank Holding Companies	Bank Deposits ($ Billions)
1955	117	$ 11.6
1965	550	$ 15.1
1968 (September 1)	684	$ 17.8
1968 (December 31)	691	$ 31.9
Banks announcing plans to formulate one-bank holding companies (September 1–December 31, 1968)	76	$ 71.8
1970	1,318	$191.0

Source: U.S. Congress (1969).

1970 Amendments to the Bank Holding Company Act of 1956 and the Role of Geographic and Product Diversification

Although avoidance of Regulations D and Q was an important consideration in bank holding company funding and formations during the late 1960s and early 1970s, the desire to achieve greater product and geographic diversity continued to play an important role in bank holding company growth. It will be remembered that the Bank Holding Company Act of 1956 and related regulatory restrictions applied only to companies owning two or more banks. In early 1968 North Carolina National Bank and Wachovia Bank and Trust, N.C. announced their intentions to form one-bank holding companies. The full potential of the one-bank holding company form did not attract public attention, however, until July of 1968 when Citicorp announced its intention to become a one-bank holding company. The principal reasons Citicorp cited for becoming a one-bank holding company related to the additional flexibility to expand geographically and to offer new services. The proxy statement notes that:

> Some of the Bank's present departments or activities such as leasing, factoring, or travel services could have greater growth potential if operated by First National City Corporation directly or through subsidiaries, because geographic expansion would be easier. . . .
>
> It is also expected that the new corporate structure can be used advantageously to move into other financially oriented activities either directly or through newly formed subsidiaries, or by acquiring companies already established in such fields.

Almost immediately it was argued in the financial press (Strachan, 1968) that the virtually unlimited geographical and product diversification potential of this new conglomerate form had sparked the broad rally that occurred in the market for bank equities following Citicorp's announcement; as discussed in the previous section, a host of other major banks also announced their intention to form one-bank holding companies (Table 1).

Congress responded almost immediately to this end run around the McFadden Act and the Douglas Amendment (which restrict interstate banking), the Glass-Steagall Act provisions which separate banking and investment banking, and the general threat to the historical separation between banking and commerce. The U.S. Congress published a study in 1969 of the one-bank holding company movement and its potential problems, and legislation was introduced in both the House and Senate in mid-February of 1969. This legislative activity culminated in passage of the 1970 Amendments to the Bank Holding Company Act of 1956. (For a detailed chronology see Eisenbeis, Harris, and Lakonishok, 1982.)

These amendments subjected one-bank holding companies to the same rules and regulations as multibank holding companies and modified the criteria contained in the act for bank holding company expansion into permissible nonbanking activities. On balance, these amendments significantly narrowed the diversification possibilities for one-bank holding companies and slightly expanded those for multibank companies by allowing expansion only into those activities that were so closely related to banking to be a proper incident thereto. (See Aharony and Swary, 1981; Martin and Keown, 1981; and Eisenbeis, Harris and Lakonishok, 1982, for analyses of the effects of these changes on BHC share values.)

Since no geographic restrictions were imposed on the locations of permissible nonbanking activities, an opportunity was provided for banking organizations to avoid the limitations of the McFadden Act and Douglas Amendment, at least with respect to certain functional banking activities. It is not surprising, therefore, that many large bank holding companies have actively used nonbanking expansion to establish a physical presence throughout the country.

More recently, several states have taken more direct steps, as permitted by the Douglas Amendment to the Bank Holding Company Act of 1956, to allow out-of-state holding companies to enter their states. New York State, Massachusetts, and Maine, for example, have passed reciprocal legislation. Alaska now permits entry by out-of-state organizations, while South Dakota and Delaware have permitted acquisitions of newly chartered banks, provided certain minimum capital and other operational employment, and locational restrictions are met. (Hawke, 1982, argues that many of these restrictions may be unconstitutional.) Many large banking organizations have already established banking subsidiaries in at least South Dakota and Delaware in order to take advantage of less restrictive usury ceilings.

A second wedge was driven into the restrictions on interstate banking with passage of the Garn-St Germain Depository Institutions Act of 1982. This act permits the interstate acquisition of a thrift institution or a failing bank with assets in excess of $500 million. Many restrictions are placed, however, on the order of preference to be given to bidders for such failed banks based on their geographic location.

With respect to product diversification, the requirement of the 1970 amendments that the nonbanking activities be "closely related to banking or managing or controlling banks as to be a proper incident thereto," has resulted in only twenty-five activities (seventeen by rule making and eight by order) being approved by the Federal Reserve Board as of May 1982 (Table 2). All but four were essentially permissible for national banks at the time the activity was approved. Only two denied activities, real estate brokerage and travel agencies, were approved activities for national banks. (The latter has since been ruled impermissible for national banks by the courts.) Thus, because of legislative and regulatory restrictions, it appears that the bank holding company movement has not resulted in significant additional product diversification potential. In fact, it is probably a misnomer to call such activities "nonbanking" activities. They are really *banking activities* being carried out in separately financed departments or subsidiaries, often outside of Regulations D and Q and McFadden Act restrictions. That is, they permit the banking organization to conduct lending and other services outside of subsidiary banks that could just as well, except for certain regulatory constraints, be done by the banks directly.

A recent series of events is raising once again the issues Congress considered in passing the 1970 amendments to close the loophole in the Bank Holding Company Act of 1956 exposed by the one-bank holding company movement. To qualify as a bank under the definition in the 1970 amendments, an organization must both make commercial loans and accept demand deposits. By divesting of either activity (or spinning it off into a separate affiliation), it has proved possible for nonbanking companies to acquire chartered commercial banks and avoid the nonbanking activity restrictions of the 1956 act. Such a device has enabled Dreyfus to acquire a national bank in New Jersey and several other firms, including Shearson/American Express, to acquire commercial banks. The extent to which this loophole will be exploited or that the agencies will permit nonbanking and securities firms to acquire commercial banks remains to be seen. Even more interesting, however, is the possibility that major U.S. bank holding companies will subdivide their demand deposit business into one particular bank subsidiary and their commercial loan business into another bank subsidiary and suddenly no longer be a bank holding company for purposes of the act.

The Role of Tax Considerations in Bank Holding Company Formations

Of all the incentives to bank holding company formation, tax considerations have probably been the single most important catalyst to the formation of the majority of the nation's bank holding companies. For example, of the more than 2,300 bank holding companies in existence, more than 80 percent are one-bank holding companies. Of these, about 55 percent are single subsidiary companies (see Strover, 1978). Thus, diversification, in terms of either the product or geographic markets to be served, cannot account for the existence of these single-subsidiary holding companies.

There are several reasons why the bank holding company form might be preferable for tax purposes. These advantages stem from the fact that, if the bank holding company is properly structured, dividends received from subsidiaries are tax deductible, and a consolidated tax return may be filed for the entire organization. The tax deductibility of dividends especially benefits those who purchase control of a bank through the use of debt, and it facilitates capital injections into subsidiary banks as compared with nonsubsidiary banks. In the former case, the typical procedure is for an individual or group of individuals to borrow money to purchase a bank. They then form a bank holding company which is given the bank stock and assumes the debt in return for stock in the bank holding company. Since dividends received from a bank by the bank holding company are tax deductible, the principal on the debt can be repaid out of dividend income. Dividend income is taxed only at the bank level. In addition the bank holding company interest payments are a deductible expense (as they are for individuals). In the case of individual ownership, dividends received would first be taxed before the principal on the acquisition debt could be paid.

Since the only source of bank holding company income is typically tax-deductible dividends from subsidiaries, the bank holding company usually starts with a zero taxable income base from which interest and other expenses are subtracted. (This assumes, of course, that the parent company is not an operating company, in which case it would have other sources of income.) This results in negative taxable income for the parent. Filing a consolidated return allows the organization to offset positive taxable income in the rest of the organization. In addition, consolidation also permits operating losses in some subsidiaries to offset operating gains in others for tax purposes.

Table 2 Permissible Nonbanking Activities for Bank Holding Companies—Under Section 4(c)8 of Regulation Y (May 1, 1982)

Activities Permitted by Regulation	Activities Permitted by Order	Activities Denied by the Board
1. Extension of credit[2] Mortgage banking Finance companies, consumer sales, and commercial Credit cards Factoring	1. Issuance and sale of travelers checks[2,6]	1. Insurance premium funding (combined sales of mutual funds and insurance)
2. Industrial bank, Morris Plan Bank, industrial loan company	2. Buying and selling gold and silver bullion and silver coin[2,4]	2. Underwriting life insurance not related to credit extension
3. Servicing loans and other extensions of credit[2]	3. Issuing money orders and general purpose variable denominated payment instruments[1,2,4]	3. Real estate brokerage[2]
4. Trust company[2]	4. Futures commission merchant to cover gold and silver bullion and coins[1,2]	4. Land development
5. Investment and financial advising[2]	5. Underwriting certain federal, state, and municipal securities[1,2]	5. Real estate syndication
6. Full-payout leasing of personal or real property[2]	6. Check verification[1,2,4]	6. General management consulting
7. Investment in community welfare projects[2]	7. Financial advice to consumers[1,2]	7. Property management
8. Providing bookkeeping or data processing services[2]	8. Issuance of small denomination debt instruments[1]	8. Computer output microfilm services
9. Acting as insurance agent or broker primarily in connection with credit extensions[2]	9. Arranging for equity financing of real estate	9. Underwriting mortgage guaranty insurance[3]
10. Underwriting credit life, accident, and health insurance	10. Acting as futures commissions merchant	10. Operating a savings and loan association[1,5]
11. Providing courier services[2]	11. Discount brokerage	11. Operating a travel agency[1,2]
	12. Operating a distressed savings and loan association	12. Underwriting property and casualty insurance[1]
	13. Operating an Article XII investment company	13. Underwriting home loan life mortgage insurance
		14. Orbanco: Investment note issue with transactional characteristics
		15. Real estate advisory services

12. Management consulting for unaffiliated banks[1,2]
13. Sale at retail of money orders with a face value of not more than $1,000, travelers checks and savings bonds[1,2]
14. Performing appraisals of real estate[1]
15. Audit services for unaffiliated banks
16. Issuance and sale of travelers checks
17. Management consulting to nonbanking depository institutions

14. Executing foreign banking unsolicited purchases and sales of securities
15. Engaging in commercial banking activities abroad through a limited purpose Delaware bank
16. Performing appraisal of real estate and real estate advisor and real estate brokerage on nonresidential properties
17. Operating a Pool Reserve Plan for loss reserves of banks for loans to small businesses
18. Operating a thrift institution in Rhode Island
19. Operating a guarantee savings bank in New Hampshire
20. Offering informational advice and transactional services for foreign exchange services

---

Source: Economic Review, Federal Reserve Bank of Atlanta, April 1983.

[1]Added to list since January 1, 1975.

[2]Activities permissible to national banks.

[3]Board orders found these activities closely related to banking and denied proposed acquisitions as part of its "go slow" policy.

[4]To be decided on a case-by-case basis.

[5]Operating a thrift institution has been permitted by order in Rhode Island, California, and New Hampshire only.

[6]Subsequently permitted by regulation.

There are two other dimensions of taxation which tend to provide significant incentives for banks to form holding companies and also to spin off permissible banking activities into subsidiaries. The first relates to the ability to avoid local taxes. Income generated within a bank is taxed by the state and perhaps municipalities in which the institution is headquartered or operates. Performing the same activity in a subsidiary of a bank holding company permits the organization, in some instances, to charter the subsidiary in a state with lower taxes which then subjects the subsidiary to "doing business" taxes only in the original state. A vivid example of this type of tax avoidance is provided by the method Citicorp chose to market the rising-rate thrift notes it announced in July of 1977. The prospectus indicates that the notes were to be offered through a specially chartered, wholly-owned subsidiary of Nationwide Financial Services Corporation (Citicorp's consumer finance company subsidiary). This subsidiary was organized to avoid subjecting the parent company to taxation in the states in which the notes were to be sold and to avoid the necessity of qualifying Citicorp to do business in those states. Additionally, it also simplified meeting the technical Securities and Exchange Commission net capital rules to qualify as a broker-dealer.

Federal tax law also provides an incentive for a holding company (and/or bank) to conduct foreign business through separately chartered subsidiaries rather than through foreign branches. The incentive stems from a provision in the present tax law permitting a subsidiary of a U.S. corporation also holding a foreign charter to retain abroad indefinitely any portion of its net income rather than upstreaming it in the form of dividends. Since only repatriated income is subject to U.S. tax, there is an incentive to conduct foreign business through separately chartered subsidiaries in low-tax countries. In contrast, income earned abroad through a foreign branch is treated as if it were earned domestically and is subject to U.S. tax (and perhaps foreign tax as well). This feature of the tax law helps to explain the growth of foreign subsidiary activities of the large U.S. money center banks in Bermuda and the Cayman Islands, both of which are low-tax countries. It may also stimulate the proliferation of foreign operations in countries that would not be profitable except for the tax advantages that result. For example, until March 16, 1978, banks were able to claim full foreign tax credits for a 25 percent tax that Brazil imposed on interest that banks earned in the country. Brazilian authorities typically rebated 85 percent of the tax to the borrowers, but the bank still received a full tax credit on the paper transaction. The intent of the tax and rebate system was to stimulate investment in Brazil by reducing the interest cost on foreign loans; the borrower benefited because of the rebate, and the lender got a tax savings from its home country.

Capital Adequacy Requirements and Other Supervisory Incentives to Bank Holding Company Formation

It has already been argued that deposit rate ceilings and reserve requirements provided a significant inducement to bank holding company formations. More importantly, these regulations also provided incentives for a holding company to spin off banking activities into other parts of the organization and for a parent holding company to fund both banking and nonbanking expansion, especially during tight money periods and when interest rates are rising. As a consequence, one of the main implications of the bank holding company form of organization is that it has facilitated increased leverage of the banking entity as a whole.

Interestingly, the thrust of early bank holding company regulatory and supervisory policy has reinforced and unintentionally tended to encourage the conduct of financing and certain activities in other parts of the organization rather than within banking subsidiaries. Following the 1970 Amendments to the Bank Holding Company Act of 1956, regulatory policy was designed to compartmentalize bank holding companies into two segments—a regulated component consisting of the banking subsidiaries and the parent holding company with its nonbanking subsidiaries. The objective was to isolate and protect banks from risk and abuse and, thus, to limit deposit insurance risks flowing from the rest of the organization which was permitted to complete and operate in a less regulated and relatively unsupervised manner (see Chase, 1978). At the same time bank holding companies were expected to be ''sources of strength'' to their banking affiliates, and there was an attempt to permit any benefit from bank holding company affiliation to be downstreamed to banking subsidiaries. In particular, the issuing of debt at the parent company level and use of the proceeds to purchase equity of subsidiary banks—a practice known as double leveraging—was not only condoned but often encouraged as a means to improve the capital positioning of a bank holding company's banking subsidiaries. This double leveraging was permitted since the financing capabilities of the parent were presumably being relied upon to inject equity into subsidiary banks. As long as banking affiliates were effectively isolated by laws and regulations, such as Section 23A of the Federal Reserve Act which limits permissible transactions among affiliates and subsidiaries, it was believed that the corporate veil would not be pierced in the event of bankruptcy or other legal action and no harm would befall subsidiary banks.

Such a policy would be appropriate if it were truly possible to isolate totally bank holding company banking subsidiaries from the rest of the organization. Separation would clearly be feasible if a holding company functioned as a mutual fund and was only a passive investor, exercising no management, operational, or financial influence over independently operated firms. The available evidence, however, indicates that bank holding companies tend to operate more as integrated firms with the parent company dictating the key aspects of their banking subsidiaries' operations, such as organizational structure, financial and managerial philosophy, as well as specific functions, such as funds management, correspondent relationships, asset and liability management, capitalization, and budgets. Moreover, bank holding company nonbanking subsidiaries appear to be even more integrated and tightly controlled than their banking subsidiaries. (See Whalen, 1982A, 1982B; Rose, 1978; and Murray, 1978.)

The implication is that when bank holding companies operate as integrated firms, rather than as a collective of truly independent companies sharing only a common mutual fund-type owner, regulatory policies designed to force compartmentalization are likely in the long run to be self-defeating. The very attempt to isolate the more heavily regulated subsidiary banks from the rest of the holding company only creates further economic incentives for the organization to attempt to circumvent banking regulations and to spin off more and more activities of the banking subsidiaries into the less heavily regulated segments of the organization. The reason, of course, is that to a firm, total profits of the organization are maximized and not necessarily the profits of individual subsidiaries. Thus, it matters little to the firm where a particular function is being conducted within the organization as long as its contribution to total firm profits is optimized.

There are likely to be two major consequences of bank holding company regulatory policies designed to force compartmentalization. First, there will be a shrinking of the regulated components relative to the nonregulated components as more and more activities are shifted from regulated to less regulated segments of the organization. Second, the operational and other interdependencies within the firm are likely to increase. This is particularly the case if customer relationships are served by coordinating the products offered by a number of different subsidiaries. Moreover, the entire holding company is likely to become more of an integrated firm with respect to risk-taking than it was before because of the integration of operations and provision of services. Integration also increases the potential for regulatory conflicts when different federal and state agencies are responsible for supervising only portions of the entity.

This shifting of activities from banking to nonbanking subsidiaries poses special public policy problems when a parent company or its nonbanking affiliates issue uninsured liabilities that are close substitutes for the insured liabilities of subsidiary banks. As a greater and greater proportion of financial liabilities shift from insured to uninsured status, then the stabilizing benefits of deposit insurance will be lost unless the government chooses implicitly to extend guarantees to such claims. This, in fact, appears to be what has occurred, at least where larger troubled or failed banking organizations have been involved. With this extension of implicit guarantees to more than insured liabilities, however, also goes the legitimate concern on the part of banking regulators and the Federal Deposit Insurance Corporation for monitoring and limiting undue risk-taking in the nonbanking segments of a holding company.

To date, the regulators have responded quite predictably to the shifting of certain funding and other activities to the nonbanking components of a holding company and to the realization that a banking subsidiary cannot be isolated from what goes on in the rest of the organization. In particular, they have begun to extend banking-type supervision and regulation, on a selective basis, to formerly unregulated segments of holding companies. The objective is both to monitor and limit risk-taking and to facilitate monetary control. The application of Regulation D and Q to bank holding company commercial paper and short-term debt and the newly revised capital adequacy standards are clear examples. For larger banking organizations, capital adequacy will now be assessed on a consolidated basis, and account will be taken for the proportion of bank equity funded with subsidy debt at the parent company level.

Implications of Financial Innovation for Regulation and Supervision of Bank Holding Companies

There are several general observations and conclusions that flow, either explicitly or implicitly, from the analysis of the effects of regulation and innovation that have important implications for public policy and the future structure of the supervision and regulation of banking organizations. They highlight the need to develop a consistent framework for the supervision and regulation of financial institutions and, in particular, for bank holding companies. These implications warrant restating.

First, the evolution of bank holding companies is an integral and natural part of this broader process of regulation-induced financial innovation. Banks were moved to adopt the bank holding company form as one means to escape certain regulatory constraints, namely Regulations D and Q, restrictions on geographic and product market expansion, capital regulation, and taxation.

Second, it appears that an increasing proportion of banking activities is being conducted at the holding company level in an attempt to avoid regulation. As mentioned earlier, parent holding companies have begun to play an increasing role in the financing of both banking and nonbanking activities through commercial paper, small note sales, and debt issues. This is presumably due to attempts to avoid Regulations D and Q, and to the accommodating capital policies of the regulators. In addition, there are increasing incentives to spin off operations of subsidiary banks, both to avoid federal and local taxes as well as the prohibition on geographic expansion in restrictive state banking laws and the McFadden Act.

Third, both banks and bank holding companies have become more highly leveraged and have also tended to rely more and more on short-term, interest-sensitive sources of funds. To this extent regulation has indirectly induced more risk-taking.

Fourth, in the 1970s, the combination of higher yielding investment alternatives, accommodating tax laws, and Regulation Q ceilings has resulted in significant expansion of U.S. banks' foreign operations. Indeed, many of the major U.S. money center banks have recently been generating more of their earnings abroad than they have domestically.

Fifth, the process of financial innovation has resulted in a blurring of the distinctions among the liabilities of not only different types of depository financial institutions but also nondepository institutions. Consequently, competition has been increased.

Sixth, financial innovation has resulted in increased competition from merchants, brokerage firms, money market mutual funds, and other financial and nondepository institutions creating competitive inequities resulting from the fact that these institutions are not subject to the same regulatory costs as banking organizations. To meet this competition and to operate profitably during periods of rapidly rising rates, banking organizations have powerful incentives to conduct as many as possible of their activities in an unregulated, or less regulated, environment. Hence, they are under constant pressure to spin off activities and functions of subsidiary banks and operate through bank holding companies and nonbanking and foreign subsidiaries.

Seventh, attempts to regulate a firm such as a bank holding company, operating under a single-objective function, by dividing it into regulated and unregulated segments, will tend to induce a reshuffling of activities into the nonregulated portions of the organization whenever a regulation becomes a binding and costly constraint. The implication is that it is not practical or possible to segment risk-taking or to separate the financial health of parts of the organization from the whole. Thus, it is also not realistic to act as if significant subsidiaries of such an organization would, in most instances, be permitted by the parent to fail. The only way to truly isolate subsidiaries would be to impose regulations to make them totally independent except for the passive ownership of shares by the parent. The problem with such a policy, however, is that it would negate the basic rationale for establishing a holding company so as to take advantage of a beneficial synergistic or other relationship that might result from financial conglomeration.

Finally, so long as it is public policy to attempt to minimize the likelihood of financial crisis by insuring deposit-type liabilities, either explicitly or implicitly, then the efficacy of such insurance can only be maintained by minimizing inducements to shift funds from insured to uninsured status. Moreover, the need to monitor and control the insurer's exposure to risk suggests that any changes in the asset and liability powers of such institutions should take place within the insured entity.

Alternative Policies and Bank Holding Company Supervision and Regulation

In view of the effects of financial innovation and the risk-inducing nature of current regulatory policies on bank holding companies, it is both appropriate and necessary to explore feasible alternatives and/or reforms. In that process it is important that any new system address or consider several factors.

1. Attempts to maintain Regulations D (member bank reserve requirements) and Q (savings and time deposit interest rate ceilings) have been the root cause of many of the restrictions placed on banking organizations affecting the terms under which financial services can be provided. In addition to inducing banking organizations to form BHCs and to take on more risk, they have provided economic incentives for nonfinancial and nonregulated firms to begin to provide financial services.
2. The entry by nonregulated firms into many financial markets suggests that bank holding companies will continue to be at a competitive disadvantage unless given increased flexibility to meet that competition.
3. The financial system has had to deal over the past few years with a series of movements in which interest rates have fluctuated widely in response to changes in the rate of inflation, the level of economic activity, and government economic policy. Such cycles are potentially destabilizing unless financial institutions are free to adjust and adapt to changing conditions. There is nothing to suggest that these cycles are dampening or will occur with less frequency in the future. Added to this domestic source of financial instability is the increased vulnerability of our financial institutions to changes in world economic conditions resulting from rapid expansion abroad. The expansion of foreign banks into the U.S. as a result of the recently passed International Banking Act will only serve to integrate further both our real sectors and financial systems with those of the rest of the world.
4. Regulation which is designed to force banking organizations to operate as a collection of single, independent entities, when the organization's incentive is to operate as an integrated entity, that also does not regulate each and every part of the entity, will only result in attempts to circumvent that effort.

There are two sets of regulatory policies which, when coupled with actions to phase out and to reduce significantly the costs of reserve requirements and Regulation Q, would achieve the long-run safety and soundness goals and be responsive to the continuing destabilizing pressures affecting banking organizations. The first is to reorient supervisory attention away from primary emphasis on subsidiary banks to focus on the consolidated bank holding company as a single, regulated entity. Some steps have already been taken with the agencies' new consolidated capital adequacy standards for large banks. The second is to create a set of regulatory incentives to encourage bank holding companies to fold activities and functions back into a consolidated subsidiary bank. Each of these alternatives raises separate sets of issues with respect to regulatory and structural reform together with political issues which may affect the practical implementation of the alternatives, and these are discussed in the next section. On the other hand, both of the proposals share certain desirable common features. For example, they both imply that substantial deregulation is justifiable on equity and economic grounds. Second, they increase institutions' flexibility to adapt to changing economic conditions. Finally, they simplify the process of supervision.

Discussion of Policy Alternatives

CONSOLIDATED BANK HOLDING COMPANY FOCUS

The first alternative would reorient regulatory and supervisory policy away from primary emphasis on subsidiary banks and focus on the consolidated bank holding company as the single, decision-making entity. Taking this policy to its logical conclusion, there would be no need to be concerned, for safety and soundness reasons, with the financial relationships among subsidiaries or with maintaining their independence. Under this alternative the holding company organizations could be regulated, examined, and supervised analogous to a branch system, with the structure of the parent and its subsidiaries simply representing ways for the firm to organize its internal accounting and control procedures. If regulated in this manner, and when accompanied with general deregulation, bank holding companies could evolve into the functional equivalent of banks.

For the purpose of regulation relevant for monetary control, a bank holding company could be treated as a single entity with its consolidated liabilities subject to the same limits and reserve requirements as banks. This policy approach also would avoid the problems of attempting to sort out and reserve certain intracompany transfers and to trace the sources and uses of intrafirm transactions to determine their regulatory status. It would have the additional benefits of (1) eliminating incentives to innovate different types of intrainstitutional fund transfers and investments to avoid reserve requirement-related constraints and (2) reducing associated reporting burdens.

This single-entity approach also holds the possibility to deregulate further the industry since regulations that have been instituted to force separation or to limit transactions between and among subsidiaries would no longer be necessary. For example, Section 23A of the Federal Reserve Act could be dropped, as could regulations, supervisory conventions, rules, and reporting requirements pertaining to intercompany transfers of funds and tax liabilities. Moreover, reporting burdens for supervisory purposes could be drastically reduced, since only consolidated entity data would need to be collected.

A principal argument that would no doubt be raised against this single-entity approach is that it would require an extension of banking-type regulation to the nonbanking activities of bank holding companies. This might place the organization at a competitive disadvantage to the extent it competed with nonregulated firms. It should be remembered, however, that with only a couple of minor exceptions, the nonbanking activities of bank holding companies are really banking activities that could legally be conducted within a bank. Therefore, the single-entity approach would not really be extending regulation, but simply closing the ability of the organization to avoid regulation by use of the bank holding company form. But still the valid point does remain that regulated firms are at a competitive disadvantage relative to less regulated firms. Therefore the long-run goal should be to reduce and limit the extent that bank holding companies are constrained by regulation, to eliminate the regulatory-induced incentives for nonbanking firms to enter financial markets, and to provide banking organizations with the needed flexibility to meet changing economic conditions.

Despite the potential appeal of this approach, substantial transitional and legal problems would exist. For example, although subsidiaries might be operated as a part of a single entity, they remain legally separate in that the minority shareholders and debt holders may have claims on the resources of subsidiaries. Ownership of assets and settlement of claims might greatly complicate the resolution of failures. Also, state and local regulatory and tax policies might conflict with federal regulatory policy. There could also be the need to reevaluate federal policy toward insurance of bank holding company liabilities. Despite these problems, the general single-entity regulatory policy could shape and provide guidance to needed legislative and regulatory changes that ultimately would lead to a parent bank holding company having all the powers permitted to its subsidiaries.

The present trend in bank holding company supervision seems already to be evolving in the direction of treating a bank holding company as a consolidated entity. The Federal Reserve recently instituted a bank holding company surveillance and computer-based monitoring system that focuses almost exclusively on the holding company as a consolidated organization. Also, the chairman of the Federal Deposit Insurance Corporation and past comptroller of the currency have argued that it is not possible, because of the interrelated nature of the holding company and its subsidiaries, for them to assess the risk and financial condition of the nonmember and national bank subsidiaries of bank holding companies without also having information on the entire organization. This raises the question of the feasibility and the desirability of maintaining the present regulatory structure giving different federal agencies supervisory responsibility for only a portion of the consolidated entity. Finally, consolidated capital standards for large bank holding companies have been put in place.

CONSOLIDATED BANK SUBSIDIARY FOCUS

To avoid some of the problems—especially the legal ones—that might be associated with consolidation and regulation of bank holding companies as single entities, the second alternative policy is to provide the necessary inducements for a bank holding company to consolidate its operations into a single-bank subsidiary, which would then be regulated as a single firm. The principal areas affected for most of the nation's bank holding companies could be the financing and operations of nonbanking subsidiaries, especially those extending across state lines. The simplest way to accomplish this would be to provide banks with all the powers of their nonbanking subsidiaries. This approach has several advantages. First, as mentioned previously, the nonbanking activities involved are—with only minor exceptions—really banking activities that banks are able to engage in directly. Thus, consolidation would not be disruptive to the financial operation of a bank or to the traditional concept of what banking really is. Furthermore, nonbanking activities account for only a small proportion of banking organizations' resources (about 3 to 5 percent in the aggregate). Therefore, consolidation would be technically feasible in most cases without disrupting the organizational structure or portfolio composition of the resulting bank. Second, for the most part, inducing consolidation would involve removal or reduction of regulation. In most instances, bank holding company activities, especially financing activities, could likely be accomplished more efficiently within a bank subsidiary except for the existence of Regulation Q and other constraints making it uneconomical to do so. Third, reduction in regulation has the beneficial side effect of increasing banking organizations' flexibility, which, as was argued earlier, would be necessary if they were to meet the competition of nonbanking firms and to adjust to the stress of economic cycles. Fourth, relaxation of regulation would tend to break down the barriers that provide the incentives for nonregulated firms to offer financial services. Fifth, consolidation of a bank holding company into a bank subsidiary simplifies and reduces the burden of supervision since only a single entity would need to be examined. Under the present regulatory structure this would eliminate, or reduce substantially, the jurisdictional problems that presently exist because several banking agencies have authority over parts of existing holding companies. Finally, consolidation would focus public debate on the proper scope of banking functions, both in terms of permissible activities and also with respect to the McFadden Act, Douglas Amendment, and Glass-Steagall Act.

Interestingly, the Garn-St Germain Depository Institutions Act of 1982 has already taken a significant, though interim, step toward this second policy option by expanding the powers of bank service corporations. Under this act, banks are now permitted to establish wholly-owned bank service corporations and

1. to engage in clerical activities previously authorized by the Bank Service Corporation Act of 1962;
2. to offer any service, except deposit-taking, permitted to the parent bank; and
3. to engage in any nonbanking activity, except deposit-taking, authorized by Federal Reserve Regulation (Table 2) to bank holding companies.

The Garn-St Germain Act "McFaddenizes" those bank service corporation activities offered under authority granted to parent banks but does not similarly limit the geographic scope of other bank service corporation activities (see Hawke, Sweet, and Mierzewski, 1982).

The 1962 Act, as amended by the Garn-St Germain Act, both simplifies and complicates some of the regulatory problems for the banking agencies. For example, banks may organize bank services corporations as joint ventures with other banks and nonbanks as well.

The risk issues and supervisory implications of such joint ventures are not totally clear, especially since transactions with bank services corporations less than 25 percent owned by individual banks are not subject to Section 23A of the Federal Reserve Act. The agencies do have authority, however, to supervise and regulate these joint ventures. For majority-owned bank service corporations, banking transactions with these subsidiaries are also not subject to Section 23A, so presumably the activities of such subsidiaries will be consolidated with the parent bank for supervisory purposes. Finally, the act reduces the incentives for banks not presently part of bank holding companies to form such a company and engage in permissible nonbanking activities.

Summary and Conclusions

This chapter reviews the forces stimulating the growth of bank holding companies. It is shown that their expansion is an integral part of the broader process of financial innovation.

High and variable interest rates, inflation, and binding regulatory constraints not only have stimulated the entry of less regulated competitors (such as merchants, brokerage house and money market mutual funds) into the financial service industry, but also have induced changes in the organization of banking firms. To avoid the costs of regulation and to compete more effectively with unregulated competitors, banking organizations have exploited the potential of the bank holding company device. Traditional functions and activities have been shifted from bank subsidiaries to less regulated nonbank subsidiaries.

This trend has complicated the supervisory and regulatory process. Bank holding companies are becoming more integrated, making it more and more difficult to insulate insured bank subsidiaries from risk-taking in the rest of the organization. Furthermore, attempts to protect the insured subsidiaries by dividing a banking organization into regulated and unregulated segments, as has been proposed by the Treasury Department, are bound to be self-defeating. Whenever regulation becomes a binding and costly constraint, banking organizations will simply shift even more activities to their less regulated subsidiaries, and because it is not realistic to believe that a highly integrated firm would let a significant affiliate fail, the risk exposure of the insurance fund becomes more difficult to manage. Thus, the efficacy of deposit insurance depends upon reducing regulatory incentives to shift funding activities from insured to uninsured subsidiaries.

Two policy proposals are put forth to deal with this problem. Both involve the combination of deregulation (basically the elimination of deposits rate ceilings and the payment of interest on reserves) and treatment of banking organizations as consolidated entities for risk assessment purposes.

The ultimate conclusion is that so long as bank holding companies—and financial institutions more generally—are regulated in ways that impose costs and induce regulatory-avoidance activities by both regulated and unregulated firms, the organizational structure of financial firms and the financial system will continue to be under dynamic pressure and continue to change. This suggests that the regulatory-induced evolution of the financial system and all the regulatory, supervisory, deposit insurance, and macro monetary policy formulation problems that are attendant with that process will continue into the future unless the necessary reforms are undertaken.

BIBLIOGRAPHY

AHARONY, JOSEPH, and ITZHAK SWARY, "Effects of the 1970 Bank Holding Company Act: Evidence from Capital Markets," *Journal of Finance,* 36 (September 1981), 841–53.

BLEEKE, JOEL, and JAMES GOODRICH, *Capitalizing on Opportunities Created by Deregulation of the Banking Industry,* McKinsey & Company, Inc., September 1981.

BOYD, JOHN H., GERALD A. HANWECK, and PIPAT PITHYACHARIYAKUL, "Bank Holding Company Diversification," in *Proceedings of a Conference on Bank Structure and Competition,* Federal Reserve Bank of Chicago, 1980, pp. 105–21.

CHASE, SAMUEL B. JR., "The Bank Holding Company as a Device for Sheltering Banks from Risk," in *Proceedings of a Conference on Bank Structure and Competition,* Federal Reserve Bank Holding Companies, Golembe Associates, Inc., February 1978.

CHRISTOPHE, CLEVELAND A., *Competition in Financial Services.* New York: First National City Corporation, 1974.

CITICORP, *The Old Bank Robbers' Guide to Where the New Money Is.* New York: Citicorp, undated.

DARNELL, JAMES, "A Study of the Costs of Complying with Government Regulation," *Issues in Bank Regulation,* 5 (Winter 1982), 14.

EISENBEIS, ROBERT A., *Financial Innovation and the Role of Regulation: Implications for Banking Organization, Structure and Regulations,* Board of Governors of the Federal Reserve System, February 1980.

________, "How Bank Holding Companies Should Be Regulated," *Economic Review,* Federal Reserve Bank of Atlanta, January 1983.

EISENBEIS, ROBERT A., ROBERT S. HARRIS, and JOSEF LAKONISHOK, *Benefits of Bank Diversification: The Evidence from Shareholder Returns,* School of Business Administration, University of North Carolina, October 1982.

FISCHER, GERALD C., and CARTER H. GOLEMBE, "The Branch Banking Provisions of the McFadden Act as Amended: Their Rationale and Rationality," in *Compendium of Issues Relating to Branching by Financial Institutions,* Subcommittee on Financial Institutions of the Committee on Banking, Housing, and Urban Affairs, United States Senate, 94th Congress, 2nd Session. Washington, D.C.: U.S. Government Printing Office, October 1976.

HAWKE, JOHN D., JR., "Are State Laws Prohibiting Interstate Banking Constitutional?" *American Banker,* December 15, 1982.

HAWKE, JOHN D., JR., WILLIAM J. SWEET, JR., and MICHAEL B. MIERZEWSKI, "Revised BSC Act Offers Banks New Opportunities, *Legal Times,* December 20, 1982.

MARTIN, J. D., and A. J. KEOWN, "Market Reaction to the Formation of One-Bank Holding Companies," *Journal of Banking and Finance,* 5 (December 1981), 383–93.

MURRAY, WILLIAM J., "Bank Holding Company Centralization Policies," study prepared for the Association of Registered Bank-Holding Companies, Golembe Associates, Inc., February 1978.

RHOADES, STEVEN A., "The Effect of Bank-Holding-Company Acquisitions of Mortgage Bankers on Mortgage Lending Activity," *Journal of Business,* 48 (1975), 344–48.

———, "The Performance of Bank Holding Companies in Equipment Leasing," *Journal of Commercial Bank Lending,* 63 (1980), 53–61.

RHOADES, STEVEN A., and GREGORY E. BOCZAR, "The Performance of Bank Holding Company-Affiliated Finance Companies," Board of Governors of the Federal Reserve System, Division of Research and Statistics, Washington, D.C., Staff Study 90, 1977.

ROSE, JOHN T., "Bank Holding Companies as Operational Single Entities," in *The Bank Holding Company Movement to 1978: A Compendium,* Board of Governors of the Federal Reserve System, Washington, D.C., September 1978.

ROSENBLUM, HARVEY, and DIANE SIEGEL, "Competition in Financial Services: The Impact of Nonbank Entry," Federal Reserve Bank of Chicago, Staff Study 83–1, 1983.

SAVAGE, DONALD T., "A History of the Bank Holding Company Movement, 1900–78," in *The Bank Holding Company Movement to 1978: A Compendium,* Board of Governors of the Federal Reserve System, Washington, D.C., September 1978.

STOVER, ROGER D., "A Re-Examination of Bank Holding Company Acquisitions," *Journal of Bank Research,* 13 (1982), 101–8.

STROVER, ROBERT, "The Single Subsidiary One-Bank Holding Company," in *Proceedings of a Conference on Bank Structure and Competition,* Federal Reserve Bank of Chicago, April 27–28, 1978.

TALLEY, SAMUEL H., "Bank Holding Company Performance in Consumer Finance and Mortgage Banking," *Magazine of Bank Administration,* 52 (1976), 42–44.

U.S. Congress House of Representatives, Committee on Banking and Currency, 91st Congress, 1st Session, *The Growth of Unregistered Bank Holding Companies—Problems and Prospects.* Washington, D.C.: U.S. Government Printing Office, February 1969.

WEISBROD, STEVEN, "Economics of Scale in Commercial Banking," unpublished paper, 1980.

WHALEN, GARY, "Multibank Holding Company Organizational Structure and Performance," Federal Reserve Bank of Cleveland, Working Paper 8201, March 1982A.

———, "Operational Policies of Multibank Holding Companies," *Economic Review,* Federal Reserve Bank of Cleveland, Winter 1981–82B.

Bank Product Deregulation: Some Antitrust Tradeoffs

Elinor H. Solomon

16

Beyond the deregulation that has already taken place in financial services are foreshadowings of continued market change and proposals for further legislative deregulation. Further moves of banks into insurance and securities activities at home and abroad and further incursions of nonbank firms into traditional preserves of depository institutions seem certain. There will be pressure to give these moves and other potential changes legal blessing.

Beyond the initial flush of success of interest rate deregulation, what problems may arise to haunt us in this new world? One of the principal concerns voiced by some important participants has been its impact on the public's access to competitive markets and to prices that reflect the economic value of the resources that they use. The extent to which that concern proves to be valid will depend on how the new competition permitted by crumbling market barriers evolves over time.

The optimal long-range resolution of the short-run transition problem is approached by competition and new entry provided by erasing product limits. Application of antitrust policy and philosophy, grounded in existing legislation, should eradicate any lingering problems. However, new antitrust legislation dealing with cross-industry mergers might help prevent abuses or conflicts, as well as clarify some present ambiguous legal and economic issues.

Reprinted from *Economic Review* (May, 1984): 20-27 by permission of the Federal Reserve Bank of Atlanta and the author.

I. Hypothetical Scenarios of Market Evolution

Product deregulation could produce several alternative results:

A. The Fully Competitive Scenario.

The ideal competitive solution would produce an environment where barriers to entry erode as Congress removes remaining Glass-Steagall constraints, and technology permits all businesses to take full advantage of new opportunities. More firms, bank and nonbank alike, compete with one another head-on in broadened product markets. Technology will reduce dramatically the cost of producing and delivering these new services. Consumers will benefit fully from the new technology through lower prices and higher quality financial service at retail. If small banks and thrifts lack the necessary capital and expertise to "go it alone," they can share in the new electronic systems or buy or rent essential components without restrictions. Since competition for small institutions' respondent accounts will be intense, the necessary technological and human inputs will be available to the country bank from big city firms or correspondents for the full cluster of new financial services.

Small or specialized institutions can compensate for any cost or pricing disadvantage through special consumer services gleaned from firsthand knowledge of the local market. Empirical studies indicate the small seller can flourish despite new competition from bank leaders.[1] Whether new rivalry comes from other banks or nonbanks, the theoretical implications for competition are similar. If competitors are numerous and varied in size and focus, sellers are unlikely to develop a collusive oligopoly. Other financial institutions will stand ready to take business away from would-be collusive oligopolists if prices get out of line. Market power will not persist permanently when attempts by would-be monopolists to raise price cause consumers to shift their business to existing competitors in the broadened product market. If that fails to keep market participants in line, then new entry from all the other kinds of financial institutions now able to compete with banks will surely do so.

Suppose that dominant commercial banks in a market are pricing short-term loans in a noncompetitive way. Customers will increasingly turn to the commercial paper markets to get short-term financing of equivalent maturity, price and quality.[2] A sufficient rise in the price of bank loans will induce these customers to shift their allegiance from bank to nonbank sellers of virtually identical loan services. At the same time, given Garn-St Germain, locally limited customers can go to a local savings and loan for business loans and the related business and transactions accounts services that they require. Hence, any noncompetitive supplier will find itself thwarted by customers who can easily switch in response to noncompetitive price increases.

[1]See Alan S. McCall. "Economies of Scale, Operating Efficiencies and the Organizational Structure of Commercial Banks," *Journal of Bank Research* (Summer 1980), pp. 95-100; Paul F. Metzker, "Future Payments System Technology: Can Small Financial Institutions Compete?" Federal Reserve Bank of Atlanta, *Economic Review* (November 1982), pp. 58-67.

[2]Evelyn M. Hurley. "The Commercial Paper Market Since the Mid-Seventies," *Federal Reserve Bulletin* (June 1982) pp. 327-334.

In Diagram 1, we can visualize competition through markets at many stages of the financial "productive process" ranging from initial "seller" (the Federal Reserve Banks and Board) to ultimate consumer (the business and household user at retail several levels downstream).

We can think of competition as proceeding in many layers, from sellers of basic raw materials or clearing services upstream to banks, businesses and consumers downstream. Given deregulation plus new technology, there can be new entry all down the line. Non-banks, such as AT&T, will soon be able to compete for clearing business with the Fed banks. In markets downstream, a variety of correspondent banks and nonbank sellers will compete for small bank business. Interaction of still greater numbers of sellers is possible at retail, all offering a cluster of financial services in regional or broader markets. Merrill Lynch, American Express and Sears compete with Citicorp.

The joint benefits of technology and bank and nonbank entry accrue to each user at each level of production, from wholesale (clearing) to interbank (correspondent services) to retail (consumer and business buyers). Because none of the profits gained from scale efficiencies of the new technology get trapped at any stage of the productive process through monopoly power, the final consumer at retail gleans fully the benefits of deregulation.[3] Market forces will have triumphed. There is little for antitrust to do given such a scenario, except perhaps to monitor development in an unobtrusive way.

B. The "Lingering Pockets of Monopoly" Scenario.

Market solutions may take time. Not all thrift institutions can easily gear up to full competition for business loans (or deposits) where any lingering pockets of monopoly persist.[4]

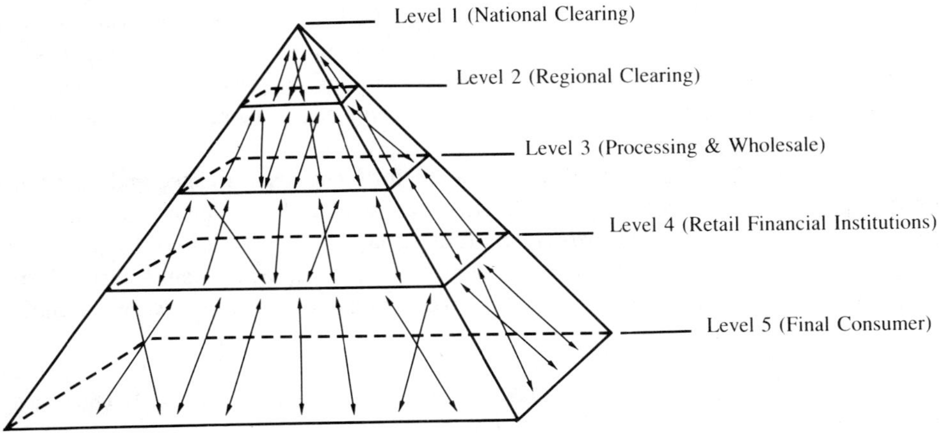

DIAGRAM 1 Levels of Financial Services Competition

[3]Benefits may flow freely downstream if, for example, arrangements or joint ventures by sellers at one level who offer, say, processing or credit card services (#3), do not contain clauses which specify prices of services at retail (#5) or discriminate against any institutional buyers at the next level (#4).

[4]The New England experience is described by Constance Dunham, "Mutual Savings Banks: Are They Now or Will They Ever Be Commercial Banks?" *New England Economic Review,* (May/June 1982) pp. 51-68.

Deregulation may impact unevenly from the deposit side according to customer sophistication or knowledge of deposit options. Banks may more rapidly raise rates paid on deposits to larger depositors with large minimum balances and collateral business. Some, but not all, of the difference in treatment of deposit accounts may reflect the different administrative cost or services bartered in return for low-cost deposits. A lack of full information about customer pricing may result in noncompetitive pricing.[5] Not all prime-based bank business loan customers are aware of below-prime market-based loan pricing. If bank customers can be clearly and permanently segmented into groups over which the bank can exercise some degree of monopoly power, price discrimination would be possible and attractive where the groups display different elasticities of demand.[6] With imperfect markets, it may be important to identify the problem and seek a practical remedy.

C. The Concentration of Resources Scenario.

Another alternative scenario suggests that the present wave of large bank and financial conglomerate mergers eventually may give rise to different, but potentially more significant, competitive difficulties. Beyond some critical "triggering point" in a merger wave, the efficiencies of large-scale production of banking services may be outweighed by possible market harm to groups of customers. At this critical point, the nature of competition is changed because a community of interest or common understanding develops between the remaining rivals.[7] The public fear of concentration of financial power is based in part upon the presumed economic clout wielded by the large and powerful.

The "deep-pocket" theory assumes that organizations with greater resources and staying power can intimidate rivals or develop anticompetitive strategies that can stick. Buyers may trust the greater reliability of a Schwab discount brokerage house allied with the Bank of America more than one standing alone, especially when the former is accompanied by extensive media hype or advertising. Or, buyers may think they stand a better chance of securing loans if they try to patronize other departments of the bank, whether or not such beliefs are well grounded.

Banks may erect a "Chinese wall" between different departments, and especially between parent bank and affiliate. But skeptics may fear conflict of interest between trust officer and loan officer, or that bank loan officers may make lower interest rate loans to long-term customers of other bank departments. The Justice Department's early Minneapolis price fixing cases found agreement between banks to charge below-prime rates to

[5]Steven Salop, "The Noisy Monopolist: Imperfect Information, Price Dispersion and Price Discrimination," *Review of Economic Studies* XLIV (October 1977), pp. 393-406.

[6]Bernard Schull, "Commercial Banks as Multiple-Product, Price-Discriminating Firms," *Banking and Monetary Studies,* pp. 351-363, P. Carson, editor 1966. Michael A. Goldberg, "The Pricing of Prime Rate," *Journal of Banking and Finance* 6 (1982), pp. 277-296. Marcelle Arak, A. S. Englander, and E. M. P. Tang, "Credit Cycles and the Pricing of the Prime Rate," Federal Reserve Bank of New York, *Quarterly Review* (Summer 1983), p. 8 and pp. 12-28.

[7]Donald Savage and Elinor Solomon, "Branch Banking: The Competitive Issues," *Journal of Bank Research,* 11 (Summer 1980), pp. 110-121.

certain respondent bank customers seeking bank acquisition financing.[8] Fears are stated also in terms of political power, and the power to influence legislation, yielding results that cannot always be measured in strictly economic terms.[9]

II. The Questions

Based on how these scenarios evolve, we can pose the following questions:

A. Are fears of undue concentration following mergers between large financial institutions exaggerated or real? If the fears materialize, can antitrust actions solve the public policy problems, given the present legal and economic underpinnings for enforcement?

B. May conflicts of interest, or alternatively, tying of scarce bank to nonbank services by the financial "supermarket" present problems? Again, what can the Antitrust Division do to resolve conflicts?

C. May all customers expect to share equally—and promptly—the benefits of deregulation and product market mixing? Will operations people (now schooled in the MBA tradition to target customer groups selectively) segment market pricing according to the price-sensitivity of customer demand? After all, customers with the greatest clout, who buy most from the financial "super-market," can threaten most effectively to leave the bank for other financial institutions if prices get out of line. Given the fact that preferred treatment to such customers may be the proper strategy for maximizing profits, what steps might the antitrust authorities wish to take to remedy pricing or allocation inequities?

One problem is to determine how the issues should be identified in economic terms. The classical microeconomic approach is implicit in modern antitrust analysis, which seeks to optimize economic efficiency and overall welfare. As long as producers gain more from a particular practice than customers lose, say from tying or price discrimination, the conditions for welfare maximization are satisfied. Any questions of income distribution, whose wealth is maximized, or whether producers gain at the expense of consumers, are left to macroeconomics, or for a political response, such as subsidies or direct grants.

[8] *United States vs. Northwestern National Bank of Minneapolis,* et al., 1964 Trade Cases #71,020 (D. Minn. 1964); *United States vs. The First National Bank of St. Paul,* et al., 1964 Trade Cases #71,021 (D. Minn. 1964) and *United States vs. The Duluth Clearinghouse Association,* et al., 1964 Trade Cases #71,022 (D. Minn. 1964) (consent decrees).

[9] Stephen A. Rhoades, *Power, Empire Building and Mergers* (Lexington Books: Lexington, Mass. 1983). Corwin Edwards, "Conglomerate Bigness as a Source of Power," in George Stigler (ed.) *Business Concentration and Price Policy* (Princeton: Princeton University Press, 1955), pp. 331-359. The Zaibatsu breakup experience in postwar Japan is instructive also. See Eleanor Hadley, *Antitrust in Japan* (Princeton, 1970).

III. Possible Solutions

A. Undue Concentration Questions.

Market solutions are always to be preferred, particularly in a period of rapid technological change. To the extent that market failures occur, there may be no one best solution to any potential problem. Our first line of defense against undue concentration is the antitrust laws, and the starting point for analysis must be the new Department of Justice Merger Guidelines.[10] They give powerful weight to economic theory in deciding which cases to litigate and how to litigate them. Judges will decide cases on the basis of economic theory and evidence to a much greater degree than earlier. Masses of data developing information on nonbank as well as bank behavior will be brought into evidence. To gauge product markets, judges may have to evaluate surveys to determine whether consumers may switch their purchases, given any hypothetical future increase in price by would-be monopolists.

1. **The Horizontal Product Merger.** Under the best of circumstances, it is difficult for the Justice Department to win antitrust cases based on hypothetical consumer behavior. Empirical difficulties of designing a reliable market survey and developing data within a realistic time frame for trial purposes are great. Defendants may argue that consumers won't know whether they will switch or not until they find themselves face to face with the reality of monopoly power. Moreover, when the prospect becomes a switch to another institutional supplier, say from banks to thrifts, or from both to money market mutuals, some consumers will be perplexed as to how to respond. They may be unfamiliar with the alternate supplier or the benefit it can offer until pushed to the wall by bad service or high prices.

   Economists can unanimously welcome the introduction of more sophisticated economic criteria as represented by the new Merger Guidelines. But that recognition puts a special burden on the antitrust authorities and especially on economists within the Antitrust Divison.[11] The new complexities of product market definition in post-Garn-St Germain markets increase the costs of effective antitrust enforcement. At the same time, economists may worry about the public policy effects of moving away from the banking ''cluster of services'' market definitions that simplify legal analysis.[12] These problems are compounded if the Antitrust Division is given sole responsibility for competitive analysis and enforcement as recommended by the Bush Task Force. Given broader markets through deregulation, however, the probabilities of competitive harm from all but the most significant mergers decrease.

[10]U.S. Department of Justice Merger Guidelines (June 14, 1982), reprinted in *Trade Regulation Report* (Commerce Clearing House) pp. 4500-05.

[11]One problem may be that mergers in small or isolated geographic markets, where nonbank entry is unattractive because of poor growth prospects, become the easiest to litigate and win. This prospect of lopsided emphasis poses a danger for effective antitrust enforcement across the board.

[12]For a statement of issues and tradeoffs see Robert A. Eisenbeis, ''Regulatory Agencies' Approaches to the 'Line of Commerce,' '' Federal Reserve Bank of Atlanta, *Economic Review* (April 1982), pp. 20-28.

The combination of more complex analysis and the economic gains brought by a broader market base should reduce the number of cases initiated, but the financial community would be ill advised to consider this as an indication that "anything goes." The Division's recent actions on the LTV-Republic merger makes clear that its continuing presence is real.[13]

2. **Product Extension Mergers.** A market extension merger is one in which a bank seeks to expand into geographic markets other than its own but often adjacent. A product extension merger is expansion into a product market often closely related to its own. Analysis is similar in both cases and can proceed in several ways.

   Suppose Citicorp decides to buy Household Finance. The Antiturst Division can analyze the merger's effects by computing Herfindahl indices in all the markets in which the two firms may now directly compete. As in any horizontal case, economists may delineate the geographic and product markets according to consumer future buying intentions in the event that prices charged by the new merged company get out of line. The Division may seek to litigate in markets where substantial overlap occurs or to require spinoffs as part of a legal settlement.

   Unfortunately, the reliability of good banking data, supplied in the past by a cooperative Federal Reserve, is not paralleled in the finance company sphere where spotty and often inconsistent data are collected by 50 state supervisory authorities. The market share data of other competing banks or finance companies and other suppliers of the same services must be secured from reluctant firms, made consistent, and factored into the market universe.

Another alternative is to go the potential competition route. Given the Department's record of Supreme Court losses in such cases, that alternative may not be appealing. With many more potential entrants in most markets, the likelihood of injury to the public on the basis of eliminating a potential competitor will decline significantly. Compared with earlier efforts, the Justice Department will have less need for and likelihood of winning.[14]

An exciting concept in the new world of interproduct competition is spatial analysis which attempts to look at many dimensions of competition simultaneously. This concept assumes that markets are not clearly separated, but that clusters of suppliers and customers compete at cluster borders where transactions costs of switching to new suppliers are lower than at the market center.[15] At the border, consumer transactions costs of purchase in alternative clusters become equalized. Suppliers must react and prices must respond competitively in both clusters, hence the "true" market expands. In this manner, just as service areas blend into broader local markets, so the local market may mesh into broader

[13]See *The Wall Street Journal,* February 16, 1984, 3. Assisant Attorney Paul McGrath said the more recent U.S. Steel Corp. bid for National Steel Corp. increased his concerns about the LTV-Republic merger, which would excessively increase concentration in three product lines.

[14]For example, *United States vs. Connecticut National Bank,* 418 U. S. 656 (1973). *United States vs. First National State Bancorporation,* 499 F. Supp. 793 (D. N. J. 1980).

[15]The literature is extensive. See, for example, B. Benson, "Spatial Microeconomics: Implications for the Relationship Between Concentration and Ownership in Bank Performance," in *Proceedings of a Conference on Bank Structure and Competition* (1980), Federal Reserve Bank of Chicago, pp. 60-85.

statewide, regional, or even national combined product-geographic markets. The new computer technology speeds this process by reducing transactions costs and disseminating product information.

While intellectually satisfying, this theory mathematically embraces the concept of product and geographic markets in intertwined multi-dimensional space. Hence, on a practical level it is unsuitable for easy empirical resolution or court use.[16]

A related and somewhat easier approach to product extension mergers would be the tentative measurement of markets as a group of concentric circle-like shapes. In a highly concentrated statewide branching state, say Oregon or Washington, the state represents an area in which banks can operate and transfer funds from within the branching organization. An EFT network may transfer funds or make short-term consumer loans for card holders over a broader multi-state region. The local market, constrained in size by convenience to depositors or small retail businesses, will represent another smaller market within the broader circumference. In product extension mergers it also may be appropriate to consider ringed areas of possible impact and to single out for analysis specific markets where damage to classes of consumers most likely will occur—bank and thrift, or bank and nonbank.

The Federal Reserve Board, in assessing mergers of large financial organizations, has often measured both statewide and local market concentration. However, except perhaps in correspondent banking markets, the state often does not represent the market area.

In states of high concentration, and generally poor bank economic performance, the state was sometimes viewed as a cluster of interconnected local markets in which monopoly power was exercised. This theory too has a counterpart for product extension mergers where substitution possibilities are close. One advantage of the "linked oligopoly" theory was that attorneys wishing to preserve the broadest range of potential horizontal and market extension antitrust possibilities could have their cake and eat it too. Markets could either be local, hence, suited for the run-of-the-mill small bank horizontal market litigation. Or, they might be viewed as concentrated clusters of interlinked local (or product) markets.

However, multi-market linkages between the same organizations do not necessarily diminish competition in markets where rivalry already is intense, as proven empirically by David D. Whitehead and Jan Luytjes (1983). Indeed, multi-market meetings may enhance the initial interfirm rivalry.[17] Modern game theory may help us understand which mergers may strengthen competition in the new world of highly interlinked product as well as geographic markets, and which may reduce or alter competition and behaviorial relation-

[16]However, Markovitz suggests that legal rules may be developed to handle specific situations in his "gravitational" spatial analysis. Richard S. Markovitz, "Predicting the Competitive Impact of Horizontal Mergers in a Monopolistically Competitive World: A Non-Market Oriented Proposal," 56 *Texas Law Review* (March 1978). "Shading" of market shares by the Antitrust Division to account for such close competition outside the primary market often reflected this view.

[17]See David D. Whitehead and Jan Luytjes, "Can Interstate Banking Increase Competitive Market Performance? An Empirical Test," *Economic Review*, Federal Reserve Bank of Atlanta (January 1984), pp. 4-10.

ships in complex and difficult to predict ways. In either case, present performance in a market must enter into analysis as a proxy for initial group interdependence.[18]

B. Tying and Conflict of Interest Questions.

It seems unlikely that the present Antitrust Division will often litigate tying or conflict of interest questions. The Division has gone on record as believing there are few circumstances where tying (or other vertical restraints on trade) are likely to reduce economic efficiency.[19]

A ''tie'' means that a customer's purchase of one product is conditioned on the purchase of another product. A bank cannot tie such nonbank services as mortgage banking to banking services such as loans in the absence of some ''leverage.'' The buyer will simply switch to another seller who does not attach strings to the purchase. Even in times of tight money, banks are unlikely to possess leverage over many bank loan customers who have other bank or nonbank financing options. But even if banks have leverage or market power over customers, independent competing suppliers of the ''tied'' products will not be hurt competitively unless ''foreclosed'' from the opportunity of selling the tied product. That implies both high concentration in the tied nonbank product and lack of easy entry—a lack of competition in both tied and tying markets. Since nonbank financial organizations such as finance companies, mortgage bankers and discount brokers tend to be less regulated than banks, with generally easier entry, the conditions conducive to a successful tie rarely exist. It is not surprising that the Justice Department has initiated few tying cases in financial markets over the years.

''Unfair advantage'' questions often focus on financing opportunities, such as a bank's superior ability to attract low-cost funds in the form of price regulated deposits. But that opportunity, if it ever existed, is shrinking as deposit rates become deregulated. The important consideration for pricing purposes is the marginal cost of funds, such as the large denomination CDs that banks must sell at market rates. Under the Bank Holding Company Act, the holding company cannot lend more than a small percentage of its assets to affiliates. If the acquired nonbank firm itself enjoys a lower financing price as an affiliate of the new bank holding company parent, that reduction may reflect administrative or marketing efficiency, or lower actual or perceived investor risk.

[18]Likelihood of a ''linked oligopoly'' developing was enhanced in one court case by suggestions of close personal contracts between leading bankers, who enjoyed discussions of common banking strategies. Merger in that litigated case was viewed as a way of eliminating the maverick local banker who did not think and act in the way of the group, thus upsetting to achievement of common goals. Rivalry was not great to begin with, whether or not collusion in a strictly legal Sherman Act sense was present. The final twist to this story was that the maverick banker decided not to go through with the merger following the ultimate Supreme Court victory after three years of litigation, and has thrived well and independently ever since.

[19]For example, William F. Baxter, ''Vertical Practices—Half Slave, Half Free,'' *Antitrust Law Journal, op. cit.*, pp. 743-754. F. M. Scherer, however, points out the technical difficulties of the new theory and its imperfect state of development, at that same Antitrust Institute, pp. 687-707.

Tying was an issue in the recent Bank of America/Schwab acquisition, in which the nation's second largest bank acquired the nation's largest discount brokerage house. The merger, approved by the Federal Reserve Board, has been appealed. The Supreme Court voted to consider the issues formally upon request of the Securities Industry Association. A Supreme Court decision will be welcome, for it may settle difficult issues of law, including Glass-Steagall Act interpretation. But because of easy entry into brokerage, careful analysis of the microeconomic issues reveals no real tying opportunity in that case.

Nor is "conflict of interest" a likely problem, since it is improbable that unsound loans will be made to discount brokerage customers to facilitate securities purchases. Bank trust departments will not accept unsound securities to help the brokerage subsidiary; Schwab will merely execute orders, not take market positions. The Bank of America may influence consumers' preferences through effective packaging of prestige associated with its many brand names and multiproduct offerings. But is that necessarily contrary to public interest? Consumers may benefit through extensive advertising of discount brokerage services, with the result that full line brokers will have to lower prices or improve service quality.

C. User Group Equity Questions.

It may well be that new competition will provide needed solutions in the world of inter-product competition and deregulation. Then we will not have to worry about esoteric measurements of equity welfare and consumer marginal utility. Even so, there is room for a continued antitrust role even if all it accomplishes is monitoring and deterrence. It is not enough simply to look at how many cases the Justice Department won vs. how many it lost in the period since 1961 when antitrust first began to be applied to financial markets. A better test would be the number of anticompetitive actions such as discrimination, price fixing or market division which did not take place because of antitrust deterrents. To that the response would be of course, how much damage the antitrust presence also did through unsolicited meddling, or dampening of normal profit and investment incentives. In either case, the problem to consider now is whether that deterrence function may in the future fail because of distorted private beliefs about the antitrust authorities' ability and readiness to do their legal job.

IV. Congressional and Regulatory Solutions

While all the economic and legal issues surrounding antitrust sort themselves out, other solutions come to mind. One would be to retain or even expand Federal Reserve authority to judge independently any major bank or nonbank acquisitions under its present bank holding company authority. Historically, the Federal Reserve Board has been more independent politically than many other branches of government. It also has a large staff of highly qualified financial economists, along with great data-gathering and econometric capabilities. To expect the Antitrust Division to understand and solve all financial competition matters in unitary isolation seems, in my view, to ask the impossible as well as to risk cyclical shifts in emphasis.

The Federal Reserve's help has been invaluable to banking antitrust enforcers, often to the distress of private parties involved. Any Board decisions are subject to Justice Department analysis and intervention through comments or active participation in regulatory proceedings, to ensure a broader economic and legal frame of reference. Court review (up to and including the Supreme Court) will continue also in contested cases. The latter, too, assures full public airing and consideration of all the issues, both legal and economic.

A final alternative is for Congress to tighten the antitrust laws and improve litigating speed. Former Assistant Attorney General John Shennefield (1979) advocated legislation designed to eliminate very large corporate mergers through acquisition of leading market positions.[20] More recently, an eminent scholar in this financial antitrust field, Stephen Rhoades, suggested legislation to limit large acquisitions. Rhoades discussed cogently the political and social as well as economic bases for accumulating and deploying power.[21] The Congress, in my view, would do well to consider these questions further for the social as well as economic payoff. Assuming the legislative route is desirable, the question is whether the Congress should act before or after relatively unencumbered free market forces have had the opportunity to sift themselves out fully. If our goal is to address the antitrust question without having to resort to divestiture, with all the potentially painful consequences of unscrambling, then Congress perhaps should look at these questions sooner rather than later.

[20]John H. Shenefield, Testimony before the Senate Committee on the Judiciary Concerning Conglomerate Mergers (March 1979).

[21]See Rhoades, *op. cit.*, footnote 10 above.

Regulatory Agencies' Approaches to the "Line of Commerce"

Robert A. Eisenbeis

17

Pressures for Change

The federal banking agencies and the courts have had a difficult time defining the relevant product line to use in bank mergers and acquisition cases. The agencies have never been particularly comfortable with the Supreme Court's delineation in the Philadelphia National Bank (PNB) and subsequent cases.* The agencies have always attempted—both before and after PNB—to take into account thrift and other competition, sometimes within, but more often than not outside, the constraints imposed by the Supreme Court decisions.

Since the Supreme Court last addressed the issue . . . [in 1975], pressures on the agencies to modify the line of commerce have heightened substantially. Numerous financial innovations and structural changes in financial markets are eroding the uniqueness of commercial banks as suppliers of demand deposits and the cluster of services that had traditionally set these institutions apart.

Moreover, these developments have reduced banks' cost advantages, and high interest rates have altered consumer preferences which had previously isolated banks from competition. The Monetary Control Act significantly broadened the deposit and asset powers of federal thrifts and authorized NOW accounts nationwide which has served to make

Reprinted with deletions from *Economic Review* (April, 1982) 25–28 by permission of the Federal Reserve Bank of Atlanta and the author.

**Editors' note: In the Philadelphia National Bank case, banking was defined as a unique line of commerce.*

banks and thrifts more homogeneous; legislation introduced during 1981 suggests that the realignment of thrift powers is not completed yet.

As interest rates have remained high, both consumers and businesses have also become more sophisticated in unbundling their use of financial services to earn the highest yields on their invested funds and to obtain credit at the most favorable rates. The growth of money market mutual funds has enabled smaller depositors to realize market rates on their savings. But the greater importance of money market funds may ultimately lie in their role in breaking down the dependence of locally limited consumers on local banks and thrifts for savings and transactional services, thus broadening the geographic scope of consumer financial markets.

The last several years have also witnessed the rapid spread of symbiotic financial arrangements in which independent firms cooperate to provide a service that could not legally or economically be offered by either firm separately. The best known example is Merrill Lynch's Cash Management Account. It combines a Merrill Lynch margin account, a Visa debit card and service arrangement provided by BancOne of Columbus, Ohio, and Merrill Lynch's money market mutual fund.

More recently, we've seen the creation of new types of financial institutions resulting from combinations of brokerage firms and other financial institutions, such as American Express-Shearson and Bache-Prudential. These institutions not only have institutionalized certain symbiotic financial arrangements, such as cash management services; they also are positioning themselves to take advantage of their freedom from reserve requirements and other regulations to offer a wide range of consumer and corporate financial, brokerage and insurance services.

Whether these new institutions will be successful remains to be seen. They are, however, able to offer potentially superior substitutes to traditional banking services and can capitalize on the fact that many bank customers have learned it can be both convenient and cost effective to obtain financial services from nonlocal and nontraditional firms. It is important to realize that these recent financial innovations and competitive structural changes which have so concerned depository financial institutions affect primarily the types of services and alternatives available to consumers. For example, Bleier and Eisenbeis (1981) argued that the MCA granted thrifts few, if any, significant powers to enable them to offer services to corporate customers; this is especially true for S&Ls. The act does grant slightly broader authority to the few federally chartered mutual savings banks to offer certain commercial services, but even here quantitative limitations have been imposed. These limitations coupled with thrifts' present financial difficulties and the problems of acquiring the necessary management expertise should limit the overall competitive significances of these changes. Similarly, the cash management and money market fund services are also directed at consumers and not to the corporate customers.

Thus, many of the events now being cited by the applicants and regulatory agencies as the rationale for a re-examination of the line of commerce issue are occurring in the retail banking submarkets. But the Supreme Court has already indicated in the Connecticut National case that "fierce" competition in such submarkets isn't sufficient to cause it to change the line of commerce definition. Thus, to base a case for a change on the need to recognize the market realities of thrift competition in consumer markets is unlikely to be particularly persuasive. In fact, the Court might be convinced that the emphasis it placed in the Connecticut National case on the cluster of services provided to commercial customers is as relevant today as it was then, especially if the Court continues to direct antitrust to the protection of affected customer classes rather than looking at competitors.

So it is tempting to cling to the more traditional line of commerce and to focus on commercial customers. Yet there are also broader policy issues, as well as some potential pitfalls, in clinging too long to such a product line definition in today's changing financial environment, when the product constitutes a decreasing portion of many banks' business.

First, what happens as bank dependence on liablility management and access to purchased monies expands as the primary source of bank funding? As commercial lending to small commercial enterprises declines as a portion of lending to consumers and large businesses, it may pay many banks to abandon the small-commercial segment of their business. That's especially true if the result is to escape—or at least reduce—antitrust scrutiny. Thus, continued reliance on the traditional antitrust approach focusing on protecting affected classes of customers in a financial environment where funds are increasingly fungible, handicaps those firms whose services happen to be included in the relevant product line.

The traditional approach provides incentive for aggressive, expansion-minded banks to abandon their activities in the relevant product lines. The long run effect may be to drive out suppliers and reduce the number of effective competitors for those very customers and in those markets the policy seeks to protect. In effect, we are forced back to one of the key public policy issues addressed in the PNB case of whether the antitrust laws should apply to banking and, if so, how?

Second, even within the traditional approach, almost any broadening of the line of commerce would have the practical effect of liberalizing the range of acquisitions that would pass muster under the antitrust laws; the broader the line of commerce, the lower the estimated concentration ratios and the lower the probability of finding a Section 7 violation. Thus, changing the line of commerce definition has the potential to precipitate a consolidation of the banking system.

At the root then, of the line of commerce issue, are three questions: What type of a consolidation movement do we want to promote, how do we want it to proceed, and what role is antitrust to play? To illustrate the potential problems, suppose the arguments of many applicants are accepted and thrifts are included in the line of commerce. Because of the present difficulties of merging banks with thrifts due to statutory prohibitions and because operating a thrift is not a permissible activity for bank holding companies, the main impact of the broader definition would be to accommodate consolidations among banking organizations. But at a time when thrifts are in such financial difficulty, do we want, as a matter of public policy, to rationalize a further skewing of the relative size distribution of the financial industry in favor of banks?

Third, the policy problems are not eased if one follows the path recommended by the Comptroller in the Northern National Bank of Presque Isle case in which multiple "product line" clusters would be analyzed. Such an approach may result in a tightening rather than a loosening of merger policy since a violation in any one of a number of relevant products lines would result in an antitrust violation. Perhaps, more importantly, however, is the increased regulatory burden that would be associated with such an approach. Data would have to be organized and collected on all the relevant product lines, not only from the merging banks, but also from all other institutions in the affected markets. At present, the only reliable data that can be organized on an approximate market basis are the FDIC Summary of Deposit data. Comparable data are not only costly to provide but also are difficult to collect and process. The problems and costs of extending such data to more than just deposits and to broaden classes of reporting institutions should not be taken lightly.

Finally, if one were to focus procedures of the FDIC and Federal Reserve Board on the competitive forces affecting banking organizations, rather than looking at affected product markets and classes of customers, the result would be a radical redirection of antitrust law from its traditional focus for all industries. In view of the large number of conglomerate acquisitions successfully evaluated using the traditional methodology, it is difficult to argue that banking is so unique and presents such difficult public policy issues as to warrant a rethinking and reorientation of antitrust policy.

The analysis of agency decisions indicated that they wrestled with the problems of delineating the relevant line of commerce long before the Supreme Court did in the PNB case. The agencies have never truly been comfortable with the Courts finding in that and subsequent cases. They have continually sought to take thrift and other competitors into account, even when such institutions were not significant suppliers of services to the relevant affected classes of customers. At the root of their difficulty is the problem of dealing with financial conglomerates which operate in many different product and geographic markets and are subject to a variety of competitive forces. As a result, the analysis they have employed has not always been consistent with that employed by the Supreme Court. The dilemma the agencies have faced has become more significant as banks have diversified into more product lines and markets, as financial innovations have broken down traditional customer relationships and dependence upon banks as suppliers of clusters of services, and as more and more diverse financial institutions have begun to offer close substitutes for banking services.

We are now faced with the problem of how to restructure the financial system and how we want the transition to that structure to proceed. In that respect, antitrust policy is but one element that needs to be considered. All the same, we should also be careful not to take the redefinition of the line of commerce too lightly or view it with the blinders of a narrow technical legal focus. For to address the line of commerce issue without regard to the broader policy issues could set the financial system on an evolutionary path that would be difficult to reverse and that might erase the gains that increased competition has brought.

The 1982 Department of Justice Merger Guidelines: Applications to Banking Mergers

Margaret E. Guerin-Calvert

18

The U.S. Department of Justice issued new guidelines for enforcement policy concerning mergers and acquisitions on June 14, 1982. The new guidelines, which replace those issued by the Department in 1968, represent some important changes and extensions from the old guidelines. The two most significant changes from the 1968 guidelines are: (1) The significantly increased specificity of the methodology for defining product and geographic markets and (2) the choice of the Herfindahl-Hirschman (''HHI'') Index, rather than the four-firm concentration ratio, as the measure of concentration in the market. Generally, the guidelines indicate that high levels of post-merger concentration in a market, coupled with significant changes in the level of concentration, are likely to result in a challenge by the Department.

Revisions to the 1968 guidelines are relevant to bank regulatory agencies' policies concerning mergers and acquisitions, because the principles underlying the Justice Department's guidelines have frequently been used by these agencies in evaluating the competitive effects of bank mergers and acquisitions. The purpose of this article, therefore, is to assess the implications of the revisions in the guidelines for bank merger analysis. Section I briefly summarizes the new Justice Department Guidelines and points out the major, substantive revisions to the 1968 guidelines. In Section II, the new guidelines are applied to banking markets; the number and nature of mergers that would violate the guidelines are

Reprinted from *Issues in Bank Regulation* (Winter, 1983): 18–25, by permission of the Bank Administration Institute and the author.

examined. Merger policy under the old and new guidelines is then compared. Section III summarizes the implications of applying the guidelines' specific standards to mergers and acquisitions of bank holding companies, and evaluates the usefulness of the guidelines as a screening device for over 2,000 mergers a year.

I. The 1982 Department of Justice Guidelines

The new guidelines have two major components: (1) Specific criteria by which product and geographic markets are defined and (2) quantitative estimates of the post-merger levels of concentration and changes in concentration due to a merger, which would prompt close antitrust scrutiny. A description of the methodology the Department of Justice will use to define product and geographic markets is a significant part of the new guidelines. This differs significantly from the amount of exposition on market definition in the 1968 guidelines, where the importance of properly defining markets was noted, but little guidance given in methodology.

Both the product and the geographic markets are defined by the use of a hypothetical 5% increase in the price of the product of the merging firms. Initially, the assumption is made that the product of the merging firms is the relevant product market. Then, the question is posed whether the merging firms would be able profitably to raise the price of their product by 5%. If consumers would shift so significant an amount of purchases to other products, such that the 5% price increase cannot be maintained, then these other products are deemed to be sufficiently close substitutes and must be included in the product market. The product market is defined when all reasonably close substitutes for the product of the merging firms have been included.

In an analogous fashion, the geographic market for the relevant product is initially assumed to be the area served by one of the merging firms. The question is then posed whether, with a 5% price increase by that firm, would consumers shift purchases in a significant amount to firms outside that area. If so, the geographic market has been defined too narrowly, and these other firms should be included. The boundaries of the geographic market are established when all the firms that could "foil" the ability of the merging firms to raise profitably the price by 5% are included.[1]

The product and geographic market definitions are the context in which the competitive effects of a merger are evaluated. The new guidelines are similar to the old guidelines in their emphasis on structural measures as predictors of the competitive outcome of a merger. The specific measure of concentration—the Herfindahl-Hirschman Index—differs,

[1]This process of hypothetical price increases has been expressed as a "foiling" concept. Lawrence White, Director of the Economic Policy Office, expresses it as follows: "Can firms in this economic area be foiled in their attempts to raise the price [by 5%] if they all got together? If they cannot be foiled, they're a market. If they can be foiled, then they're not a market, and you've got to bring the foilers in . . . ." BNA *Antitrust and Trade Regulation Report*. Vol. 42, No. 1070, at 1303 (June 24, 1981). In addition to the "significant" amount of purchases shifted, the geographic market definition methodology appears to have a second step. The profitability of maintaining the 5% price increase is also judged. The profitability of maintaining a price increase will depend on whether, despite the loss of a "significant" amount of purchases, the revenues from selling a smaller quantity at a higher price are sufficient to cover the costs of producing the smaller quantity.

however, from the four-firm concentration ratio (CR_4) used previously. While the CR_4 measures the shares (of sales or capacity) of the top four firms in the market, the HHI is the sum of the squared market shares of all firms in the industry.[2] Thus, the HHI, by weighting the shares of all firms, emphasizes the dispersion of firms' shares in an industry, rather than the dominance of the top four firms.[3]

The post-merger HHI is used in the guidelines to establish "cut points" for what are considered unconcentrated (HHI below 1000), moderately concentrated (HHI between 1000 and 1800) and concentrated (HHI greater than 1800) markets. The level of concentration in markets, coupled with the change in the level of concentration due to a merger, signal which mergers will likely be challenged.

As shown in Table 1, no mergers in unconcentrated markets are likely to be challenged. This represents a change from the 1968 guidelines where some mergers, between firms with relatively large market shares, would have been challenged in unconcentrated markets. Mergers that result in a change in the HHI of 100 or more in moderately concentrated markets or in a change in the HHI of between 50 and 100 in concentrated markets or in a change in the HHI of between 50 and 100 in concentrated markets are likely to be challenged. Other factors, such as the ease of entry or the heterogeneity of the product, which could limit the ability of firms in an industry to collude profitably, would be considered in the decision whether to challenge mergers in these categories. In concentrated markets where the change in the HHI exceeds 100, challenge is almost certain.

An application of the new guidelines could result in challenges similar in number to application of the 1968 guidelines. The shift from the four-firm concentration ratio to the HHI and the new threshold values for what is considered a highly concentrated market

Table 1 Department of Justice Guidelines for Mergers and Acquisitions

Level of HHI	HHI < 1000	1000 < HHI < 1800	HHI > 1800
Change in HHI			
ΔHHI < 50	No Challenge	No Challenge	No Challenge
50 < ΔHHI < 100	No Challenge	No Challenge	Challenge, other factors
ΔHHI > 100	No Challenge	Challenge, other factors	Challenge

[2]The HHI is expressed in the guidelines as a whole number; this follows from using shares of the firms in the industry expressed as percentages rather than decimals (*e.g.*, 20 rather than .20) and the sum of these squared numbers is thus a whole number. An HHI of 10,000 would represent a monopolistic market (*i.e.*, 100^2 = 10,000).

[3]Both the 1968 and 1982 guidelines rely on the theoretical and empirical evidence in the structure-conduct-performance literature for their use of structural measures of competition. Studies concerning the use of structural measures of concentration in manufacturing industries are reviewed in: F. M. Scherer, *Industrial Market Structure and Economic Performance,* Rand McNally, 2nd. ed. 1980; and L. Weiss, "The Concentration-Profits Relationship and Antitrust," in *Industrial Concentration: The New Learning,* H. Goldschmid, H. Mann, J. Weston, eds., Boston, Little, Brown and Co., 1971. Similar reviews concerning structure-conduct-performance studies in banking are found in: S. A. Rhoades, "Structure-Performance Studies in Banking: A Summary and Evaluation," *Staff Economic Studies,* No. 92 (Federal Reserve Board, 1977), S. A. Rhoades, "A Summary and Evaluation of Structure-Performance Studies in Banking: An Update," *Staff Studies* (Federal Reserve Board, 1982) and A. Heggestad, "Market Structure, Competition and Performance in Financial Industries: A Survey of Banking Studies," *Issues in Financial Regulation,* Edwards, ed., McGraw-Hill Book Co., 1979.

result in a small increase in the number of markets considered highly concentrated. Offsetting this to some extent is a slight increase in allowable market shares of merging firms.

II. Application of the New Merger Guidelines to Banking Markets

This section applies the structural indices of the new guidelines—the HHI and the change in the HHI—to banking markets. First, levels of concentration in banking markets are estimated. Second, changes in the level of concentration and the number and nature of mergers likely to be challenged are examined. Finally, the differences in merger enforcement policy under the old and new guidelines are analyzed.

Standard Metropolitan Statistical Areas (SMSAs) and non-SMSA counties are used as approximations for geographic markets for banking, and total deposits of banking organizations in these areas are used to calculate banking output for the product market.[4] To the extent that these proxies differ from the product and geographic markets used to analyze actual mergers, levels of concentration and thus the number of mergers predicted to violate the guidelines will vary from the actual number. It is difficult to judge whether the technique employed in this article will understate or overstate concentration levels and the number of mergers likely to be challenged. On the one hand, to the extent that nonbank organizations provide close substitutes for some or all bank products, the use of only bank total deposits will overstate both market shares and the level of concentration in the market, thus overstating the number of likely challenges.[5] On the other hand, if the geographic market for some of these products is narrower than the county or the SMSA, the shares and levels of concentration in the market will be understated.[6]

[4]Use of the product market definition methodology set out in the new guidelines may frequently lead to the disaggregation of bank services into multiple product lines, some of which have nonbank services as close substitutes. If market shares based on total bank deposits, however, are highly correlated with market shares based on a narrower product line (*e.g.*, commercial and industrial loans) for which there are few or no nonbank competitors, then the results of this study will be similar to those using the more difficult to estimate, disaggregated data. T. Watkins, in "Commercial Banking as the Relevant Line of Commerce: Does It Matter?," Federal Reserve Bank of Kansas City, paper presented at Eastern Economics Association Meeting, April 29, 1982, shows that bank deposit concentration is highly correlated with product line (*e.g.*, loans) concentration for commercial bank services. This correlation, however, does not hold up for *all* bank products when nonbank competitors are included in the product market definition. *See* C. Dunham, "Mutual Savings Banks: Are They Now or Will They Ever Be Commercial Banks?." *New England Economic Review,* May/June 1982.

[5]In practice, the amount of overstatement due to the exclusion of nonbank competitors from market share calculation could be limited by the "shading-in" of these firms. As noted in the new guidelines, it is possible that some firms do not currently provide close enough substitutes for the merging firms product to be included in the relevant product market. They may, however, still influence competition in the market or may be able, over a longer time period, to provide the relevant product. Thus, in the case of banking, the "shading-in" of thrifts, *i.e.*, accounting for the influence of firms without including their total productive capacity in the relevant product market, could reduce the number of likely challenges.

[6]While it is difficult to test the sensitivity of the conclusions to the choice of county and SMSA areas as geographic markets, the sensitivity of the conclusions to the choice of product market definitions (commercial bank deposits) can be tested by including savings and loan total deposits in total SMSA deposits. Inclusion of thrift deposits significantly reduces the number of markets considered highly concentrated. Over 20% of SMSAs are highly concentrated when savings and loan deposits are included in the market share measures, as opposed to about 50% when they are excluded.

Levels of Concentration in Banking Markets

Of the 2733 banking markets used in this study, 2386 (87%) are highly concentrated as measured by an HHI in excess of 1800 (See Table 2.)[7] Another 299 (11%) are moderately concentrated markets, and only 48 (2%) are unconcentrated. The proportion of banking markets that are highly concentrated contrasts sharply with that for manufacturing industries. Only 13% of manufacturing industries are highly concentrated, 20% are moderately concentrated and about 67% are unconcentrated.[8]

There are also significant differences between the SMSA and non-SMSA county markets: Proportionately fewer SMSA markets than non-SMSA county markets are highly concentrated. As shown in Table 2, about 50% of the 323 SMSA markets are highly concentrated; approximately 40% are moderately concentrated and the remaining 10% fall into the unconcentrated category. By contrast, nearly all (92%) non-SMSA county markets have an HHI exceeding 1800. Fewer than 1% of these nonurban markets are unconcentrated, while about 8% are moderately concentrated.

Table 2 Distribution of Concentrated, Moderately Concentrated and Unconcentrated Banking Markets

		Number of Markets		
	HHI	All Markets	SMSAs	Non-SMSA Counties
Unconcentrated	HHI < 1000	48	35	13
Moderately Concentrated	1000 < HHI < 1800	299	118	181
Highly Concentrated	HHI > 1800	2,386	170	2,216
Total		2,733	323	2,410

Market shares based on bank total deposits as of June 1981.

[7]The guidelines indicate that the *post-merger* HHI is the correct measure of concentration to employ in evaluating mergers. As it was not practically feasible to calculate post-merger HHIs for every possible merger in a market, the HHI was calculated using current (pre-merger) market shares. Thus, the estimates here of the number of markets where the HHI exceeds 1800 will consistently *underestimate* the number of markets where the post-merger HHI exceeds 1800, and constitute a lower bound estimate of the number of concentrated markets.

[8]Concentration levels for manufacturing industries were estimated from four-firm concentration ratios for four-digit SIC Manufacturing Industries. Stephen Rhoades in "Merger Guidelines, Purpose, Construction and Implementation," (mimeo, Federal Reserve Board, 1982), estimated the four-firm concentration ratios for local and regional markets for 1972, using estimates from D. Schwartzman and J. Bodoff, "Concentration in Regional and Local Industries," *Southern Economic Journal* (January 1971), pp. 343–348.

Here it is assumed that a four-firm concentration ratio of 70% is equivalent to an HHI of 1800, and a four-firm concentration ratio of 50% is equivalent to an HHI of 1000; this assumption is consistent with that employed in the new Department of Justice guidelines.

Changes in Concentration Due to Mergers

The level of post-merger concentration in markets is only one component in the decision to challenge a merger. The second component is the *change* in the level of concentration that would result from the merger. The greater the change in concentration the more likely the resulting firm can acquire market power or the greater the ability of the few large firms in the industry to collude. The new guidelines set critical levels for changes in concentration in moderately concentrated (HHI exceeding 100) and concentrated markets (HHI exceeding 50) that will prompt a challenge.

Table 3 illustrates the number of possible bank mergers that would likely be challenged under the new guidelines.[9] Possible horizontal mergers were estimated by calculating the number of possible two-firm combinations in each market, assuming that each firm merged only once and there were no inter-market mergers. Table 3 shows that there are 238,161 possible mergers in the 2733 banking markets. Of these, 132,451 (56%) would

Table 3 Application of Justice Department Guidelines to Possible Banking Mergers

Level of Concentration	Unconcentrated HHI > 1000	Moderately Concentrated 1000 < HHI < 1800	Highly Concentrated HHI > 1800
All Banking Markets (Number of Mergers) Total Number of Mergers = 238,161 Change in Concentration			
HHI > 50		55,524	22,985
50 < ΔHHI < 100	132,451	3,297	2,433
ΔHHI > 100		6,899	14,572
Total	132,451	65,720	39,990
SMSAs (Number of Mergers) Total Number of Mergers = 211,944			
HHI < 50		52,587	20,556
50 < ΔHHI < 100	131,271	1,856	975
ΔHHI > 100		2,418	2,281
Total	131,271	56,861	23,812
Non-SMSA Counties (Number of Mergers) Total Number of Mergers = 26,217			
HHI < 50		2,937	2,429
50 < ΔHHI < 100	1,180	1,441	1,458
ΔHHI < 100		4,481	12,291
Total	1,180	8,859	16,178

likely not be challenged under the new guidelines because they occur in unconcentrated markets. Another 65,720 (28%) of all possible mergers would be in moderately concentrated markets and 39,900 (18%) represent mergers in highly concentrated markets. Not all mergers in moderately concentrated and highly concentrated markets, however, would be challenged. A total of 9332 mergers (4%) fall into the category of likely, but not certain, challenge. These represent mergers in moderately concentrated markets where the change in the HHI exceeds 100 (6,899 mergers) and mergers in highly concentrated markets where the change in the HHI is between 50 and 100 (2,433 mergers). Finally, 14,572 (6%) of all mergers would be subject to more certain challenge, as they occur in highly concentrated markets and the change in the HHI from the merger exceeds 100. Thus, about 10% of all mergers would receive close antitrust scrutiny.

Again, there are differences between SMSA and non-SMSA county markets (see Table 3). In the 323 SMSA markets, there are a total of 211,944 possible mergers. Of these, over 50% would occur in unconcentrated markets and 38% would occur in moderately concentrated or concentrated SMSA markets. In moderately concentrated SMSA markets, 2,418 of a possible 56,861 mergers would likely be challenged. Of the 23,812 possible mergers in concentrated SMSA markets, about 4% would likely be challenged (because the change in the HHI is between 50 and 100). Another 10% would definitely be challenged (2,281 possible mergers) because the change in the HHI exceeds 100. Comparing these likely and more certain challenges with those mergers that would not violate the guidelines reveals that over 96% of all mergers in SMSA markets would not be challenged (see Table 3). About 3%, thus, would likely be challenged.

In contrast to the SMSA markets, a substantially greater proportion of mergers in non-SMSA counties would be challenged. The sources of this difference are: 1) The substantially greater number of concentrated markets and 2) the greater proportion of possible mergers that result in changes in the HHI exceeding 100.[10] As shown in Table 3, of 26,217 possible mergers in the 2,410 markets, only 30% would not be challenged at all. Another 23% would likely be challenged and about 47% would definitely be challenged (12,291 mergers). Thus, over 70% of all mergers in non-SMSA county markets would receive close anti-trust scrutiny, and close to 50% would likely result in suits.

Comparison of Merger Enforcement Policy Under the 1968 and 1982 Guidelines

This section compares merger enforcement policy under the new and old guidelines. As shown in Table 4, about 4,000 fewer mergers would be challenged under the 1982 guidelines as compared with the 1968 guidelines. This difference stems from two sources: 1) A slight decrease in the number of markets considered highly concentrated and 2) an increase

[9] J. Gagnon in the *New England Economic Review*, July/August (forthcoming) compares enforcement policy under the 1968 and 1982 guidelines for New England Banking markets, and uses a somewhat different methodology to reach conclusions similar to those of this paper.

[10] This is due to the smaller number of fringe or small firms in non-SMSA county markets as compared with SMSA markets.

Table 4 Comparison of Merger Policy Under 1968 and 1982 Guidelines

	All Markets			SMSAs			Non-SMSA Counties		
	Number of Markets	Number of Mergers	Number of Mergers Challenged	Number of Markets	Number of Mergers	Number of Mergers Challenged	Number of Markets	Number of Mergers	Number of Mergers Challenged
1982 Guidelines[1]									
Unconcentrated Markets	48	132,451	0	35	131,271	0	13	1,180	0
Moderately Concentrated Markets	299	65,720	6,899	118	56,861	2,418	181	8,859	4,481
Highly Concentrated Markets	2,386	39,990	17,005	170	23,812	3,256	2,216	16,178	13,749
Total Markets	2,733	238,161	23,904	323	211,944	5,674	2,410	26,217	18,230
1968 Guidelines[2]									
Unconcentrated Markets	336	208,174	9,687	152	198,009	4,086	184	10,165	5,601
Concentrated Markets	2,397	29,987	18,262	171	13,935	3,829	2,226	16,052	14,433
Total Markets	2,733	238,161	27,949	323	211,944	7,915	2,410	26,217	20,034

[1]See Table 1 for definition of markets and mergers under 1982 guidelines

[2]Unconcentrated markets determined as those where the four-firm concentration ratio (CR_4) is below 75%; concentrated markets are those where CR_4 exceeds 75%. Number of mergers challenged under the 1968 guidelines was estimated by finding those mergers where the change in the HHI exceeded 70 points in unconcentrated markets and 35 points in concentrated markets. These two estimates (35 and 70) are the midpoints of ranges estimated by the Department of Justice for purposes of converting the 1968 guidelines into a Herfindahl measurement. See Department of Justice Press Release, June 14, 1982.

in the level of market shares of the acquired and acquiring firm that triggers a possible challenge. Thus, while about 28,000 (12%) of all mergers would likely have been challenged under the 1968 guidelines, approximately 24,000 (10%) would be challenged under the 1982 guidelines.

This decrease in number of mergers challenged occurs in both SMSA and non-SMSA county markets. About 3% of all mergers in SMSA markets would be subject to challenge under the new guidelines; this contrasts with close to 4% under the 1968 guidelines.

While there is little difference in the number of non-SMSA county markets considered to be highly concentrated under the two sets of guidelines (2226 under the old guidelines and 2216 with the new), fewer mergers violate the new guidelines because of the slight increase in allowable market shares. Thus, 18,230 possible mergers (70%) in non-SMSA county markets would likely be challenged under the new guidelines while 20,034 possible mergers (76%) would have violated the old guidelines.

III. Summary and Conclusions

As the previous sections demonstrated, the new Justice Department guidelines include some important changes from the 1968 directive. Perhaps the most significant change is the lengthy exposition of the methodology for defining product and geographic markets, which was absent in the earlier guidelines, and its implications for disaggregation of bank services into multiple product lines. Less significant for banking markets is the change in absolute number of mergers likely to be challenged. About 4,000 fewer mergers would likely be subject to antitrust challenge, due primarily to a slight increase in market share levels allowed for the acquired and acquiring firms. When all banking markets are considered, about 10% of mergers would likely be challenged. This proportion of mergers subject to challenge is somewhat higher than the average for manufacturing markets, due primarily to the greater proportion of concentrated markets in banking. Thus, using the Justice Department guidelines for screening purposes would "catch" a somewhat higher proportion of mergers in banking than in other industries.

This study illustrates, however, that there are some differences among banking markets underlying the 10% figure. Due to high levels of concentration (measured by either the HHI or the four-firm concentration ratio) and the high market shares of the leading firms in markets where there are few firms, a significantly greater proportion of mergers in non-SMSA, or rural, markets would likely be challenged. Close to 70% of all mergers in these markets would be subject to close scrutiny if the guidelines were used to screen mergers. It is possible that consideration of the mitigating factors listed in the guidelines[11] could reduce the number of mergers subject to challenge in these markets. Many of these factors, however, do not seem to weigh against likely challenge of the mergers. For instance, entry into rural markets does not seem particularly easy or likely. In addition, "shading-in" of nonbank competitors in rural market merger analysis may not change significantly the levels of concentration in these markets; thrifts are frequently substantially smaller in size and more limited in scope of activities in these markets.

A more productive avenue for research on merger policy in these markets may begin with the presumption that most rural markets likely can support relatively fewer firms than urban markets (*e.g.*, less than five firms), given market size, population density and income levels. Research on the theory and application of oligopoly models or dominant firm-competitive fringe models to markets such as these rural markets would provide the basis for determining whether merger of the smaller firms in these markets is neutral or anticompetitive in effect.

Research in these areas and inclusion of the research results as modifications to the new guidelines could significantly alter the proportion of mergers likely to be challenged in these markets from its potential high of 70%, as demonstrated in this study, to a substantially lower number. This would substantially enhance the usefulness of the new guidelines for screening purposes.

[11]Such factors include the ease of entry into markets, and the likelihood that other nonbanking firms could enter and provide substitutes for bank products over a longer time period.

International Banking

V

Over the past two decades, and at a much more rapid pace in the 1970s and in the early 1980s, United States banks have substantially increased their activities abroad. In a similar though less dramatic fashion foreign banks in recent years have expanded their operations in the United States market. International banking has contributed to a more integrated international financial system and permitted a greater diversification of bank balance sheets. However, expansion into international activities exposes banks to a whole new set of risks in terms of currency and loans to customers whose credit worthiness may be difficult to establish. The activities of foreign banks in the United States have also raised questions about the equity of current regulations.

In the opening article in this section—number nineteen in this volume—Betsy B. White analyzes the factors stimulating the entry of foreign banks into United States markets and explores the supervisory and regulatory issues. White makes a strong case for placing all banks on an equitable supervisory and regulatory footing.

Article twenty by Norman S. Fieleke focuses on the critical debt problem of non-oil-exporting developing economies. This issue is of great concern to students of banking, because large money-center banks have played major roles in financing the balance of payments deficits of these economies and are now exposed to a considerable level of risk. He delineates a number of preventative measures—including better understanding of "country risk" and improved regulatory and supervisory measures.

The twenty-first article in this volume addresses the "country risk" problem broached by Fieleke. Ingo Walter investigates country risk from a portfolio-theoretic perspective. Walter calls for improved informational networks within banks and by national and international bodies as part of the country risk evaluation process.

A controversial seven-point program for reducing world banking risk is put forth by James Dean and Ian Giddy in the final article in this section. Their article, the twenty-second in this volume, was written especially for this collection. Dean and Giddy offer several innovative strategic proposals. Their brilliant essay deserves careful examination by world bankers and international banking authorities. It is included here in order to stimulate discussion and debate.

Foreign Banking in the United States: A Regulatory and Supervisory Perspective

Betsy B. White

19

The business of banking has changed substantially over the last two decades. A major aspect of this change has been the international expansion of banking operations. In the 1960s, U.S. banks moved abroad in large numbers. In the 1970s, foreign banks accelerated their expansion in this country, bringing home the effects of this change in banking.

The foreign banking presence in the United States has further stimulated competition among banks and has enhanced the international status of U.S. financial markets. But it also underscores the regulatory and supervisory issues which inevitably arise when banks move outside their home countries: What factors motivate banks to move beyond their local markets? When banks cross national boundaries, what changes in bank supervision are necessary to assure the safety and soundness of the banking system? How far does national supervisory responsibility and authority stretch? What types of regulations should apply to foreign banks in domestic markets? How do regulations affect and how are regulations affected by international banking?

Reprinted from *Quarterly Review* (Summer, 1982); 48–58 by permission of the Federal Reserve Bank of New York and the author.

International Expansion of Banking—Motivating Factors

The evolution of international banking since the early 1960s reflects changes in the economic and regulatory environments in which banks operate. By the same token, the changing nature of banking has influenced economic activity and the nature and scope of bank regulations. This article focuses on the regulatory influence on international banking, and the impact the international expansion of this business has had on regulations and supervisory practices.[1]

During the sixties, several factors combined to create incentives for U.S. banks to expand their overseas operations. First, the relative strength of the dollar stimulated American corporate investment abroad. Second, beginning in 1965, the voluntary credit restraint program imposed restrictions on lending to foreigners from domestic offices. Third, Regulation Q ceilings and reserve requirements on domestic deposits—not so onerous in low rate periods—exacted a heavy toll on domestic banking operations in the relatively high rate periods of 1966 and 1969–70.

Put another way, in the 1960s, regulation increased the cost of doing business out of domestic offices at a time when U.S. corporations and others were generating lucrative business abroad. By setting up branches in foreign countries, U.S. banks avoided the costs of these regulatory constraints. In 1960, eight U.S. banks had 102 overseas banking offices. Today 155 Federal Reserve member banks have over 700 offices abroad.

In many respects, the rapid growth of foreign banking in this country in the 1970s is a mirror image of the U.S. banking expansion abroad. The motivations and strategies stem from the same basic factors—economics and regulations. In the 1970s, foreign corporations stepped up their investment activities in this country. Foreign banks, like their U.S. counterparts in earlier years, followed suit, setting up operations in the United States to sustain and expand the corporate relationships originally established in their home countries.

Further, the dominant role of the dollar in international finance in the 1960s and 1970s made a dollar-based operation advantageous for foreign banks doing an international business. With the emergence of New York as one of the major international financial centers of the world, foreign banks set up operations here to compete in domestic money markets as well as to provide global and around-the-clock services to their clientele.

Finally, the regulatory and political climate in the United States helped attract foreign banks here in the 1970s. Until the enactment of the International Banking Act of 1978 (IBA), branches and agencies of foreign banks were supervised and regulated only at the state level. They were not subject to Federal Reserve reserve requirements, deposit interest rate ceilings, or restrictions on interstate banking.[2]

[1] In this article, *regulation* is taken to be the framework of laws and rules in which banks operate. *Supervision* refers to the enforcement of such laws and rules, especially through the oversight and examination of banks.

[2] Foreign-owned banks chartered in the United States, however, have always been subject to the same regulations as other domestic banks.

Foreign Banks in the United States

Foreign banks operate in the United States through three major types of offices: agencies, branches, and subsidiaries.[3] Branches and agencies are merely extensions of the parent bank, while subsidiaries are separately capitalized banking entities. The major difference between branches and agencies is that agencies are not allowed to accept deposits from citizens or residents of the United States.[4]

The structure of foreign banking operations in this country is summarized in Table 1. At the end of 1981, the number of branches (194) and agencies (195) were about equal. However, about two fifths of foreign bank assets were held at branches and only about one fourth at agencies. The 52 foreign bank subsidiaries accounted for about one third of foreign bank assets in this country.

The organizational form chosen by foreign banks has been greatly influenced by state and Federal laws. Prior to the IBA, licensing of branches and agencies was controlled at the state level. For example, California effectively prohibited entry by foreign branches. While California law explicitly permits the establishment of branches by foreign banks, it also requires that branches have Federal Deposit Insurance Corporation (FDIC) insurance. It was not until the passage of the IBA that the FDIC was authorized to insure branches of foreign banks.

New York State law permits foreign banks to establish branches within the state *provided* New York banks are allowed entry into the entering bank's home country. Until recently, Canadian law prohibited foreign banking operations in Canada. Consequently, Canadian banks had been limited to establishing subsidiaries and agencies in New York. Further, New York law does not allow foreign banks to operate both agencies *and* branches; the foreign bank must choose one form or the other.

The IBA authorized the Comptroller of the Currency to license Federal branches and agencies provided certain conditions are not violated. In particular, the Comptroller *cannot* issue a Federal license to a foreign bank to open an agency or branch in a state in which the bank already operates such an office under state law. Further, Federal licenses cannot be granted to establish offices in states which generally prohibit foreign branch and agency operations. The full scope of the Comptroller's authority, however, remains unclear. For example, under New York State law, foreign banks are allowed to establish branches. However, Australian banks are not allowed to establish state-licensed branches, because Australia does not allow foreign bank entry into its banking market. The Comptroller granted a Federal license to an Australian branch, because foreign branching, *per se,* is not prohibited in New York. This decision has been challenged and awaits a final ruling by the courts.

[3]Foreign banks have also established a small number of investment companies under New York State law and a large number of representative offices across the country. Investment companies are empowered to extend loans like a commercial bank and to accept credit balances but are not allowed to accept deposits. Representative offices are not allowed to conduct any banking business and serve only to disseminate information regarding parent organizations and to cultivate customer relationships. The IBA authorized foreign banks to establish Edge corporations as well. However, these institutions are restricted to doing international business and are not included in this analysis.

[4]Agencies are allowed to accept *credit balances* incidental to their customers' banking transactions. These funds are essentially clearing and compensating balances.

The organizational form chosen by a foreign bank can also depend on the type of business the bank expects to do. A foreign bank wishing to offer a full range of banking services in the United States would generally choose to establish or to acquire a subsidiary bank. Those seeking to conduct a wholesale lending business, in part funded in the United States, would generally need to open only branches. In states which do not allow foreign branching, some foreign banks have chosen to open both a subsidiary and an agency. The subsidiary provides a dollar deposit base while the agency, not subject to interstate branching restrictions or lending limits, affords considerable lending flexibility.[5] Foreign banks seeking to establish an investment outlet for dollar balances accumulated abroad might choose to establish only agencies here.

Foreign banking operations in this country are highly concentrated in New York, San Francisco, Los Angeles, and Chicago (Table 1). Oregon and Washington have long had a number of foreign banks—especially Canadian and Japanese. In recent years, Miami and Atlanta have experienced rapid growth of foreign banking offices. In choosing among states allowing foreign banking, foreign bankers have been influenced primarily by their choice of target markets. Consequently, factors such as the concentration of large corporate headquarters and trade flows have been important in determining the location of foreign banking offices in this country.

Although over 175 foreign banks from 39 countries operate offices in this country, the foreign presence in U.S. markets is dominated by banks from major industrial countries. Japanese, British, and Canadian banks operate over one third (156 of the total 441) of these offices (Table 1). Further, the number of banking offices understates the position of these banks among foreign banks in the United States. At the end of 1981, Japanese banks held one third of foreign bank assets in this country and British and Canadian banks together held over one fourth of these assets.

Banking Activities of Foreign Banks[6]

Most foreign banks in this country operate solely in the wholesale banking and money markets. Relatively few foreign banks actively seek retail business. In fact, a number of foreign banks discourage retail depositors by requiring relatively large minimum deposit balances. The retail banking markets—at least in large urban areas where foreign banks are located—are generally difficult for a foreign-named bank to penetrate. Moreover, establishing a retail business requires large investments in office space, computers, and personnel. Those investments typically show a profit only over a long time horizon. A good number of those foreign banks that have entered the retail market have done so through the acquisition of domestic banks with already established retail branch networks. Foreign agencies and branches are, therefore, by and large wholesale banking offices and should be analyzed separately from subsidiaries.

[5]Before the enactment of the IBA, foreign branches also were free from interstate restrictions.

[6]This section is based on discussions with executives at the U.S. offices of Japanese, Canadian, Swiss, French, German, and British banks and on data from the Federal Financial Institutions Examination Council's Report of Condition.

Table 1 Foreign Banking Offices in the United States
December 1981

Location of parent bank	Agencies	Branches	Subsidiaries	Total offices	Total assets (billions of dollars)
	Number of physical offices by ownership				
Japan	27	31	12	70	88.9
Canada	20	18	10	48	23.4
United Kingdom	12	19	7	38	46.2
France	7	14	1	22	16.1
Israel	6	13	3	22	4.2
Brazil	14	6	0	20	4.0
Germany	6	14	0	20	7.3
Spain	8	6	6	20	4.0
Korea	11	5	1	17	1.9
Hong Kong	8	6	1	15	12.4
Italy	5	9	1	15	10.9
Netherlands	4	7	1	12	4.8
Mexico	10	0	1	11	3.1
Switzerland	5	6	0	11	11.1
Other Asia*	23	19	2	44	1.7
Other Latin America	13	4	3	20	7.9
Australia and New Zealand	6	7	0	13	1.3
Other Europe	3	7	2	12	5.7
Middle East and Africa	7	3	1	11	0.7
Total	195	194	52	441	255.7

U.S. location	Agencies	Branches	Subsidiaries	Total offices
	Number of physical offices by state			
New York	61	113	24	198
California	96	4	20	120
Illinois	—	36	2	38
Florida	25	—	1	26
Washington	—	10	—	10
Georgia	9	—	—	9
Oregon	—	8	—	8
All other	4	23	5	32
Total numbers	195	194	52	441
Total assets (billions of dollars)	65.5	107.7	82.5	255.7

*Excludes Middle East.

The target markets of foreign agencies and branches generally are determined by their parent organizations. More often than not, all U.S. agencies and branches of a given foreign bank pursue a common strategy, sometimes even guided by common management. Therefore, to analyze the business activities of a foreign bank in this country, one should look at a consolidated balance sheet of its branches and agencies, not at individual offices.[7]

The parent organization's strategy for its U.S. operations is influenced by a variety of factors. These include the parent organization's home-country banking activities and the size and scope of its worldwide banking operations. The dollar position of affiliated offices outside the United States, the areas of expertise of the bank's management staff, and home-country laws and regulations also can play a role.

The most common motivation for entering the United States is to expand existing types of business or business relationships. Most often foreign banks are seeking:

- to service the U.S. operations of corporations operating in the home country,
- to finance trade with the home country or with other countries in which the banks have offices,
- to set up a foreign exchange operation in New York,
- to operate in the U.S. money markets, and
- to generate U.S. investment interest in the home country.

Some foreign banks provide a very broad range of services, while others focus on only one or two of these types of activities.

The decision to acquire or to establish a subsidiary bank in this country generally reflects the parent bank's overall U.S. or worldwide strategy. The activities of a subsidiary bank are managed separately at arm's length from the parent bank's other U.S. operations. Nevertheless, the subsidiary contributes to the scope of banking services a foreign bank can offer to its customers and, more often than not, the major activities of the subsidiary complement or supplement the services provided by other U.S. offices of the same bank.

The economic and business factors affecting foreign banking operations in the United states are common across banks. However, one factor—home-country laws, regulations, and practices—serves to distinguish the U.S. balance sheets of foreign banks from different countries. For example, Japanese banks are restricted in the number and types of foreign banking offices they may open.[8] Japanese banks do not have ''shell'' branches in the Caribbean as do many U.S. and other banks. Thus, Japanese agencies and branches in the United States seem to serve a somewhat broader international dollar lending role, and they have relatively more loans to non-U.S. residents than most other foreign banks. In contrast, Canadian banks book a relatively small amount of loans to nonresidents in the United States. This can be attributed, in part, to Canadian tax law which provides an incentive to book such loans at Bahamian and Cayman branches. German bank activity in the United States is influenced by home-country regulations which pertain to a bank's worldwide consolidated balance sheet. For example, German liquidity requirements—

[7]As argued below, there are several factors that can distort even such a limited consolidated balance sheet, making it unrepresentative of U.S. activities.

[8]The Japanese Ministry of Finance's criteria for granting permission to open new branches were recently eased in the broad-ranging revision of Japanese banking laws, effective April 1, 1982.

originally designed to protect the domestic depositor against loss—limit the degree to which asset and liability maturities can be mismatched. This, in effect, restricts the degree to which U.S. offices of German banks can extend long-term loans.

Many analysts have tried to assess foreign banking operations in the United States by looking at the balance sheets of different types of foreign banking offices. They have compared the composition and size of assets and liablities across branches, agencies, and subsidiaries. Such an approach has several limitations. First, as discussed previously, the agencies and branches of a given foreign bank generally have the same objectives and therefore should not be analyzed separately. Second, and probably more important, the U.S. balance sheet is only one part of the whole. Foreign bank loans to U.S. residents are not always booked in this country. For example, LIBOR-priced loans are often booked at Caribbean branches where they are funded with Eurodollar liabilities. Finally, foreign bank dollar loans to third countries may be negotiated elsewhere (for example, at the parent bank where management responsibility for such loans may lie) but booked in the United States where they are funded.

Table 2 presents the consolidated balance sheet of all U.S. agencies and branches of foreign banks at the end of 1981. Table 3 presents the same information for foreign bank subsidiaries. For the reasons cited, these figures, at best, present only a partial picture of foreign bank activity in this country. However, several observations can be made. First, loans to domestic nonfinancial entities which are booked at agencies and branches are not fully funded by deposits from domestic nonfinancial entities. That is, foreign banks do not appear to be raising funds in this country to lend abroad. Quite the contrary, foreign agencies and branches rely heavily on affiliates and the interbank market for funding. This suggests that many foreign agencies and branches serve primarily as investment outlets for dollar balances acquired by overseas offices.

A second observation is that foreign agencies and branches hold a relatively small amount of government and corporate securities. A review of individual branch and agency

Table 2 Assets and Liabilities of U.S. Agencies and Branches of Foreign Banks
December 1981

Assets	Billions of dollars	Liabilities	Billions of dollars
Loans to nonfinancial entities	80.6	Deposits due to nonfinancial entities	34.8
U.S. addressees	*(44.2)*	U.S. addressees	*(26.6)*
Foreign addressees	*(36.4)*	Foreign addressees	*(8.2)*
Claims on unaffiliated financial institutions	61.7	Liabilities to unaffiliated financial institutions†	81.0
Claims on affiliates	19.3	Liabilities to affiliates	36.5
Other assets†	7.3	Other liabilities§	20.9
Securities	4.3		
Total assets	173.2	Total liabilities	173.2

Table 3 Assets and Liabilities of U.S. Banks Owned by Foreigners
December 1981

Assets	Billions of dollars	Liabilities	Billions of dollars
Loans to nonfinancial entities	47.6	Deposits due to nonfinancial entities	53.8
U.S. addressees	*(44.2)*[¶]		
Foreign addressees	*(3.4)*[¶]		
Claims on financial institutions*	21.9	Liabilities to financial institutions[‡]	14.5
Securities	9.1	Other liabilities[§]	8.1
Other assets[†]	4.5	Capital	6.2
Allowance for possible loan loss	−0.6		
Total assets	82.5	Total liabilities and capital	82.5

Figures may not sum to totals due to rounding.

*Includes cash due from depository institutions, Federal funds sold, funds loaned under repurchase agreement to banks, and loans to financial institutions.

[†]Includes lease-financing receivables, funds loaned under repurchase agreements to nonbanks, and ''other assets'' (which include income earned on loans but not collected and other claims on nonrelated parties).

[‡]Includes deposits and credit balances due to banks, Federal funds purchased, funds borrowed from depository institutions under repurchase agreements, other liabilities to banks for borrowed money, certified and officer's checks, traveler's checks, and letters of credit sold for cash.

[§]Includes liabilities to nonbanks for borrowed money, liabilities on acceptances outstanding, funds borrowed under repurchase agreement with nondepository institutions, and ''other liabilities'' to nonrelated parties (which include expenses accrued and unpaid).

[¶]For subsidiaries with no foreign offices or less than $100 million in assets, no breakdown between foreign and domestic loans is available. All loans reported by these banks were put in the U.S. addressees category.

data suggests that most of the $4 billion in securities is owned by a relatively few New York City branches and agencies which have special expertise in U.S. securities markets. The reason most often given for the small holdings of government securities is their yield which is low relative to the funding costs faced by these banks. Further, income earned on state and local government securities, while exempt from U.S. Federal taxes, is not exempt from home-country taxation.

Finally, a comparison of agency and branch balance sheets with those of subsidiaries underscores the differences in their target markets. Subsidiaries have greater retail operations and do more domestic business than do agencies and branches. This is reflected in the relatively large portion of deposits due to non-banks. These deposits represent about 70 percent of total liabilities. Also, loans to foreigners, while only estimated, appear to be less than 5 percent of total assets. Loans to domestic nonbank entities account for about one half of total assets. In contrast, agencies and branches rely heavily on the interbank market for funding. Two thirds of their liabilities are to financial institutions. On the asset side, loans to foreigners represent about one fifth of total assets.

U.S. Regulations and Foreign Bank Activity

The regulatory and legal environment in which banks operate affects the types of business banks do and the locations in which they operate. As discussed earlier, the rapid expansion of international banking over the last two decades reflects this influence. But it has also brought about changes in banking laws and regulations. In the United States, the two most recent examples of this are the enactment of the IBA and the change in Federal regulations and state laws to encourage offshore banking in this country.

The growth of foreign banks in this country in the 1970s highlighted the descrepancy between the regulation of these institutions and the regulation of domestic banks at the Federal level. The IBA was enacted to close this gap. This legislation set in motion a series of regulatory changes which embody the principle of *national treatment* of foreign banks operating in this country. Under national treatment, to the extent reasonably possible, foreign banks are subject to the same restrictions and have the same privileges as domestic banks. To this end, the IBA restricts the expansion of interstate deposit-taking by foreign banks, subjects foreign branches and agencies to Federal Reserve reserve requirements and interest rate regulations, requires deposit insurance for branches engaged in retail banking, extends the restrictions on nonbank activities of the Bank Holding Company Act to foreign banks operating branches and agencies in the United States, and allows agencies and branches access to the discount window and to payment services provided by Federal Reserve Banks.[9]

In providing greater equality of treatment, the IBA has also affected the business of banking for foreign bankers in this country. In this respect, perhaps the most important provision of the act was the imposition of Federal Reserve reserve requirements. As these requirements have been phased in, the reserve costs to foreign banks have increased.[10] As a result, foreign banks have found it necessary to monitor and to manage their reserve positions more closely than in the past.

Further, reserve requirements have affected the relative costs of various types of funds. For example, the 3 percent reserve requirement on jumbo certificates of deposit (CDs), effective in August of this year, increases by about ⅜ percentage point the overall or "all-in" cost of CDs offered at 12 percent. Foreign bank CDs are generally priced by adding a spread to the interest rate paid by large domestic money market banks on their CDs. Consequently, foreign banks cannot adjust their CD rates (as do money center banks) to offset the increase in reserve costs if they wish to remain competitive in issuing CDs.

Some foreign bankers claim that this has necessitated charging higher loan rates, while others assert that competition prohibits higher loan rates and that their net interest margins have suffered. In either case, the relative competitive position of foreign banks in funding

[9]For a detailed description of regulatory changes resulting from the IBA, see "The International Banking Act of 1978," a report by the Board of Governors of the Federal Reserve System to the Congress, September 17, 1980. The IBA granted certain grandfather rights to foreign banks with respect to interstate banking and non-banking operations established in the United States prior to the enactment of the legislation.

[10]While some states imposed reserve requirements on foreign branch deposits, such reserves either could be held in interest-bearing form or could serve as compensating balances at correspondent banks.

and extending loans in the United States has changed. Inevitably, this will alter the future growth of their commercial lending business and may lead some banks to redirect resources to other banking activities.

In responding to the foreign bank expansion in this country, regulatory changes promulgated under the IBA generally were in the direction of greater regulatory coverage. However, the IBA also mandated a liberalization of rules governing Edge corporations to enable U.S. banks to compete more effectively with similar foreign-owned institutions. As a result, the Federal Reserve amended its regulations to allow Edge corporations to open branches nationwide and to expand their international banking services and deposit-taking ability. Keeping with the principle of national treatment, foreign banks were also permitted to own Edge corporations.

Another reduction of U.S. regulatory restrictions stemming from the expansion of international banking was the creation of international banking facilities (IBFs). Effective December 3, 1981, depository institutions operating in the United States—both foreign and domestic—were permitted to establish IBFs for the purpose of conducting international business within this country free from interest rate restrictions, reserve requirements, and FDIC insurance. Additionally, several states have enacted legislation which exempts IBF income from state and local taxes.[11]

The reaction to IBFs by foreign bankers seems to vary across nationalities. Japanese and Italian banks have shifted the most assets to their IBFs (Table 4). In large part, this probably reflects the fact that these banks do not operate ''shell'' branches in the Caribbean. Some bankers, such as the Swiss, report the appeal of U.S. country risk has led home-country customers to shift dollar deposits from third countries to IBFs to accommodate potential customer demand should it materialize—that is, to maintain their competitive position.

Supervisory Issues

When banks expand beyond their home-country boundaries, the issue of supervisory responsibility cannot be ignored. The soundness of a foreign banking organization should be of concern to both the host country and the home country. Failure of such an organization could send ripple effects throughout the financial systems of both the host country and the home country. In fact, the high degree of cross-border interbank borrowing and lending leaves no banking market completely immune to the effects of a large bank failure.

The IBA authorized, for the first time, participation in the supervision of the U.S. operations of foreign banks by Federal banking authorities. This included the authorization of the Federal Reserve to act as the residual supervisory agency to ensure a national overview of interstate activities of foreign banks. In exercising this authority, the Federal Reserve draws on examinations conducted by the primary Federal and state bank regulatory authorities. In addition, the Federal Reserve receives annual financial information on the operations of the foreign parent banking organization.

[11]For a detailed description of regulatory and tax treatment of IBFs, see Sydney J. Key and Serge Bellanger, ''International Banking Facilities: The Shape of Things to Come,'' *The World of Banking* (March-April 1982), pp. 17-23.

Table 4 Assets and Liabilities of Foreign-Owned International Banking Facilities*
December 31, 1981; In billions of dollars

Assets and liabilities	Country of ownership						
	Japan	Italy	United Kingdom	Switzerland	Germany	All others	Total
Number	48	11	9	5	8	71	152
Assets:							
Loans to nonfinancial entities	12.7	1.9	2.1	0.4	0.5	3.7	21.3
Claims on unaffiliated financial institutions	6.0	2.7	2.3	1.7	0.4	2.8	16.0
Claims on affiliates	0.2	0.1	—	—	—	0.8	1.1
Securities	0.4	†	—	—	†	†	0.5
Other assets	0.3	0.1	0.1	0.1	†	0.1	0.7
Total assets/liabilities	19.7	4.8	4.5	2.2	1.0	7.5	39.6
Liabilities:							
Deposits due to nonfinancial entities	0.7	0.5	0.2	0.1	†	1.0	2.6
Liabilities to unaffiliated financial institutions	5.7	2.1	0.1	0.4	0.1	1.2	9.6
Liabilities to affiliates	6.2	0.5	1.0	1.7	0.2	2.9	12.5
Net due to establishing institution	6.9	1.1	3.0	†	0.6	2.1	13.8
Other liabilities	0.1	0.6	0.2	†	†	0.2	1.1

*These data are included in those presented in Tables 2 and 3. Figures may not sum to totals due to rounding.

†Less than $50 million.

However, effective supervision of international banks cannot be limited to unilateral efforts by domestic authorities. It requires a cooperative effort among national supervisory authorities. A major step forward in the area of supervisory cooperation was taken in 1975 with the formation at the Bank for International Settlements (BIS) of the Committee on Banking Regulations and Supervisory Practices.[12] This Committee was formed by the central bank governors from the Group of Ten major industrial countries[13] and Switzerland to improve the coordination of national surveillance of international banking activities. Committee meetings provide a forum for the discussion of the key supervisory and regulatory issues by senior supervisory officials from the major industrial countries. And, perhaps more importantly, they provide an avenue for developing personal working relationships between supervisors, which facilitate rapid and effective cooperation should banks experience difficulties.

[12]This Committee is often referred to as the "Cooke Committee" after Peter Cooke of the Bank of England, its current chairman. A more complete review of the committee's history and its contributions is presented in W. Peter Cooke, "The Development of Co-operation between Bank Supervisory Authorities in the Group of Ten Countries, Luxembourg and Switzerland", a paper given at the International Conference of Banking Supervisors (Washington, D.C., September 24-25, 1981).

[13]The Group of Ten consists of Belgium (and Luxembourg), Canada, France, Germany, Italy, Japan, the Netherlands, Sweden, the United Kingdom, and the United States.

Effective supervision of international banks rests on two premises. First, national authorities must be *willing* to cooperate in monitoring the activities of the overseas operations of their own banks and the local operations of foreign banks. Second, authorities must be *capable* of supervising their banks' international business.

One of the first tasks of the Committee in 1975 was to develop principles for international supervisory cooperation. In particular, guidelines were needed to ensure comprehensive and coordinated surveillance of all foreign banking offices. The general statement of the Committee's views—commonly referred to as the Concordat—was endorsed by the countries represented on the Committee in December 1975.

In dividing supervisory responsibility among national banking authorities, the Concordat distinguishes between the supervision of liquidity and solvency and between the supervision of foreign branches and legally separate banking subsidiaries incorporated in a foreign country. The supervision of liquidity of all foreign offices and the solvency of subsidiaries is regarded as the primary responsibility of the host-country authorities. The supervision of solvency of foreign branches is considered to be primarily in the hands of home-country authorities.

To be fully effective, the principles set forth in the Concordat need be endorsed by supervisors worldwide. Acceptance by supervisors outside the BIS member countries has spread, but no formal endorsements have been made. Further, the effectiveness of the Concordat rests on the capability of national authorities to supervise the international activities of their banks.

Fundamental to the effective implementation of the Concordat is the timely availability of information necessary to the supervisory process. In particular, worldwide consolidated financial information is needed to assess the overall soundness of a banking institution. Good progress has been made in this area by many countries, but such data are not yet available in others. The assignment of supervisory responsibility embodied in the Concordat also requires the exchange of banking information between supervisory authorities on a confidential basis. While there is agreement that such exchanges are necessary, banking secrecy laws or regulations in some countries still impede such flows of information.

While substantial progress has been made in the area of international supervisory cooperation, the increased importance of international operations of banks has raised new areas of concern to the bank supervisor. For one, the number of banks operating in the major financial centers of the world has grown to include a broad range of institutions in both size and nationality. The phenomenal growth of international money markets and payments activity has increased the interconnectedness of the world's banking system. This interconnectedness provides a ready conduit for transmitting local financial shocks throughout the system. This aspect of the market underscores the importance of ensuring that prudential market practices, internal bank control systems, and external audit and examination procedures are in place. It is largely through the proper functioning of such safeguards that the effects of the failure of a bank or one of its customers can be contained.

Another type of concern is as much political as it is financial. The prospect that governments might exert leverage over financial institutions to achieve political objectives is not new. However, the enormous volume of cross-border and cross-currency transactions effected daily in the world banking system has magnified the riskiness of such strategies. The events in Iran, Poland, and Argentina exemplify the real exposure that such international activities bring about for banking institutions—a type of risk that is very difficult to measure and control.

Regulatory Issues

On the regulatory side, banking across national boundaries raises questions regarding the equitable treatment of banks in different markets. As mentioned previously, the United States has adopted the principle of national treatment. An alternative approach—one based on the principle of *reciprocity*—would afford foreign banks in the United States the same treatment that U.S. banks are given in the foreign banks' home countries. Adoption of a policy centered on national treatment affords greater potential for realizing the benefits of enhanced competition in our banking markets. It also minimizes the risk, inherent in a policy of strict reciprocity, of retaliatory actions by foreign governments to place additional restrictions on U.S. overseas banking operations.

By the same token, however, national treatment offers little basis for further advancement of U.S. banking interests abroad. For this reason, an argument can be made for introducing aspects of reciprocity into the regulatory process. For example, consideration of reciprocal treatment as a factor in the balancing test in the applications process might serve as one type of catalyst to providing more equitable treatment for U.S. as well as other foreign banks in other countries. From a broader perspective, however, any substantial relaxation of remaining restrictions on entry by foreign banks into national banking markets is more likely to be achieved through negotiations at an international level.

National treatment, in the form of the IBA, has taken us a long way toward more equitable treatment of banks operating in the United States. Nevertheless, regulatory differences from country to country continue to sustain disparities in the competitive opportunities facing banks both here and abroad. The three key areas of difference are geographic restrictions, capital requirements, and product line restrictions.

The IBA placed foreign banks on a more equal footing with U.S. banks with respect to the limitations on interstate banking imposed by the McFadden Act and Douglas Amendment to the Bank Holding Company Act. Further, antitrust considerations continue to limit the degree to which large *intra*state acquisitions are permitted. In effect, domestic expansion of U.S. banks is restricted. However, large foreign banks not represented in the United States are still free to expand their international operations by acquiring large U.S. banks in attractive markets. Moreover, those foreign banks having only wholesale branches are largely free to make significant acquisitions in their home state. So it follows that, unless legislative restrictions are eased, competitive considerations will continue to favor foreign banks wishing to acquire large U.S. banks—especially large troubled banks. This issue is dealt with in a limited way by legislation now pending before the Congress.[14]

[14]In particular, under S.1720, a bank holding company could, in limited and emergency circumstances, acquire a large, closed out-of-state bank.

What is perhaps more important, from a long-run competitive position, is the fact that most large international banks enjoy nationwide banking within their home country and, as such, have access to a nationwide core deposit base. Of course, neither U.S. nor foreign banks are free to branch across state lines in this country. However, this is more limiting to the growth potential of U.S. banks than their foreign competitors, since U.S. banks are not in a position to capitalize on the full market potential of their well-established retail operations.

Another dimension of home-country regulation which has an international impact is that of capital adequacy. There is general agreement that the erosion of the capital positions experienced in recent years by most major international banks should be reversed. However, there is no international consensus on the appropriate criteria for determining the adequacy of capital, or even what constitutes capital. This should not be surprising since U.S. bank supervisors are not in full agreement themselves on these issues. When different countries impose different degrees of stringency in assessing the capital adequacy of their banks, the impact on bank expansion plans can be significant. And banks with lower capital ratios can generally charge lower loan rates and obtain the same return as banks with higher capital requirements.

A third area in which domestic regulations affect international operations lies in restrictions on the types of activities in which banks can engage. For example, U.S. laws and regulations prohibit U.S. banks from engaging in commerce either at home or abroad. They also seek to maintain, at least within this country, a separation between investment and commercial banking. Most European countries do not require such separations. Rather they allow banks ''universal banking'' capabilities. For example, a German bank can provide banking services in the United States, engage in a full range of commercial and financial activities in its home country, and, through an indirect U.S non-bank subsidiary, engage in commerce here. This makes these institutions very formidable competitors of more restricted U.S. banking corporations.

Home-country regulations have not only affected the evolution of international banking but regulatory changes themselves have been influenced to an increasing degree by the multinational nature of the banking business. Banking legislation and regulation formulated before the 1960s, for good reason, focused primarily on domestic concerns and objectives. The growing importance of foreign banks in domestic markets and of banking conducted outside national regulations has necessitated a review and reevaluation of existing legal and regulatory frameworks. In the United States, the IBA was needed to fill a regulatory void created by the expansion of foreign banking activities here. And the move to allow the establishment of IBFs reflects a desire by U.S. authorities to recapture some of the banking business conducted abroad to avoid the costs of home-country regulations. The influence of foreign banking is also reflected in the 1980 revision of Canada's Bank Act and the recent liberalization of Japanese banking laws.

The restructuring of the legal and regulatory frameworks is far from complete. Domestic regulations which adversely affect banks' international competitive position are sure to come under close scrutiny, as are restrictions which apply to banks in one location but not in others. It will become increasingly difficult to sustain differences in national policy with regard to capitalization and funding practices of banks with significant international business. It will also be difficult to maintain domestic barriers separating banking from other financial services, such as investment banking activities, when both U.S. and foreign banks engage in these activities in overseas markets. These pressures for regulatory change are broadly similar to those that have characterized our dual (Federal/state and commercial bank/thrift institution) approach to banking regulation.

Summary

The rapid growth of international banking over the last two decades has been motivated and shaped by the interaction of economics and regulations. The development of extensive networks of foreign banks operating in domestic markets has served to initiate cooperation among national supervisors to develop comprehensive surveillance of international banking activities. Home-country legislation and regulation have been adapted to reflect the increasingly international nature of banking. Notwithstanding these changes, however, the continuing growth and evolution of the international banking system will remain a powerful force for further change in bank regulatory and supervisory practices.

20

International Lending on Trial

Norman S. Fieleke

That the world is undergoing its gravest financial crisis since the 1930s is now a commonplace. Less widely appreciated are the causes of the crisis, the remedies that are being adopted, and the measures that might be taken to forestall future crises. These are the topics surveyed in this article.

The Nature of the Crisis

Simply put, the crisis is a widespread failure of debtors in the poorer, or "developing," countries to pay their foreign debts on schedule. While this failure was dramatized by the extension of billions of dollars in emergency credit to Mexico last August, a problem had been apparent for some time. The number of countries in arrears on international payments had risen from 15 in 1975 to 32 at the end of 1981, at which time total arrears amounted to some $6.3 billion; and the number of developing countries reported by the World Bank as obtaining debt relief rose from 6 in 1980 to 12 in each of the years 1981 and 1982.

According to the OECD (Organization for Economic Cooperation and Development), the medium- and long-term indebtedness of some 158 developing countries and territories amounted to more than $625 billion at the end of 1982. World Bank data suggest that the

Reprinted from *New England Economic Review* (May/June, 1983). 5–13 by permission of the Federal Reserve Bank of Boston and the author.

bulk of this sum is indebtedness of public entities or is guaranteed for repayment by a public entity, but that well over $100 billion is the debt of private parties without any such guarantee. Much of this private debt is probably owed by multinational corporations operating within the developing countries.

More relevant is developing country indebtedness to commercial banks, because what might precipitate a panic would be the insolvency of major banks stemming from their inability to collect interest or principal. As can be seen from line 3 of Table 1, at the end of 1982 commercial banks and other financial institutions had about $365 billion in loans outstanding to 145 developing countries, excluding the 13 countries which belong to OPEC (Organization of Petroleum Exporting Countries). Such loans comprised about 6 percent of the total assets of the lending banks. As the table indicates, a few major borrowers—Argentina, Brazil, South Korea, and Mexico—account for most of this lending. Only one of these countries—South Korea—has met its debt obligations on schedule during the past year.

A major part of the lending to developing countries is by U.S. commercial banks, whose claims on non-OPEC developing countries amounted to more than $98 billion, or 8 percent

Table 1 Bank Lending[a] to Non-OPEC Developing Countries: Estimated Outstanding Disbursed Amounts at Year-End, 1977–1982
(In billions of dollars, unless otherwise noted)

	1977	1980	1981	1982
1. Short-term credits	37	89	110	134[b]
2. Medium- and long-term credits	82	165	195	231
A. Officially guaranteed export credits	13	33	39	49
B. Financial loans and credits	69	132	156	182[b]
3. *Total outstanding* (1 + 2)	119	254	305	365
(of which 4 countries[c], in %)	(44)	(50)	(54)	(52)

[a]International lending by commercial banks and other financial institutions, including participation of non-OECD banks in international syndicates. Data exclude bonds, shares, property and other bank assets which are not loans. They also exclude interest payable and local-currency loans. Short-term debt covers credits with an original maturity of less than one year; an unknown amount of these short-term credits is guaranteed by governments in capital-exporting countries.

[b]Assuming some consolidation of short-term debt into medium-term debt during 1982.

[c]Argentina, Brazil, S. Korea and Mexico.

Source: OECD, *External Debt of Developing Countries: 1982 Survey*, p. 43

of their total assets and 149 percent of their total shareholders' capital, at the end of June, 1982 (Table 2). The major borrowers in difficulty—Argentina, Brazil, and Mexico—had loans outstanding which amounted to more than 84 percent of the capital of the lending banks. The potential threat to solvency from developing country defaults is greater for the nine largest U.S. banks, for their loans to the non-OPEC developing countries were 222 percent of their total capital, and their loans to Argentina, Brazil, and Mexico were 113 percent of their capital (Table 3).

Table 2 U.S. Bank Claims on Non-OPEC Developing Countries

	On all countries			On Argentina, Brazil, and Mexico	
		As percent of			
End of period	In billions of dollars	Total bank assets	Total bank capital	In billions of dollars	As percent of total bank capital
1977	46.9	6.5	115	25.8	63
1978	52.2	6.3	116	26.8	59
1979	61.8	6.6	124	29.9	60
1980	75.4	7.1	132	37.0	65
1981	92.8	8.0	148	46.7	78
June 1982	98.6	8.3	149	52.4	84

Note: Data are for domestic and foreign offices of U.S. banking organizations with significant foreign banking operations. Data cover only cross-border and non-local currency lending.

Source: Board of Governors of the Federal Reserve System.

Table 3 Claims of Nine Largest U.S. Banks on Non-OPEC Developing Countries

	On all countries			On Argentina, Brazil & Mexico		
		As percent of			As percent of	
End of period	In billions of dollars	Total bank assets	Total bank capital	In billions of dollars	Total bank assets	Total bank capital
1977	30.0	8.1	163	15.6	4.2	85
1978	33.4	7.9	176	16.4	3.9	82
1979	39.9	8.2	182	18.2	3.7	83
1980	47.9	9.0	199	22.7	4.3	95
1981	57.6	10.2	220	27.4	4.9	105
June 1982	60.3	10.6	222	30.5	5.4	113

Note: Data are for domestic and foreign offices of the nine banking organizations and cover only cross-border and non-local currency lending.

Source: Board of Governors of the Federal Reserve System.

None of the banks which has been lending to the developing countries is closing its doors or reorganizing as a result of defaults in those countries, but such upheavals are not idle fears and would surely materialize in the absence of enlightened self-interest on the part of both borrowers and lenders. Paul Volcker, Chairman of the Board of Governors of the Federal Reserve System, has summarized the threat: "The situation that emerged last year was unique in its scope and potential effects. It involved several major debtors at the same time, and threatened to spread to others, weak and strong alike. It is this potential for cascading liquidity pressures, undermining the stability of the financial system, that has demanded prompt and forceful action . . . to protect the stability of the financial system as a whole and our own economy. . . . The international financial system is not separable from our domestic banking and credit system. The same institutions are involved in both markets. A shock to one would be a shock to the other. . . . We are talking about dealing with a threat to the recovery, the jobs, and the prosperity of our own country, a threat essentially without parallel in the postwar period."[1]

Because it can be very difficult, if not impossible, for creditors in one country to seize the assets of a defaulting debtor in another country, it might seem that struggling debtors would have strong incentive to repudiate their indebtedness to foreign lenders. Such is not the case, however. Private debtors who fail to honor their obligations face the prospect of a curtailment of credit and perhaps court proceedings as well. Governments which repudiated would bring upon their countries a drastic reduction in the availability of foreign credit, including credit required to finance trade flows. The trade of such nations would be further constricted by the risk that their exports might be seized in transit by foreign creditors. In addition, creditors might attach assets held abroad by repudiating governments. Thus, it is not surprising that repudiations are virtually unheard of. In fact, both borrowers and lenders have powerful incentives to avoid both repudiations and formal declarations of default and, instead, to rearrange debt repayment schedules so that neither party suffers the consequences of repudiation or its equivalent.

The unlikelihood of repudiation diminishes, but does not remove, the threat to the financial system. Creditors who do not receive timely payment from their debtors suffer an impairment of liquidity, and in extreme cases an impairment of solvency as well, whether or not the debtors repudiate. Thus, the fact that debtor governments do not repudiate—and do not go bankrupt—provides grounds for hope but not for unconcern.

It should be noted that not all developing countries are seeking to reschedule their debt. Some, including such a major borrower as South Korea, seem to be experiencing no difficulty. Still, enough countries are experiencing significant difficulties that only an ostrich would fail to perceive a general problem.

Causes

Although there are marked differences among the developing countries, the fact that debt rescheduling is common suggests that there is a common underlying cause or set of causal factors. The world recession is clearly one such cause. Because of stagnant or declining

[1]Statement before the Committee on Banking, Finance and Urban Affairs, U.S. House of Representatives, February 2, 1983.

demand, the prices of what the non-oil-exporting developing countries sell to the rest of the world have been declining, and declining more rapidly than the less flexible prices of the items they import. In 1981, the last full year for which such data are available, export prices fell by 6 percent in relation to import prices for these countries, meaning that they would have to increase the volume of their exports by about this percentage merely in order to maintain the same inflow of goods from the rest of the world. Thus, the recession has made it more difficult for the developing countries to earn the foreign exchange needed to service their debts.

Another cause of debt repayment difficulty is the sharp rise in interest rates in 1978 and 1979 and the persistence of high rates well into 1982. The average interest cost on the medium- and long-term debt of the non-OPEC developing countries rose from about 6 percent for the period 1974-1978 to more than 11 percent in 1982. This rapid rise in average interest cost occurred not only because interest rates went up but because there has been a marked decrease in the proportion of debt for which interest rates are fixed over the long term, with the result that interest rates on much outstanding debt are now frequently revised. It is estimated that the net floating-interest debt of non-OPEC, non-OECD developing countries comprised about 40 percent of their total net debt at the end of 1982, compared to only 23 percent at the end of 1978. This rise in the share of floating-interest debt reflects the effort of bank lenders to earn current market interest rates and to avoid getting locked into fixed rates of return that turn out to be well below rates later yielded in the market; bank loans (not counting export credits) now account for more than a third of the indebtedness of the non-OPEC developing countries.

The combination of declining export prices and high interest rates has made it doubly difficult for debtors in the developing countries. For example, an exporter in Brazil might well have received fewer dollars for his goods at the same time that he required more dollars to service his outstanding debt.

Fortunately for such debtors, interest rates have receded from the heights attained in 1981. Those high rates resulted from the high inflation accompanying the exorbitant oil price increases of 1979-1980 and from the ensuing anti-inflationary monetary policies adopted by some industrial countries, notably the United States. As both inflation and the restrictive policies have eased, interest rates have fallen, with significant benefits for debtors. At the end of 1982, the net floating-interest debt of non-OPEC, non-OECD developing countries was an estimated $166 billion, so that every percentage point decline in interest cost represented a saving to these countries of more than $1.6 billion; and from mid-1982 to the end of the year the relevant dollar interest rates fell by about 7 percentage points. Still, dollar interest rates remain high by historic standards, especially in relation to the declining export prices suffered by many developing nations.

While it is generally agreed that the world recession and high interest rates are important causes of the debt repayment problems of the developing countries, there is much less agreement regarding the frequent allegation that the commercial banks and the developing countries themselves have contributed heavily to the current difficulties by entering into loan agreements that were at best uneconomic, if not profligate. There is no disputing the fact that both total bank lending and net bank exposure to the non-OPEC developing countries have grown at exceptional rates in recent years. As shown by Table 1, total outstanding bank loans to these countries rose from $119 billion in 1977 to $365 billion in

1982, or 25 percent per year. For U.S. banks, total outstanding loans to these countries rose from \$46.9 billion to \$98.6 billion over roughly the same period, or by 18 percent per year, while for the nine largest U.S. banks the total grew from \$30 billion to \$60.3 billion, or 17 percent per year (Tables 2 and 3). Not only have outstanding bank loans to the non-OPEC developing countries grown very rapidly, but they have grown more rapidly than total bank assets, as illustrated by the second column of data in Tables 2 and 3.

However, to show that loan growth has been rapid is not to prove that it has been profligate. To be sure, in retrospect the managements of a number of banks no doubt wish they had been less liberal in lending to certain developing countries. Hindsight is better than foresight, especially when a recession is involved, for recessions have a way of converting seemingly sound loans into ones that any fool should have known would be unsound. On the other hand, booms do entail excesses, and many developing countries had been enjoying relatively high, if not booming, growth for some years prior to the current recession. The relevant question, then, is not whether the banks and the developing countries might now be better off if there had been less lending, but whether on the basis of the information available a few years ago they should have had the foresight to be much more conservative.

Several considerations suggest that, in general, such prescience should not have been expected. To begin with, it is natural for the non-OPEC developing countries to borrow from the rest of the world; if they truly are developing economies, they will offer profitable investment opportunities for foreign lenders and will attract net capital inflows, just as the United States did during its early development. Second, for many years the losses experienced by banks on international loans have been proportionately lower than on domestic loans.

Third, for a number of years prior to the current recession, many developing countries had compiled better records of economic growth than the industrial countries had. Fourth, widely distributed forecasts by prestigious international agencies significantly underestimated the declines in economic growth rates that were to accompany the current recession. For example, in June 1981 the IMF (International Monetary Fund) projected a growth rate of 5 percent for the non-oil developing countries for 1981, but then revised the figure downward to 2.5 percent in April 1982; similarly, at the end of 1981 the OECD projected a growth rate of 1¼ percent for the OECD countries for 1982, but then revised the figure downward to $-\frac{1}{2}$ percent at the end of 1982.

Fifth, as illustrated by Table 4, not until 1982, or 1981 at the earliest, did the officially published statistics on "creditworthiness" clearly signify a distinct deterioration for the non-oil developing countries collectively.[2] To be sure, the data initially published for 1981 (in parentheses) did show that the official monetary reserves of these countries in relation to their imports of goods and services had fallen to a comparatively low level and that debt service (payments of interest and principal) had come to claim a relatively large fraction of the receipts generated by exports; but these initial data also showed long-term external debt to be well below the highest levels attained in preceding years in relation to both exports and gross domestic production.

[2]Apart from the "deterioration" of 1974–1978, which the world weathered with little difficulty.

Table 4 Debt Indicators for Non-Oil Developing Countries Published by International Monetary Fund

Year	Official reserves as percent of imports of goods and services	Long-term external debt as percent of		Debt service on long-term external debt as percent of exports of goods and services
		Exports of goods and services	Gross domestic product	
1973	32	89	17	14
1974	22	81	16	12
1975	19	98	18	14
1976	24	103	21	14
1977	26	105	22	14
1978	27	111	24	17
1979	23	102	23	18
1980	18	93	22	16
1981	17(16)	103(96)	24(21)	21(21)
1982	17	109	25	22

Note: Reserves and debt are for end of year. Debt service consists of payments of interest and principal. Numbers in parentheses are estimates published in 1981; other data were published in 1982.

Source: International Monetary Fund, *World Economic Outlook*, 1981 and 1982.

Finally, even though bank loans outstanding to the non-OPEC developing countries continued to rise rapidly in 1981 and 1982 (Tables 1 and 2), the chart shows that the banks were not altogether oblivious to the gathering crisis, as they raised the risk premia charged on loans to Brazil, Argentina, and Mexico well before the end of 1981, and well before debt repayment problems for these countries became widely publicized. Had they taken the more severe action of refusing new loans once the crisis became apparent, they probably would have exacerbated the crisis, for reasons discussed in the next section of this article.

All of these facts suggest that the banks and the developing countries ought to be spared from blanket condemnations for failing to forestall the debt repayment problem that has materialized. On the basis of the information available as recently as two years ago, there was little reason to expect a problem of the present dimensions. This is not to deny, of course, that some lenders and borrowers were less than circumspect; indeed, one of the risks faced by prudent bank lenders is that less prudent ones will follow in their wake, for once a bank has made a loan to a country it has no means of preventing the country from subsequently incurring excessive debt, thus imperiling repayment of the originally ''prudent'' loan.

In any event, the loans were made. Aside from the issue of whether they seem justified from the perspective of information available two or three years ago, are the loans now being put to productive uses by the developing countries? Only time will tell, and the

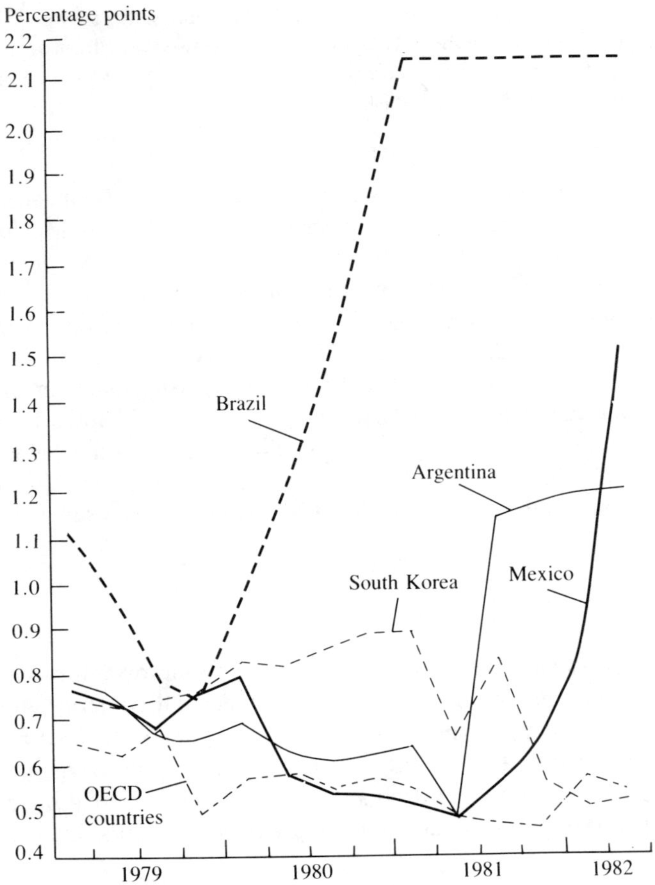

FIGURE 1 Average Loan Rate Spreads (over London Interbank Offered Rate) Charged to Selected Borrowing Countries, 1979:1Q through 1982:2Q

answer will surely vary from loan to loan and country to country. Present circumstances provide a harsh test, for it is difficult to keep invested funds working productively during a recession. For the longer term, however, on the assumption that the world economy recovers, the record offers grounds for optimism. As the World Bank has noted,

> The developing countries on the whole used borrowed funds productively during the 1970s. During that decade, the middle-income countries, which include the largest borrowers from private markets among the developing economies, performed far better than the mature industrial countries. Their gross domestic investment rose by an annual average of 7.8 percent, up from an average of 7.5 percent in the 1960s. By contrast, that growth rate fell sharply in the mature industrial economies, from an average of almost 5.9 percent to 1.6 percent a year between the

> 1960s and 1970s. . . . The difference between investment trends helps to explain why the growth of real gross domestic product in the developing countries slowed only from an annual average of 5.8 percent in the 1960s to about 5.6 percent in the unsettled 1970s, compared with a far greater deceleration of growth in the mature industrial countries from an annual average of 5.0 percent to 3.2 percent.[3]

Certainly, it is clear from Table 5 that the important "middle-income" developing countries, which include the major borrowers Argentina, Brazil, Mexico, and South Korea, were not employing foreign funds as a substitute for their own preexisting saving, or for the purpose of increasing their own immediate consumption, over the period from 1976 to 1980. On the contrary, their rate of domestic savings rose from 20 percent of gross domestic product in 1976 to 25 percent in 1980 (the last year for which data are available), so that the funds coming in from abroad contributed to the rising rate of investment in these countries rather than compensating for a decline in their saving. However, between 1979 and the early 1980s there was a sharp rise in inflation in the non-oil developing countries, partly attributable to the huge oil price increases at the time, but also attributable to expansionary policies in the developing countries which received somewhat extravagant support from foreign lenders.

Remedial Measures

A number of measures have been taken which should go far toward remedying the debt-repayment crisis. As inflation has subsided in the industrial countries and as monetary policy has been eased in some major countries, especially the United States, interest rates have dropped significantly and the U.S. economy seems on the verge of recovery. As noted in the preceding section, the decline in interest rates is a great boon to the debtor nations—and also, it might be observed, to their anxious creditors. Interest rates are still

Table 5 Gross Domestic Investment and Gross Domestic Saving as Percent of Gross Domestic Product in Middle-Income Developing Countries[1]

Year	Gross domestic investment	Gross domestic saving
1976	24	20
1977	25	24
1978	25	22
1979	26	25
1980	27	25

[1]Including Argentina, Brazil, Mexico, and South Korea.

Source: The World Bank, *World Development Report*, issues for 1978 through 1982.

[3]The World Bank, *World Debt Tables: 1982–83 Edition, p. ix.*

high in relation to the suppressed or falling export prices recorded by many of the debtors, but the widely forecast revival of U.S. economic growth, especially if accompanied by a resumption of growth in other industrial countries, would entail increased demand and higher prices for developing country exports.

Along with the policy measures taken by some industrial nations to promote economic recovery, the developing countries with major debt problems have embarked upon severe adjustment programs designed to reduce their imports and bolster their exports, thus making more foreign exchange available for the servicing of their debts. While the details of these adjustment programs vary from country to country, the programs typically include devaluation of the domestic currency in terms of foreign currencies, reduction in the growth of the domestic money supply and domestic credit and an accompanying increase in domestic interest rates, and a more restrictive fiscal policy entailing diminished government spending and higher taxation. These measures operate to reduce domestic spending on imports and to free resources for export production, which is rendered more attractive. In Argentina, Brazil, and Mexico strong emphasis has been placed on the reduction of borrowing by the government sector, and each country is committed to slashing a huge government deficit roughly in half over the course of this year alone. While in effect, such contractionary policies impose reductions in living standards already low by comparison with the industrial countries.

These adjustment measures have already borne fruit in the form of smaller trade deficits for the debtor countries, and the IMF has projected that the balance of international payments on current account for the non-oil developing countries will show a reduction in deficit of something like $20 billion in the current year. Also, the adjustment measures have helped to reassure lenders that the debtors are positioning themselves to meet their obligations, thus encouraging the lenders to cooperate by renewing loans as they come due and by sometimes extending additional credit as well. Although banks are prone to reduce their lending to a country which shows signs of debt payment difficulties, it would be counterproductive for them abruptly to terminate sizable capital flows to a debtor country and to refuse to renew outstanding loans, especially during this recessionary period, because the adjustment called for would be so harsh that few governments of debtor countries would try to impose it on their populaces. In such circumstances lenders are well advised to postpone, or reschedule, loan repayment dates, seeking payment of interest in the short run but repayment of principal only in the long run.

Both in arranging adjustment programs and the financing to support them, the IMF has played a crucial role. Banks are loath to renew credit to a nation with a severe debt problem until the nation has undertaken an adjustment program that elicits a loan from the IMF itself, which then monitors the nation's performance. On the other hand, the IMF is reluctant to make such a loan until it is assured that the proceeds will not be used merely to repay bank creditors rather than to support the adjustment program; indeed, in late 1982 the IMF informed the creditor banks of Argentina and Mexico that no new IMF financing for those countries would be forthcoming unless the banks also put up new money—which they did. Thus, the IMF has leverage over the policies of both the debtor and its creditors, and its role is pivotal.

Negotiations between a debtor country and its creditors concerning debt repayment are commonly conducted multilaterally, that is, with all creditors, or representatives of groups of creditors, present simultaneously at the negotiating sessions. Not only is this approach more efficient for the debtor than entering into separate debt rescheduling negotiations with each of its many creditors, but the approach also facilitates uniformity of treatment of the creditors. Given the recent popularity of internationally syndicated lending, it is not uncommon for hundreds of banks to be involved in debt rescheduling negotiations. As part of the rescheduling agreement, banks usually obtain higher risk premia, or "spreads," of the sort illustrated in the chart.

As with bank loans, loans by governments and international institutions are also involved in reschedulings. Moreover, governments and international institutions have been a vital source of funding for countries confronted with debt crises. For example, during the past year the Treasury Department and the Federal Reserve System in the United States have extended several billion dollars in short-term, bridging credits to Argentina, Brazil, and Mexico to help them meet their immediate liquidity requirements while adjustment and longer-term borrowing programs were being arranged. Much of this credit was extended through the Bank for International Settlements, a "central bankers' bank," which marshalled very large sums for the same borrowers from other industrial nations as well as from the United States. In addition, steps are underway to more than double the usable funds that are available to the IMF for its medium-term lending in support of adjustment programs undertaken by debtor countries.

The foregoing remedial measures are aimed chiefly at restoring the creditworthiness of the debtors in difficulty. What if, in spite of those measures, the delinquency of some debtors should undermine the liquidity of a U.S. bank? In that case, the threatened bank might turn to its central bank, the Federal Reserve System, for assistance. Provided the bank had sound collateral to pledge, it would normally be provided a loan to help it meet its own cash obligations. On the other hand, if the bank's loans to delinquent foreign debtors were deemed unrecoverable and worthless, and if writing off such loans reduced the value of the bank's assets below the level of its liabilities, the very solvency, not merely the liquidity, of the bank would then be impaired; and in such a case the bank would be obliged to close its doors unless, as commonly occurs in such instances, a takeover by another viable bank could be arranged. Bank depositors, of course, are widely insured.

Preventive Measures

Finding remedies for a crisis is good, but preventing it is better. What measures might be taken to forestall the development of international debt crises in the future?

The recent recession contributed substantially to the current crisis, and measures which averted major recessions would reduce the likelihood of future debt crises. Although it would be utopian to expect the immediate demise of the business cycle, it seems that the two major recessions of the past decade could easily have been avoided or at least substantially diminished. Even the most casual observation suggests that both were initiated largely by abrupt and unsustainable increases in the price charged by OPEC for its oil. As lesser increases probably would have been of greater benefit to OPEC itself, there is reason to hope that the experience will not be repeated.

Aside from measures to mitigate the business cycle, another class of possible preventive measures would be aimed at deterring uneconomic bank lending, or, more precisely, at bolstering the present deterrents. These measures generally call for the collection and distribution of better information both on the creditworthiness of borrowing countries and on the loan portfolios of the lending institutions, as well as for intensified governmental supervision and regulation of the lending institutions.

As for better information on the creditworthiness of borrowing countries, the need can be illustrated by the recent confusion over the amount of Argentina's foreign debt as of the end of 1982, which was estimated at between $42 billion and $43 billion by the Economy Minister early in 1983 but then declared to be $37 billion by the Governor of the Central Bank several weeks later. Other than the debtor countries themselves, sources of statistics on national indebtedness include the World Bank, the IMF, and the Bank for International Settlements. Bank lenders have expressed a need for more timely and comprehensive information than these sources now offer, and have recently established an institute to facilitate the exchange of debt statistics between commercial lenders and country borrowers. Such initiatives have the potential for providing significant social gains if it is true that loans are frequently extended—or denied—without the aid of relevant information that could be obtained at a low cost.

Data relating to the creditworthiness of a country, or to "country risk," are commonly put into the form of ratios which are used as indicators of future debt-servicing difficulties. Among such indicators are those represented in Table 4. While more timely and comprehensive information would improve the usefulness of these indicators, they would still fall short of being reliable automatic signalers of impending problems. Debt indicators resemble the leading economic indicators used to forecast business cycles in that they constitute measurement without much underlying theory but nonetheless are widely watched.

The ambiguity surrounding these indicators can easily be illustrated by reference to the oldest and most popular one, the debt service ratio. This indicator is defined as debt service payments (interest and principal) divided by earnings from exports of goods and services. The assumption is that the higher the ratio, the less capacity a country has to service additional debt. In fact, a country rarely is called upon to service its foreign debt solely from current export earnings, as foreign creditors typically reinvest rather than collect most of scheduled principal payments and make additional investments as well if the country seems creditworthy. Moreover, a rising ratio may not signify a falling debt-servicing capacity, nor a falling ratio a rising capacity. For example, a country in outright default and paying no debt service would have the lowest possible ratio, and countries can also lower the ratio by falling into arrears. The fact is that numerous countries have had debt-service ratios of between 20 percent and 70 percent without incurring serious debt-servicing difficulties, while others have been obliged to renegotiate their debt when their ratios were well below 20 percent.

More generally, all such indicators as the debt service ratio provide only half-truths about the capacity of a country to assume additional debt. Differences observed in these ratios between countries do not necessarily signify differences in creditworthiness, because nations differ in their relative ability to employ capital productively; moreover, any one country will differ in this respect over time. Thus, it is not surprising that neither simple nor sophisticated statistical techniques have been very successful in using such indicators to forecast debt servicing problems; and while better statistics would assist the banks in analyzing debt repayment prospects, equally important is the application of better analytical methods, including methods for evaluating the current and prospective quality of a country's economic management.

Another measure that might be undertaken to inhibit uneconomic bank lending would be to intensify government supervision and regulation over international lending. Indeed, at this writing this course of action is now under consideration within the United States. Moreover, in recognition of the increasing involvement of U.S. banks in foreign lending, the three Federal bank regulatory agencies—the Comptroller of the Currency, the Federal Reserve System, and the Federal Deposit Insurance Corporation—adopted in 1979 a new system for evaluating the country risk to which lending banks expose themselves. Under this system, an Interagency Country Exposure Review Committee, whose members are from the three regulatory agencies, categorizes monitored countries into four main groups: those with imminent or actual debt delinquency and those categorized as weak, moderately strong, and strong. At each bank they visit, Federal examiners then call to the management's attention those loans which the bank has outstanding to "weak" or "moderately strong" countries if the loans are above certain levels in relation to capital, as well as criticize all loans to delinquent countries. The examiners also evaluate the system employed by each bank in managing its exposure to country risk.

Such examination procedures could be supplemented by more direct government restraints over international bank lending, but such discouragement of risk-taking would entail its own risks. Even the current examination procedures "could unduly inhibit international lending," according to a recent review by the U.S. General Accounting Office (GAO). The GAO reported that the current procedures had identified (as having potential debt servicing problems) many countries which in fact did not incur payments arrearages during the year following their identification. A different approach from government examination or control would simply require fuller public disclosure by the banks of their country risk exposures, on the assumption that financial market participants themselves would then discipline or inhibit excessive risk-taking by limiting the deposits or equity capital that they placed with the more venturesome banks.

In addition to the foregoing, another set of measures designed to forestall future international debt crises would aim at securing a higher proportion of equity financing for the developing countries. Unlike the interest on debt, there is no contractual requirement for dividends to be paid on equity, so the return paid by the developing countries on such capital could legitimately be sharply reduced during a recession. Moreover, the risk of financing those countries would be spread more widely beyond the banking sector. The borrowing countries themselves could promote such a development by relaxing some of the many barriers they have erected against direct and portfolio equity investment.

Conclusion

A widespread failure of the developing countries to pay their foreign debts on schedule has aroused anxiety that large commercial bank creditors might be driven into insolvency. However, the debt repayment capacity of these countries is now being enhanced by several factors, including recent reductions in interest rates, the beginning of recovery from the global recession, the initiation of economic adjustment programs in the developing countries themselves, and the cooperation of their creditors and certain international institutions in extending interim financing.

The banks and the developing countries ought to be spared from blanket condemnations for failing to forestall the current debt crisis, because as recently as two years ago there was little reason for international borrowers and lenders to expect debt repayment problems of the present magnitude. International debt crises would be less likely in the future if recession-inducing shocks such as abrupt oil price increases could be avoided, if more timely and comprehensive information were published on the creditworthiness of borrowing countries and on the loan portfolios of lending institutions, and if a higher share of investment in the developing countries took the form of equity financing.

Country Risk, Portfolio Decisions, and Regulation in International Bank Lending

Ingo Walter

21

1. Introduction

In the growing literature on "country risk," one finds relatively little discussion of what is, or ought to be, management's ultimate objective—incorporating country-specific risk characteristics into the design of asset portfolios that are in some sense "efficient." We shall attempt to develop in this article some of the issues involved in closing this gap, both within the asset management decision process of individual banks and in the context of bank regulation.

Modern portfolio theory suggests that there are two types of risk facing any asset manager—unsystematic (diversifiable) risk, and systematic (non-diversifiable) risk. Using a stock market analogy, unsystematic risk is associated with factors affecting individual asset (share) returns. This kind of risk can be reduced, and even eliminated, by diversifying a portfolio across shares subject to different return movements in the market. Systematic risk, on the other hand, is associated with factors affecting the stock market as a whole; it influences all shares in a portfolio and is therefore non-diversifiable. The relative riskiness of a particular stock can be measured by its "beta" coefficient, the ratio of its own return volatility to the overall return volatility of the stock market as a whole. Its value to the investor depends not only on its expected returns, but also on how it would

Reprinted from *Journal of Banking and Finance* (March, 1981): 77–92 by permission of North Holland Publishing Company and the author.

affect the riskiness of the entire portfolio. Such concepts permit a skilled investor to build an "efficient" stock portfolio which maximizes returns subject to risk, given his own personal risk preferences.

Instead of stocks, banks involved in international lending have "portfolios" of cross-border exposures in different politically sovereign states. In a global context, much of this exposure is in the nature of unsystematic "country" risk and thus is diversifiable, resulting in reduced riskiness of the entire portfolio. Systematic risk, on the other hand, derives from factors affecting a number of countries simultaneously, and is less readily reduced through diversification of country exposures. Change in cross-border exposure in a particular country must be evaluated in terms of both its implications for returns and its impact on the riskiness of the bank's overall asset portfolio. An "efficient" international loan portfolio of a given risk might then be constructed once management's degree of risk aversion is known, returns on country exposures have been correctly assessed, and an attempt has been made to identify something similar in concept to individual country "betas." The risk premium associated with exposures in a particular country will tend to reflect the implicit "beta" associated with the country in question.

It is easy (and dangerous) to push this analogy too far in any mechanistic attempt to develop the principles underlying "efficient" portfolios of international bank exposures. There are a number of factors that limit the applicability of conventional portfolio theory in this particular context. For one thing, unlike the case of the stock market, the measurement of risks and returns relating to country exposures is extraordinarily difficult. It is here that the "science" of portfolio management shades into the "art" of international banking.

Still, as with any other portfolio management problem, the task facing managers of international banks is to maximize the real, economic value of their assets subject to various types of risks. One of these is linked to the political and economic fortunes of countries in which they have cross-border exposures. Returns on these assets depend on competitive factors facing a bank in the market-place for its services. What needs to be evaluated is the expected value of these returns in the future, together with elements that may influence their variance (reflecting the degree of risk).

We can express this in the form of a conventional present value equation such as the following:

$$PV_j^0 = \sum_{t=0}^{n} \frac{E(F_t)}{(1 + i_t + \alpha_t)^t}$$

where PV_j^0 is the present value of the future stream of returns to the bank related to exposure in a particular country j, $E(F_t)$ denotes the expected value of that future returns stream at time t, i_t is the risk-free discount factor representing the bank's cost of funds, and α_t represents a country risk premium, which depends on the variance of the expected future returns associated with country j relative to β_j (the beta coefficient associated with the institution involved). Prospective future developments in countries in which a bank has cross-border exposures will be reflected in the means as well as the variances of the probability distributions associated with these returns, and hence will influence both $E(F_t)$ and α_t.

2. Expected Returns in International Lending

If rational portfolio decisions in international lending depend on defensible assessments of risks and returns, it is important to develop first an accurate picture of the expected returns side $E(F_t)$. One important component is, of course, repayment of principal. A second component covers the interest returns which, in the case of floating-rate syndicated loans (comprising perhaps 40–50% of medium and long-term international financings in recent years), usually involves the spread over the three- or six-month London Interbank Offered Rate (LIBOR), or a similar floating base rate of interest. Changes in LIBOR itself tend to show up as shifts in both $E(F_t)$ and i_t, and thus cancel out, although a bank does face some residual interest-rate risk through negotiated spreads, generally fixed for the life of the loan, which may narrow or widen with future market conditions. A recent innovation, ''floating spreads,'' eliminates this residual risk as well. But principal and interest returns, properly adjusted in a time context for maturities, drawn-down schedules, and the like, represent only a part of the picture.

First, and most obvious in the case of lead managers, co-managers, agents, and others involved in the process of international loan syndication, there is a share of fees agreed upon with the borrower. These may be quite substantial, perhaps well in excess of the incremental costs involved in providing syndication services and—especially since they represent a relatively certain and immediate ''front-end'' payment—may add materially to the overall returns of banks engaged in syndicate management. On occasion, borrowers unwilling to incur higher published spreads for prestige or future market-access reasons may inflate front-end fees in order to compensate international lenders.

Second, banks often lend to a particular borrower at terms that might otherwise be considered unattractive in order to develop or maintain a ''relationship.'' This involves existing and past ties, and focuses on the expectation of future earnings from a variety of activities that include continued private and public-sector lending activities, foreign exchange transactions, deposit balances, advisory services, custodial business, and the like. There is ample evidence of the importance of the ''relationship'' factor in international lending behavior, with regular scrambles by banks to get ''close to'' the borrower within syndicates, and in the tendency for losers of syndication mandates to participate anyway in the loans in order to maintain a relationship with the borrower. Similarly, borrowers can sometimes ''encourage'' banks to participate in loans that would not otherwise be attractive by suggesting that failure to do so may lead to a loss of collateral business or pressure on their operations in host countries—thereby requiring the addition to apparent returns, in effect, of an insurance premium against possible future earnings losses elsewhere in the relationship. Particularly where the country relationship has been highly profitable in the past and/or promises to be so in the future, such anticipated ''indirect'' returns can be an important part of the total, characterized by their own profile of expected earnings.

Third, a bank's lending to a particular borrower may generate future returns with third parties that might not otherwise materialize. A major syndication may create opportunities for future trade financing or letter of credit business with home or third-country suppliers, for example. Or a particular loan can cement a relationship with a particular domestic or foreign client (''do-good'') in a way that promises additional future earnings. Once again, the ultimate returns from this source to the bank may be quite indirect and their assessment quite speculative.

It is clear, therefore, that returns of principal and interest, fees, and the remaining less tangible earnings components form a many-sided, probabilistic picture. Each element has its own time-profile and expected value, so that $E(F_t)$ in our formula is itself a highly complex composite. Each element also has its own measure of variability, so that the associated risk premium α_t is similarly complex. And often there are tradeoffs, as when the terms of loan agreements (legal documentation) are relaxed at the insistence of the borrower, thereby possibly exchanging higher expected returns in some of the aforementioned earnings components for greater risk in others. Partly for such reasons, profit attribution in international banking tends to be extraordinarily difficult, and in most banks is considered quite imperfect. For such reasons as well, the returns facing individual banks that are members of lending syndicates may well differ substantially from one to the other, particularly between banks in the management group and the rest.

3. Value of Assets Exposed to Country Risk

What kinds of eventualities associated with conditions in countries where a bank has cross-border exposure would tend to influence the real (economic) value of the exposed assets? First, the borrowing country may ultimately be unwilling or unable to effect debt service in full, the default resulting in realized accounting losses of principal and/or accrued interest which the bank must book against earnings, capital or reserves after recovering what it can through the ''right of offset'' or other means. The consequences of default for the borrower's access to international capital markets and normal channels of trade are such that this event tends to be triggered by a unique and relatively rare set of circumstances—consequences that are magnified by cross-default clauses commonly written into international loan agreements.

Second, the borrowing country may be unable to meet its external debt obligations on contractual terms and be forced to stretch-out repayment. By definition, the necessary refinancing or rescheduling under such circumstances cannot be accomplished at market terms and occurs under duress, and so the original lenders are forced to extend further credit in the hope of avoiding accounting losses in the end. This may involve an extension of maturities, a new grace period, negotiation of new facilities, an adjustment in interest spreads, or other modifications. Even if this ultimately results in increased accounting returns, if the lender under free-market conditions would have restructured his portfolio out of the exposed assets in question at any point, but cannot do so because he is locked-in, he has in fact incurred an economic loss. The real value of this particular component of his asset portfolio, in effect, has declined. The difference between *economic* and *accounting* shifts in asset values under such circumstances is not always accepted by bankers, and this may influence their reaction to the causative debt service problems and their portfolio decisions in the future.

Third, the borrowing country may be perfectly able and willing to service its external debt—successfully avoiding both default and problems leading to reschedulings or forced refinancings—yet something happens that raises the riskiness of the exposed assets from the perspective of the foreign lender. Assassination of the head of state, for example, may mean nothing at all from a debt service point of view, or it may mean eventual debt repudiation and default, or any of a number of eventualities in-between. Even though neither of our first two types of losses has been incurred by the lender, he has suffered a decline in the value of his assets insofar as he cannot immediately reallocate them in a manner consistent with his new perception of the constellation or relative risks and returns. Some such reallocation may be possible at the margin by running down exposures beginning with the very short maturities. This process, however, is usually far from the kind of instantaneous adjustment—characteristic of efficient financial markets—that is needed to avoid longer-run downward adjustment in the value of the bank's loan portfolio. Once again, bankers are reluctant to recognize such shifts, and they often ignore them in portfolio valuation and decision-making. Yet international lending to South Korea after the assassination of President Park Chung Hee, Thailand after the Vietnamese invasion of Cambodia, and Eastern Europe after the Soviet invasion of Afghanistan seems to suggest that markets are in fact responsive to shifts in "risk-classes" of countries. Thus, relative rates of change in (net) new loans in effect become a substitute for market-type portfolio adjustments.

In terms of our formula, a number of events may reduce PV_j^0. Prospective defaults can be viewed as reductions in $E(F_t)$, anticipated rescheduling or refinancing losses as forced introduction of higher-valued t's that are less than compensated for by negotiated increases in $E(F_t)$, and losses from risk-class shifts as increases in α_t. Reschedulings or forced refinancings may additionally have the effect of increasing α_t if, as a result, the country is viewed by the market as being more risky.

4. Diversification and Risk

The purpose of 'country risk assessment' is, of course, to get a fix on $E(F_t)$ and α_t—usually (as we have previously argued, mistakenly) focusing exclusively on possible threats to interest and principal. Its application to the construction of international loan portfolios is in part related to the objective of diversification, under the presumption that the α_t values for individual countries are essentially independent. If there is indeed zero correlation among returns on the country exposures in a bank's asset portfolio, it is possible for management through diversification to virtually eliminate variability in returns on international lending. The greater the degree of this correlation, the more difficult it is to do so. Yet even with some correlation in earnings variability, bank managers are in principle free to choose how much unsystematic risk to incorporate into their portfolios through the extent of diversification and the kinds of exposures incurred. Our discussion of risk and returns indicates how difficult it is to apply conventional financial theory to international bank lending. Neither the risks associated with individual country exposures nor the returns are easy to measure or identify, nor are the conventional efficient market assumptions satisfied, although movement toward ''efficient'' loan portfolios is at least conceptually possible. There are, moreover, some additional problems as well.

For one thing, risk-aversion and hence portfolio preference may be quite different as viewed by (a) an undiversified bank owner or manager, (b) a diversified stock market investor, and (c) the regulatory authorities. The first of these is well served by conventional measures of the dispersion of expected portfolio returns. The second would also have to worry about the covariance of returns on the bank's international portfolio with returns on other assets in his own portfolio—indeed, some of the affected shareholders might possibly reside outside of the bank's country of domicile. The difference between the two perspectives could be attributed to gaps in management's information about (or response to) the market's valuation of the bank's equities. The regulatory authorities, for their part, would tend to focus on the ''bankruptcy tail'' associated with different asset portfolios, given the limits of their own liability. When a bank adds a particular loan to its portfolio, therefore, its impact on the riskiness of that portfolio will depend on which of these three specific perspectives is being applied. We shall return to this point later.

A second problem, already mentioned in our earlier discussion, is that international banks are to a significant extent unable to ''buy'' and ''sell'' assets exposed to country risk. This important option, as envisaged in conventional portfolio theory, is limited to short-term exposure, which can be ''run down'' in a relatively short period of time and the assets deployed elsewhere. But the ''term exposure'' that makes up a good deal of total international lending is basically locked-in for the duration, with management unable to react through portfolio adjustment to changes in the variance of expected returns. As a result, the lender is not independent of the factors that generate the ultimate returns, as might be the case if a secondary market existed for such assets.

A third problem is that the principal and interest component of $E(F_t)$ in international loan portfolios, unlike stock or bond portfolios, may be subject to asymmetrical variance. That is, the variance of these returns may be entirely on the down-side. In conventional stock or bond portfolios, the investor can win or lose with changes in prices and interest rates. In international loan portfolios, assuming the borrower bears the interest-rate risk as in LIBOR-based loans, prospects of the bank for up-side variance in returns do not exist. As in the case of mortgage and other types of lending subject to asymmetrical variance, such truncated returns distributions tend to induce among bankers a reluctance to recognize changes in the value of their assets until losses are essentially certain. It encourages lenders to take extra care in the assessment of the down-side risks involved, design of loan documentation, assembly of syndicates, and management of ''problem'' situations. It may also give added bargaining leverage to ''problem'' borrowers in dealing with the international banks, which can itself ultimately accentuate the down-side variance of returns. The idea of asymmetrical variance, however, has to be modified if we go beyond the interest and principal components of $E(F_t)$ to take a broader view of expected returns, the prospects for which can improve significantly with a more favorable country outlook.

A fourth problem is that changes in country exposure may be ''lumpy'' in the case of banks faced with large loans representing discrete jumps in cross-border exposure, so that portfolios may be difficult to adjust at the margin. And the fact that American and certain other banks are subject to capital-based or similar lending constraints may give rise to additional limits on building efficient portfolios.

Despite such difficulties, some of the basic lessons of portfolio theory can be applied. One of these is the effects of the ability of banks to diversify and its impact on the value of their overall international loan portfolios. In one sense, the whole purpose of country risk assessment is to ascertain the covariance of expected returns on a portfolio of loans *within* a particular country. But individual country exposures in a bank's global loan portfolio may also have *in common* certain sources of risk, and this moves us closer to an application of the concept of "systematic" risk, or limits to the value of diversification in international lending.

One source of non-diversifiable risk relates to conditions in the Euromarkets as a whole. Countries requiring rollover financing may face difficulties under tight market conditions. Similarly, since the interest cost of much of the external debt of countries to international banks is linked to LIBOR, tighter international credit conditions may raise the borrowers' respective debt service (balance of payments) burdens, and thereby increase the risk associated with exposed assets in a number of countries at once. Moreover, the Euromarkets tend to be highly sensitive to the fortunes of individual countries, and serious problems in the case of one borrower may impede the ability of others to secure access to credit.

Other sources of possible covariance in returns on country exposures include conditions facing them in major export markets. This is quite clear in the case of commodity markets, where cyclical price weakness can seriously affect the terms and balances of trade of a number of countries at once—e.g., sugar, coffee, copper, and rubber. It also holds for manufactured exports, where a variety of countries may be adversely affected simultaneously by recessions and declines in import demand in principal markets, and by protectionist pressures affecting particular industry segments. Similarly, on the import side a large number of countries are clearly affected by changes in petroleum supplies and costs, and perhaps somewhat narrower analogies may be drawn for other categories of imports (food, raw materials) as well. Such risks are not totally non-diversifiable, however, since care can be taken in constructing international loan portfolios to incorporate such covariances in banks' exposure decisions.

Finally, there is the matter of the geographic distribution of country exposures. Countries in a particular region, such as Southeast Asia, may be subject to common economic or political threats. Portfolio diversification can still be achieved within such constraints. But the degree of difficulty increases when the commonalities become more prevalent, as in the case of geopolitical shocks, perceived "domino" effects, and the like.

5. Lending Decisions and Approaches to Country Risk Assessment

Despite the difficulties in measuring risks and returns, in recognizing and reacting to changes in values of country exposure in international loan portfolios, and in developing and implementing approaches to effective diversification, there is little doubt that the core lessons of portfolio theory are of substantial value in international banking. Yet exposure limits in international bank lending often seem to be set in the absence of such an overriding philosophy, and on the implicit assumption that there is zero correlation among countries, or between country conditions and the various other sources of risk we have identified. The reason may have something to do with the difficulties encountered in the country risk assessment process itself and a natural tendency to focus intensively on country-by-country analysis. A great deal has been written about this problem, and it is not necessary to review that literature once again here. The problem essentially breaks down to a matter of forecasting expected returns $E(F_t)$ and the specific sources of risk that load into our α_t variable, risk that arises out of structural (supply-side) elements, demand-side and monetary elements, external economic and political developments, as well as the quality of the national economic management and the domestic political constraints bearing upon decision-makers.

In the absence of an efficient market whose data can be analyzed, the delivery of effective country risk assessment ideally requires the employment of a true "renaissance person"—exceedingly intelligent, a holder of doctorates from respectable institutions in economics, political science, sociology, psychology and perhaps a few other fields as well, totally objective, with a great deal of common sense. In addition to being rather well-traveled, he or she is up-to-date on developments in all countries of interest to the bank (and in other countries that might affect them), and personally acquainted with key policymakers. Obviously, there are few such individuals wandering around these days. And so the question is whether international banks, *as institutions,* can in some way put together all of these qualities, using relatively "ordinary" individuals and traditional organizational linkages to assemble a superior ability to forecast the future of countries, its bearing on the real value of exposed assets, and its implications for portfolio management. Low quality estimates of $E(F_t)$ and α_t yield low quality portfolio decisions and, ultimately, second-rate performance of the bank in the competitive marketplace.

In the design of a country analysis function aiming at high-quality $E(F_t)$ and α_t estimates for use in portfolio decisions, the emphasis clearly must be on the fact that it is the beginning, not the end, of the task. Approaches that try to be overly precise risk triggering arguments among users over irrelevant points. Those that are too general may fail to concentrate on the true sources of risk in country exposure, and on the specific concerns facing a particular bank. Risk to medium- and long-term exposure requires a far more complex analysis than risk in short-term lending, yet one that is still much simpler than risk to any foreign direct investment exposure that a bank may have in a particular country.

The twin temptations of "quick and dirty" and "overloaded" country risk assessments constantly seem to confront international banks. The first approach promises mechanical short-cuts and the use of low-priced talent to grind out results at reasonable cost, but often appears to succeed only in producing nonsense—there really is no substitute for high-quality analysis, flexibility, judgement, and familiarity. The second approach may rely on well qualified internal personnel at high cost, yet encounter a dangerous narrowing of country expertise, possibly cause dissention, and create bottlenecks in the decision-making process.

The conflicting demands of country assessment—ranging from high levels of usability, auditability and comparability, and the need to capture exceedingly complex and country-specific qualitative judgments over extended periods of time, to the need to avoid abuse of the results in decision-making—probably means that there is no such thing as an "ideal" system. ''Appropriate'' systems will certainly differ for different banks. The key may reside as much on the ''human resources'' side as on the ''technology'' side. To train line bankers in using reasonably unsophisticated yet sensible country assessments properly, and in being sensitive to changing country risk profiles and sources of covariance as they go about their business, may in the end contribute more to sound portfolio decisions than comparable resources devoted to the design and implementation of more elegant systems. This would appear to follow from the view of multinational banks' general competitive advantage as ''information factories,'' to which their global operations and headquarters-affiliate links are ideally suited. Whether in systems-design or in the training function, resources devoted to the assessment of country risk clearly are subject to constraints, and there is some implicit optimum where the incremental costs in country assessment begin to outweigh the economic losses implicit in inefficient international loan portfolios.

To get the best possible fix on the critical $E(F_t)$ and α_t variables that have been the core of our discussion, the exercise of country risk assessment should be an integrated managerial process that focuses the network of information and actively involves individuals with different functions and perspectives. The exercise will thus have intangible portfolio benefits all its own, quite apart from its more visible output in the form of defensible country-by-country evaluations. Mechanization and decentralization of the country review process will tend to cut down and perhaps eliminate this benefit, and may thereby help to stifle an environment conducive to sound portfolio decisions.

Each bank's institutional information-flow and decision-making setup has its own profile, depending on such factors as the organization's size and structure. Some banks incorporate country assessments into portfolio decisions quite flexibly and informally, while others seem to rely on rigid and formalized review procedures. In some cases the review process is closely tied as well to the annual budget cycle and the allocation of lending authority to countries and regions. These again may be quite rigid in some banks, while in others they are relatively easily altered as perceived market and risk conditions change. In some banks, the determination of ''loan loss provisions'' is an integral part of the process, and affects the anticipated net profitability of loans by adjusting for risk and presumably permits improved performance evaluation within the bank's organizational framework.

While few international banks fail to maintain adequate cross-border exposure measurement, allocation, and monitoring, there seems to be far greater variability in the state of the country assessment systems themselves. Some are carefully thought through, while others are largely cosmetic or pseudo-scientific. Some are well integrated into the life of the organization, while others seem separate and even isolated. Until fairly recently, smaller U.S. banks, particularly when participating in loan syndications, tended to rely on the country evaluations of the larger money center banks. Besides being unsatisfactory from a regulatory point of view (see below), we have already noted that the appropriate risk-return calculus of lead banks is not necessarily the same as that of the smaller banks. Banks in Europe and Japan so far do not appear to have placed a great deal of emphasis on the design of formal approaches to country assessment or to incorporate them into international lending decisions, preferring instead to rely much more informally on the collective experience and wisdom of senior bank officers.

Whatever the approach, rational portfolio decisions demand that forecasts of country futures be maintained on a comparable basis—and modified in the light of covariances arising out of common export markets or sources of supply, conditions in and access to international financial markets, and regional as well as global political developments. It should also be clear that, in assessing the impact of a particular change in country exposure on the value of a bank's asset portfolio as a whole, it is not only the specific country-related variance of returns that is of importance, but also the intercountry covariance of returns, and this can easily be masked by an exclusive focus on country-specific sources of risk. And so it is possible to envision the application of the portfolio context we have developed—with risk aversion dictated by top management, correctly attributed returns estimated by line bankers, carefully defined risks to these returns estimated by formal or informal approaches to country evaluation, and covariances therein brought into the picture in the setting of exposure limits and term sublimits.

6. Regulatory Influence on Portfolio Decisions

With the growth in international lending during the 1970s came increasing concern on the part of those responsible for bank regulation and supervision that sound banking practice be maintained, including adequate information on exposure, country risk assessment, loan diversification and pricing. In terms of our earlier discussion, the regulatory function focuses exclusively on the expected value of interest and principal recovery and its variance—usually with reference to potential impairment of capital—without regard to the other types of returns relevant to bank portfolio decisions. One might therefore envision a scenario whereby influence of regulators on bank lending decisions could well move them *away from* efficient international loan portfolios, particularly since different banks have different sets of returns, access to information, perceptions of risk, and risk preferences. In the process, certain borrowers could be closed out of international credit markets who would otherwise have continued access. Is this a danger?

For American banks, losses in international lending have consistently been below domestic losses. Yet in the late 1970s, a borrower's market characterized by declining, compressed averaged spreads and lengthening average maturities "has caused concern among bankers about an erosion of documentation and lending standards. Some borrowers will no longer provide financial accounts that were standard loan documentation a couple of years ago. . . . Borrowers are demanding less stringent conditions in their loans' legal documentation, including less use of cross-default clauses."[1] Such implicit concerns about the α_t values in the equation we have been using were instrumental in moving U.S. bank regulators toward a uniform system of segregating country risks from other lending risks, and dealing with them separately in their examination reports. The emphasis has been on diversification of country exposure within a bank's international loan portfolio based on capital ratios, and on an assessment of the bank's own country risk analysis and monitoring capabilities. This new supervisory aspect necessitated agreement in November

[1] *IMF Survey*, 3 September 1979, p. 277.

1978 on a uniform country risk screening procedure by the U.S. regulatory authorities themselves, undertaken in the form of a joint effort by the Federal Reserve System, the Comptroller of the Currency, and the Federal Deposit Insurance Corporation for use by bank examiners.

In current practice, a nine-member committee of international bank examiners representing the three supervisory authorities meets several times each year to reach a consensus on the riskiness of exposure in selected countries based on a set of "briefing notes" generated by Federal Reserve economists. These, together with oral supplements, form the basis of "comments" and of the examiners' discussions with senior bank management. Although the purpose is explicitly *not* to preclude certain countries from additional U.S. bank lending, or to suggest "superior" international loan portfolios, one would suspect that the inherent "second guessing" function of the examination process is bound to have an affect on international lending decisions by influencing our α_t variable. There is the undeniable advantage of forcing the less well-managed banks to conduct independent country risk monitoring in order to justify individual exposure positions, and to pay careful attention to risks and returns in international lending. But beyond this, aversion of banks to having particular country exposures subject to "listing" or "comment" in examination reports may well drive them away from optimum loan portfolios that still meet acceptable standards of risk from a public-policy point of view by influencing relative risk premiums used in making portfolio decisions. This could involve implicit imposition of the supervisory authorities' own views of risk and diversification on the banks. Whether this consideration—together with possible flaws in the supervisory application of country analyses by bank examiners—leads to significant distortions in the international allocation of credit remains to be seen.

So far, the United States is alone in making country risk assessment an integral part of the bank examination process. Most other countries make no distinction among international lending risks pertaining to different countries, and rely almost entirely on uniform capital-asset ratios. Nor is supervisory pressure on banks to develop defensible, independent country risk assessment and monitoring systems very much in evidence outside the U.S. On the other hand, there may be a good deal of moral suasion present in the informal discussions between banks and their supervisory authorities that is an important part of the regulatory process in a number of countries. Clearly, international differences in the supervisory function, as it embodies elements of country risk, have the potential of influencing both the flow of international credit and competitive relationships in international banking.

The best recent example occurred in October 1979, when the Japanese Ministry of Finance clamped an embargo on further overseas foreign-currency lending by Japanese banks, exempting only export credits and loans for energy imports. The authorities apparently feared the vulnerability of the banks, 80% funded in the interbank market, to a repetition of the 1974 Euromarket credit squeeze. A return of the Japanese banks to the market in June 1980 was accompanied by ceilings on Euroloans, American-type lending limits, and far sharper surveillance even to the point, apparently, of imposing Ministry of Finance judgments on loan size and borrower qualifications.

There is also some movement to achieve a greater degree of international regulatory uniformity with respect to country exposure. The supervisory authorities in the United States have pushed hard to expand and refine data on cross-border exposure of American banks, and to some extent this has been paralleled by similar improvements elsewhere, including international efforts to compile and publish the relevant data. For instance, the Bank for International Settlements has assembled a great deal of information on country debt and provides guidance for national supervisory authorities on how to interpret it. The emerging consensus seems to be that authorities should apply bank supervision on a consolidated balance sheet basis, as is done in the U.S. The view is taking hold that, even though foreign subsidiaries are legally independent entities, in case of debt service problems the liabilities would nevertheless fall due to the parent bank. Both Switzerland and the United Kingdom have moved in this direction. The idea of minimum capital-asset ratios is also catching on. There is, however, no consensus on formal, systematic guidelines for diversification of loan portfolios exposed to country risk.

Besides the supervisory role at the national level, there is the possibility that country evaluations on the part of international organizations may influence the management of loan portfolios by private banks. Among the international institutions concerned with this issue are the BIS Cooke Committee of national bank supervisors, the Berne Union focusing on government export credit guarantees, and the so-called Paris Club involved in rescheduling official debt of countries in trouble. All are concerned in one way or another with assessment of country risk. While no direct links yet exist, attitudes emerging in such forums have the potential of influencing bank regulators at the national level and, through them, bank portfolio decisions.

Of possibly greater importance is the International Monetary Fund, and to a lesser extent the World Bank, which maintain detailed country evaluations used in their respective decisions on balance of payments and project financing. While these assessments are nominally confidential, important elements are available to member governments and there is the possibility that IMF opinion will gradually add a certain degree of uniformity to bank lending decisions via its links to national regulators. A strong argument can of course be made for the widest possible dissemination of data collected and analyzed by international institutions. But this hardly justifies, on either competence or portfolio grounds, undue influence of IMF staff assessments of country risk on the private banks' international lending decisions.

At the same time, in actual or potential problem situations there is great value in coordinated lending by the IMF and the banks—assuming reasonably thoughtful application of IMF conditionality. If the problems are serious enough, the banks are naturally more than anxious to have a country approach the IMF, and have been known to await the outcome of such negotiations before committing themselves to further financing. Indeed, additional bank loans may be dependent on successful discussions with the IMF, and drawdowns under such facilities carefully tied to the borrower's observance of conditions attached to parellel drawings on its IMF standby facility. In this way, added weight can be given to the IMF's influence in pressing for effective adjustment and economic discipline in deficit countries, while the implicit value of the banks' exposed assets is supported. Such parallelism, however, has so far appeared only in serious problem situations. Its extension to ordinary country lending situations could superimpose IMF country assessments upon the private banks, distorting loan portfolios by influencing risk perceptions and affecting the direction and volume of international bank lending.

7. Conclusions

Whereas assessment of country risk is itself an exceedingly difficult task, building country evaluations into the design of international loan portfolios that are in some sense "efficient" is even more complicated. Neither the risks nor the returns are clearly definable, and the assumptions underlying conventional financial theory are hardly satisfied. Nevertheless, it is important for banks to realize what they ought to be doing when they make international lending decisions, and when they throw scarce human and financial resources into country risk assessment. Portfolio theory can contribute importantly in clarifying the risks. It also helps to identify the dangers inherent in externally-imposed risk evaluations for rational portfolio decisions, particularly when they emanate from the regulatory system. At the same time, the development of informational and interactive networks within banks as part of the country evaluation process can itself lead to improved international lending decisions that implicitly embody some of the elusive portfolio concepts we have tried to focus on here.

Application of the portfolio concepts we have suggested will also help pin down the link between risk and pricing. Portfolio theory says that the riskiness of any single loan is not what is important, but rather the effect of that loan on the riskiness of the overall bank or shareholder portfolio. So, for example, loans by different banks for similar maturities to a single country might well have quite different pricing, dependent on both the nature of the "indirect" returns accruing to the lending banks and on the covariances with the total market return.

REFERENCES

CALDWELL, J. ALEXANDER and J. ANTONIO VILLAMIL, 1979, U.S. lenders are learning to discriminate, *Euromoney*, May.

DONALDSON, T. H., 1979, *Lending in international commercial banking* (Halsted-Wiley, New York).

EATON, JONATHAN and MARK GERSOVITZ, 1979, *Debt with potential repudiation: Theoretical and empirical analysis*. Mimeo. (Princeton University, Princeton, NJ).

KOBRIN, STEVEN J., 1979. Political risk: A review and reconsideration. *Journal of International Business Studies*. Sept.

KUBARYCH, ROGER M., 1980, *Portfolio approaches to managing country risk: the view from the Federal Reserve Bank of New York*. Federal Reserve Bank of New York. Mimeo, Jan.

NAGY, PANCHRAS, 1979, Quantifying country risk: A system developed by economists at the bank of Montreal. *Columbia Journal of World Business*, Jan.

PORZECANSKI, ARTURO C., 1980, The Assessment of country risk: Lessons from the Latin American experience, in: J. C. Garcia-Zamor and S. Sutin, eds. *Financing development in Latin America* (Praeger, New York).

SARGEN, NICHOLAS, 1977, Use of economic indicators and country risk appraisal, Federal Reserve Bank of San Francisco, *Economic Review,* Fall.

VAN AGTMAEL. Antoine, 1976, Evaluating the risks of lending to developing countries, *Euromoney,* April.

VOLCKER, PAUL A., 1980, *The recycling problem revisited.* Federal Reserve Board. Mimeo, March.

WALTER, INGO, 1981, International capital allocation, in: R. G. Hawkins, R. M. Levich and C. Wihlborg, eds., *Internationalization of financial markets and national economic policy* (JAI Press, Greenwich, CT).

Old and New Proposals For International Banking Safety*

James W. Dean
and
Ian H. Giddy

22

To date, there has been no international banking crash in the 1980s, despite major debt servicing problems by Poland, Mexico, Brazil, Chile and Argentina, to name only the more important. In fact, the Eurocurrency market, net of interbank loans, has continued to grow from $250 billion in 1975 to $700 billion in 1980 to over $1 trillion in 1983. The interbank market has also grown, although more slowly since mid-1982.[1] In 1983 bank profits were up, and reserves against losses were the most thickly padded in ten years.

Yet are we experiencing the calm before a storm? A significant proportion of America's financial institutions became technically insolvent when interest rates shot up in 1979–84. In addition, the full implications of interest rate volatility for Eurobanks, which have in the past relied on maturity mismatching to maintain profitability, have probably not yet been realized.[2] Moreover, rapid changes in the U.S. financial system, and in the payments and clearing mechanisms, are giving rise to the pains and problems of technological transition and heightened competition.

*This article is intended as a framework for discussion and a catalyst for debate, not a firm endorsement of each proposal put forth. Parts of it are based on Dean and Giddy (1981b) and Dean and Giddy (1981a, Section 6). We express our gratitude to Thomas Havrilesky for his helpful suggestions.

[1]For a brief history of the evolution of international banking since 1960, see Crane and Hayes (1983).

[2]However, in principle Eurobanks can now minimize maturity risk by using the Chicago, New York, London, or Bermuda Eurodollar futures markets, to which they have enjoyed access since 1981–82.

Most seriously, the banks' ability to withstand a major interruption of debt servicing may not yet have been properly tested. At the end of 1982, the loan exposure of 12 major U.S. banks to just 5 Latin American countries was over 100% of their capital base. Exposure of the 9 largest banks to the non-oil-producing developing countries as a group was a startling 221%. Crudely put, it would take the repudiation of only about half of Latin America's debt to wipe out most of the big U.S. banks. Each of the 5 Latin American countries is likely to or has experienced grave problems with debt servicing, not to mention repayment of principal. These problems are far from over. Although there has been dramatic reduction recently in domestic loan losses, bank analysts are predicting higher foreign loan losses in 1984 than in 1983. Some U.S. studies indicate that the stock markets are valuing foreign loans at only about 85% of book value.

Even the hint that a bank's capital base is threatened can force it to pay more for deposits. When Mexico declared a ninety-day loan payments moratorium in August 1982, the rate of interest on one-month deposits at U.S. banks shot up from 50 to 400 basis points over the rate on comparable Treasury bills. Moreover, a bank rumored to be in trouble can experience massive deposit runoffs, particularly in these days when large blocks of deposits are controlled by mutual funds and when banks deposit extensively with each other. Deposit runs can cause rumours of a threatened capital base to become self-fulfilling, and the pervasiveness of interbank depositing can cause difficulties to spread beyond the bank where they originated. An ultimate consequence, although most unlikely in the current context, could be a wholesale flight from international into domestic deposits or even into currency. The U.S. experience in 1929–33 dramatically attests to this possibility. Over those four years, bank failures imposed losses of about $2.5 billion on stockholders, depositors, and other creditors. However, because of a general public crisis of confidence and flight into currency, bank deposits declined by an astounding $18 billion.

Banking and regulatory arrangements may be ill-equipped to prevent such international banking crises. A fundamental defect in the present system is that offshore banking is typically free from domestic regulation yet enjoys partial protection against default losses in the form of limited lender-of-last-resort assurance from parent-country central banks. Thus, international banks can potentially externalize some of the *ex ante* costs of prudential regulation, or *ex post* costs of defaults, onto domestic banks and central banks, not even necessarily those from their parent country.

Optimally, banking regulation would be applied uniformly to on- and off-shore banks internationally. However, in a world of nationally independent regulators, the best that can be hoped for is *cooperative* enforcement of national requirements. This could involve either internationally uniform parent-country treatment or nationally uniform host-country treatment. The former has the advantage in that it removes incentives for banks to locate in the least restrictive environments. But neither arrangement completely internalizes the costs of externalities due to defaults.

Unfortunately, what we have at present is best characterized as a system of *competitive* enforcement (Giddy, forthcoming). Of the three alternatives—international uniformity, national cooperation, or national competition—this last is least desirable. Not only are default costs externalized, but incentives to deregulate competitively are relatively unchecked. And the incentives are not necessarily to deregulate domestic banking—which in many cases is needed—but rather to expand the scope of unregulated banking offshore.

The regulatory system therefore needs to be reformed in two ways (Dean, 1984). First, prudential restrictions—total quantity limitations and balance-sheet risk restraints—need to be applied more uniformly. Proposals mooted include capital requirements or offshore reserve requirements (Dean and Grubel, 1978) and internationally coordinated country-debt ceilings (Solomon, 1982). For some time, the low capital ratios enjoyed by both French and Japanese banks have been of concern (although French banks are admittedly government backed, whereas Japanese banks are kept on a tight rein and are also subject to different accounting standards). It is believed that recently the Fed has been quietly pressuring the Japanese to bring their banks more in line. The United States itself has traditionally imposed no capital requirements (except that U.S. banks may not lend more than 10% of their capital to a ''single'' borrower); but in 1983 the Fed imposed for the first time a 5% requirement and by the end of the year had successfully enforced compliance despite the fact that many of the big international banks had slipped closer to 4%. Balance sheets are also currently looking stronger in Britain and West Germany, where capital ratios are likewise up to about 5%.

Second, supervision, information disclosure, and emergency credit assurance also need to be coordinated internationally. This article is concerned largely with proposals of this latter type. We identify six ways in which the authorities could seek to avert bank runs on an international scale and recommend a seventh approach to help maintain the soundness of international interbank markets.

Present Regulatory Arrangements

The present set of regulatory arrangements governing international banking stems in large part from the concern of individual central banks with maintaining the soundness of their own large institutions. The banking supervisors of the industrial countries have escalated efforts to understand and constrain cross-border lending risks of their own banks. The monetary authorities have responded quickly to signs of weakness in major banks.

There are, however, growing signs that neither the monetary authorities nor legislatures are willing to be held ransom unconditionally to banks, borrowers, or even depositors. The package of loans put together by the Federal Reserve and the Federal Deposit Insurance Corporation to counter the deposit runoff faced by First Pennsylvania Bank in 1980 and Continental Illinois in 1984 were early warning signals of the kind of bailout to which the public sector might be held ransom. When the Penn Square Bank of Oklahoma failed in 1982, devastating repercussions were felt by Continental Illinois of Chicago through 1984, which held indirect title to much of Penn Square's oil loan portfolio. Moreover the FDIC, contrary to its custom, allowed Penn Square's uninsured depositors to lose money.

Internationally, when high interest rates and worldwide recession in the early 80s began to impair third-world borrowers' ability to repay, regulators found themselves facing a dilemma. Increased regulation was called for in order to discourage imprudent lending in the future, yet for the time being more lending and longer repayment periods (''rescheduling'') was called for to prevent imminent collapse of borrowing-country economies. In 1981, the non-oil-producing developing countries paid $55 billion in interest but were able to borrow $81 billion. By 1982, interest payments were $59 billion but new borrowing was down to $57 billion. If the banks were simply to cease extending new loans, for example to Argentina, Mexico, and Brazil alone, they would face a problem similar to the one that would confront the U.S. Congress were it compelled to turn the $210 billion fiscal deficit into an $80 billion surplus. As one expert comments, ''To expect a political feat in those countries that appears impossible for the United States is unrealistic to say the least. . . . But if they fail to produce that miracle [assuming that the banks do not resume lending to them], *de facto* default on a large scale is inevitable.'' (Cline, 1983)

In the United States, the stage was set for a game of ''chicken'' between bankers and government, with bankers refusing to lend more to problem countries unless Washington backed down on increased regulation, and Washington refusing to help bankers unless they lent more money. The *Wall Street Journal* carried headlines like ''Shootout Between Congress, Banks Develops Over Bad Foreign Loans.'' (*WSJ,* Feb. 2, 1983)

Over the first half of 1983, new international bank lending virtually ground to a halt. This was the first time since the BIS began collecting data in 1963 that the banks' external assets showed almost no increase during a half-year period. Of what lending there was, two-thirds went to borrowers in developed industrial countries, mostly corporations. Of the $4.3 billion that went to non-oil-producing developing countries, over 80% was ''involuntary''—that is, arranged in connection with IMF credits. The Fed, for example, while with one arm demanding that banks maintain higher capital ratios, has with the other stretched rules to permit them to lend more to developing countries in support of IMF rescue programs.

In short by 1983, when Congress was presented with legislation authorizing quota increases to the IMF, the issue had become not only bail-outs of domestic banks, but bail-outs of foreign governments. This issue was complicated further by Washington's evident interests in political stability in Eastern Europe and Latin America, and in some cases by borrowers' trump cards as well—for example, Mexico's oil.[3] Congress ended up approving the quota increases but was also prompted to attach an amendment instructing bank regulatory agencies (the Fed, FDIC, and Comptroller of the Currency) to formulate new and stricter regulation of international lending. The International Lending Supervision Act, passed late in 1983, imposes minimum capital requirements, new reporting requirements, limits on loan rescheduling fees, and special reserves against shaky foreign loans.

Nevertheless, despite improved supervision, qualified assurance of support, and stricter regulation, some glaring gaps remain. Arguably, some central banks have gone too far in assuring the public of their major banks' solvency. Doing so amounts to a subsidy to big banks without a countervailing disincentive to mismanagement. At the same time, certain weaknesses persist in the safety of the system as a whole. Where the legal links of parent and affiliate bank are tenuous, responsibility shifts from the parent's central bank to the

[3]See ''Money and Power: Political Effects of Debt-Crisis Moves Worry Experts,'' *Wall Street Journal,* June 30, 1983.

authorities of the host country. The resources of some host countries are obviously inadequate to the task of countering a Euromarket run. When the Luxembourg subsidiary of the Vatican's Banco Ambrosiano failed in 1982, depositors were not bailed out, either by the parent bank or the Luxembourg authorities.

Of the 500-odd banks active in the Eurocurrency interbank market, many are insufficiently important or from too small a country for their solvency to be assured. Thus the uncertainties concerning international banking stability arise from uneven and improperly priced central bank assurance to depositors. We shall now assess seven ways of building a more even foundation for the international banking system, beginning with two areas in which substantial progress is being made.

1. Supervision and Examination

Initiated under the auspices of the Bank for International Settlements in 1974, the Cooke Committee of bank supervisory authorities has advanced the American practice of extending domestic supervisory standards to banks' international activities. Overseas supervision by the U.S. authorities is itself of relatively recent vintage—the Comptroller of the Currency established an international division in 1965 and began annual onsite examinations of branches abroad in 1967. But it was not until 1973 that full consolidation of international with domestic accounts, and "transparency" of affiliates' balance sheets, were required. Other members of the BIS group, notably the British, Germans, Japanese, and Swiss, have subsequently made efforts to achieve consolidation and transparency as well as to assess country exposure, asset and liability management, and capital adequacy in relation to risky assets worldwide.

The extension of domestic supervision and examination to affiliates abroad is a logical consequence of the 1974 Basle agreement that parent banks would be expected to support foreign branches and that, if necessary, the central bank of the home country would support the parent bank. Global responsibility necessarily entails global examination and supervision by the bank regulators. Sensibly, one cannot properly assess or regulate merely the domestic operations of a bank that is managed as a global institution. Domestic constraints on bank risk can be offset readily by a higher degree of international risk-taking.

Yet the present effort is not without three important shortcomings:

1. When domestic regulations on risk and/or activities are burdensome, their extension to international banking tends to reduce the international competitiveness of the country's banks; hence the likelihood that international supervision will remain less severe than domestic supervision even if done on a consolidated basis.
2. The alternative is to seek uniformity in the supervisory constraints placed on international banks of different nationalities. While there is a natural competition-in-regulation force at work, potential and actual clashes with domestic regulations is, in practice, very difficult to achieve.
3. Much of an international bank's lending is to foreign banks. Unless they know the condition of the latter, regulators cannot fully evaluate risk exposure.

2. Disclosure and Public Information

This last problem has provided impetus to a second recent development. Along with the assignation of support and supervisory responsibility, the Cooke Committee and the *Groupe de contact* of European banking supervisors have explicitly recognized the interdependence and mutual vulnerability of each country's international banks. In recent years, members have established lines of contact to alert one another of individual banks' prospective difficulties. In addition, the group has moved toward harmonization of accounting and disclosure. In cooperation with international accounting professionals, the Cooke Committee and the EEC Commission have sought to elevate and render more transparent the norms for consolidation, loan loss provision, hidden reserves, cost of market valuation, accruals and depreciation, and levels of detail disclosed.

Despite general and growing agreement on the virtues of disclosure, one norm that remains controversial is the U.S. requirement that banks publish the size of all delinquent-country loans which exceed 1% of their total assets. Many countries argue that the U.S. practice and its attendant publicity may give country-borrowers more leverage in their debt negotiations. For example, early in 1984 there were reports that U.S. banks were under pressure to receive interest on Argentinian loans by March 31 lest they be classified as "unproductive" and therefore subject to the disclosure law. This situation supplied Argentina with the potential to argue along such lines as "We might consider meeting your March 31st deadline if you knock one eighth of a percent off the spread."

An important informational improvement came early in 1984, when the IMF's monthly *International Financial Statistics* launched a new series of country debt data that are considerably more detailed and accurate than those previously available.

The merit of this is that the more that is known by the banking community about other banks' conditions, the less likely are irrational runoffs of deposits. But even full disclosure cannot signal the unexpected or guarantee against deliberate fraud. Disclosure is evidently not enough on its own.

3. Deposit Insurance

Most observers agree that the long-established U.S. system of insuring bank deposits (up to $100,000 per account) has played a role in forestalling runs on deposits in troubled banks. During the past two decades twelve other countries have adopted insurance schemes; in particular, Germany, the United Kingdom, and the Netherlands have recently joined the club.

One proposal that has been mooted in the United States is to extend existing deposit insurance to the deposits of American banks that are booked outside the United States and to seek corresponding insurance by other Group of Ten countries. This procedure is, in fact, already done for German banks' external deposits.

The simplest way to extend coverage would be to say that any insurance that applied domestically also applied abroad. However, if the amount were limited to the small (formal) coverage that applies at home in most countries, the effect on maintaining confidence in the vast, wholesale Eurocurrency market would be negligible.

If deposit insurance coverage were made much wider and greater (e.g., 100% for deposits of all sizes), the desired effect would be achieved. But then the deposit insurance fund, however large, would fail to command confidence unless it were explicitly backed up by the central bank. This was evident as Franklin National Bank began to fail in 1974.

Thus, the internationalization of deposit insurance rests on central banks' unconditional willingness to provide back-up loans to national deposit insurance funds such as the Federal Deposit Insurance Corporation. It might be argued that this would differ little from the present state of affairs in which central banks provide implicit support to major banks.[4] There are, however, some important distinctions between the two approaches.

First, deposit insurance provides assurance only to the depositors, and not to bank managers or shareholders. Central bank bail-outs reduce the incentive for prudent management. Second, deposit insurance replaces the presumption of rescues with specific, legal, government-backed guarantees. The drawback is that doing so may remove the discipline of the market; bankers can engage in risky, leveraged lending with no fear of deposit withdrawals. The onus is, therefore, on the banking regulators to discourage excessive risk-taking.

Economists have long argued that the most efficient way to regulate insured banks is to impose a premium for the insurance commensurate with the size and riskiness of the bank. This allows some banks to specialize in the provision of high-risk, high-return investments while preserving the stability of the deposit market.

Country-by-country insurance of offshore deposits would lack complete and uniform coverage and might be hindered by over-lapping and conflicting jurisdictions. An alternative proposal has been made by Herbert Grubel (Grubel, 1979). He suggests the establishment (in Basle or Washington) of a multinational, nonprofit insurance scheme backed by major governments. Its purpose would be to "serve the multinational banking community not now covered by national schemes."

If effective, such a scheme would certainly contribute to the stability of international banking. Again, it attacks the problem of depositor confidence more directly than does a bail-out by the central bank. Yet it could work only if a great deal of regulatory power were transferred to the international agency. The IDIC would have to have both examinatory power and the right to constrain the (domestic and international) activities of commercial banks. This means a substantial loss of domestic regulatory autonomy and the creation of a supranational regulatory monolith.

The less funds and power the IDIC had, the more it would have to rely on the resources of the world's central banks to provide loans (to the IDIC or to banks directly) in the event of problems viewed as global.

Who would distinguish between local domestic problems, handled by domestic banking authorities, those that were non-domestic but isolated (to be handled by the IDIC), and

[4]In almost all the deposit insurance schemes surveyed in a recent study, the authorities have preferred to rescue banks or arrange mergers rather than to liquidate them. The result has been *de facto* 100% coverage. See Ian S. McCarthy, "Deposit Insurance: Theory and Practice," *IMF Staff Papers,* 1980, pp. 578–600.

those that were truly global in scope, to be countered by the world's central banks? Who would decide on the conditions under which such loans would be made? To grant the IDIC the necessary power and monetary resources would entail a major transfer of monetary discretion away from individual governments.

4. Supranational Lender of Last Resort

Franklin Edwards has argued that, because of the breakdown at home and abroad of product boundaries and the increased competition between markets and institutions, banking regulation has fallen behind changes in the markets. What is needed, says Edwards, is uniformity across competing financial institutions, and " . . . a supranational lender-of-last-resort facility should be established, supported by at minimum the Group of Ten central banks." (Edwards, 1980)

The value of a well-supported facility of this kind would be that it would enhance confidence in international banking, perhaps even more so than inadequately supported international deposit insurance corporations. However, many of the problems of a supranational IDIC apply to supranational lenders of last resort. The three prime issues are:

1. When would the world lender of last resort intervene to support banks, and when would support be denied? To give the supranational body decision-making power would undermine central banks' monetary control; yet without such power, the banking public would be unable to rely on the international body and would look, as before, to the individual central banks.
2. Where would the world lender of last resort get the funds to lend? If it could create credit on its own, it would be in effect a global central bank; but if it could not, it might be little more than a pretentiously titled coordinating agency. In fact, if the world lender of last resort had to borrow the funds it lent, it would not be the last resort.
3. Would the supranational lender of last resort support banks from nonparticipating countries? If not, instability could remain; but if so, a tremendous free-rider incentive would arise.

One is tempted to conclude that until the world is ready for a global central bank with centralized monetary policy and all the economic power that that entails, proposals for a supranational lender of last resort cannot be taken seriously. However, the idea continues to be touted and may be both more necessary and more plausible than it first appears. Recently, experts such as Alexander Swoboda, director of the International Center for Monetary and Banking Studies in Geneva, have argued that a fundamental problem facing international banks is the absence of secondary markets for their loans. Domestic banks have the cushion of secondary markets for their bond portfolio; and, most important, their government bills can usually be discounted with little loss at the central bank. Thus a "supranational" central bank would really mean an international discounting mechanism for banks' loan assets.

5. International Loan Insurance

In recent years several proposals have been made both in official circles and by the banking community for the development of funds and procedures to assist national governments unable to meet foreign debt payments. Some years ago the Governor of the Bank of Greece, Xenophon Zolotas, called for an insurance agency to provide guarantees for private international loans. (Zoltas, 1978a,b; Morgan Guarantee Trust, 1979). This would not only strengthen the Euromarket but "would open the commercial credit window to many low income LDCs which are today excluded from the private international capital markets because they cannot meet the creditworthiness criteria of private institutions." The guarantors of the fund would be either the private international banks themselves or the governments of industrialized countries in conjunction with the World Bank. In fact, in 1983–84, the World Bank, in an effort to increase flows of funds to developing countries, began putting together such a loan insurance plan. And at a meeting of the Group of Thirty in late 1983, Henry Wallich, a governor of the Federal Reserve Board, proposed that international banks should make "constructive" use of their currently high spreads of 2% or more over their deposit rates by putting all or part of this margin into an insurance pool.

A private country-risk insurance scheme seems to be a sound idea, for it would presumably refrain from providing guarantees on loans to profligate countries or do so only with very high premia and stringent conditions. One could argue that the multibank syndication technique already allows sufficient opportunity for spreading risk. Yet by unbundling two separable financial services—that is, by splitting the provision of funds from the assumption of risk—the scheme would allow more risk-averse banks to lend to a wider range of countries. In our view this would result in less concentration of Eurolending to a few semi-industrialized countries—Brazil, Korea, and Mexico, for example.

Of course, the fund could only succeed if it commanded the full confidence of lenders. Even a technical default could result in very onerous claims on the insurance fund, particularly if (as some argue) a default by one entity produced other defaults, perhaps because of cross-default clauses. This potential hazard may be why no such fund has arisen spontaneously.

As Zolatas recognizes, there is some doubt as to whether the industrial countries could be persuaded to underwrite risky countries' debt. There is also the question of whether government-subsidized guarantees are desirable. A loan insurance scheme sponsored by an official or semi-official international organization could *increase* the risk of the international financial system. First, because subsidized insurance (at politically negotiated premia) would enable credit to be extended at below market interest rates, LDC governments would have an incentive to borrow more than otherwise, and to invest in projects with lower yields or higher risk. Secondly, bankers, relieved of the burden of country-risk analysis, would be willing to lend in a less discriminating fashion—perhaps to inherently risky or unproductive countries.

6. What Should Be Done?

Each of the proposals presents difficulties and drawbacks. Yet much of the financial community continues to voice concern about the safety of international banking, and one hears widespread calls for prudential policies beyond the *status quo*. We have argued that government or World Bank guarantees against country risk could exacerbate present dangers. We have also argued that the transfer of sufficient monetary power to a global lender-of-last-resort or deposit insurance fund is a practical impossibility. This leaves central bank lending or national deposit insurance.

Domestically, most countries rely exclusively on their central banks to provide funds in time of crisis—in fact, until 1960, only the United States provided any form of deposit insurance for its banks. The problem with central bank bail-outs is that banks rather than depositors are protected. There is always an incentive for a failing bank to borrow from its central bank, since management's tenure and stockholders' wealth are prolonged and perhaps preserved. If bankruptcy ultimately ensues, management is not penalized for incurring central bank indebtedness; and the most stockholders can lose is the value of their shares.

Properly priced deposit insurance, on the other hand, discourages risk-taking but protects depositors. Deposit insurance premia should rise with the riskiness of a bank's asset portfolio and leverage. Deposit insurance, moreover, is a much cleaner mechanism than existing lender-of-last-resort arrangements. When the Franklin National Bank failed, the New York Fed faced problems which delayed resolution of the affair. One was that of legally "perfecting" Franklin's assets, which meant convincing debtors that the Fed now had legal authority to appropriate or redirect future interest payments. A deposit insurance scheme, by contrast, sets up clear rules for compensation.

More precisely, we advocate limited offshore depositor protection backed by the parent bank's central bank. The bank or bank subsidiary which carries the offshore deposits should be assessed a premium that is higher the riskier the bank's offshore asset portfolio—i.e., that is based on insurance principles. This insurance premium might more properly be termed a tax, since its function is not to generate an insurance fund sufficient to cover loan losses, but rather to penalize risk-taking and reward prudence. Banks would otherwise be free, within supervisory limits, to adjust their portfolios in accordance with their taste for risk.

Depositors should also be given the opportunity to choose their preferred investment position along the risk spectrum. If deposits over a certain size are not covered, or if deposits are ranked senior or junior according to their potential claim on liquidated assets, large deposits or junior deposits would then have to compensate for their higher risk by bearing higher rates of interest. Depositors could choose between low risk and low return, or the reverse.

The details of which and whose deposits were insured would quickly become public knowledge. Countries which held back on deposit insurance would find that their banks were forced into higher deposit rate tiers. Interbank depositors would react rapidly, and financial publications would cater to the nonbank market.

There would be one important qualification to the rule of home-country responsibility for deposit insurance. Certain host countries—notably the United States and Canada—have recently extended national or near-national regulatory treatment to foreign banks. In the United States and Canada this has meant the extension of domestic deposit insurance coverage to foreign banks. In these cases, insurance by the home country would be redundant.

All this is quite consistent with the present efforts at the BIS and the EEC to coordinate supervisory activities, exchange information, and act as an early warning system to alert central banks to coming problems. Supervisory cooperation is much more possible than insurance cooperation, since it is neither a call for potential philanthropy toward other countries' banks nor a demand for the *ad hoc* coordination associated with crises that an international deposit insurance scheme would require. Increased information exchange, moreover, would neatly pave the way for offshore deposit insurance schemes, since accurate loan risk assessment is the *sine qua non* of variably priced insurance.

7. A New Proposal: Interbank Credit Commitments

At the outset, we mentioned the danger that problems in one bank might spread to others through deposit runoffs. The fact that one-third or more of the typical Eurobank's assets and liabilities consist of interbank deposits accentuates this danger. Information, both hard and soft, travels very quickly in this market. The suggestion that the remaining, non-interbank two-thirds of a bank's asset portfolio is shaky can quickly cause other banks to charge it more for deposits (''tiering'') or to shut it out of the interbank market entirely. This situation can severely exacerbate a bank's initial problems. Moreover, if the problem bank is forced to default on its outstanding interbank liabilities, its problems will spread to other banks.

This reasoning points to the maintenance of a functioning interbank market during periods of uncertainty as a major means of averting a banking contraction. One way of achieving that arrangement would be to persuade participants in the world interbank market to establish a network of formal, guaranteed credit commitments to one another.

Lines of credit can be of two kinds. The interbank system presently in place is one of informal, discretionary lines extended by one bank to all other banks with which it does deposit and foreign exchange business. The second kind could be written guaranteed commitments to lend upon demand, up to specified dollar limits. These could be effective over predetermined future time periods, normally one to three years, and contain a formula for the interest rate on drawdowns. They could also carry an explicit or implicit fee. In the U.S. market for wholesale loans, such commitments already are used to reduce firms' exposure to credit rationing risk arising from ''tight credit'' policies. Typically, corporations use standby lines to back up their issuance of commercial paper.

Internationally, banks could employ similar commitments to back up uninsured deposits. Fee-based commitments are particularly well suited to the smooth absorption of isolated shocks to the international banking system because banks could sell and manage commitments on portfolio diversification principles, assuming that they would not all be used at once. Knowledge that a bank has access to such lines would forestall the ''sheer nervousness'' type of deposit runoff from less-than-top banks. Of course, they would be of little value in the event of a genuinely global, systematic shock, but such a role would not be their intention.

Some international banks, particularly those Eurobanks without ready access to a major domestic money market such as the U.S. banking system, have sought and obtained formal commitments from major domestic banks. Most, however, are unwilling to pay for a guaranteed line, relying instead on the informal lines extended by other banks; these suffice under most circumstances. Emergency, market-shrinkage possibilities are either ignored[5] or else the banks blithely rely on access to central bank credit. In fact it is plausible to reason that the dearth of guaranteed commitments between international banks is a direct result of central banks' willingness to act as lenders of last resort at non-penalty rates. An implicit, unpaid-for, open-ended line of credit with the central bank substitutes for the formal lines that the market might otherwise demand.

In effect, the central bank provides, free, what the interbank market could well supply to international banks for a fee and that domestic banks presently supply (also for a fee) to corporations. An alternative arrangement could be as follows.

The central bank would charge an annual fee for acting as lender of last resort to all banks under its aegis. The fee would be computed as a small (but above-market) percentage of all uninsured deposits of the bank, including offshore deposits. For this fee, the central bank would provide an explicit, unlimited-time line of credit in an amount equal to the uninsured deposits' value. The fee percentage would be changeable at the central bank's discretion. However, to provide banks with an incentive to develop the interbank commitment network, the central-bank line (and the fee) would be reduced by the amount of any guaranteed commitments obtained from other major banks or foreign central banks. The fee would be set high enough to induce banks to switch to interbank commitments to back up the bulk of their interbank liabilities. In other words, the central-bank fee would induce interbank lenders to offer comparable guaranteed commitments at lower rates. Eventually, central-bank facilities would be called upon only in extreme need.

The approach just delineated has several advantages over the others we have discussed—bank supervision and disclosure, lender of last resort, and deposit insurance—although it does not fully supplant any of them.

First, in contrast to its existing open-ended role of lender to troubled banks, the central bank becomes a limited lender, supplying funds rapidly and under known terms, and only when private commitments have been exhausted. The central bank need not lend individual banks one cent more than is available under its prearranged commitment. Together, the central bank and private commitments assure depositors that the bank will normally have full and continuous access to credit and not be "shut out" of the interbank market. The approach eliminates a good deal of the present vagueness about the central bank's role, whether domestic or supranational, in a liquidity crisis. The central bank need act as a general supplier of liquidity only in the event of a general run out of bank deposits into domestic currency. This transfer of funds can be done through open-market purchases of government debt from all comers at prestated prices.

Second, unlike deposit insurance, this approach allows depositors to lose money. Since loan commitments (including that of the central bank) would obviously become invalid in the event of a bank's insolvency, uninsured depositors could lose if the bank itself takes excessive risks. Hence they will avoid risky banks. Since the commitments limit the possibility of local shocks becoming global crises, systematic risk is limited and bank failures could be actuarially diversified. Central banks would continue to bear responsi-

[5]For the argument that low-probability events are ignored see Guttentag and Herring (1981).

bility for countering global shocks, and deposit insurance could be made voluntary and private. This would provide a private-sector watchdog over a bank's condition.[6]

Finally, the commitment-incentive approach would allow the dismantling of much of the present supervisory apparatus, since it would turn most of the monitoring role over to the private sector.[7] By allowing banks to fail, it would ensure shareholder vigilance, and, more important, vigilance on the part of the banks' extending commitments. Prudential discipline would thus largely be exerted by the market rather than by the authorities. Risky banks would be forced to pay a premium for credit lines and might be driven out of business or forced to moderate their portfolios. Commitments would be made subject to conditions that limit go-for-broke strategies, and lenders would impose direct constraints on capital-scarce banks.

There are, naturally, some practical problems with a scheme such as this one. The central bank would have to determine the conditions of its commitments, the fees (which would necessarily be higher for riskier banks), the eligible banks from which commitments could be obtained, and the interest rate on its loans. The most serious obstacle could be the bank's objections that commitment fees are too costly and would have to be passed on to depositors, rendering them uncompetitive. Perhaps so, but to obtain free credit facilities constitutes an unwarranted subsidy, similar to export credits. In any case, it is probable that banks which have extensive back-up credit commitments plus guaranteed access to central bank facilities would command a premium from risk-averse depositors. At the first hint of a new international banking crisis, commitment-backed banks would be the first to gain. Arguably, therefore, institution of such a scheme by one major country would provide both the example and the incentive for worldwide adoption of the commitment-network approach.

A final word: to those who protest that the present informal arrangements of central-bank backing for major international banks is working well, we counter by arguing that the assurance of central-bank bail-outs contains the seeds of crises. Until the market knows how far central banks will go, it will continue to test them. To the extent that central banks or international institutions become uncritical rescuers, they foster leaky vessels that no degree of bailing can ultimately save. The missing elements are market-related disincentives to high-return, high-risk banking. The disincentive we advocate is close to the classic Bagehot prescription: unconditional last-resort lending at penalty rates of interest. Unconditional bail-outs without such corrective disincentives will surely serve to confirm the second of Bagehot's "two great maxims of economic science":

> [T]hat the interference of government with the trade of banking is as sure to work mischief as its interference with any other trade; that the mischief will be often of the very kind which government meant to prevent, and that in trying to prevent a run it incurs great risk of causing and encouraging one (Bagehot, p. 429).

[6]Private insurers would supply deposit insurance because their risk would be limited by the guaranteed access which insured banks have to interbank and central bank credit, and by their having prior claim on the bank's assets in the event of insolvency.

[7]This should be qualified by the observation that the central bank would need to do some monitoring of the beneficiaries of its credit commitments.

REFERENCES

BAGEHOT, WALTER (1978). "The Lessons of the American Monetary Crisis," in N. St. John-Stevas, ed., *The Collected Works of Walter Bagehot,* vol. 10, London: The Economist.

CLINE, WILLIAM R. (1983). "International Debt and the Stability of the World Economy," Institute of International Economics, Washington, D.C.

CRANE, DWIGHT B., and SAMUEL L. HAYES, III (1983). "The Evolution of International Banking Competition and its Implications for Regulation," *Journal of Bank Research,* Spring, pp. 39–48.

DEAN, JAMES W. (1984). "Walking the Tightrope: Conservative and Liberal Approaches to International Banking Reform," Simon Fraser University Economics Department Discussion Paper.

______ and IAN H. GIDDY (1981a). *Averting International Banking Crises,* Monograph Series in Finance and Economics, No. 1, New York University.

______ and ______ (1981b). *Six Ways to World Banking Safety, Euromoney,* May.

______ and HERBERT G. GRUBEL (1978). "Regulatory Issues and the Theory of Multinational Banking," in Franklin R. Edwards, ed., *Issues in Financial Regulation,* New York: McGraw-Hill.

EDWARDS, FRANKLIN R. (1980). "Financial Institution and Regulatory Issues in the 21st Century: After the Crash," in Albert Verheirstraeten, ed., *Competition and Regulation in Financial Markets,* New York: Macmillan, pp. 1-13.

GIDDY, IAN H. (forthcoming). "A Theory of Bank Regulators as International Competitors," *Kredit und Kapital.*

GRUBEL, HERBERT G. (1979a). *A Proposal for the Establishment of an International Deposit Insurance Corporation,* Princeton Essays in International Finance, No. 133, July.

MORGAN GUARANTY TRUST COMPANY (1979). *World Financial Markets,* December.

MCCARTHY, IAN S. (1980). "Deposit Insurance: Theory and Practice," *IMF Staff Papers,* Sept., pp. 576–600.

SOLOMON, ANTHONY (1982). "Remarks Before the Bicentennial Financial Symposium," Federal Reserve Bank of New York, Oct. 7.

ZOLOTAS, XENOPHON (1978a). *An International Loan Insurance Scheme: A Proposal,* Bank of Greece Papers and Lectures No. 39, Athens, Bank of Greece.

______ (1978b). "A Proposal for a New Fund to Insure Against Euromarket Defaults," *Euromoney,* April, pp. 77–83.

Supervisory and Regulatory Reform

VI

The explosive geographic, product-line, and international expansion by banks and bank holding companies, featured in sections II, IV, and V of this volume, is seen by many analysts to have increased the risks assumed by bank management. As long as the underlying rationale of bank regulation is to prevent the collapse of the nation's payments mechanism, bank regulatory authorities will continue to perform the function of insuring transactions deposits. For the same reason government will continue to facilitate the rescue of troubled banks through guided mergers and lender-of-last-resort loans. Some analysts, such as Greenbaum and Higgins in section II and Eisenbeis in section IV, would argue that many of these regulatory restrictions have increased, rather than reduced, the risks assumed by banks and, ultimately, borne by taxpayers. They would contend that in today's deregulated environment some of these restrictions are so narrowly focused that they encourage risky circumvention. Other analysts indicate that such regulatory restrictions prevent the benefits of increased competition from flowing to the public.

Therefore, one is forced to conclude that if "banks" are "special," in the sense conveyed by Corrigan's article in Section IV, they will be protected. The government (and hence taxpayers) will absorb some of the risk. The pressing question today is, "What sort of regulatory restrictions provide the desired combination of publicly assumed risk and efficient and beneficial provision of depository services (liquidity) by banks?'' The articles by Greenbaum and Higgins, Kane and Horvitz in section II, the articles by Eisenbeis and Solomon in section IV, and the article by Dean and Giddy in section V offer fresh perspectives on this issue. The contributions in this section add to and complement those perspectives. A financial services environment characterized by interest-rate volatility, deregulation, and intense new geographic and product-line competition requires a fair and flexible regulatory and supervisory apparatus. Since the current system is antiquated, inequitable, and inflexible, it needs a major overhaul.

While troubled institutions still represent only a small percentage of the nation's 15,000 commercial banks, their problems and the resulting huge potential drain on the FDIC's funds have stimulated interest in monitoring the financial condition of banks. The confluence of this recent interest, new technology, and new methods of measuring risk has produced advances in surveillance techniques. In the first essay in this section, and the twenty-third in this volume, Baron H. Putnam succinctly describes the surveillance systems of the five federal regulatory agencies and presents a conceptual framework for classifying institutions according to their financial condition. This article can be read most profitably in conjunction with the essays which follow.

The bank's debt ratio is a measure of a bank's risk exposure. Excessive leverage (inadequate capital) should, through efficient surveillance, effective public disclosure, and appropriate market and regulatory reactions, discourage bank risk taking by automatically lowering the bank's rate of return. In the twenty-fourth selection of this book, James G. Ehlen, Jr., provides a thorough economic critique of both regulatory and industry views on capital adequacy. Ehlen also provides an interesting survey of recent regulatory guidelines on capital adequacy.

Methods for analyzing a bank's financial condition are useless without information. Once risks are measured, how can this information be used to influence the risk-taking activities of bank management? Recent regulatory initiatives have moved toward adding ''market discipline'' to regulators' efforts to control bank risk. The principle at work behind these initiatives is that, ideally, informed creditors and stockholders will effectively police the risk-taking activities of bank management. Gary G. Gilbert's article, the twenty-fifth in this volume, neatly evaluates the degree to which uninsured depositors and stockholders *actually do* impose such discipline on bank management and the extent to which broader disclosure could improve this corrective feedback.

The logical polar extreme of market discipline is regulatory agencies' allowing banks to fail in order to send a ''signal'' to all bank managers and thereby influence their behavior. Will greater public disclosure of a bank's financial condition—revealing the degree of likelihood of bank failure—induce creditors and stockholders to police a bank's risk-taking more closely? In the twenty-sixth article in this volume, George J. Benston answers this question by examining the incentives of stockholders, ordinary creditors, uninsured depositors, and deposit insurers to signal disapproval of bank risk-taking. He concludes that greater disclosure is of little value unless bank examination practices and surveillance techniques (reviewed by Putnam in article twenty-three) are improved.

As pointed out in many of the essays in this collection, fixed-rate deposit insurance provides banks with a subsidy in the market for acquiring funds regardless of the risks they assume in their asset-liability management. To compensate for this imbalance, regulators have long imposed asset restrictions, capital adequacy limitations, and product and geographic restrictions on insured depository institutions. In the insightful twenty-seventh article in this book, Mark J. Flannery juxtaposes the social losses from such regulations against the social gains from a safer financial system.

A simple answer to the risk-subsidizing aspect of fixed-rate deposit insurance has not been forthcoming. The proposals for reform are varied. In a comprehensive essay, number twenty-eight in this book, Larry D. Wall surveys and analyzes the proposed deposit insurance reform schemes of the three government deposit insurance agencies: the FDIC, FHLBB, and NCUA. There seems to be strong support for variable-rate deposit insurance, some type of increased disclosure and market discipline, and a reduction in coverage of large depositors.

The preceding articles point out the problem of so many bank regulatory agencies having overlapping roles in supervising, monitoring, insuring, and regulating depository institutions. For many decades bills have appeared before Congress that would consolidate regulatory functions in fewer agencies. The latest is the outcome of a study of a Committee headed by Vice President Bush. Released in 1984, the contents of the Bush Task Force's proposals are summarized in reading number twenty-nine by Gary Gilbert.

Gilbert's article, the final selection in this volume, develops the background from which to view critically the Bush proposals. He argues that the traditional difficulty of overlap and coordination among different regulatory bodies will be aggravated in the new environment of ever-expanding geographic and product lines. Gilbert contends that the Federal Reserve should be relieved of most bank supervisory duties, that supervision of state-chartered banks and one-bank holding companies be divided between the FDIC and the various state banking commissions, and that all remaining bank and bank holding companies be supervised by a new federal banking commission.

Concepts of Financial Monitoring

Barron H. Putnam

23

Prior to 1975, the financial condition of federally regulated financial institutions was determined solely through examinations. In the mid-1970s, the five financial regulatory agencies[1] conducted separate research that led to development of the surveillance (early warning) systems in place today. These systems augment the examination process by providing evaluations of regulated financial institutions' financial condition between examinations. The term "early warning system" does not necessarily mean the prediction of an emerging problem; the term explains the process by which the bank regulators can determine if the financial condition of a banking organization has changed since the last bank examination or bank holding company inspection.

The surveillance systems of the federal agencies are made up of three components: (1) computer screening to identify outlying financial organizations that fail certain ratio tests; (2) analytical reports (performance reports) that allow an analyst or examiner to perform a detailed financial analysis of a financial organization; (3) corrective action and follow-up of problems identified through the screening process.

[1]These five agencies are the Board of Governors of the Federal Reserve System, Federal Deposit Insurance Corporation, Federal Home Loan Bank Board, National Credit Union Administration and Office of the Comptroller of the Currency.

Reprinted from *Economic Review* (November, 1983): 6–13 by permission of the Federal Reserve Bank of Atlanta and the author.

Objectives and Components of Computer Monitoring Systems

The primary objective of the regulatory agencies' computer monitoring systems is to identify changes in the financial condition of institutions that they regulate in order to prevent failure. Identification allows the agencies to allocate examination resources more efficiently among problem and emerging problem institutions. The monitoring systems also help to identify specific problem areas, thus aiding off-site analysis and helping to focus examinations towards major areas of concern.

A surveillance program's screening component is designed to identify institutions whose financial condition warrants special supervisory action. There are many ways to set up a screening mechanism. Generally speaking, screening techniques employ one or more of the following procedures:

- Screening individual ratios and identifying those institutions falling in the bottom percentile of a peer group.
- Screening individual ratios and comparing them to critical values.
- Combining ratios into a composite score and ranking the institutions from best to worst based on the composite score.
- Some combination of the above.

Once institutions are classified as weak or potentially weak, an analysis is performed to determine the extent of the financial problems and their possible causes. This constitutes the second component of a computer screening system. To perform this function, the three federal bank regulatory agencies have combined their resources and devised the Uniform Bank Performance Report, comprised of 15 pages of detailed data items and financial ratios. The information is arranged to facilitate a detailed financial analysis of a bank. These reports are provided quarterly to the approximately 14,000 insured commercial banks as well as to state bank regulators and the public. They are generated on a peer group basis that takes into account the size, the number of branches, and the urban or rural location of a bank. This is probably the most detailed analytical report of its kind and it is now being used extensively by the banking industry as well as the regulators.

Once the analytical effort confirms that a serious financial problem exists, corrective action is initiated. Corrective action can vary, from a telephone conversation with management to a cease and desist order by a court. Generally speaking, if an organization's financial condition is thought to have deteriorated seriously, the examination schedule is accelerated.

Research Leading to the Development of Computer Screening Systems

Research dealing with the prediction of firm failure provided both the conceptual framework and screening ratios now utilized in many of the federal financial institutions' surveillance systems. Edward Altman's 1968 article (2) was one of the earliest studies dealing with the prediction of failure.[2] Altman's most important contribution was his use of a statistical technique called discriminant analysis to derive a single measure or value of soundness based on a multivariate equation of financial variables.

Two other important studies dealing with the prediction of bank failure, which also employed discriminant analysis, were made by David Stuhr and Robert Van Wicklen in 1974 (43) and Joseph Sinkey (37). Stuhr and Van Wicklen used examiner ratings of banks to estimate a function that would discriminate between highly rated and poorly rated banks.

Sinkey also used examination ratings to estimate his discriminant function and hypothesized that two major factors explain banking problems: the quality of management and the honesty of employees. The financial variables he tested can be divided into the following categories: (1) liquidity, (2) loan value, (3) loan quality, (4) capital, (5) efficiency and (6) sources of revenue.

Daniel Martin (24), Carol Jean Simon (36), and Leon Korobow, David P. Stuhr and Daniel Martin (19) used a model that predicted the probability of bank (credit unions in the case of Carol Jean Simon) failure. Martin pooled his data to include 58 banks that failed between 1970 and 1976 and tested 25 different ratios. He found ratios of earnings, capital adequacy, liquidity, asset quality and risk (commercial industrial loans to total loans) to be significant in predicting bank failure. Korobow, Stuhr and Martin (19), in an extension of their earlier work, used a similar model to predict whether banks would show up on the regulators' problem list. They identified variables similar to the variables discussed later in this article. Gerald Hanweck (15) and Carol Jean Simon (36) also identified variables that could be categorized under earnings, liquidity, asset quality and capital adequacy.

Appendix A summarizes the ratios identified by these authors that best explain the identification of failing institutions. A review of these variables shows a high degree of consistency between each author's findings and supports the contention that earnings, liquidity, asset quality and capital adequacy are the main determinants of variance in financial soundness and when combined into a composite score are sufficient to rank firms according to their financial condition.

Computer Surveillance Systems of the Five Financial Regulatory Agencies

The notion that an institution's financial condition can be judged based on earnings, capital adequacy, liquidity and asset quality is used in examining banks. Bank examiners assign a numerical value (ranging from 1 to 5, where 1 is the best rating) for these four criteria and for management. This rating system, called the CAMEL rating system,[3] is employed by all three bank regulatory agencies. Basically, all five criteria receive the same weights, although examiners are free to give more weight to some variables than others. Although

[2]The Altman study was preceded by studies by Taman and Beaver in 1966.

[3]The CAMEL Rating System was adopted by the three bank regulatory agencies on November 21, 1979. See Federal Financial Institutions Examination Council (FFIEC). Uniform Financial Rating System. Press Release November 21, 1979. The acronym stands for capital, asset quality, management, earnings and liquidity.

the three banking agencies have agreed upon a uniform rating system to be used by examiners for rating banks, they have not agreed on a uniform rating system to be used for rating bank holding companies, nor have they agreed on a uniform rating system to be used in the surveillance process.

All five financial regulatory agencies use a computer screening program to identify institutions that may have potential or existing problems. These agencies employ two distinct types of screening programs. The Federal Deposit Insurance Corporation (FDIC) and the National Credit Union Administration (NCUA) identify exception institutions using a critical value by comparing a reporting bank's financial ratio value to a benchmark value the regulator feels is acceptable. If an institution fails this test, it becomes a candidate for the exception list. The Federal Reserve Board (FRB) and the Office of the Comptroller of the Currency (OCC), on the other hand, screen banks using peer groups; banks falling in the bottom of the group become exception institutions. The Federal Home Loan Bank Board (FHLBB) uses both methods.

Another major difference among the agencies is in their use of a composite score (an aggregation of financial ratios) as a measure of overall financial soundness. The FHLBB, OCC and FRB use this technique, although each employs different ratios in deriving the composite score. The FDIC does not employ a composite score.

Another difference among the agencies that affects their screening programs is the frequency and detail of the reporting series from which the screening ratios are derived. Although banking agencies primarily use the reports of condition and income for screening exceptions, the degree of detail reported varies among agencies. The difference is even more pronounced because the FHLBB collects monthly data for its surveillance system, whereas the NCUA and the three banking agencies collect their data quarterly.

Table 1 lists the ratios utilized in each agency's screening programs. The ratios are

Table 1 Screening Ratios of the Federal Financial Regulatory Institutions

Ratio	Agency Using Ratio				
	FRB	FDIC	FHLBB	NCUA	OCC
Capital					
(1) Equity Capital Decrease		X			
(2) Equity Capital/Total Assets		C	X		X
(3) Retained Earnings/Average Equity Capital					X
(4) Equity Capital/Adjusted Equity Capital	X				
(5) Gross Capital/Adjusted Risk Assets	X				
(6) Reserves to Total Loans				C	
(7) Net Scheduled Items/Net Worth			X		
Profitability					
(1) Net Operating Income/Average Total Assets		C			
(2) Net Income/Assets			X		X
(3) Interest Expense on Deposits and Federal Funds Purchased and Borrowings/Total Operating Income		C			
(4) Total Expenses-(Provision for Loan Losses + Dividends)/Gross Income				C	
(5) Adjusted Return on Assets					X
(6) Net Income/Total Assets-Cash Items	X				X
(7) Total Other Earnings/Average Assets					X
(8) Gross Operating Income/Average Assets			X		
(9) Net Income/Gross Income			X		
(10) Net Operating Income/Gross Operating Income			X		

Asset Quality					
(1) Delinquent Loans/Total Assets			X		
(2) RFO and LTF's/Total Assets			X		
(3) Delinquent Loans/All Reserves				C	
(4) Delinquent Loan Ratio				C	
(5) Gross Loan Losses/NOI + Provision	X				
(6) Provision for Possible Loan Losses/ Average Assets					X
(7) Speculative Lending/Total Assets			X		
(8) Gross Charge-offs − Recoveries/ Average Loans		C			
(9) Net Scheduled Items/Total Assets			X		
Liquidity					
(1) Net Borrowings-Mortgages/Cash and Due from Banks + Total Securities Maturing in One Year or Less		C			
Interest Sensitivity and Liabilities for Borrowed Money					
(1) $100,000 or more Time Deposits + Net Borrowings/Total Loans		C			
(2) Advances + Borrowed Money/Total Savings			X		
(3) Interest-Sensitive Funds/Total Sources of Funds	X				
(4) High-Rate Savings/Total Savings			X		
Efficiency Ratios					
(1) Total Operating Expenses/Total Operating Income	X				
(2) Noninterest Expense/Total Operating Income−Interest Expense	X				
(3) Cost of Savings (YTD)/Total Savings			X		
(4) Net Interest Earnings/Average Assets					X
(5) Operating Expense/Average Assets			X		
(6) Cost of Money/Average Savings and Borrowings			X		
Change Ratios					
(1) Asset Growth Ratio			X		
(2) Change in Asset Mix					X
(3) Change in Liability Mix					X
(4) Change in Loan Mix					X
(5) Percent Change in Total Savings			X		
(6) Percent Change in Mortgage Loans			X		
(7) Percent Change in Shares (from Previous Period)				C	
(8) Percent Change in Time Deposits			C		
(9) Percent Change in Other Time Deposits			C		
(10) Loan Growth Exceeds Deposits Growth			C		
Change Ratios					
(11) Cash Dividends on Common + Preferred Stock/Net Income		C			
(12) Cash Dividends/Net Income	X				
Other Ratios					
(1) Commercial and Industrial Loans/ Total Loans, Gross	X				
(2) Mortgage Commitments/Total Assets			X		
(3) All Other Commitments/Total Assets			X		

Source: This table was derived from information provided by the five federal financial regulatory agencies. The information is as of November 1981; since that time the ratios or screening procedures could have been changed.

arranged by categories that represent the key operations of a financial institution. An "X" on the right hand side of this table indicates that the agency utilizes the ratio. The "C" value indicates that the agency utilizes a critical value in the screening program.

Determinants of Financial Soundness

Financial soundness is a measure of a company's financial condition at a certain time. On an accounting basis, financial soundness can be broken down into two parts: (1) earnings based on the income statement, and (2) net worth based on the balance sheet. The evolution of the examination process and review of research on bank failure indicate that the balance sheet can be evaluated using three key classes of variables: asset quality, liquidity, and capital adequacy. The income statement should be represented by the bottom line figure of net income. To determine financial soundness, these four categories of variables need to be aggregated into a composite score. Derivation of such a score will allow one to rank firms according to financial soundness. The aggregation process could be based on an equation where the parameters have been previously estimated or by using other techniques that allow normalization of the ratios so that they can be added into a composite score.

Earnings

Once a firm is established, earnings become the most obvious component of financial soundness. A firm cannot sustain itself long without a positive flow of income; it is from earnings that capital is retained for growth. The other variables affect earnings in one way or another. Poor asset quality can lead to write-off assets or reduced earnings. Increased leveraging usually can increase the return on stockholders' equity, but at a greater risk. By shifting to less liquid assets, perhaps extending the maturity of a security; earnings may be increased. Yet, the risk of possible insolvency is also increased.

Asset Quality

This attribute is particularly important for financial institutions because they assume both a credit and interest risk on most of their assets. Since these institutions are highly leveraged (equity capital to asset ratios range from about 5 to 10 percent), large loan or security losses can bring insolvency. High fluctuations in interest rates can cause large appreciation or depreciation in the value of long-term fixed rate assets. For financial organizations, the quality of assets will be affected both by management's control over its credit review function and by economic conditions. A look at current recessionary periods shows that nonperforming loans and loan charge-offs increased substantially during these periods. Because the quality of assets is to be reflected in the income stream, it should be included when identifying the financial condition of firms.

Conditional vs. Unconditional Risk Variables

The agency screening process attempts to identify risk that could cause an institution to encounter financial difficulties. The complexity of this risk is why many of the federal financial regulatory agencies' computer screens are as cumbersome as Table 1 illustrates. Based on a review of these screens, there appears to be a need for a better theoretical rationale for the mix of variables used. Understanding the difference between various kinds of risk relating to financial soundness can help in predicting problem or failing institutions. When predicting changes in financial condition, there are basically two types of risk variables to be considered: conditional and unconditional. Examples of unconditional risk variables are capital adequacy and liquidity. Generally speaking, firms that are highly leveraged or illiquid are thought to be riskier than firms with stronger capital and liquidity positions. Conditional risk takes into account positions whose outcomes will depend upon changing economic or structural conditions. For example, firms may purchase long-term securities that may be profitable if interest rates fall or remain stable but could lead to losses if interest rates rise (assuming no hedging). A large degree of market or product concentration may also be a conditional form of risk since a firm's profitability can depend on how economic conditions affect both its product and market area. In the case of the banking industry, bank examiners were quite aware of the effects that the poor economic conditions of 1982 had on smaller banks whose markets were concentrated in farming communities. They also saw similar financial problems for banks serving areas dependent on the auto and forestry industries.

Conditional risk variables (ratios) should not be used in standard screens without a specific set of assumptions. That is not to say that these financial variables (ratios) may not be useful in identifying firms likely to have problems. These types of ratios are better utilized in special screens that take into account projections of the direction and degree of change in economic conditions. When setting up such screens, one must also supplement the "conditional ratio screen" with an "unconditional ratio screen" that measures overall financial soundness. The need to do this is obvious; the effects of a wrong decision (as measured by the conditional ratio screen) by bank management are more likely to be absorbed by the financially strong firm (as measured by the unconditional ratio screen) than by a financially weak firm.

Liquidity

Financial firms that depend on deposits and purchased funds must have a reserve to meet unexpected deposit withdrawals or refunding needs. A sudden change in market conditions could cause funding problems for financially weak firms. Although liquidity does not appear to be the original cause of financial problems for banks, it is usually a firm's inability to meet liquidity needs that causes its ultimate demise. Measures of liquidity for financial institutions will differ from those used for industrial firms.

Capital Adequacy

A firm's equity capital plus reserves serve as a cushion to absorb losses: The lower the capital base relative to the firm's operations, the greater the risk of insolvency. We must take into consideration the earnings performance as well as the level of capital adequacy. Obviously, firms with a high return on good quality assets can assume more risk through leveraging than others with lesser return and/or asset quality having the same capital ratios. Only when earnings turn to losses does the true test of capital adequacy take place. When a firm suffers large sustained losses, capital adequacy becomes all-important.

Conclusion

To classify institutions according to their financial condition, we need a conceptual framework. Based on examination experience and previously developed early warning models, we conclude that there are four primary determinants of financial soundness: earnings, liquidity, asset quality and capital adequacy. These four determinants appear to be sufficient to rank firms according to their financial condition when they are aggregated into a composite score that takes into account the determinants' respective weights.

Appendix A
Financial Ratios Identified to Predict Failing Firms

Edward Altman (2)

- Working capital/total assets
- Retained earnings/total assets
- Earnings before interest and taxes/total assets
- Market value equity/book value of total debt
- Sales/total assets

David Stuhr and Robert Van Wicklen (43)

- Asset quality (ratio of classified and special mentioned assets to bank capital)
- Capital adequacy (capital to assets)
- Management (three variables were used, the most important of which were net operating income to assets and a debt to equity ratio)
- Asset size of bank
- Net occupancy expense to net income
- Loans to total assets ratio

Joseph Sinkey (37) 1975

- Liquidity
- Loan volume
- Loan quality
- Capital adequacy
- Efficiency
- Sources of revenue

Daniel Martin (24)

- Net income to total assets (earnings variable)
- Gross charge-offs to net operating income (asset quality)
- Expenses to operating revenues
- Loans to total assets
- Commercial loans to total loans (risk variable)
- Gross capital to risk assets (capital adequacy)

Korobow, Stuhr and Martin (20)

- Loans and leases to total sources of funds (liquidity variable)
- Equity capital to adjusted risk assets (capital adequacy)
- Operating expenses to operating revenues (income variable)
- Gross charge-offs to net income plus provisions for loan losses (asset quality)
- Commercial and industrial loans to total loans (risk variable)

BIBLIOGRAPHY

1. ALTMAN, EDWARD I. *Corporate Financial Distress: A Complete Guide to Predicting, Avoiding and Dealing with Bankruptcy*. New York: John Wiley and Sons, 1983.
2. ALTMAN, EDWARD I. "Financial Ratios, Discriminant Analysis and the Prediction of Corporate Bankruptcy," *Journal of Finance*, (September 1968) pp. 589-609.
3. ALTMAN, EDWARD I. and ARNOLD W. SAMETZ. *Financial Crises: Institutions and Markets in a Fragile Environment*. New York: John Wiley & Sons, Inc., 1977.
4. ALTMAN, EDWARD I., R. HALDEMAN and P. NARAYANAN. "ZETA Analysis: A New Model for Bankruptcy Identification," *Journal of Banking and Finance* 1, (June 1977).
5. ALTMAN, EDWARD I., ROBERT AVERY, ROBERT A. EISENBEIS and JOSEPH F. SINKEY, JR. *Application of Classification Technique in Business Banking and Finance*. Contemporary Studies in Economic and Financial Analysis, Vol. 3. Greenwich, Connecticut: Jai Press, Inc., 1981.
6. BEAVER, W. H. "Financial Ratios as Predictions of Failure," *Journal of Accounting Research* 4, (1966) pp. 71–127.
7. BEAVER, W. H. "Market Prices, Financial Ratios and the Prediction of Failure," *Journal of Accounting Research*, (Autumn 1968).
8. BENSTON, GEORGE. "How We Can Learn From Past Bank Failures," *Bankers' Magazine*, Vol. 158, (Winter 1975).

9. COLLINS, ROBERT A. and RICHMOND D. GREEN. "Statistical Models for Bankruptcy Forecasting," *Journal of Economics and Business* 34, (1982) pp. 349–354.

10. COSSLETT, STEPHEN R. "Efficient Estimation of Discrete Choice Models," In *Structural Analysis of Discrete Data with Econometric Applications,* ed. C. Manski and D. McFadden. Cambridge, Massachusetts: MIT Press, 1981.

11. EISENBEIS, ROBERT A. "Financial Early Warning Systems: Status and Future Directions," *Issues in Bank Regulation* 1(Summer 1977) pp. 8–12.

12. EISENBEIS, ROBERT A., GARY G. GILBERT and ROBERT B. AVERY. "Investigating the Relative Importance of Individual Variables and Variable Subsets in Discriminant Analysis," *Communications in Statistics* 2 (1973) pp. 205–219.

13. FLANNERY, MARK J. and JACK M. GUTTENTAG. "Identifying Problem Banks," *Proceedings of a Conference on Bank Structure and Competition, Federal Reserve Bank of Chicago* (May 3–4, 1979).

14. GHEVA, DAVID and MEIR SOKOLER. "An Alternative Approach to the Problem of Classification—The Case of Bank Failures in Israel," *Journal of Bank Research* 12 (Winter 1982) pp. 228–238.

15. HANWECK, GERALD A. "Predicting Bank Failures," Research Papers in Banking and Financial Economics, Financial Studies Section, Board of Governors of the Federal Reserve System (1977).

16. HO, THOMAS and ANTHONY SAUNDERS. "A Catastrophe Model of Bank Failure," *Journal of Finance,* (December 1980) pp. 1189–1207.

17. JOY, O. MAURICE and JOHN O. TOLLEFSON. "On the Financial Applications of Discriminant Analysis," *Journal of Financial and Quantitative Analysis* 10 (December 1975) pp. 723–739.

18. KOROBOW, LEON. "Measuring and Managing Bank Risk: Some Recent History," Paper presented to the Third International Symposium on Forecasting sponsored by the Wharton School, (June 5, 1983), Philadelphia.

19. KOROBOW, LEON and DAVID STUHR. "Toward Early Warning of Changes in Banks' Financial Condition: A Progress Report," Federal Reserve Bank of New York *Monthly Review,* (July 1975), pp. 157–165.

20. KOROBOW, LEON, DAVID STUHR and DANIEL MARTIN. "A Nationwide Test of Early Warning Research in Banking," Federal Reserve Bank of New York *Quarterly Review.* (Autumn 1977).

21. KOROBOW, LEON, DAVID STUHR and DANIEL MARTIN. "A Probabilistic Approach to Early Warning Changes in Bank Financial Condition," Federal Reserve Bank of New York *Monthly Review,* (July 1976) pp. 187–194.

22. MANSKI, CHARLES F. and STEVEN R. LERMAN. "The Estimation of Choice Probabilities From Choice Based Samples," *Econometrics* 45 (November 1977) 1977–1988.

23. MARTIN, DANIEL. "Early Warning of Bank Failure," *Journal of Finance,* 1st Quarter, 1977.

24. MARTIN, DANIEL. "Early Warning of Bank Failure: A Logit Regression Approach," *Journal of Banking and Finance* 1, 1977.

25. MEYER, P. A. and H. W. PIFER. "Prediction of Bank Failure," *Journal of Finance,* (September 1970), pp. 853–868.

26. MILLER, R.G. *Simultaneous Statistical Inference,* New York: McGraw Hill Book Company, 1966.

27. PANY, KURT and LAWRENCE F. SHERMAN. "Information Analysis of Several Large Failed Banks," *Journal of Bank Research,* (Autumn 1979), pp. 145–151.

28. PETTWAY, RICHARD H. and JOSEPH SINKEY, JR. "Establishing On-Site Bank Examination Priorities: An Early Warning System Using Accounting and Market Information," *Journal of Finance* (March 1980).
29. PETTWAY, RICHARD H. "Potential Insolvency, Market Efficiency, and Bank Regulation of Large Commercial Banks," *Journal of Finance and Quantitative Analysis* 15 (March 1980) pp. 219–236.
30. PUTNAM, BARRON. "An Empirical Model of Financial Soundness: A Case Study for Bank Holding Companies," Ph.D. Dissertation, George Washington University, Washington, D.C., (February 1983).
31. PUTNAM, BARRON. "Computer Screening Methods Employed by the Five Financial Regulatory Institutions to Identify Banks Having Actual or Potential Financial Problems," (November 13, 1981).
32. RAO, C. R. "Inference on Discriminant Function Coefficients," *Essays in Probability and Statistics,* eds. R. C. Bose et al., Chapel Hill: University of North Carolina and Statistical Publishing Society 1970, pp. 587–602.
33. ROSE, PETER S. and WILLIAM L. SCOTT. "Risk in Commercial Banking: Evidence from Postwar Failures," *Southern Economic Journal* 45, 1978, pp. 90–106.
34. SANTOMERO, ANTHONY M. and JOSEPH D. VINSO. "Estimating the Probability of Failure for Commercial Banks and the Banking System," *Journal of Banking and Finance* 1, 1977, pp. 185–205.
35. SHICK, RICHARD A. and LAWRENCE F. SHERMAN. "Bank Stock Prices as an Early Warning System for Changes in Condition," *Journal of Bank Research,* 11 (Autumn 1980) pp. 136–46.
36. SIMON, CAROL JEAN. "Predicting the Failure of Credit Unions: An Application of Multivariate Logit Analysis," Masters Thesis. Massachusetts Institute of Technology, (June 1980).
37. SINKEY, JOSEPH. "A Multivariate Statistical Analysis of the Characteristics of Problem Banks," *Journal of Finance,* (March 1975) pp. 21–38.
38. SINKEY, JOSEPH. "Identifying Large Problem/Failed Banks: The Case of Franklin National Bank of New York," *Journal of Financial and Quantitative Analysis,* 1977, pp. 779–800.
39. SINKEY, JOSEPH. "Identifying 'Problem' Banks: How Do the Banking Authorities Measure a Bank's Risk Exposure?" *Journal of Money, Credit and Banking* 10, (May 1978) pp. 184–93.
40. SINKEY, JOSEPH. *Problem and Failed Institutions in the Commercial Bank Industry,* Contemporary Studies in Economic and Financial Analysis, Vol. 4, Greenwich, Connecticut: Jai Press Inc., 1979.
41. SINKEY, JOSEPH and DAVID A. WALKER. "Problem Banks: Identification and Characteristics," *Journal of Bank Research* 5 (Winter 1975) pp. 208–17.
42. SINKEY, JOSEPH. "The Failure of United States National Bank of San Diego: A Portfolio and Performance Analysis," *Journal of Bank Research* 6 (Spring 1975) pp. 8–24.
43. STUHR, DAVID P. and ROBERT VAN WICKLEN. "Rating and Financial Condition of Banks: A Statistical Approach to Aid Bank Supervision," *Monthly Review,* Federal Reserve Bank of New York 56 (September 1974) pp. 233–38.

A Review of Bank Capital and Its Adequacy

James G. Ehlen, Jr.

24

The role of capital in banking is no different from its mission in any business endeavor. It reflects a core or base of funds permanently employed in the business that affords a sense of financial stability to the organization and the wherewithal to deal with adversity. The degree of its presence generally is viewed as a measure of relative financial strength.

In both banking and industry, the adequacy of capital is an elusive measure. Perhaps the only real determinant of adequacy is the aggregate consensus of the marketplace—that is, leverage, or the inverse of the capital ratio, should be extended until the marketplace reacts adversely and reflects concern.

This presentation will focus on the principal factors that influence the marketplace's perception of bank capital. We believe such factors are the perspective of history, regulatory guidelines, current trends, and the degree of recent stability.

However, before exploring the role of capital or reflecting on determinants of its adequacy, we need to define capital in its contemporary sense within the context of banking. Generally, or at least in an industrial context, capital suggests simply the owner's equity in the organization. Over the past decade or so, capital within the banking industry has become, due to regulatory convention, a blending of common stockholders' equity, reserves and other permanent or semi-permanent sources of funds.

Reprinted from *Economic Review* (November, 1983): 54–60 by permission of the Federal Reserve Bank of Atlanta and the author.

Capital in the Current Sense

In December 1981, the principal commercial bank regulatory agencies adopted a common definition of what constitutes capital for commercial banks. Capital was said to consist of two basic components, primary (or permanent) capital and other capital (Table 1).

Appropriately, this framework clearly separated bank capital into the permanent component and other long-term funds. Importantly, from our point of view, the permanent funds employed in the business constitute real capital, whereas the other longer-term funds do not reflect a permanent call on resources available to weather adversity and therefore take a position of lesser importance.

Other capital, in particular subordinated notes and debentures (often referred to as capital notes), became popular in the late 1960s as a device to bolster sagging overall capital ratios. Regulatory guidelines soon permitted a banking company to maintain up to one-third of its overall capital in the form of debt with an original maturity in excess of seven years.

While such a definition of capital allowed the banks to *appear* better "capitalized," it did absolutely nothing to correct the basic problem of declining equity ratios. Simply stated, banks were able to stabilize their capital ratios by progressively issuing capital notes up to the aggregate limitations. At that point, without correcting the basic reason for the declining equity capital ratio, overall capital ratios would mathematically commence to decline once again. Clearly, there is a balance sheet role for long-term funds that carry maturities in excess of normal deposits. However, we believe the role is more oriented toward our concept of liquidity rather than toward capital.

Thus, while total capital funds from a regulatory viewpoint include a variety of forms, our principal focus rests with the permanent sources of capital representing equity in the business.

The Role of Capital

Capital, or more specifically equity and reserves in a banking context, plays a rather singular role of demonstrating financial strength and stability. Basically, capital stands ready to absorb adverse financial developments that could impair the viability of continuity

Table 1

Primary (permanent) Capital
Common equity (including equity reserves)
Perpetual preferred stock
Loan-loss reserve
Other instruments with a mandatory conversion-to-common equity feature
Other Capital Items
Convertible securities
Subordinated notes and debentures
Sinking fund preferred stock

of a bank's business. It is a vital component of the on-going confidence necessary to a depository institution. Unlike other components of the balance sheet, it provides only a limited passive role in the business as a source of cost-free funds (for instance, perpetual preferred dividends are declared from earnings).

In many ways we view bank equity much like a fire extinguishing system in a modern building. It is designed to inspire confidence. If it must be used, little will be the same afterwards, but the building itself will survive.

The point is often made that banks do not fail due to inadequate capital. Such a statement is true as far as it goes. Lack of capital does not cause a failure. Failures are more often due to massive real or prospective losses on earning assets or the loss of liquidity, which itself is usually related to the perception of prospective losses. However, if the equity were sufficient to absorb the prospective losses, liquidity would likely not be threatened. After a bank failure, there is seldom residual equity available for distribution to common stockholders. Thus, while inadequate equity does not precipitate failure, it is the inevitable result of a failure. Accordingly, we conclude that a bank would not fail if capital were in fact adequate. To take this to an extreme: would a bank with 100 percent equity ever fail?

Several years ago, the New York Federal Reserve Bank employed a capital measurement plan based on a liquidation concept. The notion was that equity should be sufficient to protect depositors if it were necessary to liquidate the bank. Specific percentages were allocated to various types of risk assets. Then the adequacy of an institution's equity was measured in terms of whether the equity was sufficient to cover the percentages allocated. The concept was that the equity capital provided a cushion against the risk inherent in the bank's assets. Such an approach has its merits in that it established a specific standard. However, the standards were not flexible to changing credit or interest rate risk. More practically, the framework fell into disuse as large banks in the jurisdiction found it increasingly difficult to maintain the specified standards.

The point has on occasion been made that the strength of a financial institution and its first line of defense against adversity is earning power, with the corollary being that capital is of lesser importance. To the extent that earning power is measured in terms of profitability, or return on assets, we cannot quarrel with this.

However, unless the dividend payout ratio is uniquely high, a relatively high return on assets is almost always associated with a relatively well-capitalized bank. *Thus, it would be difficult to divorce empirically the perceived value of a high level of profitability from a well-capitalized bank. They go hand in hand.* In fact the only variable that can alter this relationship would be the rate of asset growth. And in the event of adversity, asset growth could be discretionarily controlled by management. An additional factor to remember is that adversity, almost by definition, suggests a strain on earning power. To the extent that earning power is reduced or eliminated, the focus will necessarily shift to capital.

Thus, we suggest strongly that capital plays a critical, although passive, role in maintaining the financial strength and credibility of a financial institution in the marketplace, a vital role for any institution that must rely on continuing access to funds from a wide array of sources.

Capital is often viewed as a basis for adjusting for relative degrees of business risk. That is, the greater the perceived business risk, the greater the level of capital employed in the business. It is interesting that the reverse is often true where banks with greater perceived asset risks have lower equity capital ratios. A classic example is the lower level of equity ratios among multinational banks that have the greater proportion of LDC risk exposure relative to regional banks.

Capital Adequacy and the Marketplace

With the role of capital defined as a measure of financial strength, we believe that its adequacy can only be determined by the cumulative view of the marketplace, which itself is the judge of financial strength.

Except for the influence of specific regulatory minimums or guidelines, the judgment of the marketplace tends to focus on relative rather than absolute levels.

For example, if equity ratios were appreciably lower today than they were several years ago, it would be logical for the marketplace to assume relative inadequacy. Conversely, a recently improved trend would suggest adequacy. In fact, equity ratios have generally stabilized in recent years following a decade of decline. The longer that current equity levels are maintained, the greater the perception of adequacy will become. *Stability creates a benchmark of adequacy.*

Closely related to the influence of historic trends on the marketplace's perception are the current or prospective factors influencing the stability of equity ratios or measurable shifts in the degree of risk inherent in bank portfolios.

Finally, the marketplace is strongly influenced by regulatory definitions of adequate capital, especially when they are expressed in specific terms.

Historic Perspective on Capital Ratios

Banking commentaries unsupported by actual data often refer to the declining trend of bank equity capital ratios. Equity ratios have, in fact, been relatively stable in recent years but *did* decline significantly between the mid-1960s and the mid-1970s. Average equity as a percent of average total assets has declined very modestly among money-center banks and increased slightly at regional banks over the past nine years.

However, equity capital ratios at the 25 largest banks as of year end 1976 reflected a decline of 38.9 percent from year end 1966.

As we will discuss in greater depth subsequently, maintaining equity capital ratios (except external infusions) is a mathematical function of four variables:

- return on assets (profitability),
- level of dividend payout,
- existing equity-to-asset ratio, and
- growth rate of assets.

The decline that took place in equity ratios, then, resulted because asset growth was higher than the rate of equity retention. Or, stated another way, profitability was too low to support the asset growth.

Until the early 1960s, bank asset expansion was funded principally by demand deposits and consumer savings deposits. Spreads earned on these sources of funds were large enough to allow for significant capital account growth and also to permit generally high dividends. Assuming a prime rate of 6 percent, a passbook rate of 4 percent, a capital to asset ratio of 9 percent, a reserve requirement of 5 percent, and compensating balances of 15 percent, a bank could earn 143 basis points after taxes—a 15.8 percent return on capital. Assuming no debt in the capital structure and a 50 percent dividend payout ratio, this 15.8 percent return would support equity capital account growth of approximately 8 percent.

If the dividend payout ratio were reduced to 33 percent, the return would support equity growth at 11.1 percent. At either rate, assets could expand the same amount with the equity-to-asset ratio remaining in equilibrium. Arithmetically, if the equity capital backing of assets were lower, the same level of profitability and dividend payout would support greater asset growth while equity ratios remained in equilibrium.

During the early 1970s, however, larger banks supported the bulk of their earning asset growth with certificates of deposits (CDs) and borrowed funds. Historically, it appears that the prime rate was not properly set in relation to the cost of marginal funds (CDs and other borrowings such as federal funds). Banks must have relied on an average-cost analytical framework when their emphasis should have been on marginal costs. As a result, maintaining a constant equity capital ratio through retained earnings was mathematically impossible.

From 1964–1974, the average spread between the prime rate and the composite cost of CDs and federal funds was approximately 45 basis points. Given this spread, a 5 percent reserve requirement on the CDs, a compensating balance of 10 percent, a 7 percent prime rate, a 50 percent tax rate, and a 10-basis-point cost of servicing the lending relationship, the after-tax return on such a loan would be 0.40 percent. If the compensating balance were adjusted upward to 20 percent, the return would improve to 0.88 percent. However, even an 0.88 percent return on an incremental asset could not support much asset growth if the dividend remained at 50 percent and equity ratios were as robust as was implied by the old New York Federal Reserve Bank formula, which suggests 12 percent capital backing behind risk assets. *The easy solution was to operate in disequilibrium and permit the equity-to-asset ratio to decline.*

Recent Ratio Stability and Financial Equilibrium

Since equity ratios declined to where they could be supported by the lower, but stabilized, profitability levels, both the Goldman Sachs & Co. regional and money-center indices have operated within a relatively stable range of financial equilibrium. Since 1975, the internally funded asset growth rate has more or less mirrored the actual growth rate of assets.

Accordingly, if bank profitability and capital ratios remain stable in the future, we believe that banking observers will become increasingly more sanguine in their concern over declining ratios. The record will reflect a greater degree of stability and in time the decline that took place in the 1960s will lose significance.

Regulatory Guidelines

In December 1981, the Federal Reserve Board and the Office of the Comptroller of the Currency issued specific capital adequacy guidelines for regional and community banks. They were amended in June 1983 to include multinational banks. Originally, 17 multinationals had been exempted from specific minimum ratios on the argument that their businesses were so complex as to require individual subjective analysis. However, most multinationals boosted their ratios significantly by issuing primary (equity) capital prior to their inclusion at the same minimum capital levels as the large regional banks. This suggests that low levels of equity were important reasons for their earlier exclusion.

We view regulators' action in drafting guidelines as being especially significant. It specifically establishes a definition of what constitutes capital and sets minimum standards from a regulatory point of view. Such a regulatory minimum then becomes an important benchmark for the marketplace's evaluation of adequacy. Additionally, it provides a basis for banks to utilize themselves in their corporate planning.

Historically, regulators generally relied on a peer group evaluation of capital adequacy that we believe was deficient on at least two counts. Half the banks in any given peer group were always by definition under capitalized, and the break between peer groups was highly subjective. Clearly, this system could not gain the support of financial analysts. In addition, since it dealt with a floating ratio rather than a specific analytical framework, no clear signals were sent to the marketplace regarding the regulatory view on adequacy. Thus, the new regulatory guidelines are very valuable.

Earlier we presented the regulatory definition of the two components of total bank capital: primary capital and other capital. In adopting the new guidelines, banking institutions are placed in one of three categories:

- Multinationals—as designated by their principal regulatory agency
- Regionals—all banks with over $1 billion in assets not designated as multinationals
- Community banks—all others.

For multinational and regional banks, the minimum acceptable level of primary capital is 5 percent. For community banks, the minimum standard was set at 6 percent. Regulatory agencies emphasize that in both cases these are minimum standards that should be exceeded.

For evaluating total capital adequacy, three categories have been set. Capital will be deemed adequate for Category I banks if their primary capital ratios are above the guideline minimums. Category II banks will be viewed as potentially undercapitalized and subject to extensive regulatory discussion. Category III will be considered undercapitalized and placed under continuing regulatory supervision. In applying these tests, regulatory agencies focus on consolidated entities. Thus, multibank holding companies are assessed on a consolidated basis rather than in terms of each individual bank.

Current and Prospective Trends

We argue that compliance with these new capital adequacy guidelines is now, by far, the most influential factor in the marketplace's determination of adequacy. Thus, a review of the industry's current compliance is appropriate. Table 2 shows primary and total capital expressed as a percent of total assets as of June 30, 1983, at selected banks. As a group these selected institutions exceed the minimum standards in both the primary and total capital categories.

The exceptions are among the multinationals, basically with respect to primary capital levels. Table 3 focuses in detail on the 10 largest banking companies as of June 30. Common equity equalled approximately 4 percent of total assets, the loan-loss reserves stood at 0.68 percent of assets, and other accredited forms of primary capital accounted for 0.49 percent of assets, placing the total primary capital for the group on average at 5.15 percent of total assets. Four institutions do not meet the minimum primary capital standards set by regulatory agencies. However, the shortfall is insignificant and can be met easily with "other" primary equity. Thus, as of June 1983, the industry appears to be in compliance with acceptable levels of capital adequacy.

The key question then relates to the prospects for future compliance. Here primary capital is the critical issue. Total capital is of less interest to us, since it tends to have more liquidity than capital characteristics and lacks permanence.

Focusing on primary capital and its three components, we tend to view common equity and the loan-loss reserve in concert given the obvious relationship we will address shortly. The other accepted forms of primary capital, principally perpetual preferred stock or mandatory convertible securities, are quite different. They constitute one-time capital market infusions and have no self-maintenance aspects. That is, there is no natural recurring mechanism for their growth as there is with common equity. In this regard, the important question is how much of the "other" primary capital can be included in total primary capital? We cannot answer this because we believe it can be addressed only by the marketplace. However, we believe that the important issue is not how much of an "extender" or supplement to common equity is used, but rather the level of common equity (and loan-loss reserves) itself.

Aside from external infusions, the maintenance of primary equity capital depends on the retention rate of equity expressed as a percentage of total assets and the rate of asset expansion. For example, if equity retained (net income less dividends) equals .50 percent of assets and total equity represents 5 percent of total assets, asset growth of 10 percent would be consistent with perpetual asset growth of 10 percent. Assuming the same level of retention, a faster asset growth rate implies shrinkage in the equity to asset ratio.

In aggregate the first half 1983 (annualized) asset return at the 10 largest banks was 0.58 percent. After deducting the cost of primary capital, which is the common preferred dividend and interest expense in the case of mandatory conversion notes, the retention rate was 0.35 percent of total assets. Recall the 3.99 percent asset to equity ratio as of June 30 for these same 10 banks shown in Table 3. It follows mathematically that to maintain the 3.99 percent equity to asset level, total assets can only grow at 8.75 percent. Such is not likely to be the case. *Accordingly, for the multinationals profitability must improve, or the common equity ratio is apt to decline.* Thus, although the large banks appear to be at or

Table 2 Equity Capital Ratio for 40 Selected Banking Organizations

	As a Percent of Period-End Total Assets at 6/30/83					
	Common Equity	Loan-Loss Reserve	Other Primary Capital	Total Primary Capital	Estimated Other Capital	Total Capital
Allied Bancshares	6.22%	1.01	—	7.23%	0.61%	7.84%
Bank of Boston Corp.*	4.93	0.68	—	5.61	1.62	7.23
BankAmerica Corp.	3.63	0.57	0.58	4.78	0.64	5.41
Bankers Trust N.Y. Corp.	4.06	0.64	0.92	5.62	0.60	6.22
Barnett Banks of Florida	4.90	0.66	—	5.56	2.30	7.86
Chase Manhattan Corp.	3.56	0.68	0.46	4.70	1.45	6.16
Chemical N. Y. Corp.	3.80	0.65	0.68	5.13	1.45	6.58
Citicorp	3.80	0.56	0.30	4.66	2.18	6.85
Citizens & Southern (Ga.)	5.62	0.76	—	6.39	2.00	8.39
Citizens Fidelity Corp.	6.60	0.94	—	7.53	—	7.53
Continental Illinois Corp.	4.22	0.92	—	5.14	3.10	8.25
Crocker National Corp.	4.80	0.58	0.11	5.49	0.78	6.27
First Bank System	5.19	0.65	—	5.84	2.34	8.18
First Chicago Corp.	4.06	0.61	0.71	5.38	0.88	6.27
First City Bancorp of Texas	5.43	0.71	0.04	6.18	1.44	7.62
First Interstate Bancorp	4.59	0.74	—	5.33	2.81	8.14
First Union Corp.*	4.91	0.76	0.05	5.71	0.65	6.36
InterFirst Corp.	6.10	0.74	—	6.84	2.41	9.25
Irving Bank Corp.	4.29	0.76	—	5.06	1.46	6.52
Manufacturers Hanover Corp.	3.41	0.59	0.79	4.79	4.01	8.50
Maryland National Corp.	6.15	0.67	—	6.81	4.35	11.16
Mellon National Corp.	5.12	0.89	—	6.02	2.50	8.51
Mercantile Texas Corp.	5.63	0.78	—	6.41	1.78	8.19
J. P. Morgan & Co.	4.92	0.70	0.84	6.47	0.68	7.15
National City Corp.	6.22	0.60	—	6.82	1.26	8.08
NCNB Corp.	4.81	0.62	—	5.43	2.09	7.52
Norwest Corporation*	5.18	0.74	—	5.92	7.46	13.38
PNC Financial	6.25	0.71	—	6.96	—	6.96
Rainier Bancorporation	6.19	0.80	—	6.99	—	6.99
RepublicBank Corporation	5.22	0.75	—	5.97	1.95	7.92
Republic N.Y. Corp.*	3.47	0.49	1.03	5.00	3.53	8.53
Security Pacific Corp.	4.46	0.87	—	5.33	0.64	5.97
Southwest Bancshares	5.46	0.66	—	6.12	1.67	7.79
Sun Banks	5.87	0.50	—	6.37	1.16	7.53
Texas American Bancshares	6.16	0.68	—	6.84	2.64	9.48
Texas Commerce Bancshares	5.46	0.70	—	6.16	0.29	6.45
U. S. Bancorp.	8.08	0.64	—	8.72	3.70	12.41
Valley National Corp.	5.67	0.63	—	6.30	0.67	6.97
Wachovia Corp.	6.68	0.77	0.01	7.47	0.18	7.65
Wells Fargo & Co.	4.46	0.77	—	5.23	1.24	6.47
Average	5.14	0.71	0.16	6.01	1.76	7.77

*March 31, 1983.

Source: Goldman, Sachs & Co.

Table 3 Equity Capital Ratios of Ten Largest Banking Organizations

	As a Percent of Period-End Total Assets at 6/30/83			
	Common Equity	Loan-Loss Reserve	Other Primary Capital	Total Primary Capital
BankAmerica Corp.	3.63%	0.57%	0.58%	4.78%
Bankers Trust N. Y. Corp.	4.06	0.64	0.92	5.62
Chase Manhattan Bank	3.56	0.68	0.46	4.70
Chemical N. Y. Corp.	3.80	0.65	0.68	5.13
Citicorp	3.80	0.57	0.30	4.67
Continental Illinois	4.22	0.92	—	5.14
First Chicago Corp.	4.06	0.61	0.71	5.38
Manufacturers Hanover Corp.	3.41	0.59	0.79	4.79
J. P. Morgan & Co.	4.92	0.70	0.42	6.04
Security Pacific Corp.	4.46	0.87	—	5.33
Average	3.99%	0.68%	0.49%	5.15%

Source: Goldman, Sachs & Co.

above minimum primary capital standards, we believe future maintenance of minimum standards may be a problem.

Enlarging our universe to include the regionals, common equity ratio maintenance does not appear to be as great a problem.

An interesting relationship exists between common equity and the loan-loss reserve. Historically, bank observers considered only half the loan-loss reserve a form of equity on the theory that half the reserve belonged to stockholders while the other half, having been built out of tax deductions, represented a deferred tax claim of the government. Now, with regulators giving full credit for the loan-loss reserve, it has a potential for leveraging. To build primary capital by $1 through common equity, $2 in pre-tax earnings are required. However, $2 in pre-tax earnings allocated to the loan-loss reserve results in a full $2 increase in primary capital. Thus, loan-loss reserve levels can be expected to increase over time.

Conclusion

In sum, we believe that the combined influence of the stability of capital ratios in recent years and the general compliance with the new regulatory guidelines should foster a perception of capital adequacy within the industry today.

However, looking to the future, two factors appear to be critical. One is the profitability and the other is the extent to which the marketplace will permit the use of substitutes for common equity within primary capital.

Disclosure and Market Discipline: Issues and Evidence

Gary G. Gilbert

25

Market Discipline and Sources of Bank Funding

The role and importance of disclosure in promoting greater market discipline can be judged in terms of the following criteria:

1. How much is banking currently exposed to market discipline?
2. How well does the market utilize new information to assess banking risks?
3. Does the market "tier" banks according to risk perceived on the basis of nonfinancial factors?
4. Is the market efficient in incorporating on a timely basis new information to distinguish between firm-specific risk versus industry risks?
5. Is bank behavior sensitive to market discipline?

We can evaluate these criteria separately in the major markets in which banks are funded. These include (1) large certificates of deposit (CDs) (2) interbank deposits (3) federal funds, commercial paper and bankers acceptances (4) bank stocks and (5) subordinated debt.

Reprinted from *Economic Review* (November, 1983): 70–76 by permission of the Federal Reserve Bank of Atlanta and the author.

Uninsured Deposits and Potential Market Discipline

The extent to which banks of different size are exposed to potential market discipline from uninsured depositors is shown in Table 1. As expected, the distribution is heavily skewed toward the largest banks. (When adding other uninsured liabilities to uninsured deposits, the distribution across bank size groups is roughly the same.) Approximately 74 percent of all uninsured deposits are in banks with assets over $1 billion. These represent only about 1 percent of all insured commercial banks in the United States. The smaller institutions (less than $100 million in assets), which represent 86.6 percent of all banks have, on average, less than 8.9 percent of their domestic deposits uninsured. Moreover, through 1983 only one of the 319 deposit payoffs in the FDIC's history involved the failure of a bank with more than $100 million in assets. That was the failure of Oklahoma's Penn Square Bank in 1982. Consequently, the predominance of deposits subject to potential market discipline has been in the relatively few banks that have had essentially 100 percent deposit insurance coverage in the event of failure.

While uninsured depositors represent the potential for greater market discipline, particularly for money center and regional banks, realizing this potential depends on how well these depositors scrutinize their banking relationships on the basis of new data. This, in turn, depends on their capacity and willingness to evaluate information publicly available on individual bank performance.

Since the Franklin National Bank failed in 1974, the FDIC has conducted various surveys of large depositors to determine how they evaluate their banking relationships, their sensitivity to their uninsured deposit status, and their reaction to adverse publicity.

Table 1 Distribution of Uninsured Deposits and Other Liabilities, by Bank Size (June 1982)

Asset Size	Percent of Banks	Uninsured Percent of Total Deposits (Within Size Group)	Percent of Total Uninsured Deposits (Within Size Group)	Uninsured Deposits and Other Liabilities as a Percent of Total Liabilities (Within Size Group)	Percent of Total (Within Size Group)
$10–million	14	5	0.17	7	0.12
$10–25	30	5	1	7	1
$25–50	26	8	3	10	2
$50–100	16	11	4	14	3
$100–500	11	18	12	26	10
$500–1,000	1	24	6	35	6
$1–5 billion	1	33	23	49	24
$5 billion	0.025	52	51	68	54
All	100%	28%	100%	42%	100%

Source: Federal Deposit Insurance Corporation

In 1977, the Office of Corporate Planning at the FDIC interviewed several large demand depositors at four major failed banks—Franklin National Bank, American Bank and Trust, Hamilton National Bank, and International City Bank and Trust—to analyze how large depositors affect and are affected by deposit insurance. Most of those selected had demand deposits of $100,000 or more at the four banks at the time they were closed, or shortly before. Ten were very large corporations and the remainder mostly intermediate-sized business firms. In addition, treasurers of 20 large corporations were selected randomly for telephone interviews.

In connection with the FDIC's more recent deposit insurance study, telephone interviews were conducted with 23 corporate treasurers, nine fund managers, and 13 uninsured depositors. In addition, reactions to the concept of market discipline were solicited from bankers, academicians and bank rating or analysis services.

We can generalize the results of these surveys as follows:

1. Corporate treasurers choose their banking relationships primarily on the basis of services offered, availability of financing, and convenience. Financial analysis of their banks is generally cursory. Risk of loss is not an important consideration because of the size of the financial institutions they do business with and a perception that the government will bail out the institutions if they get in trouble. Treasurers say they learn of banking problems mainly through the press. Small businesses that deal with local banks are even less sophisticated in using financial data and less knowledgeable about deposit insurance protection. Interestingly, large depositors in recent bank failures exhibit the same perceptions and reactions toward risk as depositors in bank failures of the mid-1970s.
2. There is a general concern among those surveyed that disclosure of adverse information through the press would be destabilizing and would result in a "flight to quality," possibly to larger banks.
3. Institutional investors, such as mutual funds and pension funds, are the most sophisticated in using financial data and exert the most market discipline. To qualify for investment, banks must meet size and performance requirements, which effectively limit investment to the 50 largest banks. Fund managers undertake extensive in-house analysis of banks, relying on newspapers, call reports, 10-K and 10-Q reports, and ratings services.
4. There is general agreement that broader disclosure could promote greater market discipline. Better, more timely, and more comparable information on asset quality (including foreign loans) is considered most important.

Rate "Tiering" in CD Markets

Developments in the large, negotiable CD market in the aftermath of the Franklin National Bank (1974) and Penn Square (1982) failures shed additional light on the market's efficiency in responding to greater perceived banking risks.

Evidence subsequent to the Franklin failure indicated market ''tiering,'' suggesting size served as a proxy for lower risk. This was reflected in the inability of the CD market to isolate individual banking risks on the basis of differing performance characteristics. For example, after the failure of Franklin National, CD purchasers required a return 25 basis points higher from a regional bank than from a large money center institution.[1] This was double the normal spread prior to that period. Similarly, Dwight Crane (5) found that, for the first time in many years, concern about the viability of large banks contributed to the high interest rates banks were forced to pay for CD funds. However, Crane's study of the top 30 banks in 1974 revealed a high inverse relationship between CD rates and bank size. The study found no consistent relationship between CD rates and measures of financial condition, such as the return on equity or assets, or capital ratios among banks of comparable size. Crane did find, however, an apparent relationship between the profitability of a bank in a given quarter and its CD rate. It is uncertain whether lower profitability induced higher CD rates or vice versa.

In contrast to earlier findings, preliminary FDIC analysis subsequent to the 1982 Penn Square failure reveals no tiering in CD markets. The Penn Square failure was unique in that it represented the first deposit payoff of a bank with more than $100 million in assets. At issue was whether the CD market penalized larger institutions in general because of a recognition that uninsured depositors at large failed banks could incur some losses.

An analysis of three-month and six-month rate spreads between average CD rates (for the 10 largest banks) and Treasury bill rates revealed neither a short-term nor long-term effect on the general market for large bank CDs. The average rate spreads as a percentage of Treasury bill rates were not significantly different before and after the Penn Square failure. However, for a four-month period after Penn Square, the market penalized Continental Illinois Bank, which was linked most closely with Penn Square. Continental's rates rose about 100 basis points over rates for the other money center banks. Although comparable data on CD rates were unavailable for smaller banks, there was some limited evidence that uninsured depositors and money market funds reduced their uninsured deposits, regardless of bank size, after publicized loan problems.

While the Penn Square failure itself did not appear to have a general influence on the domestic CD market, other negative events pushed risk premiums on large bank CDs to a three-year high between August and October 1982. These events included the Lombard-Wall bankruptcy and the disclosure of Mexican and Argentine debt problems. This suggested a ''flight to quality'' in the domestic CD and Treasury bill markets.

A similar pattern has been observed in the Eurodollar CD and interbank markets. These markets account for a substantial portion of uninsured deposits, and potential market discipline for large U.S. multinational banks.[2] However, the form this discipline takes may be unstable and an inefficient discriminator of individual bank performance. It has

[1]This represents a Federal Reserve Board estimate. The figure reflects the difference between the median offering rates for 30-59 day maturity CD's issued by so-called ''prime in New York'' and ''other'' banks as of September 25, 1974.

[2]Deposits in foreign offices have exhibited some volatility in the past. Partly as a result of petrodollar recycling requirements, foreign deposits increased substantially between 1975 and 1978. Since then these deposits, in the aggregate, have remained a relatively stable proportion of total deposits (around 19 percent).

been reported that such events as "Drysdale, Penn Square, and Mexico have made these markets more susceptible than ever to rumor and panic" (1). Between the end of July and the end of August 1982, the difference between three-month Eurodollar CDs and three-month Treasury bills almost doubled. During this period, Continental Illinois Bank took itself off the CD run, Banco Ambrosiano was liquidated and Mexico called in the IMF for assistance. With each new disclosure, the rate gap widened.

Like the Eurodollar CD market, the interbank Eurodeposit market is a major source of funding for international banks.[3] Adverse banking developments, such as the Bankhaus Herstatt and Franklin National Bank failures in 1974 and more recent developments have increased rate tiering or reduced credit lines for some banks in the interbank market. However, this market appears inefficient in imposing market discipline since credit rationing based on undisclosed credit lines, rather than price adjustments, is its primary means of discriminating between sound and risky banks.[4] Moreover, its inability to distinguish between "local" and "global" shocks causes the perception that one bank's problems are transmitted to other banks (11, 14, p. 17). Consequently, the interbank market is believed to "tier" credit lines less on the basis of financial statements and more on the basis of a bank's ownership status (whether it is private or public), its government's support as a lender of last resort, the bank's importance to its country, and country risk. Although banks have improved their credit analysis practices since the international banking crises of 1974, differences between nations' accounting conventions and disclosure practices still make it difficult to interpret annual reports (14, p. 18).

Uninsured Deposits and Bank Behavior

To defend the market discipline concept completely, we should be able to demonstrate that either the actual response of the private marketplace or the potential for discipline has some impact on bank risk-taking. Unfortunately, we are not aware of any studies that test banks' responses to negative signals in major funding markets such as lower stock prices, deposit outflows, or higher costs of funds. Some evidence exists, however, on the relationship between uninsured deposits and bank capital.

Studies by Peltzman (21), Mingo (19), and Gonzalez (13) used ordinary least squares regression analysis to test for a substitute relationship between the proportion of total deposits insured in a bank and its capital position or capital growth. The results are mixed. Peltzman found that, for the period 1963-65, the proportion of insured deposits was inversely related to the percentage change in bank capital, after holding structural variables constant. This suggests that a greater proportion of uninsured deposits leads to more

[3]"Reliance on interbank funding tends to be higher for smaller banks and newcomers in the international market . . . a recent study suggests that interbank deposits account for between two-thirds and three-quarters of total external and Eurocurrency deposits." *Risks in international Lending*, Group of Thirty. New York, 1982. (14, p. 16).

[4]Giddy (11) finds that individual-bank deviations from the yields on three-month Eurodollar time-deposit bid rates are not systematically related to bank sizes, profitability or capital asset ratio.

capital growth and, thus, greater market discipline. The data, however, were based on state aggregates rather than individual bank data.

In an attempt to update the Peltzman study using individual bank data, Mingo confirmed Peltzman's findings for 1970, but only for banks that were undercapitalized relative to the standards desired by appropriate regulators. To the extent that a disproportionately greater percentage of large banks may have been undercapitalized at the time, Mingo's finding may have reflected greater regulatory pressure on larger banks' capital rather than market discipline. An analysis by Gonzalez in 1974 confirmed that bank size, rather than the proportion of uninsured deposits, was influencing levels and ratios of bank capital for 1966 and 1975.

On balance, there appears to be no clear-cut evidence that bankers respond to the potential discipline of large depositors. Time-series analyses of the impact of legislative changes on deposit insurance coverage, and lags in banks' response to changes in flows of uninsured deposits, would help clarify the issues. A study of the portfolio changes of banks in response to changes in stock prices and cost of funds would also be worthwhile.

Market Discipline in Bank Capital Markets

A number of studies have been undertaken to determine the ability of debt and equity markets to evaluate banking risks. They generally question whether greater banking default risks, resulting from higher bank leverage, will require higher returns on investments in the debt and equity markets. With the exception of a few studies, evidence that the debt and equity markets distinguish bank risk based on capital levels is not pervasive. Beighley, Boyd and Jacobs (2), Peltzman (21) and Durand (7) have found that bank performance characteristics such as dividend payouts, earnings, growth, and loan loss rates explain the price of a bank's stock and its price-earnings ratio.

Further evidence of the capital markets' efficiency in responding quickly to new banking information can be derived from studies of the markets' advance response to bank failures. Pettway and Sinkey (23) studied six bank failures between 1973–1975. Analyzing trends for each bank's stock using a conventional market model, they found that, on average, the market signaled problems with these banks 33 weeks before regulatory agencies placed them on problem-bank lists.

Stover and Miller (25) found evidence that the markets for bankers acceptances, commercial paper, and federal funds also anticipated the Franklin National Bank failure. A time-series analysis of the rate spreads on each instrument and the Treasury bill rate revealed that these markets anticipated Franklin's problems about 10 months prior to failure. Importantly, the Franklin failure did not cause a permanent structural shift in risk perceptions in these markets or in the stock market (22,25).

The paucity of recent evidence leaves open the question of whether the bank debt market could be a viable source of discipline. The FDIC's deposit insurance study cites several advantages of subordinated debt in providing market discipline, saying it: (1) provides a longer-term perspective because length of maturity prevents fleeing during adversity; (2)

possesses fixed-return without receiving a benefit for increased risk; and (3) is subordinated to depositors, insured and uninsured, in the event of failure (10, Chapter III).

To summarize, the potential for bank depositors to exert "true" market discipline is limited primarily to the largest 1 percent of commercial banks. The discipline is not broad-based, but limited mainly to large institutional investors. Large depositors tend to "tier" banks based on nonfinancial factors, particularly in offshore markets. This suggests some general instability in these markets from adverse rumor or publicity attendant to banking developments. In any event, there is no clear evidence that banks are responsive to the potential instability of large uninsured depositors.

The available evidence relating to other money markets and capital markets suggests greater market efficiency. That is, these markets have been able to anticipate banking problems and react in an orderly manner. However, most of the evidence is based on a few bank failures in the mid-1970s. Updated analyses with a larger sample of bank failures would be useful to substantiate earlier findings.

Disclosure and Banking Risks

It could be argued that fuller or better quality of disclosure of bank performance might reduce the marketplace's shortcomings in providing discipline on bank risk-taking. For broader disclosure to be useful in this regard, certain conditions should be met. First, the disclosed data should provide a prior indication of deteriorating bank performance. Hopefully, this would afford "riskier" banks time to respond to market forces and to undertake remedial action. On the other hand, if the marketplace recognizes serious banking problems after the fact, it could limit the bank's ability to remedy its problems, and might even worsen its situation.

Second, the required disclosure should help the marketplace assess risks for banks of all sizes. As indicated earlier, capital markets, not deposit markets, exert the greatest market discipline. However, the Securities and Exchange Act of 1934, which requires that certain types of disclosures be sent to the public or made publicly available, applies only to relatively larger banks and bank holding companies—those registered with the Securities and Exchange Commission.[5] Collectively, these represent about 3,300 insured commercial banks, or 23 percent of the total. It should be noted that federal bank regulatory agencies recently revised their call reports to require disclosure, on a quarterly basis, of (1) past due, non-accrual and renegotiated loans; (2) a detailed breakdown of remaining maturity (repricing period) of loans and interest bearing securities, fixed and floating rate, to reflect interest rate sensitivity, and (3) information on off balance sheet transactions.[6] In addition, all commercial banks now file reports of income and condition on a quarterly basis.

[5]A description of these requirements is found in (10, Appendix C).

[6]As of this writing, new reported and disclosed information on insider loans, and other changes to the call reports, were expected in March 1984 (FDIC Bank Letter 25–83).

A third condition for effective disclosure should be proper balance between bank examination-related information and bank balance sheet statistics. A major issue is whether a regulatory agency's judgment on a bank's condition will result in an overreaction in the market and trigger bank runs. To the extent that banks are examined at different times, interbank performance comparisons based on data from examinations are less meaningful. In some cases, the information will be out of date. It has been argued that adverse classification of loans and other reported information reflect subjective, and sometimes inconsistent, judgments by examination staff and not formal determinations by the agency (10, Chapter IV, p. 11). In addition, the examiners' ability to get reliable information from banks' staffs may be undermined by disclosure of examination information.

Chapter IV of the FDIC's deposit insurance study refers to the general types of information available to regulators but not disclosed to the public. This information is contained in routine reports of examination and memoranda of the agencies regarding informal and formal administrative action to correct weaknesses that are moderately severe or worse (10, Chapter IV, pp. 11–12).

Disclosure of Examination-Related Data

Notwithstanding the practical problems in disclosing bank examination data, a number of studies have evidenced their value in predicting risk in bank loan portfolios. Although limited by the lack of rigorous statistical testing, studies have shown a positive relationship between "classified assets" (those subject to risk of nonrepayment) and eventual loan charge-offs (8, 9, 26, 27). However, these studies failed to test for the statistical significance between the charge-off experience of classified and nonclassified loans, or between classified loans and loans "past-due." The studies also failed to track systematically the path of loan classifications from "substandard" to "doubtful" to "loss."

The "before the fact" information content of examiner loan classifications is also borne out by bank failure and problem bank models. Sinkey (24) found that a low net capital ratio (total capital and reserves minus classified assets/total assets) was the best predictor of small and large bank failures in the mid 1970s. Bovenzi, Marino, and McFadden (4) provide more recent evidence of the role of classified loans as an early warning of bank failures. If the ratio of classified assets to equity capital is incorporated in a financial ratio model that distinguishes between failed and non-failed banks from 1980–1983, the proportion of bank failures identified by the model increases. This improvement in the basic model lasts two years prior to failure. Substituting the ratio of past-due loans to total assets for the ratio of classified assets to equity capital also improves the basic model's performance in predicting failures. The larger the lead time before failure, the better the "past-due" ratio performs relative to the "classified asset" ratio. Both ratios are statistically more significant than other financial ratios in the model.

Ratios such as those contained in failure prediction models are potentially more meaningful than absolute values in comparing the performance of banks of different size. While the results of these models appear to support the "before the fact" value of including examiner classifications in selected ratios for disclosure, certain qualifications are worth noting. Since the benchmark of performance is bank failure or survival, the studies do not reveal the process of deterioration and improvement of bank performance. To some extent, bank management takes remedial action when loans are criticized by examiners (26).

Some major analytical questions remain. What are the interrelations of examination and call report ratios in explaining the deterioration process? What threshold levels are considered alarming? These questions are not intended to diminish the contribution of failure prediction models, but rather to suggest further areas of research.

Adverse Disclosure and Market Stability

As noted earlier, the disclosure of examination-related data raises concern over possible market overreaction to a regulatory agency's adverse evaluation of a particular bank. The FDIC's experience is that adverse publicity, usually in the press, has resulted in deposit runoffs in some cases. Generally, though, the bank was near failure when the runoffs occurred, and the deposit drain simply hastened the inevitable.

More formal statistical analyses have tested the response of the stock market and bank depositors to adverse news. In January 1976, the New York Times disclosed the names of 35 banks on the Federal Reserve's problem list. Studies of the impact of this disclosure on bank stock prices, using conventional market models, revealed no significant change in the market's risk perceptions of these banks after disclosure (16,20). Moreover, Murphy (20) found no evidence of a ''spillover effect'' on market prices of a control group of similar-sized banks in the same geographic areas. Finally, a study by Kurtz and Sinkey (18) analyzed the reaction of depositors at small banks to unfavorable publicity based on bank irregularities such as embezzlement, fraud and misapplication of funds reported to the U.S. attorney in 1970. By examining deposit flow patterns before and after the adverse publicity, the authors concluded that the impact of disclosed bank irregularities on deposit flows was insignificant. Demand deposit withdrawals (about 10 percent) occurred for only six months after disclosure, and were partially offset by continued growth in other deposit categories. One year after disclosure, 65 percent of the banks had recouped their losses entirely.

Summary and Conclusions

The combination of high deposit insurance coverage (actual and de facto), and bank deregulation have placed an added burden on the marketplace to regulate bank behavior and discourage excessive risk-taking. There is a tendency, however, to overestimate the incentive and willingness of uninsured depositors to exert an effective and non-disruptive influence on the banking industry. On the other hand, bank capital markets and markets for purchased funds have shown some evidence of imposing such discipline, in a non-disruptive fashion, on larger institutions that are most dependent on these markets for funding.

Shortcomings of the marketplace in restraining bank risk-taking could be corrected to some degree by broader disclosure. In particular, the disclosure of bank examination data could help bank-funding markets to identify an institution's weaknesses while remedial action is still possible. The impact of such disclosure on stock prices and deposit flows may not be as disruptive as some expect. However, the disclosure of examination-related information may reduce the effectiveness of the examination process. Furthermore, the recently required bank disclosure of past-due and other nonperforming loans may serve as an effective substitute for disclosure of classified loans from examination reports.

On balance, evidence of the existence and potential of "true" market discipline is not persuasive enough to warrant its substitution for the discipline provided by regulatory agencies. While bank customers' greater perceived risk of loss from bank failure could increase incentives to impose market discipline, market participants' behavior will depend largely on the nature and scope of changes in the deposit insurance system. It is difficult to predict how pervasive the resulting market discipline would be among various banksize groups.

BIBLIOGRAPHY

1. ANDERSON, TIM and PETER FIELD. "The Tremors that Threaten the Banking System," *Euromoney,* October 1982.
2. BEIGHLEY, PRESCOTT H., JOHN BOYD, and DONALD JACOBS. "Bank Equities and Investor Risk Perceptions." *Journal of Bank Research,* Autumn 1975.
3. BENSTON, GEORGE J. and JOHN TEPPER MARLIN. "Bank Examiners' Evaluation of Credit: An Analysis of the Usefulness of Substandard Loan Data." *Journal of Money, Credit and Banking,* Vol 6, No. 1, February 1974, pp. 23–44.
4. BOVENZI, JOHN F., JAMES A. MARINO, and FRANK E. MCFADDEN. "Commercial Bank Failure Prediction Models," *Economic Review,* Federal Reserve Bank of Atlanta, November 1983.
5. CRANE, DWIGHT B. "Study of Interest Rate Spreads the 1974 CD Market," *Journal of Bank Research,* Autumn 1976.
6. DELOITTE, HASKINS, and SELLS. "The Regulation of Capital Ratios in U.S. Banking," *American Bankers Association,* January 1981.
7. DURAND, DAVID. *Bank Stock Prices and the Bank Capital Problem.* National Bureau of Economic Research, 1957.
8. Federal Deposit Insurance Corporation. "Evidence of the Ultimate Loss of Adversely Classified Loans," an unpublished paper prepared by the Division of Bank Supervision, 1976.
9. Federal Deposit Insurance Corporation. "The Classified Commercial Loan Survey: A Study of the Performance and Disposition of Adversely Classified Loans," an unpublished paper prepared by the Division of Bank Supervision, 1977.
10. Federal Deposit Insurance Corporation. *Deposit Insurance in a Changing Environment,* April 15, 1983.
11. GIDDY, IAN H. "Risk and Return in the Eurocurrency Interbank Market," presented at the Federal Reserve Board, August 1981.
12. GILBERT, GARY G. and ROGER W. WATSON. "Preliminary Analysis of Variable Rate Deposit Insurance Premiums," FDIC Internal Memorandum, September 1981.

13. GONZALEZ, GISELA A. "Effect of Uninsured Depositors on Bank Capital," an unpublished paper for the Federal Deposit Insurance Corporation, 1977.
14. Group of Thirty. *Risks in International Lending,* New York, 1982.
15. HORVITZ, PAUL M. "Elimination of Insurance Will Require More Information," *American Banker,* June 15, 1983.
16. JOHNSON, JAMES M. "The Impact of the Problem Bank Disclosure on Bank Share Prices," *Journal of Bank Research,* Autumn 1977.
17. KANE, EDWARD J. "Putting Teeth into FDIC Coverage Limitations Will Not Solve the Deposit-Insurance Problem," paper submitted to the FDIC, March 1983.
18. KURTZ, ROBERT D. and JOSEPH F. SINKEY, JR. "Bank Disclosure Policy and Procedures, Adverse Publicity and Bank Deposit Flows," *Journal of Bank Research,* Autumn 1973.
19. MINGO, JOHN. "Regulatory Influence on Bank Capital Investment," *Journal of Finance,* Vol. 30, No. 4, September 1975, pp. 1111–1121.
20. MURPHY, NEIL B. "Disclosure of the Problem Bank Lists: A Test of the Impact," *Journal of Bank Research,* Summer 1979.
21. PELTZMAN SAMUEL. "Capital Investment in Commercial Banking and Its Relationship to Portfolio Regulation," *Journal of Political Economy,* January/February 1970, pp. 1–26.
22. PETTWAY, RICHARD H. "The Effects of Large Bank Failures Upon Investors' Risk Cognizance in the Commercial Banking Industry," *Journal of Financial and Quantitative Analysis,* September 1976.
23. PETTWAY, RICHARD H., and JOSEPH F. SINKEY, JR. "Establishing On-Site Banking Examination Priorities: An Early-Warning System Using Accounting and Market Information," *Journal of Finance,* Vol. 35, No. 1, March 1980.
24. SINKEY, JOSEPH F. JR. *Problem and Failed Institutions in the Commercial Bank Industry.* Contemporary Studies in Economic and Financial Analysis, Vol. 4. Greenwich, Connecticut JAI Press Inc., 1979.
25. STOVER, ROGER D. and JAMES M. MILLER. "Additional Evidence on the Capital Market Effect of Bank Failures," *Financial Management,* Spring 1983.
26. WU, HSIU-KWANG. "Bank Examiner Criticisms, Bank Loan Defaults and Bank Loan Quality," *Journal of Finance,* Vol. 24, No. 4, September 1969, pp. 687–705.
27. ______. "Effectiveness of Bank Examiner Loan Criticisms," a paper prepared for the Comptroller of the Currency, 1977.

Financial Disclosure and Bank Failure

George J. Benston

26

Devising ways to control banks' risk-taking is an essential function of deposit insurers and other bank regulators.[1] Deposit insurance allows those who hold a majority of banks' liabilities to ignore the institutions' financial condition. The practice of merging failing banks into sound ones allows many other liability holders to act as if they were insured depositors. Many elements of market discipline that restrain other businesses are unavailable to encourage banks to limit their risk-taking. Yet, if the public-policy goals of a safe and stable financial system are to be achieved, risk-taking must be controlled.

In light of recent competitive developments that give banks more incentives to take risks, their federal insurer—the Federal Deposit Insurance Corporation (FDIC)—has recommended additional disclosure of the financial condition of individual banks to enlist the public's help in monitoring and controlling banks' risk-taking.[2] As the deposit insurance system is currently organized, however, greater disclosure is unlikely to produce greater market discipline. If shareholders expect greater returns from greater risk, they may not be induced by more information to exercise greater discipline. Banks' liability-holders are generally uninterested in banks' financial condition because they have little risk of loss.

[1]Hereafter the term ''banks'' is used to refer to depository financial institutions generally.
[2]Federal Deposit Insurance Corporation, 1983.

Reprinted from *Economic Review* (March, 1984): 5–12 by permission of the Federal Reserve Bank of Atlanta and the author.

Under these conditions, expanding disclosure may increase costs to the disclosing banks more than it will benefit the public. Changes in the present system, however, hold the potential to make increased disclosure an effective policy.

Greater disclosure of banks' financial conditions—as proposed by the FDIC—is unlikely to produce greater market discipline. Changes in the present deposit insurance system, however, might make increased disclosure effective.

Recent Concern About Bank Failures

The failure of a bank or other financial institution is but a point on a continuum of risk. At one end is the high probability that the owners will achieve a greater than expected increase in wealth; at the other is the failure of the enterprise and loss of the owners' investment. What is usually termed a bank failure is towards this other end of the continuum. In most failures, supervisory authorities generally step in and reorganize the troubled bank. This reorganization usually entails loss to the owners, the supervisory authorities and the employees, and can impose costs on uninsured depositors and other customers. Consequently, while failure is but a point on the continuum between great success and total loss, it is an important point indeed.

The phenomenon of bank failure is as old as banking itself. Therefore, we should consider first why there appears to be more supervisory interest in bank failures now than in the recent past and whether this concern seems to be justified. If one looks only at the number of banks that have failed in recent years, there seems to be reason for concern. The number of failures or FDIC-assisted mergers reflects a substantial increase. Compared with the three commercial bank failures per year from 1943 through 1974 and the 12.9 per year from 1975 into the early 1980s, the 34 in 1982 and 48 in 1983 appear worrisome. That seems particularly true considering the large number of thrift associations that have merged with the support of the Federal Savings and Loan Insurance Corporation (FSLIC) since 1980.[3] But when we recall that over 600 banks failed each year during the 1920s, the recent number seems small. Furthermore, the considerably larger number of failures during the 1920s brought no significant reforms or even vociferous demands for changes in banking supervision. It is possible, therefore, that the current increase over the post-World War II failure rate actually is desirable, since failure is a necessary attribute of dynamic, innovative markets.

However, the enactment of deposit insurance in 1933 changed the environment of the 1920s profoundly. Previously, depositors knew that their funds were at risk. Consequently, they had reason to monitor their banks. What's more, banks were not restrained legally in the interest they could pay depositors. Hence, depositors had both negative and positive reasons to assess the risks undertaken by bankers, and bankers had reason to be concerned about the depositors' perceptions.

[3]McGuirk, 1983, indicates that the FSLIC has participated in 150 assisted mergers since 1980.

Initially, federal deposit insurance did not absolve all depositors of concern about the risks that banks might take, since the amount guaranteed per account was limited at first to only $2,500. But severe restrictions on new bank charters and increased supervision reduced the risk of failure considerably. Restrictions on entry also served to increase the cost of failure to bank owners, since the value of their charters generally was greater than it would have been with free entry, and almost certainly would be lost if failure occurred.

The authorities also sought to reduce the risk of failures by maintaining and further restricting the range of products that financial institutions could offer. In particular, thrift institutions were barred from offering checking accounts, business loans unrelated to real estate, and (for the most part) consumer loans. Commercial banks were not permitted to engage in most securities underwriting and trades. These constraints kept bankers from straying beyond activities that they and their examiners knew well.[4] While these policies and practices appear to have been sufficient to prevent most failures, the environment since the late 1970s has altered this situation.

Two phenomena helped change the environment by increasing competition in markets that banks dominated. The principal one is inflation-driven high nominal interest rates. These high rates increased the opportunity value obtainable by other institutions from avoiding regulatory constraints on interest rates, thereby encouraging them to begin offering banking services. Brokerage houses, for instance, introduced money market mutual funds and interest-bearing money management accounts. The other change is more effective and less costly technology for transferring financial assets. As a consequence, third-party transfer services (in effect, demand deposits) were offered successfully by nonbanks, and government-insured deposits could be sold nationwide by brokers. The 1980 increase in insurance on accounts with balances up to $100,000 and the removal early in the 1980s of interest rate ceilings on most time deposit accounts permit people to make large investments at market interest rates without concern about the risks taken by the depository institution. The insuring agencies' long-time practice of liquidating only small institutions largely removes uninsured depositors' concern for most institutions' safety.

The entry of nonbanks into activities previously reserved to chartered and (mostly) insured banks also increased the risk of bank failure by reducing bank owners' incentives to avoid failure. This is not to say that the owners and managers of banks are indifferent to failure. But increased and then almost unrestricted entry into their markets have reduced the value of their charters. This is particularly true for banks that operate in unsheltered markets, such as the large, money center banks that face competition from a wide range of institutions, both domestic and foreign.

The Role of Disclosure

Disclosure of the financial condition and operations of individual banks has been put forth as a means of averting excessive risk-taking. Advocates contend that expanded disclosure

[4]Other reasons for and effects from imposing or continuing the restraints probably were more important (see Benson, 1982a).

can prevent or reduce risk-taking by bankers and enhance the ability of depositors and investors to assess the risks taken.

Disclosure to supervisory authorities has long been a means by which banks are regulated. In particular, banks report to the regulators their balance sheets, income statements and detailed schedules of transactions with related parties. In addition, field examinations provide the authorities with additional information. Bovenzi, et al. (1983) and Korobow and Stuhr (1983) show that this information, together with or replaced by publicly available data, can be used effectively for predicting bank failures and possible financial distress.

The general public also has relied on the release of financial information, since banks have long been required to publish their balance sheets. Many banks also have provided depositors and the general public with more detailed balance sheets and income statements voluntarily. Since 1978, banks have had to publish the income statements they file with the banking authorities. However, banks as such are not subject to the Securities Exchange Act of 1934. Therefore, only bank holding companies are required to report publicly as are other corporations.[5] As Coulson (1983) delineates, bank holding companies are required to publish detailed information about the past-due status and concentration of their loans, dealings with insiders and sources of revenue.

The question now raised by the FDIC and others is whether increased public disclosure of banks' financial operations and even of the evaluations made by examiners and supervisors would be helpful in controlling risks that banks might take. This question can be analyzed first by delineating the parties that might be interested in evaluating bank risk and then examining the nature of their concerns. As the analysis shows, their concerns are importantly different.

Four Groups Concerned About Disclosure

Four interested groups are: (1) the deposit insurers—the FDIC, Federal Savings and Loan Insurance Corporation and National Credit Union Share Insurance Funds (NCUSIF), and the other supervisory agencies closely related to them—the Comptroller of the Currency, the Federal Reserve, the Federal Home Loan Bank Board, the National Credit Union Administration, and the state banking departments; (2) uninsured depositors—those with accounts over $100,000; (3) ordinary creditors—for example, bondholders and banks with loan participations; and (4) stockholders—residual claimants to the net assets of banks.

Stockholders

They lose if their bank's managers or others perpetrate fraud upon them. This is the risk with which they are primarily concerned. Stockholders of all corporations face this risk, except that it generally is easier to remove resources from banks fraudulently, money being the most "fenceable" of assets. Hence, disclosure of loans to related parties is of interest to bank stockholders.

[5]See Coulson, 1983, for a description of the SEC's reporting requirements.

However, shareholders are not otherwise opposed to their bank taking risks, as long as the risks are offset by expected gains. Stockholders can eliminate the risk from owning any particular investment by holding a diversified portfolio of assets, though this may be costly for stockholders who have a large proportion of their assets invested in controlling interest in a smaller bank. However, when a government agency such as the FDIC or FSLIC accepts the risk of failure for a premium that is less than sufficient to cover that risk—that is, when the premium is not directly related to the risks undertaken—stockholders benefit from their banks taking greater than normal risks. It is a situation best described as "heads the stockholders win, tails the FDIC or FSLIC loses." Thus, the stockholders of banks will logically prefer risk, knowing it offers the promise of greater returns.

Disclosure of risk, then, is useful to stockholders as a means of identifying banks likely to have a greater variance of returns and to compensate shareholders for accepting that greater variance. In this regard, the stockholders benefit when they and other investors can secure information about risk conveniently and inexpensively. Thus, it is desirable to have some uniformity in the type and format of information disclosed. But stockholders also must be concerned with the cost of disclosure to the bank. This cost includes informing competitors, customers and regulators of the bank's strategies and condition when this disclosure might work against the institution. Auditing data and presenting and explaining it to users and the curious also can be costly. A management that operates a bank in the interest of its shareholders must weigh the benefits and costs of disclosure as it weighs benefits and costs of other decisions. Therefore, the authorities would seem to express their concern for the well-being of stockholders best by mandating only financial disclosure that reduces the probability and extent of fraud or of misinforming shareholders and the cost to investors of using information.[6]

Ordinary Creditors

Unlike the stockholders, who prefer non-fraud risk when compensated, creditors could be useful to the regulatory authorities as monitors of bank risk-taking. The creditors' returns are effectively limited at the top since, in the absence of capital gains resulting from unexpected changes in interest rates, they can expect to receive no more than the amount agreed to contractually. But they can lose their entire investment. Hence, they have reason to be concerned about the variance in the returns earned by banks, and will price their contracts with the banks accordingly.

Banks similarly have reason to assure their ordinary creditors that the risks undertaken will be no greater than the creditors expect. If the banks are unable to convince them, the creditors are likely to insist on interest rates that compensate them for the risks to which they might be subject. This situation is no different from that faced in any debtor-creditor

[6]See Benston 1982b, for a further explication. In any event, the usefulness of these data to security analysis is questionable. By the time the financial statements are made public, astute analysis will have ferreted out the information from other sources.

arrangement. Consequently, if a bank's management discloses honestly, it is likely to disclose voluntarily the optimal amount of financial information.[7] Management, it must be admitted, has incentive not to disclose honestly when disclosure would raise its costs of liabilities or might cause the withdrawal of uninsured deposits.

Since any additional disclosure required is likely to be more costly than beneficial (on the margin) to the creditors and to the stockholders, it would seem preferable for the regulatory authorities to forebear from imposing more rules. The authorities could benefit, though, from observing the types of data that unsecured creditors and analysts request from banks. Most importantly, the regulatory authorities could obtain information from observing the risks assessed by creditors. This information is available from the market rates at which banks' nondeposit liabilities trade. The authorities also might get continuous reports on the interest rates and fees paid by a bank to other creditors.

Uninsured Depositors

At present, in almost all banks, deposit accounts with balances of more than $100,000 are not insured. Hence, it would seem that depositors holding these accounts are a class of uninsured creditors. However, until the 1982 failure of the Penn Square Bank in Oklahoma, the government insurance agencies had in fact insured the deposit balances of almost all depositors. They did this by having the deposits of a failed bank assumed by another bank, either directly or through a merger (the practice followed for all large bank failures before and since Penn Square) or by paying off the insured depositors after many depositors with uninsured balances had been able to withdraw their funds. Consequently, most depositors have reason to believe that all their funds are, in fact, guaranteed.* Indeed, surveys reveal that depositors are little concerned with the risks taken by banks in which their funds are deposited.[8] Some evidence suggests that investors demand somewhat higher interest rates on large, negotiable certificates of deposit (CDs) issued by banks perceived to be riskier after a notable failure—for example, regional banks after Franklin National's failure and at least one large bank after the Penn Square failure.[9] Since the Penn Square liquidation, however, several deposit brokers have developed systems that allow

[7]Economies of scale from imposed disclosure requirements are exceptions to this conclusion. However, I am not aware of any conditions that are not already obviated by the effects of deposit insurance and Federal Reserve discount window and open market operations. Evidence of the existence of economies of scale might be obtained from the public's demand for such information as is published in the Federal Reserve's Uniform Bank Performance and Bank Holding Company Performance Reports, assuming that the price charged for the reports is not less than their cost of production and distribution.

**Editors' Note: The Continental Illinois crisis of 1984 further corroborates the author's conclusion here.*

[8]Gilbert, 1983 p. 71, summarizes these surveys as follows: "Corporate treasurers choose their banking relationships primarily on the basis of services offered, availability of financing and convenience. Financial analysis of their banks is generally cursory in nature. Risk of loss is not an important consideration because of the size of the institutions they do business with and the perception that the government would bail out these institutions if they get into trouble."

[9]See Gilbert, 1983, pp. 71–73.

them to distribute large time deposits in lots small enough to be insured entirely.[10] Recently proposed FDIC and FSLIC rules may eliminate these systems by limiting insurance to the first $100,000 of a deposit spread by a broker among many banks. However, opposition to these rules is strong, and brokers and depositors are both inventive and sensitive to probable losses. Whether the proposed rules will eliminate the use of broker networks to spread and effectively insure large deposits is open to question.[11]

The FDIC has proposed to encourage uninsured depositors to monitor bank risk more aggressively by paying them off in merger transactions at only the estimated value of recoveries from a troubled bank. Since the FDIC's cost of recovery would be taken off the top, uninsured depositors would in all probability get less than their deposit balances. An evaluation of that proposal is detailed by Larry Wall in this volume. Briefly, the FDIC's proposal is unlikely to be beneficial because of the different reactions of demand and time depositors.

Demand depositors with balances that they believe might be lost as a consequence of a bank failure are likely to withdraw their funds as soon as they suspect a failure.[12] These depositors have little incentive to engage in more than rumor monitoring—a condition reinforced by the lag between the end of a disclosure period and the actual disclosure of financial information. The financial system would face the prospect of bank runs, which deposit insurance was designed to prevent.

Time depositors would be at risk for balances over $100,000. But, if the FDIC's proposal to limit the insurance on brokered deposits were withdrawn or avoided, bankers and brokers could get around the proposed limitation by packaging and selling portfolios, of whatever dollar amount desired, consisting of the fully insured CDs of many banks. The removal of effective deposit insurance on some portion of CD balances above $100,000 is likely to convince them to go to this trouble.[13] Consequently, financial disclosure would play a small role with uninsured as well as insured depositors.

Deposit Insurers

Unlike others who use bank financial data, deposit insurers and the supervisory agencies on which they rely can gather information by examining records in the banks. These data

[10]See testimony of the federal regulatory agencies (J. Charles Partee, member of the Federal Reserve Board: C. T. Conover, Comptroller of the Currency, William M. Isaac, chairman of the Federal Deposit Insurance Corporation; Edwin J. Gray, chairman of the Federal Home Loan Bank Board and Edgar F. Callahan, Chairman of the National Credit Union Administration) before the Subcommittee on Financial Institutions, Supervision, Regulation and Insurance of the Committee on Banking, Finance and Urban Affairs, U. S. House of Representatives, October 27, 1983.

[11]For a detailed presentation and analysis of the spreading of deposits in insured lots by brokers and FDIC's reaction to this, see Caroline Harless. "Brokered Deposits: Issues and Alternatives," Federal Reserve Bank of Atlanta, *Economic Review*, March 1984, pp. 14–25.

[12]Technically, funds would be withdrawn when the marginal cost of a withdrawal (which is small for demand deposits) is exceeded by the expected amount of loss times the probability of loss, all in present value terms.

[13]The combination of deposit insurance, improvements in technology, expanded marketing of CDs by brokers, and de facto as well as de jure deregulation of financial services have, I believe, substantially increased the risk of bank failure. In particular, Isaac reports that "many of the 72 commercial banks that failed between February 1982 and mid-October 1983 had substantial brokered deposits. Overall, brokered deposits constituted 16 percent of the total deposits held by the 72 banks that failed." The nature of these developments and some suggestions for a solution are presented in Benston, 1984.

are reported by field examiners and are used directly by their supervisors. In recent years, researchers and supervisors have experimented with early warning surveillance systems that use data reported by banks and examiners.[14] An analysis of the effectiveness of this information in predicting bank failures should provide evidence on the usefulness of financial data, in general, for this purpose.

Some indication of the ability of bank examiners to predict trouble may be obtained from the ratings they gave banks that failed in the examination just prior to their collapse. As part of a study conducted for the Hunt Commission,[15] I reviewed the records of all commercial banks that failed from January 1959 through April 1971. (Benston, 1973, Table XIII, p. 43). Of these 56 banks, fully 59 percent had been rated "no problem." More recent evidence is presented in Bovenzi, Marino and McFadden (1983, Table 6). They related the numerical CAMEL (Capital, Assets, Management, Earnings, Liquidity) ratings given by the bank examiners to the 11, 17 and 45 banks that failed in fiscal 1981, 1982 and 1983. Banks considered to be no problem are assigned ratings of 1 or 2; banks rated 3 are "watched" by the Federal Reserve, "considered for formal administrative action" by the Comptroller, and presumably looked at closely by the FDIC; problem banks get ratings of 4 and 5.[16] The researchers report that CAMEL ratings of 1 and 2 (definitely no-problem) were given to 34 percent of the 73 banks that failed in the year prior to failure. Ratings of 1, 2 or 3 (probably no-problem) were given to 63 percent of these banks.[17] Two years before failure, 57 percent of the 60 failed banks on which researchers have data were rated by the examiners as definitely no-problem and 78 percent as definitely or probably no-problem. Thus, the examiners' record in identifying banks that will fail is far from perfect.

It also is interesting to note that the failure prediction models employed by Bovenzi, Marino and McFadden (1983) predict about as well when only publicly available information is used. They correctly predicted 64 percent of the 73 failures between July 1, 1980 and July 1, 1983 using call data available in the year before the failures. That compares with 67 percent when examination data were added to the model, 66 percent when CAMEL ratings 3, 4 and 5 were used, and only 37 percent for ratings 4 and 5. For data available two years before the failures, the model using only call data correctly predicted 50 percent of the failures. That compares with 58 percent from the model with the examination data included, 43 percent for the CAMEL ratings 3, 4 and 5 and only 22 percent for ratings 4 and 5. Thus, the more detailed and subjective examination data do not seem to add much in predicting failures.

An important reason for the imperfect forecasting ability of the early warning models that use publicly available financial data is that the principal cause of failure is fraud or misdealing. Of the 59 banks that failed from January 1959 through April 1971, fully 34 were rated "no problem" approximately one year before failure. As I reported, "a case-

[14]Bovenzi, Marino and McFadden, 1983, present a good review of much of this literature, as well as a report of their own research.

[15]The Presidential Commission on Financial Structure and Regulation.

[16]See Flannery and Guttentag, 1980, pp. 196–199 for a description and comparison of the way the three agencies use the CAMEL ratings.

Editors' Note: See also reading 23 in this volume by Putnam.

[17]Analysis of 1, 2 and 3 rated banks as reported in letter of September 19, 1983 from John Bovenzi.

by-case analysis of the non-problem rated banks that failed reveals that, in 28 or 29 of the 34 cases, failure was due to embezzlement or change of management control between examinations'' (Benston, 1973, p. 43). Fraud and self-dealing also played an important role in the failure of banks in previous periods.[18] Many of the largest bank failures in recent history also appear to have been the result of such practices. In such situations, publicly reported figures are likely to be deliberately misleading. While it seems reasonable to expect field examinations to reveal misreported data, they appear to have been relatively ineffective in this regard. One reason may be that the examiners do not audit the banks sufficiently for fraud and misreported data. Another reason is that the examiners' present performance may be as good as it should be considering the costs compared to the benefits of auditing.

Thus, without improved examination practices, the public disclosure of examination data would seem to be of little value to private analysts and investors. Indeed, considering that the examiners have the legal right to examine most of a bank's records and assuming that the examiners' efforts are cost-effective, their predictive performance suggests that more extensive public disclosure would not be worthwhile for identifying problem banks.

Were it not for the reasonable fear that bank failures will increase considerably, we might conclude that the supervisory and insurance agencies are doing as well as should be expected, given the marginal costs and benefits of improved monitoring and control of risks. Yet a number of factors are encouraging more than a few bankers to take risks deliberately. These factors include deposit insurance that removes the incentives for depositors to be concerned with banking operations and investments, the available technology that permits inexpensive packaging of insured CDs, the ability of brokers to market these CDs nationwide, consumers' increased acceptance of such investments, and the continuing deregulation of deposit banking. Consequently, a change in the present risk-monitoring procedures seems desirable.

Summary, Suggestions and Conclusions

Our analysis of the several potential users of bank financial data—stockholders, ordinary creditors, uninsured depositors, and the deposit insurers—reveals both coincidence and divergence of interests regarding the assessment of bank risk.

The stockholders' interests are consistent with the interests of the other users in the detection and prevention of fraud by banking officers. Financial data also help the investors assess risks and identify and purchase shares of riskier banks that compensate for the risk. But when the deposit insurance agencies undercharge for the risks assumed, stockholders benefit from banks seeking higher returns from riskier investments. Investors would be attracted to these banks.

Ordinary creditors, though, absorb the cost of risk; consequently, they attempt to arrange their returns to cover these costs. They have an incentive to use financial data to assess the risks. Importantly, the debtor banks have the same incentive, since they must

[18]See Benston, 1973 for details.

compensate creditors (and stockholders) for risks the creditors perceive. Consequently, the financial data that most banks provide to creditors seem likely to be the optimal quality and quantity.

Uninsured depositors, though, are not like ordinary creditors, because the deposit insurance agencies, realistically speaking, provide them with insurance. Hence, they have little reason to be concerned with the riskiness of banks in which their funds are deposited. FDIC proposals to increase their concern by explicitly denying insurance protection for a fraction of their balances over $100,000 are unlikely to be successful, at least not without cost. These proposals would enhance demand depositors' incentives to remove their funds upon a rumor of an impending bank failure. Thus, they would apply "market discipline" to the most volatile of banks' deposits. In addition, many, perhaps all, time depositors currently can package their investments in portfolios of fully insured deposits of less than $100,000 in many banks, thereby defeating the FDIC's proposal.

The deposit insurance agencies and other supervisory authorities remain those principally concerned about excessive bank risk-taking. The agencies use financial data gathered in field examinations and bank reports to assess and control the risks taken by banks. It appears, though, that they are able to predict only 37 percent to 66 percent of the failures (depending on whether a CAMEL rating of 3 is considered a prediction of failure) from financial or examination data available in the year before failure.

Increased development and use of bank surveillance models appear warranted, since they already appear to be as effective as examiners in predicting failures. At the least, the models can serve to direct the examiners' efforts towards banks that are more likely to fail. But, considering how quickly brokers can sell the insured CDs of banks that, in turn, can quickly place the funds in risky investments, more current information is needed. The insurance agencies (and their surrogates, the other supervisory authorities), might increase their requirements for continuous reporting by banks. Additionally, they might direct their field examinations more specifically towards institutions that appear to have increased their deposits quickly or to have changed investment practices or control. Indeed, as of the September 30, 1983 call report, all of the federal banking agencies require banks to report the amount of funds obtained through money brokers. Revisions proposed for the March 1984 call also require disclosure of the amounts of brokered retail deposits. The FSLIC now requires associations that are in a "supervisory status" to limit the amount of brokered funds and to submit a monthly report giving the level of such deposits and the sources and uses of the funds.

The authorities also could provide banks with information that would permit them to assess their risks better. Bankers can obtain information from and about borrowers to estimate the risk incurred. However, it is difficult for bankers to learn about the indebtedness undertaken concurrently by borrowers, particularly when these borrowers intend to be deceptive and when they increase indebtedness after the date of the balance sheet they provide to banks. Anti-trust legislation constrains banks from exchanging such information. Banks lending to countries and foreign firms have found this lack of information vexing, particularly recently. Supervisory agencies also appear to have been unaware of the extent to which several banks sometimes extended loans to a single risky borrower. While each loan might be within acceptable risk limits, the sum of a company's or country's indebtedness may not be.

It would seem desirable, therefore, for the supervisory authorities to establish a central file of indebtedness by countries and risky large borrowers. The authorities could require banks to report on their loans to such borrowers, and the information could be made available promptly to the banks (with identification of other banks excluded) and all supervisory agencies.

In addition, the authorities could look more to the private markets for indications of excessive risk-taking by banks. The bond market is one such important source of information. Changes in stock prices are a similar source, though increases in stock prices as well as decreases could signal greater risk-taking.[19] Perhaps the most important change would be to involve depositors in risk-monitoring. This could be accomplished and the considerable incentives towards risk-taking by banks brought about by deposit insurance could be mitigated by removing deposit insurance from time-dated deposits greater than, say $5,000 or $10,000 per account.[20] Insuring these balances and limiting each saver to one insured account would spare depositors the burden of determining the risk of banking. If they wished to hold larger investments free of default risk, they could purchase U.S. Treasury obligations or banks could offer privately issued insurance. The availability and cost of this insurance to banks, and the interest rates that banks would have to pay for the uninsured deposits, would provide authorities with valuable information. Probably more important is the concomitant interest of depositors and private insurers in monitoring risk-taking by banks and the banks' collateral interest in avoiding excessive risks.

In the absence of such changes in the insurance system, it is likely that additional financial disclosure, as such, will prove costly and ineffective.

REFERENCES

BENSTON, GEORGE J. "Bank Examination." *The Bulletin* (New York University Graduate School of Business Administration), pp. 89–90 May 1973.

BENSTON, GEORGE J. "Why Did Congress Pass New Financial Services Laws in the 1930s? An Alternative View," *Economic Review*. Federal Reserve Bank of Atlanta, April 1982a, pp. 7–10.

BENSTON, GEORGE J. "Security for Investors," Chapter 6, *Instead of Regulation,* Robert W. Poole, Jr., ed. *Instead of Regulation* Lexington Books (Lexington, MA, 1982b), pp. 169–205.

BENSTON, GEORGE J. "Interest on Deposits and Deposit Insurance in a Deregulated Environment," (forthcoming, *Economic Review,* Federal Reserve Bank of Atlanta).

BOVENZI, JOHN F., JAMES A. MARINO and FRANK E. MCFADDEN, "Commercial Bank Failure Prediction Models," *Economic Review,* Federal Reserve Bank of Atlanta, 68, (November 1983) pp. 14–26.

COULSON, EDMUND. "Full Disclosure: The SEC's Requirements Relating to Bank Holding Companies," *Economic Review,* Federal Reserve Bank of Atlanta, 68 (November 1983) pp. 62–69.

EHLEN, JAMES G. JR. "A Review of Bank Capital and Its Adequacy," *Economic Review,* Federal Reserve Bank of Atlanta, 68 (November 1983) pp. 54–60.

[19]The Federal Reserve Board presently monitors the security prices of about 400 bank holding companies (Putnam, 1983).

[20]See Benston, 1984, for the more fully described proposal.

FEDERAL DEPOSIT INSURANCE CORPORATION, *Deposit Insurance in a Changing Environment* Washington, D. C., 1983.

FLANNERY, MARK J. and JACK M. GUTTENTAG. "Problem Banks: Examination Identification and Supervision," in Leonard Lapidus, ed., *State and Federal Regulation of Commercial Banks*, Federal Deposit Insurance Corporation (Washington: 1980), Volume II, pp. 169–226.

GILBERT, GARY G. "Disclosure and Market Discipline Issues and Evidence," *Economic Review*, Federal Reserve Bank of Atlanta, 68 (November 1983) pp. 70–76.

HARLESS, CAROLINA "Brokered Deposits: Issues and Alternatives," *Economic Review* Federal Reserve Bank of Atlanta, 59 (March 1984).

ISAAC, WILLIAM M. "Statement on H. R. 3535, Interest on Demand Deposits; Brokered Deposits; and H. R. 4053, Compulsory Federal Deposit Insurance," presented to Subcommittee on Financial Institutions, Supervision, Regulation and Insurance of the Committee on Banking, Finance and Urban Affairs, House of Representatives, October 27, 1983.

MCGUIRK, EDWARD J. "Default Prevention, Financial Analysis and Modeling: The FSLIC Perspective," *Journal Federal Home Loan Bank Board,* 16 (October 1983) pp. 10–17.

WALL LARRY D. "The Future of Deposit Insurance: A Critique of Proposals," *Economic Review*, Federal Reserve Bank of Atlanta, 59 (March 1984).

Deposit Insurance Creates a Need for Bank Regulation

Mark J. Flannery

27

Many bank managers and owners have long complained that they are overregulated by a plethora of government agencies. The thrust of their complaint is that they could do a better job—that is, become more profitable or increase their bank's market value—if left unencumbered by regulations limiting portfolio choice, capital adequacy, holding company formations, deposit rates, and so forth. They are doubtless correct. Yet banking in the U.S. possesses institutional characteristics that require at least some of the regulations currently in place. In particular, Federal deposit insurance gives insured bankers an artificial incentive to undertake more risk than they would in an unregulated and uninsured free market. Bankers insured by the Federal Deposit Insurance Corporation (FDIC) can benefit *privately* by undertaking risks that the society as a whole considers excessive.

Restrictive bank regulations can thus be viewed as an effort to undo (or at least to limit) the distortive impact of deposit insurance on bank decisions. This view of bank regulation is certainly not all-encompassing, since numerous regulations pre-date the FDIC and others are not directly related to bank risk taking. Nonetheless, considering the impact of FDIC insurance on bank behavior can often provide a useful framework for evaluating bank regulations and regulatory reform.

Reprinted from *Business Review* (January/February, 1982) :17–27 by permission of the Federal Reserve Bank of Philadelphia and the author.

The Federal Deposit Insurance System

Congress introduced nationwide bank deposit insurance by creating the FDIC in the Banking Act of 1933.[1] By yearend 1980, 98.2 percent of all commercial banks in the U.S. were insured by FDIC. If an insured bank fails, FDIC promises to repay its depositors' losses, up to a maximum of $100,000 per account. Today, coverage extends to 79.9 percent of all bank deposit balances in the U.S. In return for this insurance coverage, each insured bank pays FDIC an annual premium set by statute at .083 percent of total deposit balances.[2] FDIC uses this income to pay its expenses (including any insurance claims from failed banks' depositors) and to maintain an adequate insurance reserve fund. After providing for operating expenses, losses, and necessary additions to its reserve fund, FDIC is required to refund 60 percent of its remaining premium income to insured banks. In recent years, such refunds have lowered the new cost of FDIC deposit insurance to .03 percent or .04 percent of a bank's total deposits—less than half the statutory rate.

As with any insurance operation, FDIC's reserve fund is its first line of defense in the event of bank failures. At yearend 1980, this fund amounted to $11 billion, or 1.16 percent of total insured deposits. Unlike private insurers, FDIC also possesses a unique second line of defense behind its reserve fund—a $3-billion credit line from the U.S. Treasury. Although the government's formal commitment to support FDIC ends here, many economists and regulators believe that the Federal Reserve and the Treasury would continue to provide almost limitless support to FDIC in the event of serious bank failures. This gives the taxpaying public a substantial indirect interest in the FDIC insurance fund's viability.[3]

Despite the fact that FDIC closely resembles private insurance companies in many regards, FDIC's fixed-rate premium structure is unusual, and this constitutes the *raison d'être* for other banking regulations. Private insurers use a variety of methods to calculate the level of premia they charge, but all have the same goal: providing adequate funds to cover future losses. Setting adequate premium levels requires an accurate assessment of the likely losses associated with each contract.

Insurance companies that cover automobiles, homes, and personal property generally charge a premium that varies with the perceived risk of the activity being underwritten. A seventeen-year-old urban male driver with three recorded accidents pays more for auto insurance than the elderly couple who live in a rural area and drive only on Sundays. Why?

[1]Although this article explicitly discusses only commercial banks, the same arguments apply to savings and loan associations, mutual savings banks, and credit unions.

[2]Note that banks with some accounts in excess of $100,000 are paying for insurance coverage their depositors won't receive. Since larger banks more often have large customers, the effective cost of their deposit insurance (per insured deposit dollar) appears higher than it is for small banks.

[3]An example of this connection between FDIC and the general public occurred in 1974. During that spring and summer, Franklin National Bank was in serious danger of failing. Rather than close the bank and pay off its insured depositors, FDIC wanted to find another bank to acquire Franklin National. To keep the troubled bank afloat while FDIC sought a suitable merger partner, the Federal Reserve Bank of New York extended sizable loans at a below-market interest rate. This action cost the Federal Reserve Bank an estimated $25 million. Since Federal Reserve operating surpluses are returned to the Treasury, U.S. taxpayers ultimately paid this cost. See Joseph F. Sinkey, "The Collapse of Franklin National Bank of New York, "*Journal of Bank Research* (Summer 1976), pp. 113–122.

Because the insurance company anticipates that the teenager is more likely to have an accident and file an insurance claim. Greater perceived risk requires higher auto insurance premia if the company is to stay in business.

Life insurance companies assess premia in a slightly more complicated fashion. Take the case of term insurance, which pays off only if the insured dies during the policy's term. Term insurance premia increase with an individual's age because, according to the annuity tables, older people are more likely to die during the contract period, exposing the insurance company to a loss. Like the automobile insurer, life insurance companies charge their higher risk customers more. At the same time, however, most insurance companies try to avoid the highest risk applicants in each age group by requiring applicants to undergo a physical examination. People in relatively poor health are denied coverage.

These examinations protect the insurance company against a phenomenon known as adverse selection. A person in poor health knows he is more likely to die than the average person his age in the general population. If all people the same age could purchase insurance for the same premium, those in worse health would be more likely to buy a policy. The average policy holder would therefore be more likely to die than the average person in the population, and the life insurance company would find itself paying for greater death benefits than it had expected from its annuity tables.[4]

The FDIC's premium structure is like the life insurance company's in one way: each bank must initially demonstrate an acceptable level of financial health in order to qualify for FDIC coverage. But the FDIC also requires frequent checkups (bank examinations) as a condition of continued coverage. This need constantly to reexamine insured banks arises because the provision of deposit insurance itself encourages the bank to become riskier than it was before becoming insured.

Distortions Caused by FDIC Insurance

Consider first a bank with no deposit insurance. If it goes bankrupt, the shareholders will lose their entire investment and depositors will be less than fully repaid. Knowing this, each potential depositor should assess the riskiness of a bank's operations.[5] While a riskier loan portfolio is likely to mean higher returns for the bank, it also raises the prospects for bankruptcy. Depositors and stockholders will require compensation for bearing that risk in the form of a higher return on their funds. Thus the willingness of bank managers to make risky loans is held in check by the concern of depositors and stockholders for the safety of their funds. Indeed, free market advocates contend that the ability of people to shift funds from one bank to another ensures that banks will undertake a socially correct amount of risk.

[4]Some insurance companies write policies for people without requiring a physical. This insurance is more expensive (has a higher premium) because the company knows it will suffer adverse selection. Healthy people are more likely to purchase lower cost policies that require a physical.

[5]Whether depositors do or can evaluate bank risk is an entirely different issue, related to the initial reasons for Federal government provision of deposit insurance. See Ian McCarthy, "Deposit Insurance: Theory and Practice," IMF *Staff Papers* (September 1980), pp. 578–600.

Now consider the impact of fixed-premium deposit insurance on the bank's risk-taking decision. It is easiest to begin with an assumption that 100 percent of all bank deposits are covered and banks have no stockholders.[6] If the bank fails, the FDIC stands ready to repay depositors in full, so depositors no longer care how risky the bank's asset portfolio really is. So long as people retain faith in the FDIC's ability to make payments, the bank's borrowing (deposit) costs are the same no matter how risky its asset portfolio. One natural check on bank risk taking has thus been eliminated. Since riskier assets offer higher expected returns and since deposit costs don't vary with the bank's perceived risk, the bank maximizes expected profits by purchasing the riskiest available assets. This decision becomes perfectly rational from the bank's private perspective once deposit insurance has been procured. In other words, *banks have a clear incentive to become more risky when the FDIC begins promising to absorb their default losses* (see Appendix).

This example overstates the argument by ignoring two important considerations. First, the bank's deposits and other liabilities are not fully (100-percent) insured by FDIC. Some depositors will therefore demand higher interest rates when the bank's underlying portfolio risk rises, making the banker's ability to profit by undertaking socially excessive risks smaller than it would be with 100-percent insurance coverage. Second, banks do have stockholders, and these owners are concerned about their risk exposure. Their aversion to risk will provide some limit to the manager's willingness to make ever riskier loans. FDIC insurance will still distort the private incentive to bear risk, however, by reducing the increase in deposit costs that would normally accompany greater bank portfolio risk.

Economists refer to distortions such as those resulting from FDIC deposit insurance as externalities, since one individual's actions affect the well-being of other people. An externality can be either good or bad. Picking up litter in a public park, for example, constitutes a good externality: the clean view is enjoyed by people *other than* the do-gooder. A factory whose chimney dumps soot onto nearby residents' drying laundry is a bad externality. The factory could burn cleaner fuel or install stack scrubbers, but these actions would mean lower profits.[7] The outcome—air pollution—illustrates how government regulation—pollution control—can improve overall social welfare even though it imposes a real burden on private parties such as factory owners.

Just as factories would ignore their polluting effects in the absence of regulation, banks will ignore the extra risk they impose on society as a result of not having to be concerned about the safety of depositors' funds. In response, bank regulators have taken steps to limit the risk that insured bankers are allowed to undertake. Effective regulations will reduce

[6]A large school of thought contends that FDIC in fact has extended insurance coverage to all bank liability holders by its decisions to arrange mergers (technically called a "purchase and assumption") rather than closing failed institutions outright. See David B. Humphrey, "100% Deposit Insurance: What Would It Cost?" *Journal of Bank Research* (Autumn 1976), pp. 192–198 or Gary Leff, "Should Federal Deposit Insurance Be 100 Percent?" *Bankers Magazine* (Summer 1976), pp. 23–30.

[7]From the factory owner's own (selfish) perspective, spewing soot is the optimal decision. It maximizes her profits. Suppose, however, it would cost $10 per year to eliminate the soot, which would make the neighbors feel $15 better off. The *socially* optimal decision would be to eliminate the soot. Pollution control laws are intended to bring about the desired result. Since the factory owner finds it privately more profitable to pollute, her profits will decline as a result of enforcing these regulations. (If profits do not decline, either the regulations are ineffective or the factory owner was operating inefficiently to begin with.) Despite the factory owner's loss, the society as a whole—factory plus neighbors—will be made better off under a proper set of pollution restrictions.

bank profits relative to what they would be without regulations (though with deposit insurance), but society should be made better off because of the diminished amount of bank risk taking.

Bank Regulations as a Response to Deposit Insurance

Many types of banking regulations can be interpreted as efforts to counteract the distortive effects of fixed-premium deposit insurance. With the introduction of one distortion (the insurance), others are required to prevent too great a departure from the socially ideal result that an unregulated market mechanism would yield. (The fact that FDIC received extensive regulatory powers in conjunction with its insurance responsibilities is consistent with this view.) Not all regulations and portfolio restrictions arise because of deposit insurance, but it often provides a useful framework for evaluating new or existing regulations.

Asset Limitations

Banks are subject to a large number of restrictions on the type or quality of assets they may hold in their portfolios. Banks may not own stocks or significant amounts of real estate; unsecured loans may not exceed 10 percent of a national bank's net worth (the lending limit); equipment leases must be conservatively valued; the quality of bank loans is evaluated carefully by bank examiners (see Bank Examinations). Recently, the Federal regulators promulgated far-reaching restrictions on bank activities in the financial futures markets that many industry observers contend limit banks' ability to profit in these markets.[8] In each instance, the regulations limit bank expansion into areas that are presumed to be relatively risky. Would bankers be better off (more profitable) without such restrictions? Almost certaintly the answer is Yes. Eliminating regulations won't make banks worse off, because they could choose the *same* portfolios if they wanted.

If banks choose new portfolios, it must be because expected profits are higher. Risk may also be increased, though, and the intent of these asset restrictions is to prevent insured banks from undertaking too much risk from society's point of view.

Capital Adequacy

A bank whose acquisition of risky assets is blocked by regulations could increase its shareholders' expected returns by lowering its equity cushion. Earnings from the same volume of assets would then accrue to a smaller number of shareholders, raising the expected return to each one. Since bank equity serves as a buffer to absorb losses, lowering the equity cushion also exposes the FDIC to greater risk. A smaller proportional loss on assets would more readily bring on bankruptcy, raising the probability of an FDIC payout.

[8]Not surprisingly, some of the futures exchanges are most critical of these regulations.

Bank regulations try to prevent this by imposing minimum capital (net worth) ratios that all banks must meet to be considered sound.

The issue of adequate bank capitalization has been hotly debated and is the subject of often bitter dispute between bankers and regulators.[9] It should be. If capital regulations did not constrain bankers (that is, lower their expected return on equity), they wouldn't complain, but neither would the regulation be successfully counteracting the distortive effects of FDIC insurance.

Bank Holding Company Permissible Activities

In some other countries, banks are closely affiliated with a myriad of financial and nonfinancial firms via holding companies or overlapping ownership and management. In the U.S., Congress has limited bank holding companies to activities "so closely related to banking as to be a proper incident thereto" (Bank Holding Company Act, 1970 Amendments). While there may be other reasons for these limitations, bank safety is a prime concern. To allow banks to become closely affiliated with firms in nonbanking lines of commerce, the regulators fear, would expose the banking subsidiary to unacceptable risks

Bank Examinations and Capital Adequacy

On-site FDIC bank examinations play an important part in identifying bank behavior that is considered overly risky. An examination evaluates many dimensions of bank operations, including liquidity, earnings, and the quality of management. In addition, asset quality and capital adequacy receive considerable attention:

> "One of the most important aspects of the examination process is the evaluation of loans, for, in large measure, it is the quality of a bank's loans which determines the risk to depositors." (*FDIC Manual of Examination Policy,* Section H, p. 1.)

> "Some qualifications are necessary, but in general the degree of protection afforded depositors is closely related to the strength of a bank's capital position. For this reason many important phases of the bank examination procedure have as their purpose the determination and analysis of a bank's capital." (*FDIC Manual of Examination Policy,* Section D, p. 1.)

Examiners' loan quality evaluations can heavily influence the level of capital considered adequate for a particular bank.

Loan losses are a routine, if unpleasant, aspect of any bank's operations. In recognition of this, bankers carry a Loan Loss Reserve in the capital

[9]For more on this subject, see Ronald Watson, "Insuring Some Progress in the Bank Capital Hassle," *Business Review,* Federal Reserve Bank of Philadelphia (July 1974), pp. 3–17, or Robert Taggart. "Regulatory Influences on Bank Capital," *New England Economic Review* (September 1977), pp. 37–46.

account. This Reserve represents the banker's best guess of the loans on her books that will not be repaid. If this evaluation is accurate, the bank's balance sheet fairly reflects the value of its assets. (In particular, bank capital—the residual difference between assets and liabilities—is correctly recorded on the balance sheet.) If the Loan Loss Reserve understates likely future losses, however, the bank's books tend to overvalue loan assets and hence overstate the true capital position.

The loan examination process constitutes an effort to verify the adequacy of the Loan Loss Reserve account. The loan examiner generally selects a subset of the bank's loan population for scrutiny, emphasizing relatively large loans and those with recent payment problems. Some examined loans will (usually) be criticized by the examiner, reflecting her opinion that the loan is somewhat unlikely to be repaid in full. In other words, the examiner does not consider the asset to be of bankable quality. The examiners take the bank's reported (book) capital position and *subtract out* a portion of the loans that have been criticized. If the bank's Loan Loss Reserve was at least sufficient to cover the examiner's estimated likely loan losses, there is no change in the bank's reported capital position. Otherwise, the bank's balance sheet overstated the true degree of protection afforded the depositors (and the FDIC). Examiners may require that some loans be written off, or that the Loan Loss Reserve account be increased through retained earnings. In any case, the regulator's determination of bank capital adequacy will be based on the reported book capital *adjusted* for the examiner's estimate of likely loan and security losses.

This connection between loan evaluation and capital adequacy can sometimes make the bank examination process acrimonious. Examiners have the primary power to criticize a bank's activities as too risky, and this criticism affects the bank's need for additional capital. Since more capital reduces the expected rate of return to equity holders, bank management views this process as intrusive. It is. Banks and the FDIC hold differing views on the issue of bank risk taking. On-site examinations constitute a prime tool by which the FDIC monitors and controls its insured banks' activities.

of at least two sorts. First, the public might confuse a troubled holding company or nonbank subsidiary firm with the bank itself and then withdraw deposits and cause a liquidity crisis. Second, the bank may extend unsound loans to other holding company subsidiary firms in an effort to forestall disaster in the nonbanking firms.

Interest Rate Ceilings.

Bank competition for selected types of deposit funds has also been limited by regulation over the years. Congress prohibited the payment of interest on demand deposit (checking) accounts in 1933, and it empowered the Federal Reserve to set maximum permissible rates payable on time and savings deposits (Regulation Q). The initial intent of both these rules was to limit bank risk taking. Banks were viewed as bidding against one another for deposit funds, then being forced to invest in risky assets in order to earn enough to cover their deposit costs.

Over the past fifteen years, financial markets developed an impressive array of devices aimed at circumventing Regulation Q. Faced with this new, unregulated competition, banks often became unable to acquire deposits in sufficient quantity at the regulated rates. While deposit rate regulation was introduced as a means of limiting bank risk exposure, it had instead become a threat to bank stability. This development was recognized by Congress when it voted in March, 1980 to eliminate Regulation Q ceilings by 1986. (This process is under the control of the Federal Depository Institution Deregulation Committee.)

It is impossible to identify precisely how much these various regulations reduce the additional risks banks take in response to their deposit insurance. The key point, however, is that insurance and regulation are *linked* activities. If one side is subjected to reforms—take deregulation as an example—then unless something is done with the present insurance scheme society will be left to bear more risk (see Reforming Deposit Insurance).

Reforming Deposit Insurance*

If the existing deposit insurance system requires such a myriad of restrictive bank regulations, why not change the system and remove the regulatory burden? Either of two significant reforms would eliminate some of the current system's distortions, but each would be difficult to implement in practice.

First, Federal deposit insurance could be eliminated entirely. Eliminating the FDIC would strengthen the impact of market forces on bank risk-taking decisions, allowing at least some bank regulations to be removed. At the same time, however, depositors would find themselves exposed to more risk, and they would have to evaluate their investment decisions more carefully. Imposing this burden on small depositors seems to contradict the initial spirit of the Federal insurance program. A middle course here would reduce the extent of FDIC coverage, for example from $100,000 back down to $20,000 or $10,000. Deposit costs would then reflect bankers' asset decisions more closely, while small savers, for whom investment and information evaluation costs are presumably most burdensome, would still benefit from insurance protection.

A second possible reform would be to make the insurance premium paid by banks vary according to the riskiness of their portfolios. (The Federal Savings and Loan Insurance Corporation has announced its intention to pursue a policy of this sort.) Just as automobile insurance companies charge more to insure unsafe drivers, riskier banks would pay a higher price for

**Editors' Note: The following article by Larry Wall surveys the latest reform proposals of the insuring agencies.*

insurance than safe banks. With a perfectly accurate method of assessing the risk of a bank's portfolio, a variable premium system would mimic the private market. It would give bankers the socially correct incentives to undertake risks while extending the benefits of Federal deposit insurance to bank depositors. The problem here is that any practical system for measuring risk would be imperfect, overestimating the risk of some activities while underestimating others. (This is also true of other existing types of insurance.) If bankers and their customers felt a particular activity was really less risky than the FDIC did, the bankers would find it unprofitable to undertake these investments because the expected return would not cover deposit costs plus the variable insurance premium. Alternatively, an FDIC premium that bankers considered too low for some particular type of risk would generate too much risk taking of this sort.

Distortions to bank asset portfolios would not disappear under a variable rate system, but they probably would be smaller. Some existing bank regulations could be modified accordingly or eliminated. Offsetting these gains, however, would be the increased complexity of determining an appropriate FDIC premium rate for each bank. Accurately comparing the effects of a risk-related FDIC premium versus the current system is a formidable task but one that bears further study.

Conclusion

Bankers benefit substantially from fixed-rate FDIC insurance, which allows them to procure a large supply of funds at a low (that is, riskless) interest rate regardless of their assets' riskiness. Severing the connection between portfolio risk and deposit costs leads banks to undertake risks they otherwise wouldn't, secure in the knowledge that they get all the benefits of a good outcome while suffering less than all of any losses that may occur. To counteract this distortion, regulators impose portfolio restrictions, capital standards, and so forth on insured banks as a means of limiting the risk the FDIC is forced to insure against. These regulations limit bankers' freedom and may reduce bank profits. Yet neither of these observations implies that the attendant regulations are socially bad, only that they are effective. If bankers felt no pain from regulators' actions, the regulations could not be affecting bank behavior!

Is there too much corrective regulation? This is a very difficult question to answer. It requires a careful comparison of society's losses (in terms of lower output) from the restrictions placed on bank decision making versus the social benefits of a safer financial environment. To date, no one has made much of an attempt to grapple with this big issue. Until some answers are generated, it will be quite difficult to say how much regulation (or deregulation) is ideal from society's point of view.

Appendix
A Simple Example of How FDIC Insurance Can Distort Bank Risk-Bearing Incentives

This example is set in a highly simplified world. The bank finances its asset acquisitions by issuing a single type of deposit liability, and it has no net worth. Uncertainty is limited to the fact that either of two possible states of the world may occur in the future. Bank assets return their higher value in the good state, and their lower value in the bad state. At the time investments are made, each future state of the world is considered equally likely to occur. (That is, each has a probability equal to 1/2.)

EXAMPLE 1: Determining the Deposit Rate and Equity Market Value.

This first example serves to illustrate the basic components of bank valuation. Assume the bank buys a one-period asset today for $900. If state number 1 occurs, the bank's asset will be worth $1,000, while in the second possible state the asset's value will be $2,000. The bank finances itself by issuing a deposit liability of $900, giving it an initial balance sheet:

Assets	Liabilities
900	900
	0 Net Worth

At the end of one time period the bank will collect on its assets, pay off the depositors, and go out of business. The riskless market rate of interest is 6 percent per year.

The value of the firm's equity can be calculated from the expected value of its future profits, assuming *risk neutrality* on the part of the owners and depositors.* First consider the depositors. Even in the bad future state of the world the bank will be able to pay off depositors their principal plus interest at the riskless rate ($954). The deposit rate will therefore be 6 percent. Risk-neutral owners will value the bank's equity at the net present value of expected future earnings after interest payments. Ignoring the discount rate:

$$\begin{aligned} \text{Value of equity} &= \tfrac{1}{2}\,(\text{profit in state 1}) + \tfrac{1}{2}\,(\text{profit in state 2}) \\ &= \tfrac{1}{2}\,(1000 - 900(1.06)) + \tfrac{1}{2}(2000 - 900(1.06)) \\ &= \$546. \end{aligned}$$

In other words, the right to receive this bank's (uncertain) end-of-period profits would be worth $546.

*A person is risk neutral if she will take a fair bet. For example, consider a game where the dealer flips a coin, promising to pay the player $1.00 if heads come up, but nothing in the event of tails. A risk-neutral person would pay up to 50¢ to play this game—the expected (mean) value of the winnings. A *risk-averse* person would pay less than 50¢; a *risk-loving* person would pay (a maximum of) more than 50¢.

EXAMPLE 2: Risk Bearing With Deposit Insurance.

Now consider the situation where the firm has the opportunity to buy an additional asset for \$300. The firm will have to borrow \$300 to acquire the asset, resulting in the balance sheet.

Assets	Liabilities
900	900
	+300
+300	
	0 Net Worth

The new asset will be worth \$100 in state number 1 and \$500 in state number 2, giving it an expected return of 0 percent [$\frac{1}{2}$ (100) + $\frac{1}{2}$ (500) = 300, the asset's purchase price]. No one should wish to purchase such an asset when the riskless market rate is 6 percent. Nonetheless, it will be shown that a bank whose deposits are insured at a fixed premium would be willing to buy this asset.

At the end of the period, the firm's total assets will be worth \$1,100 (\$1,000 for the initial asset plus \$100 for the new one) in state number 1 and \$2,500 (the initial \$2,000 plus \$500) in state number 2. Bankruptcy will result if state number 1 occurs: depositors will not be paid interest (or even repaid all the principal). FDIC insurance is now valuable to the bank's owners. Suppose FDIC promises to repay the bank's depositors in full (including interest) in return for a \$1.00 premium (.083 percent of the \$1,200 deposits). Insured depositors will lend to the bank at the riskless rate of 6 percent, making the value of equity:

$$= \tfrac{1}{2}(1100 - 1200\ (1.06) - 1) + \tfrac{1}{2}(2500 - 1200\ (1.06) - 1)$$
$$= \tfrac{1}{2}(1100 - 1273) + \tfrac{1}{2}(2500 - 1273).$$

Since expenses in the first state of the world are greater than earnings, the owners expect to receive no return for this period and will default on their obligations—that is, the firm will be declared bankrupt. (Because of deposit insurance, however, all deposits will still be paid off.) Even though the firm is worth nothing if state number 1 occurs, owners will bid a positive price for the firm's equity because profits will be positive if state number 2 occurs:

$$\text{Value of equity} = \tfrac{1}{2}(0) + \tfrac{1}{2}(2500 - 1273)$$
$$= \$613.50.$$

With deposits insured by FDIC, the owners of the bank will undertake to buy the new asset because the value of their equity rises from \$546 (without the new asset) to \$613.50. Why does this occur? Because the owners receive *all the profits* in the good state of the world but *have only limited liability* in the bad state of the world.

EXAMPLE 3: Risk Bearing Without Deposit Insurance.

Now suppose the bank's deposits are not insured. If the bad state of the world occurs, the firm goes bankrupt and the depositors as a group receive only \$1,100 for their \$1,200 of deposits. To compensate for this possible loss, the depositors must be offered a rate of return (R) in the good state of the world high enough to make their *expected* return on deposits equal to or greater than the risk-free rate. That is, for deposits of $1,200, depositors must be promised a rate R such that:

$$\tfrac{1}{2}(1100) + \tfrac{1}{2}(1200\ (1 + R)) \geq 1200\ (1 + .06)$$

$$R \geq 20.3 \text{ percent.}$$

Risk-neutral depositors would accept a promised return of 20.3 percent: risk averse depositors would demand more.

With this higher promised deposit rate, the value of the bank's equity after it purchases the $300 asset will be:

$$= \tfrac{1}{2}(0) + \tfrac{1}{2}(2500 - 1200\ (1 + .203))$$

$$= \$528.02.$$

Undertaking this new investment without deposit insurance therefore would make the firm's value drop below its initial value ($546). The bank would not invest in the asset, which is the socially correct decision.

These examples could be made considerably more realistic by increasing the number of possible future states, introducing positive net worth and several classes of depositors, allowing risk-averse depositors or bank owners, and so forth. None of these changes would alter the basic conclusions. The important implication of this example is that a *bank will undertake risky projects with a fixed-premium insurance program that it would not normally undertake*. The bank has an incentive to take on greater risks because it does not pay FDIC a premium that fully reflects the *social* cost of the bank's risk taking.

The Future of Deposit Insurance: An Analysis of the Insuring Agencies' Proposals

Larry D. Wall

28

Congress had recognized that even though deposit insurance has provided valuable benefits, the role of deposit insurance in deregulating the financial system should be reviewed. The Garn-St. Germain Act of 1982 required the Federal Deposit Insurance Corporation, the Federal Home Loan Bank Board and the National Credit Union Association to conduct such reviews, and report their recommendations. In their reports, all three agencies affirm that deposit insurance performs a valuable function, but each argues for specific reforms. . . . This article will critically evaluate the proposed reforms.

Goals of Deposit Insurance

The agencies give several reasons for deposit insurance: protection of the money supply, protection of the payments mechanism, protection of small depositors, reduction in the cost of using money, protection of small financial institutions, provision of funds to mortgage markets and encouragement of credit unions. The FDIC and FHLBB assert that the major goal of deposit insurance should be the protection of the money supply and the payments mechanism, while the NCUA places more emphasis on protecting small depositors.

Reprinted from *Economic Review* (March, 1984): 26–39 by permission of the Federal Reserve Bank of Atlanta and the author.

Review of the Agencies' Recommendations

The three insuring agencies each proposed several deposit insurance reforms. All three insuring agencies said that insurance should be reformed to provide greater incentives for insured institutions to limit their risk exposure. The agencies also made some important recommendations on other specific insurance issues.

The FDIC favored a reduction in the effective coverage of deposits to give the private sector a greater incentive to monitor bank risk. The FDIC has handled most large bank failures through the purchase and assumption method, in which a healthy bank purchases some of the assets and assumes all the deposits of the failed bank. This has had the effect of providing 100 percent deposit insurance to all deposits, including those with balances in excess of $100,000. The FDIC discussed the possibility of reducing the coverage of balances in excess of $100,000 and has subsequently announced that it will use a modified payout system at failed banks. Under this plan, when a bank fails, its uninsured depositors will receive an immediate advance equal to the amount the FDIC expects to recover for them. The FDIC would also return more money to the uninsured depositors if more funds are recovered than was expected.

The FDIC also proposed a fairly well developed variable rate deposit insurance premium plan. It said that the premium credit that banks receive should depend on their riskiness. The proposal called for a full credit for normal risk banks, a 50 percent credit for high risk banks, and no credit for very high risk banks. The FDIC expected the "vast majority of banks to be normal risk." The FDIC also provided a detailed discussion of how banks will be assigned to the three categories. The FDIC's variable rate insurance plan is not intended to influence bank risk positions, and will not do so because the size of the premium credit is too small. The FDIC does hope that its plan will bring greater equity to bank insurance premium payments by reducing the subsidy that normal banks provide to risky banks.

The FDIC argued that it should disclose supervisory actions taken against individual banks. The FDIC also argued that it should have sole responsibility for examining and insuring all banks and thrifts. If this part of the FDIC plan were implemented, then the FSLIC would be absorbed by the FDIC, which would also take over the Federal Reserve's and Comptroller of the Currency's examination responsibilities.

The FHLBB also supports variable rate deposit insurance premiums. Unlike the FDIC, however, the FHLBB wants its variable rate insurance premiums to influence insured institutions' risk exposure. The FHLBB report discussed the principles on which it would base variable rate insurance, but it did not provide any details on how its plan would work.

Private deposit insurance should be developed to provide additional coverage to government insured deposits, according to the FHLBB. The

FHLBB would have the government insure deposits up to some minimum, with private insurance covering the excess. It also suggested some cap on private insurer's liability in case of a macro-economic policy failure. The FHLBB hopes that private insurers could substitute at least in part for government regulatory agencies in controlling insured institutions' risk. The FHLBB also proposed several measures intended to make thrift owners and managers more accountable for the risk position of their institution.

The FHLBB pointed out that many of the services provided to banks by several government agencies are consolidated for thrifts in the FHLBB. The FHLBB argues that consolidation of the services, such as chartering, examining and insuring in one agency is more efficient and facilitates the handling of failures. This leads the FHLBB to conclude that the bank regulatory agencies should be rationalized before the insurance funds are consolidated. The FHLBB report was written before its current chairman, Edwin J. Gray, took over. Gray is unambiguously opposed to agency consolidation.

The NCUA proposed two measures to reduce the risk exposure of credit unions: large accounts (over $50,000) at credit unions should have insurance premiums and the first share of every credit union member should be uninsured. Most accounts at credit unions are small. The NCUA believes that the larger accounts are attracted by high interest rates at aggressive credit unions. It thinks that these aggressive credit unions are also taking on excessive risks to afford the high interest rates they pay. The NCUA would uninsure the first share of all credit union members to give members greater incentives to monitor their credit union's risk.

The NCUA believes that private insurance is at least as good as government insurance for credit unions. The agency, therefore, proposes that federal credit unions be given the option of substituting private insurance for public insurance. The NCUA also believes that its fund is inadequate and it proposes a one-time assessment from credit unions to provide more resources to the fund. Credit unions would be assessed 1 percent of their insured shares to provide additional resources to the fund.

The NCUA is opposed to consolidating its insurance fund with the other funds, arguing that credit union interests would be ignored in an agency responsible for the banking and thrift industries.

The Money Supply and the Payments System

Protecting the money supply and the payments mechanism are important functions of deposit insurance. Depository institutions have a dominant position in both; hence, insurance can protect the money supply and the payments system by protecting those depository institutions.

While economists differ on how important the money supply is to the economy, virtually all agree that a stable supply of money is essential to a smoothly operating economy.

The payments mechanism is important because it contributes to the efficient transfer of money in the economy. Cash transactions are more efficient than barter, but exchanging cash is inconvenient and expensive for many transactions. The cost of using cash can be particularly significant for large transactions. Today's payments systems (which are dominated by paper checks and wire transfers) are convenient and less expensive. Depository institutions are important because they dominate third-party payments transfer systems.

Deposit insurance, therefore, protects the money supply and the payments mechanism by maintaining public confidence in depository institutions. Depository institutions depend on public confidence. Without such confidence, depositors would withdraw their deposits. Insurance protects depository institutions by eliminating the incentive for people to redeem their deposits because it guarantees depositors that they will keep their funds, no matter what happens to their institution.

But deposit insurance does not provide complete protection of the money supply or the payments mechanism, because only depository institutions are insured. Insured depository institutions historically have had a dominant position in the money supply and payments mechanism, so the unprotected portion of both is small. This position has been eroding, however, and at some point in the future protecting insured depository institutions may not provide adequate protection to the money supply and payments mechanism.

Depository institutions' dominant position in the money supply appears to be more secure than their position in the payments system. If other features of the accounts are roughly similar, individuals have an incentive to place their money in insured depository institutions because of government deposit insurance. This incentive has only limited value, however, and individuals will move their money to nondepository institutions under the right circumstances. For example, money market mutual funds (MMMF) grew very rapidly during the late 1970s and early 1980s. MMMF growth was due in large part, however, to the interest rate restrictions imposed on depository institutions. When a money market account with no interest ceiling was authorized for insured institutions in 1982, some of the funds that had been in MMMFs returned to depository institutions. Thus, deposit insurance can help depository institutions maintain their de facto dominance of the money supply, but only if insured institutions offer competitive transaction accounts.

Depository institutions' virtually dominant position in the payments system is eroding. Depository institutions have a dominant role in checks and wire transfer, but the importance of checks in the economy is being reduced through time.[1] Non-depository firms are playing a larger role in newer technologies such as ATMs and point-of-sale networks.[2]

If depository institutions lose their dominant position in the payments system, then deposit insurance will lose its ability to protect the system and other methods will have to be found to protect the payments mechanism.

[1]See the August 1983 issue of the *Economic Review* for a discussion of the future of checks and other payments systems.

[2]For example, Penney's is planning on using its communications network to carry payments information for unaffiliated corporations. See the November 1983 issue of *Transition*.

Cost of Using Money

Deposit insurance also can reduce the information costs of using money.[3] In the absence of deposit insurance, any person or business wanting a checking account would need to evaluate the financial health of individual depository institutions. Furthermore, some individuals might be reluctant to accept checks drawn on weaker depository institutions and the cost of accepting checks would be substantial. Deposit insurance can reduce this cost by transferring the risk of loss and the responsibility for evaluating risks to the insuring body. This advantage of deposit insurance exists whether or not banks are vulnerable to financial panics. Individuals have an incentive to check on the financial health of depository institutions so long as bank failure can cause losses for depositors or those who receive checks, because banks can still fail due to insolvency.

Other Benefits of Insurance

In addition to these three general advantages, deposit insurance may benefit specific individuals and institutions. It may protect small, unsophisticated transaction account holders from loss. Many small depositors lack the ability to analyze financial institutions, and the costs of losing a small deposit can be important to them.

Deposit insurance also can help maintain the level of service in various local areas. If a depository institution fails, its community loses the services provided by the failed bank. Deposit insurance does not, however, guarantee that any community will receive a given level of service. It neither guarantees that a depository institution will be established in every community that desires one, nor that institutions will provide all the services desired by a community.

Deposit insurance also protects individuals' wealth. This raises problems, because insurance guarantees one investment, insured deposits, while leaving other forms of wealth at risk. Insuring wealth held as deposits results in those who hold a below-average proportion of their wealth in insured deposits subsidizing those who hold an above-average proportion of their wealth in insured accounts. Insuring deposits also increases the proportion of wealth placed in depository institutions. Any government deposit insurance system inherently guarantees some of the wealth of some individuals.

Some regard the ability of insurance to funnel wealth into insured institutions as an opportunity rather than a disadvantage. For example, the FHLBB notes that the FSLIC was originally created to maintain and improve the flow of funds to the housing industry, by lowering the cost of funds to institutions making mortgage loans. The question is whether deposit insurance is an efficient means of subsidy. The benefits of deposit insurance flow to all savings and loan customers whether or not Congress wants to subsidize them, including wealthy individuals who can buy unsubsidized houses. A direct subsidy would allow Congress to target its aid with greater efficiency.

Deposit insurance also provides benefits to two particular types of depository institutions: small institutions and credit unions. To the extent that depositors believe smaller institutions are riskier, in the absence of insurance they will favor larger institutions. The

[3]See Merton for a discussion of the role of deposit insurance in reducing the costs of using money.

NCUA report notes that credit union officials believe insurance benefits them by helping in the competition for funds, encouraging sponsoring organizations to create new credit unions, and allowing credit unions to venture into new activities knowing that the insurance fund will handle any severe problems.

The desirability of using deposit insurance to benefit specific institutions seems questionable. The cost to society of allowing individual institutions to fail is relatively low, according to George Benston. The real price of not allowing depository institutions to fail, Benston argues, is that it allows inefficient firms to continue operating.[4]

The Need to Reform Deposit Insurance

Deposit insurance provides several benefits to society, but it can also impose costs. The magnitude of those costs depends on the details of the deposit insurance system. At an extreme, a system of 100 percent insurance offered at no cost would provide a significant subsidy to institutions and their customers by having the government insuror absorb all risk of failure. Such a system also would encourage depository institutions to take on loans that yield a high return but are also very risky.[5] If the loans were paid off, the depository institution would profit. If the loans were not paid off, the insuror would cover the losses.

Three ways of reducing these costs of deposit insurance to society have been discussed recently: (a) some liabilities can be given less than 100 percent insurance, (b) premiums can be charged, and (c) regulations can be imposed to limit institutions' risk taking. All three methods are built into current laws providing for deposit insurance, but the agencies say that in practice these limitations have been ineffective. Each depositor is guaranteed insurance only on the first $100,000, but most cases of failure have resulted in full deposit insurance for all depositors.[6] Insurance premiums have reduced the costs by making insured institutions bear the costs of ordinary failures. The agencies note, however, that insurance premiums have not limited institutions' risk exposure because the rates charged do not vary according to the bank's risk.

The FDIC and FHLBB reports argue that regulation has limited the risk exposure of insured institutions, but their reports offer only limited evidence to support this view. Furthermore, a case can be made that the institutions' management, rather than regulation, has limited their riskiness. For example, regulations do not prevent depository institutions from taking on enormous interest rate risk, but most have avoided doing so.[7] Furthermore, regulation generates incentives to innovate with substitutes that are not covered by regulation.[8] In some cases the regulations may actually weaken the ability of deposit insurance

[4]See Tussig for an analysis of why banks should be allowed to fail. See also George Benston, "Deposit Insurance and Bank Failures."

[5]A simple demonstration of the effect of deposit insurance on banks' incentives to take risks is given in Flannery. More analytic demonstrations are given by Kareken and Wallace, Merton and Sharpe.

[6]Other liability holders, such as subordinated debt holders, do suffer losses when an insured institution fails.

[7]Those institutions that did assume large interest rate risks, primarily thrifts, did so in large part because they were required to invest in long term, fixed rate mortgages.

[8]See Kane and Eisenbeis.

to protect the money supply by inducing innovations (like money market mutual funds) by uninsured firms. Regulations that limit depository institutions also impose costs on consumers because they limit consumers' options.

Another reason why banks can be expected to become more risky in a deregulated environment is given by George Benston.* He notes that at one time many regulations protected banks from the competition of other banks and in some cases nonbank suppliers of financial services. This protection made a bank charter a valuable possession because it gave the owner an opportunity to earn an above-market rate of return. Aside from usual stockholder interest, bank owners were reluctant to take risks that might cause the bank to fail because that would mean giving up their valuable charter. Recent deregulation, however, has exposed banks to more competition and reduced banks' ability to earn an above-market rate of return. Presumably, this has lowered the value of the bank charter to its owners and increased their incentives to take risks. In other words, the franchise lost by bank owners is less valuable if their bank fails in a deregulated environment rather than in a heavily regulated environment.[9]

The old system of generally providing 100 percent de facto insurance coverage and no tiering (varying premiums according to bank risk) of insurance premiums provides an incentive for banks to take on excessive risk. Deregulation, as mentioned, may extend the problem by increasing insured institutions' ability and incentive to take risks. In this situation, some combination of increased incentives for private parties to monitor institutions' risk, risk-related premiums and increased regulation may be desirable to offset the incentives to take risk.

Critique of FDIC Insurance Reforms

The FDIC report argues that deposit insurance should protect the money supply, the payments system and small depositors. It further notes that the current flat rate premium schedule overcharges safe banks, and that the current system does not impose sufficient controls on insured institutions' risk. The FDIC report proposes that tiering insurance premiums would be more equitable, and that the risk exposure of insured institutions would be reduced if private parties had a greater stake in the failure of insured institutions. The FDIC report, therefore, suggests several proposals for placing private parties at greater risk and the agency subsequently decided to implement one of the proposals, eliminating the 100 percent de facto insurance coverage on deposits.[10] Would proposals in the FDIC report enhance protection of the money supply or the payments system? Would they reduce the degree of bank risk?

The FDIC plan to tier insurance rates is indeed more equitable to banks. The current system makes the strongest banks pay as much as the weakest banks. The FDIC does not, however, depend on risk related premiums to reduce bank risks. The proposed differences

Editor's Note: The Benston article is selection 26 in this book.

[9]This argument would be much stronger if it presented some evidence that regulation did increase the value of insured institutions' charters.

[10]FDIC plans are reported in Slater.

in insurance premiums charged by the FDIC have typically amounted to less than 4 percent of banks' operating income before taxes, a relatively small proportion. Instead, the FDIC relies on a reduction in de facto insurance coverage to reduce bank risk exposure.

The FDIC proposes to reduce the effective coverage of deposits to $100,000 in order to get large depositors to monitor the risk exposure of banks. Undoubtedly, some large depositors will evaluate bank risks and charge appropriate risk premiums as the FDIC wishes. The problem with the proposal is that large depositors can follow a variety of other strategies that will defeat the FDIC's intentions.

One of the problems is that the elimination of the de facto coverage of large depositors could provide them with more incentive to participate in bank runs. Deposit insurance reduces depositors' incentive to participate in runs by reducing their risk of loss. If insurance coverage is reduced then the incentive to participate in runs increases. The FDIC argues that its proposal does not impose large enough risks on depositors to induce bank runs. Two pieces of evidence suggest caution, however. First, large depositors already flee when an insured institution begins having financial difficulties because of the risk that the FDIC will enforce the $100,000 coverage limit.[11] Second, the FDIC estimates that its future expenses at failed banks will probably average 9 or 10 percent of the failed bank's assets. This suggests that uninsured depositors may lose a large amount of money in future bank failures.

The FDIC proposal does provide uninsured depositors with immediate access to some of their funds, a condition that might reduce the potential for bank runs based entirely on depositors' concern for liquidity. The FDIC report includes no evidence, however, that bank runs are based primarily on 'depositors' concern for liquidity. Furthermore, the potential for losses of 9 to 10 percent might motivate rapid withdrawals by large depositors.

Another problem with the FDIC proposal is that it allows large depositors to substantially reduce their risk of loss by following a strategy that weakens the stability of the entire financial system. That is, large depositors can reduce their riskiness by holding all their deposits in demand deposits and very short term deposits. If large depositors did this, they would not need to monitor their bank's condition. Uninsured depositors could substantially reduce their risk by withdrawing their deposits when they heard a rumor about the bank having financial problems or about examiners visiting the bank. If many depositors followed this strategy, then the FDIC's plan would reduce the stability of banks while the agency still would bear the most risk of failure. The number of large depositors following this strategy will be reduced if long term rates are significantly higher than short term rates, but the number will be increased if the risk of bank failures increases.

The FDIC notes that its plan may have limited effectiveness at banks with few large deposits. The plan relies on uninsured depositors to reduce banks' risk exposure. A bank could avoid uninsured depositors' discipline, however, by minimizing its number of large accounts. Banks limiting their clientele to individuals and small businesses may have few accounts with balances over $100,000. Elsewhere in this issue, Caroline Harless explains

[11] For example, Sinkey reports that $550 million in uninsured deposits were withdrawn from Franklin National prior to its failure.

how brokered deposits can be used to avoid the $100,000 limit. Thus, the uninsured deposit feature might not have much effect on the risk exposure of some banks.

These concerns do not imply that the money supply and payments system are in any danger. The Federal Reserve can still prevent a bank run from forcing banks to close by providing adequate liquidity to the financial system through open market operations. Congress and the financial system should recognize, however, that the FDIC's plans would shift more of the burden of protecting the financial system to the Federal Reserve.

Critique of FHLBB Insurance Reforms

Thrifts, the FHLBB reports says, were originally given insurance to help maintain a steady flow of funds to the mortgage markets. The report predicts that some thrifts are going to reduce their role in the mortgage markets and begin to function more like commercial banks. This change will obviate somewhat the original reason for insuring thrifts, but also will provide a new set of reasons for insurance—the same reasons given for insuring commercial banks. The FHLBB proposes several measures to reduce thrift risk exposure: variable rate insurance premiums, partial reliance on private insurance, greater emphasis on legally enforcing the fiduciary responsibility of managers and directors, encouragement of mutual organizations to convert to stock organizations, and increased emphasis on capital adequacy.

The FHLBB notes that thrift insurance helps provide funds to the mortgage markets, but it does not argue that this role in itself justifies the continuation of deposit insurance. The report says that as thrifts gain more transaction accounts, the rationale for insuring thrifts will be the same as that for insuring commercial banks. But, so far, thrifts have not attracted a large volume of transaction accounts.[12] The FHLBB also discusses the protection that insurance provides to small institutions and depositors, but does not argue that these reasons are sufficient to justify continuing insurance.

The traditional case for insuring thrifts may appear to be weak, but withdrawing insurance is not a practical alternative. Thrifts with significant transaction accounts should be insured for the same reasons that banks are insured. If insurance were limited to thrifts with significant transaction accounts, then thrifts would maintain insurance by encouraging their time and savings depositors to convert to transactions accounts. Such a conversion would result in the continued deposit insurance for thrifts, but might also increase interest rate risk exposure. Conversion of accounts would increase thrifts' interest rate risk by shortening the maturity of their deposits while doing nothing about the long term nature of their mortgages.

The FHLBB report advances risk-related insurance premiums as an important means of reducing the risk exposure of the institutions it insures. The agency acknowledges that it cannot determine what premiums an insured institution should be charged to exactly offset the risks that it imposes on the FSLIC. The report also acknowledges that the existing

[12]Transaction and Super Now Accounts were only 3.0 percent of deposits at savings and loans on March 31, 1983 according to Olin. She also reports that MMDAs accounted for 18 percent of their deposits.

empirical evidence to support such a risk-based system is weak. It nevertheless backs risk-related premiums as preferable to flat rate premiums.

Variable rate premiums charged by a government agency raise significant questions. One problem with government-determined insurance premiums is that correcting rate mispricing is costly. If a formula fails to measure risk adequately, then it can be corrected only through a costly appeal to Congress or the courts.

Another problem with variable rate government insurance is that appeals to the courts and Congress might be made on non-economic grounds. That is, the premiums set by the insuring agency might induce institutions to reduce their risk exposure, but they also might induce the institutions to look for other ways of reducing rates. Any action by a regulatory agency can be overturned by the courts or by Congress.[13] If a government agency set insurance premiums, then the premiums would be based not only on insured institutions' risk, but also on such legal and political factors.[14]

The FDIC and FHLBB reports' variable premium plans are both subject to these questions, but bear more heavily on the FHLBB plan. Problems with the FDIC premium formula are minor because the agency does not rely on risk-related premiums to control risk and because the differences in the rates charged are small. If the FHLBB risk penalties are significantly larger than those of the FDIC (which they should be given FHLBB objectives) then any problems in the FHLBB premium formula might affect thrifts' risk position and income more significantly.

The FHLBB "private insurance" proposal may increase the incentive for runs, even though it also limits private insurers' liabilities. The FHLBB cannot guarantee that private insurers will have sufficient liquid funds to meet their obligations. If depositors were unsure of a private insurance company's ability to meet its entire obligation in a timely manner, they would presumably consider withdrawing their deposits from institutions rumored to be in trouble.[15]

The FHLBB's other proposals are unlikely to affect thrift risk positions significantly. Its proposal to enforce the fiduciary responsibility of thrift managers may discourage reckless behavior, but it is a relatively blunt tool for managing thrift risk exposure. A proposal to maintain capital adequacy at thrifts remains to be specified.

[13]An example of interference from the courts is the case of Biscayne Federal Savings and Loan. The owners of Biscayne Federal fought the FSLIC closure of this institution through the courts and won a preliminary ruling in their favor although the FSLIC won on appeal several months later. An example of the use of the political process to interfere in bank regulation is the pressure applied on bank regulators with regard to past due bank loans to farmers.

[14]The Bush Commission has suggested that variable rate insurance premiums are desirable but that the agencies should rely on private sector judgments to the extent feasible. Neither of the problems with government insurance premiums are avoided by relying on private sector judgement. One government agency will still have to sift through the multitude of private sector opinions to determine an institution's risk. Many opinions of an institution's risk may be listened to, but insured institutions' premiums would still depend on the judgement of one agency. If institutions dislike that opinion, they still must engage in a costly legal or political appeal. Furthermore, if an insured institution does appeal to the courts or Congress, it can and probably will use noneconomic as well as economic arguments.

[15]This problem did occur for privately insured Mississippi savings and loans in the mid-1970s. See Left and Park for a discussion of the Mississippi experience.

The FHLBB report also mentions the desirability of thrift conversions from mutual organizations to stock organizations. Conversion would help thrifts by making it easier for them to raise new equity capital, but it is not certain that it would reduce their risk exposure. The FHLBB notes that equity holders do not lose when a mutual organization fails (since the depositors are also the shareholders) but that stockholders lose when a stock organization fails. The FHLBB report concludes, therefore, that mutuals may be less sensitive to their risk exposure than stock organizations. In a stock organization, on the other hand, the stockholders stand to benefit from successful gambles. Thus it is not obvious that stock organizations will be less risky.

Critique of NCUA Proposals

The NCUA report provides a strong case for reforming credit union share insurance. It favors allowing federal credit unions to substitute private insurance for government insurance, imposing higher premiums on large deposits, and creating a deductible for share insurance. The question is whether private insurance is an acceptable substitute for government insurance and whether higher premiums on large accounts and a deductible would reduce credit unions' risk exposure.

The NCUA report says that share insurance was originally provided to " . . . reward credit unions for a job well done and provide parity in insurance with other financial institutions." The NCUA then lists several advantages credit union officials believe they obtain from insurance. It does not specifically endorse any of the other advantages. These advantages generally embody subsidies, in one way or another, of credit unions by government insurance. The NCUA also argues that individuals should be able to have savings and transactions accounts required for routine needs at any institution without risk of loss. To meet this criterion, of course, the government would have to insure savings accounts at all institutions, which the NCUA proposes to do.

Credit union shares warrant insurance because they are a depository institution that offers a transaction account. Insuring credit union accounts would reduce the cost of using money to credit union members and would help protect the money supply.

The NCUA report maintains it is not important whether credit unions are insured by the federal government or private insurers; what matters is that they are insured. This raises the question of why government insurance of credit unions is needed if a private substitute is available. The NCUA answers that the government should be an "insurer of the last resort," maintaining that every credit union, no matter how risky, is entitled to insurance. An "insurer of the last resort" might be justified if the government wished to subsidize credit unions through share insurance or to protect wealth held at credit unions. Yet, as is noted above, subsidizing institutions and protecting wealth held in depository institutions are dubious justifications for insurance.

If the purpose of insuring credit unions, as with other depository institutions, is to protect the money supply and reduce the cost of transferring money, then private insurance is no substitute for government insurance. Private insurers' resources are limited, so these insurers are vulnerable to a loss of confidence. If shareholders lost confidence in the private insurer's ability, then the insurance would not be able to prevent a financial panic. Furthermore, depositors concerned about the safety of their money would have to evaluate both the credit union and its private insurer. Therefore private deposit insurance can neither protect the financial system from financial panic nor reduce the cost of using money to the same degree as government insurance.

The NCUA proposal to increase insurance premiums on accounts above $50,000 is not intended to affect the risk exposure of most credit unions. Whether this is a desirable measure for influencing the risk exposure of some credit unions depends on their role in our financial system. If credit unions are to become fullfledged competitors with other depository institutions, then the scaling of insurance premiums to account size would unnecessarily handicap their ability to compete. If, on the other hand, credit unions should serve only individuals of modest means, then such a scaling of premiums would both reinforce credit unions' role and reduce the risk exposure of some credit unions by discouraging them from seeking large deposits.

The proposal to eliminate insurance on the first share conflicts with the NCUA's stated purpose for deposit insurance without providing the NCUA with much protection. The agency argues that uninsuring one share would "... recreate, we believe, a greater sense of responsibility for the credit union among its members." The NCUA continues, however, that "An individual should be able to deposit a reasonable amount of funds ... without being required to constantly monitor the safety and soundness of the institution and worry about loss."[16] Thus, the proposal would have depositors (shareholders) monitor their credit union, but says that insurance is needed so that they will not have to monitor the credit union. Society benefits if people do not have to use their resources to monitor the safety of their transactions accounts. Another problem is that other depository institutions would offer fully insured accounts. If shareholders are concerned about the safety of their shares, they may shift funds to fully insured institutions. Those who decide to leave their funds in a credit union would be those least likely to care about their credit union's risk exposure.

An Alternative Reform

Deposit insurance performs several valuable functions, but a poorly structured deposit insurance system also can impose significant costs. The current system needs to be reformed, but proposals to increase depositor exposure to risk, to charge risk-related premiums and to substitute private for public insurance all have significant problems. Fortunately, other reforms could reduce deposit insurance's cost while preserving its benefits. One appealing reform idea—that banks be required to carry more subordinated debt—is contained in the FDIC report.[17] Subordinated debt holders may lose their invest-

[16]Pages 2–6 of the NCUA report.

[17]Horvitz also argues in a series of articles, which appeared in the *American Banker*, that subordinated debt is a better method of controlling bank risk.

ment if a bank fails, so they have an incentive to monitor a bank's risk. Maturity requirements could be placed on subordinated debt so that the debt, unlike demand deposits and short-term deposits, could not leave the bank at the first sign of trouble. Subordinated debt holders do not share in the benefits of bank risks that pay off, so they have no incentive to encourage the bank to take more risks.

A modest increase in required subordinated debt at insured institutions would encourage the institutions to decrease their risk exposure. A substantial increase would be even better because it would allow discipline imposed by private creditors to replace at least some of the discipline currently imposed by government regulation. Ideally, the requirements for the total of an institution's subordinated debt plus equity should be lifted to a point where the private sector bears virtually all the risk of failure. Such a shift would reduce the need for most other government safety and soundness regulations. Government regulation of institutions' equity capital position, for example, might be unnecessary. The financial markets could control depository institutions' equity capital positions as they do for most corporations.

An increase in subordinated debt seems to offer a logical long run solution, but it would take time to implement. The amount of subordinated debt that can be issued is limited by practical problems. Insured institutions' ability to sell subordinated debt is limited, as is the financial market's ability to absorb the debt.

Institutions' ability to sell the debt is limited by their financial strength and the effect subordinated debt has on the maturity of their funding. Some institutions, such as small, volunteer-run credit unions, may have problems finding investors interested in their debt. Other institutions, especially some thrifts, are currently so weak financially that few would be interested in buying their subordinated debt.

Minimum maturity requirements placed on subordinated debt could cause problems for institutions that seek to maintain some balance in the maturity of their assets and their funding.[18] Currently, bank subordinated debt is required to have an original maturity of at least seven years. Furthermore, debt with a remaining time to maturity of less than five years is not given full weight.[19] This burden on insured institutions can be reduced in several ways. The existing requirements are longer than needed if the only concern is preventing funds from leaving a bank immediately prior to failure. The insuring agencies should be able to handle problem institutions in one year or less. Insured institutions could continue to be allowed to issue floating rate subordinated debt that would reduce any potential interest rate risk problems. Insured institutions also could adjust the maturity structure of their liabilities to offset some undesirable attributes of their subordinated debt funding. Finally, the burden imposed on banks could be reduced further by giving the insuring agencies the power to allow banks to retire their subordinated debt early and to repurchase their own stock if the bank has far more equity and subordinated debt than the standards require.

[18]See Pringle for a discussion of the importance of banks' control over the maturity of their funding.

[19]These requirements are placed on subordinated debt that banks wish to include in the calculation of their total capital ratio. Subordinated debt with between 4 and 5 years to maturity is counted at 80 percent of its book value, debt with between 3 and 4 years counts 60 percent and so forth with debt maturing in less than one year being given no weight.

The financial markets probably could absorb more insured institutions' subordinated debt now, but they would need time to absorb enough subordinated debt and equity to transfer all the risk of failure to the private sector. In principle, the amount of equity plus subordinated debt needed to transfer virtually all the risk to the private sector depends on the government's policy for closing failed banks and the risk of a sudden large loss in the value of the banks' assets. If insured institutions were promptly closed when their economic worth reached zero, then the required private funds at risk would be smaller than if they were allowed to operate with negative economic worth. Similarly, if insured institutions have a well diversified asset portfolio, minimal interest rate risk and few contingent liabilities, then they will require relatively less private funds at risk because they are less likely to suffer a large sudden drop in their asset value.

The simplest solution may be to require a relatively large amount of equity plus subordinated debt, and require banks to meet certain diversification, interest rate risk and contingent liability requirements. Virtually all the risks would be shifted to the private sector if banks have equity and subordinated debt equal to 20 percent of their assets.[20] Finer calculation may reduce the percentage, which also might be lower under different examination and closing policies. Indeed, Bierwag and Kaufman point out that depositors and the FDIC would not be at risk if banks were closed immediately after their net worth fell to zero.

If 20 percent of assets were required, then a substantial amount of new issues would have to be sold. Under the proposal, commercial banks with assets in excess of $100 million would be required to increase their subordinated debt plus equity from about $104.4 billion to $361.4 billion. A number of years would be required to develop a market for the subordinated debt and equity that banks would have to sell.

A substantial increase in insured institutions' subordinated debt is desirable even if all the risks of insured institutions' failure cannot be transferred to the private sector. Admittedly an increase in the subordinated debt requirements might have higher servicing costs and they will create some problems for banks liability management. Such an increase will, however, provide an incentive for the private sector to monitor bank risk in a way that is unavoidable (unlike limitations on deposit insurance coverage). Furthermore, increases in subordinated debt requirements do not increase the incentives for bank runs.

Private Sector Discipline: What About Multinational Banks?

The FDIC report notes that uninsured depositors may exert little discipline on multibillion dollar institutions because they do not believe that such an institution would be allowed to

[20]The 20 percent of assets figure is a rough approximation of the amount banks should be required to have and is based on three elements: the FDIC's expected costs in closing failed banks, the losses borne by shareholders at failed banks and a safety margin. The FDIC's report says that the FDIC's expenses had averaged 4 percent of bank assets between 1930 and 1980, but that the average has risen to 9 percent of assets in recent years. The FDIC says that it expects its costs in the future to remain around 9 to 10 percent. The losses borne by bank equity holders and uninsured creditors vary by bank but a reasonable approximation for these losses might be 4 to 8 percent of bank assets. A 20 percent of assets standard thus exceeds probable losses at failed banks by at least a couple of percentage points. The amount of equity plus subordinated debt that is required if this alternative plan is adopted should obviously be based on a more careful analysis of expected losses at failed banks.

fail. As George Benston notes, no plan to shift risk to private creditors and insurers will be fully effective if large institutions are not allowed to fail.* Thomas Mayer analyzed the question of allowing large banks to fail and concluded that protecting depositor confidence may be an important reason for protecting large banks. He also argued, however, that such protection would not be needed if 100 percent deposit insurance existed.

Mayer's analysis suggests that the FDIC goal of protecting depository institutions from panics is inconsistent with its plan to rely on depositors to discipline insured institutions' risk position. The problems with the FDIC plan do not mean, however, that no system can be devised that simultaneously maintains depositor confidence while relying on private creditors to discipline bank risk exposure. One workable alternative would be a system of 100 percent insurance for all deposits together with a requirement for insured institutions to increase their use of subordinated debt. In this system, large banks could fail without affecting depositor confidence. Furthermore, this plan would accomplish the FDIC goal of encouraging the private sector to monitor bank risks.

Bevis Longstreth argues that large financial institutions have significant credit relationships with other financial institutions. He says allowing major institutions to fail could cause serious problems for the financial system. If large depository institutions are to be protected, one of several approaches could be taken to control their risk. One possibility is that no additional measures be taken to limit these institutions' exposure to risk. Insuring an institution's losses while allowing it to keep any profits encourages the institution to take on excessive risks. The multinational organizations might well follow this incentive.

Another possibility is that the risks could be controlled through a significant increase in regulation. This option also has problems, as evidenced by the success of money market mutual funds when bank interest payments were constrained. The money market funds were able to attract money that would otherwise have been deposited in insured institutions. This resulted in a large pool of highly liquid funds being controlled by uninsured institutions. If some financial institutions are to be insured and not others, that could raise the problem of competitive advantages for uninsured institutions.

A third possibility is that the risks could be controlled through risk-based insurance premiums. The problems with this option are that correcting errors in the government premium system would be expensive and that institutions would appeal their premiums on legal and political grounds as well as on economic grounds.

The fourth possibility is that private sector discipline could be strengthened through a dramatic increase in the equity capital standards applied to multinational institutions. An increase in the required equity capital at multinational institutions would increase private sector discipline because equity holders could suffer losses even if the institution were not closed. An increase in subordinated debt can only be an effective control on an institution's risk if the institution can fail, because subordinated creditors can suffer losses only if the institution fails. The problem with this option is that equity capital can be more costly for institutions to raise than subordinated liabilities. If multinational depository institutions were forced to raise excessive capital to replace subordinated liabilities, they might be placed at a competitive disadvantage vis-a-vis uninsured institutions.

*Editors' Note: See article 26 in this book.

Each of these options has significant disadvantages, which need to be weighed against the potential harm of closing a multinational institution.

Financial Disclosure

All three agencies believe that financial disclosure is important if the private sector is to discipline bank risk taking. None of the three agencies favors the disclosure of examination findings, but the FDIC report urges that agency actions taken against insured institutions should be disclosed. The FDIC notes that the insuring agencies' authority to mandate disclosure is limited to information the agencies need for deposit insurance. The FDIC does not want the authority to mandate further disclosure because it holds that disclosure is the bank's responsibility. Bank managers, however, have an incentive to hide their mistakes both from the bank's creditors and from stockholders. If the managers disclose their mistakes, they may receive lower bonuses or even lose their jobs. Government minimal standards would guarantee adequate disclosure.

The problem of management's incentive to hide its mistakes is not unique to depository institutions; all publicly traded firms have the same problems. The current system protects investors in public firms, including investors in bank holding companies and savings and loan holding companies, by requiring that their disclosure meet standards set by the Securities and Exchange Commission (SEC). If most of the burden for disciplining depository institutions were placed on the private sector, then the SEC's standards could provide a good model.

Adequacy of the Insurance Funds

The FDIC says that its fund is adequate, the FHLBB thinks its fund may need to be increased and the NCUA argues that its fund must be increased. These funds must be evaluated from two different perspectives: the ability of the fund to handle a financial crisis and the amount of resources contributed by insured institutions to handle non-panic failures.

A fund's ability to handle a financial crisis is important if deposit insurance is expected to prevent financial panic. To prevent such a panic, the fund should have unquestionable resources and liquidity. The alternative to relying on deposit insurance to maintain public confidence is to rely on the Federal Reserve in its role as lender of last resort (LLR). The LLR can prevent panic situations either by making loans directly to troubled institutions or by providing liquidity to the financial system after the panic begins. The Federal Reserve has the ability to create money and, therefore, can create the resources needed to handle any financial panic.

Both the FDIC and FHLBB say that insurance should protect the money supply and payments mechanism. The FDIC does not acknowledge that this function could be performed by a lender of last resort. The FHLBB does, but it contends that action by the LLR is discretionary.

The current system, however, does not rely on deposit insurance alone to protect the money supply and payments mechanism. Deposit insurance has reduced the incentive for depositors to participate in financial panics, but large commercial banks have too many uninsured deposits for insurance to stop all tendency towards panic.[21] The current system would be dependent on the LLR if the public lost confidence in large commercial banks because large accounts are not guaranteed 100 percent by insurance. The FDIC proposal to reduce effective coverage would shift even more of the responsibility for protecting the money supply and payments mechanism to the LLR. Therefore, the ability of the insurance fund to handle a financial panic is important but not crucial. The LLR, which has ultimate responsibility for protecting the system, would still be able to protect the financial system even if the insurance fund collapsed.

But there are other problems. The twin goals of preserving depositor confidence and trying to have large depositors discipline institutions are in fundamental conflict. The current system forces the LLR to choose which goal will be attained. It could expose depositors to risk by following its classical role of protecting the liquidity of the financial system in the event of a panic but ignoring the problems of individual institutions.[22] Then large depositors would occasionally lose confidence in some depository institutions. Alternatively, the LLR could protect confidence by providing loans to troubled institutions. These loans constitute a subsidy to the extent that the institutions could not borrow an equal amount on the open market at the same rate. If the market expected the LLR to provide funds at below market rates, then large depositors would be less effective in disciplining institutions.

Deposit insurance could prevent bank panics by itself if the public were confident that all deposits were insured. If the public felt that its deposits would not be at risk even if a bank failed, then it would have much less of an incentive to participate in a bank run. If 100 percent deposit insurance were adopted, the public's perception of the funds' ability to handle potential failures would be crucial. The current deposit insurance funds would be inadequate in a 100 percent insurance system because they do not guarantee that they could honor their commitments on a timely basis.

The current insurance fund system has some problems that could weaken the public's confidence in its ability to weather serious financial problems. A fundamental problem is that it relies on insurance funds. This reliance could weaken depositor confidence by leading the public to believe that deposit insurance would disappear when the funds were exhausted. Another problem with the funds is that their resources and liquidity are not guaranteed under the current system. The FDIC recognizes the desirability of increasing its resources. It currently can borrow up to $3 billion from the Treasury, but it would like to be able to borrow as much as the Secretary of the Treasury thought was needed during an emergency. The FDIC proposal still does not guarantee that it will have adequate resources

[21]The FDIC report shows that over 25 percent of the deposits at banks with assets of $1 billion or more are in accounts of $100,000 or more. The percentage of funds in accounts that are not fully insured rises to 71 percent of total deposits at banks with assets of $10 billion or more if foreign deposits are counted.

[22]See Humphrey and Keleher.

to handle any problem.[23] Furthermore, most of the insurance funds' assets are invested in Treasury securities, which may be hard to sell during a true financial panic. In order to guarantee the agencies both resources and liquidity, they must have access to as much money as it takes to handle all conceivable failures.[24]

The other dimension of the insurance funds' adequacy is their ability to meet routine failures without relying on funds from the Treasury. The FDIC and NCUA both make reasonable arguments about the ability of their respective funds to meet non-panic failures. The FHLBB does not say the FSLIC fund is inadequate, but it notes that the fund could have been exhausted if interest rates had returned to their 1981 levels for 1983 and 1984. The potential problems with the FSLIC fund are not, however, so much related to the fund's size as they are to the FSLIC's inability to close institutions with negative net economic worth. The FHLBB acknowledges that if the FSLIC had closed institutions when they first reached negative net economic worth, then the fund would never have been in danger. Instead the FSLIC waited until institutions had negative book value before closing them. No deposit insurance fund can be large enough to meet routine failures if economically bankrupt institutions are allowed to continue accumulating losses for extended periods before they are closed. Thus, there is merit in the idea that regulators use economic values rather than book (or accounting) values as much as possible.

The need for the funds to be able to handle a financial crisis is questionable. Large, uninsured depositors can lose money in a bank failure under the current and FDIC proposed systems. Therefore, these depositors have an incentive to panic regardless of the funds' ability to weather a financial crisis. If insurance were modified to protect large depositors, reforms would be needed to provide the funds with unquestionable resources and liquidity.

The agencies' recommendations appear reasonable with respect to the second dimension of fund adequacy, the ability of the fund to handle routine failures without Treasury assistance. The key point that emerges from analyzing the second dimension, however, is that regulators should use economic rather than accounting values where possible. No fund by itself can meet the losses a failed institution can generate if it is allowed to continue in operation.

Agency Consolidation

The FDIC favors consolidating the examination functions of the Office of the Comptroller of the Currency and the Federal Reserve System, and the examination and insurance

[23]Suppose as a purely hypothetical example, that several foreign countries with large debts to United States banks reneged on their debt and this made some large United States banks insolvent. The failure of several large banks could reduce the FDIC's fund to dangerously low levels.
Suppose further that the Secretary of the Treasury became obsessed with reducing the budget deficit and was unwilling to provide the FDIC with additional funds. Under these circumstances, the financial markets could become concerned about the strength of the banking system and a financial panic could begin. Even in this unlikely scenario, the financial system would not collapse because the Federal Reserve would almost certainly step in to provide liquidity to the financial system, but the FDIC would be powerless to stop such a panic.

[24]The insuring agency could be given access to the money directly by making it a part of the central bank or indirectly by giving it unlimited access to the Treasury and requiring the central bank to purchase new Treasury issues used to fund the insurance agency if necessary.

functions of the FHLBB into the FDIC. The FHLBB concedes that there is some merit in consolidating the regulatory agencies, but it argues that the banking agencies should be rationalized before any functions are taken from the FHLBB. The NCUA flatly opposes consolidation. Our evaluation may shed some light on the relationship among deposit insurance, supervision and regulation, and the Federal Reserve's role as lender of the last resort.

The relationship between the insuring agencies and the lender of last resort depends on how potential financial panics are handled. In the abstract, if the deposit insurance system and the LLR have joint responsibility for preventing financial panics, then the Federal Reserve may need an important role in bank supervision and regulation. If, on the other hand, the federal government wants to limit the effect of panics, but does not seek to prevent financial panics, then the LLR needs no supervision and regulation powers beyond those necessary to conduct monetary policy.

Complete confidence in depository institutions can be preserved by 100 percent deposit insurance or by LLR subsidies of failing institutions. In order for full insurance to be effective in maintaining depository confidence, the insuring agency must have unquestioned resources and liquidity. This implies that the Federal Reserve must be involved, because it is the only government body that can create money. At one extreme, the Fed's role might be limited to creating money at the insuring agencies' request, effectively turning monetary policy over to the insuring agency. Alternatively, the Federal Reserve could take over all of the functions of the insuring agencies and assume sole responsibility for handling financial crises.

The current deposit insurance system ultimately depends on potential LLR loans to preserve depositor confidence. Stripping the LLR of supervision and regulation functions in this environment would reduce its ability to recognize and avert potential serious problems. If an LLR without close involvement has difficulty recognizing the seriousness of potential problems, then it may underreact and fail to stop a panic situation, or overreact and provide subsidies where none are needed.

The Federal Reserve System maintains that its monetary policy responsibilities require that it be actively involved in bank supervision and regulation. Others argue that the Federal Reserve has no such need and that there is a potential conflict between the Fed's conduct of monetary policy and the Fed's bank supervision and regulation responsibilities.[25] Any redrawing of the Federal Reserve's responsibilities also will need to consider these issues.

Conclusion

Congress picked an issue ripe for action when it asked the insuring agencies to review deposit insurance. The current insurance system provides incentives to take risks, and financial deregulation may be increasing banks' ability and incentive to take risks. Congress needs to identify those functions that it wishes to have deposit insurance perform and then enact the system that will meet those functions at the lowest cost.

[25] See Peterson for a review of the literature on this potential conflict of interest.

The FDIC and FHLBB stress the protection insurance provides to the financial system, especially the money supply and payments system. Both contend that the current system provides adequate protection but needs to be adjusted to reduce the incentives for insured institutions to take risks. The FHLBB proposes to do this through variable rate government insurance and private insurance. A variable rate government insurance, however, would make depository institutions dependent on one government agency's definition of risk, a definition that might be heavily influenced by political factors. Private insurance does not seem to provide a good substitute for government insurance because its capacity to handle failures is most suspect when the insurance is most needed, during periods of significant financial problems.

The FDIC argues that placing large depositors at risk will reduce the risks taken by insured institutions while preventing financial panics. In practice, any attempt by the government to place large depositors at risk will give them substantial incentives to participate in financial panics. The FDIC proposal, thus, shifts more of the burden of protecting the financial system to the Federal Reserve. The NCUA suggests that all shareholders (depositors) should bear some of the risk. To the extent the NCUA plan succeeds in getting shareholders to monitor credit union risk, it would create the same incentives for depositor anxiety as the FDIC plan.

REFERENCES

BENSTON, GEORGE J. "Financial Disclosure and Bank Failure," *Economic Review*, Federal Reserve Bank of Atlanta, 69 (March 1984).

BENSTON, GEORGE J. "Deposit Insurance and Bank Failures," *Economic Review*, Federal Reserve Bank of Atlanta, 63 (March 1983), pp. 4–17.

BIERWAG, G. O. and GEORGE G. KAUFMAN. "A Proposal for Federal Deposit Insurance With Risk-Sensitive Premiums," *Staff Memoranda B3–3*, Federal Reserve Bank of Chicago, 1983.

EISENBEIS, ROBERT E. "Regulation and Financial Innovation Implications for Financial Structure and Competition Among Depository and Non-Depository Institutions," *Issues in Bank Regulation*, 4 (Winter 1981), pp. 15–23.

Federal Deposit Insurance Corporation, *Deposit Insurance in a Changing Environment. A study Submitted to Congress by the Federal Deposit Insurance Corporation*, Washington, D. C. (April 1983).

Federal Home Loan Bank Board. Agenda for Reforms. *A Report on Deposit Insurance to the Congress from the Federal Home Loan Bank Board*. Washington, D.C. (March 1983).

FLANNERY, MARK J. "Deposit Insurance Creates a Need for Bank Regulation," *Business Review*, Federal Reserve Bank of Philadelphia (January-February 1982), pp. 17–27.

HANESS, CAROLINE T. "Brokered Deposits: Issues and Alternatives," *Economic Review*, Federal Reserve Bank of Atlanta, 69 (March 1984).

HORVITZ, PAUL M. "Federal Deposit Insurance: Time For A Change?" *American Banker* (May 18, 1984), pp. 4, 22.

**The author would like to thank George Benston, Leonard Lapidus and Samuel Talley for valuable discussions and B. Frank King and Robert Eisenbeis for comments on an earlier draft. The views expressed are those of the author and do not necessarily reflect the opinions of the individuals cited above.*

HORVITZ, PAUL M. "Why Risk-Related Insurance Premiums Are No Answer," *American Banker* (May 26, 1984), pp. 4, 6.

HORVITZ, PAUL M. "Elimination of Insurance Will Require More Information," *American Banker* (June 15, 1984), pp. 4, 7.

HORVITZ, PAUL M. "Market Discipline Is Best Provided By Subordinated Creditors," *American Banker* (July 15, 1984), pp. 4, 8.

HORVITZ, PAUL M. "Consolidation of the Regulatory Agency Structure: Has the Time Come?" *Economic Review,* Federal Reserve Bank of Atlanta, 67 (December 1982), pp. 43–52.

HUMPHREY, THOMAS, M., and ROBERT E. KELEHER. "The Lender of Last Resort: A Historical Perspective," presented at the Cato Institute Second Annual Monetary Conference, January 20–21, 1984.

"J. C. Penney's Networking Bid," Transition 3 (November 1983), pp. 9–12.

KANE, EDWARD, J. "Accelerating Inflation, Regulation and Banking Innovation," Issues in Bank Regulation, 4 (Summer 1980). pp. 7–14.

KANE, EDWARD J. "Short-Changing the Small Saver, Federal Government Discrimination Against Small Savers During the Vietnam War," *Journal of Money, Credit and Banking,* 2 (1970), pp. 513–522.

KAREKEN, JOHN H. "Deposit Insurance Reform or, Deregulation is the Cart, Not the Horse," *Quarterly Review, Federal Reserve Bank of Minneapolis,* 7 (Spring 1983), pp. 1–9.

KAREKEN, JOHN H. and NEIL WALLACE. "Deposit Insurance and Bank Regulation: A Partial Equilibrium Exposition," *Journal of Business* (July 1978), pp. 413–438.

LEFF, GARY and JAMES W. PARK. "The Mississippi Deposit Insurance Crisis," *Bankers Magazine,* 160 (Summer 1977), pp. 74–80.

LONGSTRETH, BEVIS. "In Search of a Safety Net for the Financial Services Industry," *Bankers Magazine,* 166 (July-August, 1983), pp. 27–34.

MAYER, THOMAS. "Should Large Banks Be Allowed to Fail?" *Journal of Finance and Quantitative Analysis,* 10 (November 1975), pp. 603–610.

MERTON, ROBERT C. "Discussion," in The Regulation of Financial Institutions, Proceedings of a Conference sponsored by the Federal Reserve Bank of Boston and the National Science Foundation (October 1979), pp. 256–263.

MERTON, ROBERT C. "On the Cost of Deposit Insurance When There Are Surveillance Costs," *Journal of Business* (July 1978), pp. 439–452.

National Credit Union Administration. Credit Union Share Issuance: A Report to the Congress prepared by the National Credit Union Association, Washington, D. C. (April 1983).

OLIN, VIRGINIA K. "Changes in Deposit Account Structure: September 1982–March 1983," *Federal Home Loan Bank Board Journal* (August 1983), pp. 32–38.

PETERSON, MANFERD O. "Conflicts Between Monetary Policy and Bank Supervision," *Issues In Bank Regulation* (Autumn 1977), pp. 26–37.

PRINGLE, JOHN J. "The Capital Decision in Commercial Banks," *Journal of Finance* 29 (June 1974), pp. 779–795.

SHARPE, WILLIAM F. "Bank Capital Adequacy, Deposit Insurance and Security Values," *Journal of Financial and Quantitative Analysis* (November 1978), pp. 701–718.

SIGALE, MERWIN, "Bank Board Expects to Sell New Biscayne Within Weeks: Out of State Institutions Contenders for Florida S&L," *American Banker* (December 1, 1983), p. 20.

SINKEY, JOSEPH F., JR. Problem and Failed Institutions in the Commercial Banking Industry (JAI Press, Inc., Greenwich, Connecticut 1979), p. 156.

SLATER, KAREN. "FDIC Has New Strategy for Troubled Banks: Modified Deposit Payoff Will Increase Market Discipline, Isaac Says," *American Banker* (December 7, 1983), p. 1.

TUSSIG, A. DALE. "The Case for Bank Failure," *Journal of Law and Economics,* 10 (October 1967), pp. 129–147.

WALL, LARRY D. "The Future of Deposit Insurance: The Insuring Agencies' Proposals," *Economic Review,* Federal Reserve Bank of Atlanta, 69 (January 1984), pp. 43–57.

An Analysis of the Bush Task Group Recommendations for Bank Regulatory Reform

Gary G. Gilbert

29

Earlier this year, the Vice President's Task Group on Regulation of Financial Services proposed a reorganized structure of bank supervision and regulation. Briefly, the major recommendations for change to the present structure are as follows:

1. The establishment of a Federal Banking Agency under the Treasury Department which would regulate and supervise national banks and bank holding companies whose lead bank is a national bank. The supervision of such holding companies would also include nonbank affiliates. The Federal Banking Agency would also assume the Section 4(c)(8) powers under the Bank Holding Company Act which relates to permissible activities for bank holding companies. However, these Section 4(c)(8) powers are subject to a veto by the Federal Reserve Board by a 2/3 vote, if the Board regards the proposed changes as adversely affecting the safety and soundness of the banking system.
2. The FDIC would be removed from routine supervision of banks and would only examine troubled institutions (those with CAMEL 3, 4, 5 rated banks and a sample of other institutions). The FDIC would have cease and desist authority over all banks, would approve insurance applications for all banking institutions, would be

Reprinted from the Proceedings of the Conference on Bank Structure and Competition, April 23-25, 1984. By permission of the Federal Reserve Bank of Chicago and the author.

able to revoke insurance, and could take other enforcement actions, as necessary (e.g., remove management).

3. The Federal Reserve would continue to supervise state-chartered member banks and would take over supervisory responsibilities for state nonmember banks, other than the troubled institutions supervised by the FDIC. The Federal Reserve would also continue to regulate and supervise all bank holding companies whose lead bank is state chartered. In addition, the Federal Reserve Board would have regulatory and supervisory jurisdiction over ''international class'' bank holding companies (which will be defined later), even if the lead bank is a national bank.
4. To enhance the role of the states in bank supervision, a certification program would be established which would require transfer of much of the supervision of state-chartered banks and their holding companies to state regulators *if* state programs are judged to be equivalently reliable to those at the federal level. The standard for certification would be set by the new Federal Banking Agency, the Federal Reserve Board and the FDIC, but the Federal Reserve Board would decide on individual applications.
5. Commercial banks that passed a ''portfolio test,'' based on a certain portion of their assets in mortgage lending and other qualified assets, would be *eligible* for thrift regulation by the Federal Home Loan Bank Board and qualify for FSLIC insurance. Thrift institutions and commercial banks that did not meet this test would be subject to regulation as banks.
6. For functional regulation purposes, all securities regulations over banks and thrifts would be transferred to the Securities and Exchange Commission and all antitrust responsibilities to the Department of Justice.
7. The Federal Deposit Insurance system would be reformed to provide for risk-related insurance premiums with reliance on private sector ratings to the extent feasible, a phase-in of common minimum capital rules and accounting standards applicable to commercial banks and thrift institutions, and a reduction of the *de facto* 100% insurance coverage on deposits of large banks which traditionally have been handled by purchase and assumption transactions rather than deposit pay-offs.

It should be noted that recommendations 6. and 7. could be implemented without changing the current regulatory structure.

The stated objectives of the Bush Committee Report are to:

1. Simplify and streamline the compliance burdens on banks by reducing federal duplication of state supervisory activities.
2. Reduce overlap and duplication by reducing the number of federal agencies handling day-to-day bank supervision from three to two.
3. Strengthen holding company regulation to prevent problems from ''falling through the cracks.''
4. Preserve the dual banking system.
5. Enhance the ability of the FDIC to monitor and control its insurance risk.

These represent *proximate* goals which are similar to the objectives of other regulatory reform proposals advanced over the last few decades.[1] However, the merits of the Bush Task Force proposals depend more critically on the extent to which these goals can be met within the context of more *general* criteria for evaluating bank regulation. These criteria include: 1) protection of the nation's money supply and preserving monetary stability; 2) avoidance of excessive concentration of financial and economic resources; 3) preservation of a safe and sound banking system; and, 4) provision of adequate banking services.

Evaluating the Bush Task Force recommendations in terms of the above criteria becomes even more complicated in a rapidly changing financial services environment. For example, the Monetary Control Act of 1980 has altered the balance of benefits and costs of federal reserve membership on the one hand, and a state vs. federal charter on the other. In addition, the consolidation movement in banking is proceeding unabated. The banking industry has become increasingly diversified both geographically and organizationally, with a broader range of products being offered or proposed through legislation. These trends and developments have important implications for the financial industry and the regulatory structure within which it operates.

I. Redistribution of Regulatory Responsibilities among Federal Regulatory Agencies

The Bush Committee's recommendations for redistributing bank and bank holding company supervisory responsibilities among the Comptroller of the Currency, Federal Reserve Board, FDIC and Federal Home Loan Bank Board represent the most sweeping portion of the task force proposals. While the proposed removal of the FDIC from routine examinations appears to streamline the current system, the improvements may be more illusory than real.

Federal Reserve Board

Under most proposals for regulatory reform that have been advanced since 1962, a prerequisite is the removal of the Federal Reserve from bank supervision. However, under the Bush Committee proposals, the Federal Reserve remains firmly entrenched in the area of bank supervision. The Federal Reserve would increase its regulatory jurisdiction to 40% of bank deposits by taking over supervision of state nonmember banks, and would increase the number of banks it regulates from slightly over 1,000 to almost 10,000, or 2/3 of the banks in the United States. More notably, it would still retain 70% of the domestic assets of bank holding companies, 50% through supervision of about 50 "international class" banks, and 20% from the approximately 3,800 holding companies with state-chartered lead banks. The remaining 1,400 bank holding companies with national lead banks, representing 30% of bank holding company assets, would be turned over to the new Federal Banking Agency.

[1]For a brief summary of the proposals, see David S. Holland, "The Bank Task Group: A Critique," *Bank Expansion Reporter,* March 5, 1984, p. 14.

The Federal Reserve recently issued a "White Paper" which articulated its position on the importance of maintaining an active role in bank supervision to facilitate effective monetary policy. According to the report:[2]

> . . . monetary policy can potentially be thrown off course by disturbances or fragilities arising in the internal structure of performance of financial markets, and those disturbances may, in some instances, require a monetary response . . . But effective use of the critically important tool of crisis management is itself dependent on intimate familiarity with the operations of banks, and to a degree other financial institutions, of the kind that can only be derived from continuing the operational supervisory responsibilities. . . . On those occasions when the economic environment may require particularly forceful monetary policy action, the failure of supervisors and regulators adequately to have foreseen potential strains on depository institutions could either constrain the ability of the central bank to act vigorously to meet monetary policy objectives or create a situation in which needed monetary restraint pushes the stability of the system to and beyond the breaking point.

Implicit in this latter argument is that the examination process may sometimes be pro-cyclical to the detriment of counter-cyclical monetary policy. However, in reviewing the evidence of earlier studies, Manfred Peterson concludes that "there are elements in the examination process, particularly asset evaluation, that have at least a potential for working counter to monetary policy at various phases of the business cycle. The qualifiers are, of course, that there is little direct evidence of actual conflicts and that the overall effect of the examination process through limiting risk exposure of banks . . . may contribute directly to economic stability."[3]

A key issue is whether the data from bank examinations are systematically related to the real sector of the economy so as to be useful for the conduct of monetary policy, whether or not the examination process itself is pro-cyclical. In studying whether examination data have potential value in the formation of monetary policy, Benston and Marlin failed to find a significant relationship between the ratio of substandard loans to total loans and business-cycle turning points over the period 1953–1970.[4] An FDIC study attempted to expand upon the Benston-Marlin work by relating the substandard loan ratio and capital-to-deposit ratio, from monthly examination data, to the level of economic activity as indicated by the Department of Commerce index of coincident economic indicators. The study found no contemporaneous or lagged relationship between these examination data and the index of coincident indicators.[5]

It could be argued that the Federal Reserve has other regulatory tools, such as use of the discount window and approval authority over bank holding company acquisitions and powers, which could exert moral suasion on banking organizations to meet monetary

[2]*Federal Reserve Position on Restructuring of Financial Regulation Responsibilities,* Board of Governors of the Federal Reserve System, December 15, 1983, pp. 4–6.

[3]Manfred O. Peterson, "Conflicts Between Monetary Policy and Bank Supervision," *Issues in Bank Regulation,* Autumn 1977, p. 28.

[4]George J. Benston and John Tepper Marlin, "Bank Examiners' Evaluation of Credit: An Analysis of the Usefulness of Substandard Loan Data," *Journal of Money Credit and Banking,* February 1974.

[5]Robert Davis and Harold Nathan, "Should the Federal Reserve System Have Control of Bank Supervision and Examination Functions?," Division of Research, FDIC, 1977.

policy and other goals relating to Fed membership. However, the FDIC study recently cited found no statistical relationship between the Board of Governor's denial rates on bank holding company acquisitions and merger applications and quarterly changes in the monetary base between 1970 and 1976.[6] As far as the discount window is concerned, it should not be regarded as a major monetary tool and is no longer a major benefit of Federal Reserve membership since the Monetary Control Act has extended discount window privileges to all depository institutions holding transactions-type accounts.

Even if the Federal Reserve were to try to adapt its bank structural regulation to serve its monetary goals, one or the other could suffer significantly. Monetary policy is administered on a weekly basis in response to changing economic conditions, while bank structural regulation deals with long-term implications for the industry as a whole. Ad hoc adjustments to bank supervision would diminish the essential comparability and consistency of bank supervisory policies and practices over time.

On balance, the Bush recommendations and proposals for Federal Reserve regulation and supervision would substantially increase the amount of time and resources required for bank examination, with no demonstrable cost efficiencies, and no offsetting benefits that would accrue to monetary stability and control. Indeed, monetary policy goals and safety and soundness regulation may actually conflict.

It could be argued that the role of the Federal Reserve over state-chartered institutions will be reduced over time, anyway, as the current trend toward national chartering continues. After all, one of the major incentives for choosing a national bank charter is presumably to avoid double supervision. And, under the Bush Committee proposals, state-chartered institutions would still be subject to supervision by the Federal Reserve Board and the state regulators until state certification for examination is approved. Furthermore, the major disincentive for becoming a national bank, namely, mandatory Federal Reserve membership with the accompanying greater cost burden of Federal Reserve requirements, has been eliminated by the implementation of universal reserve requirements under the Monetary Control Act of 1980. This would reinforce incentives to choose a national charter. A banking organization operating in more than one state may prefer Federal supervision rather than having to deal with multiple state regulators.

However, the pace of national chartering may be slowed by other factors. In a number of areas the states have moved toward parity with the deregulation that has been legislated under the Monetary Control Act of 1980 and the Garn-St. Germain Act of 1982. In fact, some aspects of state regulation, such as more liberal single borrow lending limits and prospects for broader powers for state-chartered institutions in some states (e.g., South Dakota), offer advantages in choosing a state charter. In addition, as part of a 1980 study sponsored by the FDIC on state versus Federal supervision, an analysis of five strategic states found no significant differences in the cost burden of supervision of state chartered banks, which are subject to double supervision, as compared to national banks.[7]

The special segment of the banking industry proposed to remain under Federal Reserve supervision, the "international class" bank holding companies, appears justified, at least

[6]Ibid.

[7]Randall J. Miller, "On the Cost of Double Supervision for Insured State Chartered Banks," in the *Report of the Task Force on State and Federal Regulation of Commercial Banks,* FDIC, 1980.

in principle. This category would include: (1) bank holding companies with a full deposit-taking branch in a foreign country, (2) foreign bank holding companies operating in the United States, and (3) bank holding companies whose size is sufficiently large that supervisory problems affecting these institutions would have international impact. The Bush Committee defines this latter category as institutions with domestic assets equal to or greater than 0.5% of total domestic holding company assets. At present, 50 bank holding companies fulfill the criteria of "international class" set forth by the Bush Task Force. Thirty-five are bank holding companies with a lead national bank and approximately 25 of the 50 institutions hold assets which exceed the 0.5% cut off, or $12.5 billion in assets.

A reasonable rationale for Federal Reserve jurisdiction over international class institutions derives from its current role as a member of the Basle Committee on Banking Supervision and Regulatory Practices. This organization consists of the central banks in major industrialized countries which meet for purposes of increasing the coordination and uniformity of bank supervisory practices across countries that host branches, subsidiaries, and joint ventures of out-of-country organizations. While these activities at the international central banking levels suggest that U.S. bank holding companies with foreign offices should fall under Federal Reserve supervisory jurisdiction, it is not clear why bank holding companies that just happen to be large (over 0.5% of U.S. bank holding company assets) should automatically be included in the category of international class organizations. As a practical matter, any institution meeting this size cut-off would likely have some form of off-shore presence. Nevertheless, as assets grow, a greater number of institutions and a larger proportion of U.S. assets will exceed the 0.5% cut-off and fall under Federal Reserve jurisdiction. A better definition of "international class" bank holding companies for purposes of Federal Reserve Board responsibilities vis-a-vis other central banks would be some combination of scope of off-shore physical presence and proportion of assets or loans booked overseas.

Federal Banking Agency

In a major shift from the present situation, the authority to determine permissible powers of bank holding companies as under Section 4(c)(8) of the Federal Reserve Act would be shifted from the Federal Reserve Board to the new Federal Banking Agency. An interesting parallel exists between this proposal and Senator Garn's omnibus banking bill (S.2181) entitled "The Financial Services Competitive Equity Act." Senator Garn's bill attempts to prohibit affiliations between large bank holding companies and the largest insurance, real estate, securities, and other financial activities newly authorized for banks under the bill. This would be accomplished by restricting any bank holding company with domestic deposits exceeding 0.30% of total U.S. domestic deposits to acquisitions of each type of financial activity noted above which would result in no more than 25% of the bank holding company's capital. Interestingly enough, this restriction would apply to roughly the same institutions that meet the 0.5% cut-off for Federal Reserve regulation under the Bush Task Force proposal.

The single-regulator approach taken by the Bush Task Force for regulation of the bank holding company and its nonbank affiliates is implicitly based upon the rejection of the separability argument, which regards the parent and constituents of the holding company as separate operational units from a financial standpoint. The Bush Committee approach of regulating bank holding companies as single integrated entities is supported by empirical evidence and the experience of the FDIC with failed banks in holding companies. In a review of the evidence of studies through 1978, John T. Rose concludes that "bank holding companies are trying to manage their organizations as integrated entities, at least to some degree. For one thing, bank holding companies typically try to direct, through organizational structure, the management philosophy and broad operating policies of their bank and nonbank subsidiaries."[8] Rose found, however, that bank holding companies vary more widely in their integration of bank subsidiaries than they do with respect to the integration of their nonbank subsidiaries. In this regard, FDIC experience has shown that "problems in the operation of any holding company unit with the authority to use or draw on the credit standing and resources of the lead bank and the entire holding company enterprise can give rise to serious problems for constituent banks and for the lead bank in particular."[9]

The weight of the evidence, thus, supports the integrated approach to holding company regulation proposed by the Bush Task Force from a safety and soundness standpoint. However, under the proposals, regulatory control over the structure of the banking industry would become more decentralized over time. This results from the fact that *more* regulators are involved in bank holding company supervision under the Bush Task Force proposals than at present, while a greater concentration of banking resources is falling under the bank holding company umbrella.

The dual goals of preserving a safe and sound banking system and avoiding excessive concentration of banking assets in the U.S. suggests the need for more centralized bank holding company supervision than proposed by the task force. But, to some degree or another, the report delegates bank holding company regulation to the new Federal Banking Agency, the Federal Reserve Board, certified state supervisory authorities, and possibly the Federal Home Loan Bank Board (but this is not clear in the Bush recommendations). At the same time, the trend toward consolidation of banking resources within bank holding companies continues. Between 1970 and year-end 1983, the number of bank holding companies increased from 121 to 5,350. The percentage of banking offices within holding companies as a percentage of all banking offices increased from 12% to 75% over the same period. Domestic deposits in bank holding companies as a percentage of all bank deposits increased from 16% to 83%. The *American Banker* reports that the record number of mergers among the top 300 banks, which are predominantly affiliated with bank holding companies, is due primarily to the prospect of interstate banking, the difficulty for some smaller banks to compete in a deregulated environment, and changes in state banking laws which have spurred consolidation of banks within multibank holding companies.[10] Fur-

[8]John J. Rose, "Bank Holding Companies as Operational Single Entities," *The Bank Holding Company Movement to 1978: A Compendium,* A study by the Staff of the Board of Governors of the Federal Reserve System, September, 1978, p. 89.

[9]Irvine H. Sprague in testimony on S.332, Consolidated Banking Regulation Act of 1979, presented to the Committee on Government Affairs and Committee on Banking, Housing and Urban Affairs, United States Senate, February 28, 1979, p. 8.

[10]"Record Merger Activity Hikes Deposits at the Top 300 Banks," *American Banker,* March 16, 1984.

thermore, if Garn legislation were passed, it would also promote bank holding company expansion by permitting broader powers only to bank holding company affiliates and by authorizing the acquisition of savings and loan associations by bank holding companies.

For various reasons, it is likely that the future expansion within the bank holding company movement will occur primarily within the multibank holding company structure. First, the McFadden Report to Congress in 1981 recommended interstate holding company acquisitions as a transitional approach to interstate banking.[11] A review of the literature on bank holding companies, presented in the Autumn 1983 *Journal of Bank Research*, concludes that "the evidence indicates little, if any, impact of multibank holding company affiliation on the market shares of banks acquired as entry vehicles into new markets, regardless of the initial market share of the acquired bank."[12] Second, the recently established regional interstate banking pacts provide for bank holding company acquisitions of out-of-state banks within the region on a reciprocal basis. Third, interest rate deregulation and nonbank competition for funds provides an incentive for bank holding companies to operate interstate to diversify funding opportunities. One way this can be done is by establishing nonbank banks (those that accept deposits but do not make commercial loans).

As the banking system becomes more national in scope through greater interstate banking opportunities, it makes sense to locate the regulation of multibank holding companies that engage in interstate banking solely under the Federal Banking Agency. Recognizing multibank holding companies as a single integrated unit for safety and soundness considerations would require, at the very least, that state banking authorities devote considerable attention to interstate regulatory policies and practices. This would place an additional burden on the staff time and resources of state bank supervisors.

Even if all supervision of multibank holding companies were under the jurisdiction of the Federal Banking Agency, other modifications of the Bush Task Force recommendations on bank holding company supervision would be required to avoid regulatory "slippage." The problem relates to so-called mixed bank holding companies. These are multibank holding companies that include both state-chartered and nationally chartered banks. For example, in a bank holding company with a national lead bank and also a state-chartered bank, the state-chartered institution would be regulated by the Federal Reserve Board and/or the state supervisory authority, depending upon certification, while the parent, the lead bank and the nonbank affiliates would be regulated by the Federal Banking Agency. As states deregulate at a different pace than Congress, an incentive could exist for bank holding companies to maintain both state and national banks in order to give them as much legal flexibility as possible. While it is one thing to have a dual banking system that allows banks to choose which set of rules will govern them, it is not clear that allowing

[11]*Geographic Restrictions on Commercial Banking in the United States*, The Report of the President prepared under the direction of the Department of the Treasury pursuant to the International Banking Act of 1978, January 1981.

[12]Timothy J. Curry and John T. Rose, "Multibank Holding Companies: Recent Evidence on Competition and Performance in Banking Markets," *Journal of Bank Research*, Autumn 1983, p. 219.

multibank organizations to take advantage of both sets of rules simultaneously is in the public interest.

One solution would be to require the subsidiaries of a multibank holding company to have the same charter—state or federal. On the other hand, it would be preferable to find a means for regulating bank holding companies that strikes a balance between the federal interest in controlling banking structure at the interstate level and the states' interest in controlling their local banking systems. This could be accomplished in several ways. The Federal Banking Agency could regulate and supervise both federally chartered and state-chartered institutions in a mixed system for safety and soundness, while states could evaluate the performance of the state-chartered affiliates in meeting the public benefits test under Section 4(c)(8) of the Bank Holding Company Act. This test requires that the convenience, needs, and welfare of the public outweigh any expected anticompetitive effects. In support of the dual banking system, one-bank holding companies with a state-chartered bank could be regulated entirely by the state regulatory authorities, or under a divided examination program similar to that of the FDIC and 27 states. The FDIC state-federal study cited earlier found this approach to be more efficient than independent or joint examinations with the state.

The above approach would be weakened if one-bank holding companies were eligible under the Bush Task Force proposals to be regulated by the Federal Home Loan Bank Board if they met the qualifying asset test (e.g., more than 60% of assets in mortgages and other qualifying assets). An incentive for such an institution to be regulated by the Federal Home Loan Bank Board would exist if the one-bank holding company was as free of restrictions on operating powers as are one-association (unitary) savings and loan holding companies.

II. Conclusion and Recommendations

The Vice President's Task Group on Regulations of Financial Services has proposed a major restructuring of the banking regulatory system. While the objectives are worthwhile, a considerable degree of regulatory overlap would still exist under the Group's proposals. The problem stems primarily from the recommendation to broaden the supervisory responsibilities of the Federal Reserve. This redistribution of supervisory authority is in conflict with trends and developments in banking structure, particularly with regard to the multibank holding company movement.

A preferable approach would be to: 1) remove the Federal Reserve from bank supervision (except for "international class" banks and bank holding companies); 2) divide supervision of state-chartered banks and state-chartered one-bank holding companies, including nonbank affiliates, between the FDIC and certified state regulatory agencies (since the FDIC bears the ultimate risk in the event of a bank failure, it should have the ultimate responsibility for certifying individual states); and 3) place all remaining banks and bank holding companies, including nonbank affiliates, under the jurisdiction of the new Federal Banking Agency.

This proposal represents a transitional approach to a unified regulatory structure at the federal level, while preserving the dual banking system and the necessary supervisory authority of the FDIC to monitor and control its insurance risk.